Contemporary Services Marketing Management

A Reader

Edited by

Mark Gabbott and Gillian Hogg

The Dryden Press

Harcourt Brace & Company Limited

London   Fort Worth   New York   Orlando
Philadelphia   San Diego   Toronto   Sydney   Tokyo

The Dryden Press
24–28 Oval Road
London NW1 7DX

This book is printed on acid-free paper.

ISBN 0-03-099035-1

Typeset by Mackreth Media Services, Hemel Hempstead, Herts
Printed in Great Britain by WBC Book Manufacturers, Bridgend, Mid Glamorgan

Contents

Introduction

Mark Gabbott and Gillian Hogg

Considerable effort has been expended by academics over the last twenty years in establishing that services are different to other products and that these differences present special challenges to the service marketer. In their review of the development of services marketing literature Fisk, Brown and Bitner (1993) use an evolutionary metaphor. They identify a period of 'crawling out' as services marketing emerged from the goods marketing paradigm, through a 'scurrying about' phase to the present, where services marketing is 'walking erect' and demonstrating empirical and theoretical rigour. At the same time, the cross disciplinary and international nature of services research has become apparent. The nature of services and the value of taking a service orientated approach to management has been recognised outwith the specific discipline of services marketing. In this text we attempt not only to provide readers with some of the most interesting and stimulating examples of current services research, but also to provide a summary of where the discipline has come from, with a section on the Classics from the crawling out phase, which set the parameters of services research. By concentrating, in the main, on contemporary articles (which we define as since 1990) we hope to indicate where the discipline of services marketing is today. By way of an introduction it is, however, worthwhile rehearsing the basis of services marketing and reviewing the foundations upon which it is built.

DEFINITIONS OF SERVICES

The first problem with discussing service products, rather that goods, lies in defining what a service is. There is no single universally accepted definition of the term, Grönroos (1990) lists a selection of 11 definitions of the term dating from 1960 before, reluctantly, arriving at a definition which he describes as a 'blend' of those suggested by Lehtinen and Lehtinen (1982), Kotler and Bloom (1984) and Gummesson (1987):

> A service is an activity or series of activities of more or less intangible nature that normally, but not necessarily, take place in interactions between the customer and the service employee and/or physical resources or goods and/or systems of the service provider, which are provided as solutions to customer problems.
>
> Grönroos (1990) p. 27

The complexity and rather convoluted nature of this definition illustrates the problem in succinctly defining services. Gummesson (1987), referring to an unidentified source, suggests an alternative definition that is more of a criticism of attempts to find an acceptable definition

> Services are something which can be bought and sold but which you can not drop on your foot
>
> Gummesson (1987) p. 22

There is still not agreement amongst some academics as to whether the differences between goods and services are significant enough to justify the distinction. Levitt (1976) states that there are no such thing as service industries, only industries where the service component is greater or less than those in other industries. Similarly Shostack (1977) argues that there are very few 'pure' goods or services preferring a product continuum from tangible dominant goods to intangible dominant services. Any distinction is between products where the core of what is being sold is a service, with possible accompanying goods, and products where the core is a physical good where the service element is used as a product augmentation for competitive advantage.

An alternative way of regarding the definition problem in service products is presented by Rust and Oliver (1994) who conceptualise all business transactions as services, which may or may not involve a physical product. This argument is based on the idea that all products deliver some form of service, for example, a washing machine washes clothes, the washing machine is bought to deliver that service. Along with the physical product the buyer also receives service delivery, i.e. the experience of buying the washing machine, the service environment (the shop in which it is bought) and the service product which they define as the specifications of the offering. All products are, therefore, made up of these elements, centred around the physical product which is present in goods and absent in pure services. The case for considering services marketing as a separate entity is based on the belief that there are a number of common characteristics of service products which distinguish them from goods. Although the conceptualisation of the term 'services' is difficult, all products have characteristics, or attributes, that define the nature of the offering. For services these can be identified as intangibility, heterogeneity, inseparability, perishability and the concept of ownership (see, for instance, Lovelock, 1981 and Grönroos, 1978).

CHARACTERISTICS OF SERVICES

Intangibility is one of the most important characteristics of services, they do not have a physical dimension. Often services are described using tangible nouns but this obscures the fundamental nature of the service which remains intangible. Shostack (1987) points out by way of example that 'airline' means air transportation, 'hotel' means lodging rental. Berry (1980) describes a good as 'an object, a device, a thing', in contrast to a service which is 'a deed, a performance, an effort'. He argues that even though the performance of most services is supported by tangibles the essence of what is purchased is a performance; therefore, as McLuhan (1964) points out, it is the process of delivering a service which comprises the product. The implication of this argument is that consumers cannot see, touch, hear, taste or smell a service they can only experience the performance of it (Carman and Uhl, 1973; Sasser *et al.*, 1978). This makes the perception of a service a highly subjective and abstract concept.

The second characteristic of services is the inseparability of the production and consumption aspects of the transaction. The service is a performance, in real time, in which the purchaser cooperates with the provider. According to Thomas (1978) the degree of this involvement is dependent upon the extent to which the service is people based or equipment based. The inference of this distinction is that people based services tend to be less standardised than equipment based services or goods producing activities. Goods are produced, sold and then consumed, whereas services are sold and then produced and consumed simultaneously (Regan, 1963; Cowell, 1984). The inseparability of the role of service provider and consumer also relates to the lack of standardisation since the purchaser can alter both the way in which the service is delivered, as well as what is delivered, which has important implications for both the management and the evaluation of the service product.

The heterogeneity of services is also a function of human involvement in the delivery and consumption process. It refers to the fact that services are delivered by individuals and therefore each service encounter will be different by virtue of the participants or time of performance. As a consequence each purchaser is likely to receive a different service experience. The perishability of services describes the real time nature of the product. Services cannot be stored unlike goods and the absence of the ability to build and maintain stocks of the product means that fluctuations in demand cannot be accommodated in the same way as goods, i.e. in periods of excess demand more product cannot be utilised. For the purchaser of services the time at which he/she chooses to use the service may be critical to its performance and therefore to the consumers' experience. Kelley, Donnelly and Skinner (1990) make the observation that consumption is inextricably linked to the presence of other consumers and their presence can influence the service outcome.

To the above characteristics of services, Wyckham *et al.* (1975) and Kotler (1986) have identified the concept of ownership as a distinguishing feature of services. With the sale of a good the purchaser generally obtains ownership of it. By contrast in the case of a service the purchaser only has temporary access or use of it: what is owned is the benefit of the service, not the service itself, e.g. in terms of a holiday the purchaser has the benefit of the flight, hotel and beach but does not own them. The absence of ownership stresses the finite nature of services for purchasers, there is no enduring involvement in the product, only in the benefit.

PROCESS AND OUTCOME

In discussing the service product it is important to make a distinction between two principal components of the service product, the outcome, i.e. what the service is designed to achieve, and the process of delivery, i.e. how the service is delivered. It is frequently more difficult for a supplier to differentiate the outcome; for example, an accounting audit must achieve certain criteria; the outcome, audited accounts, are not easily differentiated. The purchaser requires reliability of the outcome, differentiation takes place at the process dimension, how the accounts are audited. In many services this outcome is difficult for the purchaser to evaluate, even after the service has been delivered. It is possible for the purchaser to know that the service has been delivered, but difficult to assess whether it has been delivered in the most effective way. The purchaser may not know whether the accounts were audited in the most efficient or cost effective manner; in these circumstances the way the audit takes place, the process of auditing is used to assess the competence of the auditors, i.e. financial competence is implied from the manner in which the audit is conducted. Whereas the reliability of the outcome is essential, the service supplier must deliver the core service, much of the competition in service industries takes place at the process level.

Other models have been presented which have similar bases, despite different terminology, and they all describe a process and outcome form. For instance, Grönroos (1990) refers to technical versus functional aspects, Zeithaml (1988) uses an intrinsic versus extrinsic distinction, Iacobucci *et al.* (1994) describe 'core' and 'peripheral' aspects of the service. The word pairs are not exactly interchangeable but there are strong conceptual parallels. The key factor is that in service products it is important to make a distinction between what is delivered and how it is delivered. The relationship between these two aspects is considered throughout the articles in this reader and it is the basis of most of the work on service quality and satisfaction included in Section III.

STRUCTURE OF THE READER

The reader is divided into five sections reflecting different aspects of services research. However, the sections are not intended to be inclusive, they merely provide a convenient way of presenting contemporary services research. The first section, The Classics, is the basis of the consideration of services as a separate discipline with some of the most important and, for their time, ground-breaking articles on services. This is where services research is coming from, the starting point for the subject and the foundation for the reader. The following sections, however, are reflective of current services marketing thought, in effect we have 'jumped' the intervening years. This is not to imply that the years between have not produced interesting and exciting services marketing research; readers may wish to look at Solomon, Surprenant, Czepiel and Gutman (1985) and Bitner, Boom and Tetreault's (1990) work on service encounters, Guiltinan's (1987) article on the pricing of services or Levitt's (1972 and 1976) work on services, to name but a few. However, these articles have been extensively reprinted and included in other texts; see for example, Bateson (1995). In this text we are attempting to illustrate where the discipline is in the mid 1990s and the articles chosen are all illustrative of current research in the field.

As Fisk *et al.* (1993) point out, the battle for services to be considered a separate discipline has now been won. The number of publications, conferences, teaching programmes and research centres bears witness to the fact that services are now recognised as an important and developing research area. We are now in the 'walking erect' stage of the evolution metaphor as we hope is demonstrated by the range and scope of the research represented in this reader.

REFERENCES

Bateson, J. (1995) *Managing Services Marketing*, 3rd Edn. London: Dryden Press.

Berry, L. L. (1980) 'Service Marketing Is Different', *Business* (May–June): 24–29.

Bitner, M. J., Booms, B. and Tetreault, B. (1990) 'The Service Encounter: Diagnosing Favourable and Unfavourable Incidents'. *Journal of Marketing* **54**: 71–84.

Carman, J. and Uhl, K. (1973) *Marketing: Principles and Methods*. Homewood, Ill: Irwin.

Cowell, D. (1984) *The Marketing of Services*. London: Heinemann.

Fisk, R., Brown, S. and Bitner, M. J. (1993) 'Tracking the Evolution of Services Marketing Literature'. *Journal of Retailing* **69**(No. 1): 61–103.

Grönroos, C. (1978) 'A Service Orientated Approach to Marketing Services'. *European Journal of Marketing* **12**(8), 588–601.

Grönroos, C. (1990) *Service Management and Marketing: Managing The Moments of Truth in Service Competition*. Lexington Marketing Association, Maxwell Macmillan.

Guiltinan, J. (1987) 'The Price Bundling of Services: A Normative Framework'. *Journal of Marketing* **31** (April): 74–85.

Gummesson, E. (1987) 'Lip services – A Neglected Area in Services Marketing'. *Journal of Services Marketing* (No. 1): 22.

Iacobucci, D., Grayson, K. and Ostrom, A. (1994) 'The Calculus of Service Quality and Customer Satisfaction: Theoretical and Empirical Differentiation and Integration'. *Advances in Services Marketing and Management* **3**: 1–67.

Kelley, S. W., Donnelly, J. H. and Skinner, S. J. (1990) 'Customer Participation in Service Production and Delivery'. *Journal of Retailing* **66** (No. 3): 315–335.

Kotler, P. (1986) *Principles of Marketing*, 3rd Edn. Englewood Cliffs, New Jersey: Prentice-Hall International.

Kotler, P. and Bloom, P. (1984) *Marketing Professional Services*. Englewood Cliffs NJ: Prentice Hall.

Lehtinen, U. and Lehtinen, J. (1982) *Service Quality: A Study of Dimensions*. Research Report, Helsinki, Finland.

Levitt, T. (1972) 'The Production Line Approach to Service'. *Harvard Business Review* (September/October): 41–52.

Levitt, T. (1976) 'The Industrialisation of Service'. *Harrrvard Business Review* (Sept–Oct) 63–74.

Lovelock, C. (1981) 'Why Marketing Management Needs to Be Different for Services'. In *Marketing of Services* (J. H. Donnelly and W. R. George, eds). American Marketing Association, Chicago.

Regan, W. J. (1963) 'The Service Revolution', *Journal of Marketing* 27 (July): 57–62.

Rust, R. T. and Oliver, R. L. (1994) 'Service Quality: Insights and Managerial Implications Form The Frontier'. In *Service Quality: New Directions in Theory and Practice* (R. Rust and R. Oliver, Eds). California: Sage.

Sasser, W. E., Olsen, R. P., and Wyckoff, D. D. (1978) *The Management of Service Operations*. Boston, MA: Allyn and Bacon.

Solomon, M., Surprenant, C., Czepiel, J. and Gutman, E. (1985) 'Service Encounters: An Overview'. In *The Service Encounter: Managing Employee/Customer Interaction in Service Businesses* (J. Czepiel, M. Solomon and C. Surprenant, Eds). MA: Lexington Books, 3–15.

Thomas, D. R. E. (1978) 'Strategy Is Different in Service Business'. *Harvard Business Review* (July–August): 158–165.

Wyckham, R. G., Fitzroy, P. and Mandry, G. (1975) 'Marketing of Services: An Evaluation of The Theory'. *European Journal of Marketing* **9**: 59-67.

Zeithaml, V. (1988) 'Consumer Perceptions of Price, Quality and Value: A Means-End Model and Synthesis'. *Journal of Marketing* **52** (July): 2–22.

Section I

The Classics

Services marketing management has now reached a stage in its development which demands a recognition of the special characteristics of the service product. However, this was not always the case. Academics and practitioners struggled for some time against the view that services were no different to any other class of product. As the services sector emerged in the Western economies, it was clear that new marketing tools were needed in assisting the development of a newly conceptualised product class and this is where our reader starts. We have included in this section five articles which for us represent the emergence of the services discipline and provide a necessary reference point for the consideration of more contemporary material.

The paper by Shostack (1977) has been recognised as one of the first major service marketing works. It presents a number of key ideas which have become cornerstones of the discipline. The article tackles the difficult issue of marketing semantics as an attempt to differentiate services from the dominance of the 'product orientation'. As far as the author undoubtedly moved the debate forward, the issue of definitions is still a debating point in classes and seminars across the world. The crux of the argument is the issue of 'tangibility' and Shostack argues coherently that to conceptualise services and physical products as the same, apart from intangibility, is to argue that apples are no different from oranges apart from their 'appleness'. A simple example perhaps, but one which went to the core(!) of the debate in the late 1970s and highlights the 'breaking free' aspect of this work.

The middle section of this article continues to take 'pot shots' at the prevailing marketing paradigm and this part of the work has relevance even beyond services. However, the re-conceptualisation of products as combinations of discrete elements formed into a molecular model neatly side-stepped the arguments about the classification of individual products and services. Shostack presents an holistic approach based upon a tangible/intangible continuum and this has become a classic in its own right. In the final section of the article, the author goes on to provide some suggestions about how marketers need to compensate for the problems presented by intangibility by managing peripheral cues; those things consumers experience through their five senses which characterise for them the reality of the service experience. The term 'tangibilising the intangible' changes through the discussion of physical/tangible evidence as Shostack applies it to different services contexts and their representation through advertising. In total this article summarises many of the main themes of the services marketing literature and is still considered a classic.

Unlike Shostack, the paper by Lovelock (1983) is concerned primarily with classification and has been included here to lead on from the Shostack article. Whereas Shostack dealt with services in a general way, looking for a normative approach, the work by Lovelock recognises the diversity within services and approaches the problem inductively by trying to establish commonalities across service products. This is then used as a means of engendering a cross fertilisation of ideas and activities to define some sort of boundary for services marketing. This article marks the beginning of a services classification theme in the literature continued by Lovelock, Gummesson, and Grönroos etc. While some have argued that this is a distraction from the main issues facing services, and contributes very little to the development of practice or research, the article by Lovelock is more than just a classification exercise. The statement of the five questions about services highlights some of the key issues for marketing in the services context. The matrices and accompanying text provide a great deal of clarity and detail to some of the issues highlighted by Shostack. By concentrating upon the nature of the services act, the type of relationship, degree of customisation, nature of demand and supply and finally delivery, Lovelock is able to explore a series of sub-questions through an 'insights and implications' structure. The value of this article is not so much in the classifications derived from the asking of the five questions but through the portrayal of similar services across dimensions allowing for practitioners to look beyond their own experience and draw from the experiences and activities of others.

Zeithaml (1981) presents a different perspective by concentrating upon service consumers. If one accepts the contention that service products and services marketing activity is different to that of physical products, then we must accept that consumers' responses to products are also likely to be different. This argument is still strangely alien even now in the 1990s and the amount of published research on service consumption is still relatively sparse compared to research on service products. The article presents for the first time, an attempt to explain some inherent differences in how consumers use and evaluate services as opposed to physical products. Zeithaml uses a search, experience, credence framework derived from the work of Nelson (1974) and Darby and Karni (1973). It argues that the characteristics of services suggest that they are high in experience and credence qualities but low in search qualities representing an increased difficulty for consumers in evaluation. We can criticise the framework for inadequate conceptualisation. For instance by an insufficient distinction between search and experience (i.e. when do experiences, especially of other consumers become searchable?) and between experience and credence (i.e. to what extent is there a reliance upon experience in determining credence?). However, this framework has been influential in guiding research on consumer behaviour and services in general and service evaluation in particular. The article is structured around eleven hypotheses which Zeithaml presents as axiomatic for the service consumers. In the absence of any empirical work the hypotheses remain in their propositional form, but have intuitive appeal. These hypotheses are grouped into information search, evaluative criteria, size and composition of the evoked set, perceived risk, adoption of innovations, brand loyalty and attribution of dissatisfaction which covers a considerable amount of consumer behaviour of interest to marketers. The article finishes with a series of recommendations for service marketers in respect of the hypotheses.

Grönroos (1978) provides insights from services companies as to how the marketing mix is planned and applied bearing in mind the characteristics of the service product. The article is also notable for its observations about service marketing management which, even though it was written nearly twenty years ago, are still relevant today. The article presents three dimensions which the author believes are central to the development of a contextualised marketing mix. It uses a series of three case studies to provide supporting evidence for the importance of accessibility, the human element in service delivery and the provision of auxiliary (or augmented) service offerings. It is suggested that these elements relate directly to the consumer's experience of the service product and must therefore be integral to the task of marketing planning.

The final article by Rathmell is truly a classic, being published in 1966. Its status though is not just in terms of its age, for the content of this article shows quite clearly how the early debate over the definition and classification of services was framed. It is included here as an example of the early service marketing research formulated as a discussion of issues related to service products. Many of the ideas which subsequently became important in services research are contained here, such as the difficulty in conceptualising products comprising both goods and services, the nature of service satisfaction, and the goods–service continuum. The final section of the article identifies a number of service characteristics which can still guide current debate and a call for research in the area which has certainly been responded to.

CONTENTS

1

Breaking Free from Product Marketing

G. Lynn Shostack

New concepts are necessary if service marketing is to succeed. Service marketing is an uncharted frontier. Despite the increasing dominance of services in the US economy, basic texts still disagree on how services should be treated in a marketing context.[1]

The heart of this dispute is the issue of applicability. The classic marketing 'mix', the seminal literature, and the language of marketing all derive from the manufacture of physical goods. Practicing marketers tend to think in terms of products, particularly mass-market consumer goods. Some service companies even call their output 'products' and have 'product' management functions modeled after those of experts such as Procter and Gamble.

Marketing seems to be overwhelmingly product-oriented. However, many service-based companies are confused about the applicability of product marketing, and more than one attempt to adopt product marketing has failed.

Merely adopting product marketing's labels does not resolve the question of whether product marketing can be overlaid on service businesses. Can corporate banking services really be marketed according to the same basic blueprint that made *Tide* a success? Given marketing's historic tenets, there is simply no alternative.

Could marketing itself be 'myopic' in having failed to create relevant paradigms for the service sector? Many marketing professionals who transfer to the services arena find their work fundamentally 'different', but have a difficult time articulating how and why their priorities and concepts have changed. Often, they also find to their frustration and bewilderment that 'marketing' is treated as a peripheral function or is confused with one of its components, such as research or advertising, and kept within a very narrow scope of influence and authority.[2]

This situation is frequently rationalized as being due to the 'ignorance' of senior management in service businesses. 'Education' is usually recommended as the solution. However, an equally feasible, though less comforting, explanation is that service industries have been slow to integrate marketing into the mainstream of decision-making and control because marketing offers no guidance, terminology, or practical rules that are clearly *relevant* to services.

Reprinted with permission from *Journal of Marketing*, Vol. 41, April, pp. 73–80
© 1977 American Marketing Association

MAKING ROOM FOR INTANGIBILITY

The American Marketing Association cites both goods *and* services as foci for marketing activities. Squeezing services into the Procrustean phrase 'intangible products',[3] is not only a distortion of the AMA's definition but also a complete contradiction in terms.

It is wrong to imply that services are just like products 'except' for intangibility. By such logic, apples are just like oranges, except for their 'appleness'. Intangibility is not a modifier; it is a state. Intangibles may come with tangible trappings, but no amount of money can buy physical ownership of such intangibles as 'experience' (movies), 'time' (consultants), or 'process' (dry cleaning). A service is rendered. A service is experienced. A service cannot be stored on a shelf, touched, tasted or tried on for size. 'Tangible' means 'palpable', and 'material'. 'Intangible' is an antonym, meaning '*im*palpable', and '*not* corporeal'.[4] This distinction has profound implications. Yet marketing offers no way to treat intangibility as the core element it is, nor does marketing offer usable tools for managing, altering, or controlling this amorphous core.

Even the most thoughtful attempts to broaden the definition of 'that which is marketed' away from product synonymity suffer from an underlying assumption of tangibility. Not long ago, Philip Kotler argued that 'values' should be considered the end result of 'marketing'.[5] However, the text went on to imply that 'values' were created by 'objects' and drifted irredeemably into the classic product axioms.

To truly expand marketing's conceptual boundaries requires a framework which accommodates intangibility instead of denying it. Such a framework must give equal descriptive weight to the components of 'service' as it does to the concept of 'product'.

The complexity of marketed entities

What kind of framework would provide a new conceptual viewpoint? One unorthodox possibility can be drawn from direct observation of the marketplace and the nature of the market 'satisfiers' available to it. Taking a fresh look, it seems that there are really very few, if any, 'pure' products or services in the marketplace.

Examine, for instance the automobile. Without question, one might say, it is a physical object, with a full range of tangible features and options. But another, equally important element is marketed in tandem with the steel and chrome – i.e. the service of transportation. Transportation is an *independent* marketing element; in other words, it is not car-dependent, but can be marketed in its own right. A car is only *one* alternative for satisfying the market's transportation needs.

This presents a semantic dilemma. How should the automobile be defined? Is General Motors marketing a *service*, a service that happens to include a *by*-product called a car? Levitt's classic 'Marketing Myopia' exhorts businessmen to think in exactly this generic way about what they market.[6] Are automobiles 'tangible services'? It cannot be denied that both elements – tangible and intangible – exist and are vigorously marketed. Yet they are, by definition, different qualities, and to attempt to compress them into a single word or phrase begs the issue.

Conversely, how shall a service such as airline transportation be described?

Although the service itself is intangible, there are certain very real things that belong in any description of the total entity, including such important tangibles as interior decor, food and drink, seat design, and overall graphic continuity from tickets to attendants' uniforms. These items can dramatically affect the 'reality' of the service in the consumer's mind. However, there is no accurate way to lump them into a one-word description.

If 'either-or' terms (products vs. service) do not adequately describe the true nature of marketed entities, it makes sense to explore the usefulness of a new *structural* definition. This broader concept postulates that market entities are, in reality, *combinations of discrete elements* which are linked together in molecule-like wholes. Elements can be either tangible or intangible. The entity may have either a tangible or intangible nucleus. But the whole can only be described as having a certain dominance.

Molecular model

A 'molecular' model offers opportunities for visualization and management of a total market entity. It reflects the fact that a market entity can be partly tangible *and* partly intangible, without diminishing the importance of either characteristic. Not only can the potential be seen for picturing and dealing with multiple *elements*, rather than a *thing*, but the concept of dominance can lead to enriched considerations of the priorities and approach that may be required of a marketer. Moreover, the model suggests the scientific analogy that if market entities have multiple elements, a deliberate or inadvertent change in a *single* element may completely alter the entity, as the simple switching of FE_3O_2 to FE_2O_3 creates a new substance. For this reason, a marketer must carefully manage all the elements, especially those for service-based entities, which may not have been considered previously within his domain.

DIAGRAMMING MARKET ENTITIES

A simplified comparison demonstrates the conceptual usefulness of a molecular modeling system. In Figure 1, automobiles and airline travel are broken down into their major elements. As shown, these two entities have different nuclei. They also differ in dominance.

Clearly, airline travel is intangible-dominant; that is, it does not yield physical ownership of a tangible good. Nearly all of the other important elements in the entity are intangible as well. Individual elements and their combinations represent unique satisfiers to different market segments. Thus:

- For some markets – students, for example – pure transport takes precedence over all other considerations. The charter flight business was based on this element. As might be expected during lean economic times, 'no frills' flights show renewed emphasis on this nuclear core.
- For business travelers, on the other hand, schedule frequency may be paramount.
- Tourists, a third segment, may respond most strongly to the combination of in-flight and post-flight services.

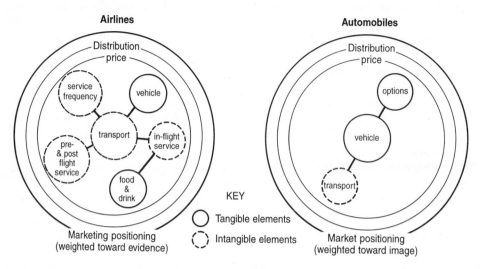

Figure 1. Diagram of market entities.

As the market entity of airline travel has evolved, it has become more and more complex. Ongoing reweighting of elements can be observed, for example, in the marketing of airline food, which was once a battleground of quasi-gourmet offerings. Today, some airlines have stopped marketing food altogether, while others are repositioning it primarily to the luxury markets.

Airlines vs. automobiles

In comparing airlines to automobiles, one sees obvious similarities. The element of transportation is common to both, as it is to boats, trains, buses, and bicycles. Tangible decor also plays a role in both entities. Yet in spite of their similarities, the two entities are not the same, either in configuration or in marketing implications.

In some ways, airline travel and automobiles are mirror opposites. A car is a physical possession that renders a service. Airline travel, on the other hand, cannot be physically possessed. It can only be experienced. While the inherent 'promise' of a car is service, airline transportation often promises a Lewis Carroll version of '*product*', i.e. *destination*, which is marketed as though it were physically obtainable. If only tropical islands and redwood forests *could* be purchased for the price of an airline ticket!

The model can be completed by adding the remaining major marketing elements in a way that demonstrates their function vis-a-vis the organic core entity. First, the total entity is ringed and defined by a set value or price. Next, the valued entity is circumscribed by its distribution. Finally, the entire entity is encompassed according to its core configuration, by its public 'face', i.e. its positioning to the market.

The molecular concept makes it possible to describe and array market entities along a continuum, according to the weight of the 'mix' of elements that comprise them. As Figure 2 indicates, teaching services might be at one end of such a scale,

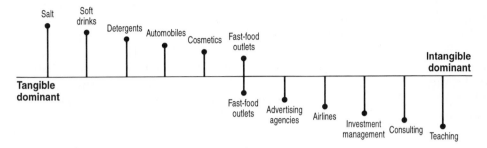

Figure 2. Scale of market entities.

intangible or I-dominant, while salt might represent the other extreme, *tangible or T-dominant.* Such a scale accords intangible-based entities a place and weight commensurate with their true importance. The framework also provides a mechanism for comparison and market positioning.

In one of the handful of books devoted to services, the author holds that 'the more intangible the service, the greater will be the difference in the marketing characteristics of the service.'[7] Consistent with an entity scale, this axiom might now be amended to read: *the greater the weight of intangible elements in a market entity, the greater will be the divergence from product marketing in priorities and approach.*

Implications of the molecular model

The hypothesis proposed by molecular modeling carries intriguing potential for rethinking and reshaping classic marketing concepts and practices. Recognition that service-dominant entities differ from product-dominant entities allows consideration of other distinctions which have been intuitively understood, but seldom articulated by service marketers.

A most important area of difference, is immediately apparent, i.e. that service 'knowledge' and product 'knowledge' cannot be gained in the same way.

A *product* marketer's first task is to 'know' his product. For tangible-dominant entities this is relatively straight-forward. A tangible object can be described precisely. It is subject to physical examination or photographic reproduction or quantitative measure. It can not only be exactly replicated, but also modified in precise and duplicate ways.

It is not particularly difficult for the marketer of *Coca-Cola,* for example, to summon all the facts regarding the product itself. He can and does make reasonable assumptions about the product's behavior, e.g. that it is consistent chemically to the taste, visually to the eye, and physically in its packaging. Any changes he might make in these three areas can be deliberately controlled for uniformity since they will be tangibly evident. In other words, the marketer can take the product's 'reality' for granted and move on to considerations of price, distribution, and advertising or promotion.

To gain *service* 'knowledge', however, or knowledge of a service element, where does one begin? It has been pointed out that intangible elements are dynamic, subjective, and ephemeral. They cannot be touched, tried on for size, or displayed on a shelf. They are exceedingly difficult to quantify.

Reverting to airline travel, precisely what *is* the service of air transportation to the potential purchaser? What 'percent' of airline travel is comfort? What 'percent' is fear or adventure? What *is* this service's 'reality' to its market? And how does that reality vary from segment to segment? Since this service exists only during the time in which it is rendered, the entity's true 'reality' must be defined experientially, not in engineering terms.

A new approach to service definition

Experiential definition is a little-explored area of marketing practice. A product-based marketer is in danger of assuming he understands an intangible-dominant entity when, in fact, he may only be projecting his *own* subjective version of 'reality'. And because there is no documented guidance on acquiring service-knowledge, the changes for error are magnified.

Case example

One short-lived mistake (with which the author is familiar) occurred recently in the trust department of a large commercial bank. The department head, being close to daily operations, understood 'investment management' as the combined work of hundreds of people, backed by the firm's stature, resources, and long history, With this 'reality' in mind, he concluded that the service could be better represented by professional salesmen, than through the traditional, but interruptive use of the portfolio manager as main client contact.

Three salesmen were hired, and given a training course in investments. They failed dismally, both in maintaining current client relationships and in producing new business for the firm. In hindsight, it became clear that the department head misunderstood the service's 'reality' as it was being experienced by his clients. To the clients, 'investment *management*' was found to mean 'investment *manager*', i.e. a single human being upon whom they depended for decisions and advice. No matter how well prepared, the professional salesman was not seen as an acceptable substitute by the majority of the market.

Visions of reality

Clearly, more than one version of 'reality' may be found in a service market. Therefore, the crux of service-knowledge is the description of the major *consensus realities* that define the service entity to various market segments. The determination of consensus realities should be a high priority for service marketers, and marketing should offer more concrete guidance and emphasis on this subject than it does.

To define the market-held 'realities' of a service requires a high tolerance for subjective, 'soft' data, combined with a rigidly objective attitude toward that data. To understand what a service entity is to a market, the marketer must undertake more initial research than is common in product marketing. More important, it will be research of a different kind than is the case in product marketing. The marketer must rely heavily on the tools and skills of psychology, sociology and other behavioral sciences – tools that in product marketing usually come into play in determining *image*, rather than fundamental 'reality'.

In developing the blueprint of a service entity's main elements, the marketer might find, for instance, that although tax return preparation is analogous to 'accurate mathematical computation' within his firm, it means 'freedom from responsibility' to one segment of the consuming public 'opportunity for financial savings' to another segment, and 'convenience' to yet a third segment.

Unless these 'realities' are documented and ranked by market importance, no sensible plan can be devised to represent a service effectively or deliberately. And in *new* service development, the importance of the service-research function is even more critical, because the successful development of a new service – a molecular collection of intangibles – is so difficult it makes new-product development look like child's play.

Image vs. evidence – the key

The definition of consensus realities should not be confused with the determination of 'image'. Image is a method of *differentiating* and *representing* an entity to its target market. Image is not 'product', nor is it 'service'. As was suggested in Figure 1, there appears to be a critical difference between the way tangible- and intangible-dominant entities are best represented to their markets. Examination of actual cases suggests a common thread among effective representations of services that is another mirror-opposite contrast to product techniques.

In comparing examples, it is clear that consumer product marketing often approaches the market by enhancing a physical object through abstract associations. *Coca-Cola*, for example, is surrounded with visual, verbal and aural associations with authenticity and youth. Although *Dr. Pepper* would also be physically categorized as a beverage, its *image* has been structured to suggest 'originality' and 'risk-taking', while *7-up* is 'light' and 'buoyant'. A high priority is placed on linking these abstract images to physical items.

But a service is already abstract. To compound the abstraction dilutes the 'reality' that the marketer is trying to enhance. Effective service representations appear to be turned 180° *away* from abstraction. The reason for this is that service images, and even service 'realities', appear to be shaped to a large extent by the things that the consumer can comprehend with his five senses – tangible things. But a service itself cannot be tangible, so reliance must be placed on *peripheral* clues.

Tangible clues are what allow the detective in a mystery novel to surmise events at the scene of a crime without having been present. Similarly, when a consumer attempts to judge a service, particularly before using or buying it, that service is 'known' by the tangible clues, the tangible evidence, that surround it.

The management of tangible evidence is not articulated in marketing as a primary priority for service marketers. There has been little in-depth exploration of the *range* of authority that emphasis on tangible evidence would create for the service marketer. In product marketing, tangible evidence is primarily the product itself. But for services, tangible evidence would encompass broader considerations in contrast to product marketing, *different* considerations than are typically considered marketing's domain today.

Focusing on the evidence

In *product* marketing, many kinds of evidence are beyond the marketer's control and are consequently omitted from priority consideration in the market positioning process. Product marketing tends to give first emphasis to creating *abstract* associations.

Service marketers, on the other hand, should be focused on enhancing and differentiating 'realities' through manipulation of *tangible* clues. The management of evidence comes first for service marketers, because service 'reality' is arrived at by the consumer mostly through a process of deduction, based on the total impression that the evidence creates. Because of product marketing's biases, service marketers often fail to recognize the unique forms of evidence that they *can* normally control and fail to see that they should be part of marketing's responsibilities.

MANAGEMENT OF THE ENVIRONMENT

Environment is a good example. Since product distribution normally means shipping to outside agents, the marketer has little voice in structuring the environment in which the product is sold. His major controllable impact on the environment is usually product packaging. Services, on the other hand, are often fully integrated with environment; that is, the setting in which the service is 'distributed' *is* controllable. To the extent possible, management of the physical environment should be one of a service marketer's highest priorities.

Setting can play an enormous role in influencing the 'reality' of a service in the consumer's mind. Marketing does not emphasize this rule for services, yet there are numerous obvious examples of its importance.

Physician's offices provide an interesting example of intuitive environmental management. Although the quality of medical service may be identical, an office furnished in teak and leather creates a totally different 'reality' in the consumer's mind from one with plastic slipcovers and inexpensive prints. Carrying the example further, a marketer could expect to cause change in the service's image simply by painting a physician's office walls neon pink or silver, instead of white.

Similarly, although the services may be identical, the consumer's differentiation between 'Bank A Service' and 'Bank B Service' is materially affected by whether the environment is dominated by butcher-block and bright colors or by marble and polished brass.

By understanding the importance of evidence management, the service marketer can make it his business to review and take control of this critical part of his 'mix'. Creation of environment can be deliberate, rather than accidental or as a result of leaving such decisions in the hands of the interior decorators.

Integrating evidence

Going beyond environment, evidence can be integrated across a wide range of items. Airlines, for example, manage and coordinate tangible evidence, and do it better than almost any large service industry. Whether by intuition or design, airlines do *not* focus attention on trying to explain or characterize the service itself. One never sees an ad that attempts to convey 'the slant of takeoff', 'the feel of acceleration', or 'the aerodynamics of lift'. Airline transport is given shape and form through consistency of a firm's identification, its uniforms, the decor of its planes, its graphics, and its advertising. Differentiation among airlines, though they all provide the same service, is a direct result of differences in 'packages' of evidence.

Some businesses in which tangible and intangible elements carry equal weight emphasize abstractions and evidence in about equal proportions. McDonald's is an excellent example. The food *product* is associated with 'nutritious' (two all-beef, etc.), 'fun' (Ronald McDonald) and 'helpful' ('We Do it All for You', 'You Deserve a Break Today'). The main *service* element, i.e. fast food preparation, is tangibly distinguished by uniformity of environment, color, and style of graphics and apparel, consistency of delivery (young employees), and the ubiquitous golden arches.

Using the scale developed in Figure 2, this concept can be postulated as a principle for service representation. As shown in Figure 3, once an entity has been analyzed and positioned on the scale, the degree to which the marketer will focus on either tangible evidence or intangible abstractions for market positioning will be found to be *inversely related to the entity's dominance.*

The more intangible elements there are, the more the marketer must endeavor to stand in the consumer's shoes, thinking through and gaining control of *all* the inputs to the consumer's mind that can be classified as material evidence.

Some forms of evidence can seem trivial until one recognizes how great their impact can be on service perception. Correspondence is one example. Letters, statements, and the like are sometimes the main conveyers of the 'reality' of a service to its market; yet often these are treated as peripheral to any marketing plan. From the grade of paper to the choice of colors, correspondence is visible evidence that conveys a unique message. A mimeographed, non-personalized, cheaply offset letter

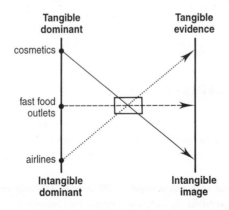

Figure 3. Principle of market positioning emphasis.

contradicts any words about service quality that may appear in the text of that letter. Conversely, engraved parchment from the local dry cleaner might make one wonder about their prices.

Profile as evidence

As was pointed out in the investment management example, services are often inextricably entwined with their human representatives. In many fields, a person is perceived to *be* the service. The consumer cannot distinguish between them. Product marketing is myopic in dealing with the issue of *people as evidence* in terms of market positioning. Consumer marketing often stops at the production of materials and programs for salesmen to use. Some service industries, on the other hand, have long intuitively managed human evidence to larger ends.

Examples of this principle have been the basis for jokes, plays, and literature. 'The Man in the Grey Flannel Suit', for example, was a synonym for the advertising business for many years. Physicians are uniformly 'packaged' in smocks. Lawyers and bankers are still today known for pin-stripes and vests. IBM representatives were famous for adhering to a 'White Shirt' policy. Going beyond apparel, as mentioned earlier, McDonald's even achieves age uniformity – an extra element reinforcing its total market image.

These examples add up to a serious principle when thoughtfully reviewed. They are particularly instructive for service marketers. None of the above examples were the result of deliberate market planning. McDonald's, for instance, backed into age consistency as a result of trying to keep labor costs low. Airlines are the single outstanding example of consciously-planned standards for uniformity in human representation. The power of the human evidence principle is obvious, and the potential power of more deliberately controlling or structuring this element is clear.

Lest this discussion be interpreted as an advocacy of regimentation, it should be pointed out that management of human evidence can be as basic as providing nametags to service representatives or as complex as the 'packaging' of a political candidate, whose very words are often chosen by committee and whose hair style can become a critical policy issue. Or, depending upon what kind of service 'reality' the marketer wishes to create, human representation can be encouraged to display *non-conformity*, as is the case with the 'creative' departments of advertising agencies. The point is that service marketers should be charged with tactics and strategy in this area, and must consider it a management responsibility.

SERVICES AND THE MEDIA

As has been previously discussed, service elements are abstract. Because they are abstract, the marketer must work hard at making them 'real', by building a case from tangible evidence. In this context, media advertising presents a particularly difficult problem.

The problem revolves around the fact that media (television, radio, print) are one step removed from tangibility. Media, by its McLuhanesque nature, abstracts the physical.

Even though product tangibility provides an anchor for media representation because a product can be *shown*, media still abstract products. A photograph is only a two-dimensional version of a physical object, and may be visually misleading. Fortunately, the consumer makes the mental connection between seeing a product in the media and recognizing it in reality. This is true even when a product is substantially distorted. Sometimes, only part of a product is shown. Occasionally, as in recent commercials for *7-up*, the product is *not* shown. However, the consumer remembers past experience. He has little difficulty recognizing *7-up* by name or remembered appearance when he sees it or wants to buy it.

Thus, media work *with* the creation of product image and *help* in adding abstract qualities to tangible goods. Cosmetics, for example, are often positioned in association with an airbrushed or soft-focus filmed *ideal* of beauty. Were the media truly accurate, the wrinkles and flaws of the flesh, to which even models are heir, might not create such an appealing product association.

Making services more concrete

Because of their abstracting capabilities, the media often make service entities more *hazy*, instead of more *concrete*, and the service marketer must work *against* this inherent effect. Unfortunately, many marketers are so familiar with product-oriented thinking that they go down precisely the wrong path and attempt to represent services by dealing with them in abstractions.

The pages of the business press are filled with examples of this type of misconception in services advertising. In advertisements for investment management, for instance, the worst examples attempt to describe the already intangible service with *more* abstractions such as 'sound analysis', 'careful portfolio monitoring', 'strong research capability', etc. Such compounded abstractions do *not* help the consumer form a 'reality', do *not* differentiate the service and do *not* achieve any credibility, much less any customer 'draw'.

The best examples are those which attempt to associate the service with some form of *tangible evidence*, working against the media's abstracting qualities. Merrill Lynch, for instance, has firmly associated itself with a clear visual symbol of bulls and concomitant bullishness. Where Merrill Lynch does not use the visual herd, it uses photographs of *tangible physical booklets*, and invites the consumer to write for them.

Therefore, the final principle offered for service marketers would hold that *effective media representation of intangibles is a function of establishing non-abstract manifestations of them.*

CONCLUSION

This article has presented several market-inspired thoughts toward the development of new marketing concepts, and the evolution of relevant service marketing principles. The hypotheses presented here do not by any means represent an exhaustive analysis of the subject. No exploration was done, for example, on product vs. service pricing or product vs. service distribution. Both areas offer rich potential for creative new approaches and analysis.

It can be argued that there are many grey areas in the molecular entity concept, and that diagramming and managing according to the multiple-elements schema could present considerable difficulties by virtue of its greater complexity. It might also be argued that some distinctions between tangible and intangible-dominant entities are so subtle as to be unimportant.

The fact remains that service marketers are in urgent need of concepts and priorities that are relevant to their actual experience and needs, and that marketing has failed in evolving to meet that demand. However unorthodox, continuing exploration of this area must be encouraged if marketing is to achieve stature and influence in the new post-Industrial Revolution services economy.

NOTES

1. See, for example, McCarthy, E. J. (1971) *Basic Marketing: A Managerial Approach*, 4th edn. Homewood, IL: Richard D. Irwin, p. 303, compared to Stanton, W. J. (1971) *Fundamentals of Marketing*, 3rd edn. New York: McGraw-Hill, p. 567.
2. See George, W. R. and Barksdale, H. C. (1974) 'Marketing Activities in the Service Industries'. *Journal of Marketing* **38** (October, No. 4): 65–70.
3. *The Meaning and Sources of Marketing Theory* (1965) Marketing Science Institute Series. New York: McGraw-Hill, p. 88.
4. *Webster's New Collegiate Dictionary* (1974) Springfield, MA: G&C Merriam Company.
5. Kotler, P. (1972) 'A Generic Concept of Marketing'. *Journal of Marketing* **36** (April, No. 2): 46–54.
6. Levitt, T. H. (1960) 'Marketing Myopia'. *Harvard Business Review* **38** (July–August): 45–46.
7. Wilson, A. (1972) *The Marketing of Professional Services*. New York: McGraw-Hill, p. 8.

2

Classifying Services to Gain Strategic Marketing Insights

Christopher H. Lovelock

INTRODUCTION

Developing professional skills in marketing management requires the ability to look across a broad cross-section of marketing situations, to understand their differences and commonalities, and to identify appropriate marketing strategies in each instance. In the manufacturing sector many experienced marketers have worked for a variety of companies in several different industries, often including both consumer goods and industrial firms. As a result, they have a perspective that transcends narrow industry boundaries.

But exposure to marketing problems and strategies in different industries is still quite rare among managers in the service sector. Not only is the concept of a formalized marketing function still relatively new to most service firms, but service industries have historically been somewhat inbred. The majority of railroad managers, for instance, have spent their entire working lives within the railroad industry – even within a single company. Most hoteliers have grown up in the hotel industry. And most hospital or college administrators have remained within the confines of health care or higher education, respectively. The net result of such narrow exposure is that it restricts a manager's ability to identify and learn from the experience of organizations facing parallel situations in other service industries – and, of course, from marketing experience in the manufacturing sector. Conversely, marketers from the manufacturing sector who take positions in service businesses often find that their past experience has not prepared them well for working on some of the problems that regularly challenge service marketers (Knisely, 1979; Lovelock, 1981; Shostack, 1977).

This article argues that development of greater sophistication in services marketing will be aided if we can find new ways to group services other than by current industry classifications. A more useful approach may be to segment services into clusters that share certain relevant marketing characteristics – such as the nature of the relationship between the service organization and its customers or patterns of demand relative to supply – and then to examine the implications for marketing action.

Reprinted with permission from *Journal of Marketing*, Vol. 47, Summer, pp. 9–20

After briefly reviewing the value of classification schemes in marketing, the article summarizes past proposals for classifying services. This is followed by presentation and discussion of five classification schemes based on past proposals, or on clinical research. In each instance examples are given of how various services fall into similar or different categories, and an evaluation is made of the resulting marketing insights and what they imply for marketing strategy development.

THE VALUE OF CLASSIFICATION IN MARKETING

Hunt (1976) has emphasized the usefulness of classification schemes in marketing. Various attempts have been made in the past by marketing theorists to classify goods into different categories. One of the most famous and enduring is Copeland's (1923) classification of convenience, shopping and speciality goods. Not only did this help managers obtain a better understanding of consumer needs and behavior, it also provided insights into the management of retail distribution systems. Bucklin (1963) and others have revised and refined Copeland's original classification and thereby been able to provide important strategic guidelines for retailers. Another major classification has been between durable and nondurable goods. Durability is closely associated with purchase frequency, which has important implications for development of both distribution and communications strategy. Yet another classification is consumer goods versus industrial goods: this classification relates both to the type of goods purchased (although there is some overlap) and to product evaluation, purchasing procedures and usage behavior. Recognition of these distinctions by marketers has led to different types of marketing strategy being directed at each of these groups. Through such classification the application of marketing management tools and strategies in manufacturing has become a professional skill that transcends industry divisions.

By contrast, service industries remain dominated by an operations orientation that insists that each industry is different. This mind set is often manifested in managerial attitudes that suggest, for example, that the marketing of airlines has nothing at all in common with that of banks, insurance, motels, hospitals or household movers. But if it can be shown that some of these services do share certain marketing relevant characteristics, then the stage may be set for some useful cross-fertilization of concepts and strategies.

How might services be classified?

Various attempts have been proposed in the past for classifying services and are outlined, with brief commentaries, in Table 1. But developing classification schemes is not enough. If they are to have managerial value, they must offer strategic insights. That is why it is important to develop ways of analyzing services that highlight the characteristics they have in common, and then to examine the implications for marketing management.

This article builds on past research by examining characteristics of services that transcend industry boundaries and are different in degree or kind from the

Table 1. Summary of previously proposed schemes for classifying services

Author	Proposed classification schemes	Comment
Judd (1964)	(1) Rented goods services (right to own and use a good for a defined time period) (2) Owned goods services (custom creation, repair or improvement of goods owned by the customer) (3) Nongoods services (personal experiences or 'experiential possession')	First two are fairly specific, but third category is very broad and ignores services such as insurance, banking, legal advice and accounting.
Rathmell (1974)	(1) Type of seller (2) Type of buyer (3) Buying motives (4) Buying practice (5) Degree of regulation	No specific application to services – could apply equally well to goods.
Shostack (1977)[a] Sasser et al.[a] (1978)	Proportion of physical goods and intangible services contained within each product 'package'	Offers opportunities for multiattribute modeling. Emphasizes that there are few pure goods or pure services.
Hill (1977)	(1) Services affecting persons vs. those affecting goods (2) Permanent vs. temporary effects of the service (3) Reversibility vs. nonreversibility of these effects (4) Physical effects vs. mental effects (5) Individual vs. collective services	Emphasizes nature of service benefits and (in 5), variations in the service delivery/consumption environment.
Thomas (1978)	(1) Primarily equipment based (a) automated (e.g. car wash) (b) monitored by unskilled operators (e.g. movie theater) (c) operated by skilled personnel (e.g. airline) (2) Primarily people-based (a) unskilled labor (e.g. lawn care) (b) skilled labor (e.g. repair work) (c) professional staff (e.g. lawyers, dentists)	Although operational rather than marketing in orientation, provides a useful way of understanding product attributes.
Chase (1978)	Extent of customer contact required in service delivery (a) high contact (e.g. health care, hotels, restaurants) (b) low contact (e.g. postal service, wholesaling)	Recognizes that product variability is harder to control in high contact services because customers exert more influence on timing of demand and service features, due to their greater involvement in the service process.
Kotler (1980)	(1) People-based vs. equipment-based (2) Extent to which client's presence is necessary (3) Meets personal needs vs. business needs (4) Public vs. private, for-profit vs. nonprofit	Synthesizes previous work, recognizes differences in purpose of service organization.

Continued overleaf

Table 1. – *(continued)*

Author	Proposed classification schemes	Comment

Lovelock (1980)	(1) Basic demands characteristics
	  – object served (persons vs. property)
	  – extent of demand/supply imbalances
	  – discrete vs. continuous relationships between customers and providers
	(2) Service content and benefits
	  – extent of physical goods content
	  – extent of personal service content
	  – single service vs. bundle of services
	  – timing and duration of benefits
	(3) Service delivery procedures
	  – multisite vs. single site delivery
	  – allocation of capacity (reservations vs. first come, first served)
	  – independent vs. collective consumption
	  – time defined vs. task defined transactions
	  – extent to which customers must be present during service delivery
		Synthesizes previous classifications and adds several new schemes. Proposes several categories within each classification. Concludes that defining object served is most fundamental classification scheme. Suggests that valuable marketing insights would come from combining two or more classification schemes in a matrix.

*These were two independent studies that drew broadly similar conclusions.

categorization schemes traditionally applied to manufactured goods. Five classification schemes have been selected for presentation and discussion, reflecting their potential for affecting the way marketing management strategies are developed and implemented. Each represents an attempt to answer one of the following questions:

1. What is the nature of the service act?
2. What type of relationship does the service organization have with its customers?
3. How much room is there for customization and judgment on the part of the service provider?
4. What is the nature of demand and supply for the service?
5. How is the service delivered?

Each question will be examined on two dimensions, reflecting my conclusion in an earlier study (Lovelock, 1980) that combining classification schemes in a matrix may yield better marketing insights than classifying service organizations on one variable at a time.

WHAT IS THE NATURE OF THE SERVICE ACT?

A service has been described as a 'deed, act or performance' (Berry, 1980). Two fundamental issues are at whom (or what) is the act directed, and is this act tangible or intangible in nature?

As shown in Figure 1, these two questions result in a four-way classification

What is the nature of the service act?	Who or what is the direct recipient of the service?	
	People	Things
Tangible actions	Services directed at people's bodies: ● health care ● passenger transportation ● beauty salons ● exercise clinics ● restaurants ● haircutting	Services directed at goods and other physical possessions: ● freight transportation ● industrial equipment repair and maintenance ● janitorial services ● laundry and dry cleaning ● landscaping/lawn care ● veterinary care
Intangible actions	Services directed at people's minds: ● education ● broadcasting ● information services ● theaters ● museums	Services directed at intangible assets: ● banking ● legal services ● accounting ● securities ● insurance

Figure 1. Understanding the nature of the service act.

scheme involving (1) tangible actions to people's bodies, such as airline transportation, haircutting and surgery; (2) tangible actions to goods and other physical possessions, such as air freight, lawn mowing and janitorial services; (3) intangible actions directed at people's minds, such as broadcasting and education; and (4) intangible actions directed at people's intangible assets, such as insurance, investment banking and consulting.

Sometimes a service may seem to spill over into two or more categories. For instance, the delivery of educational, religious or entertainment services (directed primarily at the mind) often entails tangible actions such as being in a classroom, church or theater: the delivery of financial services may require a visit to a bank to transform intangible financial assets into hard cash; and the delivery of airline services may affect some travelers' states of mind as well as physically moving their bodies from one airport to another. But in most instances the core service act is confined to one of the four categories, although there may be secondary acts in another category.

Insights and implications

Why is this categorization scheme useful to service marketers? Basically it helps answer the following questions:

1. Does the customer need to be *physically* present:
   (a) throughout service delivery?
   (b) only to initiate or terminate the service transaction (e.g. dropping off a car for repair and picking it up again afterwards)?
   (c) not at all (the relationship with the service supplier can be at arm's length through the mails, telephone or other electronic media)?

2. Does the customer need to be *mentally* present during service delivery? Can mental presence be maintained across physical distances through mail or electronic communications?
3. In what ways is the target of the service act 'modified' by receipt of the service? And how does the customer benefit from these 'modifications'?

It is not always obvious what the service is and what it does for the customer because services are ephemeral. By identifying the target of the service and then examining how it is 'modified' or changed by receipt of the service act, we can develop a better understanding of the nature of the service product and the core benefits that it offers. For instance, a haircut leaves the recipient with shorter and presumably more appealingly styled hair, air freight gets the customer's goods speedily and safely between two points, a news radio broadcast updates the listener's mind about recent events, and life insurance protects the future value of the insured person's assets.

If customers need to be physically present during service delivery, then they must enter the service 'factory' (whether it be a train, a hairdressing salon, or a hospital at a particular location) and spend time there while the service is performed. Their satisfaction with the service will be influenced by the interactions they have with service personnel, the nature of the service facilities, and also perhaps by the characteristics of other customers using the same service. Questions of location and schedule convenience assume great importance when a customer has to be physically present or must appear in person to initiate and terminate the transaction.

Dealing with a service organization at arm's length, by contrast, may mean that a customer never sees the service facilities at all and may not even meet the service personnel face-to-face. In this sort of situation, the outcome of the service act remains very important, but the process of service delivery may be of little interest, since the customer never goes near the 'factory'. For instance, credit cards and many types of insurance can be obtained by mail or telephone.

For operational reasons it may be very desirable to get the customer out of the factory and to transform a 'high-contact' service into a 'low-contact' one (Chase, 1978). The chances of success in such an endeavor will be enhanced when the new procedures also offer customers greater convenience. Many services directed at *things* rather than at people formerly required the customer's presence but are now delivered at arm's length. Certain financial services have long used the mails to save customers the inconvenience of personal visits to a specific office location. Today, new electronic distribution channels have made it possible to offer instantaneous delivery of financial services to a wide array of alternative locations. Retail banking provides a good example, with its growing use of such electronic delivery systems as automatic teller machines in airports or shopping centers, pay-by-phone bill paying, or on-line banking facilities in retail stores.

By thinking creatively about the nature of their services, managers of service organizations may be able to identify opportunities for alternative, more convenient forms of service delivery or even for transformation of the service into a manufactured good. For instance, services to the mind such as education do not necessarily require attendance in person since they can be delivered through the mails of electronic media (Britain's Open University, which makes extensive use of television and radio broadcasts, is a prime example). Two-way communication hookups can make it possible for a physically distant teacher and students to interact directly where this is necessary to the educational process (one recent Bell System advertisement featured a chamber music class in a small town being taught by an instructor several hundred miles away). Alternatively, lectures can be packaged and sold as books, records or videotapes. And in programmed learning exercises can be developed in computerized form, with the terminal serving as a Socratic surrogate.

WHAT TYPE OF RELATIONSHIP DOES THE SERVICE ORGANIZATION HAVE WITH ITS CUSTOMERS?

With very few exceptions, consumers buy manufactured goods at discrete intervals, paying for each purchase separately and rarely entering into a formal relationship with the manufacturer. (Industrial purchasers, by contrast, often enter into long-term relationships with suppliers and sometimes receive almost continuous delivery of certain supplies).

In the service sector both household and institutional purchasers may enter into ongoing relationships with service suppliers and may receive service on a continuing basis. This offers a way of categorizing services. We can ask, does the service organization enter into a 'membership' relationship with its customers – as in telephone subscriptions, banking and the family doctor – or is there no formal relationship? And is service delivered on a continuous basis – as in insurance, broadcasting and police protection – or is each transaction recorded and charged separately? Figure 2 shows the 2 × 2 matrix resulting from this categorization, with some additional examples in each category.

Insights and implications

The advantage to the service organization of a membership relationship is that it knows who its current customers are and, usually, what use they make of the services

Nature of service delivery	Type of relationship between the service organization and its customers	
	Membership relationship	No formal relationship
Continuous delivery of service	insurance telephone subscription college enrollment banking American Automobile Association	radio station police protection lighthouse public highway
Discrete transactions	long-distance phone calls theater series subscription commuter ticket or transit pass	car rental mail service toll highway pay phone movie theater public transportation restaurant

Figure 2. Relationships with customers.

offered. This can be valuable for segmentation purposes if good records are kept and the data are readily accessible in a format that lends itself to computerized analysis. Knowing the identities and addresses of current customers enables the organization to make effective use of direct mail, telephone selling and personal sales calls – all highly targeted marketing communications media.

The nature of service relationships also has important implications for pricing. In situations where service is offered on an ongoing basis, there is often just a single periodic charge covering all services contracted for. Most insurance policies fall in this category, as do tuition and board fees at a residential college. The big advantage of this package approach is its simplicity. Some memberships, however, entail a series of separate and identifiable transactions with the price paid being tied explicitly to the number and type of such transactions. While more complex to administer, such an approach is fairer to customers (whose usage patterns may vary widely) and may discourage wasteful use of what are perceived as 'free' services. In such instances, members may be offered advantages over casual users, such as discounted rates (telephone subscribers pay less for long-distance calls make from their own phones than do pay phone users) or advance notification and priority reservations (as in theater subscriptions). Some membership services offer certain services (such as rental of equipment or connection to a public utility system) for a base fee and then make incremental charges for each separate transaction above a defined minimum.

Profitability and customer convenience are central issues in deciding how to price membership services. Will the organization generate greater long term profits by tying payment explicitly to consumption, by charging a flat rate regardless of consumption, or by unbundling the components of the service and charging a flat rate for some and an incremental rate for others? Telephone and electricity services for instance, typically charge a base fee for connection to the system and rental of equipment, plus a variety of incremental charges for consumption above a defined minimum. On the other hand, Wide Area Telephone Service (WATS) offers the convenience of unlimited long-distance calling for a fixed fee. How important is it to customers to have the convenience of paying a single periodic fee that is known in advance? For instance, members of the American Automobile Association (AAA) can obtain information booklets, travel advice and certain types of emergency road services free of additional charges. Such a package offers elements of both insurance and convenience to customers who may not be able to predict their exact needs in advance.

Where no formal relationship exists between supplier and customer, continuous delivery of the product is normally found only among that class of services that economists term 'public goods' – such as broadcasting, police and lighthouse services, and public highways – where no charge is made for use of a service that is continuously available and financed from tax revenues. Discrete transactions, where each usage involves a payment to the service supplier by an essentially 'anonymous' consumer, are exemplified by many transportation services, restaurants, movie theaters, show repairs and so forth. The problem of such services is that marketers tend to be much less well-informed about who their customers are and what use each customer makes of the service than their counterparts in membership organizations.

Membership relationships usually result in customer loyalty to a particular service supplier (sometimes there is no choice because the supplier has a monopoly). As a marketing strategy, many service businesses seek ways to develop formal, ongoing relations with customers in order to ensure repeat business and/or ongoing financial support. Public radio and television broadcasters, for instance, develop membership clubs for donors and offer monthly program guides in return: performing arts organizations sell subscription series: transit agencies offer monthly passes; airlines create clubs for high mileage fliers; and hotels develop 'executive service plans' offering priority reservations and upgraded rooms for frequent guests. The marketing task here is to determine how it might be possible to build sales and revenues through such memberships but to avoid requiring membership when this would result in freezing out a large volume of desirable casual business.

HOW MUCH ROOM IS THERE FOR CUSTOMIZATION AND JUDGMENT?

Relatively few consumer goods nowadays are built to special order, most are purchased 'off the shelf'. The same is true for a majority of industrial goods, although by permutating options it is possible to give the impression of customization. Once they have purchased their goods, of course, customers are usually free to use them as they see fit.

The situation in the service sector, by contrast, is sharply different. Because services are created as they are consumed, and because the customer is often actually involved in the production process, there is far more scope for tailoring the service to meet the needs of individual customers. As shown in Figure 3, customization can proceed along at least two dimensions. The first concerns the extent to which the characteristics of the service and its delivery system lend themselves to customization; the second relates to how much judgment customer contact personnel are able to exercise in defining the nature of the service received by individual customers.

Some service concepts are quite standardized. Public transportation, for instance, runs over fixed routes on predetermined schedules. Routine appliance repairs typically involve a fixed charge, and the customer is responsible for dropping of the item at a given retail location and picking it up again afterwards. Fast food

Extent to which customer contact personnel exercise judgment in meeting individual customer needs	Extent to which service characteristics are customized	
	High	Low
High	legal services health care/surgery architectural design executive search firm real estate agency taxi service beautician plumber education (tutorials)	education (large classes) preventative health programs
Low	telephone service hotel services retail banking (excl. major loans) good restaurant	public transportation routine appliance repair fast food restaurant movie theater spectator sports

Figure 3.   Customization and judgment in service delivery.

restaurants have a small, set menu; few offer the customer much choice in how the food will be cooked and served. Movies, entertainment and spectator sports place the audience in a relatively passive role, albeit a sometimes noisy one.

Other services offer customers a wide choice of options. Each telephone subscriber enjoys an individual number and can use the phone to obtain a broad array of different services – from receiving personal calls, from a next-door neighbor to calling a business associate on the other side of the world, and from data transmission to dial-a-prayer. Retail bank accounts are also customized, with each check or bank card carrying the customer's name and personal code. Within the constraints set down by the bank, the customer enjoys considerable latitude in how and when the account is used and receives a personalized monthly statement. Good hotels and restaurants usually offer their customers an array of service options from which to choose, as well as considerable flexibility in how the service product is delivered to them.

But in each of these instances, the role of the customer contact personnel (if there are any) is somewhat constrained. Other than tailoring their personal manner to the customer and answering straightforward questions, contact personnel have relatively little discretion in altering the characteristics of the service they deliver; their role is basically that of operator or order taker. Judgment and discretion in customer dealings is usually reserved for managers or supervisors who will not normally become involved in service delivery unless a problem arises.

A third category of services gives the customer contact personnel wide latitude in how they deliver the service, yet these individuals do not significantly differentiate the characteristics of their service between one customer and another. For instance, educators who teach courses by lectures and give multiple choice, computer scored exams expose each of their students to a potentially similar experience, yet one professor may elect to teach a specific course in a very different way from a colleague at the same institution.

However, there is a class of services that not only involves a high degree of customization but also requires customer contact personnel to exercise judgment concerning the characteristics of the service and how it is delivered to each customer. Far from being reactive in their dealings with customers, these service personnel are often prescriptive: users (or clients) look to them for advice as well as for customized execution. In this category the locus of control shifts from the user to the supplier – a situation that some customers may find disconcerting. Consumers of surgical services literally place their lives in the surgeon's hands (the same, unfortunately, is also true of taxi services in many cities). Professional services such as law, medicine, accounting and architecture fall within this category. They are all white collar 'knowledge industries', requiring extensive training to develop the requisite skills and judgment needed for satisfactory service delivery. Deliverers of such services as taxi drivers, beauticians and plumbers are also found in this category. Their work is customized to the situation at hand and in each instance, the customer purchases the expertise required to devise a tailor-made solution.

Insights and implications

To a much greater degree than in the manufacturing sector, service products are 'custom-made'. Yet customization has its costs. Service management often represents an ongoing struggle between the desires of marketing managers to add value and the goals of operations managers to reduce costs through standardization. Resolving such disputes, a task that may require arbitration by the general manager, requires a good understanding of consumer choice criteria, particularly as these relate to price/value trade-offs and competitive positioning strategy. At the present time, most senior managers in service businesses have come up through the operations route: hence, participation in executive education programs may be needed to give them the necessary perspective on marketing to make balanced decisions.

Customization is not necessarily important to success. As Levitt (1972, 1976) has pointed out, industrializing a service to take advantage of the economies of mass production may actually increase consumer satisfaction. Speed, consistency and price savings may be more important to many customers than customized service. In some instances, such as spectator sports and the performing arts, part of the product experience is sharing the service with many other people. In other instances the customer expects to share the service facilities with other consumers, as in hotels or airlines, yet still hopes for some individual recognition and custom treatment. Allowing customers to reserve specific rooms or seats in advance, having contact personnel address them by name (it is on their ticket or reservation slip), and providing some latitude for individual choice (room service and morning calls, drinks and meals) are all ways to create an image of customization.

Generally, customers like to know in advance what they are buying – what the product features are, what the service will do for them. Surprises and uncertainty are not normally popular. Yet when the nature of the service requires a judgment-based, customized solution, as in a professional service, it is not always clear to either the customer or the professional what the outcome will be. Frequently, an important dimension of the professional's role is diagnosing the nature of the situation, then designing a solution.

In such situations those responsible for developing marketing strategy would do well to recognize that customers may be uneasy concerning the prior lack of certainty about the outcome. Customer contact personnel in these instances are not only part of the product but also determine what that product should be.

One solution to this problem is to divide the product into two separate components, diagnosis and implementation of a solution, that are executed and paid for separately. The process of diagnosis can and should be explained to the customer in advance, since the outcome of the diagnosis cannot always be predicted accurately. However, once that diagnosis has been made, the customer need not proceed immediately with the proposed solution: indeed, there is always the option of seeking a second opinion. The solution 'product', by contrast, can often be spelled out in detail beforehand, so that the customer has a reasonable idea of what to expect. Although there may still be some uncertainty, as in legal actions or medical treatment, the range of possibilities should be narrower by this point, and it may be feasible to assign probabilities to specified alternative outcomes.

Marketing efforts may need to focus on the process of client-provider interactions. It will help prospective clients make choices between alternative suppliers, especially where professionals are concerned, if they know something of the organization's (or individual's) approach to diagnosis and problem-solving, as well as client-relationship style. These are considerations that transcend mere statements of qualification in an advertisement or brochure. For instance, some pediatricians allow new parents time for a free interview before any commitments are made. Such a trial encounter has the advantage of allowing both parents to decide whether or not a good match exists.

WHAT IS THE NATURE OF DEMAND AND SUPPLY FOR THE SERVICE?

Manufacturing firms can inventory supplies of their products as a hedge against fluctuations in demand. This enables them to enjoy the economies derived from operating plants at a steady level of production. Service businesses cannot do this because it is not possible to inventory the finished service. For instance, the potential income from an empty seat of an airline flight is lost forever once that flight takes off, and each hotel daily room vacancy is equally perishable. Likewise, the productive capacity of an auto repair shop is wasted if no one brings a car for servicing on a day when the shop is open. Conversely, if the demand for a service exceeds supply on a particular day, the excess business may be lost. Thus, if someone cannot get a seat on one airline, another carrier gets the business or the trip is cancelled or postponed. If an accounting firm is too busy to accept tax and audit work from a prospective client, another firm will get the assignment.

But demand and supply imbalances are not found in all service situations. A useful way of categorizing services for this purpose is shown in Figure 4. The horizontal axis classifies organizations according to whether demand for the service fluctuates widely or narrowly over time; the vertical axis classifies them according to whether or not capacity is sufficient to meet peak demand.

Organization in Box 1 could use increases in demand outside peak periods, those in Box 2 must decide whether to seek continued growth in demand and capacity or to continue the status quo, while those in Box 3 represent growing organizations that may need temporary demarketing until capacity can be increased to meet or exceed current demand levels. But service organizations in Box 4 face an ongoing problem of trying to smooth demand to match capacity, involving both stimulation and discouragement of demand.

Extent to which supply is constrained	Extent of demand fluctuations over time	
	Wide	Narrow
Peak demand can usually be met without a major delay	1 electricity natural gas telephone hospital maternity unit police and fire emergencies	2 insurance legal services banking laundry and dry cleaning
Peak demand regularly exceeds capacity	4 accounting and tax preparation passenger transportation hotels and motels restaurants theaters	3 services similar to those in 2 but which have insufficient capacity for their base level of business

Figure 4.   What is the nature of demand for the service relative to supply?

Insights and implications

Managing demand is a task faced by nearly all marketers, whether offering goods or services. Even where the fluctuations are sharp, inventories cannot be used to act as a buffer between supply and demand, it may still be possible to manage capacity in a service business – for instance, by hiring part time employees or renting extra facilities at peak periods. But for a substantial group of service organizations, successfully managing demand fluctuations through marketing actions is the key to profitability.

To determine the most appropriate strategy in each instance, it is necessary to seek answers to some additional questions:

1. What is the typical cycle period of these demand fluctuations?
   - predictable (i.e. demand varies by hour of the day, day of the week or month, season of the year).
   - random (i.e. no apparent pattern to demand fluctuations).
2. What are the underlying causes of these demand fluctuations?
   - customer habits or preferences (could marketing efforts change these?)
   - actions by third parties (for instance, employers set working hours, hence marketing efforts might usefully be directed at those employers).
   - nonforecastable events, such as health symptoms, weather conditions, acts of God and so forth – marketing can do only a few things about these, such as offering priority services to members and disseminating information about alternative services to other people.

One way to smooth out the ups and downs of demand is through strategies that encourage customers to change their plans voluntarily, such as offering special discount prices or added product value during periods of low demand. Another approach is to ration demand through a reservation or queuing system (which basically inventories demand rather than supply). Alternatively, to generate demand in period of excess capacity, new business development efforts might be targeted at prospective customers with a countercyclical demand pattern. For instance, an accounting firm with a surfeit of work at the end of each calendar year might seek new customers whose financial year ended on June 30 or September 30.

Determining what strategy is appropriate requires an understanding of who or what is the target of the service (as discussed in an earlier section of this article). If the service is delivered to customers in person there are limits to how long a customer will wait in line: hence strategies to inventory or ration demand should focus on adoption of reservation systems (Sasser, 1976). But if the service is delivered to goods or to intangible assets, then a strategy of inventorying demand should be more feasible (unless the good is a vital necessity such as a car, in which case reservations may be the best approach).

HOW IS THE SERVICE DELIVERED?

Understanding distribution issues in service marketing requires that two basic issues be addressed. The first relates to the method of delivery. Is it necessary for the customer to be in direct physical contact with the service organization (customers may have to go to the service organization, or the latter may come to the former), or can transactions be completed at arm's length? And does the service organization maintain just a single outlet or does it serve customers through multiple outlets at different sites? The outcome of this analysis can be seen in Figure 5, which consists of six different cells.

Nature of interaction between customer and service organization	Availability of service outlets	
	Single site	Multiple set
Customer goes to service organization	theater barbershop	bus service fast food chain
Service organization comes to customer	lawn care service pest control service taxi	mail delivery AAA emergency repairs
Customer and service organization transact at arm's length (mail or electronic communications)	credit card company local TV station	broadcast network telephone company

Figure 5.   Method of service delivery.

Insights and implications

The convenience of receiving service is presumably lowest when a customer has to come to the service organization and must use a specific outlet. Offering service through several outlets increases the convenience of access for customers but may start to raise problems of quality control as convenience of access relates to the consistency of the service product delivered. For some types of services the organization will come to the customer. This is, of course, essential when the target of the service is some immovable physical item (such as a building that needs repairs or pest control treatment, or a garden that needs landscaping). But since it is usually more expensive to take service personnel and equipment to the customer than vice versa, the trend has been away from this approach to delivering consumer services (e.g., doctors no longer like to make house calls). In many instances, however, direct contact between customers and the service organization is not necessary; instead, transactions can be handled at arm's length by mail or electronic communications. Through the use of 800 numbers many service organizations have found that they can bring their services as close as the nearest telephone, yet obtain important economies from operating out of a single physical location.

Although not all services can be delivered through arm's length transactions, it may be possible to separate certain components of the service from the core product and to handle them separately. This suggests an additional classification scheme: categorizing services according to whether transactions such as obtaining information, making reservations and making payment can be broken out separately from delivery of the core service. If they can be separated, then the question is whether or not is is advantageous to the service firm to allow customers to make these peripheral transactions through an intermediary or broker.

For instance, information about airline flights, reservations for such flights and purchases of tickets can all be made through a travel agent as well as directly through the airline. For those who prefer to visit in person, rather than conduct business by telephoning, this greatly increases the geographic coverage of distribution, since there are usually several travel agencies located more conveniently than the nearest airline office. Added value from using a travel agent comes from the 'one-stop shopping' aspect of travel agents; the customer can inquire about several airlines and make car rental and hotel reservations during the same call. Insurance brokers and theater ticket agencies are also examples of specialist intermediaries that represent a number of different service organizations. Consumers sometimes perceive such intermediaries as more objective and more knowledgeable about alternatives than the various service suppliers they represent. The risk to the service firm of working through specialist intermediaries is, of course, that they may recommend use of a competitor's product!

DISCUSSION

Widespread interest in the marketing of services among both academics and practitioners is a relatively recent phenomenon. Possibly this reflects the fact that marketing expertise in the service sector has significantly lagged behind that in the manufacturing sector. Up to now most academic research and discussion has centered on the issue, 'How do services differ from goods?' A number of authors including Shostack (1977). Bateson (1979) and Berry (1980) have argued that there are significant distinctions between the two and have proposed several generalizations for management practice. But others such as Enis and Roering (1981) remain unconvinced that these differences have meaningful strategic implications.

Rather than continue to debate the existence of this broad dichotomy, it seems more useful to get on with the task of helping managers in service businesses do a better job of developing and marketing their products. We need to recognize that the service sector, particularly in the United States, is becoming increasingly competitive (Langeard et al., 1981), reflecting such developments as the partial or complete deregulation of several major service industries in recent years, the removal of professional association restrictions on using marketing techniques (particularly advertising), the replacement (or absorption) of independent service units by franchise chains, and the growth of new electronic delivery systems. As competition intensifies within the service sector, the development of more effective marketing efforts becomes essential to survival.

The classification schemes proposed in this article can contribute usefully to management practice in two ways. First, by addressing each of the five questions posed earlier, marketing managers can obtain a better understanding of the nature of their product, of the types of relationships their service organizations have with customers, of the factors underlying any sharp variations in demand, and of the characteristics of their service delivery systems. This understanding should help them identify how these factors shape marketing problems and opportunities and thereby affect the nature of the marketing task. Second, by recognizing which characteristics their own service shares with other services, often in seemingly unrelated industries, managers will learn to look beyond their immediate competitors for new ideas as to how to resolve marketing problems that they share in common with firms in other service industries.

Recognizing that the products of service organizations previously considered as 'different' actually face similar problems or share certain characteristics in common can yield valuable managerial insights. Innovation in marketing, after all, often reflects a manager's ability to seek out and learn from analogous situations in other contexts. These classification schemes should also be of value to researchers to whom they offer an alternative to either broad-brush research into services or an industry-by-industry approach. Instead, they suggest a variety of new ways of looking at service businesses, each of which may offer opportunities for focused research efforts. Undoubtedly there is also room for further refinement of the schemes proposed.

REFERENCES

Bateson, J. E. G. (1979) 'Why We Need Service Marketing'. In *Conceptual and Theoretical Developments in Marketing* (O. C. Ferrell, S. W. Brown and C. W. Lamb, Eds). Chicago: American Marketing Association, pp. 131–146.

Berry, L. L. (1980) 'Services Marketing is Different'. *Business Week* (May–June): 24–29.

Bucklin, L. (1963) 'Retail Strategy and the Classification of Consumer Goods'. *Journal of Marketing* 27 (January): 50.

Chase, R. B. (1978) 'Where Does the Customer Fit in a Service Operation?'. *Harvard Business Review* 56 (November–December): 137–142.

Copeland, M. T. (1923) 'The Relation of Consumers' Buying Habits to Marketing Methods'. *Harvard Business Review* 1 (April): 282–289.

Enis, B. M. and Roering, K. J. (1981) 'Services Marketing: Different Products, Similar Strategies'. In *Marketing of Services* (J. H. Donnelly and W. R. George, Eds). Chicago: American Marketing Association.

Hill, T. P. (1977) 'On Goods and Services'. *Review of Income and Wealth* 23 (December): 315–338.

Hunt, S. D. (1976) *Marketing Theory*. Columbus, OH: Grid.

Judd, R. C. (1964) 'The Case for Redefining Services'. *Journal of Marketing* 28 (January): 59.

Knisely, G. (1979) 'Marketing and the Services Industry'. *Advertising Age* (January 15), 47–50; (February 19), 54–60; (March 19), 58–62; (May 15), 57–58.

Kotler, P. (1980) *Principles of Marketing*. Englewood Cliffs, NJ: Prentice-Hall, Inc.

Langeard, E., Bateson, J. E. G., Lovelock, C. H. and Eiglier, P. (1981) *Services Marketing: New Insights from Consumers and Managers*. Cambridge, MA: Marketing Science Institute.

Levitt, T. (1972) 'Production Line Approach to Service'. *Harvard Business Review* 50 (September–October): 41.

Levitt, T. (1976) 'The Industrialization of Service'. *Harvard Business Review* 54 (September–October): 63–74.

Lovelock, C. H. (1980) 'Towards a Classification of Services'. In *Theoretical Developments in Marketing* (C. W. Lamb and P. M. Dunne, Eds) Chicago: American Marketing Association, pp. 72–76.

Lovelock, C. H. (1981) 'Why Marketing Management Needs to Be Different for Services'. In *Marketing of Services* (J. H. Donnelly and W. R. George, Eds). Chicago, IL: American Marketing Association.

Rathmell, J. M. (1974) *Marketing in the Service Sector*. Cambridge, MA: Winthrop.

Sasser, W. E. Jr. (1976) 'Match Supply and Demand in Service Industries'. *Harvard Business Review* 54 (November–December): 133.

Sasser, W. E. Jr., Olsen, R. P. and Wyckoff, D. D. (1978) *Management of Service Operations: Text and Cases*. Boston: Allyn & Bacon.

Shostack, G. L. (1977) 'Breaking Free from Product Marketing'. *Journal of Marketing* **41** (April): 73–80.

Thomas, D. R. E. (1978) 'Strategy Is Different in Service Businesses'. *Harvard Business Review* **56** (July–August): 158–165.

3

How Consumer Evaluation Processes Differ Between Goods and Services

Valarie A. Zeithaml

Services account for a large and growing proportion of economic activity. Providers of medical and legal services, haircuts, day care, entertainment, and education, among others, will proliferate to meet the growing demands for leisure and spending which accompany a rising standard of living. The primary objective of these service producers will be identical to that of all marketers: to develop and provide offerings that satisfy consumer needs, thereby ensuring their own economic survival.

To achieve this objective, service providers will need to understand how consumers choose and evaluate their offerings. Unfortunately, most of what is known about consumer evaluation processes pertains specifically to goods. The assumption appears to be that services, if not identical to goods, are at least similar enough in the consumer's mind that they are chosen and evaluated in the same manner. I propose to refute this assumption by showing that services' unique characteristics necessitate different consumer evaluation processes from those used when assessing goods.

SERVICES: SEARCH VERSUS EXPERIENCE VERSUS CREDENCE PROPERTIES?

One framework for isolating differences in evaluation processes between goods and services is the classification of qualities of goods proposed by economists Philip Nelson (1970) and Darby and Karni (1973). Nelson distinguishes between two categories of qualities of consumer goods: search qualities, attributes which a consumer can determine prior to purchasing a product; and experience qualities, attributes which can only be discerned after purchase or during consumption. Search qualities include attributes such as color, style, price, fit, feel, hardness, smell, while experience qualities include characteristics such as taste, wearability, purchase satisfaction. Some goods (e.g. clothing, furniture, and jewelry) are high in search qualities, for their attributes can be almost completely determined and evaluated prior to purchase. Other goods and services (e.g. vacations and restaurant meals) are high in experience qualities, for their attributes cannot be known or assessed until they have been purchased and are being consumed. Darby and Karni (1973) add to Nelson's two-way classification system a third category of qualities of goods, *credence* ✳ *qualities*, which are characteristics which the consumer may find impossible to evaluate even after purchase and consumption. Examples of offerings high in credence qualities include appendix operations and brake relinings on automobiles. Few consumers possess medical or mechanical skills sufficient to evaluate whether these services are necessary or are performed properly, even after they have been prescribed and produced by the seller.

Figure 1 arrays goods and services high in search, experience and credence qualities along a continuum of evaluation ranging from 'easy to evaluate' to 'difficult to evaluate'. At the left end of the continuum are goods high in search qualities, easiest to evaluate even before purchase. In the center are goods and services high in experience qualities, more difficult to evaluate because they must be purchased and consumed before assessment is possible. At the right end of the continuum are goods and services high in credence qualities, most difficult to evaluate because the consumer may be unaware of or may lack sufficient knowledge to appraise whether the offerings satisfy given wants or needs even after consumption.

The major premise of this paper is that most goods fall to the left of this continuum, while most services fall to the right due to three distinguishing characteristics. These distinguishing characteristics – intangibility, nonstandardization, and inseparability of production and consumption – make services more difficult to evaluate than goods. Difficulty in evaluation, in turn, forces consumers to rely on different cues and processes when evaluating services.

Several scholars detail the characteristics which distinguish services from products (Bessom, 1973; Rathmell, 1974; Eiglier *et al.*, 1977). *Intangibility* pertains to the

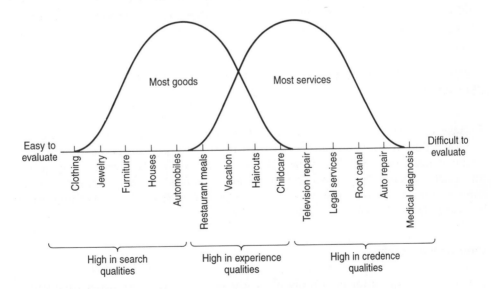

Figure 1. Continuum of evaluation for different types of products.

inability of services to be seen, felt, tasted, or touched in the same manner in which goods can be sensed. Services cannot be displayed, physically demonstrated or illustrated; therefore, they possess few search qualities and many experience qualities. *Nonstandardization* entails the inability of a producer to provide consistent performance and quality with a service. Since services cannot be inventoried, performance depends to some extent on level of demand; in periods of high demand, a service provider may not spend as much time or exert as much effort as in periods of low demand. Quality also may change from day to day because different employees perform the service, or because each employee's skills and moods vary. Nonstandardization results in high experience qualities, for consumers cannot be certain about performance on any given day, even if they use the same service provider on a regular basis. *Inseparability of production and consumption* constitutes the final characteristic which distinguishes goods and services. While tangible goods are produced, sold, and then consumed, services are sold, then produced and consumed simultaneously (Regan, 1963). Because of this inseparability, the buyer usually participates in producing the service, thereby affecting the performance and quality of the service. A doctor's accurate diagnosis, the desired haircut from a salon, effective stain removal from a dry cleaner – all these depend on the consumer's specification, communication, and participation in the production of the service. The quality of most services, and their ability to satisfy the consumer, depend not only on how well the service provider performs, but also on how well the consumer performs.

In sum, the inseparability, nonstandardization, and tangibility of services lead them to possess few search qualities and many experience qualities. Credence qualities also dominate in many services, especially those provided by professionals and specialists. While consumers may find it easy to evaluate the performance of everyday services (e.g. restaurant meals, housekeeping, or lawn care) prior to consumption, they may find it impossible to judge those performed by professionals and specialists with extensive training or experience in a specialized skill (e.g. medical diagnosis, television repair, or estate settlement).

SERVICES; SOME HYPOTHESES ABOUT CONSUMER EVALUATION PROCESSES

Because experience and credence qualities dominate in services, consumers may employ different evaluation processes than those they use with goods, where search qualities dominate. Specific areas where characteristics of services may lead to divergent evaluation processes are: information search, evaluative criteria, size and composition of the evoked set of alternatives, perceived risk, adoption of innovations, brand loyalty, and attribution of dissatisfaction.

Information search

Consumers obtain information about products and services from personal sources (e.g. friends or experts) and from nonpersonal sources (e.g. mass or selective media). When purchasing goods, consumers employ both nonpersonal sources since both effectively convey information qualities.

When purchasing services, on the other hand, consumers may seek to a greater extent on personal sources for several reasons. First, mass and selective media can convey information about search qualities but can communicate little about experience qualities. By asking friends or experts about services, however, the consumer can obtain information vicariously about experience qualities. Second, nonpersonal sources may not be available because: (1) many service providers are local, independent merchants with neither the experience nor the funds for advertising; (2) 'cooperative' advertising, or advertising funded jointly by the retailer and the manufacturer, is used rarely with services since most local providers are both producer and retailer of the service; and (3) professional associations banned advertising for so many years that some professionals and consumers tend to resist its use even though it is now permitted. Third, since consumers can discover few attributes prior to purchase of a service, they may feel greater risk to be associated with selecting an alternative. Given this risk, they may depend to a greater extent on sources such as word-of-mouth which they may perceive to be more credible and less biased.

Researchers suggest that personal sources might be more appropriate in situations where experience qualities dominate. Robertson (1971) claimed that personal influence becomes pivotal as product complexity increases and when objective standards by which to evaluate the product decrease (i.e. when experience qualities are high). Eiglier and Langeard et al. (1977) revealed that managers in four service industries believe word-of-mouth to have a great influence in services. Finally, many researchers (among them Perry and Hamm, 1969; Cunningham, 1967; Arndt, 1967) confirmed that the credibility of personal sources encourages their use in situations of high perceived risk.

Hypothesis 1: Consumers seek and rely more on information from personal sources than from nonpersonal sources when evaluating services prior to purchase.

Consumers may find post-purchase evaluation more essential with services than with goods because services possess experience qualities which cannot be adequately assessed prior to purchase. The dissonance-attribution model of audience response to communication (Ray, 1973) describes the situation which frequently occurs when consumers select services: (1) the consumer selects from among virtually indistinguishable alternatives; (2) through experience, the consumer develops an attitude toward the service; and (3) after the development of an attitude, the consumer learns more about the service by paying attention to messages supporting his choice. In contrast both to the learning response model and the low-involvement model (Ray, 1973), where consumers seek information and evaluate products prior to purchase, as they do with tangible goods, the dissonance-response model represents the case of services where most evaluation follows purchase.

Hypothesis 2: Consumers engage in greater post-purchase evaluation and information seeking with services than with products.

Hypothesis 3: Consumers engage in most post-purchase evaluation than pre-purchase evaluation when selecting and consuming services.

Criteria for evaluating quality

When purchasing goods, the consumer employs multiple cues to judge quality, among them style, color, label, feel, package, brand name, and price. When purchasing services, the consumer is limited to a small number of cues; in many cases, the only cues available on which to judge quality are the service's price and the physical facilities which house the service.

Plumbing, housekeeping, and lawn care are examples of services where price may be the only pre-purchase indicator of quality. Research (Tull, 1964; Olander, 1970; McConnell, 1968) demonstrates that when the price is the only information available, consumers use it to assess quality.

With other services (e.g. haircuts, legal aid, dental services, and weight reduction), consumers may base decisions about quality on the tangible evidence of the services: the physical facilities. Thus they may examine the offices, personnel, equipment, and paraphernalia used to perform the service in order to evaluate quality. The importance of physical facilities for this purpose has been emphasized by Eiglier *et al.* (1977), Bessom (1973), and others.

Hypothesis 4: Consumers use price and physical facilities as the major cues to service quality.

Evoked set

The evoked set of alternatives, that group of products which a consumer considers acceptable options in a given product category, is likely to be smaller with services than with goods. One reason for the reduced set involves differences in retailing between goods and services. To purchase goods, consumers generally shop in retail stores which display competing products in close proximity, clearly demonstrating the alternatives from which a consumer may select. To purchase services, on the other hand, the consumer visits a retail establishment (e.g. a bank, a dry cleaner, or a hair salon) which offers only a single 'brand' for sale. A second reason for the smaller evoked set is that consumers are unlikely to find more than one or two stores providing the same services in a given geographic area, whereas they may find numerous retail establishments in that same area carrying the identical manufacturer's product. A third reason for a smaller evoked set is the difficulty of obtaining adequate pre-purchase information about services.

Faced with the difficult task of collecting and evaluating experience qualities, consumers may satisfice by selecting the first acceptable alternative rather than maximize by considering and evaluating all available alternatives.

Hypothesis 5: The consumer's evoked set of alternatives is smaller with services than with products.

For nonprofessional services, consumers' decisions often entail choices between performing the services for themselves and hiring someone else to perform them. Working wives may choose between cleaning their own homes or hiring housekeepers, between altering their families' clothes or taking them to a tailor, even between staying home to take care of the children or engaging a day care center to provide child care. Many other services, including lawn care, tax preparation, and restaurant meals, involve decisions where consumers may consider themselves as sources of supply.

Hypothesis 6: For many nonprofessional services, the consumer's evoked set frequently includes self-provision of the service.

Innovation diffusion

The rate of diffusion of an innovation depends on consumer's perceptions of the innovation with regard to five characteristics: relative advantage, compatibility, communicability, divisibility, and complexity (Rogers, 1962). A product which has a relative advantage over existing or competing products, that is compatible with existing norms, values, and behaviors, that is communicable, and that is divisible (i.e. that can be tried or tested on a limited basis) diffuses more quickly than others. A product which is complex, i.e. difficult to understand or use, diffuses more slowly than others.

Considered as a group, services are less communicable, less divisible, more complex, and probably less compatible than goods. They are less communicable because they are intangible (e.g. their features cannot be displayed, illustrated, or compared) and because they are often unique to each buyer (as in a medical diagnosis or dental care). Services are less divisible because they are usually impossible to sample or test on a limited basis (e.g. how does one 'sample' a medical diagnosis? a lawyer's services in settling a divorce? even a haircut?). Services are frequently more complex than goods because they are composed of a bundle of different attributes, not all of which will be offered to every buyer on each purchase.

Finally, services may be incompatible with existing values and behaviors, especially if consumers are accustomed to providing the services for themselves. As an illustration, consider a novel day care center which cooks breakfast for children so that parents can arrive at work early. Mothers accustomed to performing this service for their children may resist adopting the innovation because it requires a change in habit, in behavior, even in values.

Hypothesis 7: Consumers adopt innovations in services more slowly than they adopt innovations in goods.

Perceived risk

Eiglier *et al.* (1977) report that French managers believe the level of perceived risk to be higher for consumers purchasing services as opposed to physical goods. While some degree of perceived risk probably accompanies all purchase transactions, more risk would appear to be involved in the purchase of services than in the purchase of goods because services are intangible, nonstandardized, and are usually sold without guarantees or warranties.

First, the intangible nature of services and their high levels of experience qualities imply that services generally must be selected on the basis of less pre-purchase information than is the case for products. Since research (Cox and Rich, 1967; Spence *et al.*, 1970; and others) suggests that a decrease in the amount and/or quality of information usually is accompanied by a concomitant increase in perceived risk, the purchasing of services may involve more perceived risk than the purchasing of goods.

Second, consumers may perceive more risk to be associated with the purchase of services because they are nonstandardized. Even though a consumer may have purchased the same service (e.g. haircut) many times in his or her lifetime, there will always be recurring uncertainty about the outcome and consequences each time the service is purchased.

Third, service purchases may involve more perceived risk than product purchases because, with few exceptions, services are not accompanied by warranties or guarantees. Dissatisfied service purchasers can rarely 'return' a service, since they have already consumed it by the time they realize their dissatisfaction.

Finally, many services (e.g. medical diagnosis or pest control) are so technical or specialized that consumers possess neither the knowledge nor the experience to evaluate whether they are satisfied, even after they have consumed the service.

Hypothesis 8: Consumers perceive greater risks when buying services than when buying products.

Brand loyalty

The degree to which consumers are committed to particular brands of goods or services depends on a number of factors: costs of changing brands, the availability of substitutes, the perceived risk associated with the purchase, and the degree to which they have obtained satisfaction in the past. Because it may be more costly to change brands of services, because it may be more difficult to be aware of the availability of substitutes, and because higher risks may accompany services, consumers may tend to be more brand loyal with services than with goods.

Greater search costs and monetary costs may be involved in changing brands of services than in changing brands of goods. Because of the difficulty of obtaining information about services, consumers may be unaware of alternatives or substitutes to their brands, and may be uncertain about the ability of alternatives to increase satisfaction over present brands. Monetary fees may accompany brand switching in many services: Physicians often require complete physicals on the initial visit; dentists sometimes demand new X-rays; and day care centers frequently charge 'membership fees' at the outset to obtain long-term commitments from consumers.

If consumers perceive greater risks with services, as is hypothesized above, they probably depend on brand loyalty to a greater extent than when they purchase products. Bauer (in Cox, 1967) stated that brand loyalty is a 'means of economizing decision effort by substituting habit for repeated, deliberate decisions' and suggested that it functions as a device for reducing the risks of consumer decisions. He predicted a strong correlation between degree of perceived risk and brand loyalty, and his prediction has been supported by research in perceived risk (Cunningham, 1967; Roselius, 1971; Sheth and Venkatesan, 1968).

A final reason why consumers may be more brand loyal with services is the recognition of the need for repeated patronage in order to obtain optimum satisfaction from the seller. Becoming a 'regular customer' allows the seller to gain knowledge of the consumer's tastes and preferences, ensures better treatment, and encourages more interest in the consumer's satisfaction. Therefore, a consumer may exhibit greater brand loyalty in order to cultivate a satisfying relationship with the seller.

Hypothesis 9: Brand switching is less frequent with services than with products.

Attribution of dissatisfaction

When consumers are disappointed with purchases – because the products did not fulfill the given needs, because they did not perform satisfactorily, or because they were not worth the prices – they may attribute their dissatisfaction to a number of different sources, among them the producers, the retailers, or themselves. Because consumers participate to a greater extent in the definition and production of services, they may feel more responsible for this dissatisfaction when they purchase services than when they purchase goods. As an example, consider a female consumer purchasing a haircut; receiving the cut she desires depends in part upon her clear specification of her needs to the stylist. If disappointed she may blame either the stylist (for lack of skill) or herself (for choosing the wrong stylist or for not communicating her own needs clearly).

The quality of many services depends on consumer definition: a doctor's accurate, diagnosis requires a conscientious case history and a clear articulation of symptoms; a dry-cleaner's success in removing a spot depends on the customer's knowledge of its cause; and a tax preparer's satisfactory performance relies on the receipts saved by the consumer. Failure to obtain satisfaction with any of these services may not be blamed completely on the retailer or producer, since the consumer must adequately perform his or her part in the production process also.

With products, on the other hand, a consumer's main form of participation is the act of purchase. The consumer may attribute failure to receive satisfaction to her own decision-making error, but she holds the producer responsible for product performance. Goods usually carry warranties or guarantees with purchase, emphasizing that the producer believes that if something goes wrong, it is not the fault of the consumer.

Hypothesis 10: Consumers attribute some of their dissatisfaction with services to their own inability to specify or perform their part of the service.

Hypothesis 11: Consumers may complain less frequently about services than about products due to their belief that they themselves are partly responsible for their dissatisfaction.

SERVICES: STRATEGIC IMPLICATIONS FOR MARKETERS

If research confirms that hypotheses about services, service providers may need to alter their marketing mixes to recognize different consumer evaluation processes. The high levels of experience and credence qualities postulated to be characteristic of services require alternative approaches to information provision, pricing, new service introduction, and other marketing strategies.

Information provision. If consumers employ personal sources more frequently than nonpersonal sources when seeking information about services prior to purchase, the marketer's task may be to reduce the proportion of advertising in the promotional mix. Alternatively, the marketer may want to use advertising to stimulate and simulate word-of-mouth communication (e.g. through testimonial advertisements or by developing advertising high in controversial value) (Kotler, 1980). If consumers seek more post-purchase information with services, the marketer's task may be to concentrate communication efforts to reduce dissonance after purchase.

Quality image. The potential importance of price and physical facilities as indicators of service quality suggests that marketers should manipulate these cues to their own advantage. If marketers desire to position services as high-quality offerings, for example, they may need to set a price above that of competing services. They might also want to match their physical facilities to the desired impression of quality (Bessom, 1973) so that the tangible evidence of the service provides the appropriate atmosphere.

The consumer as competitor. Nonprofessional service providers today must recognize that they often replace or compete with the consumer, which may imply more exacting standards from the consumer and more individualized, personal attention from the service provider. Consumers know what they expect from providers of housecleaning or lawn care or day care because they know what they are accustomed to providing for themselves. The alert service marketer will be certain to research consumers' expectations and demands in such situations.

Innovation diffusion. Marketers may need to concentrate on incentives to trial when introducing new services. The awareness–interest–evaluation stages of the adoption process may best be bypassed because of the difficulty and inefficiency of communicating information about intangibles. Offering free visits, dollars-off coupons, and samples may be appropriate strategies to speed diffusion of innovations in services.

Reduction of perceived risk. The hypothesized increase in perceived risk involved in purchasing services suggests the use of strategies designed to reduce risk. Where appropriate, guarantees of satisfaction may be offered. To the extent possible, service providers should emphasize employee training and other procedures to standardize their offerings, so that consumers learn to expect a given level of quality and satisfaction.

Implications of strong brand loyalty. The fact that one's own customers may be brand loyal with services is not a problem; the fact that the customers of one's competitors may be difficult to capture, however, may create special challenges. Marketers may need to direct communications and strategy to the customers of competitors, emphasizing attributes and strengths which one firm possesses and its competitors lack.

SUMMARY AND CONCLUSION

Service's unique characteristics of intangibility, nonstandardization, and inseparability lead them to possess high levels of experience and credence properties, which, in turn, make them more difficult to evaluate than tangible goods. Eleven specific hypotheses about differences in consumer evaluation processes between services and goods were offered, accompanied by strategic implications for marketers.

REFERENCES

Arndt, J. (1967). 'Word-of-Mouth Advertising and Information Communication'. In *Risk Taking and Information Handling in Consumer Behavior* (D. F. Cox, Ed.). Boston: Division of Research, Harvard University.

Bessom, R. M. (1973) 'Unique Aspects of Marketing Services'. *Arizona Business Bulletin* **9**(November): 8–15.

Cox, D. F. and Rich, S. U. (1967) 'Perceived Risk and Consumer Decision Making – The Case of Telephone Shopping'. In *Risk Taking and Information Handling in Consumer Behavior* (D. F. Cox, Ed.). Boston: Division of Research, Harvard University.

Cunningham, S. M. (1967) 'Perceived Risk in Information Communications'. In *Risk Taking and Information Handling in Consumer Behavior* (D. F. Cox, Ed.). Boston: Division of Research, Harvard University.

Darby, M. R. and Karni, E. (1973) 'Free Competition and the Optimal Amount of Fraud'. *Journal of Law and Economics* **16** (April): 67–86.

Eiglier, P., Langeard, E., Lovelock, C. H., Bateson, E. G. and Young, R. F. (1977). *Marketing Consumer Services: New Insights.* Cambridge, MA: Marketing Science Institute.

Kotler, P. (1980) *Marketing Management: Analysis, Planning and Control.* Englewood Cliffs, NJ: Prentice Hall.

McConnell, J. D. (1968) 'Effect of Pricing on Perception of Product Quality'. *Journal of Applied Psychology* **52** (August): 300–303.

Nelson, P. (1970) 'Advertising as Information'. *Journal of Political Economy* **81** (July–August): 729–754.

Olander, F. (1970) 'The Influence of Price on the Consumer's Evaluation of Products'. In *Pricing Strategy* (B. Taylor and G. Wills, Eds). Princeton, NJ: Auerbach Publishers.

Perry, M. and Hamm, B. C. (1969) 'Canonical Analysis of the Relationship Between Socioeconomic Risk and Personal Influence in Purchase Decisions'. *Journal of Marketing Research* **6** (August): 351–354.

Rathmell, J. M. (1974). *Marketing in the Service Sector.* Cambridge, MA: Winthrop.

Ray, M. L. (1973) 'Marketing Communications: The Hierarchy-of-Effects'. Unpublished research paper 180, Stanford University, August.

Regan, W. J. (1963) 'The Service Revolution'. *Journal of Marketing* **27** (July): 57–62.

Robertson, T. S. (1971). *Innovative Behavior and Communication.* New York: Holt, Rinehart and Winston.

Roselius, T. 'Consumer Rankings of Risk Reduction Methods'. *Journal of Marketing* **35**: (January): 56–61.

Rogers, E. M. (1962). *Diffusion of Innovations.* New York: The Free Press.

'Service Industries: Growth Field of '80's'. (1980). *U.S. News and World Report,* March 17, 80–84.

Sheth, J. N. and Venkatesan, M. (1968) 'Risk-Reduction Processes in Repetitive Consumer Behavior'. *Journal of Marketing* **5** (August): 307–310.

Spence, H. E., Engel, J. F. and Blackwell, R. D. (1970) 'Perceived Risk in Mail-Order and Retail Store Buying'. *Journal of Marketing Research* **5** (August): 307–310.

Tull, D., Boring, R. A. and Gonsoir, M. H. (1964) 'A Note on the Relationship of Price and Imputed Quality'. *Journal of Business* **37** (April): 186–191.

4

A Service-Orientated Approach to Marketing of Services

Christian Grönroos

THE PROBLEM

Service companies are less marketing-orientated than firms which are marketing physical goods, according to reports on service marketing.[1] Some prominent Swedish firms have recently, after several meetings in 1975 and 1976, reported that there are severe marketing problems in the service sector in comparison with goods marketing.[2] The main difference between marketing goods and services was found to be the difficulty of developing a concrete, tangible service offering. Most marketing problems discussed by the service companies came out of this conclusion.

It has even been said that service marketing has failed.[3] The research which I have been conducting among companies in several service industries in Sweden and in Finland has confirmed the view that marketing services is a difficult task. Moreover, it has also been said that the existing marketing literature has little aid to offer companies in service industries. This view should not be surprising. Marketing literature and research almost completely take their examples from goods industries. Therefore, the problems relevant to this area of business have been investigated very thoroughly indeed. Marketing scholars have, however, been very little interested in the problems of firms in service industries. Examples of the marketing problems and the marketing planning situation of these industries are very seldom discussed by researchers or treated in marketing texts.

The service sector has thus been forgotten to a great extent.[4] The re-defining of the product concept seems to be the only radical development of service marketing. Products became goods and services indicating that services are by no means without interest. However, this may have been quite fatal. It seems as if marketing scholars have been tempted to deal with service marketing and goods marketing using the same concepts, models and frames of reference. As marketing focusing on the problems of companies producing physical goods has been developed to a high degree of sophistication, marketers seem to have come to believe that this progress

Reprinted with permission from *European Journal of Marketing*, Vol. 12, No. 8, pp. 588–601 would be a gain to service firms as well. Many writers do, however, point out that service marketing must differ from goods marketing, but, nevertheless, no radical effort to develop a marketing theory, or even some marketing concepts, for service firms aiming at solving their problems seems to have been made.[5] I think that companies in the service industries deserve a better treatment by marketing scholars.

The purpose of this article

A good deal of the marketing problems of service companies may be caused by the lack of a theory of its own for service marketing. The purpose of the present article is to discuss this matter and to suggest a hypothetical framework for an important part of such a theory, i.e. the marketing mix planning. Some empirical evidence supporting the hypotheses will also be accounted for.

The most severe problems of service marketing are, in my opinion, to be found in connection with the planning of a marketing mix. I believe that this part of marketing planning is the main victim of the goods-orientation in marketing research. In this context I am mainly concentrating on *the development of a concrete service offering as part of a service marketing mix planning process*, whereas the marketing variables not to be considered part of the offering – the 'product' of service firms – are not discussed in any detail. Moreover, I am mainly interested in marketing services to consumer markets.

MARKETING OF SERVICES – THE MARKETING MYOPIA OF TODAY

The service marketing confusions

There are, in my opinion, at least three confusions of service marketing, which can to a great extent be blamed for the situation of service marketing. I believe that marketing of services can be labelled the marketing myopia of today. Yet the proportion of GNP coming from the service industries, and the proportion of all employees working in this sector of business, is approaching 50% in most developed societies, and the percentage is in fact over 50% in the most developed ones.

These confusions of service marketing are (1) the faltering service concept, (2) the opinion that everybody is in service, and (3) the view that marketing research helping companies in goods industries would help service firms equally well.

The service concept itself is confusing. No distinction is made between services as objects of marketing and services as marketing variables, i.e. as means of competition when marketing goods. Such a distinction must, in my opinion, definitely be made. Marketing of services concerns services in the first sense of the concept. The service is the *object* of marketing, i.e. *the company is selling the service as the core of its market offering.* When services are treated as a means of competition, the core of the selling proposition is a physical good, not a service. Then it is not service marketing, and the planning situation can be coped with by means of the traditional concepts and models of marketing literature.

The faltering service concept may well be a result of the idea of a goods–service continuum. All offerings may, it is said, be described by the continuum with pure goods at one extreme and pure services at the other, and with most offerings falling somewhere between these points.[6] This continuum concept mixes the two service concepts separated above. From a marketing planning point-of-view the continuum does not exist, or at least it is highly misguiding to the marketer. It gives the impression that every offering basically is the same, and can be planned in a similar manner applying the same planning instruments. In my opinion an offering concerns either goods, with or without service support (transport, maintenance, repair, etc.), or services, which may be pure services which make it possible to use goods or which are accompanied by goods (car rental, hotel, inclusive tours, etc.).

The same company may, of course, be engaged in both goods marketing and service marketing. Every firm must, however, in every planning situation, analyse the planning problem, and try to find out whether it is developing a service offering or a goods offering. A definite borderline between these two kinds of offerings cannot be drawn in a goods-service continuum. The problem must be solved *in situ* by the marketer.

Sometimes combinations of equally important goods and service elements are marketed. This marketing planning situation, systems selling, is, however, out of the scope of the present article.

Is everybody really in service?

It has become popular to consider all marketing to be service marketing. Consumers, it is said, are not buying goods or services, but the value satisfaction of offerings.[7] Consequently, there are no goods industries or service industries, but industries with varying degrees of service components, and, thus, everybody is in service.[8]

This seems to be another confusion of service marketing. The present marketing literature normally maintains that there is nothing like marketing of goods and marketing of services, but there is just marketing of goods (and services). So it also, although not on the same grounds, supports the view that everybody is in the same sort of business. Yet companies in the service sector still seem to be in trouble with their marketing.

It is, of course, reasonable to consider both goods and services to be bought by consumers in order to give some service or value satisfaction. And companies marketing physical goods would certainly many times be better off by concentrating more on the needs of the consumers and less on the tangible good itself in their marketing planning. Every consumer can perhaps be said to be in service, but certainly not every enterprise. To state that every industry is a service industry would indicate, from a marketing planning point-of-view, that the planning situation, and the tools, concepts, and models used are the same for service companies as for firms marketing goods. But, the marketing planning situation is, in my opinion, different when marketing services than when marketing physical goods.

If the marketing planning situation differs between service industries and goods industries, which I think it does, *the planning instruments developed to assist in solving the problems of goods industries may well not be applicable when planning service marketing.* However, it is most frequently said that the concepts and models used by companies in goods industries can equally well be applied by service firms. I think that there is enough empirical evidence to prove this opinion to be wrong and just another confusion of service marketing. A theory of service marketing is needed. The traditional marketing does not offer service companies appropriate planning tools.

Characteristics of services

I do not intend to add a definition of my own to the range of more or less unsatisfactory definitions already existing. I believe that it is quite impossible to find one final definition. One can, for instance, use a rather traditional one suggested by Judd in the 1960s:

> Marketed Services – A market transaction by an enterprise of an entrepreneur where the object of the market transaction is *other than* the transfer of ownership (or title, if any) of a tangible commodity.[9]

In my opinion, it would be more fruitful to find out in what respects services differ from goods, and to examine the implications for marketing planning caused by the characteristics of services.

Several characteristics can be found, but I am here going to stress only three, which I think are vital to service marketing planning. Perhaps the most important characteristic of a service is its *intangibility*. The customer cannot feel, taste, smell, or see a service before he buys it. One cannot make a thorough evaluation of a service. However, such an evaluation seems often to be desirable for most consumers, so they evaluate what they can: the interior of a restaurant, the appearance of the air hostesses, the behaviour of the bank clerks.[10]

Of course, it is not always easy to evaluate physical goods either, but the point is that they can be physically evaluated, i.e. there is something tangible to evaluate. Services cannot be evaluated as such, so they must be transformed to concrete offerings, which can be evaluated and compared to those of the competitors. If the firm does not manage this process, the customers will, in an unguided manner, pick out tangible attributes which *are* the service in the customers' mind.

Another essential characteristic of services is the *production/consumption interaction* in most service businesses. Services cannot be separated from the producer, and the producer and the seller are the same organisation.[11] A service is considered to be consumed as it is produced. Thus, producing and marketing are very interactive processes, too. Both activities are simultaneously performed by the same persons in a service company. Moreover, the inseparability of services is said to make only direct distribution possible. In fact, no normal distribution could be possible, as there is nothing tangible to distribute using the usual channels of distribution.[12]

A third characteristic of services is the *lack of ownership and transaction of ownership* when dealing with services. One does not own anything, when one has purchased a service. One is only given the right to use things, and as symbols of the lack of ownership one may get tickets, certificates, value coupons, etc.

As a summary, it seems obvious that services do differ from goods as objects of marketing. Therefore, services cannot be treated like goods in a marketing planning context. *A new service marketing mix concept is needed.*

Weaknesses of the traditional goods-orientated marketing mix concept

As a simultaneous analysis of all marketing variables in the same context is not usually possible, the marketing mix models, like McCarthy's four P's and Lipson and Darling's subcomponent model, have been developed. Different submixes are thought to be planned separately, and, finally, blended into a total marketing mix. Only the product mix must, in some way, be already shaped, before detailed pricing, distribution, and communication planning can take place.

This is a way of planning an efficient marketing mix for physical goods, and the models are developed for goods marketing. No matter how sophisticated such models are, they take for granted that it is possible to plan submixes, which afterwards can be co-ordinated into one total mix. This is possible, if there is a tangible product involved. Then there is something to develop, to price, to distribute, and to communicate about. That is, in goods marketing there is a tangible core around which the offering can be developed in a manner reflected by the traditional marketing mix models. In service marketing there is no such tangible core. It simply is not possible to plan separate submixes, which can be blended into one total marketing mix. Therefore, the traditional marketing mix concept developed for goods marketing is likely to fail in service marketing planning. This may be the main reason why service firms are less marketing-orientated than other companies.

PLANNING THE SERVICE OFFERING

The accessibility of services

Only direct distribution was earlier mentioned to be possible for service firms, because of the close production/consumption interaction. It may seem so when viewing the matter strictly in the goods sense of the distribution concept. I do believe, however, that a more innovative approach to distribution of services is called for. It seems to me as if the traditional concept ought not to be applied to service marketing at all. Instead of being a useful means of competition it becomes an unnecessary burden to the marketer.

In my opinion *the accessibility of a service* is a much more promising concept for service firms. Resources influencing accessibility are, for example, human resources, machines, offices, buildings, and other physical things as well as extra services. These resources can be managed by the marketer, and they are all aimed at making the service quickly and conveniently accessible to the consumers.

The difference between the concept of distribution channels and the concept of physical distribution does not seem meaningful in the context of services. For example, a guide may be considered part of the channel of distribution for inclusive tours. Without him much experience and many views and facts, which are part of the tours, would not be accessible to the consumers. At the same time he also distributes this part of the service; that is, he performs physical distribution.

Applying the traditional concept it may be difficult to view a person like the guide as a part of the channel of distribution, and he certainly is not performing any physical distribution, because there is nothing tangible to distribute. In terms of accessibility, the guide is, however, a manageable resource making it possible for the customers to consume the service.

I believe that the concept of accessibility can improve the understanding of service marketing in at least two ways. First, it stresses all parts of the service offering, which the consumers may recognise as the service. The service itself is intangible, but the resources – both human and non-human – influencing the accessibility transform the service into a concrete offering, which is accessible to the consumers and can be evaluated by them in comparison with competing offerings. These resources can therefore be labelled *bearers of the service*, because they bring out the service to the market.

Such elements of the service offering are, for instance, the location of a bank, the interior of a bank office or travel agency office, means of transportation and their condition, the interior and exterior of a restaurant, the waiters, ticket-collectors on buses and trains, bank clerks and cashiers, barbers, cheques, pass-books, tickets, computer and telecommunication networks, etc. These elements are indeed of many kinds but they all have two essential features in common: they promote the accessibility of the services, and they can be managed and used as a means of competition by the marketer.

Secondly, I believe that by applying the accessibility concept, service marketing has a chance of breaking free from the burden of the traditional distribution concept.[13] Direct distribution will then by no means be the only way of making the service accessible to the consumers. Insurance vending machines and franchise arrangements used by hotel and catering enterprises are examples of an innovative development of the resources influencing the accessibility.[14]

The human resources

The consumers of a service will almost always see and meet some representative of the service firm sometimes during the purchasing and/or consumption process. Nearly all employees, irrespective of their place in the organisation, will, on the other hand, at least occasionally get in touch with the customers. Therefore, the manner in which the bank manager, the bank clerk, the travel agency representative, the telephone receptionist, the tour guide, the barber, or the waiter treats the customers, what he says, and how he behaves are very critical to the view of the service which the consumers get. *Almost every single person in a service firm is, therefore, acting as a salesman and is engaged in the personal market communication efforts of the company.*

The human resources of a service firm are also part of the accessibility system of a service, and this fact makes the personnel even more vital to the company and its marketing planning. Thus, *the administration of the human resources must be considered an important means of competition in service marketing.* Marketing training – especially concerning communication and selling – is a much greater task and involves many more people in service industries than in goods industries. For a company producing and marketing physical goods it is satisfactory if the marketing staff is properly trained and the salesmen know how to sell. In a service company almost every employee belongs to the 'marketing department'. This is a fact that must be recognised, e.g. when engaging employees and planning personnel training programmes. And this goes for the financial manager of a bank as well as for the waiter of a restaurant and the telephone receptionist of an airline company.

As so many people in service firms are engaged in marketing tasks, their behaviour influences the success of the company to a great extent. Therefore, it is important to be aware of the *internal marketing task of service firms*, i.e. a service must first be successfully marketed to the personnel, so that the employees accept the service offering and thoroughly engage in performing their marketing duties. Otherwise the service may easily turn out to be a failure in relation to its ultimate target markets.

The importance of the administration of the personnel and of the internal marketing process to the success of service companies is not, I believe, quite recognised today. Frequently the employees have not been engaged to perform any marketing tasks but merely to produce the services. Therefore, it will not be an easy task for a service firm to manage its human resources in a more marketing-orientated manner. First the attitude of the personnel must be changed so that the employees accept that they are not only producers of a service, but, simultaneously, are also engaged in selling the very same service.

The personal market communication and selling tasks performed by the personnel are bearers of the service as well as the resources influencing the accessibility, because the performance of the representatives of the firm is also an element of the service offering, which brings out the intangible service to the market and can be considered by the consumers instead of the service itself.

Auxiliary services

The accessibility of a service may be influenced by offering extra services. For instance, the bank clerk may fill out forms and supermarkets may offer large parking areas in order to help the customers. But, furthermore, services can be offered as separate means of competition. Such auxiliaries are, for example, hotel booking and inclusive tours arrangements offered by airline companies and coffee offered by barbers' shops.

Sometimes a service may be an extra service influencing the accessibility for one consumer and an auxiliary service for another. Someone may choose to go by train instead of by bus, because he can have his lunch in the restaurant of the train, whereas someone else may take the train just because he enjoys the excellent meals served. But he does not actually have to eat anything.

An auxiliary service is not a bearer of the service, because it does not bring out the service to the market. But it is promoting the service, and it is certainly considered part of the service offering by the consumers.

Intra-corporate elements of the service

In the marketing planning process service firms cannot separate the different kinds of marketing mix variables, as frequently is done in marketing of physical goods. In particular, the personal market communication, as part of the administration of human resources, and the resources influencing the accessibility are extremely close to each other and to the intangible service itself.

As a matter of fact, the personal communication and the accessibility of services may be viewed as parts of the service offered to the target markets, i.e. as parts of the 'product' of service industries. They fulfil the function as bearers of the service, which bring out the intangible service to the markets as a concrete service offering, i.e. as a product. Moreover, the auxiliary services offered are from the consumers' point-of-view also part of the service offering. They are, too, shaping the service which the customers evaluate and eventually perhaps buy.

The bearers of the service and the auxiliary services are *intra-corporate elements of the service,* because the marketer can maintain full control over them. Figure 1 shows how the bearers and the auxiliary services are linked together and to the core of the offering, i.e. to the intangible idea of the service.

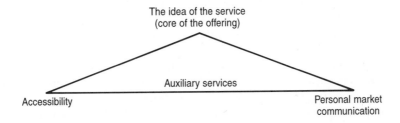

Figure 1. Intra-corporate elements of the service.

The figure illustrates how integrated the planning of marketing variables must be in service marketing. Product development is in fact quite another task than one usually thinks about, when applying the product development concept to service marketing in the goods-orientated sense of the concept.

Companies in service industries have to recognise that product development involves many more activities than one traditionally believes it does. *Development of the resources influencing the accessibility, the administration of human resources, and the development of auxiliary services are parts of the product development process.*[15] By accepting such a view services companies can, I believe, achieve considerable improvements in their marketing performance.

THE CONSUMERS AS ACTIVE PARTICIPANTS IN MARKETING

Usually the consumers are only considered to have needs which are unknown to them or relatively badly satisfied by existing products, and they either buy the product offered to them or do not buy it. They take part in the product development process only in a *passive* manner by having unsatisfied needs. They are not considered as actively shaping the product. Consumer tests and test marketing may be used, but these are actually rather passive ways in which the consumers can influence the product. Only the competitors on the market are thought of as actively influencing the performance of marketing.

When marketing services the situation of the marketer is, however, somewhat different. The traditional view of the consumers' role in the marketplace is an unnecessary restriction on the development of marketing. While this view may express the situation of a goods marketer, service companies have to make other considerations as far as the behaviour of the consumer is concerned.

The consumers are actively taking part in shaping the service offering, i.e. in product development.[16] This is due to the production/consumption interaction, which is characteristic of the service industries, and to the fact that several consumers and/or potential consumers simultaneously are on the same spot either consuming, purchasing, or planning to purchase the service. The consumers influence both the accessibility of a service and the communication about the service, and their influence can be either desirable or undesirable.

A consumer may, for instance, cause queues in a bank, thus causing the quality of the bank's services to deteriorate, or he may be part of the atmosphere in a music hall, thus improving the quality of the concert. He may also be telling potential consumers of, for instance, the restaurant of a hotel, that he, by experience, knows that it is a dull place, thus changing the communication about the restaurant in an unfavourable manner. He may on the other hand enthusiastically encourage others to visit the hotel restaurant, thus making a desirable impact on the communication.

Companies in service industries should, therefore, consider the consumers, not only the competitors, to be elements in the market actively influencing marketing planning. From the consumers' point-of-view, the other consumers, who simultaneously are making their purchasing decision and/or consuming the service, are part of the service itself. The service marketer has to recognise this fact, and include also this active role of the consumers in his marketing planning.

Moreover, the consumer himself can be considered part of the service he buys and consumes. His expectations and acting certainly influence the behaviour of the human representatives of the service firm. Thus, the quality of the service varies according to the behaviour of the consumer. The attitude of the consumers towards the service and towards the organisation producing and marketing the service must from the very beginning be kept favourable, and if the consumer happens to become disappointed, immediate action is called for.

Such activities are also important means of competition in the service industries. And the consumers of a service can be considered *extra-corporate elements of the service.* In Figure 2 these elements have been added to the intra-corporate dimensions of services.

The continuous line in the figure connecting the idea of the service, the accessibility, the personal market communication, and the auxiliary services with each other indicates that these elements of the service can be directly controlled and managed by the marketer. The dotted line connecting the consumers with the two bearers of the service shows that the consumers may influence both of them, but that the behaviour of the consumers can be controlled only indirectly by the marketer. But the line also stresses the point that the behaviour of the consumer is still, in some way, manageable.

The marketer can in advance anticipate possible patterns of behaviour of the consumers in order to be able to eliminate undesirable effects on both the accessibility and the communication.[17] And he should also be prepared to take advantage of favourable consumer influence, which is improving the quality of the service.

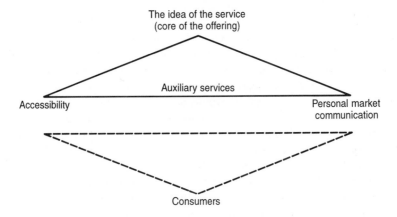

Figure 2. An extensive view of the service.

SOME EMPIRICAL SUPPORT

The study

In order to test the hypothetical view of the service offering put forward in this article, I have during the winter 1976/77 made twelve case studies of marketing planning procedures of successful companies in several service industries in Sweden and in Finland. The information was gathered by means of a two-stage interviewing procedure. First a questionnaire was mailed to the firms, and, in the second stage, the answers were supplemented by personal interviews with the persons responsible for the marketing planning.

My case studies reveal an amazingly uniform picture of the problems of the service firms, and, moreover, of the planning behaviour and the marketing variables applied by the firms. Every company, *irrespective of industry*, seems to have similar problems, mainly those of the intangibility of the services and of developing a concrete offering out of the intangible service. The tools used were also very similar, although varying terms were used.

I am not going to account for all case studies in this article. I will just present two cases, here labelled *inclusive tours marketing* and *barber's shop marketing*. Adding more cases to these would not give any new empirical evidence.

The case of inclusive tours marketing

A company offering inclusive tours for holidaymakers is operating around an intangible idea of, for example, recreation, change of milieu, experiences, excitement, and adventures. 'We sell a week of power. The consumer purchases a position where he can order others to serve him, where he is the employer, not the employee'.

In order to transform the intangible service into concrete offerings varying kinds of means are used. These means usually also make the service accessible to the consumers, but some of them are mere auxiliary services. The traditional ticket has been replaced by a travel certificate, which is issued and printed out by a computer, at the time when the tour is ordered. The computer facilitates quick and detailed booking information with a minimum of mistakes, thus giving the consumers an impression of exactness and security. 'People are not sure of what service they actually will get. In this way we give them, in advance, a concrete written specification of which services they have bought.' The travel certificate serves as an allround ticket, thus not only in a tangible manner symbolising the service, but also minimising the amount of papers and forms usually needed and, therefore, making the service more conveniently and easily accessible to the consumers.

The hotel, the airline company, and the type of aircraft used, as well as various kinds of auxiliary services, such as meals included in the tour and trips arranged on destination, are also part of the service which the company offers. Because of these resources the inclusive tours become accessible to the consumers. They are thus shaping the service, which the consumers get.

The human resources of the company are considered vitally important to the marketing performance. For example, the manager, the people behind the desk in the booking offices, and the guides are essential to the accessibility. The employees are carefully selected and trained. The performance of the personnel is considered to a great extent to shape the service which is offered. The guides are especially vital, 'because it is the guide who sells the next tour'. As long as the tour lasts the guides are in contact with the consumers, and they are more or less the last contact which the consumers have with the service and the company. If something goes wrong, it is the guides who, as representatives of the firm, have to be capable of reshaping the service so that quality is maintained and the consumers will remain satisfied.

The employees of the firm are performing market communication and selling tasks, and the better they know the destination of a tour, the better they sell. Clearly, the administration of the human resources of the company and the training of the personnel are important to marketing.

The consumers are considered part of the service offering. 'Our image keeps drinkers away, which makes the tours more comfortable to the other consumers'. The consumers also sometimes take part in the communication about the services. One single person may get all the others to complain of something without really having any reason. 'But there can be a person, who gets everybody on an auxiliary trip by enthusiastically telling them that he was on that trip last time and it was marvellous'.

The corporate image is considered important to marketing, because consumers buy the company as well as a certain tour. A favourable and attractive image is vital to the accessibility. If the image is unfavourable, the consumers may not even be interested in recognising other means of competition used by the firm.

To sum up, one can in this case notice the importance of the bearers of the intangible service to marketing. The resources influencing the accessibility and the personal market communication and selling by the personnel, as well as the auxiliary services offered, are marketing variables shaping the service offerings. Furthermore, the consumers are actively influencing the services and taking part in the communication about it.

The case of barber's shop marketing

A barber's shop offers intangible services concerning personal care, relaxation, etc. In order to transform the intangible services to concrete offerings various means are used.

It is important that the shop is located near people, on busy streets. The interior and exterior of the shop are also vital to the success of the firm. The windows of the shop are not covered, so that the people passing by can easily see what is going on inside the shop. This is a way of making the services of the barber's shop more concrete. 'We wish to create an atmosphere which pleases the customers. Our customers shall enjoy their stay with us'. Colours and music are important to the milieu and used in order to achieve the right atmosphere.

The people working in the shop and their capability of doing a good job according to the taste and wishes of the customers are perhaps the most important part of the accessibility of the services. They have to be well-trained, but, moreover, their appearance is also considered vital. They are uniformly dressed, and the uniforms are now and then changed.

The behaviour of the personnel is important too: not only how they do the job, but also what they are talking about and how they are doing it. The human resources are part of the service which the consumers get, and the administration of these resources is important to the success of the barber's shop. 'If our employees are satisfied with their job and enjoy the place, they will do a better job, and then our customers will enjoy our services even more'.

Auxiliary services are offered to some extent. Coffee is served and magazines are available. To minimise the waiting time, the shop actively tries to get its customers to book time in advance. This diminishes the risks of getting irritated customers and of lost business because of queues in the shop.

As a summary, one can notice the extreme importance of the bearers of the intangible barber services. The location, the way in which the shop is planned, the employees and their behaviour as producers and salesmen of the services are all parts of the services, which the consumers buy. Moreover, auxiliary services are offered, and the behaviour of the consumers is to some extent managed by the barber's shop.

CONCLUSIONS

The concepts and models for marketing mix planning of today do not seem applicable to companies in service industries. The case studies, both those presented here and the other studies, too, point out how much more integrated the planning of the marketing variables must be in comparison to the traditional marketing mix models. The 'product' of service firms is extremely complicated, and, therefore, the product development process involves elements normally not considered when discussing the topic.

The bearers of the service, i.e. the resources influencing the accessibility of the service and the personal market communication, are integrated parts of the service as well as possible auxiliary services. This fact makes the planning of these intra-corporate elements of the service offering parts of product development. Furthermore, the service is also shaped by the consumers, thus actively, as an extra-corporate element of the service, having an impact on the marketing planning.

The corporate image seems to be very important to service firms, because the consumers almost always get in touch with the very company offering the service. The image is thus part of the accessibility and one of the very first things the consumers may think about. A favourable image may be vital for the firm's attempts to attract customers, whereas an undesirable image may keep people from even being interested in noticing other means of competition.

Marketing variables, which do not seem to be part of the service, have not been considered in this article. However, I believe that they can be grouped into two main categories labelled *pricing* and *non-interactive market communication*, which mainly consists of advertising, publicity, and other possible means of communication where there is no production/consumption interaction between representatives of the service company and the consumers.

A lot of research has still to be done; e.g. a consumer study, the purpose of which will be to find out whether consumers really evaluate and purchase the same service offerings as indicated by the hypothetical view of the elements of the service put forward in this article and supported by the present case studies.

NOTES AND REFERENCES

1. George, W. R. and Barksdale, H. C. (1974) 'Marketing Activities in the Service Industries'. *Journal of Marketing* (October) 65; Bessom, R. M. and Jackson, D. R., Jr. (1975) 'Service Retailing: A Strategic Marketing Approach'. *Journal of Retailing* (Summer): 84; and Holloway, R. J. and Hancock, R. S. (1973) *Marketing in a Changing Environment.* New York: John Wiley & Sons, pp. 55–56: 'Marketing has not yet become an important function for most service institutions . . . Perhaps we will see the service industries become more marketing-conscious in the decade ahead.'
2. Back, R. (Ed.) (1975) *Erfagruppverksamheten.* Report from Marknadstekniskt Centrum, Stockholm, Sweden, 1976.
3. Levitt, T. (1972) 'Product-line Approach to Service'. *Harvard Business Review* (September–October): 43.
4. Wilson, A. (1975) *Professional Services and the Market Place,* Report from Marknadstekniskt Centrum, No. 4, Stockholm, Sweden, p. 5.
5. There are some efforts to create new concepts, though: for example, the suggestion of a concept of marketing intermediaries in the context of services by Donnelly, J. H., Jr. (1976) 'Marketing Intermediaries in Channels of Distribution for Services'. *Journal of Marketing* (January): 57.
6. Rathmell, J. M. (1966) 'What is Meant by Services?' *Journal of Marketing* (October): 33–34.
7. Levitt, T. (1974) *Marketing for Business Growth.* New York: McGraw-Hill, p. 8.
8. Levitt, T. 'Product-Line Approach to Service', *op, cit.,* pp. 41–42.
9. Judd, R. C. (1964) 'The Case for Redefining Services'. *Journal of Marketing* (January): 59. This definition makes it possible to distinguish between the three main categories of services: the right to possess and use a product (Rented Goods Services); or 2, the customer creation of, repair, or improvement of a product (Owned Goods Services); or 3, no product element but rather an experience or what might be termed experimental possession (Non-Goods Services).' (*ibid.,* p. 59). Marketing of services should only be concerned with services of the first and third category. Owned Goods Services are normally, but not necessarily always, means of competition when marketing goods.

10. Wyckham, R. G., Fitzroy, P. T. and Mandy, G. D. (1975) 'Marketing of Services: An Evaluation of the Theory'. *European Journal of Marketing* No. 1: p. 61.
11. Stanton, W. J. (1975) *Fundamentals of Marketing.* Tokyo: McGraw-Hill Kogakusha, p. 551.
12. George and Barksdale, *op. cit.*, p. 67.
13. Donnelly, J. H. Jr. *op. cit.* Intermediaries replacing the goods-orientated distribution concept suggested by Donnelly are any extra-corporate entity between the producer and the consumers which makes the service available and/or more convenient for the consumers. This certainly is a contribution to service marketing, but he does not, however, include intra-corporate resources with the same purpose, which, in my opinion, is too restricting when expanding the distribution concept in order to help service firms.
14. A very important part of the service firm is the corporate image. Consumers of physical goods seldom have to see or meet the producing company. Normally they deal with wholesalers and retailers. But the consumers of services nearly always get in touch with the service producing firm. This makes the firm part of the accessibility of the service. Therefore, the corporate image of the service firm may be of vital importance to marketing. If the consumers do not consider the image favourable and attractive, they will perhaps not even be interested in noticing the other means of competition of the company.
15. In some cases personal market communication can be viewed solely in a communication context and not as part of the service. The performance of a professional salesman, who is only thought of as a salesman by the customers, and not as part of the accessibility system, may be planned separately in the same context as advertising and other means of impersonal communication. However, in marketing to consumer markets personal communication is rarely just communicating about the service offering; it is almost always also shaping the service itself.
16. See Eiglier, P. and Langeard, E. (1976) *Principes de politique marketing pour les enterprises de services,* L'Institute d'Administration des Enterprises, Université d'Aix-Marseille, Decembre, who make this interesting suggestion.
17. For instance, the *demarketing* concept suggested by Kotler, P. and Levy, S. J. (1971) 'Demarketing, yes, demarketing'. *Harvard Business Review* (November–December) could be applied in this context.

5

What is Meant by Services?

John M. Rathmell

Certain concepts and phrases still exist in conventional marketing thought without their meaning being challenged, even though conditions surrounding their origin have changed. The classification of consumer goods into convenience, shopping, and specialty categories is one example;[1] channels of distribution is another.[2]

The ubiquitous phrase 'goods and services' is a special example. Most marketers have some idea of the meaning of the term 'goods'; these are tangible economic products that are capable of being seen and touched and may or may not be tasted, heard, or smelled.

But 'services' seem to be everything else; and an understanding of them is not clear. For example, convenience foods have 'built-in services'. Are they services in contrast with goods? A business publication refers to a giant retailer's new services: leased beauty salons and restaurants, telephone ordering, and in-home selling. Are these institutional rearrangements really services?

And what about service businesses that do not require heavy investment in plant and equipment? Railroads? Light and power utilities?

MARKETING'S 'GOODS' ORIENTATION

The marketing discipline has a strong 'goods' orientation. In academic courses in marketing, tangible goods are considered, but rarely services to any extent. Yet services represent an area of economic activity that accounts for 30 to 40% of consumer dollar expenditures!

Similarly, many retailers and manufacturers tend to think only in terms of tangible goods; relatively few have broadened their conception of a product to include services. There are exceptions, of course: Sears, Roebuck & Company's entry into the insurance industry, mutual funds, and interior-decorating; the automobile manufacturer's interest in repairing, financing, and leasing.

So, it is refreshing that in recent years American Marketing Association national

Reprinted with permission from *Journal of Marketing*, Vol. 30, October, pp. 32–36 conferences have included sessions on utility and financial marketing, and that the Association also has sponsored special-interest conferences in these areas of marketing.

Also, others have prescribed usage of terms rightfully marketing's responsibility. Thus, the US Department of Agriculture continues to include food-processing costs as a marketing expense, even though this practice was challenged many years ago.[3] The US Department of Commerce has assumed responsibility for blocking out the 'services' category, and thus has made a useful contribution to our knowledge of economic activity. However, does its distinction between 'goods and services' hold up from the marketing viewpoint?[4] How about the following distinctions?

- Food and clothing are goods; housing is a service.
- Automobiles are goods; airline tickets represent a purchase of a service.
- Fuel oil is a good; gas is a service.
- Religious and welfare activities contributions are services.

GOODS AND SERVICES DISTINGUISHED

A useful distinction can be made between (1) *rented-goods services*; (2) *owned-goods services*; and (3) *non-goods services*. Also we might think of *marketed services* as market transactions by an enterprise or entrepreneur where the object is other than the transfer of ownership of a tangible commodity.[5]

One implicit distinction is to consider a good to be a noun and a service a verb – a good is a thing and a service is an act. The former is an object, an article, a device, or a material, whereas the latter is a deed, a performance, or an effort. When a good is purchased, the buyer acquires an asset; when a service is purchased, the buyer incurs an expense.

Another test to distinguish a good from a service is the nature of the product's utility. Does the utility for the consumer lie in the physical characteristics of the product, or in the nature of the action or performance?

Applying this test, there are very few pure products and pure services. The satisfaction, or utility, deriving from a work of art, such as a painting or sculpture, lies solely in the good itself. The benefit, or utility, arising from legal counsel proceeds exclusively from the service rendered. In the former, no act is performed; in the latter, no good is involved.

Apart from these extremes, most goods, whether consumer or industrial, require supporting services in order to be useful; most services require supporting goods in order to be useful.

GOODS–SERVICES CONTINUUM

Economic products lie along a goods–service continuum, with pure goods at one extreme and pure services at the other, but with most of them falling between these two extremes.

This mixed characteristic is suggested by both Table 1 and Figure 1, even though quite broad categories are considered. Some are primarily goods with service support, whereas others are primarily services with goods support. Most goods are a complex of goods and facilitating services; most services are a complex of services and facilitating goods.

Table 1. Personal consumption expenditures by type of product[a]

	1959 %	1964 %
Food and tobacco:		
Goods	100.0	100.0
Services	0.0	0.0
Clothing, accessories, and jewelry:		
Goods	89.1	89.8
Services	10.9	10.2
Personal care:		
Goods	55.3	56.8
Services	44.7	43.2
Housing:		
Goods	0.0	0.0
Services	100.0	100.0
Household operation:		
Goods	59.1	57.9
Services	40.9	42.1
Medical care and death expenses:		
Goods	23.3	21.4
Services	76.7	78.6
Personal business:		
Goods	0.0	0.0
Services	100.0	100.0
Transportation:		
Goods	75.5	77.2
Services	24.5	22.8
Recreation:		
Goods	66.4	68.5
Services	33.6	31.5
Private education and research:		
Goods	0.0	0.0
Services	100.0	100.0
Religious and welfare activities:		
Goods	0.0	0.0
Services	100.0	100.0
Foreign travel and remittances net:		
Goods	50.3	39.5
Services	49.7	60.5
Total personal consumption expenditures:		
Goods	61.4	59.2
Services	38.6	40.8

[a]Derived from *Survey of Current Business*, Vol. 45 (November, 1965), pp. 20–23.

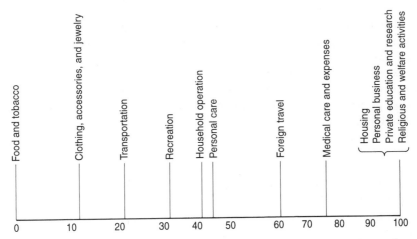

Figure 1. Per cent of major classes of personal consumption expenditures allocated to services, 1964. (Source: *Survey of Current Business*, Vol. 45 (November, 1965), pp. 20–23).

This mixed nature of most economic products is well illustrated by the leasing transaction. If a product is purchased, it is a good; but if it is rented or leased, the rentee or lessee acquires a service.

Yet for the service to have any meaning whatever a goods component must also be present. Service would contribute time and place utility; the good would be the physical commodity made available and the service would be the act of making it available for a prescribed period of time as an alternative to outright purchase.

MARKETING CHARACTERISTICS OF SERVICES

The basic question is – *What are the marketing characteristics of services?* Here are 13 answers:

1. Unlike a good, where monetary values are stated in terms of a price, services are more likely to be expressed as *rates, fees, admissions, charges, tuition, contributions, interest, and the like.*

2. In many types of service transactions, *the buyer is a client rather than a customer of the seller*; the client, when buying a service, figuratively or literally places himself 'in the hands' of the seller of the service. Consider, for example, the relationship between the student and the college, the patient and the hospital or physician, the passenger and the carrier. The buyer is not free to use the service as he wishes, as would be the case in the purchase of a good; he must abide by certain prescripts laid down by the seller in order for the service to make any contribution.[6]

3. The various marketing systems in the services category have taken on *highly differentiated characteristics.* Although contrasts do exist in those marketing systems that have evolved for different types of physical goods, they are primarily differences of degree. In the case of services, the marketing of recreation bears

little resemblance to the marketing of medical service. As additional examples, there is no apparent relationship between the marketing system for shoe-repair service and for hospital service.

4. Since services are acts or processes and are produced as they are consumed, they *cannot be inventoried*, and there can be no merchant middleman since only 'direct' sales are possible. In a number of instances, agent intermediaries are utilized in the marketing of services: insurance and travel agents, for example.

5. The question may be raised as to *the economic nature* of certain products in the services category, for example, payments to charitable and religious bodies and non-profit educational institutions. Are the church on the corner, the college on the hill, and the United Fund Agency downtown economic entities on the supply side? Certainly they compete for the consumer's dollar.

6. There appears to be a *more formal* or *professional approach to the marketing of many services* (not all, by any means) – for example, financial, medical, legal, and educational services.

7. Because services cannot be mass-produced, *standards cannot be precise.* Although service producers may be standardized, their actual implementation will vary from buyer to buyer. Perhaps there will be a standardization of services through the increasing use of service technology at the expense of personalized service, especially in medicine and education; and this would mean that services will follow goods from custom to mass production and standardization.[7]

8. *'Price-making' practices vary greatly* within the services category. Utility and transportation rates are rigidly controlled by public agencies; interest rates display characteristics of price leadership; and some service charges are established on the basis of what the traffic will bear.

9. Economic concepts of supply and demand and costs are difficult to apply to a service because of its *intangible nature.* Moreover, values of some services are difficult to fix. What is the value of the service of a lawyer or a physician in a losing cause as compared with a successful one?

10. *Most fringe benefits* take the form of services: pensions, insurance, unemployment benefits, eye and dental care, psychiatric service; seldom are benefits in the form of goods (such as turkeys at Christmas).[8] If benefits are created by the employer, in a marketing sense he is selling a product (in lieu of higher wages) to a market segment, his own employees. If the service is created by an outside specialist, such as a life insurance company, the employer is an agent (in a marketing sense) between the seller–creator of the service and the buyer–consumer.

11. There appears to be *limited concentration in the services sector of the economy.* There are few service chains; carriers and utilities are regulated.

12. Until recently, *service firms failed to differentiate between the production and marketing of services.* Performance was equivalent to marketing the service.

13. In the case of services, *symbolism derives from performance* rather than from possession.

Industrial services

The significance of industrial services in the economy is indicated in the data in Table 2.

Table 2.   Magnitude of some industrial services[a]

Type of service	Gross and personal expenditures	Industrial expenditures
Engineering and other professional services		$2 966 000 000
Business services (not elsewhere classified)		$8 492 000 000
Corporate sales: telephone, telegraph, etc.	$10 929 000 000	
Less personal consumption expenditures: telephone, telegraph, etc.	−4 720 000 000	$6 209 000 000
Corporate sales: electric and gas utilities	$20 197 000 000	
Less personal consumption expenditures: electricity and gas	−8 422 000 000	$11 775 000 000
Corporate sales: railroads	$10 382 000 000	
Less personal consumption expenditures: railway (including commutation)	−454 000 000	$9 928 000 000

[a]*Survey of Current Business*, Vol. 44 (July, 1964), pp. 16 and 28. Net figures represent corporate sales not only to business but also to government, institutions, agriculture, etc.

Services of government

The greatest marketer of services in the United States is government. The public sector is becoming a major supplier of that which was once the domain of private enterprises or private institutions. Consider Medicare, urban renewal and slum clearance, public parks and recreational areas, public higher education, and publicly-owned utilities.

   Moreover, private sellers of many services are much more controlled by public agencies than are private sellers of goods. It is not much of an exaggeration to say that the mixed economy is divided on a goods–service axis. It is conceivable that most consumer services (excluding personal-care services) eventually will be purchased from public bodies, whereas consumer goods will continue to be purchased from private enterprise.

THE SERVICE CHALLENGE FOR MARKETING

Table 1 shows services are a major component in the economy. McKittrick sees them not only diverting income flow away from manufacturing but also pressuring wages upward because of their relatively greater price increases.[9] Others have cited the lower efficiency in the personal-services sector because of the lower quality of labor in services production, as compared with goods production, and because of the limited opportunities for mechanization.[10]

   The distribution of goods is within the province of marketing. But is there the same consensus regarding amusements, health services, and hotels? Should they be treated vertically, within the respective industries and professions – or horizontally, under the marketing umbrella?

In this connection: How are the public services marketed? Are there public marketing institutions and procedures? When is the transaction completed? What is the price? What are the terms of sale? The recent promotion campaign to sell the voluntary provision in Medicare to 20 million eligible citizens represents one of the first major attempts to market a government service.

CONCLUSION

The increasing percentage of consumer expenditures allocated to intangibles deserves special attention. This is especially true of the marketing of services by public agencies.

But what are services? Certainly any comprehensive approach to the study of services marketing must begin at the conceptual level.

NOTES AND REFERENCES

1. Holton, R. H. (1958) 'The Distinctions Between Convenience Goods, Shopping Goods, and Specialty Goods'. *Journal of Marketing* **23** (July): 53–56, and (1959) 'What is Really Meant by "Specialty Goods"?' *Journal of Marketing* **24** (July): 64–66; Luck, D. J. (1959) 'On the Nature of Specialty Goods'. *Journal of Marketing* **24** (July): 61–64.
2. McVey, P. (1960) 'Are Channels of Distribution What the Textbooks Say?' *Journal of Marketing* **24** (January): 61–65.
3. Beckman, T. N. and Buzzell, R. D. (1955) 'What is the Marketing Margin for Agricultural Products?' *Journal of Marketing* **20** (October): 166–168.
4. *Survey of Current Business* (1964) **44** (July): 16.
5. Judd, R. C. (1964) 'The Case for Redefining Services'. *Journal of Marketing* **28** (January): 58–59, at p. 59.
6. For an interesting discussion of relations between clients and client-serving organizations see Bidwell, C. E. and Vreeland, R. S. (1963) 'Authority and Control in Client-serving Organizations'. *The Sociological Quarterly* **4** (Summer): 231–242.
7. Regan, W. J. (1963) 'The Service Revolution'. *Journal of Marketing* **27** (July): 57–62, at pp. 61–62.
8. 'Why Union Eyes Are on Fringes'. (1964) *Business Week* (September 12): 60.
9. McKittrick, J. B. (1962) 'The Nature of the Involvement of Marketing Management in the Profit Failure'. In *Marketing Precision and Executive Action* (C. H. Hindersman, Ed.). Chicago: American Marketing Association, pp. 75–88, at pp. 81–82.
10. 'Why Service Workers are Less Productive'. (1964) *Business Week* (November 14): 156.

Section II

The Service Experience

In this section of the reader we present some contemporary work considering elements of the service experience. It has been argued that services are no more than an experience, and as such the management of the service experience is the essence of service management. In the first article by Grove, Fisk and Bitner (1992) the authors present a means of understanding experiences based upon a drama perspective referred to as dramaturgy. This approach uses a theatrical metaphor to explore elements of the consumer's service experience. After identifying a number of parallels between the service product and drama, which includes the existence of roles, scripts and actors in both settings, the authors go on to consider how the drama metaphor can be used to investigate the delivery of the service product. By focusing upon four critical dimensions – the actors, the setting, the audience and the performance – this article is able to demonstrate that the metaphor can be meaningfully extended to the development of service strategy. The attraction of this work is the holistic nature of the framework which allows for an informed analysis of the consumer's service experience. It also presents opportunities for both a new descriptive vocabulary and a means of classifying elements of the service product. In total, this approach has many attractions not least the ease of access to service terminology. However, the authors also provide a caution. First, that the dramaturgy approach does not have universal application and second, that the notion of acting can sometimes be confused with insincerity. It may be, for instance, that total rehearsal of the performance removes an important part of experience such as variation, customisation and the need to be individually responsive. Continuing the metaphor, why pay more for first and last nights if all performances are the same?

There has been an almost implicit acceptance that services are 'riskier' than physical goods due to their intangibility and the nature of their delivery. But when looking for evidence of this in the large perceived risk and uncertainty literature there appears to be almost no mention of it. The article by Murray and Schlacter (1990) presents for the first time evidence that services do indeed invoke heightened perceptions of risk and perceptions of variability. The article draws upon perceived risk literature associated with physical products to present a series of eight hypotheses which are then sequentially examined through empirical work based upon an experimental methodology. The importance of this work is in the rigorous examination of risk as applied to service products and in the presentation of the conclusions. The first outcome of the research results is that risk reduction strategies associated with service products must be focused upon employees, encouraging continuity of personal relationships and thereby reducing the perception of variability. Second, that the methodology adopted allows for some operationalisation of 'goods' and 'services' constructs and finally that there exists differentiation among service products in consumers minds, i.e. that they are not a generic class.

The theme of differential responses by consumers is continued in the paper by Hui and Bateson (1991). The authors explore in some detail components of the service encounter in order to explain the impact of the physical setting upon consumer evaluations. The article concerns the role of perceived control which is described as the perceived ability to demonstrate competence, superiority and mastery over the environment. It is argued that this is a crucial variable in mediating the consumer's emotional and behavioural response to both the physical environment in which a service is delivered and the service personnel. The authors use two situational variables to pursue their hypotheses – consumer density (crowding) and consumer choice (degree of discretion) – to investigate the evaluation of the encounter and to assess approach–avoidance response. For those with a quantitative leaning the mechanics of the analysis are worth the effort in terms of understanding the basis of the proposed model. For those without such a leaning the article presents an integrated model which supports the contention that perceived control does have explanatory power in explaining the effects of consumer choice and consumer density on consumer evaluations of the service. The article ends with a discussion of the possible managerial responses to the conclusions drawn and an agenda for research concentrated upon the investigation of pleasurable versus unpleasurable experiences.

The paper by Gabbott and Hogg (1994) is intended as a general review of the main issues facing researchers and practitioners in locating the study of service consumption. Its inclusion here is to present evidence that consumers' experiences are highly dependent upon how and what they perceive. This is achieved by taking the defining characteristics of services and examining their impact upon information search, comparison and evaluation. The general issues are then used to provide some indication of the practical problems facing consumers when interacting with service products and in evaluating their service experiences. In the first section it is proposed that objective prepurchase information about services is difficult to obtain and there is a natural tendency for consumers to look to others to provide detail on the service experience as a source of both additional and verification information. In the second section the article re-emphasises the importance of peripheral or tangible cues used to approximate missing product information. Finally the article turns to the problem of evaluation, specifically the issue of credence and the role of experience in building credence. In conclusion the article provides a discussion of both consumer and service provider responses to the identified issues.

The final paper in this section, by Bitner, Booms and Mohr (1994), considers one of the most important elements in the service experience for consumers: the service employee. The basis of the article is that in order to fully understand the service encounter behaviour needs to be analysed from both the employee's and the customer's perspective in order to establish the events and types of behaviours which contribute to satisfaction and dissatisfaction. Apart from tackling the immensely complex area of interpersonal behaviour the authors also adopt an unusual but highly effective methodology. The authors present a theoretical perspective based upon how people use role expectation and scripts to formalise their behaviours, pointing to the importance of both as variables in explaining differences in expectations between customers and employees. Similarly the existence of self-serving attribution bias would also partially explain differences in perceptions of the encounter between groups. The critical incident methodology highlights a number of important differences in perception between the encounter participants and focuses upon the issue of 'problem customers' both in terms of their impact upon staff and their own encounter. The article finishes with a good discussion of the managerial implications of the research which points to the central importance of front-line staff in mediating the consumer's experience.

CONTENTS

6

Dramatizing the Service Experience:
A Managerial Approach

Stephen J. Grove, Raymond P. Fisk and Mary Jo Bitner

INTRODUCTION

The growth of the services economy has been widely documented and discussed. Seventy-one percent of the US GNP is produced by service industries (US Bureau of Census, 1988). Furthermore, 'service sector jobs are now a soaring seventy-two percent of all US employment' (Heskett, 1986, p. 3). The expanding interest in services marketing and management is partially related to economic trends such as the deregulation of various service industries, the growth of franchising, the relaxation of professional association standards, and computerization and technological innovation (Lovelock, 1984, 1988).

Services managers have recognized that they face several challenges unique to the nature of service products. First, supply and demand management is much more difficult than in physical goods industries (Lovelock, 1984; Sasser, 1976; Zeithaml, Parasuraman and Berry, 1985). Second, quality control in services marketing is elusive due to the inability to standardize and imperfect human performance (Bateson, 1989; Bitner and Zeithaml, 1988; Brown and Swartz, 1989; Parasuraman, Zeithaml and Berry, 1988; Zeithaml, Berry and Parasuraman, 1988; Ziethaml, Parasuraman and Berry, 1985). Third, it is difficult to calculate the costs of services, which makes pricing services a formidable task (Dearden, 1978; Guiltinan, 1987; Zeithaml, Parasuraman and Berry, 1985). Other contemporary services marketing issues include concerns over how to organize service systems (Kingman-Brundage, 1989; Shostack, 1984a, 1984b, 1987), how to portray the service encounter (Czepiel, Solomon and Surprenant, 1985; Solomon *et al.*, 1985), how to understand the service environment (Baker, 1987), how to personalize services (Surprenant and Solomon, 1985, 1987) and how to incorporate internal marketing strategies (Grönroos, 1985, 1990).

The search for services marketing generalizations has lagged behind the investigation of specific service industry issues. In 1985, only 17% (340 of 1991) of

Reprinted with permission from *Advances in Services Marketing and Management*, Vol. 1, pp 91–121.
© 1992 JAI Press Inc.

the American Marketing Association's services marketing bibliography (Fisk and Tansuhaj, 1985) addressed general conceptual insights while 83% was industry specific. In a recent computerized expansion of the services marketing bibliography (Fisk, Tansuhaj and Crosby, 1988) the general conceptual literature had eroded to slightly less than 15% (574 of 3910) of total services marketing literature. In short, conceptualizations and frameworks are needed that demonstrate common characteristics across services, distinguish services from physical goods marketing and address what Shostack (1984a) has termed 'descriptive language problems'. In addition, new taxonomies are needed that serve to summarize existing knowledge and provide direction for future research (e.g. Murphy and Enis, 1986). Also, conceptualizations and frameworks are needed that can facilitate the understanding and control of services marketing.

In recent years, several marketing scholars have acknowledged the 'drama-related' dimensions associated with services marketing. For instance, Lovelock (1981) argued that services marketers must perform several 'roles', among which are the services marketer as 'dramatist' and 'choreographer'. Berry (1981) detailed the efficacy of the Disney Corporation's practice of using show business terms such as 'cast member', 'onstage' and 'show' to describe its various operations at Disneyland and Walt Disney World. In addition, Grönroos (1985) has suggested that services are essentially 'performances', a sentiment echoed by Berry, Zeithaml and Parasuraman (1985) who argue that 'the manner in which the service is performed can be a crucial component of the service from the consumer's point of view' (p. 46). Others (Lovelock *et al.*, 1981; Booms and Bitner, 1982) have stressed the often subtle, yet pervasive influence of a service's physical 'setting'. In fact, 'it plays much the same role as packaging does for manufactured goods' (Booms and Bitner, 1982, p. 39). In short, many 'drama' aspects of services marketing can be recognized and ultimately managed.

The goal of this article is to demonstrate that (1) the drama metaphor is applicable to the marketing management of service organizations and (2) the drama metaphor framework can be utilized to enhance the understanding and control of services marketing and management. The drama metaphor is uniquely suited to managing services marketing phenomena because it captures the dynamics of the human interactions that occur. First, the drama metaphor is presented and explained. Second, an approach to dramatizing the services marketing mix that emerges from a '7 Ps' approach to services (Booms and Bitner, 1981) is presented. Third, two strategic models are developed that apply the drama tools, and service industry examples are explicated to clarify the applications of the strategic models. Fourth, strategic guidelines for services managers are presented. Finally, several contributions to services marketing thought, as well as several cautions concerning the drama framework, are discussed.

METAPHOR

A metaphor is described by Nisbet (1969, p. 4) as a way of proceeding from the known to the unknown by transferring the qualities of familiar objects to objects that are unfamiliar due to their remoteness or complexity. Poets, philosophers, socio-linguists and others have long recognized the power of the metaphor as a descriptive and analytical device. By presenting a symbolically rich message that evokes from its receiver details or 'chunks' of information lacking in a literal translation of the message, the metaphor creates a vivid mental image. As such, the metaphor often succeeds at capturing and communicating the experiential and/or processual characteristics of many phenomena that resist comprehension through logic and words alone. Whether it is applying the concept of a 'machine' to an organization structure, categorizing stock market investors as 'bulls' and 'bears', or depicting the researcher as a 'detective', the metaphor moves beyond the literal to describe and connect unfamiliar topics (Ortony 1975), generate analysis and hypotheses (Morgan, 1980) and, in some instances, serve as the basis for entire schools of thought (Arndt, 1985; Morgan, 1980). The next sections explore the drama metaphor, marketing metaphors and drama as a marketing metaphor for services.

The drama metaphor

The proposition that human behavior is drama has a rich historical tradition. Centuries ago, William Shakespeare (1600) accentuated the theatrical nature of human behavior when he wrote, 'All the world's a stage, and all the men and women merely players.' More recently, writers such as Kenneth Burke (1945, 1950, 1968), Erving Goffman (1959, 1967, 1974), R. S. Perinbanayagam (1974), Gregory Stone (1962) and a host of others have described the dramatic aspects of social interaction. Implicit in these observations is the perspective that people are symbol users who interact with others based on the meanings assigned to different features present at a behavioral setting.

The drama metaphor does not 'seek to discover or to impute to human behavior causal kinds of relations ... the concern is simply to describe the process of human behaving' (Brissett and Edgley, 1975, p. 4). In a manner similar to that of actors in a theatrical production, people utilize various dramatic devices in their everyday interactions to convey desired information. As such, any object or action, including properties of the physical environment, language, gestures, expressions, etc., may be used to influence another's perception and assessment of an interactive situation and, ultimately, his/her response to it. Just as one's understanding of a movie or theatrical production develops as the plot unfolds, one's definitions of reality emerge as actions occur and meanings are assigned to the many signs and symbols found in the behavioral setting. Social reality, then, is not simply like drama – it *is* drama insofar as it is a communication and symbolic discourse that involves articulation, definition and interactive processes (Perinbanayagam, 1974, p. 533).

Within the discipline of sociology the metaphor of human behavior as drama serves as the basis for the general school of thought called 'dramaturgy'. Perhaps best articulated through the networks of Goffman (1959, 1967, 1974), dramaturgy has spawned a depiction of social behavior as theatrical 'performances' among 'actors' who present themselves and their actions in such a way as to create a desired 'impression' one 'gives' and 'gives off' before an 'audience', in what is termed 'the front region'. Through the 'rehearsal' of performances away from the audience's view in the 'back region', aspects of the social 'actors' presentation are worked out, so a general coherence exists among 'the settings, appearance and manner' (Goffman,

1959, p. 25) that ultimately contributes to an authentic, sincere and/or believable performance.

In essence, the drama metaphor argues that the development and maintenance of a definition of an interaction relies on the audience's input as well as the actors' presentation. Through all of this, performances are viewed as tenuous, fragile processes, which can be disrupted by even minor mishaps such as unintended gestures or slips of behavior.

Marketing metaphors

Marketers have only recently begun to explore the use of metaphors as conceptual tools (Arndt, 1985; Zikmund, 1982; Stern, 1988), despite the fact that the use of metaphors is common in marketing (Zikmund, 1982). For example, phenomena such as the evolution of retailing, the pattern of a product's sales over time, the path that a product takes as it moves to market and the desired combination of marketing variables are vividly and compactly represented by the metaphors of a '*wheel* of retailing', a 'product *life cycle*', a '*channel* of distribution' and a 'marketing *mix*', respectively. A recent metaphor, which has gained significant popularity within the business literature, is the depiction of the marketing enterprise as warfare (e.g. Duro and Sandstrom, 1987; Kotler and Singh, 1981; Michaelson, 1987; Ries and Trout, 1986).

Drama as a marketing metaphor for services

Several parallels can be easily drawn between the concerns of a services manager and the proposition that drama is a metaphor for human behavior. For example, both are concerned with the strategies and tactics employed by participants to create and maintain a desirable impression before an audience, and both recognize that one way to accomplish this is through the careful management of 'expressions given and given off' by the actors and the physical setting of their behavior. Paralleling the insights of many services marketing scholars, Goffman (1959) observes that performances serve

> ...mainly to express characteristics of the task that is performed and not the characteristics of the performers. Thus, one finds that service personnel, whether in profession, bureaucracy, business, or craft enliven their manner with movements which express proficiency and integrity, but whether this manner conveys about them, often its major purpose is to establish a favorable definition of their services or product (p. 77).

Can the drama metaphor provide a way to understand and control service experiences? The remainder of this article argues that due to numerous similarities between the characteristics of service experiences and the elements comprising dramatic analysis, depicting services via the drama metphor is a logical and stimulating exercise that provides both a vocabulary and a conceptual framework for communicating and understanding services marketing and management.

DRAMATIZING THE SERVICES MARKETING MIX

The notion of the marketing mix refers to the tools or activities that are essential to marketing and that enable an enterprise to communicate with and satisfy its target markets. More specifically, the 'mix' term is intended to convey the importance of blending these tools in various desirable combinations. Traditionally, the marketing mix has been conceived as consisting of '4 Ps': *product, price, promotion* and *place* (McCarthy, 1960).

Booms and Bitner (1981) argued for the expansion of the marketing mix for services beyond the original '4 Ps'. Because services are often produced and consumed simultaneously and because customers frequently interact directly with the organization's personnel, the service manager has additional controllable elements with which to communicate and satisfy customers. Booms and Bitner (1981) proposed that these additional variables should be recognized in a broader marketing mix for services that captures the social and physical context of services by adding three additional 'Ps' (p. 48):

- *Participants* – 'All human actors who play a part in service delivery and thus influence the buyer's perceptions' (personnel and other customers).
- *Physical evidence* – 'The environment in which the service is assembled and where the firm and the customer interact.'
- *Process of service assembly* – 'The actual procedures, mechanisms, and flow of activities by which the service is delivered.'

It has become generally accepted that the services marketing mix is different from the traditional marketing mix. Cowell (1985) included Booms and Bitner's '3 New Ps' in his services marketing textbook. Meanwhile, Magrath (1986) has proposed '3 New Ps' for services marketing that are quite similar (personnel, physical facilities and process management) to those of Booms and Bitner. Prus and Frisby (1987) have also advocated two similar new Ps: people and process. In addition, continued support for the '3 New Ps' for services marketing has come from Bitner and Zeithaml (1988). The drama metaphor helps clarify the unique marketing management significance of the '3 New Ps' as proposed by Booms and Bitner.

Major drama concepts are analogous to the '3 New Ps' and can be utilized to operationalize their management. As shown in Table 1, the term 'participants' is analogous to the theatrical terms of 'actors' and 'audience', 'physical evidence' is analogous, to the 'setting' and 'process of service assembly' is analogous to the 'performance'. As with many marketing management concepts, these drama concepts embody a strong change agent orientation. Moreover, Bell (1981) has

Table 1. Drama analogues to 'Three New Ps'

Three new Ps	Drama
Participants	Actors/Audience
Physical evidence	Setting
Process of service assembly	Performance

argued that services are uniquely suited to remixing the marketing mix during the consumption of the service. The most easily remixed elements of the services marketing mix are the '3 New Ps': *participants, physical evidence* and *process of service assembly*. The drama perspective provides a framework uniquely suited for remixing these '3 New Ps' of the services marketing mix.

But will the use of these drama analogues facilitate operationalizing the management of the '3 New Ps?' Two strategic models will assist in the investigation of this question.

STRATEGIC MODELS

In approaching the service experience as drama four critical drama elements need examination: (1) the actors (personnel) whose presence and actions define the service; (2) the audience (customers) to whom the service is directed; (3) the physical setting in which the experience occurs; and (4) the service performance itself. Each of these elements represents an essential component that contributes to the service experience. Drama is the product of actors and the enactment of their roles, the scenery and staging of the action, and the audience and its involvement; the service experience is defined by similar features. First, strategic models that incorporate these drama elements are presented. Second, each drama element is examined in detail, which includes consideration of how these elements are commonly manifested in various service industries and examples of how specific service organizations have distinguished themselves by emphasizing one or more of the drama elements.

The service experience as drama

Figure 1 presents a generic model of the service experience as drama. The broadest level of the model is the setting. The setting is basically the background to the model

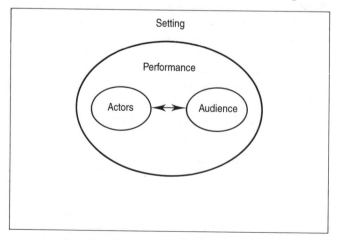

Figure 1. The service experience as drama.

and it encompasses all the dimensions embodied in the service's physical environment. The remaining components of the model represent the foreground. As depicted, the foreground concerns people and represents the social context of the model. The actors and audience are positioned at the model's center to emphasize that a service performance is largely a product of their interaction within the context of a particular setting. The bi-directional arrow between actors and audience represents the interdependence of the two entities in determining the service performance. The service performance is a unique type of restricted marketing exchange (Bagozzi, 1975) in which the actors' offering is both a response to and determinant of the audience behavior and vice versa.

While any service that involves face-to-face contact between the service provider(s) and the customer(s) within a market-controlled environment can be represented by Figure 1 (e.g. hospitals, hotels, restaurants, airlines, etc.), it is the strategic combination of these components that characterizes the nature of a particular service. For example, one hotel may strive to create an upscale service experience through careful attention to the setting's physical evidence and atmospherics, well-rehearsed scripts on the part of the actors, and a concerted effort to monitor and control the audience. Another hotel might seek a low-priced, 'no frills' service performance by reducing or altering its emphasis on the theatrical elements.

The service performance cube

Figure 2 presents a model that depicts the relative importance of the three theatrical elements comprising a service performance using a three-dimensional plus – minus structure (a '+' indicates more importance while a '−' indicates less importance). In this context, importance refers to the degree of significance that can be attributed to the drama element. The 'service performance' embraces and is a function of the

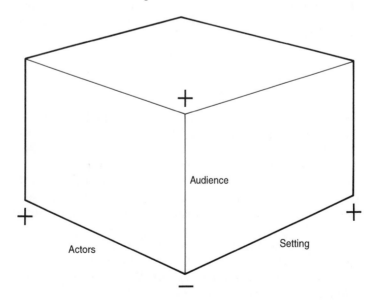

Figure 2. The service performance cube.

dimensions of actors, audience and setting. Hence, the management of these three theatrical elements affects the nature of the service performance. Each part of the 'service performance cube' can be managed before the performance begins. For any given service organization, managers may employ varying degrees of emphasis on the three dimensions of the cube. For example, until recently, women giving birth were served by hospitals that delivered babies in sterile settings, without the father present and with the physician in complete control of the delivery. Women demanded better 'settings' and more involvement of family 'audience' members and the health care system slowly responded. Today, a woman is more likely to deliver her baby by natural childbirth methods in a hospital's 'birthing' room resplendent with reminders of home. In addition, the father is typically present and assisting during the delivery. This contemporary version of childbirth represents a 'dramatically' different position on the service performance cube than the older method.

While variations in the relative importance of the various theatrical elements may be recognized within specific service industries, it is possible to identify modal responses to the elements that distinguish one service industry from another. For example, restaurants typically must attend to the potential impact of each of the theatrical components of a service experience while most motion picture theaters – despite requiring similar attention to the setting and audience components – probably are not as directly affected by the impact of the actor component (ticket takers, ushers, etc).

The 'service performance cube' offers potential insights into the positioning of services organizations. An organization may 'position' itself in terms of its emphasis on actors, audience or setting. Moreover, the 'service performance cube' can be used to facilitate identifying market niches for new services or adaptations of existing services.

The following discussion further explicates the drama elements of actors, audience, setting and performance and provides numerous specific service organization examples to clarify the many ways these drama elements can be manifested.

The actors

Just as the success of a theatrical production relies largely on the expertise and credibility of those on stage, a satisfying service experience for many services is determined largely by the service's contact personnel. From the audience's (consumer's) perspective, those delivering the service may represent the service itself; their 'technical skills' (what they do) and their 'functional skills' (how they do it) are observed and evaluated and become prime indicators of the service's quality (Grönroos, 1985). Consequently, just as theatrical performers must attend to a variety of considerations in the interest of a successful show, service 'actors' are obliged to attend to several critical dimensions of their role in the service's performance to foster the proper impression or desired definitions of the service.

Among the dramaturgical dimensions of the contact personnel that are particularly relevant for a service's evaluation are the actors': (1) appearance and manner, termed 'personal front' by Goffman (1959); (2) skill in playing their parts or performing their routines in the service's delivery; and (3) commitment to the service performance. The actors' appearance and manner consist of such personal information as dress, grooming and demeanor, which help to form the identity, mood and/or attitudes conveyed to others (Solomon, 1985; Stone, 1962). Attention to these aspects of the service personnel's presentation is one means of 'tangibilizing' a service (Berry, 1980) and can help establish consumer expectations prior to a service's performance. The skill displayed by the actors in fulfilling their service roles refers to a myriad of considerations such as competence, courtesy, knowledge, reliability and communicative abilities, all of which have been identifed as important determinants of service quality (Parasuraman, Zeithaml and Berry, 1985). How the contact personnel perform their parts in the service production contributes to the consumer's total impression of the service reality (Shostack, 1977; Zeithaml, Parasuraman and Berry, 1985).

Intimately related to one's skillful service role enactment is one's level of commitment to the service's performance. Commitment may be evidenced by the actor's determination to learn his/her part correctly, to sustain the service's impression even under conditions of personal duress and to recognize, plan for and respond to the audience's particular needs or desires (Bitner, Booms and Tetreault, 1990). Motivation for such a commitment may be the by-product of a service organization's 'internal marketing' effort (Berry, 1980; Grönroos, 1985; Sasser and Arbeit, 1978), which instills a consumer-orientation and stresses the sanctity of producing a quality service. When combined, these three dimensions of the actors' presentation affect the audience's perception of the service delivery process, a determination that ultimately influences the assessment of the service's excellence (Berry, 1980; Parasuraman, Zeithaml and Berry, 1985; Sasser, Olsen and Wyckoff, 1978; Surprenant and Solomon, 1985).

Since services typically vary with respect to the degree of direct personal contact between the service personnel and the consumer, the relative importance of the actors and their attention to dramaturgical dimensions will vary commensurately. Service organizations such as hospitals, restaurants, resorts and the like, which offer a high degree of contact between the service employees and consumers, are particularly affected by the actors' dramaturgical acumen. Services, such as public utility companies or automatic transfer machines (ATMs), which involve little or no direct personal contact between the service and the customer are obviously less affected. Furthermore, it is likely that the actors' impact will be felt more greatly in those services characterized by repeated contact with the customer, such as banking or medical services, or those services in which there is little or no other contact with the organization other than interaction with an employee at the organization's boundary, such as is the case with express mail companies and travel and insurance agencies. It is also quite important to recognize the potentially great impact of the actors' dramaturgical presentation in those services in which the contact personnel have discretion in determining the nature of the service and how it is delivered, such as education, medical services, legal services and the like. In each of these circumstances, the actors are likely to be scrutinized closely by their audience as evidence tangibilizing the service and determining its excellence.

It is apparent from this discussion that many industries exist in which the actors or contact personnel are inherently important in determining customer perceptions of the service. For example, a patient's evaluation of medical service received in a hospital is closely tied to perceptions of physician and nursing staff technical expertise as well as the functional, or process quality, of interactions with these same contact personnel. In the case of hospitals, it is almost impossible to separate the patient's evaluation of the service from his/her perceptions of the actors who deliver it. Indeed, as far as the patient is concerned, the actors, doctors, nurses, etc.) *are* the service.

In other industries, the importance of the actor may not be as obvious as it is with medical services. In such industries, an opportunity for an organization often arises to distinguish itself from its competitors by emphasizing the role of contact personnel in determining service quality. This is a notion discussed by Berry, Parasuraman and Zeithaml (1988) as the 'people factor'. Scandinavian Airlines System (SAS) has successfully implemented this approach and has gained competitive strength by stressing the personal service component of the marketing mix. SAS has accomplished this by allowing its employees far greater discretion than is typical in the airline industry (Carlzon, 1987). SAS employees are trained to 'serve the customer' and are given almost free reign to interpret what that means for each customer. The result is more satisfied customers and happier employees. Clearly, SAS has demonstrated the importance of the actor component of the services marketing mix.

The audience

A second strategic component in the depiction of the service experience as drama is the audience in whose presence the service is delivered. Since the customer must be present for many services to occur (e.g. airlines, dental treatment, etc.), one of the often cited characteristics of services is the inseparability of production from consumption (Berry, 1980; Judd, 1964; Lovelock, 1981, 1983; Regan, 1963; Shostack, 1977). As Berry, Zeithaml and Parasuraman (1985) contend, for many services, customers are 'in the factory' where they observe and 'consume' the service firsthand as it is delivered.

The condition of inseparability underscores the impact an audience may have on a service performance. The customer receiving the service or other customers present at the service experience may exercise a profound influence over a service's delivery and/or outcome (Booms and Bitner, 1981; Carman and Langeard, 1980; Langeard *et al.*, 1981; Lovelock, 1983; Martin and Pranter, 1989; Parasuraman, Zeithaml and Berry, 1985, 1988). Crowding, unruly or unanticipated behavior on the part of others sharing the service or an unwillingness or inability to cooperate with the service production on the part of the individual customer can destroy a service performance.

In short, just as the audience of a theatrical production has a responsibility to participate in the staging of the show by accepting certain rules or standards of behavior, the customers of a service are similarly obliged. As a member of the audience, not only must the customer refrain from undermining another's service experience, but he or she must also strive to enable the actors to perform at their best. This means that the customer must be informed and educated as to the expectations and requirements demanded of one as a service participant (e.g. the proper protocol and procedures to evoke a satisfying service) and cooperate accordingly (e.g. provide service personnel with the necessary inputs to perform their tasks adequately) (Bowen, 1986; Mills and Morris, 1986). Whether it is learning how to use an ATM correctly, giving a physician an accurate account of one's symptoms or responding to the rights and privileges of others sharing a service, the audience plays an active role in the service production. Through it all, the service customer – like his/her theater patron counterpart – is expected to accept tacitly the dramaturgical rule that the 'show must go on' by tolerating minor imperfections of the service performance in the interest of the overall production.

As the strategic component, the audience is an important element to consider under several conditions. Beyond those circumstances in which a high degree of direct contact with the service is involved (as discussed previously), the audience's importance also increases when a self-service feature is added to the service (ATMs, fast-food, etc.). In such cases, the audience is instrumental in determining the service's outcome (Lovelock and Young, 1979; Silpakit and Fisk, 1985). The importance of the audience is similarly evident in those services characterized as requiring a high degree of personalization (insurance, legal advice) since the audience must provide the proper inputs (e.g. communication of needs, special wants, etc.) to ensure a satisfying performance by the actors (Berry, 1983). Increased audience importance is also found among those services that cater to several or many customers simultaneously (restaurants, entertainment, etc.) since other customers can influence one's service experience and satisfaction (Grove and Fisk, 1983; Lovelock, 1983; Martin and Pranter, 1989).

Organizations skillful in their management of customer participation and customer–customer interactions can improve the value of the service from the customer's point of view. In cases when a high degree of customer participation is required, organizations can embrace their service by teaching customers their role in the service script. Bateson (1985) has argued that a clear understanding of the service script and one's part in it will increase consumers' perceptions of control of the situation insofar as they can predict the unfolding of events. Ultimately, an increased sense of control results in more satisfied customers.

Many successful service organizations have recognized the importance of educating their customers to ensure correct performance of the script. Obvious examples include various self-service restaurants where signs and verbal directions from employees help to move customers through the different steps required to create their meals. Signs on tables and doors help to ensure that customers will also clean up after themselves. Another example is the extensive effort that was required to educate bank customers in the proper use of ATMs when the devices were first introduced. To enhance their adoption, it was necessary to familiarize customers with the new technology properly, as well as aid them in overcoming the depersonalization of a formerly personal service.

Less obvious examples of customer education occur in many professional services in which clients must provide accurate information to the professional in order to receive the service they need. Professional organizations that do a good job communicating the service script and what is required of the client go a long way toward ensuring quality service outcomes. For example, an individual who goes to Hyatt Legal Services to have a will written enacts a different script than one who seeks the assistance of a 'downtown' law firm for the same purpose. In either case, clear communication of the client role is essential to the service outcome. Another interesting example in the professional service area occurs with hospital surgery services. Many hospitals now thoroughly educate the patient prior to surgery regarding post-surgery events, including how he or she will feel following surgery and the procedures that will be used. Knowing what will happen and knowing one's role in the process may increase a patient's sense of perceived control and satisfaction.

The other issue faced in managing the 'audience' or the participants relates to managing customer–customer interactions. Presumably, if all customers understand the script and enact their parts properly, there should be no conflicts among participants. A good example is the Benihana restaurant chain where interaction among customers is part of the service concept. Customers are seated in groups of eight to 10 around a central cooking area where the Japanese chef prepares each meal. Often, customers are seated next to complete strangers – a circumstance that might cause social distress in some other situations. Yet, this is the accepted 'script' at Benihana and a distinguishing characteristic of the restaurant's success.

However, many service organizations atract a variety of market segments that may each be enacting slightly different scripts. This is often the case for recreational and hospitality services such as ski resorts and hotels, among others. A hotel may be simultaneously serving a large trade show convention, a group of businesswomen, families on vacation and newleywed couples on their honeymoons. Each of these customer types has different needs and purposes for being at the hotel and probably contrasting scripts as well. To minimize potential clashes among their different customer groups, many hotels try to separate physically the market segments or encourage them to use the hotel at different times. Education of the customers as to the various scripts that may be operating may also help. For example, letting the businesswomen know what time of day the trade show conventioneers will be checking out and offering them an alternative check-out time might avoid unnecessary delays and complaints.

The setting

A third strategic component in the model of services as theater is the physical setting in which the service performance occurs. As in the staging of a theatrical production that relies on scenery, props and other physical cues to create desired impressions, a service may employ a myriad of devices to do likewise. In the words of Shostack (1977), the 'setting can play an enormous role in influencing the "reality" of a service in the consumer's mind' (p. 78).

As depicted in Figure 1, the setting embraces various features which surround the service interaction that transpires between the actors and the audience. Marketers have long recognized the potential importance of the physical environment for defining and facilitating the service exchange (Baker, 1987; Booms and Bitner, 1982; Grove and Fisk, 1983; Sherowksi, 1983; Shostack, 1977; Upah and Fulton, 1985; Zeithaml, 1981; Zeithaml, Parasuraman and Berry, 1985). Among a setting's features that may influence the character of a service are the colors or brightness of the service's surroundings; the volume and pitch of sounds employed/present within the setting; the scents, movement, freshness and temperature of the air; the use of space; the style and comfort of the furnishings; the setting's design and cleanliness; and a host of other 'atmospherics' (Kotler, 1973). All these represent evidence or tangible clues that help determine a service's reality.

Just as conditions exist under which the strategic components of service actors and audience become more important, conditions arise under which the service's setting increases in its impact. For example, the setting is likely to be more important when the time a consumer spends in the organization's environment is substantial, as may be the case with hospitals, hotels/resorts or air travel. A longer duration of contact with the service environment amplifies the potential effect of the setting's features.

The setting also increases in importance when the nature of a service may be distinguished by its environment. For instance, although they represent the same generic services, Motel 6 and Westin Hotels, Steak and Ale and Ponderosa Steakhouses, or Hyatt Legal Services and a 'downtown' law firm are usually perceived as quite different, partially due to setting characteristics. Relatedly, the importance of the setting increases when an intended market segment may be identified through a service's physical environment, as is often attempted by retail stores, restaurants or hotels. In such a circumstance, the setting provides cues that are designed to attract and appeal to a specific type of audience. For example, the settings of Chuck E. Cheese versus Pizza Hut pizza parlors are created to target quite different audiences.

Finally, a service's setting may prove to be extremely important for those special cases in which the audience is unfamiliar with the service offered and/or have few (if any) other cues upon which to judge the service. Organizations that market new service concepts are wise to rely on physical cues to simplify, tangibilize and communicate information about their offerings. In such circumstances, the physical environment may provide valuable information and indicators of quality that can facilitate consumer understanding of the service in question.

In summary, much like the theatrical production that relies on scenery and other physical cues to help define the stage action, the nature of a service in many cases is intimately tied to the environment in which it occurs. Recognizing and responding to this proposition may better enable service marketers to devise and implement the service reality they desire.

Despite the potential impact of environmental design on the audience's perceptions of the service, most design decisions are based on aesthetics from a professional designer's point of view) or on operational efficiencies. The customer, or ultimate user of the facility, is rarely consulted directly. Yet the 'atmospherics' of a service may be as important in determining the image of the organization as any variable in the services marketing mix. Many successful service organizations have recognized this power and have distinguished themselves by creative management of their physical facilities. Physical facilities can be used effectively to accomplish a variety of marketing goals, including communicating a new concept, repositioning an organization in the eyes of its target market or attracting new market segments (Booms and Bitner, 1982).

For example, when Speedi Lube started in Seattle, Washington, the owners knew they were offering an unfamiliar service to consumers. The concept of an efficient 10-minute, no-appointment-necessary, efficient car lubrication and oil change was unknown to car owners. To communicate clearly the new concept to potential customers, Speedi Lube made use of every element of physical evidence at its disposal. It communicated efficiency through crisp and clear exterior signage, tidy employee uniforms and an organized shop area painted in bright colors. It also tangibilized its service through use of a graphic schematic on the waiting room wall that showed customers exactly what was being done to their car. Further tangible evidence was provided in a checklist given to the customer showing all services performed. All this was very different from what most car owners were used to finding at corner service stations, and it served to make a new service concept a reality.

Many service organizations have been successful in repositioning themselves through skillful use of physical evidence. Facing increasing competition, a number of banks have hired retail consultants to help reposition themselves as consumer-oriented organizations with a variety of services to offer. Bank One is an example of this approach (Weiner, 1986). Bank One's interior space is no longer divided between a row of tellers on one side and imposing desks on the other, the traditional layout for a bank. Rather, a number of smaller boutiques, similar to a retail store, separate real estate services from stock brokerage, from travel services, etc. On the other side of the bank are the bank's core services: three tellers, an automated teller machine and a new accounts desk. Creative packaging of products and appealing displays are used to attract new market segments and to increase business and loyalty among old customers. All these changes in the physical decor and layout are intended to reposition the bank as a multi-service 'store' rather than a traditional bank. Thus, the setting of the service's delivery helps to define its dramatic performance.

The performance

Applying the drama metaphor to services marketing depicts the service experience as a performance in which the dramaturgical components of actors, audience and setting combine to create and sustain a service definition. Since services are processual in nature, the service definition emerges over time in response to the blending of the various components and their manifestations (see Figure 1). In the quest to present a credible and forceful service performance, it is important to coordinate the evidence provided by the actors and the setting and involve the audience adequately in the service's staging. A theatrical production adorned by magnificent scenery is likely to fail if the actors' skills are poor, just as the artful enactment of actors' roles may be for naught if the production's staging is remiss. So too, a service performance is doomed if key dramatic components do not support one another or are not responsive to the audience. It is also important to seek consistency among the dramaturgical elements over the duration of a service encounter and from one encounter to the next. Maintaining congruity between the actors' manner, actions and appearance and the cues from the service's physical environment in the performance can help establish a clear defination of a service. For example, a retail bank seeking an image of stability and competence is advised to determine from the audience's perspective the appropriate aspects to stress in the actors' and setting's contribution to a service performance that articulate such a definition. These should then be implemented so as to complement one another and fashion a single service reality. Service organizations such as McDonald's and Marriott are good examples of operations with well-defined images of service excellence based largely on the coordination and consistency of the dramaturgical components.

Further contributing to a quality performance is a strong customer-orientation as evidenced, among other things, by actively monitoring and adapting to the audience's responses to the unfolding service drama. This involves the willingness and capacity of the service actors (contact personnel and those working in the back region) to recognize the subtle (or not so subtle) cues of the audience's satisfaction with various aspects of the emerging service action and adjust the performance accordingly. Whether it is altering one's role, playing down aspects of one's service presentation, adjusting the physical environment or undertaking some other action in response to perceived audience desires, such adaptations reflect the adaptive character of a service performance.

DRAMA STRATEGY GUIDELINES

The underlying premise of the '3 New Ps' (*participants, physical evidence* and *process of service delivery*) is that each of the new Ps can aid in achieving marketing goals and thus should be managed as elements of the organization's strategy (Booms and Bitner, 1981). Given that the drama metaphor is analogous actors'/audience' roles, the setting and the performance are developed in this section as a means to improving management of the '3 New Ps'. This section also offers strategic guidelines for international services marketing.

The drama metaphor offers numerous conceptual insights that foster managerial direction and control of the drama dimensions of service organizations. Considerable managerial preparation is possible to address the actors'/audience's roles as well as service setting concerns. The service performance is harder to frame and requires careful managerial monitoring of the service experience as it unfolds.

Improving the actors'/audience's roles

Five strategies for improving the actors'/audience's roles are suggested: (1) audition the service actors; (2) employ scripting; (3) train and rehearse; (4) develop performance teams; and (5) select and train the audience.

Audition the service actors

Like holding an audition for a play, the service organization should develop methods of employee selection that go beyond the simple interview. Possible approaches include using simulation techniques (Schneider and Schecter, 1988) and having prospective employees role play job behaviors, particularly interactions with customers. A related method of employee selection might utilize videotapes to present prospective service actors with role playing situations similar to ones they may encounter on the job (Jones and Decotiis, 1986). An important aspect of 'auditioning' service worker actors is the recognition that some people are not right for parts that put them in front of an audience (Davidson, 1978; Hogan, Hogan and Busch, 1984; Schneider and Schecter, 1988).

Employ scripting

In some situations, careful scripting of plans and procedures for service actors can be implemented. In this context, a script would consist of a detailed plot of the appropriate behavior(s) in a given situation, yet not necessarily the exact words to be spoken. Determination of the various enactments to include among the scripts would be based largely on the audience's expectations (Smith and Houston, 1983, 1985; Surprenant and Solomon, 1987) and the behaviors necessary to fashion a credible performance. Such scripts would be especially useful for routine service behaviors. For example, a life insurance firm could create a script of procedures for day-to-day office activities. Also, emergency scripts would be quite circumspect to ensure a satisfactory service performance under conditions of duress. For instance, it might be advisable for insurance firms to create emergency scripts of procedures for handling the unexpected death of a policyholder. Overall, the service organization might find it valuable to develop a repertoire of scripts for each service actor, as well as for anticipated service encounters.

Train and rehearse

When theatrical actors are training and rehearsing, they have the goal of flawless performances. The actors engage in intensive rehearsals to reach this goal. Following this example, services marketers should consider developing elaborate training and rehearsal procedures for service actors. This could include extending the training process beyond simply the indoctrination of new service workers. In addition, the training and rehearsal should focus on those service employees who operate backstage, as well as those whose actions are visible to the audience in the front region. While some service organizations want their employees to perform identical behaviors for all customers, others expect their employees to be able to adapt to the needs of the customer (Surprenant and Solomon, 1987). Both circumstances require training; however, as a general rule, more complex services necessitate improvisation by the service actors. Jazz improvisation makes a good analogy here. The best jazz improvisation is not done by novices but by experienced musicians. Service organizations that expect their employees to improvise should invest in considerable training. Relatedly, the service actors who succeed at delivering a superb performance are likely to have spent some time rehearsing their parts.

Develop performance teams

Another way to enhance a service production is to create and nurture performance teams that combine the talents of highly skilled service actors (mentors) with those new to the service arena (apprentices). A similar approach is to organize the work force into a small cast of highly skilled service workers, some of whom are designated as primary players while others are supporting players (Hare, 1985). For some more complex services it might also be beneficial to utilize an 'understudy' arrangement in which the new service worker is afforded the opportunity to develop his/her skills 'at the feet' of one more experienced. This would be done prior to casting the new service actor in a frontstage part and would ostensibly increase the likelihood of a successful production by the performance team when the neophyte enters the service stage. In essense, developing teamwork requires the service organization to invest time, money and confidence in its employees. An important aspect of the performance team is the development and coordination of clearly defined parts/routines that each member of the team performs. Managing this effort is similar to directing the stage production.

Select and train the audience

Every service organization wants to select an appreciative audience for its performances. Many traditional marketing ideas are available that facilitate the selection of a target market and the promotion to it. Also, once an audience has been selected, it may become necessary to train it in order to support the performance (Bowen, 1986; Mills and Morris, 1986). As Zeithaml (1981) has stated, 'The quality of most services and their ability to satisfy the consumer depend not only on how well the service provider performs, but also on how well the consumer performs' (p. 187).

For many services, knowledgeable and cooperative participation by the audience is as much a factor affecting service performance as the service's setting or actors. For example, a successful outcome from one's encounter with an ATM or a self-service gas pump depends on one's willingness and ability to use the technology. Furthermore, a doctor's diagnosis or a hair stylist's perm relies on accurate information provided by the service customer. The willingness of the audience members to cooperate among themselves can have an impact also (Martin and Pranter, 1989). Knowledge of and adherence to the rules of conduct and protocol concerning appropriate audience behavior is necessary to enhance the service experience for one and all (e.g. airline service, restaurants, etc.). Nevertheless, few service organizations actually train their patients, clients, patrons, customers, etc.

One approach to training the audience might involve identifying those customers who have not previously patronized the service. If customers are new, efforts can be made to educate them as to customer role expectations in the service production. Enhancing the first service experience for new customers is likely to increase the probability of their repeat patronage. A variety of props, setting changes and other devices are available to enhance the customers' orientation to the service (Wener, 1985) and their role in its performance (Lovelock and Young, 1979; Martin and Pranter, 1989; Solomon *et al.*, 1985).

Improving the setting

Three strategies for improving the services setting can be applied: (1) experimenting with the service setting; (2) frontstage versus backstage decisions; and (3) managing tangible evidence.

Experimenting with the service setting

Because the setting is managerially controllable, service providers can experimentally test variations in setting just as manufacturers of physical goods spend millions of dollars to test product improvements and variations (Farrell, 1984). Field testing new setting choices in local markets may be possible for many nationwide service organizations. Field tests have the advantage of providing a 'real world' test of the setting. Where actual field tests are not feasible, the use of full-size experimental models, scale models, computer models, drawings, slides or photographic simulations can be used to gather customer input prior to design implementation. As an example, the Marriott Corporation tested preliminary design concepts for the Marriott Courtyard Hotels in a warehouse. It is crucial that the design of service settings should be a function of a customer and employee orientation and not just the orientations of architects, interior designers and service firm managers. In all cases, the setting should be sufficiently versatile to allow for growth and change in service delivery. The service setting needs to work for both customers and employees (Baker, Berry and Parasuraman, 1988).

Frontstage versus backstage decisions

The services manager must decide which aspects of the organization's service should be performed on the frontstage (in the audience's full view) and which should be attended to backstage (away from the audience's inspection). In those service operations where it is difficult to meet customer expectations of frontstage service delivery excellence, service managers may find it prudent to move such aspects to the back region. A niche may be developed in this manner also (e.g. the fabled automat restaurants). If a service organization wants to move backstage dimensions of service production to the frontstage, it requires greater attention to other performance components, such as the actors' roles and their scripts, the audience's participation and the setting's physical cues. Moving backstage activities to the frontstage has proven a successful strategy for restaurants that offer self-serve salad bars or that cook food in view of the customers. Benihana Restaurants (discussed previously) has established a competitive niche by having the chef cook the food at the table. Not surprisingly, food preparation at Benihana has become an elaborately staged performance.

Managing tangible evidence

The goal in managing tangible evidence should be the presentation of a cohesive, coherent image. One important component of the tangible evidence is the physical appearance of service employees. Many service organizations (airlines, hotels, restaurants, hospitals, law firms, etc.) have uniforms (costumes) their employees are expected to wear (Solomon, 1985). Few of these organizations have actively researched how their customers and employees respond to these uniforms. A second important component is the use of props. Every service industry has certain props that readily identify its business. Consider how easy it is to identify the service industry that is associated with the following props: stethoscope, chalkboard, bar tray and scissors. While props may seem trivial, they are actually an effective means of symbolically creating the image of the service, as well as instrumentally delivering it. Service organizations can search for props that provide both the most powerful images and the most effective means of delivering the service. As an example, life insurance firms that invest in portable computers for their agents, allowing them to do all calculations and procedures while visiting clients' homes, are using props effectively.

Improving performance

Three procedures for improving performance are available: (1) test new performances; (2) document performances; and (3) critique performances.

Test new performances

It may be expensive to test new performance alternatives, but it is less expensive than a full-scale launch of a new service performance without a 'dress rehearsal'. The goal here is to develop an organizational tradition of constantly testing 'new routines'. Such an approach may be compared to that of a comedian who regularly tests new jokes because the old jokes have become too familiar. Few service organizations can afford the complacency of a static service performance. It may take the public longer to become bored with an old service performance than an old joke, but eventually it will happen.

Document performances

Services organizations should seek to document the performances of their employees. One of the simplest methods of doing this is the use of observation by management, similar to what Peters and Austin (1985) discuss as 'Management by Wandering Around' and 'naive listening'. The biggest hazard of this approach is that the manager's observation may disrupt the service performance. Perhaps a more effective and objective observational technique would be the use of audio and/or videotaping to document the service performance. Audio and videotaping have the advantage of providing a relatively permanent and unbiased record of the service performance. The audio or videotape can be closely examined to determine strengths or weaknesses in the service production. One caveat, however, concerns the appropriateness of observing customers without their knowledge or permission. The ethics related to such documentation should be carefully considered. As an effective substitute for observation, customer recollection of critical service performances can be used to document and track performance (Bitner, Booms and Tetreault, 1990).

Critique performances

The goal of critiquing performances is to maximize the performance of all service employees. As a result, two practices are desirable: (1) reward excellent performance and (2) correct poor performance. Rewarding excellent performance is a powerful motivator not only to the excellent performer but also to those employees who aspire to excellent performance. The reward can be modest and the recongition enthusiastic. A plaque or a small cash gift is probably sufficient. Correcting poor performance is more difficult. When a service employee makes a mistake it can have dangerous consequences. The rash strategy would be to fire the employee in an extremely public way. This would serve to terrorize the remaining staff. The wiser strategy would be privately showing the employee how to avoid the mistake. Most employees want to perform well and give good service (Schneider, 1980).

International guidelines

The drama metaphor can also be employed to develop services marketing guidelines for the many service organizations that are heavily engaged in international services trade. Drama is an ancient art form and is universally practiced in modern cultures. Hence, the drama metaphor is readily communicable across cultural boundaries. Furthermore, the drama metaphor may make it conceptually easier for services marketers to understand the importance of adapting the 'play' to different cultures.

All the drama strategy guidelines presented previously in this section can be applied internationally. The general drama structure will not change, but the management of actors, audience, setting and performances will need to vary in different cultures. Goffman (1959) noted the tremendous dramaturgical variation from one culture to the next. The common vocabulary offered by the drama framework may serve as a basis for analyzing and adapting services marketing systems from one cultural setting to the next.

CONTRIBUTIONS AND CAUTIONS

Four contributions from adopting the drama metaphor are advanced and four cautionary warnings are raised.

Contributions

The drama metaphor offers four contributions to services marketing and management thought and practice by providing a (1) holistic framework; (2) design tool; (3) classification scheme; and (4) descriptive vocabulary.

Holistic framework

The drama model offers managers a holistic framework that simultaneously combines all '3 New Ps' – participants, physical evidence and process of service assembly – into the services marketing mix. Much like the original metaphor of the marketing 'mix', the drama model suggests a combination of ingredients that can be optimally blended to achieve different goals. The drama framework is then a multidimensional tool for comprehending and evaluating the service experience. The drama model offers an appealing representation of marketing transactions as persuasive and entertaining without sacrificing the ability to control the transaction.

Design tool

The drama metaphor can serve as a tool for planning, coordinating and implementing specific service designs. A major approach to service design is blueprinting (Kingman-Brundage, 1989; Shostack, 1984a, 1984b, 1987). While not part of the drama metaphor, blueprinting is a powerful tool for making the various drama components (actors, audience, setting, performance, etc.) more transparent. In addition, used in conjunction with blueprinting, the drama metaphor offers managers directions for (1) the different emphases to place on service components (e.g. low contact services should stress 'setting' to increase perceptions of service quality); (2) the amount and type of attention to devote to recruiting, selecting, training and controlling service workers (e.g. high contact services need actors with strong dramatic skills); (3) the influence that customer expectations have on service quality levels (e.g. patrons demanding high quality dictate a greater attention to detail in service delivery).

Classification scheme

A third contribution is the provision of a structural model that may be applied across different services, thereby responding to a need identified by several services scholars (Lovelock, 1983; Shostack, 1984a; Upah, Berry and Shostack, 1983). The 'service performance cube' (see Figure 2) provides a basis for analyzing and grouping similar services (e.g. those services that emphasize elaborate settings compared to those with minimal investment in setting, those services that require highly trained actors versus those requiring minimally trained actors and those services that are performed before an active audience rather than a passive audience), potentially leading to a cross-fertilization of concepts and strategies (Lovelock, 1983). In addition, this classification scheme facilitates the identification of unserved market niches and offers assistance in manipulating the services mix to capture the niche.

Descriptive vocabulary

Finally, the drama metaphor offers a vocabulary for translating and communicating the various characteristics of any particular service, thereby fostering an understanding of its nature. For example, the metaphor can be used to describe a specific service as one in which standardized 'routines' are important as a marketing technique, one in which skilled actors contribute greatly to the credibility of the 'performance' and so on. Furthermore, used as a training device, the drama framework provides a working vocabulary derived from a social phenomenon familiar to most individuals and easy to communicate to service employees.

Cautions

Four serious cautions are necessary concerning adopting the drama metaphor: the importance of authenticity, the need for adaptability, the need for appropriateness and the range of applicability.

The importance of authenticity

To many people, the drama metaphor may carry the dangerous connotation of superficial 'just acting' behaviors. The 'Have a Nice Day' phrase so dutifully mouthed by the employees of many service businesses is woefully insincere. It is imperative that the customer believes in the performance. If the public believes that a service business is presenting a 'false front', it will quickly take its patronage elsewhere. Services marketers should recognize the importance of honest actors and authentic performances.

The need for adaptability

A second hazardous connotation of the drama metaphor is that of 'canned' performances. Many dramas are rigidly scripted and may convey the image of a fixed product. Managers should consider the need for adaptability and should pursue strategies that maximize the adaptability of the service experience. Service organizations can best fulfill the marketing concept by striving to maintain the adaptability of an 'ethic of service' rather than the precision of an 'ethic of efficiency' (Schneider and Bowen, 1984). Whenever possible, rather than following a fixed script, the service worker should be encouraged to adapt the performance to the needs of the audience.

The need for appropriateness

Third, services marketers and managers should recognize the need for appropriateness. Grotesque, grating or vulgar performances are likely to yield negative consumer reviews and may 'close early'. Attractive, soothing or refined performances are likely to be 'held over by popular demand'. In short, service performances must be well tailored to the tastes and expectations of the service audience.

The range of applicability

As a last caution, the drama metaphor does not apply equally well to all services. Grove and Fisk (1989) argue that the range of applicability of the drama metaphor to services marketing management is determined by the size of the consumer audience and the degree of contact between the service performer and the consumer. Hence, the drama metaphor is weakly applicable to those services whose consumers are physically removed from the service provider and interacting via mail, telephone or computer. However, the drama metaphor applies quite well to services serving large consumer audiences and/or providing significant contact between service performer and consumer.

CONCLUSION

The drama metaphor and the application of its theatrical constructs to service experiences unites the '3 New Ps' of Booms and Bitner (1981) and can be utilized to operationalize the management of them. As was shown in Table 1, the term 'participants' is analogous to the theatrical terms of 'actors' and 'audience', 'physical evidence' is analogous to the 'setting', 'process of service assembly' is analogous to the 'performance'. Two strategic models were proposed that facilitate understanding the applications of drama constructs to services marketing and numerous strategic guidelines were offered.

As a conceptual tool, the drama framework addresses many well-known services marketing issues by demonstrating the implicit and explicit relationships among the service organization, its customers, its employees and its physical properties. As with any metaphor, the description of services in dramatic terms facilitates communication and analysis of the phenomenon at hand and can be used to generate researchable propositions. Ultimately, application of the drama metaphor to services marketing provides a holistic framework, a design tool, a classification scheme and a vocabulary for promoting the understanding and management of service experiences.

ACKNOWLEDGMENTS

The authors thank Jerry Goolsby, University of South Florida, Carol Surprenant, University of Rhode Island, and Joshua Wiener, Oklahoma State University for their helpful comments on earlier drafts of this article.

REFERENCES

Arndt, J. (1985) 'On Making Marketing Science More Scientific: Role of Orientations, Paradigms, Metaphors and Puzzle Solving'. *Journal of Marketing* **49** (Summer): 11–23.
Bagozzi, R. (1975) 'Marketing as Exchange'. *Journal of Marketing* **39** (October): 32–39.
Baker, J. (1987) 'The Role of the Environment in Marketing Services: The Consumer Perspective'. In *The Services Challenge: Integrating for Competitive Advantage* (J. Czepiel, C. Congram and J. Shanahan, Eds). Chicago: American Marketing Association, pp. 79–84.
Baker, J., Berry, L. and Parasuraman, A. (1988) 'The Marketing Impact of Branch Facility Design'. *Journal of Retail Banking* **10** (2): 33–42.
Bateson, J. (1985) 'Perceived Control and the Service Encounter'. In *The Service Encounter: Managing Employee/Customer Interaction in Service Businesses* (J. Czepiel, M. Solomon and C. Surprenant, Eds). Lexington, MA: Lexington Books, pp. 67–82.
Bateson, J. (1989) *Managing Services Marketing: Text and Readings*. Hinsdale, IL: Dryden Press.

Bell, M. (1981) 'Tactical Service Marketing and the Process of Remixing'. In *Marketing of Services* (J. Donnelly and W. George, Eds). Chicago: American Marketing Association, pp. 163–167.

Berry, L. (1980) 'Services Marketing is Different'. *Business* **30** (May–June): 24–29.

Berry, L. (1981) 'The Employee as Customer'. *Journal of Retail Banking* **3** (March): 33–40.

Berry, L. (1983) 'Relationship Marketing'. In *Emerging Perspectives in Services Marketing* (L. Berry, G. Shostack and G. Upah, Eds). Chicago: American Marketing Association, pp. 25–28.

Berry, L., Ziethaml, V. and Parasuraman, A. (1985) 'Quality Counts in Services, Too'. *Business Horizons* **28** (May–June): 44–52.

Berry, L., Parasuraman, A. and Zeithaml, V. (1988) 'The Service-Quality Puzzle'. *Business Horizons* **31** (September–October): 35–43.

Bitner, M. and Zeithaml, V. (1988) 'Fundamentals in Services Marketing'. In *Add Value to Your Service* (C. Surprenant, ed.). Chicago: American Marketing Association, pp. 7–12.

Bitner, M., Booms, B. and Stanfield Tetreault, M. (1990) 'The Service Encounter: Diagnosing Favorable and Unfavorable Incidents'. *Journal of Marketing* **54** (January): 71–84.

Booms, B. and Bitner, M. (1981) 'Marketing Strategies and Organizational Structures for Service Firms'. In *Marketing of Services* (J. Donnelly and W. George, Eds), Chicago: American Marketing Association, 47–51.

Booms, B. and Bitner, M. (1982) 'Marketing Services by Managing the Environment'. *The Cornell Hotel and Restaurant Administration Quarterly* **23** (May): 35–39.

Bowen, D. (1986) 'Managing Customers as Human Resources in Service Organizations'. *Human Resource Management* 25: 371–383.

Brissett, D. and Edgley, C. (1975) *Life As Theatre: A Dramaturgical Sourcebook.* Chicago: Aldine Publishing Co.

Brown, S. and Swartz, T. (1989) 'A Gap Analysis of Professional Service Quality'. *Journal of Marketing* **53** (April): 92–98.

Burke, K. (1945) *A Grammar of Motives.* New York: Prentice-Hall, Inc.

Burke, K. (1950) *A Rhetoric of Motives.* New York: Prentice-Hall, Inc.

Burke, K. (1968) 'Dramatism'. In *International Encyclopedia of the Social Sciences, VII.* New York: Macmillan, pp. 445–452.

Carlzon, J. (1987) *Moments of Truth.* Cambridge, MA: Ballinger Publishing Company.

Carman, J. and Langeard, E. (1980) 'Growth Strategies for Service Firms'. *Strategic Management Journal* 1 (January–March): 7–22.

Cowell, D. (1985) *The Marketing of Services.* London: W. Heinemann.

Czepiel, J., Solomon, M. and Surprenant, C. (Eds) (1985) *The Service Encounter: Managing Employee/Customer Interaction in Service Businesses.* Lexington, MA: Lexington Books.

Davidson, D. (1978) 'How to Succeed in a Service Industry: Turn the Organization Chart Upside Down'. *Management Review* **67** (April): 13–16.

Dearden, J. (1978), 'Cost Accounting Comes to Service Industries'. *Harvard Business Review,* **56** (September–October): 132–140.

Duro, R. and Sandstrom, B. (1987) *The Basic Principles of Marketing Warfare.* Chichester, England: John Wiley & Sons.

Eiglier, P. and Langeard, E. (1977) 'A New Approach to Service Marketing', in *Marketing Consumer Services: New Insights* (P. Eiglier, E. Langeard, C. Lovelock, J. Bateson and R. Young, Eds). Cambridge, MA: Marketing Science Institute, pp. 31–58.

Farrell, K. (1984) 'Franchise Prototypes'. *Venture* (January): 108–113.

Fisk, R., Tansuhaj, P. and Crosby, L. A. (eds) (1985) *Services Marketing: An Annotated Bibliography.* Chicago: American Marketing Association.

Fisk, R., Tansuhaj, P. and Crosby, L. A. (eds) (1988) *SERVMARK: The Electronic Bibliography of Services Marketing Literature.* Tempe, AZ: First Interstate Center for Services Marketing, Arizona State University.

Goffman, E. (1959) *The Presentation of Self in Everyday Life.* New York: Doubleday and Co.

Goffman, E. (1967) *Interactional Ritual.* Garden City, NJ: Doubleday and Co.

Goffman, E. (1974) *Frame Analysis: An Essay on the Organization of Experience.* New York: Harper and Row.

Grönroos (1985) '*Internal Marketing* – Theory and Practice'. In *Services Marketing in a Changing*

Environment (T. Bloch, G. Upah and V. Zeithaml, Eds). Chicago: American Marketing Association, pp. 41–47.

Grönroos, C. (1990) *Service Management and Marketing: Managing the Moments of Truth in Service Competition*. Lexington, MA: Lexington Books.

Grove, S. and Fisk, R. (1983) 'The Dramaturgy of Services Exchange: An Analytical Framework for Services Marketing'. In *Emerging Perspectives on Services Marketing* (L. Berry, G. Shostack and G. Upah, Eds). Chicago: American Marketing Association, pp. 45–49.

Grove, S. and Fisk, R. (1989) 'Impression Management in Services Marketing: A Dramaturgical Perspective'. In *Impression Management in the Organization* (R. Giacalone and P. Rosenfeld, Eds). Hillsdale, NJ: Lawrence Erlbaum Associates, pp. 427–438.

Guiltinan, J. (1987) 'The Price Bundling of Services: A Normative Framework'. *Journal of Marketing* **51** (April): 74–85.

Hare, A. (1985) *Social Interaction as Drama*. Beverly Hills, CA: Sage Publications, Inc.

Heskett, J. (1986) *Managing in the Service Economy*. Boston: Harvard Business School Press.

Hogan, J., Hogan, R. and Busch, C. (1984) 'How to Measure Service Orientation'. *Journal of Applied Psychology* **69** (1): 167–173.

Johnson, E. (1969) 'Are Goods and Services Different? An Exercise in Marketing Theory', Ph.D. Dissertation, Washington University.

Jones, C. and Decotiis, T. (1986) 'A Better Way to Select Service Employees: Video-Assisted Testing'. *Cornell Hotel and Restaurant Administration Quarterly* **27** (August): 68–73.

Judd, R. (1964) 'The Case for Redefining Services'. *Journal of Marketing* **28** (January): 58–59.

Kingman-Brundage, J. (1989) 'The ABC's of Service System Blueprinting'. In *Designing a Winning Service Strategy* (M. Bitner and L. Crosby, Eds). Chicago: American Marketing Association, pp. 30–33.

Kotler, P. (1973) 'Atmospherics as a Marketing Tool'. *Journal of Retailing* **49** (Winter): 48–64.

Kotler, P. and Singh, R. (1981) 'Marketing Warfare'. *Journal of Business Strategy* 1(Winter): 30–41.

Langeard, E., Bateson, J. Lovelock, C., and Eiglier, P. (eds) (1981) *Marketing of Services: New Insights from Consumers and Managers*. Cambridge, MA: Marketing Science Institute.

Lovelock, C. (1981) 'Why Marketing Management Needs to be Different for Services'. In *Marketing of Services* (J. Donnelly and W. George, Eds). Chicago: American Marketing Association, pp. 5–9.

Lovelock, C. (1983) 'Classifying Services to Gain Strategic Marketing Insights'. *Journal of Marketing* **47** (Summer): 9–20.

Lovelock, C. (1984) *Services Marketing: Text, Cases, and Readings*. Englewood Cliffs, NJ: Prentice-Hall, Inc.

Lovelock, C. (1988) *Managing Services: Marketing Operations, and Human Resources*. Englewood Cliffs, NJ: Prentice-Hall, Inc.

Lovelock, C. and Young, R. (1979) 'Look to Consumers to Increase Productivity'. *Harvard Business Review* **57** (May–June): 168–178.

Lovelock, C., Langeard, E., Bateson, J. and Eiglier, P. (1981) 'Some Organization Problems Facing Marketing in the Services Sector'. In *Marketing of Services* (J. Donnelly and W. George, Eds). Chicago: American Marketing Association, pp. 168–171.

Magrath, A. J. (1986) 'When Marketing Services, 4 Ps Are Not Enough'. *Business Horizons* **29** (May–June): 44–50.

Martin, C. and Pranter, C. (1989) 'Compatibility Management: Customer-to-Customer Relationships in Service Environments'. *Journal of Services Marketing* **3** (Summer): 6–15.

McCarthy, E. (1960) *Basic Marketing: A Managerial Approach*. Homewood, IL: Richard D. Irwin, Inc.

Michaelson, G. (1987) *Winning the Marketing War*. Lantham, MD: Abt Books.

Mills, P. and Morris, J. (1986) 'Clients as Partial Employees of Service Organizations: Role Development in Client Participation'. *Academy of Management Review* **11** (4): 726–735.

Morgan, G. (1980) 'Paradigms, Metaphors, and Puzzle Solving in Organizational Theory'. *Administrative Science Quarterly* **25** (December): 605–622.

Murphy, P. and Enis, B. (1986) 'Classifying Products Strategically'. *Journal of Marketing* **50** (July): 24–42.

Nisbet, R. (1969) *Social Change and History.* London: Oxford University Press.

Ortony, A. (1975) 'Why Metaphors are Necessary and Not Just Nice'. *Educational Theory* **25** (Winter): 45–53.

Parasuraman, A., Berry, L. and Zeithaml, V. (1983) 'Service Firms Need Marketing Skills'. *Business Horizons* **26** (November–December): 28–31.

Parasuraman, A., Zeithaml, V. and Berry, L. (1985) 'A Conceptual Model of Service Quality and Its Implications for Future Research'. *Journal of Marketing* **49** (Fall): 41–50.

Parasuraman, A., Zeithaml, V. and Berry, L. (1988), 'SERVQUAL: A Multiple-Item Scale for Measuring Consumer Perceptions of Service Quality'. *Journal of Retailing* **64** (Spring): 12–40.

Perinbanayagam, R. S. (1974) 'The Definition of the Situation: An Analysis of the Ethnomethodological and Dramaturgical View'. *The Sociological Quarterly* **15** (Autumn): 521–541.

Peters, T. and Austin, N. (1986) *A Passion for Excellence.* New York: Warner Books.

Prus, R. and Frisby, W. (1987) 'Marketplace Dynamics: The P's of 'People' and 'Process''. In *Advances in Consumer Research* (M. Wallendorf and P. Anderson, Eds). Provo, UT: Association for Consumer Research. pp. 61–65.

Regan, W. J. (1963) 'The Service Revolution'. *Journal of Marketing* **27** (July): 57–62.

Ries, A. and Trout, J. (1986) *Marketing Warfare.* New York: McGraw-Hill, Inc.

Sasser, W. (1976) 'Match Supply and Demand in Service Industries'. *Harvard Business Review* **54** (November–December): 133–140.

Sasser, W. and Arbeit, S. (1978) 'Selling Jobs in the Service Sector'. *Business Horizons* 19 (June): 61–65.

Sasser, W., Olsen, R. and Wyckoff, D. (1978) *Management of Service Operations: Text, Cases, and Readings.* Boston: Allyn and Bacon.

Schneider, B. (1980) 'The Service Organization: Climate is Crucial'. *Organizational Dynamics* **9** (Autumn): 52–65.

Schneider, B. and Bowen, D. (1984) 'New Services Design, Development and Implementation and the Employee'. In *Developing New Services* (W. George and C. Marshall, Eds). Chicago, IL: American Marketing Association, pp. 82–101.

Schneider, B. and Schecter, D. (1991) 'The Development of a Personnel System for Service Jobs'. In *Service Quality: Multidisciplinary and Multinational Perspectives* (S. Brown, E. Gummesson, B. Edvardsson and B. Gustavsson, Eds). Lexington, MA: Lexington Books.

Shakespeare, W. [1600] (1954) *As You Like It* (S. C. Burchell, Ed.). New Haven, CT: Yale University Press.

Sherowski, H. (1983) 'Marketing Through Facilities Design'. In *Emerging Perspectives on Services Marketing* (L. Berry, G. Shostack and G. Upah, Eds). Chicago: American Marketing Association, pp. 134–136.

Shostack, G. (1977) 'Breaking Free From Product Marketing'. *Journal of Marketing* **41** (April): 73–80.

Shostack, G. (1984a) 'A Framework for Services Marketing'. In *Marketing Theory: Distinguished Contributions* (S. Brown and R. Fisk, Eds). New York: John Wiley and Sons, pp. 250–261.

Shostack, G. (1984b) 'Designing Services that Deliver'. *Harvard Business Review* **62** (January–February): 133–139.

Shostack, G. (1987) 'Service Positioning Through Structural Change'. *Journal of Marketing* **51** (January): 34–43.

Silpakit, P. and Fisk, R. (1985) ''Participatizing' the Service Process: A Theoretical Framework'. In *Services Marketing In A Changing Environment* (T. Bloch, G. Upah and V. Zeithaml, Eds). Chicago: American Marketing Association, pp. 117–121.

Smith, R. (1985) 'A Psychometric Assessment of Measures of Scripts in Consumer Memory'. *Journal of Consumer Research* **12** (September): 214–224.

Smith, R. and Houston, M. (1983) 'Script-Based Evaluations of Satisfaction With Services'. In *Emerging Perspectives on Services Marketing* (L. Berry, G. Shostack and G. Upah, Eds). Chicago: American Marketing Association, pp. 59–62.

Solomon, M. (1985) 'Packaging the Service Provider'. *Service Industries Journal* 5 (March), 64–72.

Solomon, M. *et al.* (1985) 'A Role Theory Perspective on Dyadic Interactions: The Service Encounter'. *Journal of Marketing* **49** (Winter): 99–111.

Stern, B. (1988) 'Medieval Allegory: Roots of Advertising Strategy for the Mass Market'. *Journal of Marketing* **52** (July): 84–94.

Stone, G. (1962) 'Appearance and the Self'. In *Human Behavior and Social Process* (A. Rose, Ed.). Boston: Houghton-Mifflin, pp. 86–117.

Surprenant, C. and Solomon, M. (1985) 'Dimensions of Personalization'. In *Services Marketing In A Changing Environment* (T. Bloch, G. Upah and V. Zeithaml, Eds). Chicago: American Marketing Association, pp. 56–59.

Surprenant, C. and Solomon, M. (1987) 'Predictability and Personalization in the Service Encounter'. *Journal of Marketing* **51** (April): 86–96.

Upah, G. and Fulton, J. (1985) 'Situation Creation in Services Marketing'. In *The Service Encounter: Managing Employee/Customer Interaction in Service Businesses.* (J. Czepiel, M. Solomon and C. Surprenant, Eds). Lexington, MA: Lexington Books, pp. 255–263.

Upah, G., Berry, L. and Shostack, G. (1983) 'Emerging Themes and Directions for Services Marketing'. In *Emerging Perspectives on Services Marketing* (L. Berry, G. Shostack and G. Upah, Eds). Chicago: American Marketing Association, pp. 139–141.

US Bureau of the Census (1988). *Statistical Abstract of the United States: 1989.* 109th edition, Washington, DC.

Weiner, S. (1986) 'Banks Hire Retailing Consultants for Help in Becoming Financial-Products 'Stores''. *Wall Street Journal* May 20: 33.

Wener, R. (1985) 'The Environmental Psychology of Service Encounters'. In *The Service Encounter: Managing Employee/Customer Interaction in Service Businesses* (J. Czepiel, M. Solomon and C. Surprenant, Eds). Lexington, MA: Lexington Books, pp. 101–112.

Zeithaml, V. (1981) 'How Consumer Evaluation Processes Differ Between Goods and Services'. In *Marketing of Services* (J. Donnelly and W. George, Eds). Chicago: American Marketing Association, pp. 186–190.

Zeithaml, V. (1982) 'The Acquisition, Meaning and Use of Price Information by Consumers of Professional Services'. In *Marketing Theory: Philosophy of Science Perspectives* (R. Bush and S. Hunt, Eds). Chicago: American Marketing Association, pp. 237–241.

Zeithaml, V., Parasuraman, A. and Berry, L. (1985) 'Problems and Strategies in Services Marketing'. *Journal of Marketing* **49** (Spring): 33–46.

Zeithaml, V., Berry, L. and Parasuraman, A. (1988) 'Communication and Control Processes in the Delivery of Service Quality'. *Journal of Marketing* **52** (April): 35–48.

Zikmund, W. (1982) 'Metaphors as Methodology'. In *Marketing Theory: Philosophy of Science Perspectives* (R. Bush and S. Hunt, Eds). Chicago: American Marketing Association, pp. 75–77.

7

The Impact of Services versus Goods on Consumers' Assessment of Perceived Risk and Variability

Keith B. Murray and John L. Schlacter

INTRODUCTION

In view of the dominant role of the service sector in the industrialized economies of the world, services marketing represents a phenomenon of substantial interest. To date, however, much of the attention in services has been concerned with making a theoretical case that services are conceptually different from goods and that these differences point to special marketing management considerations (Eiglier and Langeard, 1977; Judd, 1964; Rathmell, 1966; Lovelock, 1983; Ziethaml, Parasuraman and Berry, 1985). Unfortunately, the empirical – in contrast to theoretical – basis for distinguishing key differences in substance or marketing strategy is limited.

Despite the call for a balance between qualitative and quantitative approaches to theory construction and validation (Arndt, 1985; Bagozzi, 1984; Brinberg and Hirschman, 1986; Deshpande, 1983), the development of services marketing thought has been heavily dependent on conceptual elaborations. Furthermore, empirical demonstration and verification of service marketing literature has been largely confined to nonexperimental research (Biehal, 1983; Swartz and Stephens, 1984). Compared to empirical research involving nonservice products, experimentation which examines service marketing phenomena appears to be derived from operationally ad hoc definitions and spontaneous operationalizations of the service construct (e.g. Guseman, 1981; George, Weinberger and Kelly, 1985; George *et al.*, 1984; Lewis, 1976; Weinberger and Brown, 1977). Thus, conclusions from experimental data, such as they exist, are divergent and the opportunity for replication is problematic.

Clearly, then, what is needed – as the discipline matures in this area – is a more rigorous research approach regarding services, one which can provide a process for replication and verification (Uhl and Upah, 1983). To this end, the present research

K. B. Murray and J. L. Schlacter, *Journal of the Academy of Marketing Science*, Vol. 18, No. 1, pp. 51–65, copyright © 1990 by Academy of Marketing Science
Reprinted by permission of Sage Publications, Inc.

contributes to our understanding of goods/services, in three ways. First, an issue of considerable importance to marketers, perceived risk, is addressed. While a rich literature exists which examines this concept in the context of traditional product marketing, far less effort has been devoted to the examination of perceived risk as it relates to services. No research has attempted to bridge the gap between goods and services marketing by examining the relationship of consumers' perceived risk for service relative to goods.

Second, this research extends extant services marketing thought by introducing a technique for operationalizing the service construct, for validating the construct and for using the construct in an experimentally controlled design to examine the phenomenon of perceived risk in a goods/services context. This approach responds specifically to the discipline's call for empirical examination of services marketing.

Finally, the independent variable in this study, goods/services products, is empirically determined based upon a market definition of product. Research results offer support for the notion that (1) products exist along a goods/services continuum (Johnson, 1969; Levitt, 1980; Shostack, 1977), and (2) that services are perceived by consumers as possessing inherently more risk and variability.

REVIEW OF THE LITERATURE

An elaborate marketing literature exists in which perceived risk is recognized as a fundamental concept in consumer behavior (Bauer, 1960; Bettman, 1973; Cox, 1967; Jacoby and Kaplan, 1972; Kaplan, Szybillo and Jacoby, 1974; Lutz and Reilly, 1973; Perry and Hamm, 1969; Roselius, 1971; Ross, 1972; Shiffman, 1972). Although there has been evidence that consumers may evaluate and purchase services in a different manner, compared to goods (Davis, Guiltinan and Jones, 1979; Johnson, 1969; Lewis, 1976; Weinberger and Brown, 1977), there has been relatively limited research published which examines the relative risk perceptions of services. The results of only two studies (Guseman, 1981; George et al., 1984; George, Weinberger and Kelly, 1985) have been disseminated in marketing publications which address this important topic and indicate that some consumer-related differences may occur. However, these research findings point to conflicting conclusions and neither empirical approach is without qualifications in terms of the research design employed.

The early Guseman (1981) study points to a difference in risk perception between services and goods, with services found to be riskier. In this particular study, the risk perceptions of ten goods (hosiery, butter/margarine, cough drops, felt-tip markers, tape recorders, bed mattresses, small personal leather goods, paint brush roller, wood stands, and typewriters) were contrasted to ten services (appliance repair, motel lodging, medical treatment, commercial bank services, clothes cleaning, motion pictures, spectator sports, dance instruction, auto rental, and apartment rental). Using a mail questionnaire directed to 'the lady of the home' and a total sample of 192 women, Guseman (1981) found significant differences between types of products in an aggregate measure of risk.

While Guseman's (1981) findings are consistent with theoretical predictions of marketing scholars (e.g. Ziethaml, 1981) there are signiciant problems with the experimental design of the study. First, the stimulus products, although selected at random from the Standard Industrial Classification Code Book, lack homogeneity in terms of several key, consumer-relevant considerations. Intuitive analysis of both within- and between-product group comparisons strongly suggests large differences in terms of importance, cost, involvement, and familiarity to the consumer. It is not unreasonable to expect that such differences, as they may occur, would have a significant impact on the evaluative and risk perceptions of subjects (e.g. Claxton, Fry and Portis, 1974; Jacoby and Kaplan, 1972). Specifically, it is possible to attribute significant perceived risk differences between product groupings in this study to any or all of these other rival influences on the product evaluation by subjects. Furthermore, Guseman's (1981) study exerts little experimental control over subject behavior with respect to questionnaire completion. Generalizations, such as may be possible, are only applicable to female perceptions of risk. Also, although the study is laudable in its focus on a significant topic, more specific measures of perceived risk are available and relevant.

In a later study, George, Weinberger and Kelly (1985) and George et al. (1984) attempt to examine risk perceptions between goods and services using a mall intercept format whereby 94 subjects rated eight products (four goods and four services) on seven risk dimensions. Attempting to control for 'homogeneity' of products on a 'tangible/intangible continuum', four product 'sets' were designated by the researchers (eye glasses/eye exam; color TV/TV repair; carpeting/carpet cleaning; quartz watch/watch repair) whereby each paired 'good' and 'service' was presumably equivalent and equidistant (relative to an assumed continuum of products) with regards to tangibility/intangibility considerations. These research findings suggest that earlier generalizations about services being higher on all risk categories may not be entirely justified, that risk differences between goods and services may not exist.

The empirical approach of this study (George, Weinberger and Kelly, 1985; George et al., 1984), while addressing some of the previous experimental shortcomings of Guseman (1981), merits careful examination. Specification, the study, by fiat, declares that certain product stimuli are 'services' and others are 'goods'. While there is some face validity associated with each respective designation, the stimuli are clearly vulnerable to debate. An intuitive selection of product stimuli belies an absence of explicit criteria associated with operationalizing the construct for either goods or services. Lacking an objective means of construct determination, it is arguable that several operationalizations are such that the declared 'service' retains a 'goods' component, and vice versa. Furthermore, the derivation of a product 'continuum' lacks explication and also appears to be strictly intuitive in nature, thus making replication – a hallmark of the scientific process – difficult.

While pairwise comparisons suggest a degree of 'relatedness' among the selected products, several problems encountered by Guseman (1981) persist. An absence of experimental and/or statistical controls is evident and may have significantly influenced the data. Several aspects merit brief mention: expected cost differences between pairwise products were not explicitly identified nor controlled for, despite evidence that financial cost considerations have been shown to influence risk perceptions (Jacoby and Kaplan, 1972); no specific control for subject familiarity of product experience is reported; sample composition considerations appear to have been minimized, despite the call for more uniform, homogeneous samples in cases involving theory validation/falsification (Calder, Phillips and Tybout, 1981); and, the lack of sufficient context for the rating task required of the subjects.

In short, the need for additional research which addresses the process and criteria for the inclusion of product stimuli in a test of perceived differences between goods and services is apparent. Consequently, this article will address this aspect of services marketing research and will proceed to describe the findings of an experiment which focuses on the perceived risk and perceived variability of goods and services.

Conceptualization of goods and services in marketing research

While a good can be conceptualized, at least in part, as a physical entity composed of tangible attributes which buyers purchase to satisfy specific wants and needs, the problems associated with the definition of a service have persisted to plague services research. Nonetheless, services marketing theorists have established a fairly broad consensus as to what characterizes service products (for example, Zeithaml, Parasuraman, and Berry, 1985). Generalizations characterizing services include intangibility, simultaneity of production and consumption, inseparability, and nonstandardization. As an outgrowth of these conceptualizations, marketing thought has implicitly pointed to (1) the existence of an intrinsic dichotomy between market offerings of goods and services; and (2) the notion that marketing knowledge is inherently biased toward the marketing of goods and, therefore, not necessarily applicable in the service sector of marketing (for example, Bateson, 1977; Lovelock 1979; Shostack 1977).

Despite the persuasive character of services marketing literature, some argue that there are few substantive differences between services and a generic concept of product marketing (Brown and Fern, 1981; Wyckham, Fitzroy and Mandry, 1975). Scholars have proposed that consumers make expenditures not for goods and/or services but, instead, for value satisfactions they believe are bestowed by what they are buying (Enis and Roering, 1981; Hollander, 1979; Levitt, 1969, 1980) and that products have varying degrees of tangibility–intangibility and 'service' associated with them (Levitt, 1981). Proponents of this view argue that goods-type and service-type products are not necessarily mutually exclusive.

One approach to resolving the conflict between traditional marketing thought and services marketing literature is to suggest a model that proposes the arrangement of all products along a continuum based on dimensions by which classical goods–services distinctions theoretically are made. Since *all* products can be observed to possess common properties, or dimensions (e.g. Johnson, 1969), the difference between products conventionally referred to as 'goods; or 'services' lies in the relative proportions that a particular product may have of each specific dimension (e.g. intangibility, nonstandardization, etc.) as well as the perceived dominance of each dimension relative to all other dimensions involved in defining products. Indeed, marketing scholars support the concept of a spectrum to meaningfully arrange products, based on their perceived attributes (Aspinwall, 1961; Rathmell, 1966; Shostack, 1977).

In short, a simple characterization of services qua services (and, implicitly, goods qua goods) is, at best, a crude generalization of the true nature of products and it is imperative that empirical research efforts in the services area explicitly recognize and incorporate measures which address this issue. Thus, this paper proposes that (1) there is a continuous range of products, rather than a simple, categorical dichotomy, and (2) premised on consumer perceptions, products can be meaningfully arrayed to reflect important marketing/purchase differences (Shostack, 1977).

THEORY AND HYPOTHESES: SERVICE RISK AND VARIABILITY

Perceived risk is a multi-dimensional construct (e.g. Jacoby and Kaplan, 1972; Kaplan, Szybillo and Jacoby, 1974; Roselius, 1971) which implies that consumers experience pre-purchase uncertainty as to type and degree of expected loss resulting from the purchase and use of a product (Bauer, 1960; Cox, 1967). Types of risk include financial performance, physical, psychological, social and convenience loss (e.g. Jacoby and Kaplan, 1972; Kaplan, Szybillo and Jacoby, 1974; Roselius, 1971). In risk theory literature, degree of risk is determined using a variety of approaches (Ross, 1972) and essentially involves the expected relative risk associated with a product purchase.

A number of predictions can be made which directly flow from the service marketing and consumer behavior literature with respect to risk and product variability. As noted previously, services have been typically associated with greater degrees of intangibility, simultaneity of production and consumption, and direct provider–consumer contact and, indirectly, nonstandardization (e.g. Johnson, 1969; Rathmell, 1966; Zeithaml, 1981; Zeithaml, Parasuraman and Berry, 1985). In view of these elements, the amount and/or quality of information available for services is diminished, and the amount of perceived risk is expected to be elevated (e.g. Cox and Rich, 1964; Spence, Engel and Blackwell, 1970). While there is necessarily some degree of risk which accompanies all purchases, it is predicted that more risk is associated with services than with goods (Guseman, 1981; Lewis, 1976; Zeithaml, 1981). The following hypothesis, therefore, is offered:

H_1: Consumers will perceive greater overall pre-choice risk for services than for goods.

In contrast to goods, many services typically involve costs which cannot be fully determined by the consumer in advance of the purchase decision, contributing to the uncertainty of outcome and, at the very least, a heightened degree of financial loss to the consumer. For virtually all nonservice market offerings, price is established prior to the purchase event and consumption; for services, however, this is not always possible, since many services are associated with variable completion times and/or component elements that are not completely identifiable in advance of the completion of the product, both of which might affect product cost.

For services where the price is standardized in advance of the purchase event, the actual benefits of the transaction are nonetheless variable. While the cost may be known prior to the decision to buy, actual product benefits are difficult to fully ascertain prior to purchase. Thus, even for services when costs are fixed, the nonstandardization of services leads to uncertainty with respect to the real costs and performance of the product. Consequently, the following predictions are possible:

H_2: Consumers will perceive greater pre-choice financial risk for services than for goods.

H_3: Consumers will perceive greater pre-choice performance risk for services than for goods.

Although not true for all services, most entail some degree of human involvement as an integral part of the product. Furthermore, in addition to possible direct contact between the service provider and consumer, the service environment typically can include other individuals as well. Contact with others increases the opportunity for interactions of a sensitive or potentially embarrassing nature (e.g. consumer uneasiness at expressing dissatisfaction or indecision, consumer fear of asking nairve or foolish questions). For many purchases associated with nonservice products, the potential for this type of conflict is reduced, if for no other reason than the fact that the consumption of the product is not frequently at the purchase or provision site. Thus, it can be predicted that the relatively high degree of provider/customer involvement associated with simultaneity of production and consumption for services leads to the increased opportunity for social risk, the potential loss of esteem, respect, and/or friendship offered to the consumer by other individuals. Therefore,

H_4: Consumers will perceive greater social risk for services than for goods.

Several remaining types of risk have not been specifically addressed in current services marketing literature. These forms of risk include convenience, physical, and psychological loss. Convenience risk addresses loss of time and effort associated with achieving satisfaction with a purchase; physical risk addresses product safety and possible danger or harm related to product purchase or use; and, psychological risk relates to possible loss of self-image or self-concept as a result of product purchase or use. Without clear evidence in the literature for these remaining dimensions of perceived risk, the following predictions can be tested against acceptance of the null hypothesis:

H_5: Consumers will perceive no difference in pre-choice convenience risk between services and goods.

H_6: Consumers will perceive no difference in pre-choice physical risk between services and goods.

H_7: Consumers will perceive no difference in pre-choice psychological risk between services and goods.

Closely related to the concept of perceived risk is the notion of product benefit variability. Benefit variability can be associated with the inability to standardize many services (Booms and Bitner, 1981). From a managerial perspective, factors influencing product variability include channel length and distribution configuration, the demand level, involvement of new or different service personnel and/or other customers in the service system, consumer cooperation, and other similar factors (Bateson, 1979; Eiglier and Langeard, 1977; Lovelock, 1981; Sasser, 1976). Mills and Margulies (1980) attribute this nonstandardization of services to the inability of service providers to isolate the 'technical' core of the 'manufacturing process' of services.

Thus, despite the opportunity for customized, individual-specific product benefits, other factors influence the ability of the provider to render benefits in a consistent, uniform nature. Consequently, there is expected to be particular uncertainty on the part of the consumer relative to the degree of positive and/or negative utility associated with a service (Berry, 1984; Rathmell, 1974). Therefore, it is predicted that

H_8: Consumers will perceive services to have greater variability than goods.

These hypotheses are intended to test the prediction that goods and services are associated with important consumer differences with respect to specific risk and product variation perceptions. Collectively they represent a synthesis of current marketing literature with respect to services marketing concepts.

METHODOLOGY

Previous experimental service marketing studies have assumed a priori products are 'services' and that others are 'goods' (e.g. Guseman, 1981; Weinberger and Brown, 1977; George, Weinberger and Kelly, 1985). However, research efforts predicated on this approach to product definition present theoretical difficulties (Peter, 1981), since conclusions premised on assumed operationalizations are necessarily suspect. Consequently, procedures are required whereby a respondent sample evaluates products in advance of the experiemental manipulation, in order to determine whether the products are typically perceived as goods or services. To that end, a survey was undertaken to establish a range of products against which to subsequently test hypotheses relating to consumer risk perceptions of goods and services.

Phase 1: pre-experimental study

Selection of products for the main study. A large population of products was identified to be subsequently rated in terms of their respective goods/services components. Sources for the initial list of products included *The Simmons Study of Media and Markets,* the consumer *Yellow Pages* of a large US urban metropolitan area, and the *US Census Standard Industrial Classification.* Products were selected on the basis of their inclusion in consumer product categories for both goods and services as defined by each of the sources. A judgment sample of 235 product categories was collected.

A sample of 145 consumers, drawn from the population of the main study was asked to rate products, irrespective of any designation as 'goods' or 'services', in terms of their relative goods or services qualities on a seven-point fixed interval scale from 'Has extreme "goods" properties' to 'Has extreme "service" properties'. An arithmetic mean was computed for each rated product which permitted the arrangement of the entire sample of products to be rank–ordered in terms of their relative placement along a goods–services continuum. Product ratings took place after subjects had been given a brief description of six criteria (relative to tangibility, simultaneity of production and consumption, standardization, buyer participation, importance of the producer and perishability (see Murray, 1986)) by which marketing literature typically distinguishes goods from services. To diminish respondent fatigue and bias, survey subjects were asked to rate sequentially a random subsample of no more than 50 products of the 235 initially identified.

To increase the precision of the product construct factors, pre-experimental subjects were asked to rate the perceived monetary value, or expected financial cost, associated with each product in terms of a seven point interval scale. In the determination of the factors of the subsequent experiment, the specific selection of products was limited to those falling in the expected cost range of $20 to $50. Since there is a direct correlation between cost and overall risk (e.g. Jacoby and Kaplan, 1972), this was expected to increase control of an important extraneous risk factor. To further increase experimental precision, the degree of a subject's familiarity with each product was measured by his or her rating on a seven-point interval scale. Only those products for which respondents expressed at least moderate familiarity were included in the final sample of products.

Products falling within the specific monetary value and familiarity range were arrayed along a goods–services continuum based on the mean score for each product. For purposes of this study, services were considered to be those products receiving a rating greater than 6.0 on a seven-point scale; goods were considered to be those products receiving a score of less than 2.0. Products characterized by roughly equal degrees of goods and service attributes were those falling in a mid-range of 3.5 to 4.5. Five goods, five services, and five 'mixed' products were then selected as the independent variables for the study. The use of a sample of products was intended to increase the stability of the dependent measures (Minium, 1978).

Table 1 shows a partial array of the survey data for these critical regions and, specifically, the products selected as factors of the independent variable.

Phase 2: controlled experiment

The purpose of this phase of the research was to experiementally assess the differing impact of goods and services on consumer perception of risk and expected product variability.

Experimental design

The specific formulation proposed in this study is that of a completely balanced block (repeated measures) design with nested factors in a hierarchical arrangement. From an experimental perspective, this design minimizes error variance and obtains a relatively precise estimate of treatment effects, thereby obtaining a more powerful test of a false null hypothesis (Green, 1973; Kirk, 1982). Pretests of the data collection instrument showed that confounding effects atributable to reactivity or order effects were not present with the design employed.

Sample

A total of 273 experimental sets were distributed to university students at a large, urban university in the southwestern US. However, 17 questionnaire forms were not

Table 1. Partial pre-test product rating data

Product	Good–service continuum value (1–7)	Expected product cost ($)
Low perceived service identity level of independent variable		
Windbreaker jacket	1.3	25.00
Tennis racket	1.4	41.40
Barbecue grill	1.4	47.70
Small elecric vacuum cleaner	1.5	39.60
Pocket camera	1.6	21.30
Mean product value:	1.4	35.00
Moderate perceived service identity level of independent variable		
Auto re-upholstery (including installation)	3.5	43.40
Smoke detector/alarm	3.5	25.30
Furniture rental, sofa	3.6	31.50
Auto muffler (including installation)	3.8	49.10
Restaurant meal	4.3	21.50
Mean product value:	3.7	34.16
High perceived service identity level of independent variable		
Teeth cleaning by a dentist or hygienist	6.0	35.40
Income tax advice and preparation	6.1	39.50
Auto wheel alignment	6.1	24.60
Professional interior decoration advice	6.3	37.30
Eye exam	6.6	36.50
Mean product value:	6.2	34.66

completed, properly, resulting in 256 acceptable response sets for tabulation and analysis. Of the sample, 120 subjects were males (46.9%) and 136 females (53.1%). The mean age of the sample subject was 23.8 years, with a standard deviation of 3.4.

Sample size for the proposed study was derived using an estimation approach based on expected mean differences of dependent measure scores with an adjusted confidence level of 95% and a 0.05 bound on the error of estimation. Table 2 shows the layout of the design and the accompanying sample utilized.

Procedures

To test the proposed hypotheses, the sample of young adult consumers was administered written purchase scenarios involving consumer products systematically varied and randomly selected from the 15 product stimuli isolated in the pre-test survey. Three levels of the independent variable (that is, product groups varying in goods/services characteristics) were administered to each subject in a role-playing context.

The hypothetical purchase scenario employed was adapted from Lutz and Reilly (1973) and Locander and Hermann (1979) and conforms to Bettman's (1972) concept of inherent risk for products varying in service attributes. The decision context of the purchase scenario was of a non-emergency nature, since purchase

Table 2. Experimental design: balanced complete block with repeated measures

| | Level of service characteristics of product administered as the independent variable[a] | | | | | | | | | | | | | | | |
| | High 5 products | | | | | Moderate 5 products | | | | | Low 5 products | | | | | |
Number of respondents	1	2	3	4	5	6	7	8	9	10	11	12	13	14	15	n
1–47	●					●					●					47
48–96		●					●					●				49
97–151			●					●					●			55
152–209				●					●					●		58
210–256					●					●					●	47
																n = 256
Replications:	47	49	55	58	47	47	49	55	58	47	47	49	55	58	47	= 768

[a]Products represent empirically determined stimuli used as the independent variable in the study. Five product stimuli were selected from three disparate portions of a goods–services continuum. Subjects corresponding to numbers in left-most column were exposed to one product stimulus from each sample of five for each level. The product stimuli correspond to those identified in Table 1.

decisions reflecting emergency circumstances may involve abbreviated information search processes (Wright, 1974). While scenario stimuli are employed in current marketing research (e.g. Jackson, Keith and Burdick, 1984; Mowen et al., 1985; Puto, Patton and King, 1985), a number of considerations specifically favored the use of a role-playing methodology. This approach offered the opportunity to (1) incorporate existing and accepted risk operationalizations and scales (e.g. Bettman, 1972, 1973; Jacoby and Kaplan, 1972; Locander and Hermann, 1979; Lutz and Reilly, 1973; Perry and Hamm, 1969; Peter and Ryan, 1976; Zikmund and Scott, 1973); (2) use advanced statistical analysis of the data, including the assessment of the reliability and validity of dependent measures (e.g. Churchill, 1979b; Leigh, 1983; Smith, 1982) and their interactions (e.g. Punj and Stewart, 1983); and (3) to implement a repeated measures MANOVA design, thus maximizing the degree of experimental control over a wide range of important consumer purchase determinants.

The experimental treatments consisted of three levels of the independent variable from five potential product stimuli for each level, resulting in hypothetical situations. The sets of 15 feasible treatments were identical except for the product to be 'purchased'. Respondents were randomly assigned to treatment order of the independent variable and were presented with one factor from each level of the independent variable. Thus, respondents engaged in a projective purchase task for three products systematically varied in terms of relative 'serviceness'.

Statistical analysis

The data of this research were analyzed by multivariate analysis of variance (MANOVA) procedure. As an extension of the classical MANOVA model to cases in which more than a single criterion variable is involved. MANOVA permits tests of differences involving correlated, multiple response variables, precluding the need to meet the assumption of compound symmetry required by the conventional analysis of a repeated measures design (LaTour and Miniard, 1983). The merits of this statistical technique for this type of research have been explained in detail and cogently defined by Green (1973), Wind and Denny (1974), and Green and Tull (1978) and implemented by Locander and Hermann (1979). SPSSX statistical software was used to carry out these procedures.

Measures of the dependent variables

Immediately following exposure to each of the three projective purchase scenarios, subjects completed a self-administered questionnaire designed to measure product risk and variability for each respective product stimulus. Each construct was assessed using multiple measures to enhance conceptual validity (e.g. Cook and Campbell, 1975; Campbell and Fiske, 1959). Specifically, questionnaire items measured subject response on 14 dependent variables: seven measures of perceived product risk (financial, performance, social, psychological, convenience, physical, and overall loss) and perceived product return (financial, performance social psychological, convenience, physical, and overall gain). Covariate measures of respondent age, sex and experience with the product class were also collected. in addition, the data collection instrument included appropriate manipulation checks to verify the intended effect of the independent variable.

Perceived risk. Although the literature reflects a wide variety of measures of perceived risk, the measures employed in this research were intended to collect data on inherent risk (Bettman, 1973). Consistent with other risk research (e.g. Jacoby and Kaplan, 1972; Perry and Hamm, 1969; Reselius, 1971; Schiffman, 1972; Zikmund and Scott, 1973), this study involved a number of specific factors associated with perceived risk in the purchase decision-making process. Perceived risk measures were derived from previous risk research literature (e.g. Jacoby and Kaplan, 1972; Peter and Tarpey, 1975; Roselius, 1971), although it was necessary to slightly modify item statements to accommodate products of a service nature. Six fixed interval scales were constructed and scored 1 to 7 (low to high loss). Overall perceived risk scores were obtained by summing across each of the six loss dimensions for each respondent relative to each product type rated.

Product variability. A measure of product variability is derived from the net perceived return model of Peter and Tarpey (1975) which proposes that consumer decision-making strategies are motivated by not only minimization of risk, but also the maximization of positive utility. A perceived return model is formulated identically to the perceived risk model, except for a focus on positive instead of negative utilities; conceptually, however, the two models are independent. While the net perceived gain model of Peter and Tarpey (1975) suggests that consumer decisions are based on net valences between positive and negative factors associated with a product or brand, this study, by contrast, adapts the net return model to reflect the absolute perceived valences associated with a product. In effect, this model is a combination of the risk and return models, the purpose of which is to quantify the perceived variability of the product utility. Products with comparatively greater degrees of both positive and/or negative valence imply greater respondent 'uncertainty' with regard to product perception and, implicitly, the expectation of variability. Products with minimal perceived risk and/or gain are expected to be associated with small values of product variability. Bettman (1973) provides support for this inference.

Based on Peter and Tarpey (1975), items measuring specific types of perceived return were composed of six fixed interval scales and scored 1 to 7 and measure perceived financial, social, psychological, convenience, physical, and performance gain. Overall product return was obtained by summing across each of the six gain dimensions with respect to each hypothetical product purchase.

In addition to dependent measures associated with risk and variability, covariate measures tapping respondent gender, age and product experience were employed.

RESULTS

Analysis of the experimental manipulations

To test the efficacy of the product factors identified in pre-test procedures in terms of relative service attributes, a manipulation check of the independent variable showed that the factor levels of products had been significantly varied in the context of the experimental setting. Using a seven point scale, the ratings of each group of products were 6.32, 3.77, and 1.75 for service products, service-good product combinations, and goods products, respectively. Across all factors of the independent variable, the MANOVA F value for difference among the three levels of the independent variable was significant ($F = 1290.00$, $p < .000$) as were all planned comparisons using a Bonferroni multiple comparison t test approach for contrasts among the three means.

A seven point fixed response scale was used to measure respondent familiarity with the factors of the independent variable included in the research. The product familiarity mean score across all subjects and factors was 4.58 with a standard deviation of 1.653. Familiarity scores were 4.44, 4.44, and 4.85, respectively, for high, moderate, and low levels of the independent variable. These data suggest that the sample of products used in the experimental setting were familiar to the respondents.

Although the economic risk with respect to the perceived cost of each experimental operationalization (that is, each product stimulus) was not specifically examined in the experimental setting due to questionnaire length and subject fatigue considerations, the pre-test data indicated that the average perceived product cost for high, moderate, and low-service-attribute products was $35.66, $34.16, and $35.00, respectively. These data suggest that for the population sampled the economic risk across factors associated with the levels of the independent variable was controlled for with respect to approximate perceived cost equivalence.

Measurement validation

Since multiple items were used to measure risk and variability constructs, the reliability of each measurement scale was assessed consistent with the assumptions of domain sampling theory (Churchill, 1979a). Coefficient alpha data for perceived risk, perceived return, and respondent product experience were computed. All values revealed acceptable correlations with true scores and were consistent with Nunnally's (1967) alpha values for these operationalizations. These data are summarized in Table 3.

Table 3. Validation analysis of dependent and covariate measures

Service level	Model components	Cronbach's alpha
A. Internal consistency estimates of perceived risk		
High	Mean risk	.861
Moderate	Mean risk	.797
Low	Mean risk	.802
Across all levels	Financial loss	.522
	Performance loss	.577
	Physical loss	.412
	Psychological loss	.607
	Social loss	.525
	Convenience loss	.764
	Overall mean	.877
B. Internal consistency estimates of perceived benefit		
High	Mean return	.804
Moderate	Mean return	.839
Low	Mean return	.814
Across all levels	Financial gain	.600
	Performance gain	.576
	Physical gain	.639
	Psychological gain	.475
	Social gain	.644
	Convenience gain	.723
	Overall mean	.878
C. Internal consistency estimates of subjects' product experience		
High		.924
Moderate		.895
Low		.905
	Mean coefficient alpha value	.817

FINDINGS

The study hypotheses were concerned with the effects of goods and services on respondents' perception of general and specific measures of risk as well as perception of product variability.

Overall perceived risk

Hypothesis 1 predicted that overall perceived risk would be greater for services than for goods. MANOVA procedures indicated that services were associated with greater perceived risk ($F = 15.44$, $p < .000$). Bonferroni t tests to compare dependent measures among all levels of the independent variable were performed, with the overall alpha level set at .05 for each set of comparisons. The results of this test indicated that no significant differences were detected between the low and moderate levels of the independent variable, although there was directional support for the hypothesis. There were significant differences between the moderate and high levels of the independent variable ($t = 4.18$, $p < .000$) and between the low and high levels ($t = 5.40$, $p < .000$).

Thus support for Hypothesis 1 was encountered, leading to the rejection of the null hypothesis that there are no risk differences between goods and services.

Expected financial risk

Hypothesis 2 predicted that services would be associated with greater perceived financial risk than would goods. This variable was assessed with a measure derived from previous research examining risk phenomena (Brooker, 1984; Jacoby and Kaplan, 1972; Kaplan, Szybillo and Jacoby, 1974). While there was directional support for this prediction, the analysis failed to provide statistical ($F = 2.106$, $p < .124$) support at the $a < .05$ level.

Expected performance risk

Hypothesis 3 predicted that expected performance risk would be greater for services than for goods. This variable was assessed with a measure derived from previous research examining risk phenomena (Brooker, 1984; Jacoby and Kaplan, 1972; Kaplan, Szybillo and Jacoby, 1974). The MANOVA statistical analysis failed to support the stated hypothesis ($F = 1.075$, $p < .343$). Although the data points of the dependent variable suggest a nonlinear relationship, there is some directional support for the outcome predicted.

Expected social risk

Hypothesis 4 proposed that services are associated with greater social risk than goods. This variable was assessed with a measure derived from previous research examining risk phenomena (Brooker, 1984; Jacoby and Kaplan, 1972; Kaplan, Szybillo and Jacoby, 1974). Results of the MANOVA analysis indicate that services are associated with greater expected social risk ($F = 4.713$, $p < .010$). Bonferroni t tests between the low and moderate level of the independent variable were not significant. However, the comparisons between moderate and high ($t = 2.990$, $p < .001$) and low and high ($t = 2.430$, $p < .008$) were statistically significant.

Expected convenience risk

Hypothesis 5 tests the null hypothesis that there are no differences in perceived convenience risk between goods and services. This variable was assessed with a measure derived from previous research relative to convenience risk phenomena (Roselius, 1971). The null hypothesis was rejected in view of a significant MANOVA F statistic ($F = 16.574$, $p < .000$). Bonferroni t test statistics were not significant at the $a = .05$ level between low and moderate levels of the independent variable ($t = .630$, $p < .250$). However, contrasts between the moderate and high levels ($t = 4.919$, $p < .000$) and low and high levels ($t = 5.173$, $p < .000$) of the independent variable were significant.

Expected physical risk

Hypothesis 6 predicts that subjects would not perceive a difference in expected physical risk between goods and services. This variable was assessed with a measure derived from previous research examining perceived physical risk (Brooker, 1984; Jacoby and Kaplan, 1972; Kaplan, Szybillo and Jacoby, 1974). The MANOVA F test ($F = 27.452$, $p < .000$) was significant as were the Bonferroni t tests of planned comparisons among all means. These findings preclude acceptance of the null hypothesis and provide support for the notion that respondents perceive services as having greater perceived physical risk.

Expected psychological risk

Hypothesis 7 tests the null hypothesis with respect to differences in perceived psychological risk between goods and services. This variable was assessed with a measure derived from previous research examining perceived psychological risk (Brooker, 1984; Jacoby and Kaplan, 1972; Kaplan, Szybillo and Jacoby, 1974). Statistical analysis of the data indicates a significant MANOVA F value ($F = 7.966$, $p < .000$). Bonferroni t tests among means show a significant difference at the .05 level among all means. Consequently, the null hypothesis was rejected, suggesting that services are associated with greater perceived psychological risk.

Perceived product variability

Hypothesis 8 makes the prediction that subjects perceive services to have greater variability than goods. The measure of the dependent variable in this test is the sum of the absolute ratings of respondents for perceived loss and perceived gain across all six measures of risk and return.

The MANOVA F test ($F = 9.410$, $p < .000$) was significant, indicating that goods and services are associated with differences in perceived product variability. Thus, the prediction of the hypothesis was supported by the data, that services are associated with greater perceived variability. Bonferroni t tests among the means reveal no significant differences between the low and moderate lives of the independent variable. However, significant t tests were found between the moderate and high ($t = 3.323$, $p < .000$) and low and high ($t = 4.377$, $p < .000$) levels of the independent variable.

A summary of the stated hypotheses and mean response scores for Hypotheses 1 through 8 is shown in Table 4.

Table 4. Review of hypotheses focus and experimental results

A. Summary of the empirical findings of the service variables		
Hypothesis	Focus of prediction	Empirical evidence that service products effect significant differences
1	Overall risk	Yes
2	Financial risk	No, despite directional support
3	Performance risk	No, despite directional support
4	Social risk	Yes
5	Convenience risk	Yes
6	Physical risk	Yes
7	Psychological risk	Yes
8	Product variability	Yes

B. Summary of the statistical results								
Variable	Level of independent variable: Low	Medium	High	MANOVA F value	Significance level	Bonferroni t test ($p < .05$) L-M	M-H	L-H
Type of risk								
Overall	3.456	3.544	3.931	15.449	.000	No	Yes	Yes
Financial	4.185	4.225	4.454	2.106	.124	–	–	–
Performance	4.480	4.394	4.583	1.075	.343	–	–	–
Social	2.520	2.409	2.830	4.713	.010	No	Yes	Yes
Convenience	4.074	4.152	4.762	16.575	.000	No	Yes	Yes
Physical	2.669	3.157	3.630	27.452	.000	Yes	Yes	Yes
Psychological	2.777	2.965	3.293	7.966	.000	No	Yes	Yes
Perceived product variability	3.675	3.722	3.938	9.410	.000	No	Yes	Yes

DISCUSSION

This research suggests that product attributes can influence risk perceptions. That respondents would find services to have greater risk than goods, Hypothesis 1, was supported by that data. Consistent with the predictions of Zeithaml (1981) these data indicate that consumers make significant risk distinctions based on product attributes vis-a-vis a goods–services continuum. Although these findings have been previously suggested by services marketing literature, this research offers empirical support with experimental evidence.

Hypotheses 2 and 3 predicted, respectively, that greater financial risk and performance risk would be associated with services. Though these hypotheses did not achieve statistical significance, there was directional support for the predictions. Post hoc analysis using a model which included the covariate of respondent product experience did reject the hypothesis for respondents with low product experience in the case of both predictions. Specifically, it was found that for respondents who reported low-product experience, perceived performance and financial risk was significantly elevated for services compared to goods. Alternatively, high product experience respondents perceived no significant differences for these types of risk across all levels of the independent variable. These findings are consistent with the theoretical implications of the model proposed by Zeithaml (1981), which, for naive consumers, points to the absence of search qualities for services.

Hypothesis 4 predicts that services are associated with increased social risk. The data confirmed this expectation and are consistent with service marketing literature which points to direct provider-consumer contact which, in turn, suggests the potential for conflict (Bateson, 1979; Eiglier and Langeard, 1977).

Hypotheses 5, 6 and 7 test the null hypothesis and predict no difference in perceived risk with respect to convenience, physical safety, and psychological risk, respectively. For each dimension of risk, the null hypothesis was rejected and the data point to significantly increased perceived convenience, safety, and psychological risk associated with the purchase of services.

Hypothesis 8 predicts that the perceived loss/gain variability is greater for services than for goods. This hypothesis was confirmed in support of the theoretical expectation that services are associated with increased nonstandarization in comparison to goods (Bateson, 1979; Booms and Bitner, 1981; Eiglier and Langeard, 1977).

CONCLUSIONS AND RECOMMENDATIONS

The findings of this research indicate that consumers perceive services to be more risky than goods across several types of risk and more variable in nature. A number of managerial and theoretical implications flow from these conclusions.

Managerial implications

In view of significant differences in consumers' perceived risk, the data suggest a prolonged consumer adoption and diffusion process for services and implicitly point to a need for marketing activities specifically intended to reduce risk. Several examples of marketing considerations are offered. Since services are frequently associated with greater levels of human interaction, the management of customer-contact personnel seems to be a particularly appropriate focus of marketers to decrease the opportunity for social and/or psychological loss to the consumer. The data suggest the need for service marketers to develop personnel screening and supervision techniques which specifically focus on identifying and cultivating skilled service providers who will minimize social risk for consumers.

In view of the role of experience in diminishing some types of perceived risk, service marketers may need to adopt strategies which specifically encourage consumer trial of the service product. Such strategies imply the need to offer services of an introductory nature, ideally at a reduced cost. Exposure to the service product of even a limited nature would permit the service consumer to acquire some 'experience' in evaluating personnel, product benefit, and the purchase context generally, thus reducing uncertainty and perceived risk. This strategy by the service provider would specifically address financial and performance risk considerations. This approach is consistent with Zeithaml (1981) and Young (1981) who argue that consumers find post-purchase evaluation more essential with services than with goods, since services possess experience qualities, which cannot be adequately assessed in advance of purchase.

Because of consumer perception of higher variability associated with services, a marketing mix strategy for services demands special attention to increased product uniformity. While the nature of many services is dependent upon the environment and other individuals in the service system benefit uniformity can be advanced by ensuring the standardization of key factors in the service delivery process. These factors would include provider emphasis on promoting uniformity of the service context in terms of the physical setting and environmental conditions, generally. Insofar as possible, the service firm should seek to facilitate the continuity of interpersonal relationships between provider and consumer, thus diminishing the opportunity for the service customer to attribute variation in the service product to involvement with new or unfamiliar personnel. Also, since tangible cues appear to be relevant to the consumer prior to service purchase, tangible cues provided to the consumer after the service sale may be surrogate indicators of product uniformity. Examples of 'tangibilized', post-purchase cues include a documented 'personalized' financial plan (in the case of financial services), printed suggestions to be carried out by the consumer which serve to enhance the service benefit (following consultation with a physician, landscape architect, or tax advisor), a trinket or memento symbolizing a pleasant visit (to a restaurant, pediatrician, sports event, etc.), or a before-sleep snack in the form of a chocolate mint placed on a turned-down pillow (by a hotel or cruise firm).

Efforts to smooth product variation – and the perception of variation – should be complemented by measures which ensure minimal satisfaction levels to consumers by means of guarantees, money back offers, and similar augmented product strategies. Such measures would diminish financial risk in the face of heightened levels of uncertainty concerning product variability and, ultimately, utility for the prospective service consumer. Beyond these measures, service providers need to subtly yet consciously seek to manage expectations in such a way that consumer expectancies will be consistent with the delivered service utility.

Theoretical implications

While services marketing literature suggests that services are more risky, this study represents an advance in a test of risk differences between services and goods and provides experimental evidence that services are perceived to be more risky across several specific dimensions. These specific measures go beyond previous research and extend the discipline's understanding of consumer risk perceptions across goods and services. When respondent product experience is accounted for, the data show that all risk factors are significantly elevated for services. Thus, the study offers specific empirical evidence of differential consumer risk for all dimensions across a wide range of goods and services. In addition, confirmation of the prediction that services are perceived to be associated with greater variability represents a further substantiation of extant marketing theory.

The contributions of the present study are significant in view of the attempt of this research to quantitatively and empirically define service and goods products and the subsequent effort to experimentally assess the influence of such types of products on consumer perception and behavior. While there have been few attempts at empirical research in this area, the literature in this regard has been largely conceptual in nature and has not empirically identified products and services. However, this study is significant in its application of an experimental methodology to a research area in which conceptual or survey approaches have predominated, or in which the operationalization and control of the service variable from the perspective of the consumer lacks definitional and operational rigor. Specifically, this research demonstrates that it is possible to operationalize the concept of 'services' and 'goods' with sufficient articulation so that (1) as a variable it can be manipulated and (2) its variation as an independent variable can be reliably verified by naive subjects.

Second, in contrast to dependence on a single product or product class, the present research was able to incorporate a wide range, or 'sample', of products in the experimental paradigm. Since the experimental factors were not drawn from a defined universe, theoretical 'generalizations' of the findings, in a strict sense, are not possible. However, the use of many different products to operationalize the independent variable suggests a wider application of the findings than would otherwise be possible with other, more narrowly focused research paradigms.

Third, the degree of experimental and statistical control associated with this paradigm is noteworthy. Control of the product factors in terms of perceived cost and respondent familiarity represents an important step in not only service marketing research, but also research associated with consumer risk perception. The analytic procedures represent a significant contribution to specifically controlling important individual differences which otherwise exert a confounding influence on dependent measures.

Future research directions

More experimental research in consumer behavior with respect to services is needed. A key issue relates to the development of adequate measures of consumer behavior involving services. Further study in the area should also seek to extend the scope of this study to include other product factors and sample populations from other consumer goods. While the findings here seem to show some consistency within the samples of factors of the independent variable and with the sample of subjects, the tentative conclusions with respect to perceived risk and variability need to be tested for their applicability to other factors and use groups.

It is also important that these findings be tested in a real world setting (that is, in terms of actual purchases of real products) to determine their true implications. A research context for evaluating actual consumer responses would conceivably entail the collection of data from a large sample of consumers with respect to their perceptions and behavior toward products varying in service attributes. With proper data collection and statistical controls, as suggested by this study, it would be possible to make a more deliberate determination of the importance of these data, based on actual purchase behavior of consumers.

REFERENCES

Arndt, J. (1985) 'On Making Marketing Science More Scientific: Role of Orientations, Paradigms, Metaphors, and Puzzle Solving'. *Journal of Marketing* 49: 11–23.

Aspinwall, L. (1961) *Four Marketing Theories*. Boulder, CO: University of Colorado.

Bagozzi, R. P. (1984) 'A Prospectus for Theory Construction in Marketing'. *Journal of Marketing* 48: 11–29.

Bateson, J. E. G. (1977) 'Do We Need Service Marketing'. In *Marketing Consumer Services: New Insights* (P. Eiglier, E. Langeard, C. H. Lovelock, J. E. G. Bateson and R. F. Young Eds). Cambridge, MA: Marketing Science Institute.

Bateson, J. E. G. (1979) 'Why We Need Service Marketing'. In *Conceptual and Theoretical Developments in Marketing* (O. C. Ferrell, S. W. Brown and C. W. Lamb, Jr., Eds). Chicago: American Marketing Association.

Bauer, R. A. (1960) 'Consumer Behavior As Risk-taking'. In *Dynamic Marketing for a Changing World*. Chicago: American Marketing Association, 389–393. Cited by Donald F. Cox (Ed.), *Risk-taking and Information-handling in Consumer Behavior*. Boston: Harvard University Press, 1967.

Berry, L. L. (1984) 'Services Marketing is Different'. In *Services Marketing* (C. H. Lovelock, Ed.). Englewood Cliffs, NJ: Prentice-Hall.

Berry, L. L., Shostack, G. L. and Upah, G. D. (1983) 'Preface'. In *Emerging Perspectives on Services Marketing* (L. L. Berry, G. L. Shostack and G. D. Upah, Eds). Chicago: American Marketing Association.

Bettman, J. R. (1972) Perceived Risk: A Measurement Methodology and Preliminary Findings'. In *Proceedings*, Third Annual Conference of the Advances in Consumer Research (M. Venkatesan, Ed.). College Park, MD: Association for Consumer Research.

Bettman, J. R. (1973) 'Perceived Risk and Its Components: A Model and Empirical Test'. *Journal of Marketing Research* 10: 184–189.

Bettman, J. R. (1979) *An Information Processing Theory of Consumer Choice*. Reading, MA: Addison-Wesley.

Biehal, G. J. (1983) 'Consumers' Prior Experience and Perceptions in Auto Repair Choice'. *Journal of Marketing* 47: 82–91.

Booms, B. H. and Bitner, M. J. (1981) 'Marketing Strategies and Organization Structures for Service Firms'. In *Marketing of Services* (J. H. Donnelly and W. R. George, Eds). Chicago: American Marketing Association.

Brinberg, D. and Hirschman, E. C. (1986) 'Multiple Orientations for the Conduct of Marketing Research: An Analysis of the Academic/Practitioner Distinction'. *Journal of Marketing* 50: 161–173.

Brooker, George, (1984) 'An Assessment of an Expected Measure of Perceived Risk'. In *Advances in Consumer Research* Vol. 11 (T. C. Kinnear, Ed.). Urbana, IL: Association for Consumer Research.

Brown, J. R. and Fern, E. F. (1981) 'Goods vs. Services Marketing: A Divergent Perspective'. In *Conceptual and Theoretical Developments in Marketing* (O. C. Ferrell, S. W. Brown and C. W. Lamb, Jr, Eds). Chicago: American Marketing Association.

Calder, B. J., Phillips, L. W. and Tybout, A. M. (1981) 'Designing Research for Application'. *Journal of Consumer Research* 8: 197–207.

Campbell, D. and Fiske, D. (1959) 'Convergent and Disciminant Validation by the Multitrait-Multimethod Matrix'. *Psychological Bulletin* 56: 81–105.

Churchill, G. A., Jr. (1979a) *Marketing Research*. Hinsdale, IL: Dryden Press.

Churchill, G. A., Jr. (1979b) 'A Paradigm for Developing Better Measures of Marketing Constructs'. *Journal of Marketing Research* 16: 64–73.

Claxton, J. D., Fry, J. N. and Portis, B. (1974) 'A Taxonomy of Prepurchase Information Gathering Patterns'. *Advances in Consumer Behavior* 1: 35–42.

Cook, T. and Campbell, D. (1975) 'The Design and Conduct of Experiment and Quasi-Experiments in Field Settings'. In *Handbook of Industrial and Organizational Research* (M. Dunnette, Ed.). Chicago: Rand McNally & Company, pp. 233–321.

Cox, D. F. (1967) *Risk-taking and Information Handling in Consumer Behavior.* Boston: Harvard University.

Cox, D. F. and Rich, S. V. (1964) 'Perceived Risk and Consumer Decision-making – The Case of Telephone Shopping'. *Journal of Marketing Research* **1**: 32–39.

Eiglier, P. and Langeard, E. (1977) 'A New Approach to Service Marketing'. In *Marketing Consumer Services: New Insights* (P. Eiglier, E. Langeard, C. H. Lovelock, J. E. G. Bateson and R. F. Young, Eds). Cambridge, MA: Marketing Science Institute, pp. 33–58.

Enis, B. M. and Roering, K. J. (1981) 'Services Marketing: Different Products, Similar Strategy'. In *Marketing of Services* (J. H. Donnelly and W. R. George, Eds). Chicago: American Marketing Association, pp. 1–4.

Davis, D. L., Guiltinan, J. P. and Jones, W. H. (1979) 'Service Characteristics, Consumer Search, and the Classification of Retail Services'. *Journal of Retailing* **3**: 3–23.

Deshpande, R. (1983) '"Paradigms Lost". On Theory and Method in Research in Marketing'. *Journal of Marketing* **47**: 101–110.

George, W. R., Weinberger, M. G., Tsou, B. and Kelly, J. P. (1984) 'Risk Perceptions: A Reexamination of Services Versus Goods'. In *Proceedings* (D. M. Kline and A. E. Smith, Eds). Boca Raton, FL: The Southern Marketing Association and Florida Atlantic University.

George, W. R., Weinberger, M. G. and Kelly, J. P. (1985) 'Consumer Risk Perceptions: Managerial Tool for the Service Encounter'. In *The Service Encounter: Managing Employee/Customer Interaction in Service Businesses* (J. A. Czepiel, M. R. Solomon and C. F. Surprenant, Eds). Lexington, MA: Lexington Books.

Green, P. E. (1973) 'On the Design of Multiattribute Choice Experiments Involving Large Number of Factors or Factor Levels'. In *Advances in Consumer Research, Vol. 1* (S. Ward and P. Wright, Eds). Urbana, IL: Association for Consumer Research.

Green, P. E. and Tull, D. S. (1978) *Research for Marketing Decisions.* Englewood, NJ: Prentice-Hall, Inc.

Guseman, D. S. (1981) 'Risk Perception and Risk Reduction in Consumer Services'. In *Marketing of Services* (J. H. Donnelly and W. R. George, Eds). Chicago: American Marketing Association, pp. 200–204.

Hollander, S. C. (1979) 'Is There a Generic Demand for Services?'. *MSU Business Topics* **3**: 41–46.

Jacoby, J. and Kaplan, L. B. (1972) 'The Components of Perceived Risk'. In *Proceedings, Third Annual Conference* (M. Venkatesan Ed.). Urbana, IL: Association for Consumer Research.

Jackson, D. W., Jr., Keith, J. E. and Burdick, R. K. (1984) 'Purchasing Agents' Perceptions of Industrial Buying Center Influence: A Situational Approach'. *Journal of Marketing* **48**: 75–83.

Johnson, M. E. (1969) Are Goods and Services Different? An Exercise in Marketing Theory. Unpublished dissertation. Washington University.

Judd, R. C. (1964) 'The Case for Redefining Services'. *Journal of Marketing* **28**: 58–59.

Kaplan, L., Szybillo, G. J. and Jacoby, J. (1974) 'Components of Perceived Risk in Product Purchase: A Cross-Validation'. *Journal of Applied Psychology* **59**: 287–291.

Kirk, R. E. (1982) *Experimental Design: Procedures for the Behavioral Sciences,* Belmont, CA: Brooks/Cole Publishing.

Langeard, E. (1983) 'Service Marketing in Europe and the USA'. In *Emerging Perspectives on Services Marketing* (L. L. Berry, G. L. Shostack, and G. D. Upah, Eds). Chicago: American Marketing Association, pp. 5–8.

LaTour, S. A. and Miniard, P. W. (1983) 'The Misuse of Repeated Measures Analysis in Marketing Research'. *Journal of Marketing Research* **20**: 45–57.

Leigh, J. H. (1983) 'Reliability and Validity Assessment of Patterns of Information Source Usage'. In *Advances in Consumer Research, Vol. 10*, (R. P. Bagozzi and A. Tybout, Eds). Ann Arbor, MI: Association for Consumer Research, pp. 673–678.

Levitt, T. (1969) 'Improving Sales Through Product Augmentation'. *European Business* **21**: 5–12.

Levitt, T. (1980) 'Marketing Success Through Differentiation – Anything'. *Harvard Business Review* **58**: 83–92.

Levitt, T. (1981) 'Marketing Intangible Products and Product Intangibles'. *Harvard Business Review* **59**: 94–102.

Lewis, W. F. (1976) An Empirical Investigation of the Relationship Between Services and Products in Terms of Perceived Risk. Unpublished dissertation. University of Cincinnati, OH.

Locander, W. B. and Hermann, P. W. (1979) 'The Effects of Self-Confidence and Anxiety on Information Seeking in Consumer Risk Reduction'. *Journal of Marketing Research* **16**: 268–278.

Lovelock, C. L. (1979) 'Theoretical Contributions from Services and Nonbusiness Marketing'. In *Conceptual and Theoretical Developments in Marketing* (O. C. Ferrell, S. W. Brown and C. W. Lamb, Jr., Eds). Chicago: American Marketing Association, pp. 147–163.

Lovelock, C. L. (1981) 'Why Marketing Management Needs to Be Different for Services'. In *Marketing Services* (J. H. Donnelly and W. R. George, Eds). Chicago: American Marketing Association, pp. 5–9.

Lovelock, C. H. (1983) 'Classifying Services to Gain Strategic Marketing Insights'. *Journal of Marketing* **47**: 9–20.

Lutz, R. J. and Reilly, P. J. (1973) 'An Exploration of the Effects of Perceived Social and Performance Risk on Consumer Information Acquisition'. In *Advances in Consumer Research, Vol. 1* (S. Ward and P. Wright, Eds). Urbana, IL: Association for Consumer Research, pp. 393–405.

Mills, P. K. and Margulies, N. (1980) 'Toward a Core Typology of Service Organization'. *Academy of Management Review* **5**: 255–265.

Minium, E. W. (1978) *Statistical Reasoning in Psychology and Education.* New York: John Wiley & Sons.

Mowen, J. C., Keith, J. E., Brown, S. W. and Jackson, D. W. Jr. (1985) 'Utilizing Effort and Task Difficulty Information in Evaluating Salespeople'. *Journal of Marketing Research* **22**: 185–191.

Murray, K. B. (1986) 'An Empirical Determination of Service Products and Consumer Perception of Their Relative Risk'. Working Paper 86–50, College of Business Administration, Northeastern University.

Nunnally, J. C. (1967) *Psychometric Theory.* New York: McGraw-Hill.

Park, C. (1976) 'The Effect of Individual and Situation-related Factors on Consumer Selection-related Factors on Consumer Selection of Judgmental Models'. *Journal of Marketing Research* **13**: 144–151.

Perry, M. and Hamm, B. C. (1969) 'Canonical Analysis of Relations Between Socioeconomic Risk and Personal Influence in Purchase Decisions'. *Journal of Marketing Research* **6**: 351–354.

Peter, J. (1979) 'Reliability: A Review of Psychometric Basics and Recent Marketing Practices'. *Journal of Marketing Research* **6**: 351–354.

Peter, J. (1981) 'Construct Validity: A Review of Basic Issues and Marketing Practices'. *Journal of Marketing* **18**: 133–145.

Peter, J. and Ryan, M. J. (1976) 'An Investigation of Perceived Risk at the Brand Level'. *Journal of Marketing Research* **13**: 184–188.

Peter, J. and Tarpey, L. X. (1975) 'A Comparative Analysis of Three Consumer Decision Strategies'. *Journal of Consumer Research* **2**: 29–37.

Punj, G. N. and Stewart, D. W. (1983) 'An Interaction Framework of Consumer Decision Making'. *Journal of Consumer Research* **10**: 181–196.

Puto, C. P., Patton, W. E. III and King, R. H. (1985). 'Risk Handling Strategies in Industrial Vendor Selection Decisions'. *Journal of Marketing* **49**: 89–98.

Rathmell, J. M. (1966) 'What is Meant by Services'. *Journal of Marketing* **30**: 32–36.

Rathmell, J. M. (1974) 'Marketing in the Services Sector, Cambridge, MA: Winthrop.

Roselius, T. (1971) 'Consumer Rankings of Risk Reduction Methods'. *Journal of Marketing* **35**: 56–61.

Ross, I. (1972) 'Perceived Risk and Consumer Behavior: A Critical Review'. In *Advances in Consumer Research, Vol. 2* (M. J. Schlinger Ed.). Urbana, IL: Association for Consumer Research, pp. 1–19.

Sasser, W. E. (1976) 'Match Supply and Demand in Service Industries'. *Harvard Business Review* **54**: 133–141.

Schiffman, L. G. (1972) 'Perceived Risk in New Product Trial by Elder Consumers'. *Journal of Marketing Research* **9**: 106–108.

Shostack, G. L. (1977) 'Breaking Free from Product Marketing'. *Journal of Marketing* **41**: 73–80.

Shostack, G. L. (1978) 'The Service Marketing Frontier'. In *Annual Review of Marketing 1978* (G. Zaltman, Ed.). Chicago: American Marketing Association, pp. 373–388.

Smith, S. M. (1982) 'Providing Information for the Consumer Search Process'. In *Advances in Consumer Research, Vol. 9* (A. Mitchell, Ed.). Ann Arbor, MI: Association for Consumer Research, pp. 244–246.

Spence, H. E., Engel, J. F. and Blackwell, R. D. (1970) 'Perceived Risk in Mail-order and Retail Store Buying'. *Journal of Marketing Research* 7: 364–369.

Swartz, T. A. and Stephens, N. (1984) 'Information Search for Services: The Maturity Segment'. In *Advances in Consumer Research, Vol. 11* (T. C. Kinnear, Ed.). Provo, UT: Association for Consumer Research, pp. 244–249.

Uhl, K. P. and Upah, G. D. (1983) 'The Marketing of Services: Why and How Is It Different?'. In *Research in Marketing, Vol. 6* (J. N. Sheth, Ed.). Greenwich, CT: JAI Press, pp. 231–257.

Weinberger, M. G. and Brown, S. W. (1977) 'Difference in Information Influences: Services vs. Goods'. *Journal of the Academy of Marketing Science* 5: 389–402.

Wind, Y. and Denny, J. (1974) 'Multivariate Analysis of Variance in Research on the Effectiveness of TV Commercials'. *Journal of Marketing Research* 11: 136–142.

Wright, P. (1974) 'The Harassed Decision Maker: Time Pressures, Distractions, and the Use of Evidence'. *Journal of Applied Psychology* 59: 555–561.

Wyckham, R. G., Fitzroy, P. T. and Mandry, G. D. (1975) 'Marketing of Services: An Evaluation of Theory'. *European Journal of Marketing* 9: 59–67.

Young, R. F. (1981) 'The Advertising of Consumer Services and the Hierarchy of Effects'. In *Marketing of Services* (J. H. Donnelly and W. R. George Eds). Chicago: American Marketing Association, pp. 196–199.

Zeithaml, V. A. (1981) 'How Consumer Evaluation Processes Differ Betweem Goods and Services'. In *Marketing of Services* (J. H. Donnelly and W. R. George, Chicago: American Marketing Association, pp. 186–190.

Zeithaml, V., Parasuraman, A. and Berry, L. L. (1985) 'Problems and Strategies in Services Marketing'. *Journal of Marketing* 49: 33–46.

Zikmund, W. G. and Scott, J. E. (1973) 'A Multivariate Analysis of Perceived Risk, Self-confidence and Information Sources'. In *Proceedings of the Fourth Annual Convention of the Association for Consumer Research* (S. Ward and P. Wright, Eds). Urbana, IL: Association for Consumer Research, pp. 406–416.

8

Perceived Control and the Effects of Crowding and Consumer Choice on the Service Experience

Michael K. Hui and John E. G. Bateson

The production and consumption of services generally involve a series of interactions between consumers and both the contact personnel and the settings that are provided by service organizations (Eiglier and Langeard, 1977). From these interpersonal (contact personnel and consumer) and human–environment (consumer and service setting) interactions, consumers attempt to get their needs and wants satisfied. This organization–consumer interface is commonly known as the service encounter (Czepiel, Solomon and Surprenant, 1985). We draw the distinction between this tangible series of interactions and the service experience, which is defined as the consumer's emotional feelings during the service encounter.

It has been suggested that perceived control is a crucial determinant of the quality of the two types of interactions (interpersonal and human environment) that institute the service encounter. For example, Schutz (1966) has proposed that human social behaviors are driven by three kinds of interpersonal needs, including control. He suggests that a feeling of control is essential to having satisfactory interactions with other people. Similarly, in environmental psychology, Proshansky, Ittelson and Rivlin (1974) have suggested that people tend to feel and behave more positively when they perceive that there is more control in the environment.

Drawing heavily from environmental psychology, this article explores and empirically demonstrates the contribution of the perceived-control concept to understanding the service experience and explaining the effects of consumer density (the number of consumers that are present in a service setting) and consumer choice (whether it is a person's own decision to enter into and stay in a service encounter) on the service experience. We conducted an experimental study to test the basic proposition that the consumer's perceived control in the service encounter has considerable impact on the service experience. Two situational features of the service encounter, consumer density and consumer choice, were manipulated in the experiment, and their effects on the consumer's emotional and behavioral responses to the encounter were examined. All the hypothesized relationships were integrated into a single theoretical model. The model provides substantial insights in explaining consumer's favorable or unfavorable responses to the service encounter and their reactions to crowding in different service settings.

PERCEIVED CONTROL AND THE SERVICE EXPERIENCE

Control is widely accepted as a human driving force and has often been defined as the need to demonstrate one's competence, superiority, and mastery over the environment (White, 1959). According to Averill (1973), the concept of control has been operationalized in three different ways: behavioral control, cognitive control, and decisional control. Behavioral control refers to the 'availability of a response which may directly influence or modify the objective characteristics of an event' (Averill, 1973, p. 293). Cognitive control has been broken down into predictability and cognitive reinterpretation of a situation. Finally, decisional control refers to 'choice in the selection of outcomes or goal' (Averill, 1973, p. 289).

Empirical evidence has shown that increased perceived control exerts a significant, positive impact on human physical and psychological well-being; this includes physiological responses (see, e.g. Szpiler and Epstein, 1976), task performance (see, e.g. Burger 1987), tolerance of pain and frustration (see, e.g. Sherrod et al., 1977), self-report of distress and anxiety (see, e.g. Staub, Tursky and Schwartz, 1971), and physiological well-being (see, e.g. Langer and Rodin, 1976). A review of these studies (e.g. Langer, 1983) indicates that, in environmental psychology, the concept of perceived control has been used in both laboratory and field settings. From the perspective of the service encounter, the most relevant studies have been those experiments that were performed in hospitals, homes for the aged, and supermarkets.

In studies of both hospitals and homes for the aged, the dependent measures have been physiological and psychological well-being. For example, Langer, Janis and Wolfer (1975) related experimentally manipulated cognitive control to the pre- and postoperative stress of surgical patients. They showed that control-enhancing manipulations, such as cognitive reappraisal of anxiety-provoking events, had positive benefits for well-being. Langer and Rodin (1976) showed that enhanced personal responsibility (behavioral and decisional control), such as opportunity to control time of eating and visitors, resulted in happier and more active nursing-home residents. In a follow-up study, the control-induced residents were found to live longer as well (Rodin and Langer, 1977). Langer and Saegart (1977), in their pioneering field quasi experiment, manipulated perceived control and then measured emotional (e.g. satisfaction) and behavioral (e.g. success in shopping) outcomes. Although they did not measure perceived control directly, they argued that their manipulations of density and warnings about the effects of density would directly influence control. All of the studies described above suggest that a consumer's perceived control can have considerable impact on the service experience (Bateson, 1985) and lead to our first hypothesis.

H₁: In the service encounter, any situational or interpersonal characteristic that increases consumers' perceived control will positively affect emotional and, in turn, behavioral responses to the encounter.

To test such a hypothesis requires the selection of suitable situational or interpersonal characteristics that influence the consumer's perceived control. For this study, we have chosen to focus on two situational characteristics: consumer choice and consumer density. Because of the very limited use of the perceived control concept in consumer behavior settings (and, therefore, a lack of data to guide us), it was important to choose characteristics that had proven impact in environmental psychology and that could reasonably be adapted to consumer settings. The next section reviews the theoretical pedigree of the chosen variables.

CONSUMER CHOICE AND CONSUMER DENSITY

Consumer choice

Existing literature suggests that perceived choice (the perception that an experience or outcome is caused by a person's own decision) can result in positive psychological and behavioral outcomes (Wortman, 1975). As noted earlier, Averill (1973) has argued that perceived choice is one important type of control, or, in his terms 'decisional control'. Thus, providing choice can increase perceived decisional control that should in turn increase the amount of overall perceived control. According to this model, therefore, any emotional or behavioral effects that are caused by the availability of alternative choices can be considered as outcomes of perceived control. In environmental psychology, choice has commonly been operationalized as whether it is a person's own decision to enter into or stay in a situation (Averill, 1973). Accordingly, our second hypothesis is formulated as follows.

H₂: Providing the consumer with a choice of whether to stay in the service situation will result in higher perceptions of control.

Consumer density

Stokols (1972) has asserted that there is a need to distinguish between the terms 'density' and 'crowding'. Density refers to the physical condition, 'in terms of spatial parameters' (Stokols, 1972, p. 275). On the other hand, perceived crowding is an unpleasant feeling that is experienced by an individual. More important, perceived control has been argued as a key intervening variable between density and crowding (Schmidt and Keating, 1979).

Proshansky et al. (1974) have suggested that density is a key determinant of an individual's perceived control in a particular setting. Density can facilitate or obstruct desired behaviors; the influence it has will then determine the individual's perception of crowding. For example, Rodin, Solomon and Metcalf (1978) ʰ shown that high perceived crowding results when density reduces an indiv' ability to perform a desired action. Nonetheless, there is considerable showing that perceived crowding is also a direct function of density (e.g. Langer and Saegart, 1977). This finding is not unexpected since perceived crowding refers to the 'the negative subjective experience of certain density levels' (Rapoport, 1975, p. 134). Our third hypothesis captures all the above-mentioned relationships.

H$_3$: In a service setting, density affects consumers' perceived crowding directly and indirectly through perceived control.

In line with the existing conceptualization that perceived crowding is a negative subjective experience (e.g. Stokols, 1972), the fourth hypothesis relates perceived crowding to emotional and behavioral outcomes.

H$_4$: In a service encounter, consumers' perceived crowding negatively affects emotional and, in turn, behavioral responses to the encounter.

A summary of hypotheses 1–4 can be represented by a model as presented in Figure 1. Empirical evidence has shown that the relationship between density and pleasure can vary between different settings (McClelland and Auslander, 1978). A high-density bar or restaurant is interpreted as less unpleasant than a high-density bank or retail outlet. According to Figure 1, one possible explanation for the above finding is that perceived control as a function of density varies between settings. Our fifth hypothesis captures this relationship.

H$_5$: The relationship between density and perceived control varies with the service setting.

The hypothesized model (Figure 1) also suggests a more stringent test of the intervening role of perceived control between density and perceived crowding. Given that perceived crowding is a function of perceived control, any situational determinant of the consumer's perceived control (e.g. consumer choice) is expected

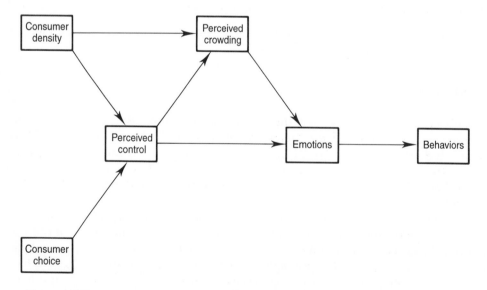

Figure 1. Effects of consumer density and consumer choice on the service experience.

to influence the consumer's perceived crowding. The sixth hypothesis is therefore formulated as follows:

H_6: In a service setting of any density level, consumers' perceived crowding is a function of any situational determinant of perceived control.

METHOD

Research design

An experimental study was conducted to test our six research hypotheses. In the study, consumer choice in the service encounter and consumer density of the service setting were manipulated independently, and their effects on the consumer's psychological and behavioral responses to the service encounter were examined. The manipulation of these two characteristics of the encounter provides a more powerful test of hypothesis 1. If a simple one-characteristic relationship can be mediated by a change in another characteristic, and this can be shown to be due to changes in perceived control, then the true intervening nature of perceived control is demonstrated.

To test hypothesis 5, we also included two service settings, a bank and a bar, in the study. Results of a pilot study indicated that people tend to believe that consumer density has less negative impact on the service experience in a bar setting than in a bank setting. Most respondents said that they would not mind staying in a high-density bar but that they would definitely try to avoid a high-density bank. In short, a 3 (consumer density: high, medium, and low) × 2 (consumer choice: choice and no choice) × 2 (service setting: bank and bar) experimental factorial design was employed. Consumer density and consumer choice were nonrepeated factors whereas service setting was a repeated factor.

Consumer density was operationalized through color slides that portrayed three different numbers of consumers in a medium-sized branch of a bank and a country bar. Prior studies have shown that slides can adequately represent the environment (e.g. Hershberger and Cass, 1974). To encompass known peaks and troughs in the number of consumers, a total of 50 slides were taken by a camera fixed at a corner of the bank. Since the camera was fixed at the same position, the only difference between the slides was the number of consumers that were inside the bank. Another 50 slides were also taken in the bar by the same method.

The consumer-density level represented in each of the 100 slides (50 from each setting) was determined by a procedure adapted from McClelland and Auslander (1978). Three individuals rated all the slides on two physical dimensions: number of people (in absolute number) and number of people per unit area (1–10 rating). Of the 100 slides, the interrater reliability, estimated by the Spearman–Brown formula (Tinsley and Weiss, 1975), was .94 for number of people and .96 for number of people per unit area. For each slide, raters' scores were summed for each of the two physical dimensions. A linear composite of the two-dimension scores then determined the consumer-density level that was represented in the slide. Finally, the three bank slides showing the highest, average, and lowest density levels were used in the experimental study to represent the high-, medium-, and low-density settings, respectively. Three bar slides were chosen in the same way.

Written scenarios were employed to operationalize the choice treatments and to describe the features of various service situations. To illustrate how the choice manipulation was created, consider the two bank scenarios used in the study.

Bank scenario 1 (choice). 'It is quarter to three on Friday afternoon and Mr Y is in a bank to transfer money from his saving to his checking account. The transfer can also be done through the cash dispensing machine outside the bank but he decides to use the cashier. Of course, he can always change his mind and use the machine instead or he can come back next week because the money is not urgently needed. However, he sticks to his original decision and stays in the bank until the transfer is done. The slide we are going to show you depicts the interior of the bank while Mr Y is there.'

Bank scenario 2 (no choice). 'It is quarter to three on Friday afternoon and Mr Y is in a bank to transfer money from his deposit to his current account. The transfer can also be done through the cash dispensing machine outside the bank but the machine is temporarily out of service. He can't come back later because the bank is going to close and the money is desparately needed to cover a check he has already written. Hence, he has to use the cashier and stay in the bank until the transfer is done. The slide we are going to show you depicts the interior of the bank while Mr Y is there.'

In the context of a laboratory experiment, it is very difficult to manipulate perceived choice in the service encounter directly. Decisions to 'come back later' are difficult to operationalize. Instead, all respondents saw the given density situation, and the scenarios were used to manipulate their perceived choice. The situations described by the written scenarios can be regarded as service-encounter analogues of Glass and Singer's (1972) manipulation of choice. In their studies, a stressful stimulus (e.g. electric shock) was delivered to all subjects. Half of the subjects, however, were given an option to avoid or escape from the stimulus, but they were asked not to do so as long as they found the stimulus bearable. As a result, no subject selected the escape or avoid option and, therefore, both the choice and no-choice subjects experienced the same stressful stimulus. Nonetheless, the findings indicated that the choice subjects felt and behaved significantly better than the no-choice subjects.

The same principle was employed in designing the written scenarios. Despite the fact that Mr Y ends up facing the same crowd of people, his presence in the service situation is more his own decision in the choice scenario than it is in the no-choice scenario. According to hypothesis 2, the two written scenarios are expected to produce a difference in the subjects' perceived choice and, hence, perceived control. A similar approach was adopted in the development of the two bar scenarios (see the Appendix).

The use of a hypothetical figure in the scenarios is based on the work of Havlena and Holbrook (1986). They suggest that there are two advantages to using hypothetical consumers (e.g. Mr Y, as in the bank scenarios) in written scenarios: '(a) to provide a projective task and thereby to discourage social desirability effects, and (b) to avoid problems involving individual differences in reactions to specific types of activities' (Havlena and Holbrook, 1986, p. 396).

The benefit of using hypothetical consumers was confirmed in a pretest of the written scenarios. When a projective task was not used, a number of respondents complained that the described situations would never happen to them and, hence, that it was difficult for them to judge their reactions to the situations.

Methodology

Subjects were recruited from various churches and a public housing estate located in London, England, and through an advertisement in a free local newspaper. A total of 115 people between the ages of 25 and 40 participated in the study.

Concurrent experimental sessions were conducted in three different lecture rooms that were of similar size and design. In each room, two envelopes were left in front of each available seat. Each envelope contained a questionnaire, the front page of which consisted of either a choice scenario or a no-choice scenario as described above. Each subject was randomly assigned to a seat in one of the three experimental rooms.

At the beginning of each experimental session, the experimenter announced that the main objective of the study was to examine human reactions to daily social situations. The subjects were asked to open the first envelope and read the scenario on the first page of the questionnaire. After one minute, the first slide, showing the same service setting that was described in the scenario at one of the three (high, medium, and low) consumer-density levels, was projected on a screen. The subjects then reported the hypothetical consumer's feelings in the situation as described by the scenario and shown in the slide. After the last subject had finished, the whole procedure was repeated again for the second service situation. Each session lasted from 50 to 70 minutes.

Dependent measures

A self-administered questionnaire measured the five dependent variables: perceived choice, perceived control, perceived crowding, pleasure, and approach-avoidance. The last two variables were drawn from the Mehrabian and Russell (1974) model of environmental reactions to represent the consumer's emotional and behavioral responses to the service encounter, respectively. Three emotional dimensions (pleasure–displeasure, dominance–submissiveness, arousal–unarousal) are included in the model, but existing evidence reveals that pleasure–displeasure tends to be the dimension that produces the most direct and strongest effect on approach-avoidance (Donovan and Rossiter, 1982; Mehrabian and Russell, 1974).

Perceived choice was measured using two simple questions. For the bank setting, the two questions were: 'How much choice do you think Mr Y has in deciding when to transfer the money?' and 'How much choice do you think Mr Y has in deciding how to transfer the money?' These questions were used as a manipulation check of the choice treatments.

Five seven-point semantic differential scales were included in one section of the questionnaire. Mehrabian and Russell's (1974) scale of dominance and Glass and Singer's (1972) scale of helplessness were combined as a semantic differential indicator of perceived control (CTL1). Both dominance and helplessness have been considered as closely associated with or alternative labels for perceived control (Russell and Mehrabian, 1976; Seligman, 1975). This section also contained Mehrabian and Russell's (1974) scale of pleasure (PLE1), a scale of perceived crowding (CRD) that was developed from review of the crowding literature (stuffy–not stuffy, cramped–uncramped, crowded–uncrowded, free to move–restricted, and spacious–confined), and a single item (choice–no choice) that was used as a second measure of perceived choice (PCHOICE2). To avoid response bias, the direction of half of the items in each scale was reversed. The items were mixed and the order of presentation was randomized.

Another section of the questionnaire consisted of three seven-point Likert-type scales. One of the scales, adapted from the studies conducted by Newcomb and Harlow (1986) and Fleming, Baum and Weiss (1987), was included as the second measure of perceived control (CTL2). Two other scales, adapted from Mehrabian and Russell's (1974) scale of approach-avoidance, measured desire to stay (DSTAY) and desire to affiliate (DAFF). The final scale was a third measure of perceived choice (PCHOICE3). This scale, developed from the choice literature, included statements like, 'It is his own decision to stay in the situation.'

In the last section of the questionnaire, 27 emotional terms were given. The respondents were asked to describe the service experience that was shown and described in the written scenario by checking a seven-point scale (from 'not at all' to 'extremely so') for each term. Twenty-four of the terms were used by Havlena and Holbrook (1986) to measure the eight basic emotion components that were identified by Plutchik (1980); each component was operationalized by three emotional terms. One more component, comfort, was added to this study. This component was also operationalized by three emotional terms: calm, peaceful, and relaxed. The 27 emotional terms form a perfect two-dimensional (pleasure–displeasure; arousing–unarousing) circumplex model as proposed by Russell and Pratt (1980). The terms were mixed, and the order of presentation was randomized. The ratings obtained on the pleasure dimension were converted into a second indicator of pleasure (PLE2) through Bush's (1972) successive-interval scales of adjectives denoting feelings.

RESULTS

The experiemental sessions produced 107 and 112 completed questionnaires for the bank and the bar settings, respectively. A two-way analysis of variance of perceived choice as a function of the two experimental variables revealed a significant choice main effect in both settings. The two choice scenarios produced significantly higher perceived-choice ratings than did the two no-choice scenarios in both settings (for the bank, $F(1,101) = 175.18$, $p < .001$; for the bar, $F(1,106) = 112.51$, $p < .001$). Neither the density main effect nor the interaction was significant. The findings indicated that the choice manipulation was effective.

The data were then analyzed through the structural equations model shown in Figure 2. The model was proved to be identified through a procedure suggested by

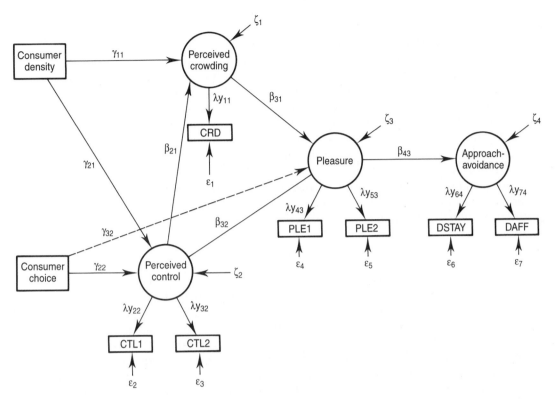

Figure 2. Structural equations model. The dashed line signifies a relationship not included in the hypothesized model (M-1) but found to be significant in the analysis (M-2).

Bagozzi (1980). Perceived choice was omitted for a more parsimonious model and because of the powerful manipulation check. With either set of data, a Cronbach α of .9 was obtained for the one scale used to measure perceived crowding (CRD). Therefore, the measurement error (ϵ_1) and correspondence loading (λ_{y11}) of CRD were fixed at .10 ($1 - \alpha$) and .95 (the square root of α), respectively, in the analysis.

Testing the hypothesized model

Multisample LISREL (Jöreskog and Sörbom, 1989) was used to test the hypothesized model. This method allowed simultaneous analysis of the data that were obtained from the two settings, and, hence, any similarity or difference in the estimated values of the parameters between the two settings could be explored. The structural equation model (M-1) gave a chi-square value of 63.89 ($df = 50$; $p = .090$), a goodness-of-fit index (GFI) of .936, and a root mean square residual (RMR) of .039 for the bank setting, and a GFI of .946 and a RMR of .031 for the bar setting. The findings suggested that M-1 produced a reasonable fit in both settings (Bagozzi and Yi, 1988).

Rival model A

A modification index of significant size, however, was obtained for the paramter γ_{32} (the causal path between choice and pleasure) in both settings. This finding suggested that there may exist a direct choice effect on pleasure. The parameter γ_{32} was therefore set free in another multisample LISREL analysis. The modified model produced a chi-square value of 50.03 ($df = 48$; $p = .393$). Compared with M-1, the modified model (M-2) has two degrees of freedom less, but its chi-square value was also 13.86 smaller. Since the difference between the chi-square values of two nested models also forms a chi-square distribution (Bagozzi, 1980), we can therefore conclude that M-2 is a better model than M-1 ($\chi^2 = 13.86$, $df = 2$, $p < .01$). A direct choice effect on pleasure (represented by the dotted line in Figure 2) was therefore added to our original hypothesized model in the subsequent analysis. A conceptual rationalization for this path is included in the Discussion.

Rival model B

As shown in Figure 2, no direct relationship is hypothesized between perceived control and approach-avoidance responses. Pleasure is assumed to be an intervening variable through which perceived control influences approach-avoidance. We made two changes to M-2 to test this assumption. First, the causal path between perceived control and approach-avoidance was set free. Second, the causal path between perceived control and pleasure was fixed at zero. The rival model produced a chi-square value of 175.03 ($df = 48$, $p < .000$), which indicated a poor fit. Therefore, a direct relationship from perceived control to approach-avoidance was not supported by our findings.

Rival model C

Another interesting rival model draws from the argument that the direction of causality between perceived control and perceived crowding may, in fact, be reversed. In other words, a strong correlation between the two variables may indicate that perceived control is a function of perceived crowding rather than the opposite, as we hypothesized. The causal path between perceived crowding and perceived control was therefore reversed in another multisample LISREL analysis, but the modified model (M-4) produced a poor fit with the data ($\chi^2 = 79.29$, $df = 48$, $p = .003$). Accordingly, the argument that high perceived crowding causes low perceived control was not supported.

Comparison between two settings

This part of the analysis was concerned with the stability of the estimated parameters across the two settings. When the values of all the parameters were constrained to be identical between the two settings, the structural equations model (M-5) produced a chi-square value of 82.30 ($df = 69$, $p = .131$). A less restrictive model (M-6), one that allowed the values of all the γ parameters to vary between the two settings, produced a chi-square value of 68.14 ($df = 65$, $p = .371$). The two chi-square values suggested that M-6 produced a significantly better fit than did M-5 ($\chi^2 = 14.16$, $df = 4$, $p < .01$).

Estimated values of parameters

A summary of all the multisample LISREL models that were tested in our analysis is presented in Table 1. Two of the models, M-2 and M-6, undoubtedly produce the best fit with our data. Note that the only difference between M-2 and M-6 is that, in the latter model, all the parameters, other than the γ's, were constrained to be identical between the two settings. Since the chi-square difference between M-2 and M-6 was not significant ($\chi^2 = 18.11$, $df = 17$, $p = NS$) and for the sake of simplicity, we therefore used the LISREL estimates of M-6 (Table 2) in testing our six hypotheses.

As shown in Table 2, except γ_{21} of the bar setting, the estimated values of all the other path coefficients are significantly different from zero at least at the .05 level. The two path coefficients, β_{32} and β_{43}, confirm that perceived control is a positive determinant of pleasure, which, in turn, exerts a positive effect on approach-

Table 1. Goodness-of-fit indicators for the structural equation models

Model	Description	χ^2	df	p	GFI	RMR
M-1	Hypothesized model	63.89	50	.090	.946[a] .936[b]	.031[a] .039[b]
M-2	M-1 plus a direct choice effect on pleasure	50.03	48	.393	.948[a] .957[b]	.032[a] .033[b]
M-3	Modification of M-2; a direct effect from perceived control to approach-avoidance	175.03	48	.000	.872[a] .875[b]	.121[a] .079[b]
M-4	Modification of M-2; perceived control as a function of perceived crowding	79.29	48	.003	.922[a] .936[b]	.130[a] .099[b]
M-5	Modification of M-2; all the parameters are constrained to be identical between the two samples	82.30	69	.131	.920[a] .922[b]	.074[a] .067[b]
M-6	Modification of M-2; except the γ's, all the parameters are constrained to be identical between the two samples	68.14	65	.371	.931[a] .938[b]	.043[a] .047[b]

GFI = goodness-of-fit index; RMR - root mean square residual.
[a]Data are for bar scenarios.
[b]Data are for bank scenarios.

Table 2. LISREL estimates of M-6

Parameters	Estimated values
λ_{y11}	.950[a]
λ_{y22}	1.000
λ_{y32}	.901 (15.78)***
λ_{y43}	1.000
λ_{y53}	.991 (24.56)***
λ_{y64}	1.000
λ_{y74}	.749 (9.63)***
β_{12}	−.661 (−10.25)***
β_{31}	−.126 (−2.78)*
β_{32}	.781 (10.93)***
β_{43}	.863 (17.11)***
γ_{11}:	
Bar	.529 (7.42)***
Bank	.398 (5.35)***
γ_{21}:	
Bar	.128 (1.76)+
Bank	−.218 (−2.92)*
γ_{22}:	
Bar	.604 (8.04)***
Bank	.446 (5.82)***
γ_{32}:	
Bar	.126 (2.32)*
Bank	.194 (3.82)***

Data are maximum likelihood estimates. For the sake of simplicity, only the estimated values of the λ_y, β, and γ parameters are presented. Numbers inside the parentheses are the t values of the estimates. Estimates without a t value are fixed parameters.
[a]A Cronbach α of .9 is obtained for the scale of perceived crowding. The λ_{y11} is fixed at a value equal to the square root of the obtained α value.
+$p < .10$.
*$p < .05$.
***$p < .001$.

avoidance (Hypothesis 1). A highly significant γ_{22} also indicates that perceived control is a positive function of consumer choice (Hypothesis 2).

The excellent fit of the structural equations model also supports the hypothesis that perceived crowding is both a direct and an indirect function of consumer density (Hypothesis 3). Moreover, a significant negative β_{31} and a significant positive β_{43} support the hypothesized relationships between perceived crowding, pleasure, and approach-avoidance (Hypothesis 4). The estimated values of γ_{21} confirm that density has a different impact on perceived control in the bar setting than in the bank setting (Hypothesis 5). In fact, a negative estimate of the parameter is obtained with the bank data, while a positive estimate, although only marginally significant ($t = 1.76$, $p < .10$), is obtained with the bar data.

Finally, the LISREL results show that perceived crowding is a negative function of perceived control (β_{12}), which, in turn, is a positive function of consumer choice (γ_{22}). Accordingly, perceived crowding is expected to be a negative function of consumer density (Hypothesis 6). As shown in Table 3, in either the bank or the bar setting, the choice subjects reported significantly lower perceived crowding than did their no-choice counterparts at all three density levels (for the bank, $F(1,101) = 13.50$, $p < .001$; for the bar, $F(1,106) = 18.73$, $p < .001$).

Table 3. Mean scores of perceived crowding as a function of density and choice

Consumer density	Choice	No choice
Bank:[a]		
Low	3.96	4.88
Medium	5.21	5.87
High	5.73	6.35
Bar:[b]		
Low	3.58	4.31
Medium	4.01	5.50
High	5.00	5.60

Perceived crowding measured with a 1–7 rating. Higher score indicates higher perceived crowding.
[a]Choice main effect: $F(1,101) = 13.50$, $p < .001$; density main effect: $F(2,101) = 22.85$, $p < .001$; choice-density interaction: $F(2,101) = .22$, NS.
[b]Choice main effect: $F(1,106) = 18.73$, $p < .001$; density main effect: $F(2,101) = 14.69$, $p < .001$; choice-density interaction: $F(2,106) = 1.67$, NS.

DISCUSSION AND CONCLUSIONS

The findings of this study strongly support the hypothesized model (Figure 1) and confirm the power of concept of perceived control in explaining the effects of consumer choice and consumer density on the emotional and behavioral outcomes of the service encounter.

Perceived control and consumer emotions and behaviors

Variation in the subject's perceived control that was caused by consumer choice and consumer density was found to exert a considerable effect on pleasure and approach-avoidance. Moreover, the fact that choice can mediate the influence of density on perceived crowding and pleasure adds support to the significance of perceived control and vindicates the use of two manipulations of perceived control.

The confirmation of Hypothesis 1 suggests that the perceived-control concept can contribute to exploring different ways to create a more pleasant service experience. Giving more choice to the consumer in the service encounter is one alternative. For example, drawing heavily from the concepts of control and choice, Mills and Krantz (1979) have allowed blood donors to choose which arm is used. This manipulation has been found to ameliorate significantly donors' experiences in blood transfusion centers. In fact, greater consumer choice is considered to be one crucial benefit of service customization, a common competitive strategy that is employed by service organizations (Surprenant and Solomon, 1987).

One limitation of this study is that the service experience was examined in a rather narrow context, in the sense that only two particular features of the service encounter were manipulated. To confirm the role of perceived control as a crucial dimension of the service experience, researchers need to investigate the power of the concept in explaining a wide variety of pleasant and unpleasant service experiences.

Perceived control and crowding

Our results also demonstrate that perceived control is a powerful concept in explaining the consumer's reactions to consumer density in the service environment. The confirmation of Hypothesis 6 suggests that any negative outcomes of high consumer density can be minimized by returning some control to the consumer. Our results show that a greater degree of choice can lower the consumer's perceived crowding in the service encounter. Other authors have suggested that similar effects can be obtained from providing situational and emotional information (Baum, Fisher and Solomon, 1981), distraction and attribution (Worchel, 1978), and architectural and interior design (Baum and Valins, 1977).

Perceived control can also be used to explain the previous finding that density produces positive emotional and behavioral effects in some settings and negative effects in other settings (Freedman, 1975). In both the bank and bar settings, there is a positive relationship between density and perceived crowding (γ_{11}), and a negative relationship between perceived control and perceived crowding (β_{12}). However, the sign of the relationship between density and perceived control (γ_{21}) varies with the setting. In the bank setting, high density is associated with lower perceived control, but in the bar setting, high density is associated with higher control. Thus, density can directly influence pleasure in a negative manner, but this can be counteracted by a positive association through perceived control.

Two existing theories can be used to explain a positive relationship between density and perceived control. According to manning theory (Wicker, 1984), every setting requires an optimal number of occupants to function effectively; then the setting is said to be adequately 'manned'. A high-density bar may be more adequately manned than a low-density bar and, hence, may offer higher levels of perceived control. The concept of behavior–environment fit (Michelson, 1970) provides an alternative explanation. People may feel that they have more control in the high-density bar simply because the setting is more compatible with their situational goals, say, to have an exciting evening after a monotonous day of hard work (Argyle, Furnham and Graham, 1980).

A possible confounding effect

The only unexpected finding obtained in this study is a direct relationship between choice and pleasure. Conceptually, this finding can be attributed to a possible confounding effect that was created by the two choice scenarios. When the subjects were told that Mr X decides to stay in the noisy bar or Mr Y decides to use the cashier, they might infer that the hypothetical consumer is a person who enjoys disco music or prefers to deal with human tellers. The two no-choice scenarios, on the other hand, did not contain any clues about the personal disposition of the hypothetical consumer (Jones and Davis, 1965).

The subjects' conditioned responses to the situations that were described in the scenarios might also contribute to a direct choice effect on pleasure. For example, subjects might have learned from previous experience that a situation like a cash-dispensing machine temporarily out of service is unpleasant. Consequently, spontaneous negative responses may have been likely when a similar service situation was described to the subjects during the experimental sessions.

APPENDIX

Bar scenarios used in the experimental study

Bar scenario 1 (choice). 'It is eight o'clock on Thursday evening, and Mr X is with one of his friends in a country pub for a drink and a chat. Disco music is being played in one of the two separated lounges in the pub. When they first arrive, Mr X and his friend decide to stay in the music lounge. Since the music is very noisy, they know beforehand they have to shout when chatting with each other in the lounge. Of course, they can always change their minds and go the quieter lounge but they stay in the music lounge until they leave an hour later. The slide we are going to show you depicts the interior of the lounge while Mr X and his friend are there.'

Bar scenario 2 (no choice). 'It is eight o'clock ... a chat. There are two lounges in the pub. Disco music is being played in both lounges so that they have to shout when chatting with each other. It is impossible for them to go to another pub because it is the only one in the area. They stay there for an hour as Mr X's friend is very keen for a drink. The slide we are ... are there.'

ACKNOWLEDGMENTS

The authors wish to thank Russell Belk for his comments on an earlier draft of this article, and three anonymous reviewers for their patience and insights. This research was funded by a grant from the Marketing Science Institute.

REFERENCES

Argyle, M., Furnham, A. and Graham, J. A. (1980) *Social Situations.* Cambridge: Cambridge University Press.
Averill, J. R. (1973) 'Personal Control over Aversive Stimuli and Its Relationship to Stress'. *Psychological Bulletin* **80** (4): 286–303.

Bagozzi, R. P. (1980) *Causal Models in Marketing*. New York: Wiley.

Bagozzi, R. P. and Yi, Y. (1988) 'On the Evaluation of Structural Equation Models'. *Journal of Academy of Marketing Science* **16** (1): 74–94.

Bateson, J. E. G. (1985) 'Perceived Control and the Service Encounter'. In *The Service Encounter: Managing Employee/Customer Interaction in Service Business* (J. A. Czpiel *et al.*, Eds). Lexington, MA: Lexington, 67–82.

Baum, A. and Valins, S. (1977) *Architecture and Social Behavior: Psychological Studies of Social Density*. Hillsdale, NJ: Erlbaum.

Baum, A., Fisher, J. D. and Solomon, S. K. (1981) 'Type of Information, Familiarity, and the Reduction of Crowding Stress'. *Journal of Personality and Social Psychology* **40** (1): 11–23.

Burger, Jerry M. (1987) 'Increased Performance with Increased Personal Control: A Self-Presentation Interpretation'. *Journal of Experimental Social Psychology* **23** (4): 350–360.

Bush, L. E. II (1972) 'Successive-Intervals Scaling of Adjectives Denoting Feelings'. *JSAS Catalog of Selected Documents in Psychology* **2**: 140.

Czepiel, J. A., Solomon, M. R. and Surprenant, C. F. (1985) *The Service Encounter: Managing Employee/Customer Interaction in Service Businesses*. Lexington, MA: Lexington.

Donovan, R. J. and Rossiter, J. R. (1982) 'Store Atmosphere: An Environmental Psychology Perspective'. *Journal of Retailing* **58** (Spring): 34–57.

Eiglier, P. and Langear, E. (1977) 'Services as Systems: Marketing Implications'. In *Marketing Consumer Services: New Insights* (P. Eiglier *et al.*, Eds). Cambridge, MA: Marketing Science, pp. 83–103.

Flemming, I., Baum, A. and Weiss, L. (1987) 'Social Density and Perceived Control as Mediators of Crowding Stress in High-Density Residential Neighborhoods'. *Journal of Personality and Social Psychology*, **52** (5), 899–906.

Freedman, J. L. (1975) *Crowding and Behavior*. San Francisco: Freeman.

Glass, D. C. and Singer, J. E. (1972) *Urban Stress: Experiments on Noise and Social Stressors*. New York: Academic Press.

Havlena, W. J. and Holbrook, M. B. (1986) 'The Varieties of Consumption Experience: Comparing Two Typologies of Emotion in Consumer Behavior'. *Journal of Consumer Research* **13** (December): 394–404.

Hershberger, R. G. and Cass, R. C. (1974) 'Predicting User Responses to Buildings'. In *Man-Environment Interactions: Evaluations and Applications, Part II* (D. H. Carson, Ed). Stroudsburg, PA: Dowden, Hutchison & Ross, pp. 117–134.

Jones, E. E. and Davis, K. (1965) 'From Acts to Dispositions: The Attribution Process in Person Perception'. In *Advances in Experimental Social Psychology*, Vol. 2 (L. Berkowitz, Ed.). New York: Academic Press, pp. 219–266.

Jöreskog, K. G. and Sörbom, D. (1989) *LISREL 7 User's Reference Guide*. Mooresville, IN: Scientific Software.

Langer, E. J. (1983) *The Psychology of Control*. Beverly Hills, CA: Sage.

Langer, E. J. and Rodin, J. (1976) 'The Effects of Choice and Enhanced Personal Responsibility for the Aged: A Field Experiment in an Institutional Setting'. *Journal of Personality and Social Psychology* **34** (2): 191–198.

Langer, E. J. and Saegart, S. (1977) 'Crowding and Cognitive Control'. *Journal of Personality and Social Psychology*, **35** (3): 175–182.

Langer, E. J., Janis, I. L. and Wolfer, J. A. (1975) 'Reduction of Psychological Stress in Surgical Patients'. *Journal of Experimental Social Psychology* **11** (2): 156–165.

McClelland, L. and Auslander, N. (1978) 'Perceptions of Crowding and Pleasantness in Public Settings'. *Environment and Behavior* **10** (4): 535–553.

Mehrabian, A. and Russell, J. A. (1974) *An Approach to Environmental Psychology*. Cambridge, MA: MIT Press.

Michelson, W. (1970) *Man and His Urban Environment: A Sociological Approach*. Reading, MA: Addison-Wesley.

Mills, R. T. and Krantz, D. S. (1979) 'Information, Choice and Reactions to Stress: A Field Experiment in a Blood Bank with Laboratory Analogue'. *Journal of Personality and Social Psychology* **37** (4): 608–620.

Newcomb, M. D. and Harlow, L. L. (1986) 'Life Events and Substance Use among Adolescents:

Mediating Effects of Perceived Loss of Control and Meaninglessness in Life'. *Journal of Personality and Social Psychology* **51** (3): 564–577.

Plutchik, R. (1980) *Emotion: A Psychoevolutionary Synthesis.* New York: Harper & Row.

Proshansky, H. M., Ittelson, W. H. and Rivlin, L. G. (1974) 'Freedom of Choice and Behavior in a Physical Setting'. In *Environmental Psychology* (H. M. Proshansky *et al.*, Eds). New York: Holt, Rinehart & Winston, pp. 170–181.

Rapoport, A. (1975) 'Toward a Redefinition of Density'. *Environment and Behavior* **7** (2): 133–158.

Rodin, J. and Langer, E. J. (1977) 'Long-Term Effects of a Control-relevant Intervention'. *Journal of Personality and Social Psychology* **35** (12): 897–902.

Rodin, J., Solomon, S. K. and Metcalf, J. (1978) 'Role of Control in Mediating Perceptions of Density'. *Journal of Personality and Social Psychology* **36** (9): 988–999.

Russell, J. A. and Mehrabian, A. (1976) 'Some Behavioral Effects of the Physical Environment'. In *Experiencing the Environment* (S. Wapner, S. B. Cohen and B. Kaplan, Eds). New York: Plenum, pp. 5–18.

Russell, J. A. and Pratt, G. (1980) 'A Description of the Affective Quality Attributed to Environment'. *Journal of Personality and Social Psychology* **38** (2): 311–322.

Schmidt, D. E. and Keating, J. P. (1979) 'Human Crowding and Personal Control: An Integration of Research'. *Psychological Bulletin* **86** (4): 680–700.

Schutz, W. C. (1966) *The Interpersonal Underworld.* Palo Alto, CA: Science & Behavior.

Seligman, M. E. P. (1975) *Helplessness.* San Francisco: Freeman.

Sherrod, D. R., Hage, J. N., Halpern, P. L. and More, B. S. (1977) 'Effects of Personal Causation and Perceived Control on Responses to an Aversive Environment: The More Control, The Better'. *Journal of Experimental Social Psychology* **13** (1): 14–27.

Staub, E., Tursky, B. and Schwartz, G. E. (1971) 'Self-Control and Predictability: Their Effects on Reactions to Aversive Stimulation'. *Journal of Personality and Social Psychology* **18** (2): 157–162.

Stokols, D. (1972) 'On the Distinction between Density and Crowding: Some Implications for Future Research'. *Psychological Review* **79** (3): 275–278.

Surprenant, C. F. and Solomon, M. R. (1987) 'Predictability and Personalization in the Service Encounter'. *Journal of Marketing* **51** (April): 86–96.

Szpiler, J. A. and Epstein, S. (1976) 'Availability of an Avoidance Response as Related to Autonomic Arousal'. *Journal of Abnormal Psychology* **85** (1): 73–82.

Tinsley, H. E. A. and Weiss, D. J. (1975) 'Inter-rater Reliability and Agreement of Subjective Judgements'. *Journal of Counseling Psychology* **22** (4): 358–376.

White, R. W. (1959) 'Motivation Reconsidered: The Concept of Competence'. *Psychological Review* **66** (5): 297–333.

Wicker, A. W. (1984) *An Introduction to Ecological Psychology.* Monterey, CA: Brooks/Cole.

Worchel, S. (1978) 'Reducing Crowding without Increasing Space: Some Application of an Attributional Theory of Crowding'. *Journal of Population* **1** (3): 216–230.

Wortman, C. B. (1975) 'Some Determinants of Perceived Control'. *Journal of Personality and Social Psychology* **31** (2): 282–294.

9

Consumer Behaviour and Services: A Review

Mark Gabbott and Gillian Hogg

INTRODUCTION

Since the early work of Judd (1964), Rathwell (1966) and Levitt (1972) there has been increasing attention paid to the marketing of services. This interest has been motivated by a recognition of the importance of the 'services sector' and a need to understand the problems of marketing services more explicitly. Early work by Sasser *et al.* (1978) provided a clear articulation of the characteristics of services which distinguished them from goods and these provided an agenda for considering how the nature of services marketing differed from that of goods, as well as highlighting some of the problems associated with adopting goods marketing terminology and concepts.

The dominant feature of the existing literature on the marketing of services is its implicit management orientation, a concentration on how services are, or should be, marketed. This approach makes a fundamental assumption which this article seeks to challenge, specifically that consumer behavior is unaffected by the nature of the product. While research into the consumption of services is sparse, this literature has already established a number of areas where the characteristics of services make accepted forms of consumer behaviour problematic. This article reviews the current services and consumer behaviour literature in order to clarify the main issues for consumers in obtaining information about services, comparing alternative service provision and evaluating the service encounter. Until the mid-1980s the dominant theoretical paradigm in consumer behaviour was the information processing approach. More recently, experiential and behavioural perspectives have been recognized as providing realistic alternatives to the information processing approach. While these perspectives may provide a means to amplify our understanding of consumer behaviour and services, the discussion in this article will take place using the information processing model in order to provide a means to synthesize service marketing and consumer behaviour literatures. This analysis highlights a number of aspects of consumer behaviour which need to be considered by service marketers.

PRODUCTS, GOODS AND SERVICES

As a first stage it is necessary to make a distinction between products, goods and services. Marketing theory has been dominated by concepts and terminology derived from the marketing of goods. This orientation has endured despite a recognition that services have a number of unique characteristics. In as much as goods and services both provide benefits and customer satisfaction, they have both been described as products in the widest sense of the word (Cowell, 1991; Enis and Reoring, 1981) which has allowed services literature to develop based upon a sound marketing literature. However there has also been a tendency to use the terms 'goods' and 'products' interchangeably with little attention paid to the service dimension which may have far-reaching implications for marketers. If it is accepted that services do have distinguishing characteristics, such as those identified by Lovelock (1981) and Booms and Bitner (1981) for example, then it is necessary to restate and understand the differences between a product, which can include both a good and service element, and a good which is defined purely in terms of its physical properties.

Most definitions of services are still framed in terms of differences with goods. The distinction is provided on the basis of a comparison of the dominant characteristics of each (Schifman and Kanuk, 1991; Regan, 1963; and Blois, 1974). However, as Foxall (1985) points out, if services are seen not as a separate entity but only as a different type of product, the differences identified between goods and services are not fundamental but merely classificatory. What is needed is an appreciation of the dimensions of services which place different demands on both the purchaser and the provider.

As a way of highlighting the inadequacy of discriminating between goods and services Levitt (1972) argues that there is no such thing as a service industry, only industries where service components are greater. The distinction is between suppliers where the core of what they are selling is a service and suppliers that use a service element associated with a goods element as a competitive advantage, a theme developed by Gronroos (1978). The corollary of this argument is that all purchases of goods involve an element of service. Shostack (1977) argues that there are very few 'pure' products or services and describes a product continuum from tangible dominant goods to intangible dominant services. However, even within this approach there is a service element which is still indistinct from the good. Kotler (1991) provides structure to the continuum by identifying four distinct categories of offer: purely tangible goods, tangible goods with accompanying services, a major service with accompanying goods and services and pure services. A common feature of these approaches is a recognition that services have a number of distinguishing characteristics. These characteristics have been identified as: intangibility, inseparability, heterogeneity, perishability and ownership (Sasser et al., 1978; Shostack, 1977; Grönroos, 1978).

SERVICE CHARACTERISTICS

Intangibility is one of the most important characteristics of services, they do not have a physical dimension. Often services are described using tangible nouns but this obscures the fundamental nature of the service which remains intangible. Shostack (1987) for instance points out that 'airline' means air transportation, 'hotel' means lodging rental. Berry (1980) argues that even although the performance of most services is supported by tangibles the essence of what is purchased is a performance, therefore as McLuhan (1964) points out, it is the process of delivering a service which comprises the product. The implication of this argument is that consumers cannot see, touch, hear, taste or smell a service they can only experience the performance of it (Carman and Uhl, 1973; Sasser *et al.*, 1978). The second characteristic of services is the inseparability of the production and consumption aspects of the transaction. The service is a performance, in real time, in which the consumer cooperates with the provider, Bell (1981). According to Thomas (1978) the degree of this involvement is dependent upon the extent to which the service is people-based or equipment-based. The inference of this distinction is that people-based services tend to be less standardized than equipment-based services or goods producing activities. Goods are produced, sold and then consumed, whereas services are sold and then produced and consumed simultaneously (Regan, 1963; Cowell, 1984). The inseparability of the role of service provider and consumer also refers to the lack of standardization since the consumer can alter both the way in which the service is delivered, as well as what is delivered, which has important implications for the process of evaluation.

The heterogeneity of services is also a function of human involvement in the delivery and consumption process. It refers to the fact that services are delivered by individuals to individuals and therefore each service encounter will be different by virtue of the participants or time of performance. As a consequence each consumer is likely to receive a different service experience. The perishability of services describes the real time nature of the product. Services cannot be stored unlike goods and the absence of the ability to build and maintain stocks of the product means that fluctuations in demand cannot be accommodated in the same way as goods, i.e. in periods of excess demand more product cannot be utilized. For the consumer of services the time at which the consumer chooses to use the service may be critical to its performance and therefore the consumers experience. Kelley *et al.* (1990) make the observation that consumption is inextricably linked to the presence of other consumers and their presence can influence the service outcome.

To the above characteristics of services, Judd (1964), Wyckham *et al.* (1975) and Kotler (1982) have identified the concept of ownership as a distinguishing feature of services. With the sale of a good the purchaser generally obtains ownership of it. By contrast in the case of a service the purchaser only has temporary access or use of it: what is owned is the benefit of the service, not the service itself, i.e. in terms of a holiday the consumer has the benefit of the flight, hotel and beach but does not own them. The absence of ownership stresses the finite nature of services for consumers, there is no enduring involvement in the product only in the benefit.

These separate characteristics which distinguish a service from a good have formed the basis of most analyses of services marketing. However, very few attempts have been made to consider these characteristics together in order to investigate their joint effect upon consumers' behaviour. Simply, we know that intangibility creates a problem for consumers in evaluation and choice, we also know that heterogeneity presents an impediment to learning and routinizing behaviour but the combined effect of service characteristics are still not clearly understood.

CONSUMER BEHAVIOUR AND SERVICES

With the developing interest in services and services marketing it might be expected that the consumer behaviour literature would include references to the evaluation and consumption of intangibles. However, there are very few examples of published work which refer explicitly to the consumption characteristics of services. There would appear to be an assumption, consistent with the interchangeability of terminology, that consumer behaviour related to goods is the same as that related to products, i.e. the difference between goods and services is insignificant. In the case of products where the 'good' element is dominant this may be a valid assumption, but for products where the dominant characteristic is the service intangibility this assumption denies the significant impact upon consumption behaviour of the characteristics identified above.

As a vehicle for examining likely differences in consumer behaviour and services, a simple process model of consumer behaviour will be used, drawn from the dominant information processing perspective. This view implies that consumers first search for information about possible alternatives and attributes, selected alternatives are then compared on the basis of these attributes and once consumption has occurred the product is re-evaluated. Under each of these three process headings the services and consumer behaviour literature will be reviewed in order to provide some indication of the likely consumer responses to the problems presented by services.

Information search

The literature on consumer information activity in relation to goods is large and concentrates upon classifying the various sources of information (e.g. Beales et al., 1981; Engel et al., 1986; Westbrook and Fornell, 1979; Fletcher, 1987), the ability to assimilate information from these sources (e.g. Jacoby et al., 1974; Miller, 1956; Keller and Staelin, 1987; Summers, 1974; Wilkie, 1974; Jacoby, 1984; Muller, 1984); the motivation for external search behaviour and the extent of that behaviour (e.g. Johnson and Russo, 1984; Urbany et al., 1989; Bucklin, 1966; Moore and Lehlann, 1980). The characteristics of services which we believe place an additional information burden on consumers are associated with information sources used, the nature of information available from each source and the consumers response to that information.

Commonly two types of consumer information sources are referred to: internal and external sources. The search of internal sources of information is characterized by Bettman (1979b) as a scan of memory. When faced with a purchase decision consumer first examine memory for information which may be relevant to the decision (Jacoby et al., 1978). This information may be the result of previous experiences, which constitute a body of knowledge about, or an attitude toward, a product or a product class. If previous service experience is available this is an extremely credible source even if it is recognized that the experiences which comprise this information are event-specific and may not provide any clear indication as to future performance. The work carried out by Murray (1991) provided some support for this and pointed to a preference for internal sources of information in evaluating services.

Where information gained from previous experience is not available to consumers, or the information already held is considered insufficient to discriminate between different offerings, then the consumer may be motivated to search for information externally. This external information search implies a conscious recognition of the need for more decision-relevant information. The extent of external search is said to be dependent upon a number of factors, such as product category experience, product complexity or the degree of buyer uncertainty. On each of these dimensions, services are likely to prompt significant external search effort. In itself, this does not indicate any specific differences in the consumption behaviour related to services with that of goods. An alternative approach suggested by Murray (1991) is that in considering the degree of external information search it is inadequate to merely analyse the absolute number of sources used but more productive to assess source effectiveness.

The effectiveness of information available from external sources is related to the nature of services. Nelson (1970) identifies experience and search qualities of products where search qualities are those product attributes which can be almost completely determined and evaluated prior to purchase, for example, colour, size, price, etc. Experience qualities are those attributes which cannot be known or assessed prior to purchase but are determined during or after consumption. The more tangible the product the more dominant are the search qualities and the more intangible the less information is available before consumption. Services are therefore high in experience qualities and low in search qualities.

The implication for the consumer is that experiential information is perhaps the most difficult to obtain pre-purchase. The only sources of this type of information are pre-purchase trial, observation or reliance upon the experiences of others (Locander and Hermann, 1979). Pre-purchase trial is not an option in the case of services since they are produced as they are consumed and they therefore have to be experienced in total before they can be assessed, for instance it is not possible to try a haircut before purchase. Observation is equally unreliable as a source of information since the service is intangible and the participation of any other individual gives no guarantee of a repeated performance. As a consequence a number of authors (e.g. Murray, 1991) suggest that consumers look towards personal sources of information. This positions is supported by Zeithaml (1981) who suggests that the need for experience information of the service prompts a reliance upon word-of-mouth sources as they are perceived to be more credible and less biased. This is also consistent with the work of Robertson (1970), Eiglier *et al.* (1977) and Urbany and Weilbacker (1987) who indicate that word-of-mouth sources are pivotal in relation to services. As a consequence we can say that where service is a dominant element of a product, consumers face a number of problems, primarily in acquiring and using their own knowledge and also that the external environment cannot provide appropriate objective information. The likely response is an increased reliance on personal sources of information.

Comparison

The process of information search leads the consumer to an evoked set of alternatives that will form the basis of comparison and choice. The difficulties of obtaining effective pre-purchase information about services is likely to result in a smaller evoked set in services than goods. Zeithaml (1981) suggests that because of the nature of services and the difficulties in obtaining effective information consumers tend to be more loyal once they have found an acceptable alternative, for instance in the case of professional services like solicitors; indeed, if the consumer has previous experience of a service the evoked set may be as small as one (see Johnston and Bonama 1981). However if the internal information is negative or the consumer does not have experience on which to base the choice then the size of evoked set will be dependent upon the effectiveness of the external information that was available. There are various models of how consumers choose between available alternatives in different situations, such as Bettman (1979a), Grether and Wilde (1984), Wright (1975) and Fletcher and Hastings (1983). The common component of these models is a set of attributes. There are two identifiable problems for consumers in defining attribute sets in relation to services, problems of identifying attributes and problems of making comparisons on the basis of these attributes.

All products have attributes or defining characteristics, in the case of goods these attributes are tangible, can be determined in advance of purchase and common to all consumers purchasing the product. By contrast in the case of services the attributes of provision are intangible, cannot be determined in advance of purchase and are not common to all consumers, i.e. the individual consumers' needs are accommodated by their involvement in the service delivery, for example, in the case of hairdressing where the consumer is involved in describing and modifying the service outcome. In the absence of any tangible indications of what the service will be like consumers must use other means of comparing services in the pre-purchase phase. Shostack (1977) and Berry (1980) point to the subsequent reliance upon peripheral tangible cues to predict quality. The more intangible dominant the service the fewer clues are likely to be available, Levitt (1981) suggests that in these circumstances it is necessary for consumers to establish metaphors for tangibility or cues that help them to 'tangibilize the intangible', in order that they may create a credible expectation. Various authors have pointed to the role of the environment in which the consumption of the service takes place in providing these metaphors or cues such as Bitner (1992) or Lewis (1991). These would include corporate wear, decor, appearance of service providers, standard of equipment or furnishing and all may be used to approximate the missing tangible product information (Gabbott, 1991). The key problem for the consumer is identifying the cues which will most accurately predict the nature of the service experience.

The second issue for consumers is in comparing service alternatives on the basis of common attributes. Services cannot be compared simultaneously, but can only be compared in series, not parallel, i.e. a consumer cannot put two services side by side at any one time. Added to this time dimension is the problem of heterogeneity. The absence of truly common attributes implies that services are non-comparable products. Johnson (1984) suggests that faced with non-comparable product alternatives the consumer will search for the basis of a comparison by moving to more abstract product attributes, e.g. necessity, social status or entertainment value. In the case of services non-comparability is likely to evoke a reverse form of abstraction where services are compared on increasingly material or tangible criteria until there is little left to compare other than the service provider as the ultimate physical embodiment of the service.

Another characteristic of service dominant products is that some attributes are bargainable in the sense that they are determined between provider and consumer. Brucks and Shurr (1990) define bargaining as a process whereby two or more parties mutually define one or more attribute values for a product. For instance, in the case of insurance services the terms of the offering are negotiated before delivery. The bargainable nature of some service attributes serves to emphasize the uncertainty of the comparison process. This factor also has implication for the number of alternatives compared where bargainability reduces the number of alternatives as well as significantly reducing the number of attributes used in the comparison process.

Evaluation

A critical stage in the consumption process is the evaluation of the product after consumption as a means of building experience and knowledge as well as learning about the product class. Any product is evaluated on the basis of whether it fulfils the pre-determined need and whether the outcome meets the consumer's expectations about how the need should have been fulfilled. In this sense there is a pre-determined standard against which to compare the outcome. Several researchers have made a distinction between objective and perceived quality in evaluating products, e.g. Zeithaml (1988). Objective quality refers to the technical superiority or excellence of a product against measurable and verifiable standards. Garvin (1983) describes this as evaluation based upon amounts of specific attributes or ingredients, for example, weight, colour or size. Perceived quality can be defined as the consumers' judgement about a product's overall excellence or superiority. Quality is defined solely in terms of the consumer's perception which is a much more use-orientated approach to evaluation and is closer to the definition of service quality proposed by Zeithaml et al. (1990) as 'meeting or exceeding customer expectations'. The determination of satisfaction or dissatisfaction is therefore on the basis of a comparison between perceived quality and expected quality of the service experience.

Parasuraman et al. (1991) suggest that there is a fundamental expectation of a service; which is that it provides what it promises, i.e. accountants produce accurate accounts and dry cleaners produce clean clothes. This fundamental expectation has been described as a reliability dimension of service by Parasuraman et al. (1991) and by Gronroos (1991) as the technical quality dimension. This basic expectation generally relates to the more tangible elements of a product and as such it can be measured by the consumer in a reasonably objective manner. Swan and Comb (1976) make a similar point using the term instrumental performance to describe a minimum level of quality.

In the case of goods, what has been received is evident before its performance is evaluated. By comparison services are produced as they are consumed therefore the difference between goods and service elements of a product is that the consumer of a service evaluates how a service is received before it is clear what has been received. Once the service performance is complete it is conceivable that satisfaction with how the service was delivered will be reviewed. This makes the process of evaluating performance, i.e. determining satisfaction or dissatisfaction much more complex in the case of services.

The problem with this approach comes when consumers do not have the knowledge or experience to evaluate what they have received or that their expectations of what they wanted from the service are not clear. Darby and Karni (1973) refer to these as the credence qualities, these are characteristics of a product that the consumer finds difficult to evaluate even after purchase and consumption. In these circumstances how a service was delivered may be used to evaluate what was delivered, this is referred to by Gronroos as the functional quality, or by Swan and Comb (1976) as expressive performance. Parasuraman *et al.* (1991) refer to both as process dimensions and argue that these dimensions are usually evaluated as the service is delivered. Process dimensions have been described as service responsiveness (willingness to help), assurance (knowledge and courtesy of providers), and empathy (the caring individualized relationship between provider and consumer) and the signs, symbols and artifacts of delivery (signposting, decor, personal presentation) (Zeithaml, 1981; Bitner, 1992). These dimensions added to the reliability of the delivered service and form five dimensions of service quality identified by Zeithaml *et al.* (1990). This research suggests that although reliability ('the what') is important in meeting customer expectations the process dimensions ('the how') are the most important in exceeding customer expectations. The 'how' dimensions are almost invariably associated with the individual service provider.

In terms of satisfaction, the way in which the consumer participates in the service will influence his evaluation of the service received. Customers may be required to participate in the definition and production of the service and may therefore feel personally involved in the success or failure of the outcome (Zeithaml, 1981). If a consumer cannot or does not clearly articulate or understand their own requirements, or has formed unrealistic expectations of the service then they may feel that some responsibility for the failure was their own. Therefore the process of evaluating services in terms of satisfaction and dissatisfaction is a shared responsibility between provider and consumer.

DISCUSSION

This article has suggested that acquiring information, choice and the evaluation of services present a number of problems for consumers. These problems are derived from the nature of services in particular their intangibility and their heterogeneity. In the first stage of the simple process model, information is difficult to obtain since the service is intangible and there is no objective information that the consumer can obtain other than relying upon personal experience. However, since service experiences vary across consumers and across time so experience information either from self or others can only be a guide to future performance rather than a predictor. Other information gained from search has to be tempered by the evaluation of the source of the information. As such information effectiveness for the consumer of services is questionable.

The second problem for consumers is in comparing service alternatives. Again intangibility and heterogeneity present the main impediments to the effective assessment of future performance. What is being assessed in the case of a service is the perceived benefit from the service rather than the service itself. The consumer is choosing between their own subjective assessments of the likely service outcome. Comparison is hampered further by the heterogeneity of service provision and the difficulties in identifying or generating attributes upon which to base a choice. Finally, once the service has been initiated either by purchase, by acceptance or instruction there are problems in evaluating what is being, or what has been provided. In this context the role of expectations are pivotal. It has been argued that failure to achieve satisfaction from a service is as much the responsibility of the consumer as the provider in not identifying precise needs, yet it must also be recognized that consumers may not have a precise set of needs to communicate and this is central to the delivery of satisfaction and benefit.

The description of services as problematic for consumers is a theme which is common across a broad range of literature. Most suggestions propose marketing responses tackling some of the fundamental characteristics of services. These include making services appear less intangible by focusing upon physical dimensions, or less heterogeneous through standardized delivery or by recognizing the importance of word-of-mouth information sources using such techniques as personal endorsement. However, little attention has been paid to the likely consumer responses to the problems presented by services.

Responses

It is generally accepted that consumers are ultimately seeking to simplify or routinize their purchase decisions at the same time as minimizing the level of risk attached to the outcome. In relation to goods two key responses have been identified: first, the reliance upon product cues which are used to approximate missing information or predict likely outcomes and second, the reliance upon inertia or loyalty built upon satisfaction in order to routinize the consumption decision. However, both these responses need to be examined in the light of the characteristics of services.

Existing work on product cues associated with goods has tended to concentrate upon the identification of cues used by the consumer. A number of studies have identified brand name, origin or price as active cues. The basis of this analysis is that goods have a finite number of available attributes which can serve as pre-purchase clues for the consumer. In the case of services the range of cues is much wider since they are present in all tangible accompaniments to the service, i.e. provider, artifacts, premises or goods components. If the range of cues available pre-purchase is wider than that associated with goods and the cues are also uniquely associated with each service. The presence of variable cues both within service products and across service products do not provide support for the simplification function of cues for the consumer. A second implicit assumption associated with product cues is the ability to justify or prove their worth. Since tangible cues vary from provider to provider and form a small part of the service experience, the effectiveness of individual cues is likely to vary from provider to provider. Finally, product cues in relation to goods are used pre-purchase and their value assessed post-purchase. Where services are concerned the delivery may take place at a different time, with a different provider, with different tangibles or in a different place to the purchase transaction. As a result cues used to evaluate a service pre-purchase may be different to those used to evaluate during delivery or even after delivery has taken place.

The second response of consumers in relation to goods is brand or product loyalty which is one form of routinizing purchase behaviour. In the case of services loyalty can only be placed with the provider of the service rather than the service itself, i.e. it is theoretically impossible to obtain the same service from a different provider. Loyalty is built up from a series of successful service encounters with the same provider and the number of consumers with successful encounters builds reputation. An aspect of loyalty in relation to services which is different to that of goods is the potential to cement a relationship between customer and provider. We have identified above the inability in some circumstances of the consumer to accurately vocalize or identify needs and expectations. Subsequent service encounters allow needs and expectations of the consumer to be synchronized with the abilities and performance of the provider. This process of repeat purchasing is likely to result in the continued and increment strengthening of service relationships where the consumer is able to take full advantage of the potential benefits offered. In the case of goods the relationship is likely to plateau once all benefits have been experienced and may in some circumstances start to decline. It is evident that this continued relationship also produces a sense of ownership over the service with consumers referring to 'my accountant', 'my hairdresser', or 'my mechanic'. Equally this may have an impact upon attribution in the case of failure. The amount of investment in the relationship may lead consumers to rationalize failures on the basis of 'just a bad day', since they have experienced better or that it is their own fault in not correctly communicating needs. Either way relationships are likely to be more stable in the case of services than goods.

CONCLUSION

This article has investigated the implications for consumer behaviour presented by services as opposed to goods. It has concluded that services present a number of problems for consumers and also that suggested consumer responses in relation to goods may not be applicable to services. Specifically that there is a body of knowledge which explains consumer behaviour in relation to goods and that this body of knowledge suggest problems for consumers in choosing and evaluating services. It also suggests a number of responses to these problems which are again derived from this goods perspective. The final consideration is that the whole argument is being framed within the rational information processing perspective of consumer behaviour. Either consumer problems in relation to services need to be more fully explored within this framework or research will need to move outside this perspective perhaps towards examining the personal relationship between provider and consumer such as the degree of empathy or sympathy or explore the alternative behavioural perspectives. These may provide a means to integrate service design, service encounter and service consumption which emerge as crucial to service marketing. This article has endeavoured to concentrate upon consumer behaviour rather than re-iterate the managerial implications of service characteristics which form the basis of a substantial part of the services literature. It is our contention that unless consumer behaviour and in particular consumer responses to the problems associated with service are clarified, service marketing may be in danger of pursuing provider-oriented solutions to the problems perceived to be faced by consumers rather than truly understanding the nature of consumer decision processes or the reality of consumer behaviour.

REFERENCES

Beales, H., Mazis, M. Salop, S. and Staelin, R. (1981) 'Consumer Search and Public Policy'. *Journal of Consumer Research* **8** (June): 11–22.

Bell, M. L. (1981) 'A Matrix Approach to the Classification of Marketing Goods and Services'. In *Marketing of Services* (J. H. Donnelly and W. R. George, Eds). Chicago: AMA.

Berry, L. L. (1980) 'Services Marketing is Different'. *Business* (May–June): 24–29.

Bettman, J. R. (1979a) *An Information Processing Theory of Consumer Choice*. Massachusetts, Addison Wesley.

Bettman, J. R. (1979b) 'Memory Factors in Consumer Choice: A Review'. *Journal of Marketing* **43**: 37–53.

Bitner, M. J. (1992) 'Servicecapes: The Impact of Physical Surroundings on Customers and Employees'. *Journal of Marketing* **56**: 57–71.

Blois, K. J. (1974) 'The Marketing of Services: An Approach'. *European Journal of Marketing* **8** (Summer): 137–145.

Booms, B. H. and Bitner, M. J. (1981) 'Marketing Strategies and Organizational Structures for Service Firms'. In *Marketing of Services* (J. H. Donnelly and W. R. George, Eds). Chicago: AMA.

Brucks, M. and Schurr, P. (1990) 'The Effects of Bargainable Attributes and Attribute Range Knowledge on Consumer Choice Processes'. *Journal of Consumer Research* **16** (March): 409–419.

Bucklin, L. (1966) 'Testing Propensities to Shop'. *Journal of Marketing* **30** (January): 22–27.

Carman, J. and Uhl, K. (1973) *Marketing: Principles and Methods*. Homewood, IL: Irwin.

Cowell, D. (1984). *The Marketing of Services*. London: Heinemann.

Cowell, D. W. (1991) 'Marketing Services'. In *The Marketing Book* (M. J. Baker Ed.). Oxford, Butterworth Heinemann.

Darby, M. R. and Karni, E. (1973) 'Free Competition and the Optimal Amount of Fraud'. *Journal of Law and Economics* **16** (April): 67–86.

Eiglier, P., Langeard, E., Lovelock, C., Bateson, J. and Young, R. (1977) *Marketing Consumer Services: New Insights*. Cambridge, MA: Marketing Science Institute.

Engel, J., Blackwell, R. and Miniard, P. (1986) *Consumer Behaviour*. New York: Dryden.

Enis, B. M. and Roering, K. (1981) 'Services Marketing: Different Products, Similar Strategies'. In *Marketing of Services* (J. H. Donnelly and W. R. George, Eds). Chicago: AMA.

Fletcher, K. and Hastings, W. (1983) 'The Relevance of the Fishbein Model to Insurance Buying'. *Service Industries Journal* **3** (No. 3): 296–307.

Fletcher, K. (1987) 'Consumers Use and Perceptions of Retailer Controlled Information Sources'. *International Journal of Retailing* **2** (No. 3): 59–66.

Foxall, G. (1985) 'Marketing is Service Marketing'. In *Marketing in the Service Industries*. London: Frank Cass.

Gabbott, M. (1991) 'The Role of Product Cues in Assessing Risk in Second Hand Markets'. *European Journal of Marketing* **25** (No. 9): 38–50.

Garvin, D. (1983) 'Quality on the Line'. *Harvard Business Review* **61** (Sept–Oct): 65–73.

Grether, D. and Wilde, L. (1984) 'An Analysis of Conjunctive Choice: Theory and Experiments'. *Journal of Consumer Research* **10** (March): 373–385.

Gronroos, C. (1978) 'A Service Orientated Approach to Marketing Services'. *European Journal of Marketing* **12** (No. 8): 589.

Gronroos, C. (1991) *Strategic Management and Marketing in the Services Sector*. Studentlitteratur: Lund, Sweden.

Jacoby, J. (1984) 'Perspectives on Information Overload'. *Journal of Consumer Research* **10** (March).

Jacoby, J., Chestnut, R. and Fisher, W. (1978) 'A Behavioural Process Approach to Information Acquisition in Nondurable Purchasing'. *Journal of Marketing Research* **15** (No. 3, August): 532–544.

Jacoby, J., Speller, D. and Berning, C. (1974) 'Brand Choice Behaviour as a Function of Information Load: Replication and Extension'. *Journal of Consumer Research* **1**: 33–42.

Johnson, E. and Russo, J. E. (1984) 'Product Familiarity and Learning New Information'. *Journal of Consumer Research* **11** (June): 542–550.

Johnson, M. (1984) 'Consumer Choice Strategies for Comparing Noncomparable Alternatives'. *Journal of Consumer Research* **11** (December): 741–753.

Johnston, W. and Bonoma, T. (1981) 'Purchase Process for Capital Equipment and Services'. *Industrial Marketing* **4**: 253–264.

Judd, R. C. (1964) 'The Case for Redefining Services'. *Journal of Marketing* **28**: 59–73.

Keller, K. and Staelin, R. (1987) 'Effects of Quality and Quantity of Information on Decision Effectiveness'. *Journal of Consumer Research* **14** (September): 200–213.

Kelley, S. W., Donnelly, J. H. and Skinner, S. J. (1990) 'Customer Participation in Service Production and Delivery'. *Journal of Retailing* **66** (No. 3): 315–335.

Kotler, P. (1982) *Principles of Marketing.* New Jersey: Prentice-Hall.

Kotler, P. (1991) *Marketing Management.* New Jersey: Prentice-Hall.

Levitt, T. (1972) 'Production-line Approach to Service'. *Harvard Business Review* (Sept–Oct): 41–52.

Levitt, T. (1981) 'Marketing Intangible Products and Product Intangibles'. *Harvard Business Review* **59** (May–June): 94–102.

Lewis, B. (1991) 'Service Quality: An International Comparison of Bank Customers' Expectations and Perceptions'. *Journal of Marketing Management* **7**: 47–62.

Locander, W. and Hermann, P. (1979) 'The Effect of Self-confidence and Anxiety on Information Seeking in Consumer Risk Reduction'. *Journal of Marketing Research* **19**: 268–274.

Lovelock, C. (1981) 'Why Marketing Management Needs to be Different for Services'. In *Marketing of Services* (J. H. Donnelly, and W. R. George, Eds). Chicago: AMA.

McLuhan, M. (1964) *Understanding Media.* New York: McGraw-Hill.

Miller, G. (1956) 'The Magical Number Seven Plus or Minus Two, Some limitations on our Capacity for Processing Information'. *Psychological Review* **63** (No. 2).

Moore, W. L. and Lehmann, D. (1980) 'Individual Differences in Search Behaviour for a Nondurable'. *Journal of Consumer Research* **7** (December): 296–307.

Muller, T. (1984) 'Buyer Response to Variation in Product Information Load'. *Journal of Applied Psychology* **69** (No. 2, May).

Murray, K. (1991) 'A Test of Services Marketing Theory: Consumer Information Acquisition Activities'. *Journal of Marketing* **55** (January): 10–25.

Nelson, P. (1974) 'Advertising as Information'. *Journal of Political Economy* **81** (July–August): 729–754.

Parasuraman, A., Berry, L. and Ziethaml, V. (1991) 'Understanding Customer Expectations of Service'. *Sloan Management Review* (Spring): 39–48.

Rathwell, J. M. (1966) 'What is Meant by Services?' *Journal of Marketing* **30**: 32–36.

Rathwell, J. M. (1974) *Marketing in the Services Sector.* Cambridge, MA: Winthrop.

Regan, W. J. (1963) 'The Service Revolution'. *Journal of Marketing* **27** (July): 57–62.

Robertson, T. S. (1970) *Innovative Behaviour and Communication.* New York: Holt, Rheinhart and Winston.

Sasser, W. E., Olsen, R. P. and Wyckoff, D. D. (1978) *The Management of Service Operations.* Boston, MA: Allyn & Bacon.

Schiffman, L. and Kanuk, L. (1991) *Consumer Behaviour,* 4th Edition. New Jersey: Prentice-Hall.

Shostack, G. L. (1977) 'Breaking Free From Product Marketing'. *Journal of Marketing* **41**: 73–80.

Shostack, G. L. (1987) 'Service Positioning Through Structural Change'. *Journal of Marketing* **51**: 34–43.

Summers, J. (1974) 'Less Information is Better'. *Journal of Marketing Research* **XI** (November): 467–468.

Swan, J. and Comb, L. (1976) 'Product Performance and Consumer Satisfaction: A New Concept;. *Journal of Marketing* **40** (April): 25–33.

Thomas, D. R. E. (1978) 'Strategy is Different in Service Businesses'. *Harvard Business Review* (July–August): 158–165.

Urbany, J. and Weilbacker, D. (1987) 'A Critical Examination of Nelson's Theory of Information and Consumer Behaviour'. In *AMA Educators Conference Proceedings* (S. Douglas *et al.* Eds). Chicago: AMA.

Urbany, J., Dickson, P. and Wilkie, W. (1989) 'Buyer Uncertainty and Information Search'. *Journal of Consumer Research* **16** (September): 208–215.

Westbrook, R. A. and Fornell, C. (1979) 'Patterns of Information Source Usage Among Durable Goods Buyers'. *Journal of Marketing Research* **16** (August): 303–312.

Wilkie, W. L. (1974) 'Analysis of Effects of Information Load'. *Journal of Marketing Research* **XI** (November): 462–466.

Wright, P. (1975) 'Consumer Choice Strategies: Simplifying or Optimising'. *Journal of Marketing Research* **12** (February): 60–67.

Wyckham, R., Fitzroy, P. and Mandry, G. (1975) 'Marketing of Services: An Evaluation of Theory'. *European Journal of Marketing* **9** (No. 1): 59–67.

Zeithaml, V. (1988) 'Consumer Perceptions of Price, Quality and Value: A Means–End Model and Synthesis'. *Journal of Marketing* **52** (July): 2–22.

Zeithaml, V. (1981) 'How Consumer Evaluation Processes Differ Between Goods and Services'. In *Marketing of Services* (J. H. Donnelly and W. R. George, Eds). Chicago: AMA.

Zeithaml, V., Parasuraman, A. and Berry, L. (1990) *Delivering Quality Service.* New York: Collier Macmillan.

10

Critical Service Encounters: The Employee's Viewpoint

Mary Jo Bitner, Bernard H. Booms and Lois A. Mohr

The worldwide quality movement that has swept the manufacturing sector over the last decade is beginning to take shape in the service sector (*Business Week*, 1991; Crosby, 1991). According to some, the shift to a quality focus is essential to the competitive survival of service businesses, just as it has become essential in manufacturing (Heskett *et al.*, 1994; Schlesinger and Heskett, 1991).

Service quality researchers have suggested that 'the proof of service [quality] is in its flawless performance' (Berry and Parasuraman, 1991, p. 15), a concept akin to the notion of 'zero defects' in manufacturing. Others have noted that 'breakthrough' service managers pursue the goal of 100% defect-free service (Heskett, Sasser and Hart, 1990). From the customer's point of view, the most immediate evidence of service occurs in the service encounter or the 'moment of truth' when the customer interacts with the firm. Thus, one central goal in the pursuit of 'zero defects' in service is to work toward 100% flawless performance in service encounters. Here, flawless performance is not meant to imply rigid standardization, but rather 100% satisfying performance from the customer's point of view. The cost of not achieving flawless performance is the 'cost of quality', which includes the costs associated with redoing the service or compensating for poor service, lost customers, negative word of mouth, and decreased employee morale.

Although more firms are realizing the importance of service quality and customer satisfaction, it is not always clear how to achieve these goals. Situations arise in which quality is low and the problem is recognized by both the firm (i.e. employees) and the customer, but there may be disagreement on the causes of the problem and the appropriate solutions. In service encounters such disagreements, sure to diminish customer satisfaction, underscore the importance of understanding the types of events and behaviours that cause customers to be satisfied or dissatisfied. Because the service encounter involves at least two people, it is importance to understand the encounter from multiple perspectives. Armed with such understanding, firms are better able to design processes and educate both employees and customers to achieve quality in service encounters.

Reprinted with permission from *Journal of Marketing*, Vol. 58, October, pp. 95–106
© 1994 American Marketing Association

Previous research in the context of the restaurant, hotel, and airline industries identified categories of events and behaviors that underlie critical service encounters from the customer's point of view (Bitner, Booms and Tetreault, 1990; hereafter BBT). The primary purpose of this study is to examine the contact employee's perspective of critical service encounters and to understand, in the context of the same three industries, the kinds of events and behaviors that employees believe underlie customer satisfaction. The employee perspective is then compared with BBT to gain insight into any disparities in perspectives. A second purpose of the study is to evaluate the usefulness of the classification scheme developed by BBT (1990). If the scheme is conceptually robust, it should hold for different respondent groups.

The research is guided by the following questions:

- From the contact employee's point of view, what kinds of events lead to satisfying service encounters for the customer? What causes these events to be remembered favorably?
- From the contact employee's point of view, what kinds of events lead to dissatisfying service encounters for the customer? What causes these events to be remembered with distaste?
- Do customers and employees report the same kinds of events and behaviors leading to satisfaction and dissatisfaction in service encounters?

Before presenting the empirical study, we discuss relevant research and theory.

CUSTOMER AND CONTACT EMPLOYEE VIEWPOINTS

Frontline personnel are a critical source of information about customers. There are two basic ways that customer knowledge obtained by contact employees is used to improve service: (1) Such knowledge is used by the contact employees themselves to facilitate their interactions with customers and (2) It is used by the firm for making decisions. First, employees often modify their behavior from moment to moment on the basis of feedback they receive while serving customers. Schneider (1980) argues that people who choose to work in service occupations generally have a strong desire to give good service. To the extent that this is true, contact personnel can be expected to look frequently for cues that tell them how their service is received by customers. The more accurate their perceptions are, the more likely their behavioral adjustments are to improve customer satisfaction.

Second, because contact personnel have frequent contact with customers, they serve a boundary-spanning role in the firm. As a result, they often have better understanding of customer needs and problems than others in the firm. Researchers have theorized and found some evidence that open communication between frontline personnel and managers is important for achieving service quality (Parasuraman, Berry, and Zeithaml, 1990; Zeithaml, Berry and Parasuraman, 1988). Schneider and Bowen (1984) argue that firms should use information gathered from contact personnel in making strategic decisions, especially decisions regarding new service development and service modifications.

It seems reasonable to conclude that accurate employee understanding of customers enables both the employee and the firm to adjust appropriately to customer needs. However, previous research correlating customer and employee views of service is sparse and offers mixed conclusions. Schneider and Bowen (1985) and Schneider, Parkington and Buxton (1990) found high correlations ($r = .63$ and $r = .67$, respectively) between employee and customer attitudes about overall service quality in a bank setting. Their results are contradicted, however, in a study by Brown and Swartz (1989). These researchers gathered data on patient experiences with their physicians and compared them with the physicians' perceptions of their patient's experiences. The differences they found were rather large and inversely related to overall patient satisfaction.

Another study of 1300 customers and 900 customer service professionals conducted by Development Dimensions International found differences in perceptions between the two groups (*Services Marketing Newsletter*, 1989). Customer service professionals in that study consistently rated the importance of particular service skills and competencies and their actual performance higher than customers rated the same skills and competencies. Similarly, Langeard and colleagues (1981) found that field managers at two banks tended to overestimate (compared with customer ratings) the importance of six broad service delivery dimensions. Other studies have found differences when comparing customer and employee evaluations of business situations using scenarios and role playing in product failure contexts (Folkes and Kotsos, 1986), a complaint context (Resnik and Harmon, 1983), and the context of retailer respondents to customer problems (Dornoff and Dwyer, 1981).

We would therefore expect, on the basis of these studies, to find similarities in employee and customer views of the service encounter, but we would expect significant differences as well. Role, script, and attribution theories provide conceptual bases for these expectations.

THEORETICAL EXPLANATIONS

Role and script theories

Similarities in how customers and employees view service encounters are most likely when the two parties share common rule expectations and the service script is well defined (Mohr and Bitner, 1991; Solomon *et al.*, 1985). A *role* is the behavior associated with a socially defined position (Solomon *et al.*, 1985), and *role expectations* are the standards for role behavior (Biddle, 1986). In many routine service encounters, particularly for experienced employees and customers, the roles are well defined and both the customer and employee know what to expect from each other.

In addition, many types of service encounters, such as seating customers in a restaurant, are repeated frequently throughout a person's life, resulting in strong, standardized, and well-rehearsed scripts (i.e. structures that describe appropriate sequences of role behaviors) (Schank and Abelson, 1977). When service encounters have strong scripts, the employee and customer are likely to share expectations about the events that will occur and the order of occurrence. They are less likely to share ideas about subscripts, which are prescriptions for handling what Schank and Abelson describe as 'obstacles and errors', two types of interferences that may occur in otherwise predictable scripts.

Role and script theory, combined with the routine nature of many service encounters, suggests that customers and employees are likely to share a common perspective on service experiences. It is also clear that differences in perspective may arise when roles are less defined, a participant is unfamiliar with expected behaviors, or interferences require the enactment of complex or less routine subscripts.

Attribution theory

Dissimilarities in viewpoint may arise when service encounter partners have conflicting views of the underlying causes behind the events, that is, when their attributions differ. Research shows that there are many biases in the attribution process (Fiske and Taylor, 1984). Most clearly relevant for the perception of service providers and customers is the self-serving attribution bias. This is the tendency for people to take credit for success (i.e. to give internal attributions for their successes, a self-enhancing bias) and deny responsibility for failure (i.e. to blame failure on external causes, a self-protecting bias). Given these biases we would expect employees to blame the system or the customer for service failures, whereas the customer would be more likely to blame the system or the employee. The result would be different views of the causes of service dissatisfaction. It is less clear that this bias would operate in the case of a service encounter success. Although the desire for self-enhancement might lead both the employee and customer to give themselves credit for the success, the fact that the customer is paying the firm for a service would probably preclude the bias on the customer's side. Overall, then, the self-serving attribution bias leads to the expectation that the perspectives of the employee and customer will differ more in service failure than in service success situations.

Both empirical research and theory suggest that similarities as well as differences in perspectives are likely to occur between service encounter participants. Role and script theories suggest that in relatively routine situations such as the ones studied, there will be strong similarities in perspective. However, attribution biases suggest that there will also be significant differences in viewpoint. We explore to what extent the perspectives of contact personnel and those of customers are different. And, to the degree that they are different, the data provide insight into the nature of these disparities.

METHOD AND ANALYSIS

Data collection

Data were collected using the critical incident technique (CIT), a systematic procedure for recording events and behaviors that are observed to lead to success or failure on a specific task (Ronan and Latham, 1974), in this case, satisfying the customer. (For more detailed discussions of the method, see BBT; Flanagan, 1954; Wilson-Pessano, 1988): Using the CIT, data are collected through structured, open-ended questions, and the results are context analyzed. Respondents are asked to report specific events from the recent past (within 6 to 12 months). These accounts provide rich details of firsthand experiences in which customers have been satisfied or dissatisfied. Because respondents are asked about specific events rather than generalities, interpretation, or conclusions, this procedure meets criteria established by Ericsson and Simon (1980) for providing valuable, reliable information about cognitive processes. Researchers have concluded that when used appropriately (Flanagan, 1954; Wilson-Pessano, 1988), the critical incident method is reliable in terms of stability of the categories identified across judges, valid with respect to the content identified, and relevant in that the behaviors illuminated have proven to be important to the success or failure of the task in question (Ronan and Latham, 1974; White and Locke, 1981).

Hotel, restaurant, and airline employees were interviewed and asked to recall critical service encounters that caused satisfaction or dissatisfaction for customers of their firms. Thirty-seven trained student interviewers collected the data – 781 total incidents. Each one recruited a minimum of ten employees from among the same three industries studied in BBT, asking each employee to describe one incident that was satisfactory and one that was dissatisfactory from the customer's point of view.

Because all the interviewers were employed in the hospitability sector, they recruited fellow employees and employees of establishments with which they were familiar. They were instructed not to interview fellow students. The refusal rate was negligible. The incident sample represented 58 hotels, 152 restaurants, and 4 airlines. On average, the employees providing the incidents had 5.5 years of working experience in their respective industries. The employees ranged in age from 16 to 64 (mean age 27) and were 55% female and 45% male. The instructions to the employees being interviewed were as follows:

Put yourself in the shoes of customers of your firm. In other words, try to see your firm through your customers' eyes.
Think of a recent time when a customer of your firm had a particularly satisfying (dissatisfying) interaction with yourself or a fellow employee. Describe the situation and exactly what happened.

They were then asked the following questions:

1. When did the incident happen?
2. What specific circumstances led up to this situation?
3. Exactly what did you or your fellow employee say or do?
4. What resulted that made you feel the interaction was satisfying (dissatisfying) from the customer's point of view?
5. What should you or your fellow employee have said or done? (for dissatisfying incident only)

To be used in the analysis, an incident was required to (1) involve employee-customer interaction, (2) by very satisfying or dissatisfying from the customer's point of view, (3) be a discrete episdoe, and (4) have sufficient detail to be visualized by the interviewer. Seven incidents failed to meet these criteria, leaving 774 incidents (397 satisfactory and 377 dissatisfactory).

Classification of incidents

The incident classification system developed by BBT was used as a starting point for sorting the data with the assumption that, to the degree that customers and employees remember satisfying and dissatisfying encounters in the same way, the same classification system should be appropriate. Incidents that could not be classified within the original scheme would then provide evidence for differences in perspective.

One researcher trained in the classification scheme coded the incidents. Any that did not fit into the scheme were put aside. This researcher and a second then worked together on categorizing this group of 86 incidents (11% of the total). These incidents were read and sorted, combined, and resorted until a consistent coding scheme was developed that combined similar incidents into distinct, meaningful categories. When the new categories were labeled and the two researchers achieved concensus on assignment of the incidents, the new cateogires (one major group with four sub-categories) were added to the original classification system.

A set of complete coding instructions was then written (see Appendix A). They included general instructions for coders, operational definitions of each category, and decision rules for assigning incidents to categories. These are procedures recommended by Perreault and Leigh (1989) for improving the reliability of judgment-based data. The coding instructions were used to train a third researcher who had not participated in the categorization decisions. This researcher then coded the 774 employee incidents, providing an interjudge reliability check on the classification system. Discrepancies between the first and third researchers' assignments were resolved by the second researcher.

The interjudge agreement between the first and third researchers was 84% for the satisfying incidents and 85% for the dissatisfying incidents. These figures are respectably high, especially considering that the classification system in this study contains 16 categories. The percentage agreement statistic probably underestimates interjudge reliability in this case because this statistic is influenced by the number of coding categories (i.e. the more categories, the lower the percentage agreement is likely to be) (Perreault and Leigh, 1989). For this reason, two other measures of interjudge reliability were calculated. Cohen's κ, which corrects for the likelihood of chance agreement between judges, was found to be .816 for the satisfying and .823 for the dissatisfying incidents. Perreault and Leigh (1989) argue, however, that κ is an overly conservative measure of reliability because it assumes an a priori knowledge of the likely distribution of responses across categories. To correct for this they designed an alternative index of reliability, I_r, appropriate for marketing data. Rather than contrasting interjudge agreement with an estimate of chance agreement, I_r is based on a model of the level of agreement that might be expected given a true (population) level of reliability. Furthermore, the index focuses on the reliability of the whole coding process, not just on the agreement between judges. I_r was found to be .911 and .914 for the satisfying and dissatisfying incidents, respectively.

RESULTS AND DISCUSSION

The categories of events and behaviors that employees believe underlie their customers' satisfaction and dissatisfaction in service encounters are identified and discussed first. Then the results are compared with customer perceptions using the BBT data.

Classification of employee-reported incidents

The critical incident classification system based on incidents gathered from customers (BBT) consists of three major groups of employee behaviors that account for all satisfactory and dissatisfactory incidents: (1) employee response to service delivery system failures, (2) employee response to customer needs and requests, and (3) unprompted and unsolicited employee actions. Of the 774 employee incidents, 668 were classified into one of these three groups and the 12 categories within them. The incidents were very similar in detail to those provided by customers. (See BBT for detailed descriptions of the groups and categories and sample incidents.)

Eighty-six encounters (11% of the total) did not fit any of the predetermined groups. These incidents were categorized into one major group labeled 'problem customer behavior' and they were added to the categorization scheme as 'Group 4'. In these cases, the coders could not attribute the satisfaction and dissatisfaction to an action or attitude of the employee – instead, the root cause was the customer. Such customers were basically uncooperative, that is, unwilling to cooperate with the service provider, other customers, industry regulations, and/or laws. These situations created problems for the employees, and rarely were they able to deal with them in such a way as to bring about customer satisfaction; only three of these incidents were satisfactory.

Within the problem customer behavior group, four categories emerged (Table 1 provides examples of incidents from the four new categories):

1. *Drunkenness* – The employee perceives the customer to be clearly intoxicated and creating problems such as harassing other customers nearby, giving the employee a hard time, or disrupting the atmosphere of the establishment:;

2. *Verbal and physical abuse* – The customer verbally and/or physically abuses either the employee or other customers;

3. *Breaking company policies or laws* – The customer refuses to comply with policies or laws, and the employee attempts to enforce compliance; and

4. *Uncooperative customers* – The customer is generally rude and uncooperative or unreasonably demanding. From the employee's perspective, the customer is unwilling to be satisfied, no matter what is done for him or her.

The employee's view of satisfactory versus dissatisfactory encounters

Here we examine the frequencies and proportions of employee accounts in the four groups and 16 categories as shown in Table 2. It should be noted that the frequencies and proportions shown in the table reflect numbers of reported events. The actual frequency of occurrence of the type of event represented by a particular group or category cannot be inferred from the data. Nor can greater importance be inferred by greater frequencies in a particular category (Wilson-Pessano, 1988). The data are shown in full in Table 2; however, our discussion focuses on the four major groups. To facilitate understanding, the employee-reported incidents are

Table 1. Group 4 sample incidents: problem customers

Dissatisfactory	Satisfactory
A. Drunkenness	
An intoxicated man began pinching the female flight attendants. One attendant told him to stop, but he continued and then hit another passenger. The copilot was called and asked the man to sit down and leave the others alone, but the passenger refused. The copilot then 'decked' the man, knocking him into his seat.	A person who became intoxicated on a flight started speaking loudly, annoying the other passengers. The flight attendant asked the passenger if he would be driving when the plane landed and offered him coffee. He accepted the coffee and became quieter and friendlier.
B. Verbal and physical abuse	
While a family of three was waiting to order dinner, the father began hitting his child. Another customer compalined about this to the manager who then, in a friendly and sympathetic way, asked the family to leave. The father knocked all the plates and glasses off the table before leaving.	None
C. Breaking company policies or laws	
Five guests were in a hotel room two hours past checkout time. Because they would not answer the phone calls or let the staff into the room, hotel security staff finally broke in. They found the guests using drugs and called the police.	None
D. Uncooperative customer	
When a man was shown to his table in the nonview dining area of the restaurant, he became extremely angry and demanded a window table. The restaurant was very busy, but the hostess told him he could get a window seat in a half hour. He refused to wait and took his previously reserved table, but he complained all the way through the dinner and left without tipping.	None

THE SERVICE EXPERIENCE   157

Table 2. Group and category classification by type of incident outcome (employees only)

| | Type of Incident Outcome | | | | | |
| | Satisfactory | | Dissatisfactory | | Row total | |
Group and category	No.	%	No.	%	No.	%
Group 1. Employee-responses to service-delivery system failures						
A. To unavailable service	31	7.8	37	9.8	68	8.8
B. To unreasonably slow service	23	6.0	48	12.7	71	9.2
C. To other core service failures	55	13.9	110	29.2	165	21.3
Subtotal, Group 1	109	27.5	195	51.7	304	39.3
Group 2. Employee responses to customer needs and requests						
A. To 'special needs' customers	80	20.2	14	3.7	94	12.1
B. To customer preferences	99	24.9	43	11.4	142	18.3
C. To admitted customer error	11	2.8	0	0.0	11	1.4
D. To potentially disruptive others	6	1.5	5	1.3	11	1.4
Subtotal, Group 2	196	49.4	62	16.4	258	33.3
Group 3. Unprompted and unsolicited employee actions						
A. Attention paid to customer	43	10.8	6	1.6	49	6.3
B. Truly out-of-the ordinary employee behavior	25	6.3	28	7.4	53	6.8
C. Employee behaviors in the context of cultural norms	7	1.8	3	.8	10	1.3
D. Gestalt evaluation	0	0.0	0	0.0	0	0.0
E. Performance under adverse circumstances	14	3.5	0	0.0	14	1.8
Subtotal, Group 3	89	22.4	37	9.8	126	16.3
Group 4. Problematic customer behavior						
A. Drunkenness	3	0.8	16	4.2	19	2.5
B. Verbal and Physical Abuse	0	0.0	9	2.4	9	1.2
C. Breaking company policies or laws	0	0.0	16	4.2	16	2.1
D. Uncooperative customer	0	0.0	42	11.1	42	5.4
Subtotal, Group 4	3	0.8	83	22.0	86	11.1
Column total	397	51.3	377	48.7	774	100%

summarized and ranked according to the percentage of incidents in the four major incident groups:

Distribution of dissatisfactory incidents

Rank order	Group:	*Percentage*
1	Group 1: Response to failures	51.7
2	Group 4: Problem customers	22.0
3	Group 2: Response to requests	16.4
4	Group 3: Unprompted action	9.8

Distribution of satisfactory incidents

Rank order	Group:	*Percentage*
1	Group 2: Response to requests	49.4
2	Group 1: Response to failures	27.5
3	Group 3: Unprompted action	22.4
4	Group 4: Problem customers	.8

When employees were asked to report incidents resulting in customer dissatisfaction, they tended to describe problems with external causes such as the delivery system or inappropriate customer behaviors. By far the largest number of dissatisfactory incidents were categorized in Group 1 (response to delivery system failures), with the next largest proportion falling into Group 4 (problem customers). These results are not unexpected given what attribution theory suggests. When things go wrong, people are more likely to blame external, situational factors than to attribute the failing to their own shortcomings. A modest number of dissatisfactory incidents were found in Group 2. In many of these cases, the employees implied that they were unable to satisfy customer needs due to constraints placed on them by laws of their own organization's rules and procedures, again placing the blame on an external source. The smallest percentage of dissatisfactory incidents were classified in Group 3, which reflects spontaneous negative employee behaviors (e.g. rudeness, lack of attention). Again, this is consistent with the bias toward not blaming oneself for failures.

The largest proportion of satisfactory incidents, from the employee's point of view, occurred in response to customer needs and requests (Group 2). Almost half of particularly satisfying customer encounters reported by employees resulted from their ability to adjust the system to accommodate customer needs and requests. Success is attributed in these cases to the employee's own ability and willingness to adjust. The next largest proportion of satisfactory incidents were categorized in Group 1. This is an interesting set of incidents, because each one began as a failure but ended as a success because of the ability of the employee to recover. Employees clearly remember their ability to recover in failure situations as a significant cause for ultimate customer satisfaction. A relatively modest (when compared with the customer view) number of satisfactory incidents were categorized as unprompted and unsolicited employee actions (Group 3). Perhaps employees do not view their own behavior as 'spontaneous', but they instead remember them in association with a specific external cause (e.g. a customer need, a service failure). Finally, there were virtually no satisfactory incidents categorized in the problem customer group (Group 4). This makes sense, because it is difficult to imagine a very problematic customer leaving the encounter feeling satisfied except under highly unusual circumstances.

Comparing customer and employee views

Table 3 combines data from the current study with the original BBT data for purposes of comparison. Because the employees and customers in these two studies all described different incidents, conclusions from employee–customer comparisons are exploratory, and the explanations are somewhat speculative. Although we rely on role and attribution theories to explain the differences we observed, it is possible that these differences could be due to sampling variations of differences in the incident pool from which the two groups drew. However, given the care taken in collecting the data to avoid systematic biases, that both studies were conducted in the same city using the same three industries, and that many of the same firms were the source of incidents in both studies, we have confidence in our theoretical explanations of the results.

Table 3. Comparison of employee and customer responses: incident classification by type of incident outcome[a]

| Groups | Type of Incident Outcome | | | | Row total | |
| | Satisfactory | | Dissatisfactory | | | |
	No.	%	No.	%	No.	%
Group 1. Employee responses to service delivery system failures						
Employee Data	109	27.5	195	51.7	304	39.3
Customer Data	81	23.3	151	42.9	232	33.2
Group 2. Employee responses to customer needs and requests						
Employee Data	196	49.4	62	16.4	258	33.3
Customer Data	114	32.9	55	15.6	169	24.2
Group 3. Unprompted and unsolicited employee actions						
Employee Data	89	22.4	37	9.8	126	16.3
Customer Data	152	43.8	146	41.5	298	42.6
Group 4. Problematic customer behavior						
Employee Data	3	0.8	83	22.0	86	11.1
Customer Data	0	0.0	0	0.0	0	0.0
Column total						
Employee Data	397	51.3	377	48.7	774	100%
Customer Data	347	49.6	352	50.4	699	100%

[a]Customer response data from Bitner, Booms and Tetreault (1990).

A large majority of the employee incidents from the current study could be categorized in the original three groups and 12 categories, suggesting strong similarities in the way employees and customers report the sources of satisfaction and dissatisfaction in service encounters. Recall that these are relatively routine service encounters and in both studies the respondents were experienced service participants. Even so, the addition of a fourth group and the significant differences in frequencies and proportions of incidents found in the groups suggest that there are dissimilarities in what they report as well. Hierarchical log-linear analysis of Table 3 shows a significant three-way interaction between group (1, 2, 3, or 4), type of outcome (satisfactory or dissatisfactory), and incident source (employee or customer) (LR χ^2 change = 8.17; p = .04). There is also a significant two-way interaction between group and incident source (LR χ^2 change = 263.31; $p <$ .0001). Because of the significant three-way interaction, the results are discussed separately for satisfactory and dissatisfactory incidents.

Within the dissatisfactory incident classifications, customers and employees have relatively similar proportions in Groups 1 and 2. The significant interaction is caused by Group 3, which is dominated by customer incidents, and Group 4, which contains incidents reported by employees only. These results are very consistent with expectations based on attribution biases. Employees are highly unlikely to describe customer dissatisfaction as being caused by their own predispositions, attitudes, or spontaneous behaviors. Customers, on the other hand, will be likely to blame the employee rather than anything they themselves might have contributed. This is clearly reflected in the observation that customers report no dissatisfactory incidents caused by their own problem behaviors (Group 4).

The differences in how customers and employees report satisfactory encounters are provocative as well, albeit less exteme. Again, this is consistent with attribution theory, which predicts larger differences in perceptions in failure than in success situations. Within the satisfactory incidents, Groups 1 and 4 are equally represented for both customers and employees. The significant interaction is the result of Group 2 being dominated by employee incidents and Group 3 being dominated by customer incidents.

IMPLICATIONS FOR RESEARCHERS

Generalizability of the service encounter classification scheme

The importance and usefulness of robust classification schemes for theory development and practical application have been discussed by social scientists (e.g. McKelvey, 1982) and marketing scholars (e.g. Hunt, 1991; Lovelock, 1983). Yet we have few such frameworks in marketing, primarily because the classification schemes that have been proposed have rarely been subjected to empirical validation across times and contexts.

This study represents one contribution in a program of research designed to test the validity and generalizability of a scheme for categorizing sources of service encounter satisfaction and dissatisfaction (BBT). If the scheme holds in different settings (e.g. different industry contexts, or in internal as well as external encounters) and across different respondents (e.g. customers versus providers, customers in different cultures), then the scheme can be viewed as more robust and of greater theoretical as well as practical value. Other studies have reported that the three major groups of behaviors identified by BBT are also found in a retail context (Kelley, Hoffman and Davis, 1993) and a study of 16 consumer services (Gremler and Bitner, 1992). Through replication, the framework becomes more valuable in identifying generalizable 'service behaviors'.

The results of our research indicate that all the categories found in the original customer-perspective study were also found when employees were asked to report except 'problem customers'. The addition of this new group provides a more complete classification system that can be further examined in other contexts.

Problem customers

A primary contribution of this research effort is the empirically based finding that unsatisfactory service encounters may be due to inappropriate customer behaviors – the notion that sometimes customers are wrong. Others have suggested the existence of problem customers (e.g. Lovelock, 1994; Schrage, 1992; Zemke and Anderson, 1990). Lovelock for example, suggests the term 'jaycustomers' to label customers who 'misconsume' in a manner similar to jaywalkers who cross streets in unauthorized places. Our research provides empirical evidence that these difficult customer types do exist and in fact can be the source of their own dissatisfaction.

Although no one really believes customers are always right, firms have policies that pretend this is so, and managers urge and demand that customer contact employees treat customers as if they are always right. Needless to say, such avoidance leads to stresses and strains for managers and frontline personnel alike and potentially bigger problems for firms. (See Hochschild, 1983, for a discussion of personal and organizational impacts of nonauthentic ways of dealing with customers). With a better understanding of problem customers can come better methods for eliminating or dealing with the underlying causes of the problems.

This area is ripe with important research questions, such as the following: What types of problems do customers cause? What are the most frequent problems? What types of customers tend to be problem customers? Under what circumstances do customers create either more or fewer problems? And, from a management viewpoint, what can be done to identify problem customers, and how can and should employees deal with them?

This initial research represents a start at addressing some of these questions and the beginnings of a typology of problem customer behaviors. The categories of behaviors discovered are not surprising given the nature of the industries studied. Each service involves the possible serving of food and drink – including alcoholic beverages. In each service the customers are in close physical proximity for extended periods of time. Restaurant, airline, and hotel customers are many times in tight public spaces that put them cheek to jowl with other customers. Personal social interactions are carried out in front of other customers who are most often strangers. And, as mentioned previously, the types of encounters studied here are all relatively routine and commonly experienced. Finally, customers frequently have transaction-based encounters with the service personnel rather than long-term relationship-based encounters. It is assumed that these circumstances influenced the nature of the subcategories of problems identified in Group 4. Thus, although we believe that the major problem customer group will surface whenever employees are asked to relate instances of dissatisfactory encounters, further research is needed to identify other subcategories within the group and relate problem types to service industry conditions, circumstances, and customer segments.

Although we have identified problem customers by exploring the sources of customer dissatisfaction, there may be other types of 'wrong customers'. For example, even when customers do not misbehave, they may not be good relationship customers for the organization because they do not meet the target market profile, they are not profitable in the long term, or in some cases they may not be compatible with the service provider in terms of personality or work style (Lovelock, 1994; Zeithaml and Bitner, 1995). It is beyond the scope of this article to discuss the full conceptualization of wrong customers, but it may be fruitful for researchers in the future to incorporate the misbehaving customers we have identified into this more extensive conceptual scheme.

Theory implications

Role and script theories suggest that customers and employees in routine, well-understood service transactions will share parallel views of their roles and the expected sequence of events and behaviors. The types of service encounters studied here and in the original study do represent frequently encountered and routine services. Shared views of the encounter should result in common notions of the sources of customer satisfaction and dissatisfaction. The fact that 89% of the employee incidents could be classified in the original classification scheme suggests that customers and employees do indeed report incidents with most of the same sources of satisfaction and dissatisfaction.

An interesting issue for further research is whether the overall strong similarity of views between customers and employees would result if the industries studied were ones in which the scripts were less routine and well practiced.

Results of the study indicate that though employees and customers do report many of the same sources of customer satisfaction and dissatisfaction, there are also significant differences. These disparities show up in the distribution of incidents across the major groups, and the differences were most dramatic for the dissatisfactory service encounters. The self-serving attribution bias suggests explanations for why some of these differences were observed.

MANAGERIAL IMPLICATIONS

Using the classification scheme

One purpose of this study was to evaluate the soundness of the classification scheme developed by BBT in a distinctive context. Through the addition of the problem customer grouping, the framework is now more complete, and the scheme itself can provide a starting point for a company or industry to begin identifying with greater specificity the events and behaviors peculiar to its own setting. For example, the framework has been used for proprietary purposes in medical and travel agent contexts. In these cases, the companies began with the existing groups in the classification scheme and fleshed out the categories with useful specifics that could be employed in service training or service re-design.

The customer is not always right

In the industries studied here, problem customers were the source of 22% of the dissatisfactory incidents. This group may be even larger in industries in which the customer has greater input into the service delivery process (e.g. health care, education, legal services).

Several implications are suggested by the problem customer group. First, managers must acknowledge that the customer is not always right, nor will he or she always behave in acceptable ways. Contact employees who have been on the job any period of time know this, but frequently they are being told that the 'customer is king' and are not given the appropriate training and tools to deal with problem customers. Employees need appropriate coping and problem-solving skills to handle customers as well as their own personal feelings in these situations. Employees can also be taught to recognize characteristics of situations (e.g. unexpected peaks in demand, inordinate delays) and anticipate the moods of their customers so that some potential problem situations can be avoided completely or alleviated before they accelerate.

To provide employees with the appropriate training and skills for working with problem customers, the organization must clarify its position regarding such customers. A basic problem customer strategy might be conceptualized as ranging along a continuum from 'refuse to serve them' to 'satisfy them at all costs'. For example, some car rental companies have attempted to refuse customers with bad driving histories by checking records in advance and rejecting bad-risk drivers (Dahl, 1992). In a different context, some Madison Avenue ad agencies say that 'some accounts are so difficult to work with that they simply cannot – or will not – service them' (Bird, 1993). Although organizations have intuitively recognized that not all customer segments are right for the firm and that each individual customer is not right all the time, some are beginning to acknowledge these facts more explicitly and are attempting to quantify the impact of problem or 'wrong' customers on profitability and organizational stress.

Beyond the need to develop employee skills, there is the need for 'training' customers so that they will know what to expect and appropriate behaviors in given situations. For example, some upscale resorts that offer highly discounted rates in nonpeak seasons find that their discount customers, who may not be accustomed to the 'rules of behavior' appreciate information on what to wear and other expected behaviors while at the resort. In other more complex and less familiar service situations (e.g. professional services), customers may truly appreciate knowing more about their role in the service process and the behaviors and information that are needed from them to make the service succeed (Bloom, 1984). It has been suggested that by treating customers as 'partial employees' they can learn to contribute to the service in ways that will enhance their own satisfaction (Bowen, 1986).

Employees as sources of customer data

Previous research has suggested that contact employees are good sources of information on customer attitudes (Schneider and Bowen, 1985; Schneider. Parkington and Buxton, 1980). Our study confirms these findings insofar as employees of hotels, restaurants, and airlines report all the same categories of customer satisfaction and dissatisfaction reported by customers in the same industries. However, we would caution against relying too much on contact employee interpretations of customer satisfaction for two reasons. First, although they report the same basic categories, the proportions of incidents found in the categories are significantly different from those reported by customers. Second, in some industries in which service encounters are less routine, contact employees may not be as accurate in their assessment of customer expectations and satisfaction (see Brown and Swartz, 1989).

Employee desire for knowledge and control

It is apparent in reading the incidents that contact employees *want* to provide good service and are very proud of their abilities to do so. This pride comes through in the large percentage of satisfactory incidents found in Group 2, in which employees' own skills, abilities, and willingness to accommodate customer needs were the sources of customer satisfaction. Balancing out this sense of pride are a large number of frustrating incidents in which employees believe they cannot for some reason recover from a service failure or adjust the system to accommodate a customer need. These reasons usually stem from lack of basic knowledge of the system and its contraints, inability to provide a logical explanation to the customer, cumbersome bureaucratic procedures, poorly designed systems or procedures, or the lack of authority to do anything.

Reliability is critical

The data show that a majority of the dissatisfactory incidents reported by employees resulted from inadequate responses to service delivery system failures. This result, together with other research reporting service reliability as the single most important dimension used by consumers to judge service quality (Parasuraman, Zeithaml and Berry, 1988, 1990), implies a need for service process and system analysis to determine the root causes of system failures (Kingman-Brundage, 1989; Shostack, 1984, 1987). Systems can then be redesigned and processes implemented to ensure higher reliability from the customer's point of view. The best way to ensure satisfaction, however, is not to have a failure in the first place.

CONCLUSION

The research suggests that many frontline employees do have a true customer orientation and do identify with and understand customer needs in service encounter situations. They have respect for customers and a desire to deliver excellent service. Oftentimes the inability to do so is governed by inadequate or poorly designed systems, poor or nonexistent recovery strategies, or lack of knowledge. When employees have the skills and tools to deliver high-quality service, they are proud of their ability to do so.

We also learned from employees that customers can be the source of their own dissatisfaction through inappropriate behavior or being unreasonably demanding. We suspect that this new group of dissatisfactory incidents caused by problem customers would surface in any service industry and that its existence represents a strategic challenge for the organization as well as an operational real-time challenge for service employees. In a time when 'customer is king' is the stated philsophy of most forward-thinking organizations, acknowledgment that wrong customers exist, coupled with creative thinking about customer roles and management of customer expectations, may considerably deepen understanding of and ability to cultivate customer relationships.

APPENDIX A: INSTRUCTIONS FOR CODERS

Overview

1. You will be provided with a set of written critical service encounter events. Each 'story' or 'event' is recorded on a standardized questionnaire. Two types of questionnaires were used, one for satisfying interactions and one for dissatisfying interactions.

2. Each service encounter questionnaire reflects the events and behaviors associated with an encounter that is memorable because it is either particularly satisfying or particularly dissatisfying. The respondents were employees of restaurants, airlines and hotels. However, they were asked to take the customer's point of view in responding to the questions. Thus, the data reflect employees' remembrances of times when customers had particularly dis/satisfying encounters with their firms.

3. You will be asked to categorize each incident into one of 16 categories, based on the key factor that triggered the dis/satisfactory incident. Sorting rules and definitions of categories are detailed below.

4. It is suggested that you read through each entire service encounter before you attempt to categorize it. If an incident does not appear to fit within any of the 16 categories, put it aside. In addition, do not attempt to categorize incidents that do not meet the basic criteria. An incident must: (A) include employee-customer interaction, (B) by very satisfying or dissatisfying from the customer's point of view, (C) be a discrete episode, and (D) have sufficient detail to be visualized by the interviewer.

Coding rules

Each incident should be categorized within one category only. Once you have read the incident, you should begin asking the following questions in order to determine the apropriate category. Definitions of the categories are attached.

1. Is there a service delivery system failure? That is, is there an initial failure of the core service that causes the employee to respond in some way? Is it the employee's response that causes the event to be remembered as highly satisfactory or dissatisfactory?

If the answer is *yes*, place the incident in Group 1. Then ask, what type of failure? (A) unavailable service; (B) unreasonably slow service; (C) other core service failures.

If the answer is *no*, go on to question 2.

2. Is there an explicit or implicit request or need for accommodation or extra services? That is, is the customer asking (either explicitly or implicitly) that the system be somehow adjusted to accommodate him/her? Is it the employee's response that causes the event to be remembered as highly satisfactory or dissatisfactory?

If the answer is *yes*, place the incident in Group 2. Then ask what type of need/ request is triggering the incident: (A) 'special needs' customer, (B) customer preferences; (C) admitted customer error; (D) potentially disruptive other customers.

If the answer is *no*, go on to question 3.

3. Is there an unprompted and unsolicited action on the part of the employee that causes the dis/satisfaction? That is, does a spontaneous action or attitude of the employee cause the dis/satisfaction? (Since this follows rules 1 and 2, it obviously implies that there is no service failure and no explicit/implicit request.)

If the answer is *yes*, place the incident in Group 3. Then, ask what type of unprompted and unsolicited action took place: (A) attention paid to customer; (B) truly out-of-the-ordinary action; (C) employee behaviors in the context of cultural norms; (D) gestalt evaluation; (E) exemplary performance under adverse circumstances.

If the answer is *no*, go to question 4.

4. Does the dis/satisfaction stem from the actions/attitudes/behaviors of a 'problem customer'? That is, rather than the dis/satisfaction being attributable to an action or attitude of the employee, is the root cause actually the customer?

If the answer is *yes*, place the incident in Group 4. Then, ask what type of behavior is causing the problem: (A) drunkenness; (B) verbal/physical abuse; (C) breaking/resisting company policies or laws; (D) uncooperative customer.

If the answer is *no*, put the incident aside.

CIT classification system – definitions

Group 1. Employee response to service delivery system failure (failure in the core service, e.g. the hotel room, the restaurant meal service, the flight, system failures).

A. Response to unavailable service (services that should be available are lacking or absent, e.g. lost hotel room reservation, overbooked airplane, unavailable reserved window table).
B. Response to unreasonably slow service (services or employee performances are perceived as inordinately slow). (Note: When service is both slow and unavailable, use the *triggering* event).
C. Response to other core service failures (e.g. hotel room not clean, restaurant meal cold or improperly cooked, damaged baggage).

Group 2. Employee response to customer needs and requests (when the customer requires the employee to adapt, the service delivery system to suit his/her unique needs; contains either an explicit or inferred request for customized (from the customer's point of view) service).

A. Response to 'special needs' customers (customers with medical, dietary, psychological, language, or sociological difficulties; children; elderly customers).
B. Response to customer preferences (when the customer makes 'special' requests due to personal preferences; this includes times when the customer requests a level of service customization clearly beyond the scope of or in violation of policies or norms).
C. Response to admitted customer error (Triggering event is a customer error that strains the service encounter, e.g. lost tickets, incorrect order, missed reservations).
D. Response to potentially disruptive others (when other customers exhibit behaviors that potentially strain the encounter, e.g. intoxication, rudeness, deviance).

Group 3. Unprompted and unsolicited employee actions (events and behaviors that are truly unexpected from the customer's point of view, not triggered by a service failure, and show no evidence of the customer having a special need or making a special request).

A. Attention paid to customer (e.g. making the customer feel special or pampered, ignoring or being impatient with the customer).
B. Truly out-of-the-ordinary employee behavior (particularly extraordinary actions or expressions of courtesy, or profanity, inappropriate touching, violations of basic etiquette, rudeness).
C. Employee behaviors in the context of cultural norms (norms such as equality, honesty, fairness, discrimination, theft, lying, or refraining from the above when such behavior was expected).
D. Gestalt evaluation (no single feature stands out, instead 'everything went right' or 'everything went wrong'.
E. Exemplary performance under adverse circumstances (when the customer is particularly impressed or displeased with the way an employee handles a stressful situation).

Group 4. Problematic customer behavior (customer is unwilling to cooperate with laws, regulations, or the service provider; this includes rudeness, abusiveness, or a general unwillingness to indicate satisfaction with the service regardless of the employees' efforts).

A. Drunkenness (in the employee's perception, the customer is clearly intoxicated and creating problems, and the employee has to handle the situation).

B. Verbal and physical abuse (the customer verbally and/or physically abuses either the employee or other customers, and the employee has to handle the situation).

C. Breaking/resisting company policies or laws (the customer refuses to comply with policies (e.g. showing airplane ticket to the flight attendant before boarding) or laws (e.g. use of illegal drugs in the hotel room), and the employee has to enforce compliance).

D. Uncooperative customer (customer is generally rude and uncooperative or extremely demanding; any efforts to compensate for a perceived service failure are rejected; customer may appear unwilling to be satisfied; and the employee has to handle the situation).

ACKNOWLEDGMENTS

The authors gratefully acknowledge the support of the First Interstate Center for Services Marketing and the College of Business, Arizona State University, in conducting this research. The helpful comments of three anonymous *JM* reviewers are also appreciated.

REFERENCES

Berry, L. L. and Parasuraman, A. (1991) *Marketing Services.* New York: The Free Press.

Biddle, B. J. (1986) 'Recent Developments in Role Theory'. *Annual Review of Sociology* **12**: 67–92.

Bird, L. (1993) 'The Clients That Exasperate Madison Avenue'. *Wall Street Journal* (November 2): B1.

Bitner, M. J., Booms, B. H. and Tetreault, M. S. (1990) 'The Service Encounter: Diagnosing Favorable and Unfavorable Incidents'. *Journal of Marketing* **54** (January): 71–84.

Bloom, P. N. (1984) 'Effective Marketing for Professional Services'. *Harvard Business Review* (September/October): 102–110.

Bowen, D. E. (1986) 'Managing Customers as Human Resources in Service Organizations'. *Human Resource Management* **25** (3): 371–383.

Brown, S. W. and Swartz, T. A. (1989) "A Gap Analysis of Professional Service Quality'. *Journal of Marketing* **53** (April): 92–98.

Business Week (199), Special Issue on Quality.

Crosby, L. A. (1991) 'Expanding the Role of CSM in Total Quality'. *International Journal of Service Industry Management* **2** (2): 5–19.

Dahl, J. (1992) 'Rental Counters Reject Drivers Without Good Records'. *Wall Street Journal* (October 23): B1.

Dornoff, R. J. and Dwyer, F. R. (1981) 'Perceptual Differences in Market Transactions Revisited: A Waning Source of Consumer Frustration'. *The Journal of Consumer Affairs* **15** (Summer): 146–157.

Ericsson, K. A. and Simon, H. A. (1980) 'Verbal Reports as Data'. *Psychological Review* **87** (May): 215–250.

Fiske, S. T. and Taylor, S. E. (1984) *Social Cognition.* Reading, MA: Addison-Wesley.

Flanagan, J. C. (1954) 'The Critical Incident Technique'. *Psychological Bulletin* **51** (July): 327–358.

Folkes, V. S. and B. Kotsos (1986) 'Buyers and Sellers' Explanations for Product Failure: Who Done It?'. *Journal of Marketing* **50** (April): 74–80.

Gremler, D. and Bitner, M. J. (1992) 'Classifying Service Encounter Satisfaction Across Industries'. In *Marketing Theory and Applications* (C. T. Allen *et al.*, Eds). Chicago: American Marketing Association, pp. 111–118.

Heskett, J. L., Jones, T. O., Loveman, G. W., Earl Sasser, Jr., W. and Schlesinger, L. A. (1994) 'Putting the Service-Profit Chain to Work'. *Harvard Business Review* (March/April): 164–172.

Heskett, J. L., Earl Sasser, Jr., W. and Hart , C. W. L. (1990) *Service Breakthrough.* New York: The Free Press.

Hochschild, A. R. (1983) *The Managed Heart.* Berkeley, CA: University of California Press.

Hunt, S. (1991) *Modern Marketing Theory.* Cincinnati, OH: South-Western Publishing Company.

Kelley, S. W., Hoffman, K. D. and Davis, M. A. (1993) 'A Typology of Retail Failures and Recoveries'. *Journal of Retailing* **69** (4): 429–452.

Kingman-Brundage, J. (1989) 'The ABC's of Service System Blueprinting'. In *Designing a Winning Service Strategy* (M. J. Bitner and L. A. Crosby, Eds). Chicago: American Marketing Association, pp. 30–33.

Langeard, E., Bateson, J. E. G., Lovelock, C. H. and Eiglier, P. (1981) *Services Marketing: New Insights from Consumers and Managers.* Cambridge, MA: Marketing Science Institute.

Lovelock, C. (1983) 'Classifying Services to Gain Strategic Marketing Insights'. *Journal of Marketing* **47** (Summer): 9–20.

Lovelock, C. (1994) *Product Plus.* New York: McGraw-Hill.

McKelvey, B. (1982) *Organizational Systematics: Taxonomy, Evolution, Classification.* Berkeley, CA: University of California Press.

Mohr, L. A. and Bitner, M. J. (1991) 'Mutual Understanding Between Customers and Employees in Service Encounters'. In *Advances in Consumer Research*, Vol. 18, R. H. Holman and M. R. Solomon, Eds. Provo, UT: Association for Consumer Research, 611–617.

Parasuraman, A., Berry, L. L. and Zeithaml, V. A. (1991) 'Refinement and Reassessment of the SERVQUAL Scale'. *Journal of Retailing* **67** (4): 420–450.

Parasuraman, A., Zeithaml, V. and Berry, L. L. (1988) 'SERVQUAL: A Multiple-Item Scale for Measuring Consumer Perception of Service Quality'. *Journal of Retailing* **64** (Spring): 12–40.

Parasuraman, A., Zeithaml, V. and Berry, L. L. (1990) 'An Empirical Examination of Relationships in an Extended Service Quality Model'. Report No. 90–122. Cambridge, MA: Marketing Science Institute.

Perreault, W. D., Jr. and Leigh, L. E. (1989) 'Reliability of Nominal Data Based on Qualitative Judgments'. *Journal of Marketing Research* **26** (May): 135–148.

Resnik, A. J. and Harmon, R. R. (1983) 'Consumer Complaints and Managerial Response: A Holistic Approach'. *Journal of Marketing* **47** (Winter): 86–97.

Ronan, W. W. and Latham, G. P. (1974) 'The Reliability and Validity of the Critical Incident Technique: A Closer Look'. *Studies in Personnel Psychology* **6** (Spring): 53–64.

Schank, R. C. and Abelson, R. P. (1977) *Scripts, Plans, Goals and Understanding.* New York: John Wiley and Sons, Inc.

Schlesinger, L. A. and Heskett, J. L. (1991) 'The Service-Driven Service Company'. *Harvard Business Review* (September/October): 71–81.

Schneider, B. (1980) 'The Service Organization: Climate is Crucial'. *Organizational Dynamics* (Autumn): 52–65.

Schneider, B. and Bowen, D. E. (1984) 'New Services Design, Development and Implementation and the Employee'. In *Developing New Services* (W. R. George and C. Marshall, Eds). Chicago: American Marketing Association, 82–101.

Schneider, B. and Bowen, D. E. (1985) 'Employee and Customer Perceptions of Services in Banks: Replication and Extension'. *Journal of Applied Psychology* **70** (3): 423–433.

Schneider, B., Parkington, J. J. and Buxton, V. M. (1980) 'Employee and Customer

Perceptions of Service in Banks'. *Administrative Science Quarterly* **25** (June): 252–267.

Schrage, M. (1992) 'Fire Your Customers'. *Wall Street Journal* (March 16): A8.

Services Marketing Newsletter (1989) 'Recent Study Shows Gap Between Customers and Service Employees on Customer Service Perceptions'. 5 (Summer), 1.

Shostack, G. L. (1984) 'Designing Services That Deliver'. *Harvard Business Review* (January/February): 133–139.

Shostack, G. L. (1987) 'Service Positioning Through Structural Change'. *Journal of Marketing* **51** (January): 34–43.

Solomon, M. R., Surprenant, C., Czepiel, J. A. and Gutman, E. G. (1985) 'A Role Theory Perspective on Dyadic Interactions: The Service Encounter'. *Journal of Marketing* **49** (Winter): 99–111.

White, F. M. and Locke, E. A. (1981) 'Perceived Determinants of High and Low Productivity in Three Occupational Groups: A Critical Incident Study'. *Journal of Management Studies* **18** (4): 375–387.

Wilson-Pessano, S. R. (1988) 'Defining Professional Competence: The Critical Incident Technique 40 Years Later'. American Institutes for Research, invited address to the Annual Meeting of the American Educational Research Association, New Orleans.

Zeithaml, V. A., Berry, L. L. and Parasuraman, A. (1988) 'Communication and Control Processes in the Delivery of Service Quality'. *Journal of Marketing* **52** (April): 35–48.

Zeithaml, V. A. and Bitner, M. J. (1995) *Services Marketing*. New York: McGraw-Hill.

Zemke, R. and Anderson, K. (1990) 'Customers From Hell'. *Training* (February): 25–33.

Section III

Service Quality and Satisfaction

Service quality is at the centre of any discussion about service marketing management. The conceptualisation of service quality, its relationship to satisfaction, and methods of measuring it, have been a central theme of the services literature over the past 15 years. Whilst there may be general agreement that the evaluation of services is more subjective than tangible goods and, therefore, that an understanding of consumers is central to understanding service quality, there has been less agreement about how to operationalise service quality as a construct. Service quality remains illusive, difficult to define and measure. There is not even general agreement about the meaning of quality. In particular, the close conceptual links between satisfaction and quality have led to considerable disagreement about whether and how these two dimensions are related. Much of this debate had centred around the direction of causality, i.e. whether service quality is an antecedent to satisfaction or whether it is a wider concept, developed as a result of a number of satisfying experiences over time. As Parasuraman (1993) pointed out, the issue is complicated by the fact that the terms are often used interchangeably and have both been operationalised using the same disconfirmation of expectations paradigm (i.e. the idea that customers hold expectations about a service and their subsequent evaluations are based on whether these expectations are confirmed or not). The relationship between satisfaction and quality is raised in a number of the articles in this section and is representative of a recurrent theme in the service quality literature. Holbrook (1994) goes so far as to suggest that 'issues regarding the meaning of the word "quality" appear to pose considerable barriers to clear thinking. In order to remove some of these barriers, this section considers two main themes of service quality research, the development of a measurement tool that can be used by firms to assess the quality of the service they provide, and the relationship between operatinalisations of service quality and customer evaluations.

We start by presenting the most commonly used, and abused, service quality measurement tool: SERVQUAL. The impact of Parasuraman, Zeithaml and Berry's work on contemporary service management literature cannot be underestimated. The central idea of their work is the notion of 'gaps' between the expectations of service and subsequent perceptions of what is delivered. These gaps are located throughout the organisation between front line staff, customers and managers. The identification of ten dimensions of service quality, later refined to five – reliability, assurance, tangibles, empathy and responsiveness (RATER) – has dominated the literature in the field of service quality. Much of the research in this area since Parasuraman, Zeithaml and Berry introduced SERVQUAL in 1988 has been concerned with validating or challenging the construct. Two key articles that challenge the gaps model are included in this section: Cronin and Taylor's (1992) paper, which argues for performance based measures and presents a variant SERVPERF scale, and an article by Teas (1993), who questions the conceptual and operational validity of the perceptions minus expectations framework. However, you may wish to refer to the January 1994 edition of the *Journal of Marketing* in which Parasuraman, Zeithaml and Berry respond to these criticisms and Cronin and Taylor and Teas reply.

In contrast, Frank Buttle's (1996) review of SERVQUAL concentrates on systematically examining the theoretical, operational and statistical criticisms of the SERVQUAL scale and raises a number of directions for future research in the area of service quality measurement. These discussions represent marketing academics grappling with the intricacies of service quality in order to present a recognised and accepted basis for the advancement of research and the improvement of practice.

The following two articles in this section address an alternative perspective on the service quality debate, the extent to which consumers behavioural intentions are influenced by the service quality that they receive. Boulding *et al.* (1993) are concerned with identifying the ways in which customer expectations are formed and the consequences of these upon purchase behaviour. In contrast Bolton and Drew (1991) consider how customers assess value and suggest a multi-stage model of service evaluation. The model proposes that service satisfaction, quality perception and value are interlinked into an overall evaluation which is affected by actual performance. These streams of service quality research are not independent and taken together provide an overview of current conceptualisations of service quality research in the consumer arena. The final article considers quality in the context of industrial services, specifically how industrial buyers can build relationships via service quality. The importance of quality as a factor in relationship building is the basis of much of the literature on relationship marketing (see, for instance, Christopher, Payne and Ballantyne 1991). The Holmlund and Kock (1995) article in this section discusses this in terms of the level of quality necessary to meet the firm's goals. The authors stress the economic service quality dimension which is of vital importance in industrial situations and permeates all business transactions.

CONTENTS

11

SERVQUAL: A Multiple-Item Scale for Measuring Consumer Perceptions of Service Quality

A. Parasuraman, Valarie A. Zeithaml and Leonard L. Berry

Intensifying competition and rapid deregulation have led many service and retail businesses to seek profitable ways to differentiate themselves. One strategy that has been related to success in these businesses is the delivery of high service quality (Rudie and Wansley, 1985; Thompson, DeSouza and Gale, 1985). Delivering superior service quality appears to be a prerequisite for success, if not survival, of such businesses in the 1980s and beyond.

Unlike goods quality, which can be measured objectively by such indicators as durability and number of defects (Crosby, 1979; Garvin, 1983), service quality is an abstract and elusive construct because of three features unique to services: intangibility, heterogeneity, and inseparability of production and consumption (Parasuraman, Zeithaml and Berry, 1985). In the absence of objective measures, an appropriate approach for assessing the quality of a firm's service to measure consumers' perceptions of quality. As yet, however, no quantitative yardstick is available for gauging these perceptions.

The purpose of this article is twofold: (1) to describe the development of a multiple-item scale for measuring service quality (called SERVQUAL) and (2) to discuss the scale's properties and potential applications. The basic steps employed in constructing the scale closely parallel procedures recommended in Churchill's (1979) paradigm for developing better measures of marketing constructs. Figure 1 provides an overview of the steps.

This article is divided into five sections. The first section delimits the domain of the service-quality construct and describes the generation of scale items (Steps 1, 2 and 3 in Figure 1). The second section presents the data-collection and scale-purification procedures (Steps 4 through 9) while the third section provides an evaluation of the scale's reliability and factor structure (Step 10). The next section deals with assessment of the scale's validity (Step 11). The final section discusses potential applications of the scale.

Reprinted with permission from *Journal of Retailing*, Vol. 64, No. 1, pp. 12–40.
© 1988 JAI Press Inc.

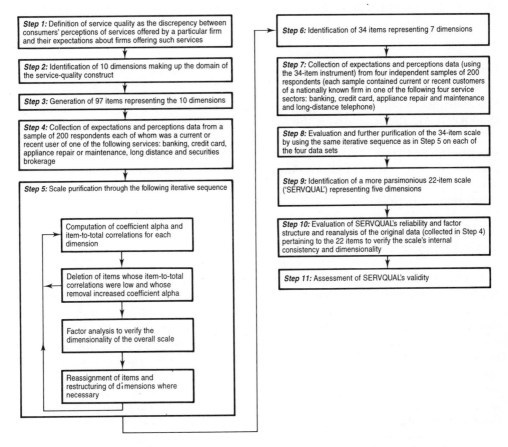

Figure 1. Summary of steps employed in developing the service quality scale.

DOMAIN OF THE SERVICE-QUALITY CONSTRUCT

In deploring the inadequacy of measurement procedures used in the marketing discipline Jacoby (1978) wrote:

> Many of our measures are developed at the whim of a researcher with nary a thought given to whether or not it is meaningfully related to an explicit conceptual statement or the phenomena or variable in question. In most instances, our concepts have no identity apart from the instrument or procedures used to measure them. (p. 92).

The need for scale development to be preceded by, and rooted in, a sound conceptual specification of the construct being scaled has been emphasized by other scholars as well (e.g. Churchill, 1979; Peter, 1981). The conceptual foundation for the SERVQUAL scale was derived from the works of a handful of researchers who have examined the meaning of service quality (Sasser, Olsen and Wyckoff, 1978; Gronroos, 1982; Lehtinen and Lehtinen, 1982) and from a comprehensive qualitative research study that defined service quality and illuminated the dimensions along which consumers perceive and evaluate service quality (Parasuraman, Zeithaml and Berry, 1985).

Conceptualization of service quality

The construct of quality as conceptualized in the services literature and as measured by SERVQUAL, the scale that is the focus of this article, involves perceived quality. Perceived quality is the consumer's judgment about an entity's overall excellence or superiority (Zeithaml, 1987). It differs from objective quality (as defined by, for example, Garvin, 1983 and Hjorth-Anderson, 1984); it is a form of attitude, related but not equivalent to satisfaction, and results from a comparison of expectations with perceptions of performance.

Perceived quality versus objective quality

Researchers (Garvin, 1983; Dodds and Monroe, 1984; Holbrook and Corfman, 1985; Jacoby and Olson, 1985; Zeithaml, 1987) have emphasized the difference between objective and perceived quality. Holbrook and Corfman (1985), for example, note that consumers do not use the term quality in the same way as researchers and marketers, who define it conceptually. The conceptual meaning distinguishes between mechanistic and humanistic quality: 'mechanistic (quality) involves an objective aspect or feature of a thing or event; humanistic (quality) involves the subjective response of people to objects and is therefore highly relativistic phenomenon that differs between judges' (Holbrook and Corfman, 1985, p. 33). Garvin (1983) discusses five approaches to define quality, including two (product-based and manufacturing-based) that refer to objective quality and one (user-based) that parallels perceived quality.

Quality as attitude

Olshavsky (1985) views quality as a form of overall evaluation of a product, similar in many ways to attitude. Holbrook concurs, suggesting that quality acts as a relatively global value judgment. Exploratory research conducted by Parasuraman, Zeithaml and Berry (1985) supports the notion that service quality is an overall evaluation similar to attitude. The researchers conducted a total of twelve focus group interviews with current or recent consumers of four different services – retail banking, credit card, securities brokerage, and product repair and maintenance. The discussions centred on issues such as the meaning of quality in the context of the service in question, the characteristics the service and the provider should possess in order to project a high quality image, and the criteria customers use in evaluating service quality. Comparison of the findings from the focus groups revealed that, regardless of the type of service, customers used basically the same general criteria in arriving at an evaluative judgement about service quality.

Quality versus satisfaction

Oliver (1981) summarizes current thinking on satisfaction in the following definition: '[satisfaction is a] summary psychological state resulting when the emotion surrounding disconfirmed expectations is coupled with the consumer's prior feelings about the consumption experience' (p. 27). This and other definitions (e.g Howard and Sheth, 1969; Hunt, 1979) and most all measures of satisfaction relate to a specific transaction. Oliver (1981) summarizes the transaction-specific nature of satisfaction, and differentiates it from attitude, as follows:

> Attitude is the consumer's relatively enduring affective orientation for a product, store, or process (e.g. customer service) while satisfaction is the emotional reaction following a disconfirmation experience which acts on the base attitude level and is consumption-specific. Attitude is therefore measured in terms more general to product or store and is less situationally oriented. (p. 42).

Consistent with the distinction between attitude and satisfaction, is a distinction between service quality and satisfaction: perceived service quality is a global judgment, or attitude, relating to the superiority of the service, whereas satisfaction is related to a specific transaction. Indeed, in the twelve focus group interviews included in the exploratory research conducted by Parasuraman, Zeithaml and Berry (1985), respondents gave several illustrations of instances when they were satisfied with a specific service but did not feel the service firm was of high quality. In this way, the two constructs are related, in that incidents of satisfaction over time result in perceptions of service quality. In Oliver's (1981) words, 'satisfaction soon decays into one's overall attitude toward purchasing products'.

Expectations compared to perceptions

The writings of Sasser, Olsen and Wyckoff (1978); Gronroos (1982); and Lehtinen and Lehtinen (1982), and the extensive focus group interviews conducted by Parasuraman, Zeithaml and Berry (1985), unambiguously support the notion that service quality, as perceived by consumers, stems from a comparison of what they feel service firms should offer (i.e. from their expectations) with their perceptions of the performance of firms providing the services. Perceived service quality is therefore viewed as the degree and direction of discrepancy between consumers' perceptions and expectations.

The term 'expectations' as used in the service quality literature differs from the way it is used in the consumer satisfaction literature. Specifically, in the satisfaction literature, expectations are viewed as *predictions* made by consumers about what is likely to happen during an impending transaction or exchange. For instance, according to Oliver (1981), 'It is generally agreed that expectations are consumer-defined probabilities of the occurrence of positive and negative events if the consumer engages in some behavior' (p. 33). In contrast, in the service quality literature, expectations are viewed as desires or wants of consumers, i.e. what they feel a service provider *should* offer rather than *would* offer.

Dimensions of service quality

Exploratory research of Parasuraman, Zeithaml and Berry (1985) revealed that the criteria used by consumers in assessing service quality fit 10 potentially overlapping dimensions. These dimensions were tangibles, reliability, responsiveness, communication, credibility, security, competence, courtesy, understanding/knowing the customer, and access (a description of the dimensions can be found in Parasuraman, Zeithaml and Berry, 1985, p. 47). These 10 dimensions and their descriptions served as the basic structure of the service-quality domain from which items are derived for the SERVQUAL scale.

Generation of scale items

Items representing various facets of the 10 service-quality dimensions were generated to form the initial item pool for the SERVQUAL instrument. This process resulted in the generation of 97 items (approximately 10 items per dimension). Each item was recast into two statements – one to measure expectations about firms in general within the service category being investigated and the other to measure perceptions about the particular firm whose service quality was being assessed. Roughly half of the statement pairs were worded positively and the rest were worded negatively, in accordance with recommended procedures for scale development (Churchill, 1979). A seven-point scale ranging from 'Strongly Agree' (7) to 'Strongly Disagree' (1), with no verbal labels for scale points 2 through 6, accompanied each statement (scale values were reversed for negatively worded statements prior to data analysis). The expectation statements were grouped together and formed the first half of the instrument. The corresponding perception statements formed the second half. An abbreviated version of the instrument, containing a set of expectation statements (labeled as E's) and a corresponding set of perception statements (labeled as P's), along with directions for responding to them, is included in the appendix. Negatively worded statements are identified by a minus sign within parentheses in the appendix.

DATA COLLECTION AND SCALE PURIFICATION

The 97-item instrument was subjected to two stages of data collection and refinement. The first stage focused on: (1) condensing the instrument by retaining only those items capable of discriminating well across respondents having differing quality perceptions about firms in several categories, and (2) examining the dimensionality of the scale and establishing the reliabilities of its components. The second stage was primarily confirmatory in nature and involved re-evaluating the condensed scale's dimensionality and reliability by analyzing fresh data from four independent samples. Some further refinements to the scale occurred in this stage.

Data collection, first stage

Data for initial refinement of the 97-item instrument were gathered from a quota sample of 200 adult respondents (25 years of age or older) recruited by a marketing research firm in a shopping mall in a large metropolitan area in the

Southwest of the USA. The sample size of 200 was chosen because other scale developers in the marketing area had used similar sample sizes to purify initial instruments containing about the same number of items as the 97-item instrument (e.g. Churchill, Ford and Walker, 1974; Saxe and Weitz, 1982). The sample was about equally divided between males and females. Furthermore, the respondents were spread across five different service categories – appliance repair and maintenance, retail banking, long-distance telephone, securities brokerage, and credit cards. These categories were chosen to represent a broad cross-section of services that varied along key dimensions used by Lovelock (1980, 1983) to classify services. For each service category, a quota of 40 recent users of the service was established. To qualify for the study, respondents had to have used the service in question during the past three months.

Screened and qualified respondents self administered a two-part questionnaire consisting of a 97-statement expectations part followed by a 97-statement perceptions part. For the first part, respondents were instructed to indicate the level of service that should be offered by firms within the service category in question. For the second part, respondents were first asked to name a firm (within the service category) that they had used and with which they were most familiar. Respondents were then instructed to express their perceptions about the firm.

Scale purification, first stage

The 97-item instrument was refined by analyzing pooled data (i.e. data from all five service categories considered together). The pooling data was deliberate and appropriate because the basic purpose of this research stage was to develop a concise instrument that would be reliable and meaningful in assessing quality in a variety of service sectors. In other words, the purpose was to produce a scale that would have general applicability.

Purification of the instrument began with the computation of coefficient alpha (Cronbach, 1951), in accordance with Churchill's (1979) recommendation. Because of the multidimensionality of the service-quality construct, coefficient alpha was computed separately for the 10 dimensions to ascertain the extent to which items making up each dimension shared a common core.

The raw data used in computing coefficient alpha (and in subsequent analyses) were in the form of difference scores. Specifically, for each item a difference score Q (representing perceived quality along that item) was defined as $Q = P - E$, where P and E are the ratings on the corresponding perception and expectation statements, respectively. The idea of using difference scores in purifying a multiple-item scale is not new. This approach has been used in developing scales for measuring constructs such as role conflict (Ford, Walker and Churchill, 1975).

The values of coefficient alpha ranged from .55 to .78 across the 10 dimensions and suggested that deletion of certain items from each dimension would improve the alpha values. The criterion used in deciding whether to delete an item was the item's corrected item-to-total correlation (i.e. correlation between the score on the item and the sum of scores on *all other* items making up the dimension to which the item was assigned). The corrected item-to-total correlations were plotted in descending order for each dimension. Items with very low correlations and/or those whose correlations produced a sharp drop in the plotted pattern were discarded. Recomputations of alpha values for the reduced sets of statements and examination of the new corrected item-to-total correlations led to further deletion of items whose elimination improved the corresponding alpha values. The iterative sequence of computing alphas and item-to-total correlations, followed by deletion of items, was repeated several times and resulted in a set of 54 items, with alpha values ranging from .72 to .83 across the 10 dimensions.

Examining the dimensionality of the 54-item scale was the next task in this stage of scale purification and was accomplished by factor analyzing the difference scores on the 54 items. The principal axis factoring procedure (Harman, 1967) was used and the analysis was constrained *a priori* to 10 factors. When the 10-factor solution was rotated orthogonally, no clear factor pattern emerged. Many of the items had high loadings on several factors, thereby implying that the factors may not be independent of one another. Moreover, some degree of overlap among the 10 conceptual dimensions was anticipated by the researchers who initially identified and labeled the dimensions (Parasuraman, Zeithaml and Berry, 1985). Therefore the 10-factor solution was subjected to oblique rotation (using the OBLIMIN procedure in SPSS-X) to allow for intercorrelations among the dimensions and to facilitate easy interpretation.

The oblique rotation produced a factor-loading matrix that was by and large easy to interpret. However, several items still had high loadings on more than one factor. When such items were removed from the factor-loading matrix, several factors themselves became meaningless because they had near-zero correlations with the remaining items, thereby suggesting a reduction in the presumed dimensionality of the service-quality domain. Furthermore, the highest loadings of a few of the remaining items were on factors to which they were not originally assigned. In other words, the factor loading suggested reassignment on some items.

The deletion of certain items (and the resultant reduction in the total number of factors or clusters of items) and the reassignment of certain others necessitated the recomputation of alphas and item-to-total correlations and the reexamination of the factor structure of the reduced item pool. This iterative sequence of analyses (Step 5 in Figure 1) was repeated a few times and resulted in a final pool of 34 items representing seven distinct dimensions. The alpha values and factor loadings pertaining to the 34-item instrument are summarized in Table 1.

As shown in Table 1, five of the original 10 dimensions – tangibles, reliability, responsiveness, understanding/knowing customers, and access – remained distinct. The remaining five dimensions – communication, credibility, security, competence, and courtesy – collapsed into two distinct dimensions (D4 and D5), each consisting of items from several of the original five dimensions. The average pairwise correlation among the seven factors following oblique rotation was .27. This relatively low correlation, along with the relatively high factor loadings shown in Table 1, suggested that service quality might have seven fairly unique facets.

The high alpha values indicated good internal consistency among items within each dimension. Moreover, the combined reliability for the 34-item scale, computed by using the formula for the reliability of linear combinations (Nunnally, 1978), was

Table 1. Summary of results from first stage of scale purification

Dimension	Label	Reliability coefficients (alphas)	Number of items	Factor loadings of items on dimensions to which they belong[a]
Tangibles	D1	.72	4	63 75 62 47
Reliability	D2	.83	5	74 56 73 71 47
Responsiveness	D3	.84	5	60 73 59 76 66
Communication Credibility Security Competence Courtesy	D4	.79	4	35 53 66 56
	D5	.85	7	41 62 47 50 75 52 54
Understanding/ Knowing Customers	D6	.85	4	80 76 62 77
Access	D7	.78	5	57 50 75 52 71
Reliability of linear combination (Total-scale reliability)		.94		

[a]Numbers are the magnitudes of the factor loadings multiplied by 100. The loadings of items on dimensions to which they did not belong were all less than .3. The percentage of variance extracted by the seven factors was 61.7%.

quite high (.94). Therefore, the 34-item instrument was considered to be ready for further testing with data from new samples.

Data collection, second stage

To further evaluate the 34-item scale and its psychometric properties, data were collected pertaining to the service quality of four nationally known firms: a bank, a credit-card company, a firm offering appliance repair and maintenance services, and a long-distance telephone company. For each firm, an independent shopping-mall sample of 200 customers 25 years-of-age or older were recruited by a marketing research firm in a major metropolitan area in the East. To qualify for the study, respondents had to have used the services of the firm in question within the past three months. Each sample was divided about equally between males and females. As in the first stage of data collection, questionnaires were self-administered by qualified respondents.

Scale purification, second stage

A major objective of this stage was to evaluate the robustness of the 34-item scale when used to measure the service quality of the four firms. Therefore the data from each of the four samples analyzed separately to obtain alpha values (along with corrected item-to-total correlations) and a factor-loading matrix following oblique rotation of a seven-factor solution. The results from each sample facilitated cross-validation of the results from the other samples.

The results of the four sets of analyses were quite consistent, but differed somewhat from the first-stage findings summarized in Table 1. Specifically, two differences emerged. First, the corrected item-to-total correlations for several items (particularly among items making up the dimension labeled D4 and D7 in Table 1) and the alphas for the corresponding dimensions were lower than those obtained from the first stage. Second, the factor-loading matrices obtained from all four analyses showed much greater overlap between dimensions D4 and D5, and between dimensions D6 and D7. Because these differences occurred consistently across four independent samples and data sets, further purification of the 34-item scale was deemed necessary.

A few items with relatively low item-to-total correlations were deleted. Furthermore, as suggested by the factor analyses, the items remaining in D4 and D5, as well as those in D6 and D7, were combined to form two separate dimensions. For each sample, alpha values were recomputed for the reduced set of five dimensions and a factor analysis (involving extraction of five factors followed by olique rotation) was performed. In examining the results of these analyses, an iterative sequence similar to the one shown in Step 5 in Figure 1 was followed. This procedure resulted in a refined scale ('SERVQUAL') with 22 items spread among five dimensions (D1, D2, D3, a combination of D4 and D5, and a combination of D6 and D7). The expectation and perception statements in the final SERVQUAL instrument are shown in the appendix.

An examination of the content of the final items making up each of SERVQUAL's five dimensions (three original and two combined dimensions) suggested the following labels and concise definitions for the dimensions:

Tangibles: Physical facilities, equipment, and appearance of personnel
Reliability: Ability to perform the promised service dependably and accurately
Responsiveness: Willingness to help customers and provide prompt service
Assurance: Knowledge and courtesy of employees and their ability to inspire
                  trust and confidence
Empathy: Caring, individualized attention the firms provides its customers

The last two dimensions (assurance and empathy) contain items representing seven original dimensions – communication, credibility, security, competence, courtesy, understanding/knowing customers, and access – that did not remain distinct after the two stages of scale purification. Therefore, while SERVQUAL has only five distinct dimensions, they capture facets of all 10 originally conceptualized dimensions.

SERVQUAL'S RELIABILITY AND FACTOR STRUCTURE

Table 2 shows the component and total reliabilities of SERVQUAL for each of the four samples. The reliabilities are consistently high across all four samples, with the possible exception of a couple of values pertaining to the tangible dimension. The total-scale reliability (i.e. reliability of linear combination) is close to .9 in each of the four instances.

Results of the factor analyses of data from the four samples are summarized in Table 3. The overall patterns of factor loading are remarkably similar across the four independent sets of results. With few exceptions, items assigned to each dimension consistently have high loadings on only one of the five factors extracted. The distinctiveness of SERVQUAL's five dimensions implied by the results in Table 3 was further supported by relatively low intercorrelations among the five factors – the average pairwise correlations between factors following oblique rotation were .21, .24, .26 and .23 for the bank, credit card, repair and maintenance, and long-distance telephone samples, respectively.

As an additional verification of the reliabilities and factor structure of SERVQUAL, the first-stage data set that resulted in the 34-item instrument with seven dimensions was reanalyzed after deleting the 12 items that dropped out during the second stage of scale purification. The results of this reanalysis are summarized in Table 4 and reconfirm the high reliabilities and dimensional distinctiveness of the scale. The average pairwise correlation among the five factors following oblique rotation was .35.

It is worth noting that the interative procedure used to refine the initial instrument was guided by empirical criteria and by the goal of obtaining a concise scale whose items would be meaningful to a variety of service firms. The reliabilities and factor structures indicate that the final 22-item scale and its five dimensions have sound and stable psychometric properties. Moreover, by design, the iterative procedure retained only those items that are common and relevant to all service

Table 2. Internal consistencies of the five service-quality dimensions following second stage of scale purification

| Dimension | Label | Number of items | Reliability coefficients (alphas)[a] | | | | Items[b] |
			B	CC	R&M	LDT	
Tangibles	F1	4	.52	.62	.64	.64	Q1 Q2 Q3 Q4
Reliability	F2	5	.80	.78	.84	.74	Q5 Q5 Q6 Q7 Q8 Q9
Responsiveness	F3	4	.72	.69	.76	.70	Q10 Q11 Q12 Q13
Assurance	F4	4	.84	.80	.87	.84	Q14 Q15 Q16 Q17
Empathy	F5	5	.71	.80	.72	.76	Q18 Q19 Q20 Q21 Q22
Reliability of Linear Combination (Total-Scale Reliability)			.87	.89	.90	.88	

[a] B = bank; CC = credit card company; R&M = repair and maintenance company; LDT = long distance telephone company.
[b] The item numbers correspond to those of the expectation and perception statements in the appendix.

firms included in the study. However, by the same token, this procedure may have deleted certain 'good' items relevant to some but not all firms. Therefore, while SERVQUAL can be used in its present form to assess and compare service quality across a wide variety of firms or units within a firm, appropriate adaptation of the instrument may be desirable when only a single service is investigated. Specifically, items under each of the five dimensions can be suitably reworded and/or augmented to make them more germane to the context in which the instrument is to be used.

Table 3. Factor loading matrices following oblique rotation of five-factor solutions[a]

FACTOR LOADINGS

Items	Bank					Credit card company					Repair and maintenance company					Long distance telephone company				
	F1	F2	F3	F4	F5	F1	F2	F3	F4	F5	F1	F2	F3	F4	F5	F1	F2	F3	F4	F5
Q1	34	28	—	—	—	36	—	35	—	—	34	—	—	—	—	42	—	—	—	—
Q2	64	—	—	—	—	70	—	—	—	—	70	—	—	—	—	72	—	—	—	—
Q3	39	—	—	28	—	52	—	—	—	—	53	—	—	—	—	51	—	—	—	—
Q4	28	—	—	28	—	52	—	—	—	—	65	—	—	—	—	59	—	—	30	—
Q5	—	72	—	—	—	—	54	—	—	—	—	73	—	—	—	—	52	—	—	—
Q6	—	63	—	—	—	—	43	27	—	—	—	51	—	—	—	—	40	—	—	—
Q7	—	71	—	—	—	—	87	—	—	—	—	84	—	—	—	—	79	—	—	—
Q8	—	80	—	—	—	—	83	—	—	—	—	88	—	—	—	—	59	—	—	—
Q9	—	39	—	—	—	—	49	—	—	—	—	29	—	30	—	—	54	—	—	—
Q10	—	—	37	—	—	—	—	43	—	26	—	—	56	—	—	—	—	39	—	—
Q11	—	—	55	—	—	—	—	48	—	—	—	—	52	—	—	—	—	43	—	—
Q12	—	—	62	—	—	—	—	54	—	—	—	—	74	—	—	—	—	92	—	—
Q13	—	—	69	—	—	—	—	33	—	—	—	—	71	—	—	—	—	53	—	—
Q14	—	—	—	68	—	—	—	—	65	—	—	—	—	86	—	—	—	—	69	—
Q15	—	—	—	84	—	—	—	—	76	—	—	—	—	89	—	—	—	—	81	—
Q16	—	—	—	72	—	—	—	—	73	—	—	—	—	65	—	—	—	—	61	—
Q17	—	—	—	64	—	—	—	—	61	—	—	—	—	64	—	—	—	—	66	—
Q18	—	—	—	—	37	—	—	—	—	64	—	—	—	—	42	—	—	—	—	59
Q19	—	—	—	—	48	—	—	—	—	72	—	—	—	—	61	—	—	—	—	79
Q20	—	—	—	—	41	—	—	—	—	63	—	28	34	—	46	—	—	—	—	55
Q21	—	—	—	—	33	—	—	—	—	59	—	—	—	—	32	—	—	—	—	36
Q22	—	—	—	—	68	—	—	—	—	64	—	—	—	—	61	—	—	—	—	59

[a] All numbers in the table are magnitudes of the factor loadings multiplied by 100. Loadings that are .25 of less are not shown. The percentage of variance extracted by five factors in the bank, credit card, repair and maintenance, and long-distance telephone samples were 56.0%, 57.5%, 61.6%, and 56.2%, respectively.

Table 4. Reanalysis of first stage data for the five-dimensional scale

Dimension	Label	Number of items	Reliability coefficients (alphas)	Items	Factor loadings of items on dimensions to which they belong[a]
Tangibles	F1	4	.72	Q1	69
				Q2	68
				Q3	64
				Q4	51
Reliability	F2	5	.83	Q5	75
				Q6	63
				Q7	71
				Q8	75
				Q9	50
Responsiveness	F3	4	.82	Q10	51
				Q11	77
				Q12	66
				Q13	86
Assurance	F4	4	.81	Q14	38
				Q15	72
				Q16	80
				Q17	45
Empathy	F5	5	.86	Q18	78
				Q19	81
				Q20	59
				Q21	71
				Q22	68
Reliability of linear combination (total-scale reliability)			.92		

[a] Numbers are magnitude of the factor loadings multiplied by 100. The loadings of items on dimensions to which they do not belong were all less than .3. The percentage of variance extracted by the five factors was 63.2%.

ASSESSMENT OF SERVQUAL'S VALIDITY

SERVQUAL's high reliabilities and consistent factor structures across several independent samples provide support for its trait validity (Campbell, 1960; Peter, 1981). However, while high reliabilities and internal consistencies are necessary conditions for a scale's construct validity – the extent to which a scale fully and unambiguously captures the underlying, unobservable, construct it is intended to measure – they are not sufficient (Churchill, 1979). The scale must satisfy certain other conceptual and empirical criteria to be considered as having a good construct validity.

The basic constructual criterion pertaining to construct validity is face of content validity. (Does the scale appear to measure what it is supposed to? Do the scale items capture key facets of the unobservable construct being measured?) Assessing a scale's content validity is necessarily qualitative rather than quantitative. It involves examining two aspects: (1) the thoroughness with which the construct to be scaled and its domain were explicated and (2) the extent to which the scale items represent the construct's domain. As discussed in earlier sections, the procedures used in developing SERVQUAL satisfied both these evaluative requirements. Therefore the scale can be considered to possess content validity.

The scale's validity was also assessed empirically by examining its convergent validity, i.e. the association between SERVQUAL scores and responses to a question that asked customers to provide an overall quality rating of the firm they were evaluating. Respondents in the second stage of data collection rated the service firm's overall quality (referred to hereafter as 'Overall Q') by checking one of four categories – excellent, good, fair, poor. The correspondence between the Overall Q ratings and the SERVQUAL scores was examined using one-way ANOVA. The treatment variable in the ANOVA's was Overall Q – with three categories instead of four because very few respondents checked 'poor', thereby necessitating creation of a combined 'fair/poor' category. The dependent variable was the average difference score (i.e. perception-minus-expectation score) on each SERVQUAL dimension as well as on the total SERVQUAL scale (separate ANOVA's were conducted for each dimension and for the total scale). Significant ANOVA results were investigated further using Duncan's multiple range test to identify significant differences across the Overall Q categories. The results of these analyses for each of the four samples are summarized in Table 5 under the heading 'Overall Q'.

The numbers reported in Table 5 are average SERVQUAL scores within each Overall Q category, measured on a −6 to +6 score on which the higher (less negative) the score, the higher is the level of perceived service quality. In each of the four samples, the combined SERVQUAL score for those in the 'excellent' category is significantly higher (less negative) than for those in the 'good' category. Furthermore, respondents in the 'good' category have a significantly higher combined SERVQUAL score than those in the 'fair/poor' category. A similar pattern of findings is evident for the scores on the individual SERVQUAL dimensions as well. The strength and persistence of the linkage between the Overall Q categories and the SERVQUAL scores across four independent samples offer strong support for SERVQUAL's convergent validity.

SERVQUAL's validity was further assessed by examining whether the construct measured by it was empirically associated with measures of other conceptually related variables. Respondents in each sample answered two general questions that provided measures of variables (labeled 'Recommend' and 'Problem' in Table 5) which one could expect to be related conceptually to perceived service quality: (1) whether the respondents would recommend the service firm to a friend and (2) whether they had ever reported a problem with the services they received from the firm. Respondents answering yes to the first (Recommended) question and no to the second (Problem) question could be hypothesized to perceive higher service quality than other respondents. As Table 5 shows, the results are consistent with this hypothesis. These findings provide additional support for SERVQUAL's validity.

Table 5. Significant differences in mean scale values for respondents – segmented according to the variables overall Q, recommend and problem[a]

Individual scale dimensions	Overall Q			Recommend		Problem	
	Excellent	Good	Fair/Poor	Yes	No	Yes	No
Bank							
Tangibles	-0.04^b	-0.52^c	-1.08^d	-0.41^b	-0.98^c	-0.75^b	-0.46^b
Reliability	-0.25^b	-0.96^c	-2.30^d	-0.82^b	-2.21^c	-1.55^b	-0.92^c
Responsiveness	-0.32^b	-0.97^c	-1.54^c	-0.74^b	-1.81^c	-1.22^b	-0.84^b
Assurance	-0.49^b	-1.03^c	-1.98^d	-0.88^b	-2.12^c	-1.52^b	-0.96^c
Empathy	-0.30^b	-1.02^c	-1.52^c	-0.76^b	-1.88^c	-1.07^b	-0.91^b
Combined scale	-0.22^c	-0.92^c	-1.61^d	-0.72^b	-1.77^c	-1.22^b	-0.80^c
Sample size	46	112	40	164	33	47	151
Credit card company							
Tangibles	0.06^b	-0.61^c	-0.79^c	-0.39^b	-0.80^c	-0.76^b	-0.29^c
Reliability	-0.42^b	-0.94^c	-2.32^d	-0.82^b	-2.50^c	-1.42^b	-0.82^c
Responsiveness	-0.08^b	-1.13^c	-1.71^c	-0.75^b	-2.59^c	-1.31^b	-0.77^b
Assurance	-0.59^b	-1.31^c	-2.29^d	-1.08^b	-2.83^c	-1.49^b	-1.15^b
Empathy	-0.50^b	-1.38^c	-1.94^c	-1.03^b	-2.77^c	-1.62^b	-1.01^b
Combined scale	-0.32^b	-1.10^c	-1.79^d	-0.83^b	-2.27^c	-1.29^b	-0.83^c
Sample size	60	112	28	183	17	50	149
Repair and maintenance company							
Tangibles	-0.15^b	$-0.40^{b,c}$	-0.86^c	-0.36^b	-0.85^b	-0.58^b	-0.34^b
Reliability	-0.48^b	-1.30^c	-3.20^d	-1.14^b	-3.48^c	-2.14^b	-1.18^c
Responsiveness	-0.08^b	-1.08^c	-2.41^d	-0.83^b	-2.54^c	-1.71^b	-0.80^c
Assurance	-0.33^b	-1.35^c	-2.84^d	-1.16^b	-2.91^c	-2.04^b	-1.13^c
Empathy	0.15^b	-1.11^c	-2.17^d	-0.85^b	-2.19^c	-1.67^b	-0.74^c
Combined scale	-0.16^b	-1.07^c	-2.30^d	-0.88^b	-2.40^c	-1.65^b	-0.85^c
Sample size	45	114	40	168	30	65	132
Long distance telephone company							
Tangibles	-0.08^b	-0.44^c	-0.50^c	-0.26^b	-0.95^c	-0.42^b	-0.26^b
Reliability	-0.45^b	-1.42^c	-2.53^d	-1.05^b	-2.71^c	-1.54^b	-1.03^c
Responsiveness	-0.30^b	-1.43^c	-1.90^c	-1.00^b	-2.03^c	-1.46^b	-0.86^c
Assurance	-0.39^b	-1.45^c	-2.10^d	-1.00^b	-2.64^c	-1.62^b	-0.87^c
Empathy	-0.33^b	-1.19^c	-2.10^d	-0.86^b	-2.34^c	-1.16^b	-0.90^b
Combined scale	-0.30^b	-1.15^c	-1.83^d	-0.83^b	-2.13^c	-1.24^b	-0.76^c
Sample size	69	104	25	178	19	78	120

[a] Numbers are *mean values* on a scale ranging from -6 to $+6$, on which zero implies that consumer perceptions and expectations coincide, negative values imply that perceptions fall short of expectations, and positive values imply that perceptions exceed expectations.

[b,c,d] Means with the *same* superscripts are not significantly different. Means with *different* superscripts are significantly different.

APPLICATIONS OF SERVQUAL

It is difficult to identify any retailers that offer no services whatsoever. Some retailers offer facilitating services, such as sales assistance and delivery, to help sell goods. Some retailers sell services directly, in addition to offering facilitating services. Some retailers sell only services. Quality of service is an important issue for all these retailers. Competing goods retailers (department stores, supermarkets) may sell many identical products and quality of service is a primary means of competitive differentiation. Retailers that sell any services (telephone companies, airlines) have little to offer if their service is poor (Berry, 1986).

SERVQUAL is a concise multiple-item scale with good reliability and validity that retailers can use to better understand the service expectations and perceptions of consumers and, as a result, improve service. The instrument has been designed to be applicable across a broad spectrum of services. As such, it provides a basic skeleton through its expectations/perceptions format encompassing statements for each of the five service-quality dimensions. The skeleton, when necessary, can be adapted or supplemented to fit the characteristics or specific research needs of a particular organization.

SERVQUAL is most valuable when it is used periodically to track service quality trends, and when it is used in conjunction with other forms of service quality measurement. A retailer, for example, would learn a great deal about its service quality and what needs to be done to improve it by administering both SERVQUAL and an employee survey three or four times a year, plus systematically soliciting and analyzing customer suggestions and complaints. The employee survey should include questions concerning perceived impediments to better service, e.g. what is the biggest problem you face trying to deliver high-quality service to your customers? If you could be president for a day, what one change would you make in the company to improve quality of service?

SERVQUAL can be used to assess a firm's quality along each of the five service dimensions by averaging the difference scores on items making up the dimensions. It can also provide an overall measure of service quality in the form of an average score across all five dimensions. Because meaningful responses to the perception statements require respondents to have some knowledge of or experience with the firm being researched, SERVQUAL is limited to current or past customers of that firm. Within this constraint, a variety of potential applications are available.

One potential application of SERVQUAL is to determine the *relative importance* of the five dimensions in influencing customers' overall quality perceptions. An approach for doing this is to regress the overall quality perception scores on the SERVQUAL scores for the individual dimensions. The results of such a regression analysis for the four companies in the present study are shown in Table 6 (the dependent variable was overall Q, coded as excellent = 4, good = 3, fair = 2, and poor = 1).

The adjusted R^2 values are statistically significant in all four cases and are also quite respectable, particularly in view of the fact that the dependent variable had only four categories, and the first three accounted for most of the responses. A striking result in terms of the relative importance of the five dimensions in predicting overall quality in that reliability is consistently the most critical dimension. Assurance is the second most important dimension in all four cases. Tangibles is more important in

Table 6. Relative importance of the five dimensions in predicting overall quality

Dimension	Standardized slope coefficient	Significance level of slope[a]	Adjusted R^2
Bank			
Tangibles	.13	.07	.28 ($p < .00$)
Reliability	.39	.00	
Responsiveness	.07	.35	
Assurance	.13	.09	
Empathy	.01	.89	
Credit card company			
Tangibles	.07	.26	.27 ($p < .00$)
Reliability	.33	.00	
Responsiveness	.12	.11	
Assurance	.17	.02	
Empathy	.04	.58	
Repair and maintenance company			
Tangibles	.04	.48	.52 ($p < .00$)
Reliability	.54	.00	
Responsiveness	.11	.09	
Assurance	.16	.02	
Empathy	.01	.81	
Long-distance telephone company			
Tangibles	.08	.17	.37 ($p < .00$)
Reliability	.45	.00	
Responsiveness	.12	.09	
Assurance	.15	.03	
Empathy	.02	.78	

[a] Significance levels are for two-tailed tests.

the case of the bank than in the other three firms, while the reverse is true for responsiveness. Empathy is the least important dimension in all four cases. However, the relatively small magnitudes of the regression coefficients for empathy and their lack of statistical significance should be interpreted with caution because empathy did have a statistically significant simple correlation with overall quality, ranging from .20 in the case of the bank to .40 in the case of the repair and maintenance company. Empathy also had significant correlations of the same order of magnitude with reliability and assurance (the two most important dimensions), thereby implying that its importance in the regression analyses may have been masked somewhat by possible multicollinearity. Therefore, while empathy is apparently the least important of the five SERVQUAL dimensions, it is by no means *un*important.

Another application of the instrument is its use in categorizing a firm's customers into several perceived-quality segments (e.g. high, medium, and low) on the basis of their individual SERVQUAL scores. These segments then can be analyzed on the basis of (1) demographic, psychographic and/or other profiles; (2) the relative importance of the five dimensions in influencing service quality perceptions; and (3) the reasons behind the perceptions reported. For example, suppose a department store found that a large number of SERVQUAL respondents falling in the 'medium' perceived-quality group fit its prime target market based on demographic and psychographic criteria. Suppose further that reliability and assurance were found to be the most important quality dimensions and, based on perception-expectation gap scores for items concerning these dimensions, the items relating to record-keeping accuracy and behavior of contact personnel revealed the biggest gaps. With these data, the department store's management would understand better what needs to be done to improve its image in the eyes of a very important group – customers within the firm's prime target markets who give the firm 'medium' service quality scores and who are in position to either respond to improved service from the firm or defect to the competition.

SERVQUAL can also be used by multi-unit retail companies to track the level of service provided by each store in the chain. By asking respondents to indicate the particular store in the chain with which they are most familiar, and to provide perceptions responses for that unit, the researcher can compare each store's average SERVQUAL score with the scores from other stores. Service quality scores can then be a factor in store manager performance appraisals and compensation, among other uses. Also, SERVQUAL scores for the individual stores can be used to group outlets into several clusters with varying quality images. A careful examination of the characteristics of the stores in the different clusters may reveal key attributes that facilitate – or hinder – the delivery of high quality service.

A retailer can also use SERVQUAL to assess its service performance relative to its principal competitors. The two-section format of the instrument, with separate expectation and perception sections, makes it convenient to measure the quality of several firms simply by including a set of perception statements for each firm. The expectations section does not have to be repeated for each firm. For example, a supermarket chain could include its two principal competitors in a total market survey, asking respondents to provide perception ratings for each of the companies with which they have shopping experience. A retailer that uses SERVQUAL to identify the most salient service quality dimensions for its target markets, and to compare itself to the competition in terms of strengths and weaknesses on these particular dimensions, will certainly have a sense of what its priorities should be with regard to service quality.

In summary, SERVQUAL has a variety of potential applications. It can help a wide range of service and retailing organizations in assessing consumer expectations about and perceptions of service quality. It can also help in pinpointing areas requiring managerial attention and action to improve service quality. In addition, we hope the availablility of this instrument will stimulate much-needed empirical research focusing on service, quality and its antecedents and consequences.

ACKNOWLEDGEMENT

The research reported in this article was made possible by a grant from the Marketing Science Institute, Cambridge, MA.

APPENDIX: THE SERVQUAL INSTRUMENT[a]

Directions: This survey deals with your opinions of _____ services. Please show the extent to which you think firms offering _____ services should possess the features described by each statement. Do this by picking one of the seven numbers next to each statement. If you strongly agree that these firms should possess a feature, circle the number 7. If you strongly disagree that these firms should possess a feature, circle 1. If your feelings are not strong, circle one of the numbers in the middle. There are no right or wrong answers – all we are interested in is a number that best shows your expectations about firms offering _____ services.

E1. They should have up-to-date equipment.
E2. Their physical facilities should be visually appealing.
E3. Their employees should be well dressed and appear neat.
E4. The appearance of the physical facilities of these firms should be in keeping with the type of services provided.
E5. When these firms promise to do something by a certain time, they should do so.
E6. When customers have problems, these firms should be sympathetic and reassuring.
E7. These firms should be dependable.
E8. They should provide their services at the time they promise to do so.
E9. They should keep their records accurately.
E10 They shouldn't be expected to tell customers exactly when services will be performed. (−)[b]
E11. It is not realistic for customers to expect prompt service from employees of these firms.(—)
E12. Their employees don't always have to be willing to help customers.(−)
E13. It is okay if they are too busy to respond to customer requests promptly.(−)
E14. Customers should be able to trust employees of these firms.
E15. Customers should be able to feel safe in their transactions with these firms' employees.
E16. Their employees should be polite.
E17. Their employees should get adequate support from these firms to do their jobs well.
E18. These firms should not be expected to give customers individual attention.(−)
E19. Employees of these firms cannot be expected to give customers personal attention.(−)
E20. It is unrealistic to expect employees to know what the needs of their customers are.(−)
E21. It is unrealistic to expect these firms to have their customers' best interest at heart.(−)
E22. They shouldn't be expected to have operating hours convenient to all their customers.(−)

Directions: The following set of statements relate to your feelings about XYZ. For each statement, please show the extent to which you believe XYZ has the feature described by the statement. Once again, circling a 7 means that you strongly agree that XYZ has that feature, and circling a 1 means that you strongly disagree. You may circle any of the numbers in the middle that show how strongly your feelings are. There are no right or wrong answers – all we are interested in is a number that best shows your perceptions about XYZ.

P1. XYZ has up-to-date equipment.
P2. XYZ's physical facilities are visually appealing.
P3. XYZ's employees are well dressed and appear neat.
P4. The appearance of the physical facilities of XYZ is in keeping with the type of services provided.
P5. When XYZ promises to do something by a certain time, it does so.
P6. When you have problems. XYZ is sympathetic and reassuring.
P7. XYZ is dependable.
P8. XYZ provides its service at the time it promises to do so.
P9. XYZ keeps it records accurately.
P10. XYZ does not tell customers exactly when services will be performed.(−)

P11.   You do not receive prompt service from XYZ's employees. ($-$)
P12.   Employees of XYZ are not always willing to help customers. ($-$)
P13.   Employees of XYZ are too busy to respond to customer requests promptly. ($-$)
P14.   You can trust employees of XYZ.
P15.   You feel safe in your transactions with XYZ's employees.
P16.   Employees of XYZ are polite.
P17.   Employees get adequate support from XYZ to do their jobs well.
P18.   XYZ does not give you individual attention. ($-$)
P19.   Employees of XYZ do not give you personal attention. ($-$)
P20.   Employees of XYZ do not know what your needs are. ($-$)
P21.   XYZ does not have your best interests at heart. ($-$)
P22.   XYZ does not have operating hours convenient to all their customers. ($-$)

[a] A seven-point scale ranging from 'Strongly Agree' (7) to 'Strongly Disagree' (1), with no verbal labels for the intermediate scale points (i.e. 2 through 6), accompanied each statement. Also, the statements were in random order in the questionnaire. A complete listing of the 34-item instrument used in the second stage of data collection can be obtained from the first author.
[b] Ratings on these statements were reverse-scored prior to data analysis.

REFERENCES

Berry, L. L. (1986) 'Retail Businesses Are Service Businesses'. *Journal of Retailing* **62** (Spring): 3–6.

Campbell, D. T. (1960) 'Recommendation for APA Test Standards Regarding Construct, Trait or Discriminant Validity'. *American Psychologist* **15** (August): 546–553.

Churchill, A., Jr (1979) 'A Paradigm for Developing Better Measures of Marketing Constructs', *Journal of Marketing Research,* **16** (February), 64–73.

Churchill, G. A., Jr., Ford, N. M. and Walker, O. C. Jr. (1974) 'Measuring the Job Satisfaction of Industrial Salesmen'. *Journal of Marketing Research* **11** (August): 254–260.

Cronbach, L. J. (1951) 'Coefficient Alpha and the Internal Structure of Tests'. *Psychometrika* **16** (October): 297–334.

Crosby, P. B. (1979) *Quality is Free: The Art of Making Quality Certain.* New York: New American Library.

Dodds, W. B. and Monroe, K. B. (1984) 'The Effects of Brand and Price Information on Subjective Product Evaluations'. *Advances in Consumer Research XII.*

Ford, N. M., Walker, O. C, Jr. and Churchill, G. A., Jr. (1975) 'Expectation-Specific Measures of the Intersender Conflict and Role Ambiguity Experienced by Industrial Salesmen'. *Journal of Business Research.* **3** (April): 95–112.

Garvin, D. A. (1983) 'Quality on the Line'. *Harvard Business Review.* **61** (September–October): 65–73.

Gronroos, C. (1982) *Strategic Management and Marketing in the Service Sector.* Helsingfors: Swedish School of Economics and Business Administration.

Harman, Harry, H. (1967) *Modern Factor Analysis,* 2nd edn. Chicago: The University of Chicago Press.

Hjorth-Anderson, C. (1984) 'The Concept of Quality and Efficiency of Markets for Consumer Products. *Journal of Consumer Research* **11** (September): 708–718.

Holbrook, M. B. and Corfman, K. P. (1985) 'Quality and Value in the Consumption Experience: Phaldrus Rides Again'. In *Perceived Quality* (J. Jacoby and J. Olson, Eds). Lexington, Massachusetts: Lexington Books, pp. 31–57.

Howard, J. and Sheth, J. (1969) *The Theory of Buyer Behavior.* New York: John Wiley and Sons.

Hunt, K. (1979) *Conceptualization and Measurement of Consumer Satisfaction and Dissatisfaction.* Cambridge, Mass: Marketing Science Institute.

Jacoby, J. (1978) 'Consumer Research: A State of the Art Review' *Journal of Marketing* **42** (April): 87–96.

Jacoby, J. and Olson, J. (Eds) (1985) *Perceived Quality.* Lexington, Massachusetts: Lexington Books.

Lehtinen, U. and Lehtinen, J. R. (1982) 'Service Quality: A Study of Quality Dimensions'. Unpublished working paper, Helsinki: Service Management Institute, Finland OY.

Lovelock, C. H. (1980) 'Toward a Classification of Services'. In *Emerging Perspectives on Service Marketing* (L. L. Berry, G. L. Shostack, G. Upah, Eds). Chicago: American Marketing Association, pp. 72–76.

Lovelock, C. H. (1983) 'Classifying Services to Gain Strategic Marketing Insights'. *Journal of Marketing* 47 (Summer): 9–20.

Nunnally, J. C. (1978) *Psychometric Theory*, 2nd edn. New York: McGraw Hill Book Company.

Oliver, R. (1981) 'Measurement and Evaluation of Satisfaction Process in Retail Settings'. *Journal of Retailing* 57 (Fall): 25–48.

Olshavsky, R. W. (1985) Perceived Quality in Consumer Decision Making: An Integrated Theoretical Perspective. In *Perceived Quality* (J. Jacoby and J. Olson, Eds.). Lexington, Massachusetts: Lexington Books.

Parasuraman, A., Zeithaml, V. and Berry, L. (1985) 'A Conceptual Model of Service Quality and Its Implications for Future Research'. *Journal of Marketing* (Fall): 41–50.

Peter, J. P. (1981) 'Construct Validity: A Review of Basic Issues and Marketing Practices'. *Journal of Marketing Research* 18 (May): 133–145.

Rudie, M. J. and Wansley, H. B. (1985) 'The Merrill Lynch Quality Program'. In *Services Marketing in a Changing Environment* (T. Bloch, G. Upah, and V. A. Zeithaml, eds). Chicago, IL: American Marketing Association.

Sasser, W. E. Jr., Olsen, R. P. and Wyckoff, D. D. (1978) *Management of Service Operations: Text and Cases.* Boston: Allyn & Bacon.

Saxe, R. and Weitz, B. A. (1982) 'The SOCO Scale: A Measure of the Customer Orientation of Salespeople'. *Journal of Marketing,* 19 (August): 343–351.

Thompson, P., DeSouza, G. and Gale, B. T. (1985) *The Strategic Management of Service Quality.* Cambridge, MA: The Strategic Planning Institute, PIMSLETTER No. 33.

Zeithaml, V. (1987) *Defining and Relating Price, Perceived Quality, and Perceived Value,* Report No. 87–101. Cambridge, MA: Marketing Science Institute.

12

Measuring Service Quality:
A Reexamination and Extension

J. Joseph Cronin Jr. and Steven A. Taylor

Service industries are playing an increasingly important role in the overall economy of the United States (Bateson, 1989; Ginzberg and Vojta, 1981; Koepp, 1987). In fact, the proportion of the US population employed in the service sector increased from 30% in 1900 to 74% in 1984 (Bateson, 1989). Koepp (1987) suggests that this sector is continuing to increase, as 85% of all the new jobs created since 1982 have been in service industries. Bateson (1989) further suggests that the growing importance of the service sector is not limited to the United States, as services currently account for 58% of the total worldwide GNP. There even appears to be executive consensus in the United States that service quality is one of the most important problems facing management today (Blackiston, 1988; Cound, 1988; Cravens, 1988; Langevin, 1988; Sherden, 1988).

Interest in the measurement of service quality is thus understandably high and the delivery of higher levels of service quality is the strategy that is increasingly being offered as a key to service providers' efforts to position themselves more effectively in the marketplace (cf. Brown and Swartz, 1989; Parasuraman, Zeithaml and Berry, 1988; Rudie and Wansley, 1985; Thompson, DeSouza and Gale, 1985). However, the problem inherent in the implementation of such strategy has been eloquently identified by several researchers: service quality is an elusive and abstract construct that is difficult to define and measure (Brown and Swartz, 1989; Carman, 1990; Crosby, 1979; Garvin, 1983; Parasuraman, Zeithaml and Berry, 1985, 1988; Rathmell, 1966). In addition, to date the important relationships between service quality, customer satisfaction, and purchasing behavior remain largely unexplored.

Our research has two objectives. First, we suggest that the current conceptualization and operationalization of service quality (SERVQUAL) is inadequate. The SERVQUAL scale is based on Parasuraman, Zeithaml and Berry's (1985) gap theory, which suggests that the difference between consumer's expectations about the performance of a general class of service providers and their assessment of the actual performance of a specific firm within that class drives the perception of service quality. However, little if any theoretical or empirical evidence supports the relevance of the

Reprinted with permission from *Journal of Marketing*, Vol. 56, July, pp. 55–68.

expectations–performance gap as the basis for measuring service quality (Carman, 1990). In fact, the marketing literature appears to offer considerable support for the superiority of simple performance-based measures of service quality (cf. Bolton and Drew, 1991a,b; Churchill and Suprenant, 1982; Mazis, Ahtola and Klippel, 1975; Woodruff, Cadotte and Jenkins, 1983). We therefore develop and test a performance-based alternative to the SERVQUAL measure.

The second objective is to examine the relationships between service quality, consumer satisfaction, and purchase intentions. Though these relationships have been discussed theoretically (cf. Bitner, 1990; Bolton and Drew, 1991a,b; Brown and Swartz, 1989; Parasuraman, Zeithaml and Berry, 1988; Zeithaml, Parasuraman and Berry, 1990), they have not been subjected to a thorough empirical test. In particular, the purpose of the second phase of our study is to provide managers and researchers more information about (1) the causal order of the relationship between service quality and customer satisfaction and (2) the impact of service quality and customer satisfaction on purchase intentions. Simply stated, the managers of service providers need to know how to measure service quality, what aspects of a particular service best define its quality, and whether consumers actually purchase from firms that have the highest level of perceived service quality or from those with which they are most 'satisified'.

After presenting theoretical background, we describe our research methods and results. We then discuss our findings and explore their implications for management and for future research. Finally, we examine the limitations of our study.

THEORETICAL BACKGROUND

Service quality has been described as a form of attitude, related by not equivalent to satisfaction, that results from the comparison of expectations with performance (Bolton and Drew, 1991a; Parasuraman, Zeithaml and Berry, 1988). A close examination of this definition suggests ambiguity between the definition and the conceptualization of service quality. Though researchers admit that the current measurement of consumers' perceptions of service quality closely conforms to the disconfirmation paradigm (Bifner, 1990; Bolton and Drew, 1991a), they also suggest that service quality and satisfaction are distinct constructs (Bitner, 1990; Bolton and Drew, 1991a,b; Parasuraman, Zeithaml and Berry, 1988). The most common explanation of the difference between the two is that perceived service quality is a form of attitude a long-run overall evaluation, whereas satisfaction is a transaction-specific measure (Bitner, 1990; Bolton and Drew, 1991a; Parasuraman, Zeithaml and Berry, 1988). Parasuraman et al. (1988) further suggest that the difference lies in the way disconfirmation is operationalized. They state that in measuring perceived service quality the level of comparison is what consumer *should* expect, whereas in measures of satisfaction the appropriate comparison is what a consumer *would* expect. However, such a differentiation appears to be inconsistent with Woodruff, Cadotte and Jenkins' (1983) suggestion that expectations should be based on experience norms – what consumer *should* expect from a given service provider given their experience with that specific type of service organization.

Thus, the service literature has left confusion as to the relationship between consumer satisfaction and service quality. This distinction is important to managers and researchers alike because service providers need to know whether their objective should be to have consumers who are 'satisfied' with their performance or to deliver the maximum level of 'perceived service quality'. The importance of this issue has led to several recent efforts to clarify the relationship between satisfaction and service quality (cf. Bitner, 1990; Bolton and Drew, 1991a,b; Parasuraman, Zeithaml and Berry, 1985, 1988).

Initially Parasuraman *et al.* (1985, 1988) proposed that higher levels of perceived service quality result in increased consumer satisfaction, but more recent evidence suggests that satisfaction is an antecedent of service quality (cf. Bitner, 1990; Bolton and Drew, 1991a,b). In particular, Bitner has demonstrated empirically a significant causal path between satisfaction and service quality in a structural equation analysis. In a second study, Bolton and Drew (1991a) used the common assumption that service quality is analogous to an attitude as a basis to suggest that satisfaction is an antecedent of service quality. Specifically, Bolton and Drew posit that perceived service quality ($ATTITUDE_t$) is a function of a consumer's residual perception of the service's quality from the prior period ($ATTITUDE_{t-1}$) and his or her level of (dis)satisfaction with the current level of service performance (CS/D_t^1)[1]. This notion suggests that satisfaction is a distinct construct that mediates prior perceptions of service quality to form the current perception of service quality.

$$ATTITUDE_t = g(CS/D_t, ATTITUDE_{t-1}) \qquad (1)$$

Bolton and Drew (1991a) indicates this relation implies that the disconfirmation process, expectations and performance all should have a significant impact on consumers' current perceptions of service quality. However, their results suggest that perceived service quality is strongly affected by current performance and that the impact of disconfirmation is relatively weak and transitory.

Finally, Bolton and Drew (1991b) extend the discussion of the relationship between satisfaction and service quality by proposing the following structural equations.

$$Service\ Quality = q_o\ (CS/D_t, Disconfirmation) \qquad (2)$$

$$CS/D_t = c(Disconfirmation, Expectations, Performance) \qquad (3)$$

To gain more insight into Bolton and Drew's findings, and into how service quality should be measured, we next briefly examine the satisfaction and attitude literatures.

Implications from the satisfaction and attitude literatures

A major problem in the literature is the hesitancy to call perceived service quality an attitude. The literature's position is typified by Parasuraman, Zeithaml and Berry's (1988) description of service quality as '...similar in many ways to an attitude' (p. 15). Researchers have attempted to differentiate service quality from consumer satisfaction, even while using the disconfirmation format to measure perceptions of service quality (cf. Bitner, 1990; Carman, 1990; Grönroos, 1990; Heskett, Sasser and Hart, 1990; Parasuraman, Zeithaml and Berry, 1988; Zeithaml, Parasuraman and

---

[1] CS/D_t = Consumer Satisfaction/Dissatisfaction.

Berry, 1990). However, this approach is not consistent with the differentiation expressed between these constructs in the satisfaction and attitude literatures.

Oliver (1980) suggests that attitude (ATT) is initially a function of expectations (EXP) [$ATT_{t1} = f(EXP)$] and subsequently a function of the prior attitude toward and the present level of satisfaction (SAT) with a product or service [ATT_{t2} $f(ATT_{t1}$, $SAT_{t2})$]. Purchase intentions (PI) then are considered initially to be a function of an individual's attitude toward a product or service [PI_{t1} $f(ATT_{t1})$], but subject to modification due to the mediating effect on prior attitude of the satisfaction inherent in subsequent usages [PI_{t2} $f(ATT_{t2})$ $f(ATT_{t1}$, $SAT_{t2})$]. Thus, Oliver suggests that consumers form an attitude about a service provider on the basis of their prior expectations about the performance of the firm, and this attitude affects their intentions to purchase from that organization. This attitude then is modified by the level of (dis)satisfaction experienced by the consumer during subsequent encounters with the firm. The revised attitude becomes the relevant input for determining a consumer current purchase intentions.

If one considers service quality to be an attitude, Oliver's (1980) study suggests that (1) in the absence of prior experience with a service provider, expectations initially define the level of perceived service quality, (2) upon the first experience with the service provider, the disconfirmation process leads to a revision in the initial level of perceived service quality, (3) subsequent experiences with the service provider will lead to further disconfirmation, which again modifies the level of perceived service quality, and (4) the redefined level of perceived quality similarly modifies a consumer's purchase intentions toward that service provider.

Hence, Oliver's research suggests that service quality and consumer satisfaction are distinct constructs, but are related in that satisfaction mediates the effect of prior-period perceptions of service quality to cause a revised service quality perception to be formed. Satisfaction thus rapidly becomes part of the reviewed perception of service quality. This logic is consistent with Bolton and Drew's (1991a) findings and also calls into question the use of the disconfirmation framework as the primary measure of service quality, because disconfirmation appears only to mediate, not define, consumers' perception of service quality.

If in fact service quality is to be conceptualized as 'similar to an attitude', perhaps more information could be generated for managers and researchers alike if the measurement of the construct conformed to an attitude-based conceptualization. A review of alternative attitude models suggests that the 'adequacy-importance' forms is the most efficient model to use if the objective is to predict behavioral intention or actual behavior (Mazis, Ahtola and Klippel, 1975). In this models, an individual's attitude is defined by his or her importance-weighted evaluation of the performance of the specific dimensions of a product or service (see Cohen, Fishbein and Ahtola, 1972). However, experimental evidence indicates that the performance dimension alone predicts behavioral intentions and behavior at least as well as the complete models (Mazis, Ahtola and Klippel, 1975). This finding suggests using only performance perceptions as a measure of service quality.

A study by Churchill and Surprenant (1982) also partially supports the efficacy of using only performance perceptions to measure service quality. They conducted two experiments to examine the effects of expectations, performance, and disconfirmation on satisfaction. The results of one experiment suggested that performance alone determines the satisfaction of subjects, Woodruff, Cadotte and Jenkins (1983) contribute additional support for performance only measures of attitude. Again using the 'adequacy importance model, they indicate that assimilation contrast theory suggests that consumers may raise or lower their performance beliefs on the basis of how closely perceived performance approximates expected performance. Thus, they suggest that including importance weights and expectations only introduces redundancy. From the results of a field experiment, Bolton and Drew (1991a) also conclude the current performance ratings strongly affect attitudes whereas the effects of disconfirmation are generally insignificant and transitory. This study is particularly significant because the attitude examined is customers' perceptions of the quality inherent in a service.

Thus, the conclusion of the satisfaction and attitude literatures appear to be that (1) perceived service quality is best conceptualized as an attitude, (2) the 'adequacy-importance' model is the most effective 'attitude-based' operationalization of service quality, and (3) current performance adequately captures consumers' perceptions of the service quality offered by a specific service provider. In addition to the theoretical support for performance-based measures of service quality, practitioners often measure the determinants of overall satisfaction/perceived quality by having customers simply assess the performance of the company's business processes. Furthermore, the performance-based approach may actually be more in line with an antecedent/consequent conceptualization: that is, judgements of service quality and satisfaction appear to follow the evaluation of service provider's performance. The first objective of our study is to examine these conclusions empirically by testing a performance-based measure of service quality as an alternative to the current disconfirmation-based SERVQUAL scale.

Operationalizing service quality

The current measurement of perceived service quality can be traced to the research of Parasuraman, Zeithaml and Berry. These authors originally identified 10 determinants of service quality based on a series of focus group sessions (1985). They subsequently developed SERVQUAL (1988), which recasts the 10 determinants into five specific components: tangibles, reliability, responsiveness, assurance, and empathy (Figure 1).

The basis for identifying these five components was a factor analysis of the 22-item scale (see Appendix) developed from focus groups and from the specific industry applications undertaken by the authors (see Parasuraman, Zeithaml and Berry, 1985, 1988; and Zeithaml, Parasuraman and Berry, 1990 for a comprehensive review).

The scale development procedures employed appear to support the face validity of the 22 scale items (individual questions) included in the scale, but the issue of how the service quality measure should be constructed and whether the individual scale items actually describe five separate service quality components is problematic. In fact, some empirical evidence suggests that the proposed delineation of the five components is not consistent when subjected to cross-sectional analysis (Carman, 1990). Specifically, Carman found that some of the items did not load on the same component when compared across different types of service providers. However,

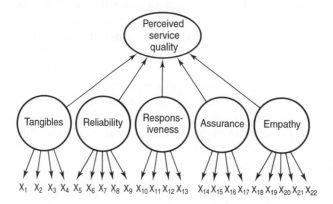

Figure 1. Service quality as conceptualized by Parasuraman, Zeithaml and Berry (1988).

though the veracity of conceptualizing the SERVQUAL scale as consisting of the five distinct components identified by Parasuraman, Zeithaml and Berry (1988) has been questioned (Carman, 1990), the validity of the 22 individual performance scale items that make up the SERVQUAL scale appears to be well supported, both by the procedures used to develop the items and by their subsequent use as reported in the literature (cf. Carman, 1990). We therefore conclude that these 22 performance items adequately define the domain of service quality and we use the same performance items to examine the proposed alternative to the SERVQUAL scale and in the analyses of the relationships between service quality, consumer satisfaction, and purchase intentions.

Research models and propositions

We investigate four specific questions that correspond to the three research steps identified in the Methods section. The first question is directed at the measurement of the service quality construct. Specifically, the ability of the more concise performance-only scale suggested by the literature review (SERVPERF, equation 6) is compared with that of three alternatives: SERVQUAL (equation 4), weighted SERVQUAL (equation 5), and weighted SERVPERF (equation 7).

$$\text{Service Quality} = (\text{Performance} - \text{Expectations}) \tag{4}$$

$$\text{Service Quality} = \text{Importance}* (\text{Performance} - \text{Expectations}) \tag{5}$$

$$\text{Service Quality} = (\text{Performance}) \tag{6}$$

$$\text{Service Quality} = \text{Importance}* (\text{Performance}) \tag{7}$$

The first proposition provides the basis for our investigation:

P_1: An unweighted performance-based measure of service quality (unweighted SERVPERF) is a more appropriate basis for measuring service quality than SERVQUAL, weighted SERVQUAL, or weighted SERVPERF.

The evaluation P_1 calls for an assessment of whether the addition of the importance weights suggested by Zeithaml, Parasuraman and Berry (1990) improves the ability of the SERVQUAL and SERVPERF scales to measure service quality and a direct comparison of the two measurement approaches. On the basis of the findings by Bolton and Drew (1991a), and the attitude and satisfaction literatures reviewed previously, the addition of importance weights is not expected to improve either scale and the SERVPERF alternative is expected to outperform the SERVQUAL scale.

The structural models identified in Figure 2 are used to further the consideration of the SERVQUAL and SERVPERF scales as well as to consider the three remaining research questions. As discussed in the literature review, the SERVPERF scale appears to conform more closely to the implications of the satisfaction and attitude literatures. Therefore, we propose that the model incorporating SERVPERF (model 2) will have a better fit (as measured by the chi square statistic and the measurement model's adjusted goodness of fit) because the performance-only form is more consistent with established theory (cf. Mazis, Ahtola and Klippel, 1975) and hence the SERVPERF measurement model should more closely approximate the theoretical model identified in Figure 2.

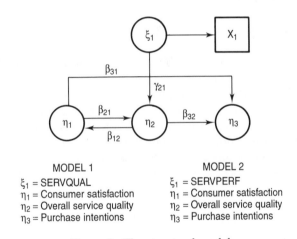

MODEL 1
ξ_1 = SERVQUAL
η_1 = Consumer satisfaction
η_2 = Overall service quality
η_3 = Purchase intentions

MODEL 2
ξ_1 = SERVPERF
η_1 = Consumer satisfaction
η_2 = Overall service quality
η_3 = Purchase intentions

Figure 2. The structural models.

The second objective of our study is to examine the relationships between service quality, consumer satisfaction, and purchase intentions. The following three additional propositions identify the questions addressed in this part of the study.

P_2: Customer satisfaction is an antecedent of perceived service quality.

P_3: Consumer satisfaction has a significant impact on purchase intentions.

P_4: Perceived service quality has a significant impact on purchase intentions.

The first question considered is the causal order of the perceived service quality–satisfaction relationship (P_2). This analysis is also based on a consideration of the structural models identified in Figure 2. Specifically, P_2 proposes that the path (B_{21}) showing consumer satisfaction as an antecedent of service quality should have a statistically significant ($p \leq .05$) LISREL estimate whereas the estimate of the reverse path (satisfaction as an outcome of service quality, B_{12}) should not be significant (cf. Bitner, 1990; Bolton and Drew, 1991a,b).

The next question investigated is whether consumers' level of satisfaction with a service provider affects their purchase intentions toward that firm (P_3). Again, the structural models are used to investigate this proposition. Specifically, in models that confirm (i.e., the theoretical model is not rejected), the LISREL estimate for the path linking satisfaction and purchase intention (B_{31}) is examined to determine whether the effect is significant ($p \leq .05$).

The final question addressed is whether consumers' perceptions of service quality affect their purchase intentions (P_4). The investigation of this proposition is identical to that of P_3 but the path of interest is between service quality and purchase intentions (B_{32}).

METHODS

Organization of the research

Step 1: Examining the dimensionality of SERVQUAL

In this step, the confirmatory factor analysis capabilities of LISREL VII were used to determine whether the 22 items that define the SERVQUAL scale have the same factor loading pattern for the firms investigated was found by Parasuraman, Zeithaml and Berry (1988). To the extent that similar factor structures are identified (see Figure 1), evidence of the responsibility of the SERVQUAL scale is produced. If the five-component structure is not confirmed, the OBLIMIN factor analysis procedure in SPSS-X and a reliability analysis can be used to assess the dimensionality and reliability of the items.

Step 2: Comparison of alternative measures of service quality

On the basis of the theoretical concerns discussed previously, we assessed three alternatives to the SERVQUAL scale. Specifically, in this step we examined the original SERVQUAL scale (equation 4), an importance-weighted SERVQUAL scale (equation 5), a performance-based approach to the measurement of service quality (SERVPERF, equation 6), and an importance-weighted version of the SERVPERF scale (equation 7). This examination proceeded in two stages. First, the ability of each of the four scales to explain variation in service quality was assessed by regressing the individual items comprising each of the alternative scales against a measure of the respondents' perceptions of the overall quality inherent in the services offered by the eight firms included in the sample (see Appendix, variable 85).

Second, each measure's theoretical support was examined in an analysis of the structural models identified in Figure 2. Specifically of interest were (1) the degree of fit of the respective models and (2) the significance of the effect on service quality attributed to each of the alternative measures (i.e. the significance of the path between the perceived service quality scale used and the overall measure of the service quality, path γ_{21}).

Step 3: Analysis of relationship between service quality, consumer satisfaction and purchase intention

The third step extended the research beyond the question of which approach to the measurement of service quality is the most appropriate. Here we considered (1) the causal order of the consumer satisfaction–service quality relationship, (2) the effect of consumer satisfaction on purchase intentions, and (3) the effect of service quality on purchase intentions. These relationships were also investigated through the analysis of the structural models identified in Figure 2. Specifically, we investigated each relationship by examining the significance of the LISREL VII estimated path coefficient that links the variables noted.

The sample

Data were gathered from personal interviews conducted in a medium sized city in the southeastern United States. A total of 660 usable questionnaires (all questions answered) were gathered randomly from consumers at their residences by trained interviewers during a two-week period in the summer of 1988. The sampling frame was the entire population of the city. Interviewers were instructed to solicit responses randomly and were assigned city areas to prevent overlap.

Responses were gathered on the service quality offered by two firms in each of the four industries: banking, pest control, dry cleaning, and fast food. Because of the length of the questionnaire, respondents were asked to evaluate only one firm. The sample size for each industry was: banking 188 (firm 1, 92 and firm 2, 96); pest control 175 (firm 1, 91 and firm 2, 84); dry cleaning 178 (firm 1, 88 and firm 2, 90); fast food 189 (firm 1, 98 and firm 2, 91). The firms and industries were chosen on the basis of the results of a convenience survey suggesting that these were the four service industries most familiar to the area's consumers. The two firms chosen within each industry were those with the largest sales volume in the city where the sample was drawn (for the banks, the number of depositors was used to qualify the firms included). Respondents were screened to determine whether they had used one of the service providers included in the study within the last 30 days. This screening ensured that the respondents were familiar with the firm whose services they were asked to evaluate.

Measures

The measures needed for the study were expectations, perceptions of performance, and importance measures to construct the four alternative measures of service quality, a direct measure of service quality, a measure of consumer satisfaction, and a purchase intentions measure. The 22 expectations (see Appendix, variables E_1–E_{22}) and performance (see Appendix, variables P_1-P_{22}) items were taken directly from the SERVQUAL scale (Parasuraman, Zeithaml and Berry, 1988). The importance weights were adapted from the wording of the expectation and performance items included in the original SERVQUAL scale (see Appendix, variables I_1–I_{22}). The direct measure of the service quality was based on responses to a 7-point semantic differential question (see Appendix, variable 85). In addition, self-report measures of consumer satisfaction and purchase intentions were constructed similarly (see Appendix, variables of 87 and 84, respectively).

RESULTS

Dimensionality, reliability, and validity of service quality measures (step 1)

Dimensionality and reliability

The first step was to examine the dimensionality of the current service quality scale (SERVQUAL) by means of a confirmatory factor analysis. Table 1 gives the results of the LISREL VII-based analysis for each of the four types of service firms (banks, pest control, dry cleaning, and fast food). These results suggest that the 5-component structure proposed by Parasuraman, Zeithaml and Berry (1988) for their SERVQUAL scale (see Figure 1) is not confirmed in any of the research samples. Specifically, the chi-square statistic universally indicates a poor fit between the theoretical and measurement models for the 5-component structure. The adjusted goodness-of-fit indices (AGFI) are also not indicative of a good fit as they range from .740 to .831.

Table 1. Confirmatory factor analysis parameter estimates for 5-factor conceptualization of service quality

Parameter	Banks	Pest control	Dry cleaning	Fast food
Chi square	308.60	486.16	402.60	364.16
d.f.	204	204	204	204
p	.000	.000	.000	.000
GFI[a]	.863	.790	.819	.849
AGFI[b]	.831	.740	.776	.813
RMSR[c]	.309	.466	.381	.515

[a] Goodness of fit.
[b] Adjusted goodness of fit.
[c] Root mean square residual.

Because the 5-factor structure was not confirmed we decided to assess the unidimensionality of the 22 items. We performed a factor analysis of the SERVQUAL and SERVPERF scales using the OBLIMIN oblique factor rotation procedure in SPSS-X. All of the items loaded predictably on a single factor with the exception of item 19 (see Table 2), which loaded very weakly in the analysis of the SERVQUAL scale and had a negative loading for both scales. It was therefore dropped and coefficient alpha for both scales and all subsamples (each industry) was recalculated. As is indicated in Table 2, the reliability in every case (coefficient alpha in excess of .800) suggests that

Table 2. Factor analysis of 22 individual dimensions of service quality

	SERVQUAL				SERVPERF			
Variable	Banks	Pest control	Dry cleaning	Fast food	Banks	Pest control	Dry cleaning	Fast food
V1	.396	.697	.577	.181	.480	.820	.692	.408
V2	.397	.368	.492	.249	.463	.652	.614	.458
V3	.477	.523	.536	.339	.557	.842	.642	.499
V4	.381	.319	.398	.055	.485	.703	.640	.384
V5	.781	.741	.736	.543	.804	.831	.774	.572
V6	.728	.753	.798	.543	.726	.828	.760	.683
V7	.826	.837	.805	.748	.822	.891	.856	.669
V8	.791	.832	.789	.679	.799	.873	.785	.679
V9	.833	.694	.654	.380	.788	.835	.626	.349
V10	.346	.467	.209	.325	.355	.532	.281	.136
V11	.568	.611	.358	.657	.640	.712	.483	.607
V12	.522	.622	.499	.706	.631	.706	.539	.672
V13	.500	.556	.392	.706	.623	.789	.538	.660
V14	.572	.622	.730	.409	.685	.785	.771	.550
V15	.817	.676	.762	.595	.815	.788	.836	.665
V16	.573	.764	.740	.641	.638	.793	.803	.689
V17	.647	.608	.673	.544	.688	.702	.666	.518
V18	.535	.563	.472	.412	.620	.762	.483	.429
V19	.337	.298	.165	.027	.677	.769	.615	.474
V20	.459	.502	.399	.422	.580	.685	.490	.485
V21	.502	.571	.522	.464	.552	.670	.703	.573
V22	.272	.420	.399	.156	.345	.598	.403	.280
Eigenvalue	7.472	8.229	7.437	5.194	9.037	12.651	9.378	6.408
Coefficient alpha[a]	.890	.901	.900	.849	.925	.964	.932	.884

[a] Item V19 excluded.

both scales can be treated as unidimensional. Thus, in the analysis that follows, the 21 retained items are either summed or averaged (to develop the four service quality scales in the LISREL VII analysis of the structural models) or they are considered as one composite set of individual measures (in the stepwise regression analysis).

Validity

The primary threat to the validity of the measures used in this study is construct validity Carmmes and Zeller (1979, p. 23) state. 'Fundamentally, construct validity is concerned with the extent to which a particular measure relates to other measures consistent with theoretically derived hypotheses concerning the concepts (or constructs) that are being measured'. They further suggest that the process of construct validation is by definition theory-laden. Churchill (1979) suggests that convergence and discriminant validity should be assessed in investigations of construct validity. Convergent validity involves the extent to which a measure correlates highly with other measures designed to measure the same construct. Therefore, we examined a correlation matrix of all items tested in models 1 and 2 (see Table 3). A high correlation between the items SERVPERF, importance-weighted SERVPERF, and

Table 3. Correlation coefficients for structural models in Figure 2

	SERVQUAL	Weighted SERVQUAL	SERVPERF	Weighted SERVPERF	Overall service quality	Satisfaction	Purchase intention
SERVQUAL	1.0000						
Weighted SERVQUAL	.9787	1.0000					
SERVPERF	.8100	.7968	1.0000				
Weighted SERVPERF	.6589	.6307	.9093	1.0000			
Overall service quality	.5430	.5394	.6012	.5572	1.0000		
Satisfaction	.5605	.5559	.5978	.5513	.8175	1.0000	
Purchase intention	.3534	.3613	.3647	.3486	.5272	.5334	1.0000

service quality indicates some degree of convergent validity. Discriminant validity involves the extent to which a measure is novel and does not simply reflect some other variable. Churchill (1979) suggests assessing discriminant validity by determining whether the correlation between two different measures of the same variable is higher than the correlation between the measure of that variable and those of any other variable. Again, an examination of the correlation matrix in Table 3 indicates discriminant validity of the research variables as the three service quality scales all correlate more highly with each other than they do with other research variables (i.e. satisfaction and purchase intentions). Hence, we suggest that the proposed performance-based measures provide a more construct-valid explication of service quality because of their content validity (i.e. use of importance weights and use of performance-based measures are arguably more theoretically sound approaches) and the evidence of their discriminant validity.

Comparison of alternative measures to service quality (Step 2)

P_1 suggests that the unweighted SERVPERF scale should capture more of the variation in service quality than any of the other identical alternatives (SERVQUAL, weighted SERVQUAL, and weighted SERVPERF). The stepwise regression analysis summarized in Table 4 affirms P_1. In all of the four service industries examined, unweighted SERVPERF explains more of the variation in the global measure of service quality (see Table 4).

In addition, a comparison of the SERVQUAL and weighted SERVQUAL scales (columns 1–4 and 5–8 of Table 4) indicates that the unweighted SERVQUAL scale explains more of the variation in service quality in three of the four industries (the exception being dry cleaning). We therefore decided to use only the unweighted SERVPERF and SERVQUAL scales in the structural analysis of the relationship between these scales, service quality, consumer satisfaction, and purchase intentions because they arguably represent the best of each of the two alternative conceptualizations of service quality.

Table 4. The variation explained by the alternative measures of service quality

	SERVQUAL				Weighted SERVQUAL				SERVPERF				Weighted SERVPERF			
	Banking	Pest control	Dry cleaning	Fast food	Banking	Pest control	Dry cleaning	Fast food	Banking	Pest control	Dry cleaning	Fast food	Banking	Pest control	Dry cleaning	Fast food
V1[1]																.256[c]
V2								.164[b]				.157[b]				
V3				.143[a]												
V4		.147[a]				.227[a]			.248[c]							
V5					.194[a]											
V6	.284[c]	.200[a]	.307[c]	.255[c]	.222[b]	.186[a]	.277[b]	.282[b]	.350[c]		.380[c]		.267[b]		.240[b]	
V7	.478[c]				.452[b]		.268[b]	.234[b]	.351[b]			.407[b]	.437[b]		.242[b]	
V8		.594[c]				.614[c]				.304[b]				.346[c]		
V9		.216[a]			.248[b]			.131[a]	.231[b]				.195[a]	.193[b]		
V10																
V11			.158[a]				.268[c]			.256[a]						
V12													.253[b]			.242[b]
V13				.141[a]								.152[a]				.194[b]
V14		.352				.329[c]		.153[a]								.130[a]
V15											.191[a]					
V16			.235[b]	.187[b]				.318[a]		.175[a]	.349[c]	.165[a]			.189[a]	
V17											.219[b]			.161[a]		
V18							.135[a]									
V19			.127[a]	.163[a]					.158[b]						.164[b]	
V20					.167[b]							.141[a]	.141[a]			
V21	.189[b]					.157[a]							.181[b]			
V22		.142														
R	.46511	.36515	.30747	.41534	.44813	.36316	.36958	.38332	.47895	.38760	.44675	.47585	.40333	.33726	.43166	.46718

Where a $p < .05$
       b $p < .01$
       c $p < .001$

V1 to V22 are the alternative scale items of service quality (see Appendix A, variables P1 to P22). Entries in the cells represent correlation coefficients. All nonsignificant coefficients are omitted.
Numbers in each cell are adjusted R's.

Relationship between service quality, customer satisfaction, and purchase intentions (Step 3)

Figure 2 identifies the two models used to investigate P_2, P_3 and P_4 and to further the comparison of the performance and disconfirmation based measures of service quality (SERVPERF and SERVQUAL respectively). Models 1 and 2 are identical with the exception that SERVQUAL is used to measure service quality in model 1 whereas SERVPERF is used in model 2. The models conceptualize a nonrecursive ('two-way') relationship between service quality and satisfaction in order to test simultaneously the effects hypothesized by Parasuraman, Zeithaml and Berry (1985, 1988) (service quality is an antecedent of customer satisfaction) and by Bitner (1990) and Bolton and Drew (1991a,b) (service quality is an outcome of customer satisfaction). In addition, the model suggests that both service quality and satisfaction affect purchase intentions.

However, before considering P_2, P_3 and P_4, we assessed the fit of the two respective models to the data (see Table 5). Model 1 (SERVQUAL) had a good fit in two of the four industries (banking and fast food) whereas model 2 (SERVPERF) had an excellent fit in all four industries. Because the only difference in the two models is the measure of service quality used (either SERVQUAL or SERVPERF), these results were interpreted as additional support for the superiority of the SERVPERF approach to the measurement of service quality.

Because of this superiority, we used model 2 to assess the strength of the relationships between service quality, consumer satisfaction, and purchase intention. This analysis suggests that (1) service quality has a significant ($p < .05$) effect on consumer satisfaction in all four samples (see Table 5, model 2, path β_{12}), (2) consumer satisfaction has a significant ($p < .05$) effect on purchase intentions in all four samples (see Table 5, model 2, path β_{31}), and (3) service quality does not have a significant ($p < .05$) impact on purchase intentions in any of the samples (see Table 5, model 2, path β_{32}). Thus, P_2 and P_3 both receive strong support from the results, though the direction of the effect observed in the consideration of P_2 is the opposite of that proposed. The analysis of P_4 afforded no support for the proposed effect.

DISCUSSION

We investigated three main questions:

- How should service quality be conceptualized and measured?
- What is the causal order of the relationship between service quality and consumer satisfaction?
- What impacts do service quality and consumer satisfaction have on purchase intentions?

In answer to the first question, the literature review and empirical results both suggest that service quality should be conceptualized and measured as an attitude. The literature clearly supports the performance-only (SERVPERF) approach. In the empirical analysis, the first step calls into question the efficacy of the 5-component

Table 5. Standardized parameter estimates for causal models

Parameter	Banking		Pest control		Dry cleaning		Fast food	
	LISREL estimate	T-Value	LISREL estimate	T-Value	LISREL estimate	T-Value	LISREL estimate	T-Value
SERVQUAL model (1)								
B_{21}	1.796	1.512	2.810	1.341	8.398	-.408	-.055	-.300
B_{12}	1.113	14.794	1.099	10.620	1.103	15.256	.904	10.566
B_{31}	.668	3.712	.646	4.247	.836	4.598	.343	2.774
B_{32}	.280	1.475	.301	2.033	.099	.542	.296	2.187
γ_{21}	2.417	2.226	2.289	1.746	7.157	.452	.812	5.325
Chi square	.000	$(p=.972)$	5.090	$(p=.024)$	4.060	$(p=.044)$	6.020	$(p=.140)$
AGFI	1.000		.863		.890		.838	
RMS	.001		.068		.061		.063	
SMC-Y_1	.664		.465		.750		.647	
Y_2	3.482		7.309		58.200		.254	
Y_3	.325		.326		.409		.260	
SERVPERF model (2)								
B_{21}	1.353	1.595	1.377	1.944	2.904	.989	.141	.845
B_{12}	1.109	14.156	1.006	11.793	1.065	17.584	.944	12.787
B_{31}	.550	3.124	.659	4.323	.837	4.598	.362	2.924
B_{32}	.374	1.979	.285	1.926	.098	.535	.282	2.069
γ_{21}	2.154	2.585	1.683	3.202	3.644	1.300	1.179	6.122
Chi square	.080	$(p=.781)$	.220	$(p=.639)$	3.290	$(p=.070)$	.230	$(p=.629)$
AGFI	.998		.994		.910		.994	
RMS	.009		.012		.044		.010	
SMC-Y_1	.657		.521		.768		.652	
Y_2	2.298		1.886		7.799		.278	
Y_3	.305		.325		.412		.266	

conceptualization of service quality offered by Parasuraman, Zeithaml and Berry (1988). The second step indicates that the SERVPERF scale explains more of the variation in service quality than does SERVQUAL. Both the literature review and the analysis of the structural models (see Figure 2 and Table 5, models 1 and 2) suggest that the SERVQUAL conceptualization is in fact flawed: (1) it is based on a satisfaction paradigm rather than an attitude model and (2) the empirical analysis of the structural model suggests that the SERVQUAL model (see Figure 2 and Table 5, model 1) confirms in only two of the four industries. Thus, the weight of the evidence clearly support the use of performance based measures of service quality.

The second question investigated is the causal order of the satisfaction service quality relationship. Much of the recent literature has suggested that satisfaction is an antecedent of service quality (cf. Bitner, 1990; Bolton Drew, 1991a,b). However, the analysis of the research model indicate that this may not be the case and provides empirical support for the notion that perceived service quality in fact leads to satisfaction as proposed by Parasuraman, Zeithaml and Berry (1985, 1988).

The third question pertains to the effects of service quality and satisfaction on purchase intentions (see Figure 2 and Table 5). The analysis of the LISREL estimates (model 2, see Table 5) suggests that satisfaction has a significant ($p < .05$) effect on purchase intentions in all four samples whereas service quality does not have such an effect in any of the four industries. From the significance tests summarized in Table 5, satisfaction appears to have a stronger and more consistent effect on purchase intentions than does service quality.

CONCLUSIONS AND MANAGERIAL IMPLICATIONS

The major conclusion from our study is that marketing's current conceptualization and measurement of service quality are based on a flawed paradigm. We present empirical and literature support suggesting that service quality should be measured as an attitude. The performance-based scale developed (SERVPERF) is efficient in comparison with the SERVQUAL scale, it reduces by 50% the number of items that must be measured (44 items to 22 items). The analysis of the structural models also supports the theoretical superiority of the SERVPERF scale (see Table 5), only the model that uses the SERVPERF scale consistently confirmed (model 2). These factors, along with the failure of the 5-component SERVQUAL model to confirm (see Table 1), support the use of a performance-based measure of service quality.

The remaining questions addressed in our study are essential managerial issues. The results suggest that service quality is an antecedent of consumer satisfaction and that consumer satisfaction exerts a stronger influence on purchase intentions than does service quality. Thus, managers may need to emphasize total customer satisfaction programs over strategies centering solely on service quality. Perhaps, consumers do not necessarily buy the highest quality service; convenience, price, or availability may enhance satisfaction while not actually affecting consumers' perceptions of service quality.

Finally (see Table 4), the results from step 1 also suggest that the scale items that define service quality in one industry may be different in another. Perhaps high involvement services such as health care or financial services have different service quality definitions than low involvement services such as fast food or dry cleaning. Managers and researchers therefore must consider the individual dimensions of service quality when making cross-sectional comparisons. Managers should also be able to adjust their marketing strategies more effectively when the full set of individual scale items are considered.

IMPLICATIONS FOR FUTURE RESEARCH

Our research has only begun to address the many issues that are important in the management of services. The findings undoubtedly raise more questions than they answer, but the questions we address – how the service quality construct should be measured and how service quality is related to consumer satisfaction and purchase intentions – are arguably among the most important concerns in service marketing.

Future studies should consider other attitude-based conceptualizations and extend beyond the four service industries sampled in our study. The nature of the relationship between consumer satisfaction and service quality appears to be an area in great need of additional exploration. Investigation of the roles of satisfaction and service quality in predicting market share also appear well directed and may enhance our understanding of the role of these constructs in the formation of purchase intentions. The failure of service quality to affect purchase intentions consistently should be a concern for both managers and researchers. Perhaps consumers do not always buy the best quality service. Might they instead purchase on the basis of their assessment of the value of the service? Perhaps future research should develop measures of service performance that utilize other criteria, such as value, for determining whether a service is purchased. Finally, our study was specific to a service context. Generalizing the results to goods industries may not be possible. The ever increasing magnitude of the service sector simply underscores the need for managers and researchers alike to increase the attention directed at the important issues in the marketing of services.

LIMITATIONS

In designing our study, we attempted to minimize its limitations. However, generalizations beyond the four specific service industries investigated are tenuous. Future studies should incorporate multiple measures of all of the constructs examined. Limiting the study to the two highest market share firms in each category may also have affected the variable distribution and, hence, the importance of the predictors. In addition, with the possible exception of banking, the services investigated are all low involvement service categories. Perceived quality may play a bigger role (in comparison with satisfaction) in high involvement situations, where a firm may need to do more than simply meet customers' 'minimum requirements'. Finally, the number of constructs other researchers could add to the models examined is probably unlimited.

APPENDIX

Expectations

This survey deals with *your opinions of* ____ *services*. Please show the extent to which you think institutions offering telephone services should possess the features described in each statement. Do this by using the scale presented below. If you strongly agree that these institutions should possess a feature, place a seven on the line preceding the statement. If you strongly disagree that these institutions should possess a feature, place a one on the line. If your feelings are not strong, place one of the numbers between one and seven on the line to properly reflect the actual strength of your feelings. There are no right or wrong answers – all we are interested in is a number that best shows your Expectations about institutions offering banking services.

1	2	3	4	5	6	7
STRONGLY DISAGREE						STRONGLY AGREE

____ E1   They should have up-to-date equipment and technology.

____ E2   Their physical facilities should be visually appealing.

____ E3   Their employees should be well dressed and appear neat.

____ E4   The appearance of the physical facilities of these institutions should be in keeping with the type of service provided.

____ E5   When these institutions promise to do something by a certain time, they should do so.

____ E6   When customers have problems, these institutions should by sympathetic and reassuring.

____ E7   The institutions should be dependable.

____ E8   They should provide their services at the time they promise to do so.

____ E9   They should keep their records accurately.

____ E10 They shouldn't be expected to tell their customers exactly when services will be performed.

____ E11 It is not realistic for customers to expect prompt service from employees of these institutions.

____ E12 Their employees don't always have to be willing to help customers.

____ E13 It is okay if they are too busy to respond to customer requests promptly.

____ E14 Customer should be able to trust employees of these institutions.

____ E15 Customers should be able to feel safe in their transactions with these institutions' employees.

____ E16 Their employees should be polite.

____ E17 Their employees should get adequate support from these institutions to do their jobs well.

____ E18 These institutions should not be expected to give customers individual attention.

____ E19 Employees of these institutions cannot be expected to give customers personal attention.

____ E20 It is unrealistic to expect employees to know what the needs of their customers are.

____ E21 It is unrealistic to expect these institutions to have their customers' best interests at heart.

____ E22 They shouldn't be expected to have operating hours convenient to all their customers.

Performance

The following set of statements relate to *your feelings about XYZ* _____. For each statement, please show the extent to which you believe XYZ _____ has the feature described by the statement. Once again, placing a seven on the line means you strongly agree that XYZ has that feature, and a one means you strongly disagree. You may use any of the number in the middle as well to show how strong your feeling are. There are no right or wrong answers – all we are interested in is a number that best shows your perceptions about XYZ, whether you use their service or not.

1	2	3	4	5	6	7
STRONGLY						STRONGLY
DISAGREE						AGREE

_____   P1   XYZ_____has up-to-date equipment.
_____   P2   XYZ_____'s physical facilities are visually appealing.
_____   P3   XYZ_____'s employees are well dressed and appear neat.
_____   P4   The appearance of the physical facilities of XYZ_____is in keeping with the type of service provided.
_____   P5   When XYZ_____promises to do something by a certain time, it does so.
_____   P6   When you have problems, XYZ_____is sympathetic and reassuring.
_____   P7   XYZ_____is dependable.
_____   P8   XYZ_____provides its services at the time it promises to do so.
_____   P9   XYZ_____keeps its records accurately.
_____   P10 XYZ_____does not tell its customers exactly when services will be performed.
_____   P11 You do not receive prompt service from XYZ_____employees.
_____   P12 Employees of XYZ_____are not always willing to help customers.
_____   P13 Employees of XYZ_____are too busy to respond to customer requests promptly.
_____   P14 You can trust employees of XYZ_____.
_____   P15 You can feel safe in your transactions with XYZ_____'s employees.
_____   P16 Employees of XYZ_____are polite.
_____   P17 Employees get adequate support from XYZ_____to do their jobs well.
_____   P18 XYZ_____does not give you individual attention.
_____   P19 Employees of XYZ_____do not give you personal attention.
_____   P20 Employees of XYZ_____do not know what you needs are.
_____   P21 XYZ_____does not have your best interests at heart.
_____   P22 XYZ_____does not have operating hours convenient to all their customers.

Importance

The following set of statements relate to *your feelings about the importance of each feature described in your decision to purchase* _____ *services*. A seven means you consider the feature very important in deciding where to purchase banking services, a one means it is very unimportant. You may place any of the numbers shown on the scale below beside each feature to indicate its importance to you. There are no right or wrong answers – all we are interested in is your perception of how important each feature is to you in your decision where to purchase banking services.

1	2	3	4	5	6	7
VERY						VERY
UNIMPORTANT						IMPORTANT

_____   I1   Up-to-date equipment.
_____   I2   Physical facilities that are visually appealing.
_____   I3   Employees that are well dressed and appear neat.
_____   I4   Physical facilities that appear to be in keeping with the type of service provided.

_____   I5   When something is promised by a certain time, doing it.
_____   I6   When there is a problem, being sympathetic and reassuring.
_____   I7   Dependability.
_____   I8   Providing service by the time promised.
_____   I9   Accurate record keeping.
_____   I10   Telling the customer exactly when the service will be performed.
_____   I11   Receiving prompt service.
_____   I12   Employees who are always willing to help customers.
_____   I13   Employees who are not too busy to respond to customer request promptly.
_____   I14   Employees who are trustworthy.
_____   I15   The feeling that you are safe when conducting transactions with the firm's employees.
_____   I16   Employees who are polite.
_____   I17   Adequate support from the firm so employees can do their job well.
_____   I18   Individual attention.
_____   I19   Employees who give you personal attention.
_____   I20   Employees who know what your needs are.
_____   I21   A firm which has your best interests at heart.
_____   I22   Convenient operating hours.

Other measures

The following set of statements relate to *your feelings about XYZ* _____. Please respond by circling the number which best reflects your own perceptions.

(Future Purchase Behavior)

(84)   In the next year, my use of XYZ____will be

1 . . . 2 . . . 3 . . . 4 . . . 5 . . . 6 . . . 7
NOT AT ALL   VERY FREQUENT

(Overall Quality)

(85)   The quality of XYZ____'s services is

1 . . . 2 . . . 3 . . . 4 . . . 5 . . . 6 . . . 7
VERY POOR   EXCELLENT

(Satisfaction)

(87)   My feelings towards XYZ____'s services can best be described as

1 . . . 2 . . . 3 . . . 4 . . . 5 . . . 6 . . . 7
VERY UNSATISFIED   VERY SATISFIED

ACKNOWLEDGEMENTS

The authors express their sincere appreciation to the editor and three anonymous *JM* reviewers for their helpful comments on previous versions of the article.

REFERENCES

Bateson, J. E. (1989) *Managing Services Marketing.* London: Dryden Press.

Bitner, M. J. (1990) 'Evaluating Service Encounters: The Effects of Physical Surroundings and Employee Responses'. *Journal of Marketing* **54** (April): 69–82.

Blackiston, G. H. (1988) 'Service Industries: A Renaissance in Quality'. *Executive Excellence.* **5** (9): 9–10.

Bolton, R. N. and Drew, J. H. (1991a) 'A Longitudinal Analysis of the Impact of Service Changes on Customer Attitudes'. *Journal of Marketing* **55** (January): 1–9.

Bolton, R. N. and Drew, J. H. (1991b). 'A Multistage Model of Customer Assessments of Service Quality and Value'. *Journal of Consumer Research* **17** (March): 375–384.

Brown, S. W. and Swartz, T. A. (1989) A Gap Analysis of Professional Service Quality'. *Journal of Marketing.* **53** (April): 92–98.

Carman, J. M. (1990) 'Consumer Perceptions of Service Quality, An Assessment of the SERVQUAL Dimensions'. *Journal of Retailing* **66** (1): 33–55.

Carmmes, E. G. and Zeller, R. A. (1979) 'Reliability and Validity Assessment'. Sage Publications Series Number 07 017. Newbury Park. CA: Sage Publications, Inc.

Churchill, G. A. Jr. (1979) 'A Paradigm for Developing Better Measures of Marketing Constructs'. *Journal of Marketing Research* **16** (February): 64–73.

Churchill, G. A. Jr. and Surprenant, C. (1982) 'An Investigation into the Determinants of Customer Satisfaction'. *Journal of Marketing Research* **19** (November): 491–504.

Cohen, J. B., Fishbem, M. and Ahtola, O. T. (1972) 'The Nature and Uses of Expectancy Value Models in Consumer Attitude Research'. *Journal of Marketing Research* **9** (November): 456–460

Cound, D. M. (1988) What Corporate Executives Think About Quality: The Results of the 1987 Gallup Survey'. *Quality Progress* **21** (2): 20–23.

Cravens, D. W. (1988) 'The Marketing of Quality'. *Incentive* **162** (11): 26–31.

Crosby, P. B. (1979) *Quality Is Free: The Art of Making Quality Certain.* New York: American Library.

Garvin, D. A. (1983) 'Quality on the Line'. *Harvard Business Review* **61** (September–October): 65–73.

Ginzberg, E. and Vojta, G. (1981) 'The Service Sector of the U.S. Economy.' *Scientific American* **244** (March): 31–39.

Grönroos, C. (1990). *Service Management and Marketing: Managing the Moments of Truth in Service Competition.* Lexington, MA: Lexington Books.

Heskett, J. L., Sasser, W. I. and Hart, W. L. (1990) *Service Breakthroughs. Changing the Rules of the Game.* New York: The Free Press.

Koepp, S. (1987). 'Pul-eeze! Will Somebody Help Me'. *Time* (February 2): 28–34.

Langevin, R. C. (1988) 'Service Quality: Essential Ingredients'. *Review of Business* **9** (3): 3–5.

Mazis, M. B., Ahtola, O. T. and Klippel, R. E. (1975). 'A Comparison of Four Multi-Attribute Models in the Prediction of Consumer Attitudes'. *Journal of Consumer Research* **2** (June): 38–52.

Oliver, R. I. (1980). 'A Cognitive Model of the Antecedents and Consequences of Satisfaction Decisions'. *Journal of Marketing Research* **17** (November): 460–469.

Parasuraman, A., Zeithaml, V. and Berry, L. (1985) 'A Conceptual Model of Service Quality and Its Implications for Future Research'. *Journal of Marketing* **49** (Fall): 41–50.

Parasuraman, A., Zeithaml, V. and Berry, L. (1988) 'SERVQUAL A Multiple Item Scale for Measuring Consumer Perceptions of Service Quality'. *Journal of Retailing* **64** (Spring): 12–40.

Rathmell, J. M. (1966). 'What Is Meant by Services'. *Journal of Marketing* **30** (October): 32–36.

Rudie, M. J. and Wansley, H. B. (1985) 'The Merrill Lynch Quality Program'. In *Services Marketing in a Changing Environment* (T. Bloch, G. Upah and A. Zeithaml, Eds). Chicago: American Marketing Association.

Sherden, W. A. (1988) 'Gaining the Service Quality Advantage'. *Journal of Business Strategy.* **9** (2): 45–48.

Thompson, P., DeSouza, G. and Gale, B. T. (1985) *The Stragegic Measurement of Quality,* Cambridge, MA: The Strategic Planning Institute, PIMSLETTER, No. 33.

Woodruff, R. B., Cadotte, E. R. and Jenkins, R. L. (1983) 'Modeling Consumer Satisfaction Processes Using Experienced-Based Norms'. *Journal of Marketing Research* **20** (August): 296–304.

Zeithaml, V. A., Parasuraman, A. and Berry, L. L. (1990) *Delivering Quality Service: Balancing Customer Perceptions and Expectations*. New York: The Free Press.

13

Expectations, Performance Evaluation, and Consumers' Perceptions of Quality

R. Kenneth Teas

The issue of service quality has received considerable attention in the marketing literature (Berry, Zeithaml and Parasuraman, 1985; Bolton and Drew, 1991; Brown and Swartz, 1989; Carman, 1990; Cronin and Taylor, 1992; Hostage, 1975; Olshavsky and Miller, 1972; Parasuraman, Zeithaml and Berry, 1985, 1988; Parasuraman, Berry and Zeithaml, 1990; Swartz and Brown, 1989; Zeithaml, 1988; Zeithaml, Berry and Parasuraman, 1988; Zeithaml, Parasuraman and Berry, 1990). Important concepts examined in some of this research involve various service 'gaps' that highlight several factors potentially affecting service quality. The service quality gap concept that has received the most attention is the 'expected service–perceived service gap' (P–E) identified by Parasuraman, Zeithaml and Berry (1985), operationally defined in terms of a 'perceptions-minus-expectations' measurement framework. Through the identification of service gaps that potentially affect customers' perceptions of service quality represents a significant contribution, the validity of the P–E service quality gap concept and corresponding measurement framework is questionable because of a number of problems involving conceptual and operational definitions of the concept of expectations and the resulting ambiguity with respect to the theoretical justification and interpretation of the P–E perceived quality framework. My purpose, therefore, is fourfold. First, the P–E service quality model is currently specified in the services marketing literature is examined and important conceptual and definitional problems are identified. Second, recent research identifying measurement validity problems concerning the operationalization of the P–E measurement framework is reviewed. Third, the P–E model and two alternative perceived quality models that are designed to address the problems associated with the P–E model are empirically tested. Fourth, implications of the conceptual issues examined in this study and of the empirical findings are explored.

Reprinted with permission from *Journal of Marketing*, Vol. 57, October, pp. 18–34.

CONCEPTUAL BACKGROUND

Definitions

Parasuraman, Zeithaml and Berry (1988, p. 16) define perceived service quality as 'a global judgement, or attitude, relating to superiority of the service'. Additionally, they link to the concepts of perceptions and expectations as follows: 'Perceived quality is viewed as the degree and direction of discrepancy between consumers' perceptions and expectations' (Parasuraman, Zeithaml and Berry, 1988, p. 1). In the services marketing literature, perceptions (P) are defined as consumers' beliefs concerning the service received (Parasuraman, Zeithaml and Berry, 1985) or experienced service (Brown and Swartz, 1989). Expectations (E) are defined by Parasuraman, Zeithaml and Berry (1988, p. 17) as 'desires or wants of consumers, i.e., what they feel a service provider should offer rather than would offer'. Parasuraman and his co-authors (1988) emphasize that the term 'expectations' is used differently in the service quality literature than it is in the consumer satisfaction literature in that service expectations (E) do not represent predictions about what service providers 'would' offer, but rather what they 'should' offer. Recently, researchers examining service quality issue have adopted the Parasuraman, Zeithaml and Berry (1985) conceptualization of expectations (Brown and Swartz, 1989; Carman, 1990).

This original definition of expectations is somewhat vague in terms of the meaning of 'should'. Recently, however, Parasuraman, Berry and Zeithaml (1990, p. 12) noted that the service expectations concept is 'intended to measure the customers' normative expectations', and that these expectations represent an 'ideal standard' of performance.

Carman (1990) also suggests that service quality expectations involve 'norms' and that these 'norms' are based on past experience.

The P–E perceived quality model

The operationalization of the quality concept in empirical studies (Parasuraman, Zeithaml and Berry, 1986, 1988; Brown and Swartz, 1989; Carman, 1990) suggests that perceived service quality can be conceptualized with the following P–E measurement model:

$$SQ_i = \sum_{j=1}^{k} W_j\,(P_{ij} - E_{ij}) \qquad (1)$$

where:

SQ_i = SERVQUAL overall perceived quality of stimulus i.
k = The number of attributes.
W_j = A weighting factor if attributes have differentiated weights.[1]
P_{ij} = Performance perception of stimulus i with respect to attribute j.
E_{ij} = Service quality expectation for attribute j that is the relevant norm for stimulus i.

---

[1] In published perceived service quality research, W_j is not included in the model and, therefore, is assumed to be equal to 1.0.

Equation (1) suggests that perceived service quality (SQ_i) increases as the differences between P_{ij} and E_{ij} increases across attributes. It is important to note that Parasuraman, Zeithaml and Berry (1988) emphasizes that this P–E service gap concept is different from the disconfirmed expectations concept in traditional consumer satisfaction/dissatisfaction models. First, the P–E gap concept represents a comparison with a norm; it does not represent a difference between predicted and received service. Exceeding the norm means how quality is received. Second, the P–E service quality concept as expressed in equation (1) is not a predictive model. It is a measurement specification in which perceived quality is equivalent to perceptions-minus-expectations.

The traditional method of operationalizating the P–E gap concept is to obtain perception and expectation scores for each attribute and calculate SQ by equation (1) with the attribute weights implicitly assumed to be equal ($W_j = 1$). For example, using the procedures described in Table 1, the P and E measures for the appeal of the physical facilities of a bank are obtained by agree/disagree (strongly agree = 7, strongly disagree = 1) ratings of the following statements:

1. Expectations (E) – 'Their physical facilities should be visually appealing'.
2. Perceptions (P) – 'XYZ's physical facilities are visually appealing'.

According to Parasuraman, Zeithaml and Berry (1986, p. 8);

> The difference between the ratings of statements like these is a measure of perceived service quality. The higher (more positive) the perception-minus-expectation score, the higher is the level of perceived service quality.[2]

The P–E measurement framework suggests the highest service quality score for an attribute occurs when the expectation score is +1 and the perception score is +7, giving a service quality score of +6 (7−1). The lowest service quality score is one in which the expectation score is +7 and the perception score is +1, giving a service quality score of −6 (1−7). If this measurement framework is valid, it should reflect constantly increasing levels of quality as scores move from −6 to +6. However, on the basis of the Parasuraman, Zeithaml and Berry (1985) definition of service expectations as ideal standards, the following discussion demonstrates that alternative conceptualizations of the ideal standard may be incompatible with the assumption that increasing P–E scores reflect continually increasing levels of perceived quality.

The ideal performance problem

Parasuraman, Berry and Zeithaml (1990) note that the SERVQUAL expectations measure is intended to measure 'normative expectations'. In a subsequent article they suggest that the SERVQUAL expectations concept 'is similar to the ideal standard in the CS/D literature' (Zeithaml, Berry and Parasuraman, 1991, pp. 3 – 4),

---

[2]Carman (1990) adopts this P–E measurement framework whereas Brown and Swartz (1989) use an 'expectations-minus-perceptions' (E–P) framework. The focus of my discussion is on the P–E procedure; however, the discussion generally applies to the E–P procedure as well.

Table 1. Standard instructions for P–E gap model measures

---

1. Expectations measures (E)

This survey deals with your opinions of _____ service. Please show the extent to which you think firms offering _____ services should possess the features described by each statement. Do this by picking one of the seven numbers next to each statement. If you strongly agree that these firms should possess a feature, circle the number 7. If you strongly disagree that these firms should possess a feature, circle 1. If your feelings are not strong, circle one of the numbers in the middle. There are no right or wrong answers. All we are interested in is a number that best shows your expectations about firms offering _____ services.

(1)   They should have up-to-date equipment.
(2)   Their physical facilities should be visually appealing.
■
■
■

(22) They shouldn't be expected to have operating hours convenient to all customers.

2. Perceptions measures (P)

The following set of statements relates to your feelings about XYZ. For each statement, please show the extent to which you believe XYZ has the feature described by the statement. Once again, circling a 7 means that you strongly agree that XYZ has that feature, and circling 1 means that you strongly disagree. You may circle any of the numbers in the middle that show how strong your feelings are. There are no right or wrong answers. All we are interested in is a number that best shows your perceptions about XYZ.

(1)   XYZ has up-to-date equipment.
(2)   XYZ's physical facilities are visually appealing.
■
■
■

(22) XYZ does not have operating hours convenient to all customers.

3. Revised expectations measures (E*)

Based on your experiences as a customer of _____ company services, please think about the kind of _____ companies that would deliver excellent quality of service. Think about the kind of _____ company with which you would be pleased to do business. Please show the extent to which you think such a _____ company would possess the feature described by each statement. If you feel a feature is not at all essential for excellent _____ companies such as the one you have in mind, circle the number 1. If you feel a feature is absolutely essential for excellent _____ companies, circle 7. If your feelings are less strong, circle one of the numbers in the middle. There are no right or wrong answers. All we are interested in is a number that truly reflects your feelings regarding _____ companies that would deliver excellent quality of service.

(1)   Excellent _____ have up-to-date equipment.
(2)   The physical facilities of excellent _____ are visually appealing.
■
■
■

(22) Excellent _____ have operating hours convenient to all customers.

---

such as

1. Miller's (1977) 'ideal expectations, defined as the wished-for level of performance'.
2. Swan and Trawick's (1980) 'desired expectations, defined as the level at which the consumer wanted the product to perform'.
3. Prakash's (1984) 'normative expectations, i.e. how a brand should perform for the customer to be completely satisfied'.

   Though Zeithaml, Berry and Parasuraman (1991) have indicated that service expectations are *similar* to these ideal standards, they have not clearly articulated the specific interpretation of the ideal standard they adopt. Accordingly, alternative interpretations are examined subsequently. It will be demonstrated that conceptualizing service expectations as ideal standards is a problem under each of the interpretations examined.

Classic attitudinal model ideal point interpretation

Since Parasuraman, Zeithaml, and Berry (1988) argue that perceived quality is an attitude, the ideal standard could be interpreted to be similar to the ideal point specified in classic ideal point attitudinal models (Ginter, 1974; Green and Srinivasan, 1978).[3] However, the P–E measurement specification as expressed in equation (1) suggests that perceived quality (Q_i) increases as P increasingly exceeds E. In contrast, ideal point attitudinal models suggest that perceived quality might decrease as P increasingly exceeds the ideal point.[4] Clearly, the SERVQUAL P–E measurement specification is not compatible with this classic ideal point interpretation of E.

Feasible ideal point interpretation

A second interpretation of the SERVQUAL ideal standard is that it represents a feasible level of performance under ideal circumstances, i.e. the best level of performance by the highest-quality provider under perfect circumstances. Under this interpretation, it could be argued that the service provider's performance might exceed this standard and that perceived quality increases accordingly as specified in equation (1).[5] However, depending on whether the attributes are vector attributes (i.e. infinite or maximum classic attitudinal model ideal points) or finite ideal point

---

[3]In these models, the ideal point is the perfect or utility maximizing level of the attribute. For example, if the attribute has a non-maximum ideal point, once the ideal point is reached, 'there are negative utility returns for further increases in the attribute' (Lilien, Kotler and Moorthy, 1992, p. 91).

[4]For example, ideal point models, such as those proposed by Ginter (1974) and Green and Srinivasan (1978), suggest that the favorableness of an evaluation of an attitude object is positively related to the closeness of the object to the ideal object. Increasingly exceeding the ideal, therefore, would be predicted by these models to be negatively, rather than positively, related to the favorableness of the evaluation.

[5]This feasible ideal concept is similar to Miller's (1977, p. 86) ideal concept which he defines as 'what performance level [the consumer]...feels might possibly be achieved by the object given ideal circumstances'.

attributes (i.e. non-infinite or intermediate classic attitudinal model ideal points), this feasible ideal point interpretation may not be justified. As an illustration, consider a one-attribute service quality situation. The SERVQUAL P–E measure of an individual's perceived quality of stimulus i is

$$SQ_i = P_i - E_i \qquad (2)$$

where

SQ$_i$ = The SERVQUAL measure of the individual's overall perceived quality of stimulus i.

P$_i$ = The individual's perceptions of the performance of stimulus i with respect to the single attribute.

E$_i$ = The individual's quality expectation norm for the single attribute – conceptualized as a feasible ideal point.

Measuring perceived quality as specified in equation (2) results in measured perceived quality (SQ$_i$) being a positive linear function of P$_i$, holding E$_i$ constant, and a negative linear function of E$_i$, holding P$_i$ constant. Assuming the attribute is a vector attribute (i.e. the classic attitudinal model ideal point is a maximum or infinite), these relationships have logical interpretations. Firest, increasing performance intensity P$_i$ levels would be increasingly close to the infinite classic ideal performance intensity; therefore, a positive relationship between perceived quality and P$_i$ is at least not illogical. Second, increasing expectancy norm intensity E$_i$ levels would be increasingly close to the classic ideal performance intensity. It is at least not illogical to assume that the perceived quality associated with a particular performance intensity P$_i$ is negatively affected when the performance norm (E$_i$), to which P$_i$ is compared, becomes increasingly close to the ideal performance intensity.

If the single attribute is not a vector attribute (i.e. the classic attitudinal model ideal-point is not a maximum value), the appeal of the 'feasible ideal point' interpretation of E is reduced. For example, consider the following modified one-attribute SERVQUAL model that includes the concept of the classic attitudinal model ideal point:

$$MQ_i = -1 \left[|\, P_i - I \,| - |\, E_i - I \,| \right] \qquad (3)$$

where P$_i$ and E$_i$ are defined in (2) and

MQ$_i$= A modified SERVQUAL measure of the quality of stimulus i.

I   = The ideal amount of the single attribute – the classic attitudinal model ideal point.

The right side of equation (3) is multiplied by -1 so that increased values of MQ$_i$ are associated with increased perceived quality. The $|\, P_i - I \,|$ component of equation (3), which replaces P$_i$ in equation (2), expresses performance as the absolute value of the distance between perceived performance P$_i$ and ideal performance I. The $|\, E_i I \,|$ component of equation (3), which replaces E$_i$ in equation (2), expresses the expectancy norm as the absolute value of the distance between E$_i$ and the ideal performance level I. The rationale for substituting $|\, P_i - I \,|$ for P$_i$ is that it is difficult to envision a positive monotonic relationship between performance intensity P$_i$ and attitude (or perceived quality) when the ideal performance level (i.e. classic attitudinal model ideal) is an intermediate level of intensity. Ideal point attitudinal models predict that increasing performance intensity beyond the intermediate classic ideal point will produce less rather than more favorable evaluations as predicted by the P–E model. However, when perceived performance is expressed as $|P_i-I|$, decreasing values of $|P_i-I|$ are associated with increasing congruence between perceived performance (P_i) and ideal performance (I). Therefore, a positive relationship between $-1|P_i-I|$ and MQ_i is at least not illogical.[6]

Similarly, it is difficult to envision a negative monotonic relationship between the expectancy norm (E_i) and perceived quality when an intermediate level of intensity is the classic attitudinal model ideal performance level.[7] However, when the normative expectation is expressed as $|E_i-I|$, decreasing value of $|E-I|$ are associated with increasing congruence between the expectancy norm (E_i) and the classic ideal (I). Therefore, a negative relationship between $-1|E_i-I|$ and MQ_i is at least not illogical. That is, it is not illogical to assume that the perceived quality MQ_i is negatively affected when performance norm E_i, to which P_i is compared, becomes increasingly close to the classic attitudinal model ideal performance intensity (I). Under the assumption that P_i is measured by the SERVQUAL perceptions scale, E_i is measured by the SERVQUAL expectation scale, and I is measured by a similar 7-point scale, the general characteristics of the MQ_i measure as specified in equation (3) are as follows:

1. When I is a maximum value (I = 7), MQ_i as specified in equation (3) is perfectly correlated with SQ_i as specified in equation (2). Therefore, the two measurement expressions are equivalent assuming maximum (or infinite) classic ideal points.

2. When $1 < I < 7$ the relationship between MQ_i, and P_i is an inverted V function when E is held constant and the relationship between MQ_i and E_i is a V function when P_i is held constant.

3. When I = 1, SQ_i and MQ_i are negatively correlated $(r = -1)$.

These properties of MQ_i demonstrate a lack of equivalence of the perceived quality measures as expressed in equation (2) and (3) under the assumption of finite classic attitudinal model ideal-point (non-vector) attributes. In addition, the inverted v function linking MQ_i and P_i and the v function linking MQ_i and E_i suggest a monotonic simplification of the non-linear relationships is not appropriate. Clearly, the SERVQUAL P–E measurement specification is not compatible with the 'feasible ideal point' interpretation of E when finite classic ideal point attributes are involved.

In summary, there are a number of complex theoretical and definitional problems associated with the SERVQUAL P–E perceived quality model. Consequently following a review of recently identified measurement validity problems associated

---

[6]Equation (3) can be rewritten as

$$MQ_i = (-1 [|P_i-I|]) - (-1 [|E_i-I|])$$

Therefore, equation (3) suggests that $-1[|P_i-I]$ and $-1[|E_i-I|]$ are positively and negatively related to MQ_i, respectively.

[7]For example, when the expectancy norm (E_i) exceeds the intermediate classic ideal intensity (I), further increases in the intensity of E_i would result in the norm being farther from the ideal point. In this situation a particular performance intensity P_i is being compared to the norm that is less attractive; consequently, the perceived quality associated with P_i would not be expected to be diminished.

with framework, alternative frameworks are developed to address the problems – particularly the ideal point problem.

OPERATIONAL DEFINITION PROBLEMS

Empirical research has identified important problems concerning the operationalization of the service expectations (E) concept. First, Parasuraman, Berry and Zeithaml (1990) suggest that the word 'should' may cause respondents to assign unrealistically high ratings to the E response scales; therefore, they propose the revised expectation E* measure described in Table 1. Second, research by Carman (1990), indicates the SERVQUAL dimensions are not 'generic' as suggested by Parasuraman, Zeithaml and Berry (1988). On the basis of the empirical results, Carman (1990) questions the validity of the expectation measure when consumers do not have 'well formed expectations'. Third, exploratory research by Teas (1993) suggests a lack of congruence between the conceptual and operational definitions of the original SERVQUAL E measure. The findings of the research indicate a considerable portion of the variance in responses to the SERVQUAL E scale is because of variance in respondents' interpretations of the question being asked rather than to variance in respondents' attitudes (Teas, 1993).[8]

Given this operational ambiguity associated with the expectations (E) concept, an important question concerns the degree to which the ambiguity has been eliminated through the revised expectation (E*) measure, which requests the respondent to focus on 'companies that would deliver excellent quality' and if specific features are 'essential' for excellent service (Parasuraman, Berry and Zeithaml, 1990, p. 46). However, definitions of 'essential', include 'indispensable', 'necessary' and 'something that is fundamental' (*American Heritage Dictionary*, 1985, p. 465). Defining the revised SERVQUAL E* this way, in conjunction with the P–E measurement specification as expressed in equation (1), suggests high performance on essential attributes (high E* scores) reflects lower quality than higher performance on attributes that are essential (low E* scores). It is difficult to envision a theoretical argument that supports this measurement specification.

ALTERNATIVE PERCEIVED QUALITY FRAMEWORKS

Clearly, there are serious conceptual and operational problems associated with the SERVQUAL P–E perceived quality measurement framework. First, if the expectation 'normative ideal standard' concept E_j is interpreted to represent a classic attitudinal model ideal point concept, a positive monotonic link between perceived quality and the SERVQUAL SQ_i as specified in equation (1) may not be expected when the attributes are finite classic attitudinal ideal-point attributes. Second, if the expectation concept is interpreted to represent a feasible ideal point, classic ideal point attitudinal models suggest possible nonmonotonic linkages between

---

[8]In a recent article, Cronin and Taylor (1992) published the results of an empirical test of the original SERVQUAL model. On the basis of a literature review and the empirical findings, they conclude that the 'current operationalization of service quality confounds satisfaction and attitude' and that performance-based measures of service quality may be more effective than the SERVQUAL P–E measure.

SERVQUAL SQ_i scores calculated by equation (1) and true perceptions of quality. Third, the SERVQUAL expectations E and revised expectations E^* are characterized by a number of operational definition problems involving such issues as operationalizing the P–E framework for inexperienced consumers, variance in respondents' interpretation of the SERVQUAL E scale, and the meaning of the revised SERVQUAL E^* concept of 'essential' features. Because of these problems, the following evaluated performance (EP) perceived quality model is developed, addressing the ideal point problem by formally incorporating the classic ideal point concept into a perceived quality model. Additionally, using the EP model as a theoretical foundation, a normed quality (NQ) model is developed that integrates the classic ideal point concept with the SERVQUAL revised expectation (E^*) concept.

Perceived quality models using an evaluated performance (EP) framework

Building on *The Dictionary of Psychology* (Chaplin, 1981) definition of quality – 'the relative goodness or excellence of anything' – Monroe and Krishnan (1985, p. 212) define perceived product quality as 'the perceived ability of a product to provide satisfaction "relative" to available alternatives'. On the basis of this definition and the assumptions that the perceived ability of the product (defined as a good or service) to deliver satisfaction can be conceptualized as the product's relative congruence with the consumer's ideal product features (conceptualized as classic attitudinal model ideal points), the proposed probabilistic evaluated performance (EP) model of perceived quality is[9]

$$Q_i = -1 \left[\sum_{j=1}^{m} W_j \sum_{k=1}^{n_j} P_{ij_k} \left| A_{j_k} - I_j \right|^t \right] 1/t \qquad (4)$$

where

Q_i = the individual's perceived quality of object i.
   Multiplying the right side of the equation by -1 results in larger values of Q_i being associated with higher levels of perceived quality.
W_j = importance of attribute j as a determinant of perceived quality.
P_{ij_k} = the perceived probability that object i has amount k of attribute j.[10]
A_{j_k} = amount k of attribute j.
I_j = ideal amount of attribute j as conceptualized in classic ideal point attitudinal models.
m = number of attributes.
n_j = number of 'amount' categories of attribute j.
t = Minkowski space parameter.[11]

---

[9]The proposed model focuses on attributes that can be defined along quantitative continuums. A potential extension of the model would be to incorporate nominal scaled attributes (e.g. color). For example of multiattribute models that mix quantitative and nominal scaled attributes, see Green and Srinivasan (1978).

[10]See Ahtola (1975) for a discussion of an attitudinal model that includes probabilities of alternative amounts or levels of multiple attributes.

[11]See Ginter (1974) for a discussion of an attitudinal model that includes the Minkowski space parameter specification.

If it is assumed that l equals 1.0, equation (4) becomes

$$Q_i = -1 \left[\sum_{j=1}^{m} W_j \sum_{k=1}^{n_j} P_{ij_k} | A_{j_k} - I_j | \right] \tag{5}$$

This perceived quality model as expressed in equation (4) or (5) posits that an individual's perceptions of the quality of the performance of object i is positively related to the weighted likelihood that the performance of object i on m performance dimensions is close to the individual's perceptions of optimal performance (the classic attitudinal model ideal) on the m dimensions. The model implies that the perceived quality of object i can be increased by (1) closing the gap between object i's performance and the ideal object's performance on one or more of the m attributes, (2) reducing the relative weights W_j for attributes characterized by large $| A_{j_k} - I_j |$ gaps, (3) increasing the relative weights W_j for attributes characterized by small $| A_{j_k} - I_j |$ gaps, (4) increasing the relative probabilities associated with the occurrence of small $| A_{j_k} - I_i |$ gaps, and (5) decreasing the relative probabilities associated with the occurrence of large $| A_{j_k} - I_j |$ gaps.

Several alternative perceived quality concepts and measures can be derived from equations (4) and (5) by making certain assumptions. For example, if it is assumed that the individual evaluates object i with perceived certainty and that object i has a constant amount of each attribute, equation (5) becomes the following nonprobabilistic evaluated performance (EP) model of perceived quality:

$$Q_i = -1 \left[\sum_{j=1}^{m} W_j | A_{ij} - I_j | \right] \tag{6}$$

where Q_i, W_j, and I_j are defined in equation (4) and A_{ij} equals the individual's perceived amount of attribute j possessed by object i. Equation (6) is similar to Ginter's (1974) 'city block' distance ideal point model.

A normal quality model

If object i is defined as the excellence norm that is the focus of the revised SERVQUAL E* concept, equations (4), (5) or (6) can be used to define the perceived quality of the excellence norm Q_e in terms of similarity between the excellence norm and the ideal object with respect to the m attributes. The quality of another object Q_i relative to the quality of the excellence norm then can be conceptualized as the 'normed quality gap' or 'normed quality' as follows:

$$NQ_i = [Q_i - Q_e] \tag{7}$$

where Q_i is defined in equation (4) and

  $NQ_i =$ Normed Quality Index for object i.
  Q_e = The individual's perceived quality of the excellence norm object.

If the excellence norm is equal to the ideal or perfect object, equation (4) suggests Q_e will equal 0 and, therefore, normed quality (NQ_i) would be equal to perceived quality (Q_i).

If the SERVQUAL normative expectations concept is respecified to be this 'excellence norm', equations (6) and (7) can be used to derive the following modified SERVQUAL model that addresses the ideal point problem by incorporating the classic ideal point concept into the model:

$$NQ_i = -1 \left[\sum_{j=1}^{m} W_j \left(|A_{ij} - I_j| - |A_{ej} - I_j| \right) \right] \qquad (8)$$

where W_j and I_j are defined in equation (4), A_{ij} is defined in equation (6), and

NQ$_i$ = Normed Quality Index for object i.
A$_{ej}$ = The individual's perceived amount of attribute j possessed by the excellence norm.

If infinite classic ideal points are assumed, equation (8) can be expressed as

$$NQ_i = \sum_{j=1}^{m} W_j (A_{ij} - A_{ej}). \qquad (9)$$

Though equation (9) is similar in structure to the original SERVQUAL model described in equation (1), it is important to note that two necessary assumptions used in the derivation of equation (9) are that all the m attributes have infinite classic ideal points and that the SERVQUAL normative expectations concept is redefined as the 'excellence norm' specified in equation (8).

EMPIRICAL TESTS

Because of the conceptual and operational problems associated with the original SERVQUAL P–E model, tests of the validity of the revised SERVQUAL P–E*, normed quality (NQ), and evaluated performance (EP) measurement models are warranted. Consequently, the empirical tests in this study focus on measurement validity issues with respect to these models. The issues examined involves the (1) conceptual-operational definition congruence of the SERVQUAL expectation and revised expectation measures (E and E*) and an ideal point measure and (2) criterion and construct validity of the original P–E, revised P–E*, NQ, and EP perceived quality measurement frameworks.

Research questions

The purpose of the empirical study is to compare alternative perceived quality measurement frameworks by examining the following issues:

1. The primary differences among the models involve the P–E model's service expectations E and E* and the EP model's ideal point (I) concepts. Since there is definitional ambiguity associated with the service expectations E and E* concepts, the question of conceptual-operational definition congruence of the service expectations (E and E*) measures and of the ideal point (I) used to operationalize the EP model is explored.

2. Weighted and unweighted versions of the following models are compared in terms of criterion and construct validity:

   a. Original SERVQUAL P–E model (equation 1) using the original expectations (E) measure,
   b. Revised SERVQUAL P–E model (equation 1) using the revised expectations (E*) measure,
   c. Nonprobabilistic ideal-point evaluated performance (EP) model (equation 6),
   d. Normed Quality Model (equation 8) using the revised expectations (E*) measure.

For the purpose of this study, the following definitions are used:

1. *Criterion validity* concerns 'the degree of correspondence between a measure and a criterion variable, usually measured by their correlation...When the criterion exists at the same time as the measure, this is called concurrent validity' (Bollen, 1989, p. 186).
2. *Construct validity* concerns the degree to which 'a measure relates to other observed variables in a way that is consistent with theoretically derived predictions' (Bollen, 1989, p. 188).

On the basis of the conceptual and operational problems associated with P–E perceived quality models in general and the expectations (E) and revised expectations (E*) concepts in particular, the following hypotheses are examined in this study:

   H_1: The criterion validity of the EP measurement framework is greater than the criterion validity of the P–E, revised P–E*, and normed quality (NQ) measurement frameworks.
   H_2: The construct validity of the EP measurement framework is greater than the construct validity of the P–E, revised P–E*, and the normed quality (NQ) measurement frameworks.

The criterion validity variable used to test H_1 is the respondent's global assessment of service quality. Because service quality can be expected to affect such factors as business growth, market share, customer preferences, and customer loyalty (Zeithaml, Parasuraman and Berry, 1990), the variables used in the construct validity test (H_2) involve shopping preferences, purchase intentions, and overall satisfaction with store services.

Research design

The data used to examine the research questions were obtained from a random sample (selected from the telephone directory) of respondents from a small midwestern city. Each of the 120 respondents, who were paid $15 for their participation in a personal interview, was assigned randomly to one of two cells and was requested to respond to a series of measurement instruments designed to operationalize the SERVQUAL P–E and revised P–E* measurement frameworks, the normed quality (NQ) measurement framework, and the evaluated performance (EP) measurement framework. The bulk of the services marketing literature examining the (P–E) quality model uses a non-transaction-specific, relationship-oriented, focus.

Consequently, the hypotheses were tested within the context of ongoing service provided by three local discount stores (K-Mart, Wal-Mart and Target). Each respondent in each of the two cells was randomly assigned one of the stores to rate on ten of the service attributes from the SERVQUAL instrument (Parasuraman, Zeithaml and Berry, 1986; Zeithaml, Parasuraman and Berry, 1990) – two attributes for each of the five general SERVQUAL dimensions.

The survey procedures[12]

The sequence of questions for the two survey cells are presented in Table 2 and a detailed discussion of the instrumentation is presented in Appendix A. As noted in Table 2, each respondent answered a series of questions measuring (1) service expectations,[13] performance perceptions, ideal points, and importance weights with respect to ten SERVQUAL service attributes and (2) overall satisfaction, preference, intentions, and perceived quality. These responses were used to test the measurement validity hypotheses. In addition, the respondents answered qualitative

Table 2. The sequence of questions

Question order		
Cell 1	Cell 2	Measure
1	3	E_{ij}: SERVQUAL expectations measures for each attribute.[a]
2	2	P_{ij}^s: SERVQUAL perceptions measures for the randomly selected store with respect to each attribute.
3	1	E_{ij}^*: SERVQUAL revised (excellence norm) measures for each attribute
4	4	P_{ij}^d: Semantic differential scale performance measures for the randomly selected store with respect to each attribute.
5	5	I_j: Semantic differential scale ideal performance measures for each attribute.
6	6	Overall satisfaction, preference, intentions, and quality measures.
7	7	Follow-up questions (which were tape-recorded) concerning reasons for 'non-extreme' E_{ij}, E^*_{ij}, and I_j ratings.
8	8	Attribute importance weights.

[a] The primary focus of the validity tests involves the SERVQUAL expectation measures. Consequently, all the SERVQUAL measures were obtained first so the process of obtaining the other measures would not have an effect on the SERVQUAL responses.

---

[12]Each model examined in this study specifies difference scores, i.e., performance–minus–expectations, performance–minus–ideal, or expectations–minus–ideal. These difference scores were operationalized by measuring the individual components and calculating the differences. This approach was selected because this is the approach used in the published literature involving the SERVQUAL measurement specification. As noted by Prakash (1984), the use of difference scores can result in low measurement reliability. Consequently, an alternative, and probably preferable, procedure that deserves attention in future research is the use of scales that are designed to capture the perceived differences directly rather than measure each component and calculating the differences. These kinds of scales are routinely used in consumer satisfaction research (Churchill and Surprenant, 1982).

[13]The SERVQUAL expectations (E) and revised expectations (E*) were stated using the formats published in Parasuraman, Zeithaml and Berry (1988) using the Parasuraman, Berry and Zeithaml (1990), respectively. The same ten attributes were used for the P_j^d, I_j, and W_j ratings.

follow-up questions, concerning their reasons for 'non-extreme' ('non-7') responses to the expectations (E and E*) and ideal point (I) rating scales, which were used to examine the issues of conceptual and operational definitions congruence. The follow-up questions focused on non-extreme responses because the SQ_i, NQ_i, and Q_i measures, as specified in equations (1), (8), and (6), respectively, are perfectly correlated when expectations (E or E*) and ideal point (I) measures are fixed at the extreme point on the scales (i.e. $E_{ij} = I_i = 7$). However, Q_i becomes less positively correlated with SQ_i as E_i or I_j scores become less extreme and SQ_i becomes less positively correlated with NQ_i as I scores become less extreme. Furthermore, responses to the SERVQUAL E measure are usually highly skewed with many mean values exceeding 6.0 (Parasuraman, Zeithaml and Berry, 1986). Consequently, focusing the follow-up questions on the non-extreme responses facilitates an analysis of those factors that are causing the variance in the ratings.

FINDINGS

I used two approaches to examine empirically the validity of the alternative perceived quality measurement frameworks tested. First, the congruence between the conceptual and operational definitions of the measures is explored qualitatively by analyzing the responses to the open-ended follow-up questions concerning the respondents' reasons for non-extreme SERVQUAL expectancy (E and E*) and ideal point (I) ratings. Second, the criterion and construct validity of the SERVQUAL P–E, the normed quality (NQ), and the evaluated performance (EP) perceived quality measurement frameworks are assessed quantitatively by testing hypotheses H_1 and H_2.

Reasons for non-extreme expectations and ideal point responses

The primary categories used for classifying responses to the follow-up questions concerning reasons for non-extreme responses to the expectations and ideal point measures were (1) not feasible, (2) sufficient, (3) not necessary, (4) less important, (5) implied less important, (6) classic ideal, (7) forecast, and (8) other. These categories were developed through a preliminary exploratory study and a preliminary evaluation of the follow-up question responses. Definitions of these categories are presented in Table 3.

Two coders were instructed to classify independently the responses according to the scheme shown in Table 3. Their instructions were to classify each response in either one category or two if the response indicated that the respondent was mentioning more than one issue. The following procedures were used to determine the ultimate classification of the responses:

1. If both coders classified the response into the same single or double categories, the response was classified according to the coders' classification.
2. If the coders disagreed on the classification, a referee coder was used to decide which classification to use. If the referee disagreed with both coders, the response was classified as an 'other' response.

Table 3. Classification categories for exploratory follow-up questions

The following categories were used to classify the tape recorded answers concerning reasons for non-extreme responses to the Expectations (E), Revised Expectations (E˙), and Ideal Point (I) Measures:

Not feasible – Not possible or not capable of being accomplished or achieved.

Sufficient – As much of the characteristics as is needed – enough or an adequate amount.

Not necessary – The response was categorized as 'Not necessary' only if the word 'necessary' was used.

Forecast – To predict, estimate, or calculate in advance. To make an estimation of conditions or events.

Less important – The response was categorized as 'less important' only if the word 'important' was used.

Implied less important – The degree to which the characteristic has value, significance, or consequence.

Classic ideal – The perfect or preferred amount of the characteristic.

Other – All responses that could not be classified in one or a combination of two of the preceding categories were classified as 'Other'.

A summary of the results of these coding procedures is presented in Table 4, and examples of coded responses are provided in Appendix B.

SERVQUAL expectations

As indicated in Table 4, a total of 454 responses to the SERVQUAL E questions were non-extreme. This represents approximately 38% of the 1200 responses to the SERVQUAL E scales (120 respondents answering 10 questions each). Approximately 39.4% of the non-extreme responses were categorized as 'not feasible' and 25.6% were classified as 'less important'. Other less frequently occurring responses included 'sufficient', 'forecast', 'classic ideal', and various double classifications such as 'not feasible/sufficient'. Approximately 8.1% of the responses were not classifiable. The patterns of responses are similar for the revised SERVQUAL E* measure.[14]

Under the assumption that the feasibility concept is congruent with the excellence norm concept of the P–E model, the 39.4% and 35% 'not feasible' classification rates for E and E* measures, respectively, represent indexes of the congruence between the conceptual and operational definitions of the measures with respect to the non-extreme answers. If the 'sufficient' and all double categories that include 'not feasible' and 'sufficient' as one of the category labels are added to these congruence

---

[14]The patterns of responses vary somewhat across the ten SERVQUAL items. For example, the 'not feasible' and/or 'sufficient' category percentages for the five SERVQUAL dimensions (two items per dimension) are 'Tangibles' (36.9%); 'Reliability' (49.2%); 'Responsiveness' (50.0%); 'Assurance' (53.7%); and 'Empathy' (65.3%). The two dimensions with the largest numbers of non-extreme responses are 'Reliability' (122 non-extreme answers across two-items) and 'Empathy' (121 non-extreme answers across two items).

Table 4. Reasons for non-extreme ('Non-7') responses to the expectations and the ideal point scales

	SERVQUAL E		Revised SERVQUAL E*		Ideal I	
	Frequency	Percentage	Frequency	Percentage	Frequency	Percentage
Not Feasible	179	39.4	151	35.0	23	15.2
Sufficient[a]	38	8.3	41	9.5	10	6.6
Not Feasible/Sufficient[a]	3	0.6	4	0.9	0	0
Not Feasible/Importance[b]	9	2.0	10	2.3	0	0
Not Feasible/Ideal	0	0	0	0	4	2.7
Sufficient[a]/Importance[b]	7	1.5	5	1.2	0	0
Sufficient/Ideal	0	0	1	0.2	9	6.0
Sufficient/Forecast	2	0.4	0	0	0	0
Less Important	116	25.6	125	28.9	34	22.5
Ideal	9	2.0	14	3.2	43	28.5
Ideal/Importance[b]	2	0.4	1	0	5	3.3
Forecast	51	11.2	47	10.9	10	6.6
Forecast/Importance[b]	1	0.2	1	0.2	0	0
Other	37	8.1	32	7.4	13	8.6
Total 'Non-7' Responses	454	100.0	432	100.0	151	100.0

[a] In this table the 'Not Necessary' and 'Sufficient' categories are combined.
[b] In this table the 'Less Important' and 'Implied Less Important' categories are combined.

indexes, the congruence percentages are 52.4% and 49.1% for the E and E* measures, respectively.

Clearly, the 'less important', 'classic ideal', and 'forecast' categories represent situations in which the respondents interpretations of the E and E* scales are not congruent with the expectations concept specified in the P–E service quality model. Approximately 39.2% and 43.5% of the E and E* follow-up responses, respectively, were classified within this group of single or double classification categories. Furthermore, as indicated in Table 5, a considerable number of respondents used these explanations. For example, the 'less important' reason was expressed by more than 50% of the respondents in their answers to at least one of the follow-up questions for the SERVQUAL E and E* measures. The 'forecast' and 'ideal' reasons were expressed by approximately 30% and 7% of the respondents, respectively. These results suggest the following potentially serious measurement validity problems:

1. *Attribute importance* – When the SERVQUAL E or E* measures are interpreted by the respondent to involve attribute importance, the P–E difference score calculation results in an inverse relationship between attribute importance and quality perceptions all else being equal. A more logical interpretation of an E or E* score in this situation is that it represents an attribute weight (W_j in equation (5) rather than a quality norm E_{ij} or E_{ij}^*). This suggests an expected positive relationship between the expectations scores and perceived quality, all else being equal.
2. *Forecast* – When the SERVQUAL E or E* measures are interpreted by the respondent to be requesting a forecast, the P–E score lacks discriminant validity with respect to the disconfirmed expectation concept specified in traditional

consumer satisfaction models. This finding, therefore, is not congruent with the Parasuraman, Zeithaml and Berry (1988) position that expectations do *not* represent performance predictions and that the concept of the P–E service quality gap is differentiated from the concept of disconfirmed expectations specified in consumer satisfaction models.

3. *Ideal* – When the SERVQUAL E or E* measures are interpreted by the respondent to involve the classic ideal point concept, classic ideal point attitudinal models suggest that the P–E score would be expected to be positively related to perceived quality only when the value of P is less than or equal to E. When P exceeds E, increased P–E scores would be expected to be negatively related to perceived quality.

These findings suggest that a considerable portion of the variance in the SERVQUAL E and E* measures is the result of measurement error induced by respondents misinterpreting the scales. A conservative estimate of the magnitude of this incongruence is 38.5% for the E measure and 43.5% for the E* measure. If double-coded categories that include 'less-important', 'ideal', or 'forecast' as one of the codes are included in the calculation, this estimated incongruence is 43.8% and 48.4% for the E and E* measures, respectively.

Ideal point measure

As indicated in Table 4, responses to the follow-up questions involving the ideal (I) attribute level measure indicate the most frequent response categories are 'ideal'

Table 5. Summary of reasons given by respondents concerning non-extreme ('Non-7') responses to the expectations and ideal point measures (the entries in the table are the percentages of respondents ($n = 120$) that expressed the reason at least one time)

Reasons for non-extreme response	SERVQUAL E percentage of respondents	SERVQUAL E* percentage of respondents	Revised Ideal I percentage of respondents
Not Feasible	72.2	71.3	13.9
Sufficient[a]	20.4	22.2	5.5
Not Feasible/Sufficient[a]	2.8	5.6	0
Not Feasible/Importance[b]	2.8	6.5	0
Not Feasible/Ideal	0	0	1.9
Sufficient[a]/Importance[b]	1.9	7.4	0
Sufficient/Ideal	0	0.9	4.6
Sufficient/Forecast	1.9	0	0
Less Important	50.9	52.8	27.8
Ideal	6.5	7.4	26.9
Ideal/Importance[b]	1.9	0.9	1.9
Forecast	31.5	30.6	7.4
Forecast/Importance[b]	0.9	0.9	0
Other	11.1	16.7	6.5

[a] In this table the 'Not Necessary' and 'Sufficient' categories are combined.
[b] In this table the 'Less Important' and 'Implied Less Important' categories are combined.

(28.5%), 'less important' (22.5%), and 'not feasible' (15.2%). Consequently, there is evidence that the ideal point measure lacks discriminate validity with respect to concepts of importance and feasibility. This is a somewhat surprising finding because the instructions specifically request the respondent to describe the ideal or perfect discount store. It is interesting to note, however, that the tendency for non-extreme responses was much smaller for the ideal point measure than it was for the expectations measures.

Hypotheses tests

The following variables derived from the survey data were used to test H_1 and H_2 (see Table 2 for listing of the survey data variables):

Q = *Global quality* and was measured by the summation of the two perceived global quality measures. The coefficient alpha for the measure is .828.

Y = *Global store preference* and was measured by the summation of the preference, overall satisfaction, and two intentions measures. The variables were summed to form one index because they were highly correlated.[15] The coefficient alpha for the summated score is .761.

S_1 = *Unweighted P–E* service quality and was calculated by combining the P^s_{ij} and E_{ij} ratings according to equation (1) and assuming $W_j = 1$.

S_2 = *Weighted P–E* service quality and was calculated by combining the P^s_{ij}, E_{ij} and W_j ratings according to equation (1).

R_1 = *Unweighted revised P–E** service quality and was calculated using the procedures for calculating S_1, except the revised E^*_{ij} was substituted for E_{ij}.

R_2 = *Weighted revised P–E** service quality and was calculated using the procedures for calculating S_2, except E^*_{ij} was substituted for E_{ij}.

NQ_1 = *Normed Quality (NQ)* and was calculated by combining P^s_{ij}, E^*_{ij}, and I_j according to equation (8) and assuming $W_j = 1$.

NQ_2 = *Normed Quality (NQ)* and was calculated by using P^s_{ij}, E^*_{ij}, I_j, and W_j according to equation (8).

EP_1 = *Evaluated Performance (EP)* service quality and was calculated by combining the P^d_{ij} and I_j ratings according to equation (6) and assuming $W_j = 1$.

EP_2 = *Weighted Evaluated Performance (EP)* service quality and was calculated by combining P^d_{ij}, I_j, and W_j ratings according to equation (6).

The degree of *criterion validity* of the SERVQUAL P–E, normed quality (NQ), and evaluated performance (EP) measurement models was assessed using the pairwise correlations between the global quality measure (Q) and each of the alternative quality measures S_1, S_2, R_1, R_2, NQ_1, NQ_2, EP_1, and EP_2. The degree of *construct validity* of the same set of measures was assessed using the pairwise correlations between the global store preference measure (Y) and each of the alternative quality measures.

---

[15]Because of the ambiguity concerning the causal link between perceived quality and consumer satisfaction, a global store preference summated scale was constructed that omitted the overall satisfaction item. The construct validity test results involving this variable were the same (in terms of statistical significance patterns) as those involving the summated scale that includes the overall satisfaction item.

H_1 and H_2 suggest the criterion and construct validity of the evaluated performance measures (EP_1 and EP_2) are greater than the criterion and construct validity of the other measures.

The criterion and construct validity coefficients are presented in Table 6 for the eight perceived quality measures examined. As indicated, the criterion validity coefficients range from .698 to .733 for the P–E measures, .688 to .701 for the NQ measures, and .778 to .806 for the evaluated performance (EP) measures. The construct validity coefficients range from .588 to .640 for the P–E measures, .576 to .622 for the NQ measures, and .720 and .753 for the EP measures.

Table 6. Criterion and construct validity coefficients[a]

Perceived quality model	Global quality Q	Global satisfaction Y
(S_1) =P–E – unweighted model[b]	$\hat{\rho}_{S_1Q}=.725$	$\hat{\rho}_{S_1Y}=.604$
(S_2) =P–E – weighted model[c]	$\hat{\rho}_{S_2Q}=.698$	$\hat{\rho}_{S_2Y}=.588$
(R_1) =Revised P–E – unweighted model[d]	$\hat{\rho}_{R_1Q}=.733$	$\hat{\rho}_{R_1Y}=.639$
(R_2) =Revised P–E – weighted model[e]	$\hat{\rho}_{R_2Q}=.713$	$\hat{\rho}_{R_2Y}=.640$
(NQ_1) =Normed Quality – unweighted model[f]	$\hat{\rho}_{NQ_1Q}=.701$	$\hat{\rho}_{NQ_1Y}=.622$
(NQ_2) =Normed Quality – weighted model[g]	$\hat{\rho}_{NQ_2Q}=.688$	$\hat{\rho}_{NQ_2Y}=.576$
(EP_1) =Evaluated Performance (EP) – unweighted model[h]	$\hat{\rho}_{EP_1Q}=.806$	$\hat{\rho}_{EP_1Y}=.753$
(EP_2) =Evaluated Performance (EP) – weighted model[i]	$\hat{\rho}_{EP_2Q}=.778$	$\hat{\rho}_{EP_2Y}=.720$

Criterion validity coefficients

1. ρ_{S_1Q} =Pairwise correlation between S_1 and Q.
2. ρ_{S_2Q} =Pairwise correlation between S_2 and Q.
3. ρ_{R_1Q} =Pairwise correlation between R_1 and Q.
4. ρ_{R_2Q} =Pairwise correlation between R_2 and Q.
5. ρ_{NQ_1Q} =Pairwise correlation between NQ_1 and Q.
6. ρ_{NQ_2Q} =Pairwise correlation between NQ_2 and Q.
7. ρ_{EP_1Q} =Pairwise correlation between EP_1 and Q.
8. ρ_{EP_2Q} =Pairwise correlation between EP_2 and Q.

Construct validity coefficients

1. ρ_{S_1Y} =Pairwise correlation between S_1 and Y.
2. ρ_{S_2Y} =Pairwise correlation between S_2 and Y.
3. ρ_{R_1Y} =Pairwise correlation between R_1 and Y.
4. ρ_{R_2Y} =Pairwise correlation between R_2 and Y.
5. ρ_{NQ_1Y} =Pairwise correlation between NQ_1 and Y.
6. ρ_{NQ_2Y} =Pairwise correlation between NQ_2 and Y.
7. ρ_{EP_1Y} =Pairwise correlation between EP_1 and Y.
8. ρ_{EP_2Y} =Pairwise correlation between EP_2 and Y.

[a] The validity coefficients are the pairwise correlations between the quality models and the global measures of perceived quality (Q) and preference (Y).
[b] The unweighted P–E model corresponds to expression (1) with $W_j=1.0$.
[c] The weighted P–E model corresponds to expression (1).
[d] The unweighted revised P–E model corresponds to expression (1) with $W_j=1.0$ and $E^*_j=E_{i}j$.
[e] The weighted revised P–E model corresponds to the expression (1) with $E^*_{i}j = E_{i}j$.
[f] The weighted normed quality (NQ) model corresponds to expression (8).
[g] The unweighted evaluated performance (EP) model corresponds to expression (6) with $W_j=1.0$.
[h] The weighted evaluated performance (EP) model corresponds to expression (6).

The results of the criterion validity test (H_1), presented in Table 7, indicate that the criterion validity coefficient for the unweighted evaluated performance (EP) measure is statistically significantly greater than the criterion validity coefficients for each of the P–E and NQ measures. The criterion validity coefficient for the weighted evaluated performance (EP) model is statistically significantly greater than the criterion validity coefficients for the weighted P–E and the unweighted and weighted NQ measures, but is not statistically significantly greater than the criterion validity coefficients for the unweighted P–E models. These findings, which partially support H_1, suggest that the EP measure is characterized by somewhat higher criterion validity than the P–E and NQ measure. However, the results indicate that the weighted models perform somewhat more poorly than the unweighted models.

The construct validity test results (H_2), presented in Table 8, indicate that H_2 is supported by all the tests. In each test the evaluated performance (EP) measure is characterized by higher construct validity than each P–E and MQ measure.

In general, these findings indicate considerable support for the hypotheses that

Table 7.   Criterion validity tests (H_1) – tests of differences between the criterion validities of the P–E, Normed Quality (NQ), and Evaluated Performance (EP) models

Hypothesis		Estimates	Correlation difference	t^a
H1.a tests (the unweighted EP model compared with the other models)				
$\rho_{EP_1Q} > \rho_{S_1Q}$	$\hat{\rho}_{EP_1Q}=.806$	$\hat{\rho}_{S_1Q}=.725$	.081	2.001[b]
$\rho_{EP_1Q} > \rho_{S_2Q}$		$\hat{\rho}_{S_2Q}=.698$	.108	2.543[c]
$\rho_{EP_1Q} > \rho_{R_1Q}$		$\hat{\rho}_{R_1Q}=.733$	.073	1.954[b]
$\rho_{EP_1Q} > \rho_{R_2Q}$		$\hat{\rho}_{R_1Q}=.713$	.093	2.313[b]
$\rho_{EP_1Q} > \rho_{NQ_1Q}$		$\hat{\rho}_{NQ_1Q}=.701$	.105	2.476[c]
$\rho_{EP_1Q} > \rho_{NQ_2Q}$		$\hat{\rho}_{NQ_2Q}=.688$	.118	2.617[c]
H1.b tests (the weighted EP model compared with the other models)				
$\rho_{EP_2Q} > \rho_{S_1Q}$	$\hat{\rho}_{EP_2Q}=.778$	$\hat{\rho}_{S_1Q}=.725$	.053	1.260
$\rho_{EP_2Q} > \rho_{S_2Q}$		$\hat{\rho}_{S_2Q}=.698$	.080	1.865[b]
$\rho_{EP_2Q} > \rho_{R_1Q}$		$\hat{\rho}_{R_1Q}=.733$	.045	1.125
$\rho_{EP_2Q} > \rho_{R_2Q}$		$\hat{\rho}_{R_2Q}=.713$	.065	1.685[b]
$\rho_{EP_2Q} > \rho_{NQ_1Q}$		$\hat{\rho}_{NQ_1Q}=.701$	.077	1.710[b]
$\rho_{EP_2Q} > \rho_{NQ_2Q}$		$\hat{\rho}_{NQ_2Q}=.688$	.090	1.945[b]

[a] The *t*-value is calculated by a formula specified by Blalock (1960, p. 317) for testing the differences between two correlations when the samples are not independent.
[b] $p < .05$ (one-tail *t*-test).
[c] $p < .01$ (one-tail *t*-test).

Table 8.   Construct validity tests (H_2) – tests of differences between the construct validities of the P–E, Normed Quality (NQ), and Evaluated Performance (EP) models

Hypothesis		Estimates	Correlation difference	t^a
H2.a tests (the unweighted EP model compared with the other models)				
$\rho_{EP_1Y} > \rho_{S_1Y}$	$\hat{\rho}_{EP_1Y}=.753$	$\hat{\rho}_{S_1Y}=.604$	.149	3.046[c]
$\rho_{EP_1Y} > \rho_{S_2Y}$		$\hat{\rho}_{S_2Y}=.588$	.165	3.530[c]
$\rho_{EP_1Y} > \rho_{R_1Y}$		$\hat{\rho}_{R_1Y}=.639$	.114	2.494[c]
$\rho_{EP_1Y} > \rho_{R_2Y}$		$\hat{\rho}_{R_2Y}=.640$	.113	2.470[c]
$\rho_{EP_1Y} > \rho_{NQ_1Y}$		$\hat{\rho}_{NQ_1Y}=.622$	.131	2.501[c]
$\rho_{EP_1Y} > \rho_{NQ_2Y}$		$\hat{\rho}_{NQ_2Y}=.576$	.177	3.661[c]
H2.b tests (the weighted EP model compared with the other models)				
$\rho_{EP_2Y} > \rho_{S_1Y}$	$\hat{\rho}_{EP_2Y}=.720$	$\hat{\rho}_{S_1Y}=.604$	.116	2.319[b]
$\rho_{EP_2Y} > \rho_{S_2Y}$		$\hat{\rho}_{S_2Y}=.588$	.132	2.661[c]
$\rho_{EP_2Y} > \rho_{R_1Y}$		$\hat{\rho}_{R_1Y}=.639$	.081	1.736[b]
$\rho_{EP_2Y} > \rho_{R_2Y}$		$\hat{\rho}_{R_2Y}=.640$	.080	1.832[b]
$\rho_{EP_2Y} > \rho_{NQ_1Y}$		$\hat{\rho}_{NQ_1Y}=.622$	.098	1.999[b]
$\rho_{EP_2Y} > \rho_{NQ_2Y}$		$\hat{\rho}_{NQ_2Y}=.576$	.144	2.843[b]

[a] See footnote [a] in Table 7.
[b] $p < .05$ (one-tail *t*-test).
[c] $p < .01$ (one-tail *t*-test).

the criterion and construct validity of the evaluated performance (EP) perceived quality measurement framework is higher than the concurrent and construct validity of the P–E and NQ measurement frameworks.

DISCUSSION

The empirical tests in this study are limited to the examination of the validity of perceived quality measures using a limited subset of the SERVQUAL items,[16] single-item indicators for satisfaction and shopping preference, and a two-item indicator for purchase intentions. In addition, the tests involve a narrow retail setting and were on the basis of data from a limited sample of respondents. Though caution is necessary in generalizing the findings, considerable evidence of problems associated with the P–E service quality framework was found; consequently, additional research examining this issue is warranted.

Conceptual issues and questions

The examination of the alternative perceived quality models suggests several conceptual questions that deserve attention in further research. For specific issues involve (1) conceptual definition ambiguity, (2) the theoretical justification of expectations in the measurement of perceived quality, (3) the usefulness of the probability specification in the evaluated performance (EP) measurement framework, and (4) the link between perceived quality and consumer satisfaction/dissatisfaction.

Expectation definition ambiguity

A review of the service quality literature and the results of this study's empirical tests indicate that it is conceptually unclear what the SERVQUAL expectations E concept represents. First, the conceptualization of E as an ideal standard suggests a possible classic attitudinal model ideal point interpretation. Under this interpretation it is theoretically unsound to assume, as specified in the P–E equation (1), that performance levels that exceed the ideal standard result in higher perceived quality than performance levels that equal the ideal standard. Second, if E is interpreted to represent a feasible ideal point concept, a positive monotonic linkage between the SERVQUAL P–E measure and perceived quality would not be expected when the attributes involved are finite ideal point (i.e. non-infinite classic ideal point) attributes. Third, the revised SERVQUAL E* measurement instructions request respondents to rate the service issues in terms of the degree to which they are

---

[16]Most of the SERVQUAL attributes can be expected to be considered to be vector attributes (infinite ideal point attributes) by most respondents (see Table 4 for exceptions). Future studies examining the validity of the P–E, NQ, and EP models should evaluate the models in situations in which there is a higher incidence of finite ideal point attributes, because in these situations the differences among the models are most pronounced.

essential. However, it is not theoretically clear why high performance on essential attributes should reflect lower perceived quality than high performance on less essential attributes, as predicted in equation (1). Clearly, each of these interpretations is not compatible with the mathematical properties of the P–E perceived quality specification. However, on the basis of the definitional frameworks suggested in the service quality literature, it is difficult to envision any definitions of the SERVQUAL expectations (E) concept that are compatible both with the mathematical properties of the P–E measurement specification and the assumption that the P–E measure is conceptually differentiated from the disconfirmed expectation concept specified in traditional consumer satisfaction/dissatisfaction models.

This definitional ambiguity is reflected in a model specified by Bolton and Drew (1991). Building on the consumer satisfaction literature, particularly Oliver (1981), they specify disconfirmed expectations to be a predictor of satisfaction. However, using Parasuraman, Zeithaml and Berry (1988) framework as a theoretical foundation, they specify the same disconfirmed expectations variable to be a predictor of perceived quality. The model, therefore, explicitly assumes that the disconfirmed expectations concepts specified by Oliver (1981) and Parasuraman, Zeithaml and Berry (1988) are identical. This assumption is incongruent with the Parasuraman, Zeithaml and Berry (1988) definitional framework, which differentiates the P–E service gap from the concept of disconfirmed expectations specified in consumer satisfaction models.

The theoretical justification of the SERVQUAL E

A second conceptual issue concerns the question of whether the service expectation concept is theoretically justified as a component of a perceived quality measure. The following are examples of issues that are linked to this question:

1. The P–E model results in various P and E values producing identical P–E scores. For example, there are seven P and E combinations that produce P–E scores equal to 0 ($P = 1$ and $E = 1$; $P = 2$ and $E = 2$...$P = 7$ and $E = 7$). A question that deserves attention in further research is whether 'tied' P–E values can be expected to correspond to equal perceived quality. The evaluated performance (EP) perceived quality model suggests these tied P–E scores would correspond to different levels of perceived quality depending on the location of the classic ideal attribute intensity levels. For example, these models suggest that assuming the ideal performance level is 6, a $P = 1$, $E = 1$ situation would correspond to a lower level of perceived quality than a $P = 6$, $E = 6$ situation.

2. In the context of a consumer evaluating the quality of a consideration set of competing service providers, a logical assumption is that the expectation (E) would be the same for each member of the consumer's consideration set. Consequently, when implementing the P–E measurement framework in this context, each respondent would supply one set of E responses and multiple sets of P responses – one set for each member of the consideration set. Using equation (1) to calculate the perceived quality (Q_1) index for the consideration set would result in the E_{ij} response vector being subtracted from each of the P_{ij} response

vectors. Consequently, for each member of the consideration set, the SERVQUAL Q_i would be perfectly correlated with the summated P_{ij} scores. Therefore, the E_{ij} component provides no information beyond that of the performance component concerning differences among the consideration set members.

Usefulness of the evaluated performance probability component

A third conceptual issue involves the usefulness of the probability component of the evaluated performance (EP) perceived quality framework. One question concerning this issue is the degree to which measures of consumer perceptions of the probabilities of various performance levels across attributes can be used to operationalize the concepts of search, experience, and credence properties. The following are examples of issues that could be examined in further research:

1. Attributes with comparable mean levels of anticipated performance can have different probability estimates associated with various specific performance levels. Management could reduce the risk associated with attributes, particularly with respect to experience or credence attributes, by using marketing programs designed to decrease the variance of the probability distributions associated with particular attributes' performance levels. This might be achieved by using performance guarantees or tangible factors that 'signal' performance predictability (e.g. physical facilities, equipment, certifications, and price).
2. Service alternatives with comparable performance (or anticipated performance) quality can be perceived by consumers to have different probability distributions with respect to performance on particular attributes. For example, experience with a service can reduce the variance of the distribution of customers' probability ratings associated with various performance levels. Inducing customers to switch service suppliers, therefore, not only requires projecting an image that the alternative service provider's performance quality exceeds the current supplier, but also that the probability distribution associated with alternative performance levels on important attributes is narrow enough so that the disability associated with perceived switching risk does not block the switching decision.

The perceived quality-consumer satisfaction link

A fourth conceptual question concerns the causal link between perceived quality and consumer satisfaction. Most research on consumer satisfaction has been on the basis of the Oliver (1981) transaction-specific focus in which satisfaction is specified as a function of disconfirmation of expectations (with expectations defined as consumers' performance forecasts). Building on this conceptualization of satisfaction and the assumption that perceived service quality is a 'global judgment or attitude', Parasuraman, Zeithaml and Berry (1988) suggest that perceived quality is a function of (caused by) satisfaction.

Significant evidence suggests the perceived quality-consumer satisfaction causal linkage may be opposite to that specified by service quality researchers. First, the

Monroe and Krishnan (1985) definition of perceived product quality as 'the perceived ability of a product to provide satisfaction', implies a quality-to-satisfaction link. Second, in a consumer satisfaction model specified by Churchill and Surprenant (1982), global performance, defined as 'overall unit quality', is specified as a predictor of consumer satisfaction. Third, the concept of a performance norm has been used in consumer satisfaction models as a comparison standard (Oliver, 1989). In general 'performance-minus-norm' disconfirmation is hypothesized to predict consumer satisfaction in these models (Woodruff, Cadotte and Jenkins, 1983).

One way to integrate these two causal perspectives is to specify two perceived quality concepts – transaction-specific quality and relationship quality – and to specify perceived transaction-specific quality as the transaction-specific performance component of contemporary consumer satisfaction models. This implies that transaction-specific satisfaction is a function of perceived transaction-specific performance quality. Furthermore, if perceived relationship quality can be assumed to be similar to the Parasuraman, Zeithaml, and Berry (1988) perceived service quality concept or to Oliver's (1981) 'base attitude level', transaction-specific satisfaction could be argued to be a predictor of perceived long-term relationship quality.

Measurement validity issues

The results of this study indicate the SERVQUAL expectations (E) and revised expectations (E*) measures lack discriminant validity with respect to the concepts of attribute importance, classic attribute ideal-points, and performance forecasts. This finding suggests a considerable portion of the variance SERVQUAL expectations measures may be because of respondents' misinterpretations of the question. Unless this measurement validity problem is corrected, it will be difficult to test the SERVQUAL measurement framework. For example, the findings of this study indicate the evaluated performance (EP) measurement framework is characterized by higher validity than the P–E and normed quality (NQ) frameworks. However, the lower validity of the P–E and NQ measurement specifications could be caused by the conceptual problems identified previously and/or to the measurement validity problems associated with the E and revised E* measures.

The findings concerning the ideal (I) component of the EP model suggest some respondent confusion in interpreting the scale. Because the intended interpretation is the 'perfect' attribute level as specified in ideal point attitude models, research is needed that focuses on increasing the discriminant validity between measures of ideal performance and the concepts of attribute importance and performance feasibility.

The research results indicate that the inclusion of attribute weights in the SERVQUAL P–E, normed quality (NQ), and evaluated performance (EP) models does not improve the validity of the models. This result is similar to the findings of other research that indicates importance weights often do not increase, and may decrease, the predictive validity of multiattribute models (Bass and Wilkie, 1973).

CONCLUSIONS

My purpose was to examine the validity of the P–E 'gap' framework as currently specified and, on the basis of this examination, develop and test alternative models of consumers' perceptions of quality. The examination of the P–E service quality model indicates a number of problems, particularly with respect to the conceptual and operational definitions of the expectations (E) and the revised expectations (E*) components of the model. These problems, in turn, create ambiguity concerning the interpretation and theoretical justification of the P–E perceived quality concept. On the basis of these problems, an evaluated performance (EP) model and a normed quality (NQ) model of perceived quality are developed and, along with the P–E model, empirically tested.

The results of a qualitative assessment of the SERVQUAL (Parasuraman, Zeithaml and Berry, 1988; Zeithaml, Parasuraman and Berry, 1990) expectation (E) and revised expectation (E*) measures indicate that the measures lack discriminant validity with respect to the concepts of attribute importance, performance forecasts, and classic attribute ideal points. This suggests a considerable portion of the variance in the SERVQUAL expectations measures may be caused by respondents' misinterpretation of the question rather than to different attitudes or perceptions. Though somewhat less pronounced, similar discriminant validity problems were found for the ideal-point measure used to operationalize the EP perceived quality model.

The results of criterion and construct validity tests indicate that, when compared to the SERVQUAL P–E and normed quality (NQ) frameworks, the evaluated performance (EP) framework is characterized by greater concurrent and construct validity. A comparison of the weighted versus unweighted models indicates that the unweighted models generally performed better than the weighted models in terms of concurrent and construct validity.

The EP model proposed here is designed to overcome some of the problems associated with the P–E gap conceptualization of service quality. Though the findings indicate that the EP model may be more valid than the SERVQUAL P–E and the NQ models, additional theoretical and empirical research is needed to further examine the question of which framework examined in this study, or perhaps another framework, is most valid and useful.

APPENDIX A

The survey instruments

1. The directions for the SERVQUAL (P^s), E$_j$), and E$_j^*$) are listed in Table 1. The ten SERVQUAL items used, which were stated as published in the literature (Zeithaml, Parasuraman and Berry, 1990; Parasuraman, Berry and Zeithaml, 1990), were

    Tangibles
    (1) XYZ has modern looking equipment.
    (2) XYZ's physical facilities are visually appealing.

Reliability
(3) When you have a problem, XYZ shows a sincere interest in solving it.
(4) XYZ performs the service right the first time.

Responsiveness
(5) Employees of XYZ give you prompt service.
(6) Employees of XYZ are never too busy to respond to your requests.

Assurance
(7) Employees of XYZ are consistently courteous.
(8) Employees of XYZ can answer your questions.

Empathy
(9) XYZ employees understand your specific needs.
(10) XYZ has operating hours convenient to all its customers.

2. The directions for the semantic differential scales were as follows:

Performance (P^d). Please read the descriptions on each end of the following scales and check the blanks that best describe your feelings towards the store listed above. You should check an end blank if a phrase is very descriptive of the store. The center blank is a neutral rating. The other blanks represent intermediate positions of slightly descriptive and quite descriptive.

Ideal (I). Please read the descriptions on each end of the following scales and check the blanks that best describe your *ideal or perfect discount store.*

The following is an example of the semantic differential scaling format:

XYZ does not have   XYZ has
modern-looking equipment ....modern-looking equipment

3. Overall perceived quality was measured by the following questions:

a. Using the scale provided, rate the overall quality of service you receive in XYZ.

Extremely Low Quality									Extremely High Quality	
0	1	2	3	4	5	6	7	8	9	10

b. XYZ provides high quality customer service (5-point 'Strongly Agree = 5/Strongly Disagree = 1' scale).

4. Shopping preferences, purchase intentions, and overall satisfaction were measured with the following 5-point 'Strongly Agree = 5/Strongly Disagree = 1' scale:

a. I am satisfied with the services I receive in XYZ.

b. I do *not* intend to shop in XYZ very often in the future (reversed coded).

c. I will purchase a large number of products in XYZ during the next year.

d. I prefer to shop at XYZ more than I do at other local discount stores.

5. The directions for the attribute importance weight measures (W_j) were as follows:

Please look over the following list and find one factor for which it would be most important to you to get excellent performance instead of poor performance. Assign 100 points to this CRITICAL FACTOR. Then consider each of the remaining factors. For each factor, how important is it for you to receive excellent service rather than poor service? If it is only half as important for this factor as it is for the CRITICAL FACTOR, assign it 50 points. In general, assign points to the factors that indicate how they compare to the critical factor in terms of the importance of getting excellent service rather than poor service. If any factors are of equal importance, assign them an equal number of points.

APPENDIX B

Example follow-up responses – perceived quality study

A. *Not Feasible*
- Not possible – no way that the clerk can understand my specific needs.
- Can't wait on everybody at once.
- Never is a bad word to use – it's not possible.
- I've gone into the store knowing exactly myself what I want.
- Can't expect it to be right every time.
- Never is a pretty strong word – it's impossible.

B *Sufficient*
- Better than half is OK.
- It doesn't have to be ultra modern.
- Good equipment, well maintained, would do just as well as modern equipment.
- They should have good equipment – but it doesn't need to be the most modern. Seven would imply they should have the most modern equipment – and I think a 6 would suffice.

C. *Not Necessary*
- I wouldn't know what modern equipment was – it's not necessary anyway.
- Not necessary to know to exact need.
- It's not absolutely necessary.

D. *Less Important*
- Not as important as other things I was ranking then.
- It's not important if you know what you want.
- I don't think the visual appearance is that important.
- The physical facilities are not as important as the people.
- The word 'all' is the problem – it's not important to me that you stay open all day and all night to serve all customers.

E. *Implied Less Important*
- Not a critical thing
- Doesn't make a big difference.
- Looks don't have much bearing.
- Doesn't matter – I don't care about this.
- I don't care what the equipment looks like.
- It just doesn't make any difference to me.
- If it's visually appealing, it doesn't really matter to me – it's the price I'm looking for.
- I don't care either way – it doesn't matter.
- It's not a major thing.
- I don't care as much about the store as I do about the products.
- As long as they have the product, it shouldn't matter what the store looks like.
- Modern looking doesn't impress me.
- It's not crucial.

F. *Ideal*
- Too modern can be a detriment – the stuff can be too advanced.
- I don't want employees to know what my needs are. They don't need to know. I like the anonymity.
- If people are overly courteous – that can make you nervous.
- Don't want my store to be machine like.
- I don't want them to open as many hours as they are now – Sundays for example.
- You can be too modern.
- I want to be left alone when I'm in the store.
- I don't what them to be too pushy.
- I don't think they should be open on Sundays.
- I don't want them to be over solicitous of me.
- It's not fair to the employees – too much pressure on the employees.

- I've been in stores where, instead of prompt service, they get to where they're on top of you bugging you all the time.
- I don't like stores that are ultra modern and gleamy chrome – I think they become rather cold.

- I don't want someone who is going to talk my head off or be over aggressive.
- I don't want a clerk at the store waiting for me to come in.
- I don't want the store employees to shake my hand when I go into the store and pat me on the back when I leave.

G. Forecast

- That's the way discount stores are.
- They just aren't.

- Unlikely to be perfect.
- All of them have pretty much good hours.
- A five is normal for a discount store – you're just not going to get perfection.

H. Examples of double classifications

1. A five rating is good enough. Being modern isn't important (Sufficient/Importance).
2. It's not that important to me – doesn't have to be perfect (Sufficient/Importance).
3. It's not important – not necessary to be perfect (Not Necessary/Importance).
4. Not necessary – my ideal would be to not be open on Sundays (Not Necessary/Ideal).
5. It's not necessary – you wouldn't get that kind of service anyway (Not Necessary/Forecast).
6. If they could satisfy me half the time I'd be satisfied – nobody's perfect (Not Feasible/Sufficient).
7. Not humanly possible – good rather than perfect is good enough (Not Feasible/Sufficient).
8. It's not possible or even necessary to understand everybody's needs – it's impossible (Not Feasible/Not Necessary).
9. Not necessary – anyway, they can't understand everyone's needs – it's impossible (Not Feasible/Not Necessary).
10. That's impossible – it's unimportant (Not Feasible/Importance).
11. Can't be perfect – anyway, it's not important (Not Feasible/Importance).
12. If it was constantly installing new modern looking equipment, they would be too busy installing new equipment to wait on customers (Not Feasible/Ideal).
13. If I think the products are good, the facilities don't have to be that good (Sufficient/Implied Importance).
14. A five is good enough – you just don't get sevens in discount stores (Sufficient/Forecast).
15. You don't get perfection in these kinds of stores – I don't care about that when I go to a Target or K-Mart (Forecast/Implied Importance).
16. It isn't important. In fact, you can overdo modern aspects (Ideal/Importance).
17. When I'm in a store, I usually prefer to be left alone. It's just not important that they know what I need (Ideal/Importance).

ACKNOWLEDGEMENTS

The author thanks the editor, three anonymous reviewers, Sridar N. Ramaswami and John G. Wacker (Iowa State University), and Jon Austin (University of Wisconsin – Madison) for their valuable comments on earlier drafts of this article.

REFERENCES

Ahtola, O. T. (1975) 'The Vector Model of Preference: An Alternative to the Fishbein Model', *Journal of Marketing Research* **12** (February): 52–59.

American Heritage Dictionary (1985) Boston: Houghton Mifflin Co.

Bass, F. and Wilkie, W. L. (1973) 'A Comparative Analysis of Attitudinal Predictions of Brand Preference'. *Journal of Marketing Research.* **10** (August): 262–269.

Berry, L. L., Zeithaml, V. A. and Parasuraman, A. (1985) 'Quality Counts in Services, Too'. *Business Horizons* **28** (May/June): 44–52.

Blalock, H. M. (1960) *Social Statistics.* New York: McGraw-Hill Book Company.

Bollen, K. A. (1989) *Structural Equations with Latent Variables.* New York: John Wiley and Sons.

Bolton, R. N. and Drew, J. H. (1991) 'A Multistage Model of Customers' Assessments of Service Quality and Value'. *Journal of Consumer Research* **17** (March): 375–384.

Brown, S. W. and Swartz, T. A. (1989) 'A Gap Analysis of Professional Service Quality'. *Journal of Marketing* **53** (April): 92–98.

Carman, J. M. (1990) 'Consumer Perceptions of Service Quality: An Assessment of the SERVQUAL Dimensions'. *Journal of Retailing* **66** (Spring) 33–55.

Chaplin, J. P. (1981) *Dictionary of Psychology.* New York: Dell Publishing Co., Inc.

Churchill, G. A., Jr and Surprenant, C. (1982) 'An Investigation into the Determinants of Customer Satisfaction'. *Journal of Marketing Research.* **19** (November): 491–504.

Cronin, J. J. Jr. and Taylor, S. A. (1992) 'Measuring Service Quality: A Re-examination and Extension'. *Journal of Marketing* **56** (July): 55–68.

Ginter, L. (1974) 'An Experimental Investigation of Attitude Change and Choice of a New Brand', *Journal of Marketing Research* **11** (February): 30–40.

Green, P. E. and Srinivasan, V. (1978) 'Conjoint Analysis in Consumer Research: Issues and Outlook'. *Journal of Consumer Research* **5** (September): 103–123.

Hostage, G. M. (1975) 'Quality Control in a Service Business'. *Harvard Business Review* (July/August): 98–106.

Lilien, G. L., Kotler, P. and Moorthy, K. S. (1992) *Market Models.* Englewood Cliffs, NJ: Prentice Hall, Inc.

Miller, J. A. (1977) 'Studying Satisfaction, Modifying Models, Eliciting Expectations, Posing Problems, and Making Meaningful Measurements'. In *Conceptualization and Measurement of Consumer Satisfaction and Dissatisfaction* (H. K. Hunt, Ed.). Cambridge, MA: Marketing Science Institute, pp. 72–91.

Monroe, K. B. and Krishnan, R. (1985) 'The Effect of Price on Subjective Product Evaluations'. In *Perceived Quality* (J. Jacoby and J. C. Olson, Eds). Lexington, MA: Lexington Books, pp. 209–232.

Oliver, R. L. (1981) 'Measurement and Evaluation of Satisfaction Processes in Retail Settings' *Journal of Retailing* **57** (Fall): 25–48.

Oliver, R. L. (1989) 'Processing of the Satisfaction Response in Consumption: A Suggested Framework and Research Propositions'. *Journal of Consumer Satisfaction/Dissatisfaction and Complaining Behavior* **2**: 1–16.

Olshavsky, R. W. and Miller, J. A. (1972) 'Consumer Expectations, Product Performance, and Perceived Product Quality'. *Journal of Marketing Research* **9** (February): 19–21.

Parasuraman, A., Berry, L. L. and Zeithaml, V. A. (1990) *An Empirical Examination of Relationships in an Extended Service Quality Model.* Cambridge, MA: Marketing Science Institute.

Parasuraman, A., Zeithaml, V. A. and Berry, L. L. (1985) 'A Conceptual Model of Service Quality and Its Implications for Future Research'. *Journal of Marketing* **49** (Fall): 41–50.

Parasuraman, A., Zeithaml, V. A. and Berry, L. L. (1986) *SERVQUAL: A Multiple-Item Scale for Measuring Consumer Perceptions of Service Quality.* Cambridge, Massachusetts: Marketing Science Institute.

Parasuraman, A., Zeithaml, V. A. and Berry, L. L. (1988) 'SERVQUAL: A Multiple-Item Scale for Measuring Consumer Perceptions of Service Quality'. *Journal of Retailing* **64** (Spring): 12–40.

Prakash, V. (1984) 'Validity and Reliability of the Confirmation of Expectations Paradigm as a Determinant of Consumer Satisfaction'. *Journal of the Academy of Marketing Science,* **12** (Fall): 63–76.

Swan, J. E. and Trawick, I. F. (1980) 'Satisfaction Related to Predictive vs. Desired Expectations'. In *Refining Concepts and Measures of Consumer Satisfaction and Complaining Behavior* (H. K. Hunt and R. L. Days, Eds). Bloomington, IN: Indiana University, pp. 7–12.

Swartz, T. A. and Brown, S. W. (1989) 'Consumer and Provider Expectations and Experiences in Evaluating Professional Service Quality'. *Journal of the Academy of Marketing Science.* **17** (Spring): 189–195.

Teas, R. K. (1993) 'Consumer Expectations and the Measurement of Perceived Service Quality'. *Journal of Professional Services Marketing* 8 (2): 33–54.

Woodruff, R. B., Cadotte, E. R. and Jenkins, R. L. (1983) 'Modeling Consumer Satisfaction Processes Using Experience-Based Norms'. *Journal of Marketing Research.* **20** (August): 296–304.

Zeithaml, V. A. (1988) 'Consumer Perceptions of Price, Quality, and Value: A Means-End Model and Synthesis of Evidence'. *Journal of Marketing Research.* **52** (July): 2–22.

Zeithaml, V. A., Berry, L. L. and Parasuraman, A. (1988) 'Communication and Control Processes in the Delivery of Service Quality'. *Journal of Marketing* 52 (April): 35–48.

Zeithaml, V. A., Berry, L. L. and Parasuraman, A. (1991) 'The Nature and Determinants of Customer Expectations of Service'. Marketing Science Institute, working paper No. 91–113, Marketing Science Institute, Cambridge, MA.

Zeithaml, V. A., Parasuraman, A. and Berry, L. L. (1990) *Delivering Quality Service Balancing Customer Perceptions and Expectations.* New York: The Free Press.

14

SERVQUAL: Review, Critique, Research Agenda

Francis Buttle

SERVQUAL: A PRIMER

SERVQUAL provides a technology for measuring and managing service quality (SQ). Since 1985, when the technology was first published its innovators Parasuraman, Zeithaml and Berry have further developed, promulgated and promoted the technology through a series of publications (Parasuraman *et al.*, 1985, 1986, 1988, 1990, 1991a, 1991b, 1993, 1994; Zeithaml *et al.*, 1990, 1991, 1992, 1993).

The ABI/Inform database 'Global edition' (September 1994) reports that service quality has been a keyword in some 1447 articles published in the period January 1992 to April 1994. By contrast SERVQUAL has been a keyword in just 41 publications. These publications incorporate both theoretical discussions and applications of SERVQUAL in a variety of industrial commercial and not-for-profit settings. Published studies include tyre retailing (Carman, 1990), dental services (Carman, 1990), hotels (Saleh and Ryan, 1992) travel and tourism (Fick and Ritchie, 1991), car servicing (Bouman and van der Wiele, 1992), business schools (Rigotti and Pitt, 1992), higher education (Ford *et al.*, 1993; McElwee and Redman, 1993), hospitality (Johns, 1993), business-to-business channel partners (Kong and Mayo, 1993), accounting firms (Freeman and Dart, 1993), architectural services (Baker and Lamb, 1993), recreational services (Taylor *et al.*, 1993), hospitals (Babakus and Mangold, 1992; Mangold and Babakus, 1991; Reidenbach and Sandifer-Smallwood, 1990; Soliman, 1992; Vandamme and Leunis, 1993; Walbridge and Delene, 1993), airline catering (Babakus *et al.*, 1993a), banking (Kwon and Lee, 1994; Wong and Perry, 1991), apparel retailing (Gagliano and Hathcote, 1994) and local government (Scott and Schieff, 1993). There have also been many unpublished SERVQUAL studies. In the last two years alone, the author has been associated with a number of sectoral and corporate SERVQUAL studies: computer services, construction, mental health services, hospitality, recreational services, ophthalmological services, and retail services. In addition, a number of organizations, such as the Midland and Abbey National banks have adopted it.

Service quality (SQ) has become an important research topic because of its apparent relationship to costs (Crosby, 1979), profitability (Buzzell and Gale, 1987; Rust and Zahorik, 1993; Zahorik and Rust, 1992), customer satisfaction (Bolton and Drew, 1991; Boulding *et al.*, 1993), customer retention (Reichheld and Sasser, 1990), and positive word of mouth. SQ is widely regarded as a driver of corporate marketing and financial performance.

SERVQUAL is founded on the view that the customer's assessment of SQ is paramount. This assessment is conceptualized as a gap between what the customer expects by way of SQ from a class of service providers (say, all opticians), and their evaluations of the performance of a particular service provider (say a single Specsavers store). SQ is presented as a multidimensional construct. In their original formulation Parasuraman *et al.* (1985) identified ten components of SQ:

1. reliability;
2. responsiveness;
3. competence;
4. access;
5. courtesy;
6. communication;
7. credibility;
8. security;
9. understanding/knowing the customer;
10. tangibles.

(See Appendix for definitions and examples.) In their 1988 work these components were collapsed into five dimensions: reliability, assurance, tangibles, empathy, responsiveness, as defined in Table 1. Reliability, tangibles and responsiveness remained distinct, but the remaining seven components collapsed into two aggregate dimensions, assurance and empathy.[1] Parasuraman *et al.* developed a 22-item instrument with which to measure customers' expectations and perceptions (E and P) of the five RATER dimensions. Four or five numbered items are used to measure each dimension. The instrument is administered twice in different forms, first to measure expectations and second to measure perceptions.

Table 1. SERVQUAL dimensions

Dimensions	Definition	Items in scale
Reliability	The ability to perform the promised service dependably and accurately	4
Assurance	The knowledge and courtesy of employees and their ability to convey trust and confidence	5
Tangibles	The appearance of physical facilities, equipment personnel and communication materials	4
Empathy	The provision of caring, individualized attention to customers	5
Responsiveness	The willingness to help customers and to provide prompt service	4

In 1991, Parasuraman *et al.* published a follow-up study which refined their previous work (1991b). Wording of all expectations items changed. The 1988 version has attempted to capture respondents' normative expectations. For example, one 1988 expectation item read 'Companies offering _____ services should keep their records accurately'. The revised wording focused on what customers would expect from 'excellent service companies'. The sample item was revised thus: 'Excellent companies offering _____ services will insist on error-free records'. Detailed wording of many perceptions items also changed. Two new items, one each for tangibles and assurance, were substituted for two original items. The tangible items referred to the appearance of communication materials. The assurance item referred to the knowledge of employees. Both references had been omitted in the 1988 version.

Analysis of SERVQUAL data can take several forms: item-by-item analysis (e.g. $P1 - E1$, $P2 - E2$); dimension-by-dimension analysis (e.g. $P1 + P2 + P3 + P4/4) - (E1 + E2 + E3 + E4/4)$, where $P1$ to $P4$, and $E1$ to $E4$, represent the four perception and expectation statements relating to a single dimension); and computation of the single measure of service quality $((P1 + P2 + P3 \ldots + P22/22) - (E1 + E2 + E3 + \ldots + E22/22))$, the so-called SERVQUAL gap.

Without question, SERVQUAL has been widely applied and is highly valued. Any critique of SERVQUAL, therefore, must be seen within this broader context of strong endorsement. What follows is a discussion of several criticisms which have been levelled at SERVQUAL elsewhere or have been experienced in the application of the technology of this author.

CRITICISMS OF SERVQUAL

Notwithstanding its growing popularity and widespread application, SERVQUAL has been subjected to a number of theoretical and operational criticisms which are detailed below:

1. Theoretical:
   - Paradigmatic objections: SERVQUAL is based on a disconfirmation paradigm rather than an attitudinal paradigm; and SERVQUAL fails to draw on established economic, statistical and psychological theory.
   - Gaps model: there is little evidence that customers assess service quality in terms of $P - E$ gaps.
   - Process orientation: SERVQUAL focuses on the process of service delivery, not the outcomes of the service encounter.
   - Dimensionality: SERVQUAL's five dimensions are not universals; the number of dimensions comprising SQ is contextualized; items do not always load on to the factors which one would a priori expect; and there is a high degree of intercorrelation between the five RATER dimensions.
2. Operational:
   - Expectations: the term expectation is polysemic; consumers use standards other than expectations to evaluate SQ; and SERVQUAL fails to measure absolute SQ expectations.

- Item composition: four or five items can not capture the variability within each SQ dimension.
- Moments of truth (MOT): customers' assessments of SQ may vary from MOT to MOT.
- Polarity: the reversed polarity of items in the scale causes respondent error.
- Scale points: the seven-point Likert scale is flawed.
- Two administrations: two administrations of the instrument causes boredom and confusion.
- Variance extracted: the over SERVQUAL score accounts for a disappointing proportion of item variances.

Each of the criticisms will be examined below.

Theoretical

Paradigmatic objections

Two major criticisms have been raised. First, SERVQUAL has been inappropriately based on an expectations-disconfirmation model rather than an attitudinal model of SQ. Second, it does not build on extant knowledge in economics, statistics and psychology.

SERVQUAL is based on the disconfirmation model widely adopted in the customer satisfaction literature. In this literature, customer satisfaction (CSat) is operationalized in terms of the relationship between expectations (E) and outcomes (O). If O matches E, customer satisfaction is predicted. If O exceeds E, then customer delight may be produced. If E exceeds O, then customer dissatisfaction is indicated.

According to Cronin and Taylor (1992, 1994) SERVQUAL is paradigmatically flawed because of its ill-judged adoption of this disconfirmation model. 'Perceived quality', they claim, 'is best conceptualized as an attitude'. They criticize Parasuraman et al. for their hesitancy to define perceived SQ in attitudinal terms, even though Parasuraman et al. (1988) had earlier claimed that SQ was 'similar in many ways to an attitude'. Cronin and Taylor observe:

> Researchers have attempted to differentiate service quality from consumer satisfaction, even while using the disconfirmation format to measure perceptions of service quality . . . this approach is not consistent with the differentiation expressed between these constructs in the satisfaction and attitude literatures.

Iacobucci et al.'s (1994) review of the debate surrounding the conceptual and operational differences between SQ and CSat concludes that the constructs 'have not been consistently defined and differentiated from each other in the literature'. She suggests that the two constructs may be connected in a number of ways. First, they may be both different operationalizations of the same construct, 'evaluation'. Second, they may be orthogonally related, i.e. they may be entirely different constructs. Third, they may be conceptual cousins. Their family connections may be dependent on a number of other considerations, including for example, the duration of the evaluation. Parasuraman et al. (1985) have described satisfaction as more situation- or encounter-specific, and quality as more holistic, developed over a longer period of time, although they offer no empirical evidence to support this contention. SQ and CSat may also be related by time order. The predominant belief is that SQ is the logical predecessor to CSat, but this remains unproven. Cronin and Taylor's critique draws support from Oliver's (1980) research which suggests that SQ and CSat are distinct constructs but are related in that satisfaction mediates the effect of prior-period perceptions of SQ and causes revised SQ perceptions to be formed. SQ and CSat may also be differentiated by virtue of their content. Whereas SQ may be thought of as high in cognitive content, CSat may be more heavily loaded with affect (Oliver, 1993).

Cronin and Taylor suggest that the adequacy-importance model of attitude measurement should be adopted for SQ research. Iacobucci *et al.* (1994) add the observation that 'in some general psychological sense, it is not clear what short-term evaluations of quality and satisfaction are if not attitudes'. In turn, Parasuraman *et al.* (1994) have vigorously defended their position, claiming that critics seem 'to discount prior conceptual work in the SQ literature', and suggest that Cronin and Taylor's work 'does not justify their claim' that the disconfirmation paradigm is flawed.

In other words, Cronin and Taylor (1994) comment that:

> Recent conceptual advances suggest that the disconfirmation-based SERVQUAL scale is measuring neither service quality nor consumer satisfaction. Rather, the SERVQUAL scale appears at best an operationalization of only one of the many forms of expectancy-disconfirmation.

A different concern has been raised by Andersson (1992). He objects to SERVQUAL's failure to draw on previous social science research, particularly economic theory, statistics, and psychological theory. Parasuraman *et al.*'s work is highly inducive in that it moves from historically situated observation to general theory. Andersson (1992) claims that Parasuraman *et al.* 'abandon the principle of scientific continuity and deduction'. Among specific criticisms are the following:

First, Parasuraman *et al.*'s management technology takes no account of the costs of improving service quality. It is naive in assuming that the marginal revenue of SQ improvement always exceeds the marginal cost. (Aubrey and Zimbler (1983), Crosby (1979), Juran (1951) and Masser (1957) have addressed the issue of the costs/benefits of quality improvement in service settings.)

Second, Parasuraman *et al.* collect SQ data using ordinal scale methods (Likert scales) yet perform analyses with methods suited to interval-level data (factor analysis).

Third, Parasuraman *et al.* are at the 'absolute end of the street regarding possibilities to use statistical methods'. Ordinal scales do not allow for investigations of common product-moment correlations. Interdependencies among the dimensions of quality are difficult to describe. SERVQUAL studies cannot answer questions such as: Are there elasticities among the quality dimensions? Is the customer value of improvements a linear or non-linear function?

Fourth, Parasuraman *et al.* fail to draw on the large literature on the psychology of perception.

Gaps model

A related set of criticisms refer to the value and meaning of gaps identified in the disconfirmation model.

Babakus and Boller (1992) found the use of a 'gap' approach to SQ measurement 'intuitively appealing' but suspected that the 'difference scores do not provide any additional information beyond that already contained in the perceptions component of the SERVQUAL scale'. They found that the dominant contributor to the gap score was the perceptions score because of a generalized response tendency to rate expectations high.

Churchill and Surprenant (1982), in their work on CSat, also ponder whether gap measurements contribute anything new or of value given that the gap is a direct function of E and P. It has also been noted that:

> while conceptually, difference scores might be sensible, they are problematic in that they are *notoriously unreliable*, even when the measures from which the difference scores are derived are themselves highly reliable (Iacobucci et al., 1994).

Also, in the context of CSat, Oliver (1980) has pondered whether it might be preferable to consider the $P - E$ scores as raw differences or as ratios. No work has been reported using a ratio approach to measure SQ.

Iacobucci *et al.* (1994) take a different tack on the incorporation of E measures. They suggest that expectations might not exist or be formed clearly enough to serve as a standard for evaluation of a service experience. Expectations may be formed simultaneously with service consumption. Kahneman and Miller (1986) have also proposed that consumers may form 'experience-based norms' after service experiences, rather than expectations before.

A further issue raised by Babakus and Inhofe (1991) is that expectations may attract a social desirability response bias. Respondents may feel motivated to adhere to an 'I-have-high-expectations' social norm. Indeed, Parasuraman *et al.* report that in their testing of the 1988 version the majority of expectations scores were above six on the seven-point scale. The overall mean expectation was 6.22 (Parasuraman *et al.*, 1991b).

Teas (1993a, 1993b, 1994) has pondered the meaning of identified gaps. For examples, there are six ways of producing $P - E$ gaps of -1 ($P = 1$, $E = 2$; $P = 2$, $E = 3$; $P = 3$, $E = 4$; $P = 4$, $E = 5$; $P = 5$, $E = 6$; $P = 6$, $E = 7$). Do these tied gaps mean equal perceived SQ? He also noted that SERVQUAL research thus far has not established that all service providers within a consideration or choice set, e.g. all car-hire firms do, in fact, share the same expectations ratings across all items and dimensions.

A further criticism is that SERVQUAL fails to capture the dynamics of changing expectation. Consumers learn from experiences. The inference in much of Parasuraman *et al.*'s work is that expectations rise over time. An E score of seven in 1986 may not necessarily mean the same as an E score in 1996. Expectations may also fall over time (e.g. in the health service setting). Grönroos (1993) recognizes this weakness in our understanding of SQ, and has called for a new phase of service quality research to focus on the dynamics of service quality evaluation. Wotruba and Tyagi (1991) agree that more work is needed on how expectations are formed and changed over time.

Implicit in SERVQUAL is the assumption that positive and negative disconfirmation are symmetrically valent. However, from the customer's perspective, failure to meet expectations often seems a more significant outcome than success in meeting or exceeding expectations (Hardie *et al.*, 1992). Customers will often criticize poor service performance and not praise exceptional performance.

Recently, Cronin and taylor (1992) have tested a performance-based measure of SQ, dubbed SERVPERF, in four industries (baking, pest control, dry cleaning and fast food). They found that this measure explained more of the variance in an overall measure of SQ than did SERVQUAL. SERVPERF is composed of the 22 perception items in the SERVQUAL scale, and therefore excludes any consideration of expectations. In a later defence of their argument for a perceptions-only measure of SQ, Cronin and Taylor (1994) acknowledge that it is possible for researchers to *infer* consumers' disconfirmation through arithmetic means (the P − E gap) but that 'consumer perceptions, not calculations, govern behavior'. Finally, a team of researchers, including Zeithaml herself (Boulding *et al.*, 1993), has recently rejected the value of an expectations-based, or gap-based model in finding that service quality was only influenced by perceptions.

Process orientation

SERVQUAL has been criticized for focusing on the process of service delivery rather than outcomes of the service encounter.

Grönroos (1982) identified three components of SQ: technical, functional and reputational quality. Technical quality is concerned with the outcome of the service encounter, e.g. have the dry cleaners got rid of the stain? Functional quality is concerned with the process of service delivery, e.g. were the dry cleaner's counter staff courteous? Reputational quality is a refection of the corporate image of the service organization.

Whereas technical quality focuses on *what*, functional quality focuses on *how* and involves consideration of issues such as the behaviour of customer contact staff, and the speed of service.

Critics have argued that outcome quality is missing from Parasuraman *et al.*'s formulation of SQ (Cronin and Taylor, 1992; Mangold and Babakus, 1991; Richard and Allaway, 1993).

Richard and Allaway (1993) tested an augmented SERVQUAL model which they claim incorporates both process and outcome components, and comment that 'the challenge is to determine which process and outcome quality attributes of SQ have the greatest impact on choice'.[2] Their research into Domino Pizza's process and outcome quality employed the 22 Parasuraman *et al.* (1988) items, modified to suit context, and the following six outcome items:

1. Domino's has delicious home-delivery pizza.
2. Domino's has nutritious home-delivery pizza.
3. Domino's home-delivery pizza has flavourful sauce.
4. Domino's provides a generous amount of toppings for its home-delivery pizza.
5. Domino's home-delivery pizza is made with superior ingredients.
6. Domino's prepared its home-delivery pizza crust exactly the way I like it.

These researchers found that the process-only item borrowed and adapted from SERVQUAL accounted for only 45% of the variance in customer choice; the full inventory, inclusive of the six outcome items, accounted for 71.5% of variance choice. The difference between the two is significant at the 0.001 level. They conclude that process-and-outcome is a better predictor of consumer choice than process, or outcome, alone.

In defence of SERVQUAL, Higgins *et al.* (1991) have argued that outcome quality is already contained within these dimensions: reliability, competence and security.

Dimensionality

Critics have raised a number of significant and related questions about the dimensionality of the SERVQUAL scale. The most serious are concerned with the number of dimensions, and their stability from context to context.

There seems to be general agreement that SQ is a second-order construct, that is, it is factorially complex, being composed of several first-order variables.[3] SERVQUAL is composed of the five RATER factors. There are however, several alternative conceptualizations of SQ. As already noted, Grönroos (1984) identified three components – technical, functional and reputational quality; Lehtinen and Lehtinen (1982) also identify three components – interactive, physical and corporate quality; Hedvall and Paltschik (1989) identify two dimensions – willingness and ability to serve, and physical and psychological access; Leblanc and Nguyen (1988) list five components – corporate image, internal organization, physical support of the service producing system, staff/customer interaction, and the level of customer satisfaction.

Parasuraman *et al.* (1988) have claimed that SERVQUAL:

> provides a basic skeleton through its expectations/perceptions format encompassing statements for each of the five service quality dimensions. The skeleton, when necessary, can be adapted or supplemented to fit the characteristics or specific research needs of a particular organization.

In their 1988 paper, Parasuraman *et al.* also claimed that 'the final 22-item scale and its five dimensions have *sound and stable psychometric properties*'. In the 1991b revision, Parasuraman *et al.* found evidence of '*consistent factor structure*... across five independent samples' (emphases added). In other words, they make claims that the five dimensions are generic across service contexts. Indeed, in 1991, Parasuraman *et al.* claimed that 'SERVQUAL's dimensions and items represent core evaluation criteria that transcend specific companies and industries' (1991b).[4]

Number of dimensions

When the SERVQUAL instrument has been employed in modified form, up to nine distinct dimensions of SQ have been revealed, the number varying according to the service sector under investigation. One study has even produced a single-factor solution.

Nine factors accounted for 71% of SQ variance in Carman's (1990) hospital research: admission service, tangible accommodations, tangible food, tangible privacy, nursing care, explanation of treatment, access and courtesy afforded visitors, discharge planning, and patient accounting (billing).[5]

Five factors were distinguished in Saleh and Ryan's (1992) work in the hotel industry – conviviality, tangibles, reassurance, avoid sarcasm, and empathy. The first of these, conviviality, accounted for 62.8% of the overall variance; the second factor, tangibles, accounted for a further 6.9%; the five factors together accounted for 78.6%. This is strongly suggestive of a two-factor solution in the hospitality industry. The researchers had 'initially assumed that the factor analysis would confirm the [SERVQUAL] dimensions but this failed to be the case'.

Four factors were extracted in Gagliano and Hathcote's (1994) investigation of SQ in the retail clothing sector – personal attention, reliability, tangibles and convenience. Two of these have no correspondence in SERVQUAL. They conclude 'the [original SERVQUAL scale] does not perform as well as expected' in apparel speciality retailing.

Three factors were identified in Bouman and van der Wiele's (1992) research into car servicing – customer kindness, tangibles and faith.[6] The authors 'were not able to find the same dimensions for judging service quality as did Berry et al.'.

One factor was recognized in Babakus et al.'s (1993b) survey of 635 utility company customers. Analysis 'essentially produced a single-factor model' of SQ which accounted for 66.3% of the variance. The authors advance several possible explanations for this unidimensional result including the nature of the service, (which they describe as a low-involvment service with an ongoing consumption experience), non-response bias and the use of a single expectations/perceptions gap scale. These researchers concluded: 'With the exception of findings reported by Parasuraman and his colleagues, empirical evidence does not support a five-dimensional concept of service quality'.

In summary, Babakus and Boller (1992) commented that 'the domain of service quality may be factorially complex in some industries and very simple and unidimensional in others'. In effect, they claim that the number of SQ dimensions is dependent on the particular service being offered.

In their revised version, Parasuraman et al. (1991b) suggest two reasons for these anomalies. First, they may be the product of differences in data collection and analysis procedures. A 'more plausible explanation' is that 'differences among empirically derived factors across replications may be primarily due to across-dimension similarities and/or within dimension differences in customers' evaluations of a specific company involved in each setting'.

Spreng and Singh (1993) have commented on the lack of discrimination between several of the dimensions. In their research, the correlation between Assurance and Responsiveness constructs was .97, indicating that they were not separable constructs. They also found a high correlation between the combined Assurance–Responsiveness construct and the Empathy construct (.87). Parasuraman et al. (1991b) had earlier found that Assurance and Responsiveness items loaded on a single factor, and in their 1988 work had found average intercorrelations among the five dimensions of .23 to .35.

In testing their revised version (Parasuraman et al., 1991b), Parasuraman and colleagues found that the four items under Tangibles broke into two distinct dimensions, one pertaining to equipment and physical facilities, the other to employees and communication materials. They also found that Responsiveness and Assurance dimensions showed considerable overlap, and loaded on the same factor. They suggested that this was a product of imposing a five-factor constraint on the analysis. Indeed, the additional degrees of freedom allowed by a subsequent six-factor solution generated distinct Assurance and Responsiveness factors.

Parasuraman *et al.* (1991a) have now accepted that the 'five SERVQUAL dimensions are interrelated as evidenced by the need for oblique rotations of factor solutions...to obtain the most interpretable factor patterns. One fruitful area for future research'; they conclude, 'is to explore the nature and causes of these interrelationships'.

It therefore does appear that both contextual circumstances and analytical processes have some bearing on the number of dimensions of SQ.

Contextual stability

Carman (1990) tested the generic qualities of the SERVQUAL instrument in three service setting – a tyre retailer, a business school placement centre and a dental school patient clinic. Following Parasuraman *et al.*'s suggestion, he modified and augmented the items in the original ten-factor SERVQUAL scale to suit the three contexts. His factor analysis identified between five and seven underlying dimensions.

According to Carman, customers are at least partly context-specific in the dimensions they employ to evaluate SQ. In all three cases, Tangibles, Reliability and Security were present.[7] Responsiveness, a major component in the RATER scale was relatively weak in the dental clinic context. Carman also commented: 'Parasuraman, Zeithaml and Berry combined their original Understanding and Access dimensions into Empathy...our results did not find this to be an appropriate combination'. In particular he found that if a dimension is very important to customers they are likely to be decomposed into a number of sub-dimensions. This happened for the placement centre where Responsiveness, Personal attention, Access and Convenience were all identified as separate factors. According to Carman, this indicates that researchers should work with the original ten dimensions, rather than adopt the revised five-factor Parasuraman *et al.* (1988) model.

There is also an indication from one piece of cross-cultural research that the scale may not always travel well. Ford *et al.* (1993) computed alphas for a SERVQUAL application in the higher education contexts of New Zealand and the USA markets which the authors describe as 'intuitively' similar. Table 2 displays the results.

These results challenge Zeithaml's (1988) claim that consumers form higher level abstractions of SQ that are generalized across contexts.

Table 2. SERVQUAL alphas in New Zealand and the USA

Dimensions	Cronbach alpha	
	USA	New Zealand
Tangibles	.7049	.6833
Reliability	.8883	.8514
Responsiveness	.8378	.8063
Assurance	.8229	.7217
Empathy	.8099	.7734

Item loadings

In some studies (e.g. Carman, 1990), items have not loaded on the factors to which they were expected to belong. Two items from the Empathy battery of the Parasuraman *et al.* (1988) instrument loaded heavily on the Tangibles factor in a study of dental clinic SQ. In the tyre retail study, a Tangibles item loaded on to Security; in the placement centre a Reliability item loaded on to Tangibles. An item concerning the ease of making appointments loaded on to Reliability in the dental clinic context, but Security in the tyre store context. He also found that only two-thirds of the items loaded in the same way on the expectations battery as they did in the perceptions battery. Carman supplies other examples of the same phenomena, and suggests that the unexpected results indicate both a face validity and a construct validity problem. In other words, he warns against importing SERVQUAL into service setting contexts without modification and validity checks.

Among his specific recommendations is the following: 'We recommend that items on Courtesy and Access be retained and that items on some dimensions such as Responsiveness and Access be expanded where it is believed that these dimensions are of particular importance'. He also reports specific Courtesy and Access items which performed well in terms of nomological and construct validity.

Carman (1990) further suggested that the factors, Personal attention, Access or Convenience should be retained and further contextualized research work be done to identify their significance and meaning.

Item intercorrelations

Convergent validity and discriminant validity are important considerations in the measurement of second-order constructs such as SERVQUAL. One would associate a high level of convergent validity with a high level of intercorrelations between the items selected to measure a single RATER factor. Discriminant validity is indicated if the factors and their component items are independent of each other (i.e. the items load heavily on one factor only).[8] Following their modified replication of Parasuraman *et al.*'s work, Babakus and Boller (1992) conclude that rules for convergence and discrimination do not indicate the existence of the five RATER dimensions.

The best scales have a high level of intercorrelation between items comprising a dimension (convergent validity). In their development work in four sectors (banking, credit-card company, repair and maintenance company, and long-distance telecommunications company) Parasuraman *et al.* (1988) found inter-item reliability coefficients (alphas) varying from .52 to .84. Babakus and Boller (1992) report alphas which are broadly consistent with those of Parasuraman, varying from .67 to .83 (see Table 3). In their 1991b version, Parasuraman *et al.* report alphas from .60 to .93, and observe that 'every alpha value obtained for each dimension in the final study is higher than the corresponding values in the...original study'. They attribute this improvement to their rewording of the 22 scale items.

Spreng and Singh (1993), and Brown *et al.* (1993) are highly critical of the questionable application of alphas to difference scores. They evaluate the reliability

Table 3. Reliability of SERVQUAL

Factor	Item	Parasuraman et al. (1988)		Babakus and Boller (1992)	
		Coefficient alpha	Item-to-total correlations	Coefficient alpha	Item-to-total correlations
Tangibles	Q1	.72	.69	.67	.38
	Q2		.68		.59
	Q3		.64		.31
	Q4		.51		.54
Reliability	Q5	.83	.75	.82	.66
	Q6		.53		.58
	Q7		.71		.59
	Q8		.75		.75
	Q9		.50		.49
Responsiveness	Q10	.82	.51	.68	.44
	Q11		.77		.44
	Q12		.66		.45
	Q13		.86		.52
Assurance	Q14	.81	.38	.83	.64
	Q15		.72		.77
	Q16		.80		.65
	Q17		.45		.58
Empathy	Q18	.86	.78	.71	.46
	Q19		.81		.46
	Q20		.59		.48
	Q21		.71		.45
	Q22		.68		.47

of SERVQUAL using a measure specifically designed for difference scores (Lord, 1963). Spreng and Singh conclude that 'there is not a great deal of difference between the reliabilities correctly calculated and the more common [alpha] calculation', an observation with which Parasuraman et al. (1993) concurred when they wrote: 'The collective conceptual and empirical evidence neither demonstrates clear superiority for the non-difference score format nor warrants abandoning the difference score format'.

Operational

Expectations

Notwithstanding the more fundamental criticism that expectations play no significant role in the conceptualization of service quality, some critics have raised a number of other concerns about the operationalization of E in SERVQUAL.

In their 1988 work, Parasuraman et al. defined expectations as 'desire or wants of consumers, i.e. what they feel a service provider *should* offer rather than *would* offer' (emphasis added). The expectations component was designed to measure 'customers' normative expectations' (Parasuraman et al., 1990), and is 'similar to the ideal standard in the customer satisfaction/dissatisfaction literature' (Zeithaml *et al.*, 1991). Teas (1993a) found these explanations 'somewhat vague' and has questioned respondents' interpretations of the expectations battery in the SERVQUAL instrument. He believes that respondents may be using any one of six interpretations (Teas, 1993b):

1. *Service attribute importance.* Customers may respond by rating the expectations statements according to the importance of each.
2. *Forecasted performance.* Customers may respond by using the scale to predict the performance they would expect.
3. *Ideal performance.* The optimal performance, what performance 'can be'.
4. *Deserved performance.* The performance level customers, in the light of their investments, feel performance should be.
5. *Equitable performance.* The level of performance customers feel they ought to receive given a perceived set of costs.
6. *Minimum tolerable performance.* What performance 'must be'.

Each of these interpretations is somewhat different, and Teas contends that a considerable percentage of the variance of the SERVQUAL expectations measure can be explained by the difference in respondents' interpretations. Accordingly, the expectations components of the model lacks discriminant validity. Parasuraman *et al.* (1991b, 1994) have responded to these criticisms by redefining expectations as the service customers would expect from 'excellent service organizations', rather than 'normative' expectations of service providers, and by vigorously defending their inclusion in SQ research.

Iacobucci *et al.* (1994) want to drop the term 'expectations' from the SQ vocabulary. They prefer the generic label 'standard', and believe that several standards may operate simultaneously; among them 'ideals', 'my most desired combination of attributes', the 'industry standard' of a nominal average competitor, 'deserved' SQ, and brand standards based on past experiences with the brand.

Some critics have questioned SERVQUAL's failure to access customer evaluations based on absolute standards of SQ. The instrument asks respondents to report their expectations of excellent service providers within a class (i.e. the measure are relative rather than absolute). It has been argued that SERVQUAL predicts that:

> customers will evaluate a service favourably as long as their expectations are met or exceeded, regardless of whether their prior expectations were high or low, and regardless of whether the absolute goodness of the [service] performance is high or low. This unyielding prediction is illogical. We argue that 'absolute' levels (e.g. the prior standards) certainly must enter into a customer's evaluation (Iacobucci et al., 1994).

Put another way, SERVQUAL assumes that an E-score of six for Joe's Greasy Spoon Diner is equivalent to an E-score of six for Michel Roux's Le Lapin French restaurant. In absolute terms, clearly they are not, Grönroos (1993) refers to a similar oddity, which he calls the bad-service paradox. A customer may have low expectations based on previous experience with the service provider; if those expectations are met there is no gap and SQ is deemed satisfactory.

Since Zeithaml *et al.* (1991) have themselves identified two comparison norms for SQ assessment ('desired service', the level of service a customer believes can and should be delivered; 'adequate service', the level of service the customer considers acceptable) it seems unlikely that the debate about the meaning of expectations is over.

Item composition

Each factor in the 1988 and 1991 SERVQUAL scales is composed of four or five items. It has become clear that this is often inadequate to capture the variance within, or the context-specific meaning of, each dimension. Carman's (1990) study of hospital services employed 40 items. Bouman and van der Wiele (1992) used 48 items in their car service research, Saleh and Ryan (1992) 33 items in their hospitality research, Fort (1993) 31 items in his analysis of software house service quality and Babakus and Mangold (1992) 15 items in their hospital research. Parasuraman *et al.* (1991b) acknowledge that context-specific items can be used to supplement SERVQUAL, but caution that 'the new items should be similar in form to the existing SERVQUAL items'.

Moments of truth

Many services are delivered over several moments of truth or encounter between service staff and customer: hotel and hospital services for example. Carman (1990) found evidence that customers evaluate SQ by reference to these multiple encounters. For example, in his hospital research he listed the three items below:

1. My discharge from the hospital was prompt.
2. Nurses responded promptly when I called.
3. My admission to the hospital was prompt.

These items did not load heavily on a single Responsiveness factor as might be expected; instead they loaded on factors which represented a particular hospital function, or moment of truth. Parasuraman *et al.*, in contrast, have declared the SQ is a more global construct, not directly connected to particular incidents.

Polarity

Of the 22 items in the 1988 SERVQUAL scale, 13 statement pairs are positively worded, and nine pairs are negatively worded. The negatives are the full set of Responsiveness and Empathy statements. Parasuraman *et al.*'s goal was to reduce systematic response bias caused by yea-saying and nay-saying. This is accepted as good normative research practice (Churchill, 1979), yet has consequences for respondents who make more comprehension errors, and take more time to read items (Wason and Johnson-Laird, 1972).

In factor analysis of SERVQUAL data, Babakus and Boller (1992) found that all negatively-worded items loaded heavily on one factor while all positively-worded items loaded on another. They also found a significant difference between the average P, E and gap scores of positively and negatively-worded items. They conclude that the wording of the items produces a 'method factor': 'Item wording may be responsible for producing factors that are method artifacts rather than conceptually meaningful dimensions of service quality'. Item wording creates data quality problems, and calls into question the dimensionality and validity of the instrument. Babakus and Mangold (1992), in their application of SERVQUAL to a hospital setting, therefore decided to employ only positively-worded statements. Parasuraman *et al.* (1991b) have responded to these criticisms by rewording all negatively-worded items positively.

Scale points

The use of seven-point Likert scales has been criticized on several grounds. Although none of these are specific to SERVQUAL applications, they bear repeating here. Lewis (1993) has criticized the scale for its lack of verbal labelling for points two to six. She believes this may cause respondents to overuse the extreme ends of the scale and suggests this could be avoided by labelling each point. Another issue is the respondents' interpretation of the meaning of the midpoint of the scale (e.g. is it a 'don't know', 'do not feel strongly in either direction' or a 'do not understand the statement' response?) Lewis is also concerned about responses which suggest there is no gap when in fact a gap does exist. For instance a respondent may have expectations of 5.4 and perceptions of 4.6 (a gap of 0.8) but when completing SERVQUAL may rate each as 5, the nearest possible response in each case. This is an example of a Type II error.

Babakus and Mangold (1992) opted to use five-point Likert scales on the grounds that it would reduce the 'frustration level' of patient respondents, increase response rate and response quality.

Two administrations

Respondents appear to be bored, and sometimes confused by the administration of E and P versions of SERVQUAL (Bouman and van der Wiele, 1992). Boredom and confusion imperil data quality.

Carman (1990) also comments on the timing of the two administrations. He is critical of Parasuraman *et al.* for asking respondents to complete the two questionnaires at a single sitting. In Parasuraman *et al.*'s 1988 work respondents were asked to report their expectations and perceptions, based on what they had experienced in the last three months. All self-reports were entirely *ex post*, a practice also criticized by Grönroos (1993). Carman also observed that it was impractical to expect customers to complete an expectations inventory prior to a service encounter and a perception inventory immediately afterwards. His solution was to collect data on the expectations–perceptions difference with a single question at a single administration, for example: 'The visual appeal of XYZ's physical facilities is (much better, better, about the same, worse, much worse) than I expected'. Lewis (1993) refers to work undertaken by Orledge who has also experimented with an alternative method of combining perceptions and expectations. He combined the two elements as in the following example:

Indicate on the scale using a 'P' how well dressed the staff of company XYZ are. On the same scale indicate using an 'E' how well dressed you expect the staff of companies in this industry to be.

smart _____ : _____ : _____ E __ : _____ : _____ : __ P__ : _____ untidy

Bouman and van der Wiele (1992) also comment on the same problem. Babakus and Boller (1992), and Babakus *et al.* (1993b) solved the problem by employing a single seven-point scale to collect gap data. Recommended earlier by Carman (1990), the scale ranged from 7 = 'greatly exceeds my expectations' to 1 = 'greatly falls short of my expectations'.

Clow and Vorhies (1993) argue:

> When expectations and experience evaluations are measured simultaneously, respondents will indicate that their expectations are greater than they actually were before the service encounter.

They contend that expectations must be measured prior to receipt of services otherwise responses will be biased. Specifically, Clow and Vorhies found that:

> Customers who had a negative experience with the service tend to overstate their expectations, creating a larger gap; customers who had a positive experience tend to understate their expectations, resulting in smaller gaps.

Variance extracted

Fornell and Larcker (1981) have suggested that 'variance extracted' should be stringently employed as a measure of construct validity. Parasuraman *et al.* (1988) reported that the total amount of variance extracted by the five RATER factors in the bank, credit card, repair and maintenance, and long-distance telephone samples was 56.0%, 57.5%, 61.6% and 56.2% respectively. Parasuraman *et al.* (1991a) report variance explained in a telephone company, insurance company 1, insurance company 2, bank 1 and bank 2 at 67.2%, 68.3%, 70.9%, 71.6% and 66.9%, respectively. When the samples are combined, variance explained is 67.9%. Babakus and Boller's (1992) utility-sector replication reported 58.3%. Carman's (1990) modified replication in the hospital sector, tyre store, business school placement centre and dental clinic reported 71%, 61%, 75% and 71% respectively. Saleh and Ryan's (1992) modified replication in the hotel sector reported 78.6%. Bouman and van der Wiele's (1992) modified replication in car servicing reported 40.7% only. Generally, the modified scales tended to produce higher levels of variance extracted. The higher the variance extracted, the more valid is the measure.

CONCLUSION

SERVQUAL has undoubtedly had a major impact on the business and academic communities.

This review has identified a number of theoretical and operational issues which should concern users of the instrument. Since the most serious of these are concerned with face validity and construct validity, this conclusion briefly reviews the nature and significance of validity.

Face validity is concerned with the extent to which a scale appears to measure what it purports to measure.

Construct validity generally:

> is used to refer to the vertical correspondence between a construct which is at an unobservable, conceptual level and a purported measure of it which is at an operational level. In an ideal sense, the term means that a measure assesses the magnitude and direction of (1) all of the characteristics and (2) only the characteristics of the construct it is purported to assess (Peter, 1981, emphases added).

In particular, the concerns about the adoption of an inappropriate paradigm, the gaps model, SERVQUAL's process orientation, and SERVQUAL's dimensionality (the four theoretical criticisms as listed earlier) are construct validity issues.

Critical face and construct validity questions which SERVQUAL researchers face are: Do consumers actually evaluate SQ in terms of expectations and perceptions? Do the five RATER dimensions incorporate the full range of SQ attributes? Do consumers incorporate 'outcome' evaluations into their assessments of SQ?

Construct validity is itself a composite of several forms of validity: nomological validity, convergent validity and discriminant validity.

Nomological validity is the extent to which a measure correlation in theoretically predictable ways with measures of different but related constructs. SQ is one of a number of apparently interrelated constructs whose precise alignments has yet to be explored. Included in the nomological net are customer (dis)satisfaction, customer retention and defection, behavioural intention, attitude to service provider or organization, and service provider or organization choice. Some research into these questions has been published (Parasuraman *et al.*, 1991b; Richard and Allaway, 1993) but the relationships have yet to be explored fully.

Convergent validity is the extent to which a scale correlates with other measures of the same construct. A high level of intercorrelation between items comprising each RATER dimension would indicate high convergent validity internal of SERVQUAL. A high level of correlation between SERVQUAL scores and a different, reliable and valid measure of SQ, would indicate a high level of external convergent validity. Discriminant validity is the extent to which a measure does *not* correlate with other measures from which it is purported to differ. If SQ evaluations were composed of five distinct RATER dimensions, one would expect little correlation between the five factors. SERVQUAL's dimensionality would be regarded as more stable if individual items loaded on to the dimensions to which they belong.

Issues to face and construct validity are of overriding importance in the development of instruments such as SERVQUAL. The operational criticisms are evidently less significant than the theoretical criticisms, and pose less of a threat to validity. The theoretical criticisms raised in this article are of such moment that the validity of the instrument must be called into question.

Despite these shortcomings, SERVQUAL seems to be moving rapidly towards institutionalized status. As Rust and Zahorik (1993) have observed, 'the general SERVQUAL dimensions...should probably be put on any first pass as a list of attributes of service'.

These criticisms indicate that there is still a need for fundamental research. There are still doubts about whether customers routinely assess SQ in terms of Expectations and Perceptions; there are doubts about the utility and appropriateness of the disconfirmation paradigm; there are doubts about the dimensionality of SQ; there are doubts about the universality of the five RATER dimensions. These are serious concerns which are not only significant for users of SERVQUAL but for all those who wish to understand better the concept of SQ.

DIRECTIONS FOR FUTURE RESEARCH

This review has raised several conceptual and operational difficulties surrounding SERVQUAL which are yet to be resolved. The following represent a set of questions which SQ researchers should address:

1. Do consumers always evaluate SQ in terms of expectations and perceptions? What other forms of SQ evaluation are there?
2. What form do customers expectations take and how best, if at all, are they measured? Are expectations common across a class of service providers?
3. Do attitude-based measures of SQ perform better than the disconfirmation model? Which attitudinal measure is most helpful?
4. Is it advantageous to integrate outcome evaluations into SQ measurement and how best can this be done?
5. Is the predictive validity of P measures of service quality better than that of P–E measures?
6. What are the relationships between SQ, customer satisfaction, behavioural intention, purchase behaviour, market share, word-of-mouth and customer retention?
7. What is the role of context in determining E and P evaluations? What context-markers do consumes employ?
8. Are analytical context markers such as tangibility and consumer involvement helpful in advancing SQ theory?
   - Do evaluative criteria in intangible-dominant services (e.g consulting) differ from those in tangible-dominant services (e.g. hotels)?
   - How does involvement influence the evaluation of SQ?
9. How do customers integrate transaction-specific or MOT-specific evaluations of SQ? To what extent are some MOTs more influential in the final evaluation than others?
10. What are the relationships between the five RATER factors? How stable are those relationships across context?
11. What is the most appropriate scale format for collecting valid and reliable SQ data?
12. To what extent can customers correctly classify items into their a priori dimensions?

Answers to questions such as these would help improve our understanding of the service quality construct and assess the value of the SERVQUAL instrument. Even in its present state SERVQUAL is a helpful operationalization of a somewhat nebulous construct.

Many of these questions require contextually sensitive qualitative research. The first question, 'Do consumers always evaluate SQ in terms of expectations and perceptions?', is perhaps best approached through in-depth case analyses of particular service encounters. The formation of expectations implies a consumer who accumulates and processes information about a high class of service providers. This would appear to make prima facie sense for high-cost, high-risk services, e.g. if purchasing a weekend break to celebrate 25 years of wedded bliss. It is as likely that expectations high in cognitive content would be formed for a low-cost, low-risk service such as a hot drink from a coffee shop? The role of context appears to have been repressed or subjugated in the present body of SERVQUAL research. Context need to be recovered.

Other questions lend themselves to multisectoral comparative analyses. For example, the question, 'Is the predictive validity of P-measures of SQ better than that of P–E measures?', is perhaps best approached in multi-sectoral study which thoroughly tests the predictive performance of P and P–E SQ measures.

Pursuit of this research agenda would surely strengthen our understanding of the meaning, measurement and management of service quality. Parasuraman, Zeithaml and Berry have undoubtedly done a splendid job of marketing SERVQUAL's measurement and management technologies. It remains to be seen whether its dominance will remain unchallenged.

NOTES

1. The mnemonic RATER is a helpful aide mèmoire, where R = reliability, A = assurance, T = tangibles, E = empathy and R = responsiveness.
2. Richard and Allaways's (1993) research was largely focused on testing SERVQUAL's predictive validity. Parasuraman *et al.* (1991b) have also tested the predictive validity of the modified SERVQUAL scale. Customers in five samples were asked three questions: Have you recently had a service problem with the company? If you have experienced a problem was it resolved to your satisfaction? Would you recommend the service firm to a friend? It was hypothesized that positive answers to these questions would be correlated negatively, positively and positively, respectively, with higher perceived SQ scores. All results were statistically significant in the hypothesized direction, lending support to the predictive validity of the instrument.
3. Babakus and Boller (1992) have expressed concern that it is unclear whether SERVQUAL is measuring a number of distinct constructs or a single, global, more abstract variable.
4. Cronin and Taylor (1992), following a test of SERVQUAL in four classes of service firm, conclude in stark contrast that 'the five-component structure proposed by Parasuraman, Zeithaml and Berry (1988) for their SERVQUAL scale is not confirmed'.
5. Babakus and Mangold's (1992) research into hospital SQ identified three factors within the expectations data, accounting for 56.2% of the variance in the item scores, two factors within the perception data (70.6%) and 'no meaningful factor structure' within the difference or gaps data.
6. Customer kindness, that is 'the front office personnel's approach to the customer and his problems, regardless of the service delivered', was the only factor to have significant relationship with future car servicing intentions, future car purchase intentions, and word-of-mouth recommendation.

7. Carman's Security factor is composed of Credibility, Security and Competence. Parasuraman *et al.* (1988) had incorporated these three components, together with Communication and Courtesy, into the factor Assurance.
8. For a discussion of construct, convergent and discriminant validity see Churchill (1979) and Peter (1981).

APPENDIX. TEN COMPONENTS OF SERVICE QUALITY

(1) *Reliability* involves consistency of performance and dependability. It also means that the firm performs the service right first time and honours its promises. Specifically, it may involve:
   - accuracy in billing;
   - performing the service at the designated time.

(2) *Responsiveness* concerns the willingness or readiness of employees to provide service. It may involve:
   - mailing a transaction slip immediately;
   - calling the customer back quickly;
   - giving prompt service (e.g. setting up appointments quickly).

(3) *Competence* means possession of the required skills and knowledge to perform the service. It involves:
   - knowledge and skill of the contact personnel;
   - knowledge and skill of operational support personnel;
   - research capability of the organization.

(4) *Access* involves approachability and ease of contact. It may mean:
   - the service is easily accessible by telephone;
   - waiting time to receive service is not extensive;
   - convenient hours of operation and convenient location of service facility.

(5) *Courtesy* involves politeness, respect, consideration, and friendliness of contact personnel (including receptionists, telephone operators, etc.). It includes:
   - consideration for the consumers property;
   - clean and neat appearance of public contract personnel.

(6) *Communication* means keeping customers informed in language they can understand, and listening to them. It may mean that the company has to adjust its language for different customers. It may involve:
   - explaining the service itself and how much the service will cost;
   - explaining the trade-offs between service and cost;
   - assuring the consumer that a problem will be handled.

(7) *Credibility* involves trustworthiness, believability, honesty. It involves having the customer's best interests at heart. Contributing to credibility are:
   - company name and reputation;
   - personal characteristics of the contact personnel;
   - the degree of hard sell involved in interactions with the customer.

(8) *Security* is the freedom from danger, risk, or doubt. It may involve:
   - physical safety;
   - financial security and confidentiality.

(9) *Understanding/knowing the customer* involves making the effort to understand the customer's needs. It involves:
   - learning the customer's specific requirements;
   - providing individualized attention.

(10) *Tangibles* include the physical evidence of the service.
  ● physical facilities and appearance of personnel;
  ● tools or equipment used to provide the service;
  ● physical representations of the service, such as a plastic credit card.

REFERENCES AND FURTHER READING

Andersson, T. D. (1992) 'Another Model of Service Quality: A Model of Causes and Effects of Service Quality Tested on a Case Within the Restaurant Industry. In (Kunst, P. and Lemmink, J., Eds), *Quality Management in Service.* van Gorcum, The Netherlands, pp. 41–58.

Aubry, C. A. and Zimbler, D. A. (1993) 'The Banking Industry: Quality Costs and Improvements'. *Quality Progress* (December): 16–20.

Babakus, E. and Boller, G. W. (1992) 'An Empirical Assessment of the SERVQUAL Scale'. *Journal of Business Research* **24:** 253–268.

Babakus, E. and Inhofe, M. (1991) 'The Role of Expectations and Attribute Importance in the Measurement of Service Quality'. In *Proceedings of the Summer Educators' Conference* (M. C. Gilly *et al,* Eds). American Marketing Association, Chicago, IL, pp. 142–144.

Babakus, E. and Mangold, W. G. (1992) 'Adapting the SERVQUAL Scale to Hospital Services: an Empirical Investigation'. *Health Services Research* **26** (2, February): 767–786.

Babakus, E., Pedrick, D. L. and Inhofe, M. (1993b) 'Empirical Examination of a Direct Measure of Perceived Service Quality Using SERVQUAL Items. Unpublished manuscript, Memphis State University, TN.

Babakus, E., Pedrick, D. L. and Richardson, A. (1993a) 'Measuring Perceived Service Quality within the Airline Catering Service Industry. Unpublished manuscript, Memphis State University, TN.

Baker, J. A. and Lamb, C. W. Jr (1993) 'Managing Architectural Design Service Quality'. *Journal of Professional Services Marketing* **10** (No. 1): 89–106.

Bolton, R. N. and Drew, J. H. (1991) 'A Multistage Model of Customers' Assessment of Service Quality and Value'. *Journal of Consumer Research* **17** (March): 375–384.

Boulding, W., Kalra, A., Staelin, R. and Zeithaml, V. A. (1993) 'A Dynamic Process Model of Service Quality: from Expectations to Behavioral Intentions'. *Journal of Marketing Research* **30** (February): 7–27.

Bouman, M. and van der Wiele, T. (1992) 'Measuring Service Quality in the Car Service Industry: Building and Testing an Instrument'. *International Journal of Service Industry Management* **3** (No. 4): 4–16.

Brown, T. J., Churchill, G. A. and Peter, J. P. (193) 'Improving the Measurement of Service Quality'. *Journal of Retailing* **69** (No. 1, Spring): 127–139.

Buzzell, R. D. and Gale, B. T. (1987) *The PIMS Principles.* Free Press, New York, NY.

Carman, J. M. (1990) 'Consumer Perceptions of Service Quality: an Assessment of the SERVQUAL Dimensions'. *Journal of Retailing* **66** (No. 1, Spring): 33–35.

Churchill, G. A. (1979) 'A Paradigm for Developing Better Measures of Marketing Constructs', *Journal of Marketing Research* **19** (February): 64–73.

Churchill, G. A. and Surprenant, C. (1982) 'An Investigation into the Determinants of Customer Satisfaction'. *Journal of Marketing Research* **19:** 491–504.

Clow, K. E. and Vorhies, D. E. (1993) 'Building a Competitive Advantage for Service Firms'. *Journal of Services Marketing* **7** (No. 1): 22–3.

Cronin, J. J. Jr and Taylor, S. A. (1992) 'Measuring Service Quality: a Reexamination and Extension'. *Journal of Marketing* **56** (July): 55–68.

Cronin, J. J. Jr and Taylor, S. A. (1994) 'SERVPERF Versus SERVQUAL: Reconciling Performance-based and Perceptions-minus Expectations Measurement of Service Quality'. *Journal of Marketing* **58** (January): 125–131.

Crosby, P. B. (1979) *Quality is Free.* McGraw-Hill, New York, NY.

Fick, G. R. and Ritchie, J. R. B. (1991) 'Measuring Service Quality in the Travel and Tourism Industry'. *Journal of Travel Research* **30** (No. 2, Autumn): 2–9.

Ford, J. W., Joseph, M. and Joseph, B. (1993) 'Service Quality in Higher Education: a Comparison of Universities in the United States and New Zealand Using SERVQUAL'. Unpublished manuscript, Old Dominion University, Norfolk, VA.

Fornell, C. and Larcker, D. F. (1981) 'Evaluating Structural Equation Models with Unobservable Variables and Measurement Error'. *Journal of Marketing Research* **18** (February): 39–50.

Fort, M. (1993) 'Customer Defined Attributes of Service Quality in the IBM Mid-range Computer Software Industry. Unpublished MBA dissertation, Manchester Business School, Manchester.

Freeman, K. D. and Dart, J. (1993) 'Measuring the Perceived Quality of Professional Business Services. *Journal of Professional Services Marketing* **9** (No. 1): 27–47.

Gagliano, K. B. and Hathcote, J. (1994) 'Customer Expectations and Perceptions of Service Quality in Apparel Retailing'. *Journal of Services Marketing* **8** (No. 1): 60–69.

Grönroos, C. (1982) *Strategic Management and Marketing in the Service Sector.* Swedish School of Economics and Business Administration, Helsinki.

Grönroos, C. (1984) 'A Service Quality Model and its Marketing Implications'. *European Journal of Marketing,* **18**: 36–44.

Grönroos, C. (1993) 'Towards a Third Phase in Service Quality Research: Challenges and Future Directions. In *Advances in Services Marketing and Management* (T. A. Swartz, D. E. Bowen and S. W. Brown, Eds). Vol. 2, JAI Press, Greenwich, CT, pp. 49–64.

Hardie, B. G. S., Johnson, E. J. and Fader, P. S. (1992) 'Modelling Loss Aversion and Reference Dependence Effects on Brand Choice. Working paper, Wharton School, University of Pennsylvania, PA.

Hedvall, M.-B. and Paltschik, M. (1989) 'An Investigation in, and Generation of, Service Quality Concepts'. In *Marketing Thought and Practice in the 1990s* (G. J. Avlonitis *et al.* Eds). European Marketing Academy, Athens, pp. 473–483.

Higgins, L. F., Ferguson, J. M. and Winston, J. M. (1991) 'Understanding and Assessing Service Quality in Health Maintenance Organizations'. *Health Marketing Quarterly* **9** (Nos 1–2): 5–20.

Iacobucci, D., Grayson, K. A. and Omstrom, A. L. (1994) 'The Calculus of Service Quality and Customer Satisfaction: Theoretical and Empirical Differentiation and Integration'. In *Advances in Services Marketing and Management, Vol. 3* (T. A. Swartz, D. E. Bowen and S. W. Brown, Eds). JAI Press, Greenwich, CT, pp. 1–68.

Johns, N. (1993) 'Quality Management in the Hospitality Industry, part 3: Recent Developments'. *International Journal of Contemporary Hospitality Management* **5** (No. 1): 10–15.

Juran, J. M. (1951) *Quality Control Handbook.* McGraw-Hill, New York, NY.

Kahneman, D. and Miller, D. T. (1986) 'Norm Theory: Comparing Reality to its Alternatives'. *Psychological Review* **93**: 136–153.

Kong, R. and Mayo, M. C. (1993) 'Measuring Service Quality in the Business-to-business Context'. *Journal of Business and Industrial Marketing* **8** (No. 2): 5–15.

Kwon, W. and Lee, T. J. (1994) 'Measuring Service Quality in Singapore Retail Banking'. *Singapore Management Review* **16** (No. 2, July): 1–24.

Leblanc, G. and Nguyen, N. (1988) 'Customers' Perception of Service Quality in Financial Institutions'. *International Journal of Bank Marketing* **6** (No. 4): 7–18.

Lehtinen, J. R. and Lehtinen, O. (1982) 'Service Quality: a Study of Quality Dimensions'. Unpublished working paper, Service Management Institute, Helsinki.

Lewis, B. R. (1993) 'Service Quality Measurement'. *Marketing Intelligence and Planning* **11** (No. 4): 4–12.

Lord, F. M. (1963) 'Elementary Models for Measuring Change'. In *Problems in Measuring Change.* (C. W. Harris Ed.). University of Wisconsin Press, Madison, WI, pp. 22–38.

McElwee, G. and Redman, T. (1993) 'Upward Appraisal in Practice: an Illustrative Example using the QUALED Scale'. *Education and Training* **35** (No. 2, December): 27–31.

Mangold, G. W. and Babakus, E. (1991) 'Service Quality: the Front-stage Perspective vs the Back Stage Perspective'. *Journal of Services Marketing* **5** (No. 4, Autumn): 59–70.

Masser, W. J. (1957) 'The Quality Manager and Quality Costs'. *Industrial Quality Control* **14**: 5–8.

Oliver, R. L. (1980) 'A Cognitive Model of the Antecedents and Consequences of Satisfaction Decisions'. *Journal of Marketing Research* **17** (November): 460–469.

Oliver, R. L. (1993) 'A Conceptual Model of Service Quality and Service Satisfaction: Compatible Goals, Different Concepts'. In *Advances in Services Marketing and Management*, Vol. 2 (T. A. Swartz, D. E. Bowen and S. W. Brown, Eds). JAI Press, Greenwich, CT, pp. 65–85.

Parasuraman, A., Berry, L. L. and Zeithaml, V. A. (1990) *An Empirical Examination of Relationships in an Extended Service Quality Model.* Marketing Science Institute, Cambridge, MA.

Parasuraman, A., Berry, L. L. and Zeithaml, V. A. (1991a) 'Perceived Service Quality as a Customer Based Performance Measure: an Empirical Examination of Organizational Barriers using an Extended Service Quality Model'. *Human Resource Management* **30** (No. 3, Autumn): 335–364.

Parasuraman, A., Zeithaml, V. and Berry, L. L. (1985) 'A Conceptual Model of Service Quality and its Implications for Future Research'. *Journal of Marketing* **49** (Autumn): 41–50.

Parasuraman, A., Zeithaml, V. and Berry, L. L. (1986) 'SERVQUAL: a Multiple-item Scale for Measuring Customer Perceptions of Service Quality'. Report No. 86–108, Marketing Science Institute, Cambridge, MA.

Parasuraman, A., Zeithaml, V. and Berry, L. L. (1988) 'SERVQUAL: a Multiple-item Scale for Measuring Consumer Perceptions of Service Quality'. *Journal of Retailing* **64** (Spring): 12–40.

Parasuraman, A., Zeithaml, V. and Berry, L. L. (1991b). 'Refinement and Reassessment of the SERVQUAL Scale'. *Journal of Retailing* **67** (No. 4): 420–450.

Parasuraman, A., Zeithaml, V. and Berry, L. L. (1994) 'Reassessment of Expectations as a Comparison Standard in Measuring Service Quality: Implications for Future Research'. *Journal of Marketing* **58** (January): 111–124.

Peter, J. P. (1981) 'Construct Validity: a Review of Basic Issues and Marketing Practices'. *Journal of Marketing Research* **18** (May): 133–145.

Reichheld, F. F. and Sasser, W. E. Jr. (1990) 'Zero Defections: Quality comes to Service'. *Harvard Business Review* (September–October): 105–111.

Reidenbach, R. E. and Sandifer-Smallwood, B. (1990) 'Exploring Perceptions of Hospital Operations by a Modified SERVQUAL Approach'. *Journal of Health Care Marketing* **10** (No. 4, December): 47–55.

Richard, M. D. and Allaway, A. W. (1993) 'Service Quality Attributes and Choice Behavior'. *Journal of Service Marketing* **7** (No. 1): 59–68.

Rigotti, S. and Pitt, L. (1992) 'SERVQUAL as a Measuring Instrument for Service Provider Gaps in Business Schools'. *Managing Research News* **15** (No. 3): 9–17.

Rust, R. T. and Zahorik, A. J. (1993) 'Customer Satisfaction, Customer Retention and Market Share' *Journal of Retailing* **69** (No. 2, Summer): 193–215.

Saleh, F. and Ryan, C. (1992) 'Analysing Service Quality in the Hospitality Industry using the SERVQUAL Model'. *Services Industries Journal* **11** (No. 3): 324–43.

Scott, D. and Schieff, D. (1993) 'Service Quality Components and Group Criteria in Local Government'. *International Journal of Service Industry Management* **4** (No. 4): 42–53.

Soliman, A. A. (1992) 'Assessing the Quality of Health Care'. *Health Care Marketing* **10** (Nos 1–2): 121–141.

Spreng, R. A. and Singh, A. K. (1993) 'An Empirical Assessment of the SERVQUAL Scale and the Relationship between Service Quality and Satisfaction. Unpublished manuscript, Michigan State University, TN.

Taylor, S. A., Sharland, A., Cronin, A. A. Jr and Bullard, W. (1993) 'Recreational Quality in the International Setting'. *International Journal of Service Industries Management* **4** (No. 4): 68–88.

Teas, K. R. (1993a) 'Expectations, Performance Evaluation and Consumers' Perceptions of Quality'. *Journal of Marketing* **57** (No. 4): 18–24.

Teas, K. R. (1993b) 'Consumer Expectations and the Measurement of Perceived Service Quality'. *Journal of Professional Services Marketing* **8** (No. 2): 33–53.

Teas, K. R. (1994) 'Expectations as a Comparison Standard in Measuring Service Quality: an Assessment of a Reassessment'. *Journal of Marketing* **58** (January): 132–139.

Vandamme, R. and Leunis, J. (1993) 'Development of a Multiple-item Scale for Measuring Hospital Service Quality'. *International Journal of Service Industry Management* **4** (No. 3): 30–49.

Walbridge, S. W. and Delene, L. M. (1993) 'Measuring Physician Attitudes of Service Quality'. *Journal of Health Care Marketing* **13** (No. 4, Winter): 6–15.

Wason, P. J. and Johnson-Laird, P. N. (1972) *Psychology of Reasoning; Structure and Content.* B.T. Batsford, London.

Woodruff, R. B., Cadotte, E. R. and Jenkins, R. L. (1983) 'Modeling Consumer Satisfaction Processes using Experience-based Norms'. *Journal of Marketing Research* **20**: 296–304.

Wong, S. M. and Perry, C. (1991) 'Customer Service Strategies in Financial Retailing'. *International Journal of Bank Marketing* **9** (No. 3): 11–16.

Wotruba, T. R. and Tyagi, P. K. (1991) 'Met Expectations and Turnover in Direct Selling'. *Journal of Marketing* **55**: 24–35.

Zahorik, A. J. and Rust, R. T. (1992) 'Modeling the Impact of Service Quality of Profitability: a Review. In *Advances in Services Marketing and Management* (T. A. Swartz, D. E. Bowen and S. W. Brown. Eds). JAI Press, Greenwich, CT, pp. 49–64.

Zeithaml, V. A. (1988) 'Consumer Perceptions of Price, Quality and Value: a Means-end Model and Synthesis of Evidence'. *Journal of Marketing* **52** (July): 22–22.

Zeithaml, V. A., Berry, L. L. and Parasuraman, A. (1991) 'The Nature of Determinants of Customer Expectations of Service'. Working paper 91–113, Marketing Science Institute, Cambridge, MA.

Zeithaml, V. A., Berry, L. L. and Parasuraman, A. (1993) 'The Nature and Determinants of Customer Expectation of Service'. *Journal of the Academy of Marketing Science* **21** (No. 1): 1–12.

Zeithaml, V. A., Parasuraman, A. and Berry, L. L. (1990) *Delivering Quality Service: Balancing Customer Perceptions and Expectations.* Free Press, New York, NY.

Zeithaml, V. A., Parasuraman, A. and Berry, L. L. (1992) 'Strategic Positioning on the Dimensions of Service Quality'. In *Advances in Services Marketing and Management*, Vol. 2 (T. A. Swartz, D. E. Bowen and S. W. Brown Eds). JAI Press, Greenwich, CT, pp. 207–228.

15

A Dynamic Process Model of Service Quality: from Expectations to Behavioral Intentions

William Boulding, Ajay Kalra, Richard Staelin and Valarie A. Zeithaml

In response to growing importance of services in the worldwide economy and the recognition by goods firms of the need to compete on service dimensions of the augmented product, several researchers have examined the problems of measuring and managing service quality (Bitner, 1990; Bolton and Drew, 1991a,b; Parasuraman, Berry and Zeithaml, 1990; Parasuraman, Zeithaml and Berry, 1985, 1988; Zeithaml, Berry and Parasuraman, 1991). In this article, we added to this literature by providing insights into both the process by which customers for judgments of service quality and the way these judgments affect subsequent behavior. Specifically, we propose and estimate a process model of service quality that (1) traces the way customers form and update their perceptions of service quality and (2) identifies the consequences of these perceptions on individual-level behavioral intention variables that affect the strategic health of the firm.

Our model development draws from the service quality, attitude and customer satisfaction literatures. We follow the lead of the service quality literature and center our attention on modeling and measuring the cumulative construct of the overall quality level of the firm's service delivery system. We take note of the similarity between the construct 'perceived service quality' from the service quality literature and the construct 'attitude toward an object' from the attitude literature. This similarity helps us generate theoretical predictions in our model of service quality. We also draw from the satisfaction literature, though we make explicit the distinction between this literature, which emphasizes consumers' perceptions of a specific transaction, and the service quality literature, which emphasizes cumulative perceptions.[1]

---

[1]Readers should not confuse the consumer satisfaction measure discussed in the popular press and measured by many corporations with the satisfaction measure used in most academic satisfaction studies. The former is usually a cumulative concept whereas the latter is transaction specific. We discuss this difference subsequently.

Reprinted with permission from *Journal of Marketing Research*, Vol. 30, February, pp. 7–27.
© 1993 American Marketing Association.

At the core of our model is the assumption that individuals' current perceptions of the service quality of a firm just after a service contact are a blend of (1) their prior expectations of what *will* and what *should* transpire during the contact and (2) the actual delivered service during the service encounter. Further, we acknowledge that consumers update their expectations whenever they receive relevant information about the service through such means as word-of-mouth, company communications; and contact with the firm's or the competitor's service delivery system.

We test our model with data from two different studies, The first was a laboratory study involving multiple service encounters within the setting of staying in a hotel. Two different prior expectations and the delivered service were manipulated. With these longitudinal data, we use standard experimental analysis to test our basic hypotheses. We then specify a formal structural model representing our conceptualization of the service quality process. Using the same experimental data, we simultaneously test our basic hypotheses and the specification of our structural equations.

The second study enables us to increase the generalizability of our results by examining the service quality process for different service by using a different research method (a field study). In the laboratory study we were able to control (and thus measure) the objective aspects of the delivered service, but in our field study we did not obtain any objective measure of the actual dimensions of the service encounter for each individual. In addition, we obtained measures of expectations and perceptions at only one point in time. Such data are common in the area of service quality where (1) customers normally are polled once to ascertain their expectations and perceptions and (2) actual service is not measured, partly because obtaining objective measures is difficult and partly because the actual service delivered normally varies from person to person (and server to server). Consequently, we develop a method of analysis based on our structural process model that controls for (removes) all unobserved, individual-specific information affecting the customer's expectations and perceptions (the actual service being one such factor) while still allowing estimation of two key parameters of our process model. Such a technique should have broad applicability to service firms that want to measure the relative influences of the two different expectations *and* the delivered service (despite the fact that it is unmeasured) on the customer's perceptions of the firm's service quality.

In addition to postulating and testing a new dynamic model of expectations and perceptions, and providing an analytic approach for estimating major portions of this model with multiple-measures data obtained at only one point in time, we add to the service quality literature in several other ways. Though other researchers have postulated the existence of different expectations, our study is the first empirical demonstration of the joint influence of our two postulated expectations in a service quality setting. We also link the satisfaction and service quality literature by showing our dynamic model of service quality to be compatible with the currently accepted definition of transaction-specific satisfaction. Further, because the major current empirical paradigm for assessing service quality (the gaps model proposed by Parasuraman, Zeithaml and Berry, 1985) and our model are a subset of a more general model, we are able to estimate the validity of these alternative conceptualizations. Finally, ours is one of the first published field studies in which individual-level data are used to examine empirically the impact of consumers' perceptions of service quality on a set of intended behaviors of strategic interest to the firm.

In the following section, we develop our structural model and generate hypotheses for empirical testing. We then estimate the parameters of this model with the two different datasets. We conclude with a discussion of our results.

MODEL DEVELOPMENT

Because our model has many of the same constructs as prior models of service quality and customer satisfaction/dissatisfaction (CS/D), we begin this section with a brief review of the dominant concepts of these two literatures. Expectations and perceptions play an important role in both literatures. In general, both literatures treat these constructs as static, at least for estimation purposes. Also, recent studies in both literatures have acknowledged the existence of multiple classes of expectations (Forbes, Tse and Taylor, 1986; Tse and Wilton, 1988; Wilton and Nicosia, 1986; Zeithaml, Berry and Parasuraman, 1991). Two main standards of expectations emerge. One standard represents the expectations as a *prediction* of future events (Gilly, 1979; Gilly, Cron and Barry, 1983; Miller, 1977; Prakash, 1984; Swan and Trawick, 1980). This is the standard typically used in the satisfaction literature. The other standard is a *normative* expectation of future events (Miller, 1977; Prakash, 1984; Swan and Trawick, 1980), operationalized as either desired or ideal expectations. This is the standard typically used in the service quality literature (Parasuraman, Zeithaml and Berry, 1988).

Though these literatures are different expectation standards, expectations and perceptions in both literatures are usually linked via the disconfirmation of expectations paradigm (Oliver, 1977, 1980). This paradigm holds that the predictions customers make in advance of consumption act as a standard against which customers measure the firm's performance (Bearden and Teel, 1983; Churchill, 1979; Day, 1977; Woodrull, Cadotte and Jenkins, 1983). In the CS/D literature this paradigm states that the higher the expectation in relation to actual performance, the greater the degree of disconfirmation and the lower the satisfaction (Bearden and Teel, 1983; Latour and Peat, 1979; Swan and Trawick, 1981; Tse and Wilton, 1988). Expectations also play a contrast, or disconfirming, role in the gaps model of service quality (Parasuraman, Zeithaml and Berry, 1985). In this model the consumer's perception of overall service quality results from a comparison between expectations and perceptions of the different components of service. With perceptions of service held fixed, the higher the expectations, the lower the perceived quality.

Our model also includes expectations and perceptions. However, it differs from the disconfirmation formulation in that we postulate that individuals' overall quality assessments, and thus behaviors, are affected only by their current perceptions of the service, and not their current expectations. These current perceptions, in turn, are the result of customers' two types of prior expectations of the service and the most recent service encounter.

In developing our conceptualization, we organize our discussion around three processes: (1) the process by which customers form and update their expectations,

(2) the process by which customers develop perceptions of the quality of specific aspects of the service delivery system as well as an overall assessment of the firm's service quality, and (3) the relationship between perceptions of overall service quality and intended behaviors. After describing each of these processes, we provide a summary of the model and its testable implications.

The process that generates expectations

Customer expectations are pretrial beliefs about a product or service (Olson and Dover, 1979). In the absence of any information, prior expectations of service will be completely diffuse. In reality, however, customers have many sources of information that lead to expectations about upcoming service encounters with a particular company. These sources include prior exposure to the service, word or mouth, expert opinion, publicity, and communications controlled by the company (e.g. advertising, personal selling, and price), as well as prior exposure to competitive services (Zeithaml, Berry and Parasuraman, 1991).

Following the example of recent work suggesting the importance of multiple expectation standards, we postulate two different classes of expectations. Consistent with the expectations-as-predictions standard often used in the CS/D literature, we propose that customers form expectations about what *will* happen in their next service encounter with a firm. We refer to these expectations as *will* expectations. We also propose that customers form expectations about what *should* happen in their next service encounter, that is, the service customers feel they appropriately deserve. This normative expectation, here-after referred to as a *should* expectation, is close in spirit to the 'what ought to happen' expectation proposed by Tse and Wilton (1988). We distinguish this *should* standard from the ideal, or desired, standard frequently used in the service quality literature (Zeithaml, Berry and Parasuraman, 1991). What customers think *should* happen may change as a result of what they have been told to expect by the service provider, as well as what the consumer views as reasonable and feasible on the basis of being told of a competitor's service or experiencing the firm's or the competitor's service. In contrast, the consumer's *ideal* expectation – what a consumer wants in an ideal sense – may be unrelated to what is reasonable/feasible and/or what the service provider tells the customer to expect. Moreover, because *ideal* expectations represent enduring wants and needs that remain unaffected by the full range of marketing and competitive factors postulated to affect the *should* expectation, we believe *ideal* expectations are much more stable over time than consumer expectations of what should occur.

We start our discussion by noting that expectations and perceptions can change over time. Also, as becomes clearer subsequently, we acknowledge that there are J unique dimensions of service quality for each of these constructs. Finally, we note that our approach is to first specify general functional relationships for the process that generates these expectations and perceptions. After testing these general relationships, we specify and test explicit functional forms. These explicit equations enable us to gain additional insights into the process as well as develop an approach for estimating the parameters of our model with cross-sectional data.

More formally, let WE_{ijt} be consumer i's *will* expectation for the jth dimension of a service just after experiencing a service contact at time t; DS_{ijt}^* be the jth component of the service delivered to person i at time t (as captured by factors such as the number of thank you's, the waiting time, etc., and where the * notation indicates a transaction-specific construct as opposed to a cumulative construct); and $\mathbf{X}_{it}$ be a vector of information variables other than the service contact influencing the person's *will* expectations of the service prior to a new service contact. We acknowledge that a person's *will* expectations just before a new service contact can differ from the expectations held just after the prior service contact because of the information $\mathbf{X}_{it}$ that enters the system between service encounters. However, in our subsequent empirical work we do not measure such information. Consequently, our approach is to control, but not explicitly model or test, for effects of external information.[2]

We hypothesize that a consumer's expectations of what will happen in subsequent contacts with the firm's service delivery system depend not only on the information obtained from the most recent service contact, but also on the expectations held just prior to the service contact. Such a formulation explicitly acknowledges that two different individuals may hold different expectations about future service contacts even when they experience an identical (in an objective sense) service encounter. This is equivalent to saying that biases are present and that these biases are due to prior expectations.

More formally, we specify the following functional relationship:

$$WE_{ijt} = f_1(WE_{ijt-1}, \mathbf{X}_{it}, DS_{ijt}^*). \tag{1}$$

Note that equation (1) assumes expectations are influenced by the actual encounter (DS_{ijt}^* in our notation) versus the consumer's perception of the actual encounter. We acknowledge that the consumer's perceptions of the *particular* service encounter may, in fact, be used to update expectations. However, if we denote this perception as $PS_{ijt}^* = g(DS_{ijt}^*)$, but also that DS_{ijt}^* is a very good proxy for PS_{ijt}^*, that is, there is a strong positive relationship between the two constructs. Because our empirical work has no direct measure of PS_{ijt}^*, we integrate out this unobserved variable, which leads us to use DS_{ijt}^* instead of PS_{ijt}^* in specifying the functional relationship given by equation (1).

In making predictions about the effects of delivered service and prior expectations on a consumer's updated expectations, we believe a Bayesian-like updating process occurs. Specifically, customers have an expectation just prior to the service contact (WE_{ijt-1}), experience a new service contact (DS_{ijt}^*), and develop a posterior prediction of future service (WE_{ijt}). Because customers are *integrating* information, this process implies that both prior information and new information will be positively related to the updated prediction. This logic leads to our first two hypotheses.[3]

H$_1$: $\partial f_1/\partial WE_{ijt-1} > 0$.
H$_1$: $\partial f_1/\partial DS_{ijt}^* > 0$.

We believe *should* expectations are influenced from three sources. Similar to *will* expectations, the customer's new *should* expectations (SE_{ijt}) will be related to the

---

[2]For a more explicit statement of how these $\mathbf{X}$ variables might influence expectations: see Boulding *et al.* (1992).

[3]All stated hypotheses are based on the assumption of 'all else equal'.

customer's prior *should* expectation (SE_{ijt-1}). Second, the *should* expectation may differ between time t and $t-1$ because of new information reaching the customer between service contacts, such as changes in price, firm communications, and competitive service delivery. We denote this new information as $\mathbf{Z}_{it}$. Third, experiences with the firm's own delivery system can lead to increases, but never decreases, in the customer's *should* expectations between time t and $t-1$.

An example of the influence of new information is when a firm raises its price and the customers shift their *should* expectations upward to reflect their belief that the service should be better than it was before the price increase. Similarly, if a firm announces that it plans to increase service over previous levels, customers may believe the firm should deliver on this promise. Also, if customers are exposed to a firm's competitor who delivers unanticipated higher levels of service, the customers may believe the firm should deliver similarly high levels of service. For example, Lexus's recent policy of replacing the car when a consumer expresses displeasure with the paint job might alter the consumers' *should* expectations level for other car manufacturers.

We believe that the delivered service influence *should* expectations only when the firm's own service delivery exceeds the individual's prior *should* expectations. Specifically, we postulate that the more the firm's actual delivered service exceeds the customer's prior *should* expectations, the more the customer will increase his or her future *should* expectations for that firm. Thus, in our Lexus example, we would postulate that if the policy of replacing the car exceeds the customer's prior *should* expectations, the customer's *should* expectations for Lexus will increase.

We state these beliefs more formally with the following functional relationship.

$$SE_{ijt} = f_2(SE_{ijt-1}, \mathbf{Z}_{it}, K_{ijt} \cdot DS_{ijt}^*), \tag{2}$$

where $K_{ijt} = 1$ when $DS_{ijt}^* > SE_{ijt-1}$, 0 otherwise. As before, we do not model the $\mathbf{Z}$ vector in any more depth because we control for, but do not measure, these factors.

More specifically, we expect SE_{ijt} to relate directly to SE_{ijt-1}, modified by $K_{ijt} \cdot DS_{ijt}^*$. This leads to our next two hypotheses.

H_3: $\partial f_2/\partial SE_{ijt-1} > 0$.
H_4: $\partial f_2/\partial K_{ijt} \cdot DS_{ijt}^* > 0$.

Equations (1) and (2) make explicit that the two types of expectations are different (albeit related) constructs, and that it should be possible to manipulate one or the other of these expectations via the $\mathbf{X}$ and $\mathbf{Z}$ vectors and different service encounters. We say more on this point in discussing our laboratory study.

Finally, we do not explicitly specify a process that generates *ideal* expectations for two reasons. First, as previously noted, *ideal* expectations are generally unchanged over time; therefore, the *ideal* expectation at time t equals the *ideal* expectation at time $t-1$. Second, we conjecture that *ideal* expectations influence *should* expectations. The $\mathbf{Z}$ vector in equation (2) could easily include information about an individual's *ideal* expectation.

The process that generates perceptions

We next explicate our conceptualization of how customers form perceptions of the service quality of a firm.[4] This formulation differs from the disconfirmation formulation most often found in the CS/D literature (Oliver, 1980) and the gap formulation found in the service quality literature (Parasuraman, Zeithaml and Berry, 1985). However, we show that the implications from our service quality model are compatible with the transaction-specific definition of satisfaction found in the CS/D literature. In addition, we test the viability of our model in relation to the gaps model. In these ways, our model begins to integrate the service quality and satisfaction literatures.

In our model, a person's perception of each of the J dimensions of service quality is conceptualized as a *cumulative* construct, denoted by PS_{ijt} that is updated each time the person is exposed to the service. We postulate that these perceptions are influenced by a person's expectations of the service as well as the most recent service encounter. We thus explicitly allow for a person to have a perceptual bias, as our model implies that two customers experiencing an identical service encounter will have different cumulative perceptions of the service if they enter the encounter with different expectations.

Stated more formally, individual i's cumulative perceptions of the jth dimension of service quality held at time t will be a blend of three factors: the person's expectations just prior to the encounter of what will happen and what should happen, and the new service encounter. The general function relationship is

$$PS_{ijt} = f_3(WE_{ijt-1}, \mathbf{X}_{it}, SE_{ijt-1}, \mathbf{Z}_{it}, DS^*_{ijt}), \qquad (3)$$

where $\mathbf{X}_{it}$ and $\mathbf{Z}_{it}$ are vectors that capture adjustments to expectations occurring between service encounters, as defined in equation (1) and (2).

We believe a person's expectations color the way he or she perceives reality. Specifically, we postulate that customers have higher expectations of what the firm *will* deliver have higher perceptions of the service after an encounter, all else equal, than those with lower *will* expectations. Conversely, customers with higher expectations of what a firm *should* deliver have lower perceptions of the service after an encounter, all else equal, than those lower *should* expectations. Finally, we believe the delivered service positively affects perceptions. These statements give rise to the following testable hypotheses.

H_5: $\partial f_3 / \partial WE_{ijt-1} > 0$.
H_6: $\partial f_3 / \partial SE_{ijt-1} < 0$.
H_7: $\partial f_3 / \partial DS^*_{ijt} > 0$.

H_5 and H_7 are based on similar logic. We believe customers average/integrate past experience with the firm which is summarized by their prior *will* expectations) and their latest service encounters in making a cumulative assessment of the service quality level of the firm. This notion leads to our hypothesizing the positive influences. We note that the role of *will* expectations is very similar to the role of the 'initial impression' in averaging models of attitude. In these attitude models, initial impressions always have a positive (assimilative) influence.

As distinguished from the assimilative role of the *will* expectations, the *should*

---

[4]Keep in mind that these perceptions are *not* the perceptions of a specific service encounter, but instead the perceptions of the service quality based on the consumer's cumulative experience with the firm's service delivery system.

expectation acts as a standard of comparison in relation to competitors. As the standard set by competitors goes up, all else equal, the firm fares less well in how it is perceived by customers. Placing our models within the context of assimilation–contrast attitude theory, we are stating that the *should* expectation provides a negative (contrast) influence on overall attitude (perceptions of quality).

Dimensions of service quality

A central construct in our model is the customer's perception of overall service quality for a firm. Recent research suggests that this quality assessment is not uni-dimensional, but instead comprises multiple abstract dimensions (Garvin, 1987; Hjorth-Anderson, 1984; Holbrook and Corfman, 1985; Maynes, 1976; Parasuraman, Zeithaml and Berry, 1985; Zeithaml, 1988). After studying four consumer service industries, Parasuraman, Zeithaml and Berry (1985, 1988) identified five dimensions: reliability, assurance, responsiveness, empathy and tangibles.

We make the assumption that customers perceive the service quality of a system in terms of these five dimensions, and also that their expectations of what *will* and *should* happen are in terms of these five dimensions. We incorporate the multidimensional aspect of overall service quality by defining the following relationship:

$$OSQ_{it} = f_4(PS_{ijt}),\qquad(4)$$

where OSQ_{it} equals individual i's overall perception of the firm's service quality at time t, and the j subscript on PS corresponds to the jth dimension of the service enumerated by Parasuraman and his co-authors. Note that we postulate that the perceptions of the J different dimensions of the service, and not the 'actual' service, directly affect the person's assessment of the overall service quality of a firm. In this way we again acknowledge that perceptual biases are present and that perceptions of reality, not 'reality' itself, affect overall attitudes and subsequent behavior.

Previous empirical work suggests that these dimensions of service all have a positive, albeit perhaps unequal, impact on overall quality perceptions. In a variety of different service businesses and industries, respondents consistently rated the dimensions of reliability as most important (Parasuraman, Berry and Zeithaml, 1990; Zeithaml, Berry and Parasuraman, 1991). Consistent with previous findings, we believe that though quality is multidimensional, reliability is the key dimension in determining overall perceptions of service quality.

Hence, we hypothesize that the different dimensions of quality are averaged together in some fashion to produce an overall assessment of quality. Further, by substituting equation (3) into equation (4), we can propose hypotheses about the role of the two different expectations and delivered service in customers' judgments of overall quality. Specifically, because the expected signs on PS_{ijt} in equation (4) are positive, we should serve the same direction of effects for the expectation and delivered service constructs as in equation (3). Consequently, we propose the following testable hypotheses.

H_8: $\partial f_4 / \partial WE_{ijt-1} > 0$.
H_9: $\partial f_4 / \partial SE_{ijt-1} < 0$.
H_{10}: $\partial f_4 / \partial DS^*_{ijt} > 0$.

The relationship between overall quality and behavioral intentions

Delivery of high service quality is presumed to relate positively to the success of the firm. Interestingly, no empirical research outside a laboratory setting has been reported that supports this relationship between service quality perceptions and behavioral outcomes of importance to the firm.[5] Unless this positive relationship exists, understanding how customers form judgments about service quality has limited managerial relevance.

We propose the following function to capture this relationship.

$$BI_{imt} = f_5(OSQ_{it}),$$ (5)

where BI_{imt} equals the mth behavioral intention (i.e. loyalty, word of mouth, etc.) for individual i at time t. We strongly believe that service quality positively affects important behavioral outcomes such as loyalty and positive word of mouth. Furthermore, we can substitute through from equations (3) and (4) to examine the indirect effects of expectations and delivered service on behavioral intentions. Because the predicted effect of overall quality in equation (5) is positive, we should observe the same predicted effects of expectations and delivered service as given for equations (3) and (4).

H_{11}: $\partial f_5 / \partial WE_{ijt-1} > 0.$
H_{12}: $\partial f_5 / \partial SE_{ijt-1} < 0.$
H_{13}: $\partial f_5 / \partial DS_{ijt}^* > 0.$

Summary

We present our full conceptual model in Figure 1, which summarizes the proposed relationships among the types of expectations, service quality perceptions, overall perceived service quality, and behavioral intentions. Individuals enter into each service transaction with an initial set of expectations about what *will* and *should* occur on each of the dimensions of service. These initial expectations and the actual delivered service then lead to cumulative perceptions of the delivered service on each dimension, as well as updated expectations for each dimension of what *will* and *should* occur in future transactions. Finally, perceptions of the dimensions of service contribute to an overall assessment of the level of service quality, which in turn leads to behavioral outcomes.

EMPIRICAL TESTING

We now turn to empirical testing in our conceptual model. We begin with an experimental study in which we manipulate the constructs delivered service, *will* expectations, and *should* expectations. We analyze the data in two stages. First, using

---

[5]In the area of customer satisfaction, a recent individual-level study found a significant and positive effect of satisfaction on customer retention (Anderson and Sullivan, 1990).

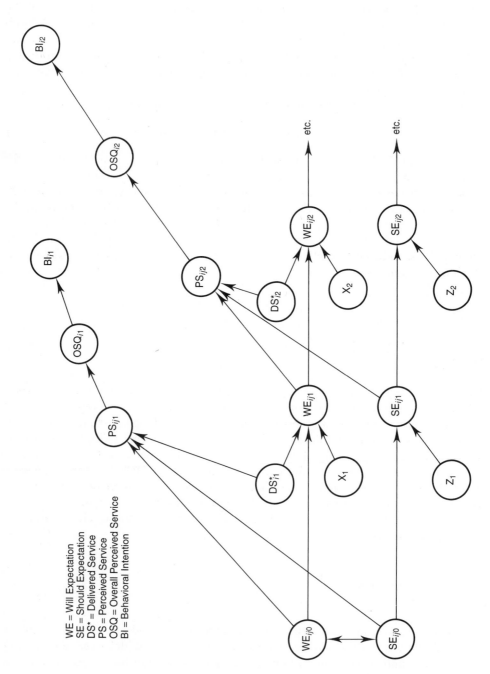

WE = Will Expectation
SE = Should Expectation
DS* = Delivered Service
PS = Perceived Service
OSQ = Overall Perceived Service
BI = Behavioral Intention

Figure 1. A dynamic process model of service quality.

standard experimental analysis, we use the data to directly test the hypotheses relating to these constructs that emerge from the five functional relationships specified previously. Second, given favorable outcomes of these tests, we specify explicit functional forms for equations (1) through (5). We than estimate this system of equations in a way that enables us to directly test the underlying process suggested by Figure 1. Importantly, this procedure also enables us to directly *test the specification of our explicit functional forms.*

As this specification test provides support for our structural model specification, we next take advantage of this information to develop a method for estimating our dynamic model with data taken at a single point in time. We than apply this approach to data collected in a second study. This second study serves three purposes. First, it increases confidence in the generalizability of our findings because a different data collection approach (a natural field setting), a different service, and a different analytic approach are used. Second, it enables us to test certain relationships that are not explored in study 1. Third, it provides an important insight into how managers can easily and effectively collect data to assess service quality.

STUDY 1

Sample and data

To test the conceptual model in Figure 1, we first used data obtained from a laboratory experiment involving two simulated visits to a hotel. Subjects were 107 business professionals, including managers and staff, located in a major metropolitan area. Eleven subjects' questionnaires were unusable because of missing data. These subjects were dropped, resulting in a sample size of 96.

Procedure

Subjects participated individually in the experiment and were assigned randomly to one of eight conditions. They were told that the purpose of the task was to find out how they evaluate hotels. A self-administered computer diskette was provided, along with instructions to start the program. Subjects were asked to assume they were to stay at a hotel during a business trip. They were then provided an overview of the task and an explanation of the stimuli. After evaluating a hypothetical restaurant to familiarize themselves with the keyboard and the task, they began and actual task.

Both *should* and *will* expectations were manipulated by providing subjects information about (1) others' perceptions of the quality of target hotel 'Alpha' they were to visit and (2) the level of service provided and the price offered by a competitor hotel. Subjects were asked to indicate the quality of hotel service they expected to receive and the quality they though they should receive. They then 'visited' the hotel. After reading a brief general description of their stay, subjects viewed information about the specific performance rating of six features provided by the hotel. Measures of quality assessment were obtained at this point, followed by two behavioral intention measures, and then measures of current *will* and *should* expectations of the level of service.

Subjects were informed they were to stay at the same hotel a second time and were provided information about this second service encounter. Measures of overall quality assessment and the two behavioral intentions and expectations measures were obtained again after this 'visit'.

Design

We used a three-factor between-subjects design. The factors were initial *will* expectations (three levels: low, medium, and high), *should* expectations (two levels: medium and high), and delivered service (two levels: low and high). Because prior research (Kalra, 1992) had indicated difficulty in manipulating *will* expectations to exceed *should* expectations, we focused our attention on obtaining data for only four of the six possible *will–should* pairs (medium *will*/high *should*; medium *will*/medium *should*; high *will*/high *should*; and low *will*/medium *should*). These four conditions were fully crossed with the two levels of service, yielding eight cells. Though incomplete, this design provides unconfounded contrasts for testing our stated hypotheses (e.g. low *will*/medium *should* vs. medium *will*/medium *should* provides and unconfounded contrast for testing effects of prior *will* expectations). Also, though subjects paid two 'visits' to a hotel, we do not use the information relating to the second 'visit' in our initial experimental analysis because the first visit affects customers' expectations, thereby negating our ability to conduct planned contrasts for the data related to the second visit. However, we do use this information to test further qualitative implications of the model when we estimate the structural system of equations.

Manipulations

Should and will expectations

On the basis of theory and results of prior experiment (Kalra, 1992), we determined that we could manipulate *should* and *will* expectations by providing information on (1) prior exposure to a competitor's service (which we provided via information on price and rated service of a competitor) and (2) price, word of mouth, and expert opinion on the object hotel (Hotel Alpha). This manipulation was done via a paragraph describing information on the subject's prior visit to a nearby competitive hotel and others' views on Hotel Alpha. Each description held fixed the Hotel Alpha price. As is seen in the discussion on the manipulation checks, this approach resulted in the four desired *will–should* combinations. For more details on these manipulations, see Boulding *et al.* (1992).

Delivered service

Half of the subjects first received comparatively high performance ratings on the six features provided in their hotel visits, and then comparatively low performance ratings in the second visit. The order was reversed for the other half of the subjects.

As we show subsequently, high performance is approximately equivalent to an 80 on our measurement scale and low performance is approximately equivalent to a 50.

Stimuli

Hotels were used as the service settings for two reasons. First, subjects were familiar with the product category. Second, hotels are typically characterized by variability in the quality of service provided during different encounters. The stimuli consisted of a constant neutral description of the stay and manipulated information about performance ratings on six features of the hotel. The features, selected on the basis of a pilot study, were noise, checkin/checkout, amenities, hotel staff, cleanliness, and bed comfort. The subjects were asked to assume that the ratings reflected their own opinions of the features associated with the hotel. Subjects could only view the ratings of the feature one at a time. They were free to examine the stimuli as long as they wanted and in any sequence. The performance ratings were displayed in the form of a bar graph anchored between 'poor' and 'excellent'.

Measures[6]

Quality assessments

Quality assessments were measured on a 100-point scale. Subjects were asked to 'describe your opinion on the overall quality of Hotel Alpha', which was anchored by the labels 'very unfavorable' and 'very favorable'. The quality assessment were obtained after both the first and second visits. Further, the question was framed so as to obtain measures of overall quality rather than satisfaction/dissatisfaction with a specific visit.

Behavioral intentions

Two questions were asked after each visit about the subject's willingness to provide favorable word of mouth and repeat business. These questions were 'How likely are you to stay again a Hotel Alpha?' and 'How likely are you to recommend Hotel Alpha to a friend?' Both questions were anchored between 'very unlikely' and 'very likely'. For purposes of analysis, we combine these two questions to form behavioral intentions scale (equally weighted). This item scale yields a Cronbach alpha value of .92.

Expectations

Will expectations associated with overall service were measured by the question 'What is your opinion on the level of service Hotel Alpha will actually provide you?' *Should* expectations were measured by the question 'What is your opinion on the

---

[6]The measures in this first experiment are at the overall service level instead of the *j*th dimension level. This is mathematically equivalent to assuming $J = 1$. Given the 'limited' exposure to the service, we found subjects were more comfortable with this more macro level of service quality.

level of service you would consider to be reasonable, or Hotel Alpha should provide?' Both questions were framed in terms of future expectations, anchored on one end by 'poor service' and on the other 'excellent service', and measured on a 100-point scale.

The same order of questions was used in all conditions, which leads to the following sequence of measures for each customer: at $t = 0$, the customer's *will* and *should* expectations; at $t = 1$ and $t = 2$, the delivered service (i.e., high or low), the customer's perceptions of the quality of the service at the hotel, his or her behavioral intentions, and updated *will* and *should* expectations.

Empirical analysis: stage 1

Expectation manipulation checks

Table 1 presents cell means for our different measures. The cell means from $t = 0$ for the *will* and *should* expectations enable us to test the effectiveness of our expectation manipulations. Because the delivered service manipulation occurs after the measures taken at $t = 0$, we can collapse the data across the two levels of delivered service. Thus, in the following discussion we combine cells 1 and 5, 2 and 6, 3 and 7, and 4 and 8.

As evidence of the success of our manipulations, the *will* expectation means are higher in cells 2 and 6 than in cells 4 and 8 ($t_{92} = 7.56$) and higher in cells 3 and 7 than in cells 1 and 5 ($t_{92} = 10.37$). As evidence of discriminant validity, the *should* expectations for cells 2 and 6 do not differ from those for cells 4 and 8 ($t_{92} = .65$),

Table 1.   Study 1 cells means[a]

Manipulations			Means of will expectations		Means of should expectations		Means of perceived service quality	Means of behavioral intention index
Expectations will/should	Service delivered	Cell	$t = 0$	$t = 1$	$t = 0$	$t = 1$	$t = 1$	$t = 1$
Med/high	High	1	50.50	64.30	89.70	91.20	62.70	61.55
			(3.69)	(8.85)	(8.72)	(7.42)	(7.99)	(15.71)
Med/med	High	2	51.36	70.00	61.36	77.27	72.27	70.68
			(10.97)	(11.18)	(11.42)	(12.91)	(10.33)	(15.12)
High/high	High	3	84.00	77.42	84.58	84.58	76.16	74.45
			(7.15)	(7.26)	(10.54)	(10.10)	(8.59)	(8.95)
Low/med	High	4	28.75	63.44	61.87	68.43	65.31	63.75
			(18.75)	(9.07)	(20.48)	(18.41)	(12.58)	(10.91)
Med/high	Low	5	54.61	53.46	86.54	83.46	52.69	45.15
			(12.65)	(16.88)	(5.56)	(12.14)	(17.27)	(18.05)
Med/med	Low	6	50.83	59.16	63.75	63.75	55.00	55.21
			(4.88)	(10.83)	(14.94)	(14.32)	(12.43)	(20.35)
High/high	Low	7	87.08	65.41	91.25	86.25	66.67	61.87
			(7.52)	(10.54)	(8.01)	(13.16)	(9.37)	(10.45)
Low/med	Low	8	26.00	39.00	57.50	66.00	48.00	37.50
			(9.07)	(11.50)	(14.95)	(14.10)	(11.83)	(14.67)

[a] Standard deviations are in parentheses.

nor do cells 1 and 5 differ from cells 3 and 7 ($t_{92} = .00$). Similarly, for the *should* expectation we note the means are higher in cells 1 and 5 than in cells 2 and 6 ($t_{92} = 6.61$). As further evidence of discriminant validity, the *will* expectation for cells 1 and 5 do not differ from those for cells 2 and 6 ($t_{92} = .55$). Consequently, we conclude that (1) we were successful in manipulating initial *will* and *should* expectations into the four desired cells, (2) were were able to identify antecedents to each expectation, and (3) the two different expectations are in fact separate constructs.

Results

Table 1 also gives cell means at $t = 1$ for the two expectations measures, as well as for the measures of overall quality and the behavioral intentions index. A series of cell contrasts enable us to test the qualitative hypotheses generated from the five specified functional relationships.[7] Table 2 indicates the relevant cell contrast that hold 'all else equal' for tests of our hypotheses, as well as the test results. As a check on our specified equations, this table also includes tests of significance for relationships not included in the equations.

Because the specified functional relationships do not contain interaction terms (with the exception of the *should* expectation equation), we first conduct joint tests of significance for all interaction terms estimable from our experimental design for equations (1), (3), and (5). We find no joint interaction effects in any of these three equations reaching significance at the .10 level.[8] Therefore, for these equations, we restrict our attention to testing for main effects.

Starting with the *will* expectations updating equation, Table 2 indicates strong support for our two main effects hypotheses. Results of the cell contrast suggest that prior *will* expectations and the delivered service both contribute positively and significantly to the updated *will* expectations, supporting H_1 and H_2. We also find marginal significance ($p = .10$) for the effect of prior *should* expectations in the *will* expectation equation. Because we do not hypothesize this relationship, we explore it in greater depth in the stage 2 analysis of our experimental data.

Turning to the *should* expectation updating equation, we note that the prior *should* expectation significantly and positively affects the updated *should* expectation (H_3). Consistent with our specification of equation 2, we find no main effect of delivered service, nor do we find an effect or prior *will* expectations. In addition, looking at differences in values between $t = 0$ and $t = 1$, we find significant support for H_4, that is, delivered service increases *should* expectations, but only if the delivered service exceeds the prior *should* expectation. This occurred only in cells 2 and 4, where the delivered service was high (approximately 80) and the prior *should* expectations were medium (approximately 60).

---

[7]As noted in footnote 6, in the context of this experiment we assume a single dimension of quality. We therefore cannot distinguish between the constructs 'perceptions' (*PS*) and 'overall quality' (*OSQ*) as laid out in equations (3) and (4). Thus, equation (3) and H_5–H_7 are redundant with equation (4) and H_8–H_{10}. In study 2 we generate separate estimates of equations (3) and (4).

[8]In the *will* expectation equation, $F_{3.88} = 2.14$; in the perceived service equation $F_{3.88} = 0.80$; and in the behavioral intentions equation, $F_{3.88} = 1.02$.

Table 2.   Hypothesis test results[a]

Hypothesis[b]	Dependent measure	Factor	Cell contrast	t-statistic[c]
H_1	WE_t	WE_{t-1}	1,5 vs. 3,7	4.08*
H_1	WE_t	WE_{t-1}	2,6 vs. 4,8	3.24*
H_2	WE_t	DS_t^*	1,2,3,5 vs. 5,6,7,8	5.99*
NH	WE_t	SE_{t-1}	1,5 vs. 2,6	1.88***
H_3	SE_t	SE_{t-1}	1,5 vs. 2,6	4.17*
NH	SE_t	WE_{t-1}	1,5 vs. 3,7	.36
NH	SE_t	WE_{t-1}	2,6 vs. 4,8	.70
NH	SE_t	DS_t^*	1,2,3,4 vs. 5,6,7,8[d]	1.30
H_4	$SE_t - SE_{t-1}$	K, DS_t^*	2,4 vs. 1,3,5,6,7,8	3.39*
H_5	PS_t	WE_{t-1}	1,5 vs. 3,7	4.16*
H_5	PS_t	WE_{t-1}	2,6 vs. 4,8	1.36***
H_6	PS_t	SE_{t-1}	1,5 vs. 2,6	1.78**
H_7	PS_t	DS_t^*	1,2,3,4 vs. 5,6,7,8	5.44*
H_{11}	BI_t	WE_{t-1}	1,5 vs. 3,7	4.26*
H_{11}	BI_t	WE_{t-1}	2,6 vs. 4,8	2.14**
H_{12}	BI_t	SE_{t-1}	1,5 vs. 2,6	2.92*
H_{13}	BI_t	DS_t^*	1,2,3,4 vs. 5,6,7,8	6.11*

[a]Given directional hypotheses, significance tests are one-tailed. For nonhypothesized relationships, significance tests are two-tailed.
[b]NH indicates not hypothesized.
[c]Calculated t-statistics are based on 88 degrees of freedom.
[d]This is a very conservative test. A less conservative test would contrast cells 1,3 vs. 5,7.
*Significant at the .01 level.
**Significant at the .05 level.
***Significant at the .10 level.

Table 2 also indicates strong support for the three main effects hypotheses relating to our perceived service equation (assuming a single dimension of quality). In support of H_5, prior *will* expectations positively and significantly influence cumulative assessments of perceived service. In support of H_6, prior *should* expectations negatively and significantly affect perceived service. Also, as predicted by H_7, delivered service positively and significantly contributes to perceptions of service quality.

Finally, it is interesting to see whether our manipulations affect the downstream behavioral intentions measures. Table 2 again provides support for all of our stated main effects hypotheses. As suggested by H_{11} and H_{12} prior *will* expectations positively and significantly influence behavioral intentions, whereas prior *should* expectations negatively and significantly influence behavioral intentions. As one would expect, and as stated by H_{13}, delivered service positively and significantly influences behavioral intentions.

In summary, our experimental data provide strong support for all of our hypothesized relationships given by equations (1) through (5) and all but one of the implicit null hypotheses. We highlight three conclusions from these analyses. First, we demonstrate conclusively that *will* and *should* expectations are different constructs. Second, we confirm that *will* expectations positively influence and *should* expectations negatively influence perceptions of quality. Third, holding fixed the delivered service, one can trace a measurable effect of two different expectations on individuals' behavioral intentions.

The preceding univariate contrasts take full advantage of the experimental design aspect of our data. Further, such contrasts require no assumptions about the specific functional forms of equations (1) through (5). A drawback of this approach, however, is that it does not allow us to estimate the magnitude of the effects. It also does not allow us to specify and test any cross-equation implications of our process model as given in Figure 1, or use the period 2 data for estimation. To accomplish these latter objectives, we must make specific assumptions about the functional forms of equations (1) through (5). However, we can directly test those assumptions. As long as these assumed functional forms are costless (i.e. they are not rejected by specification tests), we favor this approach because it yields the benefit of additional specificity.

Empirical analysis: stage 2

Specification of functional forms

In specifying our process model, we focus our attention on the functional relationships for our measured constructs, WE, SE, PS and BI. We do not specify the role of 'other' information (i.e. the $\mathbf{X}$ and $\mathbf{Z}$ vectors) in this process, because in our studies we control for (but never measure) 'other' information.[9] Consequently, we leave this part of our conceptualization to future research.

With the preceding caveat in mind, we now fully specify equation (1) (we distinguish the fully specified equation by 'S':

$$WE_{ijt} = \alpha_{jt}WE_{ijt-1} + (1 - \alpha_{jt})DS^*_{ijt} + \epsilon_{1it} \tag{1S}$$

where the parameters α_{ij} (which can assume values between 0 and 1) determines the relative weights assigned to the prior expectation and the delivered service in the updating equation, and ϵ_{1it} is an error term. This specification make equation (1S) consistent with our conceptualization of *will* expectations being updated by means of an averaging process.

We note two testable implications of this specification. First, one can test the validity of the averaging model by comparing the estimates of equation (1S), which contains a single constrained parameter, with an additive model, which would contain two unconstrained parameters. Second, there is a qualitative implication as to the value of α_{jt} over time. Specifically, as an individual accumulates more information about a service on the basis of past experience, the influence of WE_{ijt-1}, which captures this past experience, should receive more weight in relation to the most recent service encounter in generating future predictions about the service. Consequently, α_{jt} should grow larger over time.

---

[9]In study 1, no information is provided between our measurement of WE_{t-1} and the service encounter at time t. In study 2, we explicitly control for differences in the informational environment by conducting within-person analysis.

Turning to the *should* expectation updating process, we fully specify equation (2) as

$$SE_{ijt} = SE_{ijt-1} + \beta_{jt}(K_{ijt} \cdot DS^*_{ijt}) + \epsilon_{2it}, \tag{2S}$$

where β_{jt} equals an updating parameter postulated to be greater than zero and ϵ_{2it} is an error term. Unlike equation (1S), this updating formulation does *not* follow an averaging process. Instead, we believe *should* expectations follow a ratcheting process – they can go up, but they cannot go beyond prior levels.[10] More specifically, equation (2S) implies that *should* expectations equal old *should* expectations unless the latest delivered service exceeds the prior *should* expectation.

For the perception equation, we make the assumption that customers blend their prior *will* expectations with the latest service experience in a manner identical to that used to form the new *will* expectation. This averaging process is then additively blended with the consumer's *should* expectations. We represent these beliefs mathematically as

$$PS_{ijt} = \alpha_{jt}WE_{ijt-1} + (1 - \alpha_{jt})DS^*_{ijt} + \gamma_{jt}SE_{ijt-1} + \epsilon_{3it}, \tag{3S}$$

where α_{jt} is the same updating parameter as given in equation (1S), γ_{jt} is a new updating parameter with $\gamma_{jt} < 0$, and ϵ_{3it} is an error term. Such a formulation makes explicit the assimilative (averaging) role of prior *will* expectations and the latest delivered service, and the contrastive (adding) role of *should* expectations.[11]

As with equation (1S), we can test the explicit averaging assumption of (3S) by comparing the constrained one-parameter averaging process with an unconstrained two-parameter process. We can also test whether the parameter α_{jt} is the same parameter as given in equation (1S) by comparing an unconstrained estimate of this parameter with one that is constrained to equality across equations (1S) and (3S).

Note that by replacing the first two terms of equation (3S) with the left side of equation (1S), one can see the difference between an individual's current *perception* of the service and his or her current *prediction* of likely service. Specifically, these two constructs differ increasingly as the consumer's prior expectations of what service they *should* get increase. Two implications are that we expect the parameter on the *should* expectation term to be significant in equation (3S), but not to add explanatory power in equation (1S). We test both implications with all of our longitudinal data.

Because our conceptualization of the role of expectations in generating perceptions is new, we use simple examples to reconcile it with previous conceptualizations and demonstrate its intuitive appeal. First, for notational simplicity, assume that there is only one dimension of service quality. Further assume that two individuals have identical expectations of what should happen but, on the basis of prior service, the first individual predicts future service will rate a five and the second individual predicts future service will rate a seven. Given our system of equations, the implication is that individual 2's current perception is higher than individual 1's. Finally, suppose these

---

[10]Conceptually, we believe that information in the **Z** vector could cause these expectations to decrease. For example, a price decrease by the firm or learning about much higher levels of price for competitors could lower *should* expectations.

[11]An alternative theoretical basis for (3S) is that *will* expectations affect the private psychological impression of the service, whereas the *should* expectations affect the output mapping of private psychological impressions onto overt ratings of perceptions (Lynch, Chakravarti and Mitra, 1991).

two individuals simultaneously experience a new service encounter and receive identical delivered service that rates a six. We next explore three questions:

- Which of these two individuals will have higher cumulative perceptions of the quality of the firm's delivery system after the encounter?
- Which will be most satisfied with the most recent encounter?
- How are the perceptions of each individual changing over time?

According to the hypothesized relationships in equations (3S), the second individual will have a higher perception of the service because this individual combines all prior experience with the latest transaction to form a cumulative perception of the service. However, on the basis of a definition of satisfaction associated with the disconfirmation of expectations paradigm (i.e. satisfaction equals performance minus expected performance, or $DS^*_{ijt} - WE_{ijt-1}$ in our notation), the first person will be more satisfied with the most recent service encounter because this person had the lower prior *will* expectation. Finally, given the form of equation 3S, the second individual (who originally had the higher value for overall perceived quality) will show a decrease in his or her cumulative perception of quality because the last service encounter was below his or her predicted level of service. Similarly, the first individual (who had the lower value for overall perceived quality) will show an increase in cumulative perceived quality because his or her last service encounter exceeded his or her predicted level of service. In this way, our model is compatible with the CS/D disconfirmation of expectations paradigm and shows how satisfaction with a specific transaction can lead to an increase in perception of the overall service.

In a similar vein, assume two individuals with identical *will* expectations, but different *should* expectations, receive identical actual service. In this case, our model predicts that the individual with the higher expectation of what the service *should* deliver perceives the service more negatively. One way of thinking of this effect is that some individuals are more critical or demanding than others. Individuals who develop higher expectations of what service *should* occur (perhaps because of firm or competitive actions) are more difficult to please (i.e. they form more negative evaluations) than individuals with lower *should* expectations.

Finally, our model has the pleasing characteristic that improvement in the service delivery system lead to more positive service quality perception.[12] To see this effect, imagine a firm engaged in 'continuous quality improvements', a currently popular business concept. If the *will* expectation itself had a negative effect, and this expectation increased with the increasing service, a firm would have to constantly upgrade its delivered service simply to stay even with the rising expectations. Said differently, despite improved service delivery, there would be no resulting improvements in consumer perceptions of quality. In contrast, our model suggests that firms benefit from increasing consumer expectations of what service will occur. Specifically, if a firm increases expectations of what will occur by improving delivered service, the consumer will perceive a higher quality service than before the service improvements occurred, even if the service plateaus at this higher level.[13]

---

[12]This is also a characteristic of the conceptual model of Bolton and Drew (1991a).

[13]Technically, if delivered service plateaus, that is, $DS^*_t = DS^*_{t-1}$, our model yields more positive future service quality perceptions if $(1 - \alpha) > (\gamma\beta K)$.

We next specify a simple functional form suggesting that overall perceived quality is a linear combination of perceptions of different dimensions of quality.

$$OSQ_{it} = \sum_{j=1}^{5} \phi_j PS_{ijt} + \epsilon_{4it} \qquad (4S)$$

where the ϕ_j are > 0 and ϵ_{4it} represents an error term.

Our dynamic formulation as stated by equations (1S) through (4S) differs from the prevailing model of service quality, the gaps model (Parasuraman, Zeithaml and Berry, 1985). We label the gaps model a static formulation because not temporal sequencing is specified. In the static model, overall quality is represented by gap 5, which consists of perceptions minus contemporaneous *should* expectations. Gap 5 is in turn a function of gaps 1 through 4, which contain, among other things, information about actual service. Representing the static model relationship between overall perceived quality and gap 5 in equation form results in the following expression.

$$OSQ_{it} = \sum_{j=1}^{5} \Theta_j (PS_{ijt} - SE_{ijt}) + \epsilon_{6it} \text{ (the gaps model)} \qquad (6)$$

Two points should be noted about equation (6). First, because the gaps model is static, expectations prior to the service contact are assumed implicitly to equal those after the service. Thus, equation (6) is stated in terms of contemporaneous perceptions and expectations. Second, the gaps model implicitly constrains the parameters on perceptions and expectations to negative equality. A more general formulation of equation (6) allows these coefficients to vary, that is,

$$OSQ_{it} = \sum_{j=1}^{5} (\Theta_{1j} PS_{ijt} + \Theta_{2j} SE_{ijt}) + \epsilon_{7it} \qquad (7)$$

(the generalized gaps model)

Note that our dynamic specification, given by equation (4S), is also a special case of equation (7). In particular, our dynamic model formulation implies $\Theta_{1j} > 0$ and $\Theta_{2j} = 0$. In contrast, the gaps model predicts $\Theta_{1j} = -\Theta_{2j}$.

We put forward these alternative specifications of the overall quality equation to highlight our differences with the prevailing model of service quality. Because we do not obtain separate measures of perceptions and overall quality, we cannot test the different specifications by using our study 1 data. However, in study 2 we compare the validity of our formulation represented by equation (4S) with the specification given by equations (6) and (7).

Finally, we specify behavioral intentions as a single linear function of overall quality perceptions.

$$BI_m = \lambda_m OSQ_{it} + \epsilon_{5it} \qquad (5S)$$

where $\lambda_m > 0$ and ϵ_{5it} is an error term.

Empirical model and results

We have three longitudinal measures of the *will* and *should* expectations and two measures each for the perceived service, the actual service delivered, and the behavioral intentions. Therefore, we can estimate our system of equations (i.e. equations (1S), (2S), (3S) and (5S)) at two different time periods. Before doing so, however, we need to relate our obtained measures to the theoretical constructs in our structural model. In particular, we need to calibrate all of our measured constructs onto a common scale. We do this by making the arbitrary, but nonrestrictive, assumption that our measured expectations, denoted by M preceding the expectation notation (i.e. *MWE* and *MSE*), establish the metric for our empirical measures. Thus, we scale all of the other measures in relation to the measured expectations variables. We present the details of this scaling calibration in Appendix A.

The scaling calibration enable us to write our structural model in terms of measured variables. The resultant empirical model includes four scaling parameters – a, b, c and d – in addition to our structural parameters. Substituting equations (A1) through (A3) from Appendix A into equations (1S), (2S), (3S) and (5S) yields the following empirical model.

$$MWE_{it} = (1 - \alpha_t)a + \alpha_t MWE_{it-1} + (1 - \alpha_t)bMDS_{it}^* + \epsilon_{8it} \qquad (8)$$

$$MSE_{it} = \beta_t aK_{it} + MSE_{it-1} + \beta_t BK_{it} \cdot MDS_{it}^* + \epsilon_{9it} \qquad (9)$$

$$MPS_{it} = -c + (1 - \alpha_t)a + \alpha_t MWE_{it-1} + (1 - \alpha_t)bMDS_{it}^* + \gamma_t MSE_{it-1} + \epsilon_{10it} \quad (10)$$

$$MBI_{it} = -d + \lambda_t c + \lambda_t MPS_{it} + \epsilon_{11it} \qquad (11)$$

where $t = 1, 2$ for equation (8) through (11), yielding an empirical model composed of eight equations. Two points must be made about these equations. First, the coefficients of this empirical model often confound the structural and scaling parameters. For example, the intercept term in equation (8) is the product of the structural parameter $(1 - \alpha_t)$ and the scaling parameter a. Even so, we are unable to obtain at least one direct estimate of each of the structural parameters. Second, unlike the structural model parameters, none of the scaling parameters are time-subscribed because we see no reason to expect our theoretical construct scales to shift over time.

We have three goals in estimating this empirical model. First, we want to test the validity of the complete specification of our process model. Second, we want to confirm our previous qualitative findings by using a second analytic approach and an extended dataset. Finally, we want to extend our insights by examining how the information integration parameters change over time.

We start by addressing the specification issue. We do this by first estimating our empirical model by using OLS, imposing no restrictions across or within equations. Thus, for example, we do not constrain the parameters on MDS_{it}^* in equations (8) and (10) to equal one minus the parameter on MWE_{it-1} (in either equation (8) or equation (10)) times the scaling parameter b. Estimation in this manner yields estimates of 22 coefficients. As noted previously, most of the coefficients in equations

(8) through (11) do not provide direct estimates of our structural parameters. However, this procedure does yield two unconfounded estimates each for the structural parameters α_1 and α_2 and one direct estimate each for the structural parameters γ_1, γ_2, β_1, β_2, λ_1, and λ_2. These results, along with the confounded estimates, are reported in Table 3.

We make two observations about the results in Table 3. First, we note that all of the unconstrained, direct estimates of our structural parameters have the predicted direction as well as statistical significance. Second, though we subsequently formally tested for equality, we note that the two independent unconstrained estimates of α_1 and α_2 (i.e. the coefficients on MWE_{t-1} in equations (8) and (10)) are approximately equal. Table 3 indicates that the two estimates of α_1 equal .34 and .38 and the two estimates of α_2 equal .80 and .87.

Table 3. Unrestricted model estimates of equations (8)–(11) for $t = 1$ and $t = 2^a$

	Dependent variables							
	Eq.(8)		Eq.(9)		Eq.(10)		Eq.(11)	
Independent variables	$MWE_{t=1}$	$MWE_{t=2}$	$MSE_{t=1}$	$MSE_{t=2}$	$MPS_{t=1}$	$MPS_{t=2}$	$BI_{t=1}$	$BI_{t=2}$
Constant	35.79*	.33	.00	.41	47.88*	9.63	−3.41	4.73***
	(3.009)	(6.135)	(1.652)	(.961)	(4.807)	(8.095)	(5.338)	(2.667)
MWE_{t-1}	.34*	.80*			.38*	.87*		
	(.046)	(.086)			(.059)	(.113)		
MDS_t	15.00*	21.13*			14.20*	22.48*		
	(2.170)	(2.559)			(2.211)	(3.000)		
$K^*MDS_t^*$			10.37*	8.69*				
			(3.115)	(2.007)				
MSE_{t-1}			1.00^b	1.00^b	−.17**	−.24*		
			(0.0)	(0.0)	(.075)	(.093)		
MPS_t							.99*	.93*
							(.083)	(.046)
R^2	.504	.533	.288	.624	.465	.463	.602	.814

^{a} Standard errors are in parentheses.
^{b} The dependent measure in this equation equals $(MSE_t - MSE_{t-1})$.
*Significant at the .01 level.
**Significant at the .05 level.
***Significant at the .10 level.

We now formally test the numerous within- and cross-equation constraints, that is, assumptions implied by our conceptual model. An example of a cross-equation constraint is that the coefficient on MWE_{t-1} in equations (8) and (10) should be equal. An example of a within-equation constraint is forcing the three α parameters in equation (8) to equality. We impose these constraint by using SAS's nonlinear search procedure, SYSNLIN. More technically, we estimate only the four parameters (at two different points in time) of theoretical interest, α_1, α_2, γ_1, γ_2, β_1, β_2, λ_1 and λ_2, and the four scaling parameters a, b, c, and d. This results in reducing a 22-parameter model to a 12-parameter model. Because the constrained model is a subset of the unconstrained model, we can perform a likelihood ratio test based on the sums of squared errors (Amemiya, 1985). This ratio is distributed χ^2 with degrees of freedom equal to the number of imposed restrictions. The test enables us to identify whether our structural model imposes binding constraints, that is, whether we have misspecified the process by which our subjects form perceptions of quality, which in turn leads to behavioral intentions.

We find that the cross- and within-equation constraints are *not* binding. The estimated χ^2 equals 2.46, which is well below the critical χ^2 value for $p = .5$ and 10 degrees of freedom $(\chi^2_{10} = 9.34)$.[14] Thus, we come nowhere close to rejecting the underlying assumptions embedded in our process model. Though we recognize that this finding does not mean that we have specified the best possible process model, it does increase our confidence in the robustness of our specification.

Table 4 presents the fully constrained estimates of our structural model. In discussing these estimates, we first note that all of the estimates of the eight structural

Table 4. Restricted model estimates for equations (8)–(11) for $t = 1$ and $t = 2$[a]

Parameter	Estimate
α_1	.38*
	(.035)
α_2	.55*
	(.044)
β_1	.13*
	(.034)
β_2	.12*
	(.023)
γ_1	−.11**
	(.055)
γ_2	−.21*
	(.055)
λ_1	.91*
	(.042)
λ_2	.98*
	(.042)
a	49.18*
	(1.944)
b	29.41*
	(2.941)
c	−9.94**
	(4.226)
d	−11.24**
	(4.545)

[a]Standard errors in parentheses.
*Significant at the .01 level.
**Significant at the .05 level.

---

[14]Because we want to *accept* the null hypothesis that our structural model does not impose binding constraints, we use a p value of .5 to increase the power of rejecting the null hypothesis.

parameters of theoretical interest are significant and in alignment with our qualitative hypotheses. In addition, because we now obtain estimates of the scaling parameters, we note that on the 100-point expectations scale, 'low' service is estimated to equal 49.2 and 'high' service is estimated to equal 78.6 (i.e. $a = 49.2$ and $b = 29.4$).

For patterns of results over the two periods in the data, we note the increase in α_t from period 1 to 2 (from .38 to .55). This result is compatible with our hypothesis that this parameter will grow over time as customers accrue more prior experience and weight the current experience less in updating their *will* expectations and perceptions of service quality. We also note the doubling in absolute size in γ, the coefficient on the *should* expectation in the perception equation, from period 1 to period 2 (from $-.11$ to $-.21$). Though not hypothesized, this result relates to a specification issue we now address.

In particular, as another check on our specification, we include the prior *should* expectation in the *will* expectation updating equation. When we estimate this equation for time $= 1$, we find a significant coefficient on the *should* expectation variable, as one would expect given our ANOVA findings. However, at time $= 2$ this coefficient loses significance ($t_{92} = 1.07$). This result, coupled with the observation that γ_t increased in absolute size from .11 to $-.21$ over the two time periods, leads us to conclude that the strength of the customer's beliefs about what should happen became stronger as customers gained more exposure to the service situation. Consequently, their beliefs about perceptions of quality became more distinct from their beliefs about what will happen. In particular, the *should* expectation loses significance in equation (1S) (where it is hypothesized to have no effect) and becomes more significant in equation (3S) (where it is hypothesized to have a significant negative effect).

Finally, perceptions of quality strongly influence behavioral intentions. Interestingly, the parameter capturing this effect, λ, increases in size from period 1 to period 2 (.91 to .98). Though a marginal increase in size, this result warrants further investigation because it implies that over time perceptions of quality becomes increasingly important in driving behavioral intentions.

Discussion

The results reported in stage 1 and stage 2 of study 1 are very compatible with our postulated process model. We interpret these results as providing strong evidence that a person's prior *will* and *should* expectations, and the delivered service, influence a person's perceptions of quality. Moreover, our results provide strong support for our conceptualization that *will* expectations positively influence perceptions of quality and *should* expectations negatively influence perceptions of quality. These perceptions, in turn, positively influence behavioral intentions.

Perhaps of greater significance is the finding that the numerous within- (e.g. averaging of *will* expectations and delivered service in the *will* expectation updating equation) and cross-equation (e.g. the same terms appearing in the *will* expectation updating equation and the perception equation) restrictions were nonbinding. Rather than assuming we correctly specify these equations, or simply accepting the individual coefficient estimates from these equations as compatible with our conceptualization, we directly test the 'assumptions' (implied restrictions) inherent in our model. Thus, we take the unusual step of simultaneously testing the significance of the structural parameters and subjecting our structural model to a stringent specification test. *Both* of these results strongly support our conceptualization.

Given these results, we next address the generalizability of our model. We do this by presenting the results of a second study in which a very dissimilar research method (a field study) was used to assess customers' perceptions and expectations of a real service.[15] Compatible results with this second approach would provide substantial evidence that our obtained results are not due to some confound (unknown to us) associated with the laboratory experiment.

STUDY 2

Besides providing a vehicle for replicating our previous finding by a very different research approach, study 2 provides two additional sources of value. First, it enables us to estimate equations (4S), (6) and (7), which we could not do in study 1. Second, it provides a setting to explicate a research method that enables firms to track customers' evaluations of service quality, an inherently dynamic process as shown by our model, using data collected from a single point in time. This method is exceptionally valuable in that it enables managers to infer the impact of their delivered service, *without measuring* this construct. Therefore, these explorations should be of great interest to practitioners involved in measuring service quality and cumulative customer satisfaction.

Sample

The data for this study were obtained from a major study of service quality of an educational institution. This study, commissioned by the top management of the institution, was based on 177 obtained responses of the current customers of the institution. Participation by the customers was both voluntary and confidential, resulting in a 46% response rate. Monetary rewards were provided to a small set of participating customers as a result of a lottery drawing.

Operationalization of variables

Expectations and perceptions of the five dimensions of service quality were measured by 36 statements taken from SERVQUAL (Parasuraman, Zeithaml and Berry, 1988) and then modified by top managers and the research team to capture more precisely expectations and perceptions associated with an educational service. Respondents recorded these expectations and perceptions by indicating their agreement with each statement on a 1 to 7 scale. Approximately half of the sample gave expectations data

---

[15]This 'second' study was actually conducted and analyzed prior to the first (laboratory) study. However, the analysis scheme used for the second study relies on many of the assumptions tested in the laboratory study. Hence, for exposition, we reverse the order of discussion for the two studies.

Table 5. Expectations and perception scale items[a]

Reliability

    Professors and teaching assistants will grade fairly and accurately.

    Courses will be well taught.

    The staff will ensure that the MBA program runs smoothly.

    Professors will be organized and prepared for class.

    When professors promise to be available during office hours, they will be there to see
       students.

    Professors will have prior teaching experience before coming to this organization.

    Cronbach alpha:

       Expectations = .74

       Perceptions = .73

Empathy items

    Professors will give students individual attention.

    Professors will help students with personal problems and career advice.

    Students will be able to contact a professor at home.

    Professors will know what the needs of their students are.

    Professors will have their students' best interest at heart.

    Cronbach alpha:

       Expectations = .69

       Perceptions = .74

---

[a]*Should* expectations substituted the word 'should' for 'will'. Perceptions substituted the word 'are' for 'will'. Also, we report a single Cronbach alpha for expectations because the *will* and *should* contemporaneous expectations differ only by an individual-specific constant.

in the form of what customers thought *should* happen, whereas the other half of the sample gave their predictions of what *will* happen in the education process. Using the original SERVQUAL scales as a guide, and after performing factor analysis in combination with managerial judgment, we grouped the 36 questions to form multiple measures for the five dimensions of service quality (reliability, responsiveness, assurance, empathy, and tangibles). Table 5 provides the scale for two of the five dimensions, along with the Cronbach alpha values for the perception and expectation scales. Boulding *et al.* (1992) report this information for all five dimensions.

    The alpha values indicate that the reliability of all our scales equals or exceeds .60 with most exceeding .7. On the basis of this result and prior evidence of Parasuraman, Zeithaml and Berry (1988) that there are five dimensions of service quality, we formed indices by averaging the responses to the individual measures associated with a dimension. These indices are used as summary measures of the five underlying constructs in estimating equations (4S), (6) and (7).

    Overall quality of the educational service and six items of intended individual-level behaviors of strategic importance to the school were also measured. The latter measures included such items as saying positive things about the school to people outside the school, planning to contribute money to the class pledge upon graduation, and planning to recommend the school to one's employer as a place to recruit. These six behavioral intention variables were grouped into a single index measure. As evidence that these six items tap the underlying behavioral intentions construct, the Cronbach alpha is equal to .80. Finally, country of origin, gender, degree of prior work experience, first or second year in program, and area of educational concentration were measured to partially control for individual differences in the subsequent analyses. As we have no theoretical interest in these variables, we do not discuss them further, though they are included during estimation as covariates.

Estimation

Our data are similar to most service quality field study data in that they consist of a cross-section of self-reported information taken at one point in time. Consequently, they impose some limitations on direct estimation of the structural equations developed in the preceding section. Specifically, because we measure expectations variables contemporaneously with perceptions variables, we do not have measures of prior expectations.[16] Finally, we do not measure actual delivered service because any measure obtained from the customer immediately become a perception of the service, and because we were unable to match objective organization measures of actual service to the individuals receiving the service. This is a typical problem in any service setting.

Even though our particular data constrain us from directly estimating equations (1S), (2S) and (3S), we show that it is still possible to obtain consistent estimates of the two key parameters in our process model, that is, α_{jt} and γ_{jt}, as well as the parameters in equations (4S), (5S), (6) and (7), simply by using contemporaneous measures of all the relevant constructs. Moreover, these two parameter estimates enable us to perform falsifying tests on our basic structural model, as well as gain insight into the relative influences of prior *will* and *should* expectations *and* the unobserved delivered service on customers' current perceptions of the cumulative level of service quality of the five dimensions of service quality.

More specifically, we derive consistent estimates for α_{ji} and γ_{jt} from reduced-form equations that assume equations (1S), (2S), and (3S) represent the true underlying process. We justify this assumption on the basis of three points. First and foremost, results from our study 1 tests indicate that equations (1S), (2S), and (3S) are an excellent representation of the service quality process. Second, using our study 2 data, we can directly test two implications from our model by looking at the signs and magnitudes of the estimates of the two structural parameters α_{jt} and γ_{jt}. Empirical results inconsistent with hypothesized signs and magnitudes for these coefficients will indicate the nonviability of out postulated structural model. Third, we cannot come up with a plausible alternative structural model that could produce the results generated in our reduced-form modeling approach.

Our approach is to derive reduced-form equations are in terms of only observable contemporaneous variables. We start by specifying one additional nonrestrictive relationship between our two expectation constructions. Note that in a field setting there is normally a strict cross-sectional correlation between SE_{ijt} and WE_{ijt}, even

---

[16]To test for response biases due to priming with either the *will* or *should* expectations, we obtain measures of either the contemporaneous *will* expectation or the *should* expectation, but never both from the same respondent. As will become evident, this decision to ask for either *will* or *should* expectations, but not both, does not hamper our ability to obtain consistent estimates of α and γ.

though equations (1S) and (2S) do not impose any direct contemporaneous relationship between these two constructs. We capture this correlation by specifying the relationship between SE_{ij} and WE_{ij} for any arbitrary point in time, t, to be

$$SE_{ijt} = WE_{ijt} + \mu_{ijt},\tag{12}$$

where μ_{ijt} captures all individual differences at time t. Thus, μ_{ijt} includes all influence of the individual's previous experiences, factors included in the $\mathbf{X}$ and $\mathbf{Z}$ vectors for the past t periods, and individual differences associated with the degree to which a customer is critical or demanding.

Appendix B presents the derivation of our estimating equations. This derivation consists of three simple steps. First, we use equation (12) to rewrite equation (3S) completely in terms of either the *will* or the *should* expectation. We take this step because we measure either the *will* or the *should* expectation for each individual, but not both. Second, we use equation (1S) and (2S) to write these equations in terms of contemporaneous expectations. Third, by recognizing that we have N measures for each individual on each of the j dimensions of service quality (see Table 5), we utilize the multiple (repeated) measures aspect of our design and thereby remove (control for) all of the factors that are fixed for a specific individual (i.e. delivered service). This is done by 'mean-differencing' the data, as shown in Appendix B.

These three steps yield the following two reduced-form equations.

$$(PS_{ijnt} - PS_{ij \cdot t}) = \left(\frac{\alpha_{jt} + \gamma_{jt}}{\alpha_{jt}}\right)(WE_{ijnt} - WE_{ij \cdot t}) + \epsilon_{13it},\tag{13}$$

$$(PS_{ijnt} - PS_{ij \cdot t}) = (\alpha_{jt} + \gamma_{jt})(SE_{ijnt} - SE_{ij \cdot t}) + \epsilon_{14it},\tag{14}$$

where PS_{ijnt}, WE_{ijnt}, and SE_{ijnt} are the nth measure of the jth dimension for the appropriate construct for the $\cdot$ notation indicates the mean for the ith individual on the jth dimension.

In words, equations (13) and (14) state that for each individual there is a relationship between how that person responds to the nth perception question tapping dimension j relative to his or her mean response and how the same person responds to the analogous *will* and *should* expectations question relative to the respective mean response. These equations result in within-individual analyses. In particular, utilizing the multiple (repeated) measures aspect of our design enables us to control for all individual-specific factors that remain unchanged at time t. In our case, this is the actual service delivered to a given individual, the individual's 'history' and characteristics, including a person's proclivity to use a specific portion of the response scale, and any new information received prior to time t. As a result, equations (13) and (14) no longer contain any unobserved variables and consistent estimation of two coefficients, $(\alpha_{jt} + \gamma_{jt})/(\alpha_{jt})$ and $(\alpha_{jt} + \gamma_{jt})$, is possible. From these two coefficients we can fully identify the two structural parameters found in equations (1S) and (3S). (Dividing $(\alpha_{jt} + \gamma_{jt})$ by $(\alpha_{jt} + \gamma_{jt})/(\alpha_{jt})$ yields an estimate of α_{jt}. Once $\hat{\alpha}_{jt}$ is obtained, it is easy to get an estimate of γ_{it}.) These estimates can potentially falsify our original structural equations – if $\hat{\alpha}_{jt}$ is not significantly greater than zero and $\hat{\gamma}_{jt}$ is not significantly less than zero, there is strong evidence to disconfirm our conceptualization as stated in (1S), (2S) and (3S).

Results

We begin by reported the estimates for the behavioral intention equation, (5S). Similar to our study 1 results in which perceptions of quality relate positively to behavioral intentions, we find that overall perceived quality positively and significantly ($t_{146} = 2.18$) relates to the index of behavioral intentions. We next explore the relationship between overall perceived quality and the measures of the five dimensions of service quality as posited by Parasuraman, Zeithaml and Berry (1985). We start with the unconstrained form of this relationship, equation (7), which allows for different parameter values on each of the perception and expectation measures. Next, we estimate the gaps model, equation (6), which constrains the coefficient on the *j*th dimension of expectations to equal the negative of the coefficient on the *j*th dimension of perceptions. Finally, we estimate our dynamic model specification, equation (4S), which imposes the constraint that the coefficients on the expectation dimensions equal zero.[17]

We report the results of these estimates in Table 6. Column 1 of Table 6 corresponds to equation (7) and columns 2 and 3 correspond to equations (6) and (4S), respectively. We note all three equations yield results consistent with the hypothesis that the particular model being tested is statistically significant. Hence, we next explore which equation best captures reality by noting that equations (4S) and (6) are constrained versions of (7), thereby enabling us to test the implied constraints of (4S) and (6). We do so in the model comparison tests reported in the footnotes of Table 6. Specifically, the F-tests indicate that we must reject the constraint $\Theta_{1j} = -\Theta_{2j}$, but that we cannot reject the constraint $\Theta_{2j} = 0$. More generally, we reject the static formulation of the gaps model (i.e. equation 6) and its implied constraint. However, we fail to reject our dynamic model in favor of what is effectively an unconstrained version of the static gaps formulation (i.e. equation (7)). We take these results to demonstrate strong support for this part of our dynamic specification.

Finally, we use the estimates in column 4 of Table 6 to test for the relevance of all five proposed dimensions of service quality. In this model, we eliminate all but the reliability and empathy perception variables. Comparing the estimates in column 4 with those in column 3 by means of an F-test indicates that we fail to reject the two-dimensional representation of quality in favor of the five-dimensional representation.[18] Thus, column 4 represents the preferred model for overall perceived quality for our particular application. As expected, these estimates indicate that reliability is the primary driver of overall quality perceptions.

We next turn our attention to estimating the updating parameters α_{jt} and γ_{jt} via our reduced-form equations (13) and (14) for the two relevant (i.e. significant) quality perception dimensions. Before discussing these estimates, however, we test whether the perceptions obtained from respondents providing *will* expectations differ from those of respondents providing *should* expectations by running regression

---

[17]As the five dimensions of perceived service quality appear on the left side of our structural model, we tested for the necessity of two-stage (simultaneous) estimation of our overall service quality equation. This test (Hausman, 1978) revealed a recursive relationship, indicating the appropriateness of ordinary least squares estimation. This was true for the behavioral intention equations as well.

[18]We also fail to reject the parsimonious model given in column 4 in favor of the full unconstrained model given in column 1.

Table 6. Overall perceived quality of service equation estimates

Independent variables	(1) Unconstrained model	(2) Gaps model	(3) Dynamic model	(4) Limited dynamic model
Gaps		.026*		
Responsiveness		−.003		
Assurance		−.006		
Empathy		.026**		
Tangibles		−.000		
Perceptions				
Reliability	.046*		.049*	.043*
Responsiveness	−.007		−.004	
Assurance	−.007		−.008	
Empathy	.027**		.021***	.015***
Tangibles	.003		.003	
Expectations[a]				
Reliability	−.004			
Responsiveness	.008			
Assurance	.005			
Empathy	−.022			
Tangibles				
R^2	.286	.214[b]	.272[c]	.266[d]

[a]We test whether the *will* and *should* expectation variables require different coefficients in this analysis. They do not, unsurprisingly, for two reasons. First, at any given time *t*, the *will* and *should* expectations differ only by an individual-specific constant. Second, the coefficient on the contemporaneous expectation is zero, whether for *will* or *should* expectations.
[b]Significantly different from unconstrained model in the .05 level.
[c]Not significantly different from unconstrained model.
[d]Not significantly different from unconstrained model or dynamic model.
*Significant at the .01 level.
**Significant at the .05 level.
***Significant at the .10 level.

where perceptions are a function of the type of expectation measured. As we fail to find a significant coefficient on the version of the expectation measure variable for any of the perception dimensions, we infer that all of our perception data come from the same overall population.

Table 7 presents the results of our estimates of α_{jt} and γ_{jt}. First, we find that both the reliability and empathy dimensions the estimate of the *will* expectation coefficient (i.e. α_{jt}) is significantly greater than zero but less than one, as postulated.[19] Second, our two estimates of the *should* expectation coefficient (i.e. γ_{jt}) are significantly less than zero, also as postulated. Thus, our field study results are compatible with our conceptualization that prior expectations of what service *will* occur positively influence perceptions of delivered service, whereas prior

[19]Table 7 discusses how we develop significance tests.

Table 7. Reliability and empathy perception equation estimates[a]

Dependent variable	Will expectation coefficient (α_i) [b]	Should expectation coefficient (γ_i)
Reliability perception	.771*	−.513*
	(.211)	(.218)
Empathy perception	.714*	−.372*
	(.115)	(.125)

[a] Standard errors are in parentheses. A technical appendix is available from the authors upon request explaining how standard errors and significance levels were calculated. The basic idea was to use Monté Carlo techniques to calculate the distribution of $(\alpha_j + \gamma_j)/[(\alpha_j + \gamma_j)/(\alpha_j)] = \hat{\alpha}$, and $(\alpha_j + \gamma_j) - \hat{\alpha} = \hat{\gamma}_j$ and then calculate the standard deviations and fractiles of these derived distributions.
[b] Because the coefficient on delivered service equals one minus α, the implied delivered service coefficients for reliability and empathy are .229 and .286, respectively.
*Significant at the .01 level.

expectations of what service *should* occur negatively influence these perceptions. In addition, because α_{jt} also appears in equation (1S), we find support for our premise that *will* expectations are updated after a service encounter.

DISCUSSION

We present a process model of how individuals develop perceptions of a firm's service delivery system over time. By explicitly acknowledging that perceptions and expectations change over time, we are better able to explicate and test the relationships between expectations, perceptions, and intended behavior. The model is tested with data derived from two very different studies, one a longitudinal laboratory experiment and the other a field study using questionnaire data collected at one point in time. In both cases, the results are strongly compatible with all aspects of our process model.

We find the convergence of results for the two different studies very encouraging. Our model appears robust to different analytic approaches, different data collection methods, and different service settings. Thus, though one might generate specific criticisms of the individual studies, we think of none that spans both studies. Consequently, we have a strong posterior belief that our model adequately summarizes the major forces that cause customers to form and update their perceptions of a firm's overall service quality level.

These forces have major implications for any firm interested in service quality. As expected, but never empirically verified in a field setting, our results indicate that the greater customers' perceptions of a firm's overall service quality, the more likely the customers are to engage in behaviors beneficial to the strategic health of the firm (e.g. generate positive word of mouth, recommend the service, etc.).

Our research also provides insights into how firms can best increase customers' perceptions of their overall service quality. Our most important managerial insight relates to the role of expectations. The prevailing model of service quality defines perceived service quality as the gap between expectations and perceptions, and does not differentiate among types of expectations. It leads to the strategic implication that firms can try either to increase perceptions or lower expectations in their quest to increase overall service quality. Our results are incompatible with both this one-dimensional view of expectations and the gap formulation for service quality. Instead, we find that service quality is directly influenced only by perceptions. Also, increasing customer expectations of what a firm *will* provide during future service encounters actually leads to higher perceptions of quality after the customer is exposed to the actual service, all else equal. From this finding we infer that firms should manage customers' predictive expectations *up* rather than down if they want to increase customer perceptions of overall service quality. In addition, our results strongly support our premise that customers' expectations of what a firm *should* deliver during a service encounter *decrease* their ultimate perceptions of the actual service delivered, all else equal. Therefore, improved assessments of service quality can result when customers' expectations of what a firm *should* deliver are managed downward.

The issue of managerial importance, then, is how to manage both types of expectations. Ideally, one would want to simultaneously increase customers' *will* expectations and decrease their *should* expectations. At this stage of our research, we know of no activity that can ensure this result. One airline firm attempted to do this by simultaneously telling customers that all airlines had problems with guaranteeing on-time arrivals because of factors outside the airlines' control, but that they were the best at being on time. In this way the firm's ad campaign attempted to address both the *should* and *will* expectations. Whether or not this approach to managing both sets of expectations worked as intended is an empirical question.

A second approach to managing *will* and *should* expectations is for the firm to engage in activities that increase the customers' *will* expectations without a proportional increase in their expectations of what the firm *should* do. From equations (1S) and (2S), we see that providing the best possible service each and every time can increase *will* expectations but it might also increase the *should* expectations. Fortunately, our empirical evidence suggests that *will* expectations increase faster than the *should* expectations, so that the net impact on perceptions is positive. However, firms need to monitor the relative magnitudes of α, β, and γ to ensure that increases in objective service quality also result in increases in perceptions of service quality (see footnote 13 for more details). Finally, managers may be able to identify specific firm actions (other than service) that affect only the *will* or *should* expectations. Such actions would enable the firm to increase (decrease) the *will* (*should*) expectations without modifying the other.

In addition to providing managerial insights, we were able to demonstrate a method of estimating the two key parameters from our dynamic model by using survey data taken from customers at only one point in time. As a result, managers can learn about the relative importance of service delivery and customer expectations for their specific business. This determination should be very useful in assessing the relative value of trying to modify perceptions through changes in the service delivery system and the firm's communications, as well as identifying the speed with which managers can expect perceptions to change over time.

We believe our analytic approach provides managers an easily implementable method for estimating our model because it does not require measuring the actual service provided or prior expectations. However, as seen from our derivation, the estimation technique requires that (1) the surveys obtain multiple measures of perceptions and expectations, (2) all of the measures within a dimension have identical influence on that dimension, and (3) if the managers believe customers have much different levels of prior experience, they segment the customers so as to reflect the possible differences in the updating parameters.

Our research also has implications for academicians. We note a great similarity between our work on modeling perceived service quality and its impact on intended future behavior and the models of Churchill and Surprenant (1982) and Tse and Wilton (1988), who were concerned with explicating the factors that influence perceived product performance (and ultimately its impact on consumer satisfaction). As in our study 1, both of these research teams were able to measure prior expectations and the actual product performance. However, only Tse and Wilton measured two types of expectations and thus were able to obtain unbiased estimates. Their study found, analogous to our results, that prior *will* expectations and actual product performance were positively related to perceived performance. In addition, they found that prior *expectations on what consumers would ideally like to see* in the product were negatively related to perceived performance. Interestingly, they found the actual product performance variable to have a much stronger influence on perceived performance than we did in our study. This difference is not surprising given that services typically have a higher proportion of experience and credence properties than products, making service performance more difficult to evaluate than product performance. It seems likely that perceptions will be more influenced by expectations (relative to actual service) for firms with a higher content of unobservable (or fallible) quality. Along these lines, future research might assess the degree to which different industries or customers with different levels of prior experience influence the extent to which prior knowledge, new communications, or the actual service encounter dominates the process by which customers form judgments of quality.

Though we suggest conceptually, and demonstrate empirically, that customers update their expectations and perceptions, interesting aspects of this process have not been investigated. For example, the antecedents of the different expectation variables remain largely unexplored.[20] Given the need to manage *will* expectations up and the *should* expectations down, understanding the determinants of these expectations is a critical managerial issue. Also, because we can restate our equations mathematically in a variety of formats, our empirical analyses provide no evidence on the cognitive process by which customers form, store, or retrieve perceptions. Consequently, we hope that researchers utilize experimental and panel data to continue delving into the dynamic process by which customers form expectations and perceptions of service quality.

Finally, we note that our process model has the potential for broader applications. First, one might view overall service quality as a measure of the firm's service equity. Further, because the antecedents of this construct are known, measuring and managing these antecedents (e.g. expectations) can help a firm better understand

---

[20]To date we know what word-of-mouth communications and information from expert sources affect *will* expectations whereas information on the competitors and to a lesser degree word of mouth affect *should* expectations. We used this knowledge to manipulate the subjects' prior expectations in study 1.

which actions either enhance or detract from the firm's service equity and thus its ability to compete. Second, we see no reason why our process model would not apply to products as well as services. However, empirical support for this belief remains to be provided. Third, we see direct applicability of our model in better understanding, tracking, and influencing customer satisfaction as referred to in the popular press. The reason is that the measures used to reflect satisfaction are usually cumulative, versus transaction specific, and thus are analogous to our construct of perceived quality.

APPENDIX A: SCALING CALIBRATION

Our goal is to rescale all of the measures so that they have a common metric. Assume this metric is defined in terms of the measured expectations, MWE and MSE. For our measure of the delivered service construct, we note that only two levels of service, high and low, were experienced by the subjects. Let $MDS_{it} = 1$ if the service was high and $MDS_{it} = 0$ if the service was low, where MDS_{it} equals measured delivered service. Next, we define

$$DS_{it}^* = a + b\,MDS_{it}, \tag{A1}$$

where a and b are ≥ 0. This formulation enables us to convert our measure of delivered service onto the same 100-point scale as the expectation scale. Thus, the a parameter represents the metric value of low service, whereas $a + b$ represents the metric value of high service.

We also need to acknowledge that a person's measured perception, denoted MPS, may be on a different scale than the person's measured expectations. For calibration across these scales, we define

$$PS_{it} = c + MPS_{it}, \tag{A2}$$

where c is a shift parameter.

Similarly, we let the measured behavioral intention, denoted MBI, be on a different scale than the person's measured perceptions:

$$BI_{it} = d + MBI_{it}, \tag{A3}$$

where d is again a shift parameter.

APPENDIX B: DERIVATION OF ESTIMATING EQUATIONS

First, using equation (12), write equation (3S) completely in terms of either the *will* or *should* expectation:

$$PS_{ijt} = (\alpha_{jt} + \gamma_{jt})\,WE_{ijt-1} + (1 - \alpha_{jt})\,DS_{ijt}^* + \epsilon B_{1it}, \tag{B1}$$

and

$$PS_{ijt} = (\alpha_{jt} + \gamma_{jt})\,SE_{ijt-1} + (1 - \alpha_{jt})\,DS_{ijt}^* + \epsilon B_{2it}, \tag{B2}$$

These equations make it clear that even if measures of lagged expectations are available, using only one of the two lagged expectation variables to estimate the relationships between expectations and perceptions (even after controlling for actual service) will result in biased expectations coefficient estimate for that expectation (i.e. the obtained estimate is $(\alpha + \gamma)$ versus $\hat{\alpha}$ or $\hat{\gamma}$).[21]

---

[21]Most published studies linking expectations to perceptions include only one expectation in the estimating equation. If our laboratory results generalize, the equations (B1) and (B2) imply the obtained coefficients in these single-expectation models are biased.

Next, because we only observe *contemporaneous* expectations, we use equations (1S) or (2S) to rewrite equations (B1) and (B2) in terms of current values of either *WE* or *SE*.

$$PS_{ijt} = \left(\frac{\alpha_{jt} + \gamma_{it}}{\alpha_{jt}}\right) WE_{ijt} - \gamma_{jt}\frac{(1 - \alpha_{jt})}{\alpha_{jt}} DS^*_{ijt} + \epsilon_{B3it},$$ (B3)

and

$$PS_{ijt} = (\alpha_{jt} + \gamma_{jt}) SE_{ijt} + [1 - \alpha_{jt}\beta_{jt}\mathbf{K}_{ijt} - \gamma_{jt}\beta_{jt}\mathbf{K}_{ijt} - \alpha_{jt}]DS^*_{ijt} + \epsilon_{B4it}.^{22}$$ (B4)

Next, imagine that equations (B3) and (B4) have *n* subscripts indicating the individual measures for the perception and expectation constructs. Take means over the *n* items for the *i*th individual and the *j*th dimension in equations (B3) and (B4), yielding

$$PS_{ij \cdot t} = \left(\frac{\alpha_{jt} + \gamma_{it}}{\alpha_{jt}}\right) WE_{ij \cdot t} + \epsilon_{B5it},$$ (B5)

and

$$PS_{ij \cdot t} = (\alpha_{jt} + \gamma_{it}) SE_{ij \cdot t} + \epsilon_{B6it},$$ (B6)

where the · notation indicates the mean for the *i*th individual on the *j*th dimension. Subtracting equations (B5) and (B6), respectively, from equations (B3) and (B4) supplemented with the *n* subscripts produces equations (13) and (14) reported in the text.[23]

ACKNOWLEDGEMENTS

The authors thank seminar participants at MIT, Wharton and Harvard, as well as France LeClerc, Julie Edell, and especially John Lynch for their helpful comments.

REFERENCES

Amemiya, T. (1985) *Advanced Econometrics*. Cambridge, MA: Harvard University Press.
Anderson, E. W. and Sullivan, M. W. (1990) 'Customer Satisfaction and Retention Across Firms'. Presentation at the TIMS College of Marketing Special Interest Conference on Services Marketing, Nashville, TN (September).
Bearden, W. D. and Teel, J. E. (1983) 'Selected Determinants of Customer Satisfaction and Complaint Reports'. *Journal of Marketing Research* **20** (November): 21–28.
Bitner, M. J. (1990) 'Evaluating Service Encounters: The Effects of Physical Surroundings and Employee Responses'. *Journal of Marketing* **54** (April): 69–82.
Bolton, R. N. and Drew, J. H. (1991a) 'A Multi-stage Model of Customers' Assessments of Service Quality and Value'. *Journal of Consumer Research* **17** (March): 375–384.
Bolton, R. N. and Drew, J. H. (1991b) 'A Longitudinal Analysis of the Impact of Service Changes on Customer Attitudes'. *Journal of Marketing* **55** (January): 1–9.
Boulding, W. R., Staelin, R., Kalra, A. and Zeithaml, V. (1992) 'Conceptualizing and Testing a Dynamic Process Model of Service Quality'. Working Paper No. 92–121. Cambridge, MA: Marketing Science Institute.

---

[22]Note that these equations imply that use of only the contemporaneous *will* or *should* expectations in a perceptions equation results in biased estimates for these expectation variables.

[23]If one measures both *will* and *should* expectations, one can derive a third estimating equation containing both types of expectations (see Boulding *et al.*, 1992).

Cadotte, E. R., Woodruff, R. B. and Jenkins, R. L. (1987) 'Expectations and Norms in Models of Consumer Satisfaction'. *Journal of Marketing Research* **24** (August): 305–314.

Churchill, G. A., Jr. (1979) 'A Paradigm for Developing Better Measures of Marketing Constructs'. *Journal of Marketing Research* **11** (August): 254–260.

Churchill, G. A., Jr. and Surprenant, C. (1982) 'An Investigation Into the Determinants of Satisfaction Research'. *Journal of Marketing Research* **19** (November): 491–504.

Day, R. L. (1977) 'Towards a Process Model of Consumer Satisfaction'. In *Conceptualization and Measurement of Consumer Satisfaction and Dissatisfaction* (H. K. Hunt, Ed.). Cambridge, MA: Marketing Science Institute, 153–183.

Forbes, J. D., Tse, D. K. and Taylor, S. (1986) 'Toward a Model of Consumer Post-Choice Response Behavior'. *Advances in Consumer Research*, Vol. 13 (R. L. Lutz, Ed.). Ann Arbor, MI: Association for Consumer Research, 658–616.

Garvin, D. A. (1987) 'Competing on the Eight Dimensions of Quality'. *Harvard Business Review* **65**(November–December): 101–109.

Gilly, M. C. (1979) 'Complaining Consumers: Their Satisfaction with Organizational Response'. In *New Dimensions of Consumer Satisfaction and Complaining Behavior* (R. L. Day and H. K. Hunt, Eds). Bloomington, IN: School of Business Indiana University, pp. 99–107.

Gilly, M. C., Cron, W. L. and Barry, T. E. (1983) 'The Expectation-Performance Comparison Process: An Investigation of Expectation Type'. In *International Fare in Consumer Satisfaction and Complaining Behavior.* (R. L. Day and H. H. Hunt, Eds.). Bloomington, IN: School of Business, Indiana University, pp. 10–16.

Hausman, J. A. (1978) 'Specification Tests in Econometrics'. *Econometrica* **46** (November): 1251–1272.

Hjorth-Anderson, C. (1984) 'The Concept of Quality and the Efficiency of Markets for Consumer Products'. *Journal of Consumer Research* **11** (2): 708–718.

Holbrook, M. B. and Corfman, K. P. (1985) 'Quality and Value in the Consumption Experience: Phaedrus Rides Again'. In *Perceived Quality* (J. Jacoby and J. Olson, Eds). Lexington, MA: Lexington Books, pp. 31–57.

Kalra, A. (1992) 'An Empirical Validation and Transaction-Level Investigation of an Expectation-Based Process Model of Service Quality'. PhD dissertation, Duke University.

LaTour, S. A. and Peat, N. C. (1979) 'Conceptual and Methodological Issues in Consumer Satisfaction Research'. In *Advances in Consumer Research*, Vol. 6 (W. L. Wilkie, Ed.). Ann Arbor, MI: Association for Consumer Research, 431–437.

Lynch, J. G., Jr., Chakravarti, D. and Mitra, A. (1991) 'Contrast Effects in Consumer Judgments: Changes in Mental Representations or in the Anchoring of Rating Scale?'. *Journal of Consumer Research* **18** (3): 284–297.

Maynes, E. S. (1976) 'The Concept and Measurement of Product Quality'. *Household Production and Consumption* **40** (5): 529–559.

Miller, J. A. (1977) 'Studying Satisfaction, Modifying Models, Eliciting Expectations, Posing Problems, and Making Meaningful Measurements'. In *Conceptualization and Measurement of Consumer Satisfaction and Dissatisfied* (H. K. Hunt, Ed.). Bloomington, IN: School of Business, Indiana University, pp. 72–91.

Oliver, R. L. (1977) 'Effect of Expectation and Disconfirmation on Post-Exposure Product Evaluation: An Alternative Interpretation'. *Journal of Applied Psychology* **62** (April): 480–486.

Oliver, R. L. (1980) 'A Cognitive Model of the Antecedents and Consequences of Satisfaction Decisions'. *Journal of Marketing Research* **17** (November): 460–469.

Olson, J. C. and Dover, P. (1979) 'Disconfirmation of Consumer Expectations Through Product Trial'. *Journal of Applied Psychology* **64** (April): 179–189.

Parasuraman, A., Berry, L. L. and Zeithaml, V. A. (1990) 'An Empirical Examination of Relationships in an Extended Service Quality Model'. Working paper, Marketing Science Institute.

Parasuraman, A., Zeithaml, V. A. and Berry, L. L. (1985) 'A Conceptual Model of Service Quality and Its Implications for Future Research'. *Journal of Marketing* **49** (Fall): 41–50.

Parasuraman, A., Zeithaml, V. A. and Berry, L. L. (1988) 'SERVQUAL: A Multiple-Item Scale for Measuring Consumer Perceptions of Service Quality', *Journal of Retailing* **64** (Spring): 12–40.

Prakash, V. (1984) 'Validity and Reliability of the Confirmation of Expectations Paradigm as a Determinant of Consumer Satisfaction'. *Journal of the Academy of Marketing Science* **12** (Fall): 63–76.

Swan, J. E. and Trawick, F. I. (1980) 'Satisfaction Related to Predictive vs. Desired Expectations: A Field Study'. In *New Findings on Consumer Satisfaction and Complaining* (R. L. Day and H. K. Hunt, Eds). Bloomington, IN: School of Business, Indiana University, pp. 15–22.

Swan, J. E. and Trawick, F. I. (1981) 'Disconfirmation of Expectations and Satisfaction With a Retail Service'. *Journal of Retailing* **57** (Fall): 49–67.

Tse, D. K. and Wilton, P. C. (1988) 'Models of Consumer Satisfaction Formation: An Extension'. *Journal of Marketing Research* **25** (May): 204–212.

Wilton, P. C. and Nicosia, M. (1986) 'Emerging Paradigms for the Study of Consumer Satisfaction'. *European Research* **14** (January): 4–11.

Woodruff, R. B., Cadotte, E. R. and Jenkins, R. L. (1983) 'Modeling Consumer Satisfaction Processes Using Experience-Based Norms'. *Journal of Marketing Research* **20** (August): 296–304.

Zeithaml, V. A. (1988) 'Consumer Perceptions of Price, Quality, and Value: A Means-End Model and Synthesis of Evidence'. *Journal of Marketing* **52** (July): 2–22.

Zeithaml, V. A., Berry, L. L. and Parasuraman, A. (1991) 'The Nature and Determinants of Customer Expectations of Service'. Working Paper, Marketing Science Institute.

16

A Multistage Model of Customers' Assessments of Service Quality and Value

Ruth N. Bolton and James H. Drew

In recent years, companies have become convinced of the strategic benefits of quality (Phillips, Chang and Buzzell, 1983). As a result, may large companies have created quality-measurement programs that attempt to relate product and service attributes to customer evaluations of quality (Hauser and Clausing, 1988; Zeithaml, Parasuraman and Berry, 1990). In many service industries, companies have created programs that include surveys to elicit customers' assessments of service quality; a feedback loop allows service changes to be implemented and then evaluated with subsequent survey data.

In parallel with recent managerial interest in service quality measurement programs, researchers have become interested in the identification and measurement of service-quality dimensions. In their well-known article, Parasuraman, Zeithaml and Berry (1985) suggest that customers evaluate overall service quality on five underlying dimensions: tangibles, reliability, responsiveness, assurance, and empathy. In subsequent research, they developed an instrument called SERVQUAL that measures customers' perceptions of service quality (Parasuraman *et al.*, 1988).

This study explores how customers integrate their perceptions of a service to form an overall evaluation of that service. It differs from prior research concerning quality in two ways. First, it develops a *multistage* model of the determinants of perceived service quality and service value. Second, it describes how customers' expectations, perceptions of current performance and disconfirmation experiences affect their satisfaction with a service, which in turn affects their assessment of service quality and value.

The first section of this article discusses the constructs of customer satisfaction, perceived service quality, and service value and then integrates these in a multistage model of residential customers' perceptions of service performance, service quality, and service value for local telephone service. The next two sections describe how the model is operationalized as a multiple-equation system and estimated by a two-stage least squares procedure with data from customer surveys. The last two sections discuss the empirical findings and their implications.

BACKGROUND

Customer satisfaction

Market researchers distinguish between customers' satisfaction with respect to a specific transaction and their global evaluation of a service (Holbrook and Corfman, 1985; Olshavsky, 1985). Oliver (1981) argues that satisfaction is characterized by the surprise a customer experiences after a purchase (i.e. a service encounter) and that this surprise eventually becomes an input to a less dynamic attitude. Consequently, satisfaction can be considered to influence the customer's evaluation of service quality, purchase intentions, and behavior (see, e.g., LaBarbera and Mazursky, 1983).

Customer satisfaction or dissatisfaction (CS/D) is a function of the disconfirmation arising from discrepancies between prior expectations and actual performance (Cardozo, 1965; Oliver, 1980; Olshavsky and Miller, 1972; Olson and Dover, 1976). The CS/D literature demonstrates that expectations and perceptions of performance levels affect customer satisfaction directly, as well as indirectly via disconfirmation. For example, Tse and Wilton's (1988) experiments showed that perceived performance exerts a direct influence on CS/D, in addition to the influences from disconfirmation or expectations. The theoretical linkages identified in the CS/D literature are illustrated by the thin solid lines in Figure 1.

Expectations, performance evaluations, and disconfirmation do not necessarily have independent additive effects for every product or service. Churchill and Surprenant (1982) found that CS/D with a non-durable good is a function of all three constructs, whereas CS/D with a durable good is solely a function of performance evaluations. Consequently, expectations, performance evaluations, and disconfirmation are *potential* antecedents of CS/D with a service. For example, in his discussion of modes of satisfaction, Oliver (1989) proposed that customer responses concerning continuously provided services or long-lasting durables are characterized by passive expectations and, therefore, that disconfirmation will not operate unless performance is outside the range of experience-based norms. Hence, customers's assessments of continuously provided services, such as public utilities or cable television, may depend on performance evaluations only.

Service quality

Recent marketing research regarding customers' attitudes towards services has focused on perceived service quality. Perceived service quality is defined as the customer's assessment of the overall excellence or superiority of the service (Zeithaml, 1988). Parasuraman *et al.* (1985, 1988) consider that a customer's assessment of overall service quality depends on the *gap* between expectations and perceptions of actual performance levels. They propose that overall service quality is evaluated on five underling dimensions: tangibles, reliability, responsiveness, assurance, and empathy. They propose that each quality dimension can be quantified by obtaining measures of expectations and perceptions of performance levels of service attributes relevant to each dimension, calculating the difference between expectations and perceptions of actual performance on these attributes,

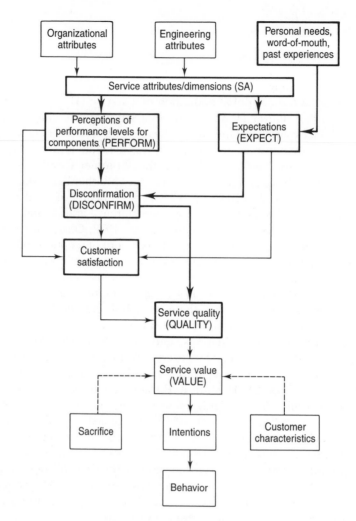

Figure 1. A multistage model of customer assessments of service quality and value.

and then averaging across attributes. They also suggest that expectations should be influenced by personal needs, word-of-mouth communications, and past experiences. The determinants of perceptions are not discussed in their model, but, presumably, they are influenced by attributes of the service-delivery process. The theoretical linkages proposed by Parasuraman *et al.* (1985) are illustrated by the double lines in Figure 1.

Both CS/D and perceived service quality are postulated to be influenced by the gap between expectations and perceptions of performance (i.e. disconfirmation). However, the CS/D literature suggests a more elaborate model in which disconfirmation, expectations, and actual performance levels affect customer satisfaction, which, in turn, becomes an input to customers' perceptions of service quality. As Figure 1 illustrates, this conceptualization implies that customers' perceptions of service quality are directly affected by disconfirmation and indirectly affected by disconfirmation, expectations, and actual performance levels (via CS/D).

Service value

On the basis of a review of previous research and on an exploratory study, Zeithaml (1988, p. 14) suggests that 'perceived value is the customer's overall assessment of the utility of a product based on perceptions of what is received and what is given'. If perceived service value is analogous to the concept of perceived product value, then Zeithaml's work suggests that service value can be considered to involve a trade-off between a customer's evaluation of the benefits of using a service and its cost. Customers' assessments of service value are hypothesized to influence purchase intentions and behavior.

A customer's assessment of value depends on sacrifice (i.e. the monetary and nonmonetary costs associated with utilizing the service) and the customer's frame of reference (Zeithaml, 1988). Thus, there should be differences in customers' assessments of service value due to differences in monetary costs, nonmonetary costs, customer tastes, and customer characteristics. The theoretical linkages among sacrifice and customer characteristics, service value, intentions, and behavior are illustrated by the broken lines in Figure 1.

A multistage model of service quality and value

The preceding paragraphs provide a conceptual framework for a model of customers' assessments of service quality and value. A customer's global assessment of a service can be decomposed into a series of interrelated stages: assessments of performance, service quality, and value. These three stages are specified algebraically as a multistage model in the tradition of the perception-preference-choice model (Urban and Hauser, 1980), the lens model (Brunswick, 1952), and information integration theory (Anderson, 1974).

Most services are multidimensional bundles of core, facilitating, and supporting services (Grönroos, 1987). For example, airline service includes core service (transportation), facilitating service (check-in procedures), and supporting service (in-flight meals). In accordance with the tradition of multiattribute modeling, the model developed here considers a customer's perception of service performance ($PERFORM_k$) to be based on an assessment of performance on particular service attributes and dimensions (e.g. reliability). That is,

$$PERFORM_k = p_k(\mathbf{SA_k}),\qquad(1)$$

where $\mathbf{SA_k}$ is a vector of perceptual ratings of attributes/dimensions that describe service k, and p_k is a function with parameters that depend on the nature of service k.

As discussed earlier, a customer's disconfirmation experiences, expectations, and perceived performance levels affect CS/D with a specific service transaction. In turn, CS/D influences the customer's global evaluation of service quality. Thus, a reduced-form model describing customers' assessments of service quality (QUALITY) is the following[1]:

$$QUALITY = q(\textbf{PERFORM, EXPECT, DISCONFIRM}), \qquad (2)$$

where **EXPECT** is a vector describing prior expectations about the performance of the component services $(k = 1, \ldots, K)$, and **DISCONFIRM** is a vector describing perceptions of the discrepancy between performance and expectations concerning the component services $(k = 1, \ldots, K)$.

After evaluating service quality, the customer assesses service value (VALUE) by trading off the quality of service versus its costs in a given situation. That is,

$$VALUE = v_0(QUALITY, \textbf{SACRIFICE, CHAR}), \qquad (3a)$$

where **SACRIFICE** is a vector of variables describing the monetary and nonmonetary costs associated with customer's utilization of the service, and **CHAR** is a vector of customer characteristics.

As illustrated in Figure 1, prior research has implicitly assumed that customers' assessment of service value depends on their assessment of service quality. In contrast, we hypothesize that customers may weight the underlying components of service quality (**PERFORM, EXPECT,** and **DISCONFIRM**) differently when assessing service value.[2] This notion can be reflected in the service-value equation in the following way:

$$\begin{aligned} VALUE = v_1(QUALITY, \textbf{SACRIFICE, CHAR,} \\ \textbf{PERFORM, EXPECT, DISCONFIRM}) \end{aligned} \qquad (3b)$$

The hypothesis that customers weight service-quality components differently when assessing service quality versus value is testable by constraining equation (3b) to equal equation (3a).

A MODEL OF CUSTOMERS' ASSESSMENTS OF TELEPHONE SERVICE

This section describes a multistage model of customers' assessments of a continuously provided service, namely, telephone service. The following paragraphs describe the three stages of the model: the formation of customer perceptions of service performance, service quality, and value.

---

[1]On the basis of Figure 1, we have the following structural equations:

$$QUALITY = q_0(CS/D, DISCONFIRM), \qquad (i)$$

$$CS/D = c(DISCONFIRM, EXPECT, PERFORM). \qquad (ii)$$

Substituting equation (ii) in equation (i), we obtain the reduced-form equation (2) shown in the text. This article focuses on customers' (relatively stable) attitudes about service quality and value; it does not model (relatively transitory) evaluations of CS/D.

[2]For example, the role of disconfirmation may be similar to the role of perceived gains and losses in Thaler's (1985) model of consumer choice. In his model, a consumer value function is defined for differences relative to a reference point (i.e. perceived gains and losses), rather than for absolute levels in a purchasing situation. He postulates that people will be more sensitive to losses than to gains, suggesting that the customer may weight negative disconfirmation more heavily than other factors in assessing service value. This theory is consistent with the notion that the customer may weight perceptions of performance levels, expectations, and disconfirmation differently in assessing quality than in assessing value.

Performance evaluations

Local telephone service is actually a bundle of services, including local-call provision, long-distance access, operator services, customer services (e.g. installation and changes), and billing services. Hence performance evaluation ($PERFORM_k$) was modeled for three component services: billing, local, and long-distance services. The explanatory variables in the BILLING, LOCAL and LONG equations are primarily extrinsic cues related to the reliability, responsiveness, assurance and empathy dimensions of overall service quality. In addition, customer perceptions of billing, local, and long-distance services are postulated to depend on past experiences at different operating companies (**LOC-SUPPLY**), which differ in plant and equipment, operating procedures, climate and geography.

The customer's perception of billing service was hypothesized to be positively related to the customer's having no billing problems in the preceding 30 days (NO-CONTACT), satisfactory resolution of the problem (SATISFY), and customer's perception of the courtesy of telephone company personnel (COURTESY).[3] That is,

$$\text{BILLING} = f_1(\text{NO-CONTACT, SATISFY, COURTESY, \textbf{LOC-SUPPLY}}). \quad (4)$$

The relevant attributes of local and long-distance service are fairly well-defined: provision of a dial tone, a correctly established connection to a dialled number, a static-free line, and no premature disconnections of calls. Hence, it was hypothesized that a customer's perceptions of local and long-distance services would be negatively related to perceptions of frequency of trouble with these four service attributes (FDIAL, FCONNECT, FSTATIC, and FCUTOFF, respectively). It was also hypothesized that the customer's perception of long-distance service would be positively related to the courtesy of telephone company personnel. Furthermore, it should depend on the particular long-distance carrier (AT & T, Sprint, or MCI; (**LD-SUPPLY**) because each carrier uses somewhat different transmission technologies. These notions can be summarized algebraically as follows:

$$\text{LOCAL} = f_2(\text{FSTATIC, FDIAL, FCONNECT, FCUTOFF, COURTESY, \textbf{LOC-SUPPLY}}), \quad (5)$$

and

$$\text{LONG} = f_3(\text{FSTATIC, FDIAL, FCONNECT, FCUTOFF, COURTESY, \textbf{LOC-SUPPLY}, \textbf{LD-SUPPLY}}). \quad (6)$$

Perceived quality

As discussed in the preceding section, a customer's assessment of service quality is postulated to depend on CS/D with the current service. In turn, CS/D depends on the perceived performance of service components, prior expectations about performance, and perceptions of the discrepancy between performance and

---

[3]Preliminary analyses indicated that specific attributes of the bill (e.g. the level of detail) did not affect assessments of billing service.

expectations (i.e. disconfirmation). However, Oliver (1989) has argued that customers' assessments of continuously provided services (such as telephone service) may depend solely on performance.

In this study, customers' evaluations of local telephone services are hypothesized to depend on performance *and* disconfirmation for two reasons. First, exploratory research confirmed that customer expectations about telephone service are not actively processed. Verbal protocols collected during in-depth interviews with 50 telephone customers yielded few speech segments concerning performance expectations (1%). Second, the deregulation of the telecommunications industry is altering the nature and level of telephone service so that residential customers may experience disconfirmation. For example, unfavorable disconfirmation occurs when the company drops free telephone and inside-wire repair. Hence, customers' assessments of telephone service quality are postulated to be a function of performance and disconfirmation, but not of expectations.

With regard to operationalizing the disconfirmation component of quality, recall that favorable or unfavorable disconfirmation was argued to arise from discrepancies between anticipated service (based on prior telephone experiences) and actual service. However, rather than measure disconfirmation for every service-quality dimension, this study measured disconfirmation with two questions that compared current telephone service with prior telephone experiences. The two questions had better/same/worse response categories (Oliver, 1981).[4] Specifically, QUALITY has hypothesized to depend on the customer's evaluation of the current provider relative to a prior local telephone service supplier (COMPARE) and the customer's assessment of the service supplier (COMPARE) and the customer's assessment of the extent of improvement in service compared with that of a year ago (IMPROVE).[5] In addition, QUALITY was postulated to depend on whether the customer's local telephone service had always been provided by the current carrier (NO CHANGE). Since positive disconfirmation should lead to higher assessments of overall service quality, the effects of these three variables were hypothesized to be positive. In addition, it was hypothesized that a customer who is a heavy user of local on long-distance service (#LOCAL, #LONG) may perceive overall service quality to be higher or lower than other customers because s/he may more opportunities for (positive or negative) disconfirmation.

Regarding the performance aspect of quality, it was postulated that a customer evaluated the overall quality of telephone service by forming intermediate perceptions of of the performance levels of component services and then weighting

---

[4]In contrast, Parasuraman *et al.* (1988) measure disconfirmation as the difference between separate measures of expectations and perceptions. Similarly, early approaches to measuring disconfirmation in the CS/D literature elicited separate measures of pre-performance judgments (i.e. expectations) and postperformance judgments, which created an artificial negative correlation between expectation and disconfirmation. Oliver (1981) points out that a better- and worse-than-expected scale is more meaningful to respondents and that is consistently has been highly correlated with satisfaction across a large number of different settings. He also points out that this scale is independent of expectation levels, which is important in multivariate analyses.

[5]A customer's ability to compare service from alternative telephone companies is an additional source of disconfirmation. The variable NO-CHANGE is a surrogate variable for this source of disconfirmation. Prior research indicated that customers who have only had service from one telecommunications provider are less discriminating (i.e. rate services more favorably).

these intermediate evaluations. Perceptions of higher levels of performance were hypothesized to be associated with higher assessments of overall quality. QUALITY was modeled as a function of the customer's assessments of the performance of seven services: billing, local and long-distance service, directory assistance (DIRECT), operator assistance (OPER), installation (INSTALL) and repair services. Not all customers utilize all services, especially repair and installation services, during a given period. Consequently, if a customer did not have experience with one of the component services (e.g. repair), his/her perceptions of that service were not elicited, and the relevant ratings variables (e.g. REPAIR) was assigned the value zero. Indicator variables (NO-DIRECT, NO-OPER, NO-INSTALL, and NO-REPAIR) were then used to represent the absence or presence of experience with a specific component. These 11 performance variables are extrinsic cues of the five quality dimensions of reliability, responsiveness, assurance, empathy, and tangibles.

The equation for overall quality can be summarized as follows:

$$\text{QUALITY} = f_4(\text{BILLING, LOCAL, LONG, DIRECT, NO-DIRECT,}$$
$$\text{OPER, NO-OPER, INSTALL, NO-INSTALL, REPAIR, NO-REPAIR,} \qquad (7)$$
$$\text{NO-CHANGE, COMPARE, IMPROVE, \#LOCAL, \#LONG}).$$

Perceived value

The VALUE equation (equation 3b) was operationalized in the following way. A residential customer's assessment of the value of telephone services will chiefly depend on an assessment of the overall quality of telephone services. However, disconfirmation and performance may be weighted differently when assessing value versus overall quality. Hence, it is hypothesized that performance perceptions of three key service variables (BILLING, LOCAL, and LONG) and disconfirmation (NO-CHANGE, COMPARE, IMPROVE, #LOCAL, #LONG) will be weighted more heavily in assessing value than in assessing quality. In other words, these variables are hypothesized to have a positive effect on VALUE in addition to the positive effect on QUALITY.

Local telephone service is usually regulated so that prices are not free to fluctuate, and the service has no direct competitor in franchised areas. Also, since the large majority of customers used the same telephone company for long periods of time, customers are unable to compare their company's service with another's service unless they have lived in a different franchised area. Consequently, a change in price for local service, rather than relative price (vis-a-vis) competitors), is more likely to affect value. However, price changes are relatively infrequent, and none occurred at the time of the study. For these reasons monetary costs are relatively unimportant for local telephone service; however, nonmonetary costs may still be important in assessing value. In addition, billing policies may affect value judgments, such as when a customer does not meet a telephone company's payment schedule and service is abruptly terminated. Note that other continuously provided services (e.g. utilities) are likely to be characterized by similar customer responses.

Since the role of monetary and nonmonetary cost in customers' assessment of perceived service value is somewhat different in this industry, income was chosen to represent the customers' relative sacrifice (i.e. budget constraints). As income increases, the cost of telephone service becomes a similar proportion of the customer's total budget, so that the customer may perceive telephone service to be less valuable to available substitutes. For example, conversing over the telephone may seem to be a less valuable form of socialization compared with travel and trips to the theater. In addition, different types of customers may attach differential value to telephone service. Customers who use their residential telephone primarily for business purposes (BUSINESS) may value telephone service more highly than customers who use the telephone primarily for social or other personal reasons. Also, older customers (AGE), heavy users (#LOCAL and #LONG), and members of larger households (#HOUSE) may value residential telephone service more highly because of their heavier reliance on telephone services. Similarly, customers who are employed outside the home (EMPLOYED) may value residential telephone service less highly since they may have access to telephone service at their place of employment. The equation for the value of residential telephone services is expressed as follows.

$$\text{VALUE} = f_5(\text{QUALITY, BILLING, LOCAL, LONG,}$$
$$\text{NO-CHANGE, COMPARE, IMPROVE, \#LOCAL, \#LONG,} \qquad (8)$$
$$\text{\#HOUSE, AGE, INCOME, BUSINESS, EMPLOYED}).$$

The operationalized form of the multistage model of telephone service quality and value is summarized by equations (4)–(8).

RESEARCH METHODS

The data base

The study utilized survey data from a systemwide (i.e. national) probability sample of 1408 residential telephone subscribers in 1985. In the survey, customers' recent telephone experiences were probed, their ratings of various service process attributes were reported, and overall service quality and value assessments were obtained. The survey elicited for component services identified by Parasuraman *et al.* (1985, 1988) using measures similar to, but not identical to, SERVQUAL. The questionnaire focused heavily on the reliability, responsiveness, assurance, and empathy dimensions. For example, the survey asked directly about the courtesy of employees, as well as about the attitudes of knowledgeability of sale representatives and other employees, to obtain measures of assurance. Ratings of the fifth quality dimension, tangibles, were not directly elicited since customer contact with the telephone company usually occurs over the telephone. Even repair and installation services do not necessarily require contact between telephone company personnel and customers.

There are two major differences between this survey and SERVQUAL. The items in this survey were framed specifically in terms of the telecommunications industry (rather than framed generically as they are in SERVQUAL). Specifically, the questions used in this study elicited ratings of intrinsic and extrinsic cues that signal service quality for telephone service. Second, unlike SERVQUAL, this survey did not measure expectations concerning service-quality dimensions. However, the survey did elicit direct measures of disconfirmation, whereas SERVQUAL does not.

Measures of constructs

Table 1 summarizes the model specification, hypotheses, and construct measures used in this research. The model consists of five equations: three performance equations, a service-quality equation, and a service-value equation. The hypothesized signs of the coefficients are shown in parentheses. The measures of the constructs are defined with the phraseology of the actual questionnaire. For example, the overall quality question is, 'Thinking just about the past 30 days, how would you rate the overall quality of services provided by your local telephone company? Would you say it is: Poor, Fair, Good or Excellent?'

Model estimation

The model of telephone-service quality and value is postulated to be a linear additive, compensatory model.[6] In assessing service quality and service value, the customer is assumed to weigh the various considerations associated with service quality, trading off lesser performance on some service attributes for greater performance on others. This specification assumes that the service is at least minimally satisfactory on all attributes (as required by public utilities commissions).

In the residential model, BILLING, LOCAL, LONG, and QUALITY appear as both dependent and predictor variables. The measurement errors in these equations may be correlated. (A positive correlation is likely because the dependent variables are measured on similar scales). Hence, a two-stage least squares estimation procedure was used (Johnston, 1972).[7]

RESULTS

The results are displayed in Table 2. The model seems to be well supported by the data. The R^2 for the equations ranges from .25 to .43, which is reasonably good explanatory power for equations estimated with cross-sectional data. (This result also compares favorably with the explanatory power of Parasuraman et al.'s (1988) OLS

---

[6]In the QUALITY equation, the coefficients of the variables describing service contacts (i.e. DIRECT, NO-DIRECT, OPER, NO-OPER, INSTALL, NO-INSTALL, REPAIR, NO-REPAIR) are interpreted in the following way. If a service contact took place (e.g. repair), customers provide a rating of the service (e.g. REPAIR), and the coefficients of that variable represents the influence of their perception of the service on their assessment of overall quality. If a service contact did not take place, customers do not provide a rating of the service (e.g. REPAIR is assigned the value zero); consequently, the influence of the rating of the service on overall quality is not estimated. However, the relevant dummy variable (e.g. NO-REPAIR) takes on the value one and the coefficient of that variable represents the increase or decrease in the customer's assessment of overall quality due to the absence of a particular service contact. (In other words, there is a shift in the intercept between users and nonusers, plus a slope effect for users only).

[7]Preliminary analyses estimated these same equations as binary logit models (which do not require interval scale properties for the dependent variable). Since the logit results were similar to the results found in this study, our assumption that the scales have interval properties does not appear to affect the results.

Table 1. Definitions of variables in the residential model

	Definition
Endogenous variables:	
BILLING	Rating of *the billing job* (e.g. *'How would you rate...?'*)
LOCAL	Rating of *local calls*
LONG	Rating of *long-distance calls*
QUALITY	Rating of *the overall quality of services provided by the local telephone company*
VALUE	*Overall value of services provided by the local telephone company, considering the amount paid for services received* (scale: 'very poor value' [1] ... 'very good value' [5])
Predictor variables:	
Equation 4:	
NO-CONTACT (+)	No billing problem in the past 30 days (yes/no)
SATISFY (+)	Satisfactory resolution of the billing problem (yes/no)
COURTESY (+)	Rating of *the courtesy of telephone company personnel*
LOC-SUPPLY (+/−)	A vector of six indicator variables representing six of the seven geographic areas
Equations[a] 5 and 6:	
FSTATIC (−)	Frequency of transmission problems (e.g. *'how often did... occur in the past 30 days?'*)
FDIAL (−)	Frequency of dial tone problems
FCONNECT (−)	Frequency of connection problems
FCUTOFF (−)	Frequency of disconnection problems
COURTESY (+)	As defined for equation (4)
LOC-SUPPLY (+/−)	As defined for equations (4)
LD-SUPPLY (+/−)	A vector of three variables representing the three major long-distance carriers: AT & T, Sprint, and MCI
Equation 7:[b]	
NO-CHANGE (+)	Local telephone service has always been provided by current provider (yes/no)
COMPARE (+)	If the respondent has ever subscribed to local service from another supplier, a comparison of the current provider with the prior provider is elicited (scale is: 'much worse' [1] ... 'much better' [5]); if not, variable is coded zero
IMPROVE (+)	Extent of improvement in telephone service compared with a year ago (scale: 'much worse' [1] ... 'much better' [5])
#LOCAL (+/−)	Frequency of local calls
#LONG (+/−)	Frequency of long-distance calls
DIRECT (+)	Rating of directory-assistance service[c]
NO-DIRECT (+)	Did not use directory-assistance service in the past 30 days (yes/no)
OPER (+)	Rating of toll/assistance operator service[c]
NO-OPER (+)	Did not use toll/assistance operator in the past 30 days (yes/no)
INSTALL (+)	Ratings of service associated with a connection or change[c]
NO-INSTALL (+)	Did not use installation service in the past 30 days (yes/no)
REPAIR (+)	Rating of repair service[c]
NO-REPAIR (+)	Did not use repair service in the past 30 days (yes/no)
Equation 8:[d]	
NO-CHANGE (+)	As defined for equation (7)
COMPARE (+)	As defined for equation (7)
IMPROVE (+)	As defined for equation (7)
#LOCAL (+/−)	As defined for equation (7)
#LONG (+/−)	As defined for equation (7)
#HOUSE (+)	*Number of persons in the household*
AGE (+)	Age category of respondent (seven-point scale)
INCOME (−)	Household income category (seven-point scale)
BUSINESS (+)	Telephone primarily used for business purposes (yes/no)
EMPLOYED (−)	Respondents employed outside the home (yes/no)

Italics indicate exact phrasing of some questions. Rating variables are coded on a four-point scale (poor/fair/good/excellent). Frequency variables are coded on a four-point scale (seldom/sometimes/often/almost always). Other scales are as indicated above. The sign in parentheses indicates the hypothesised positive (+) or negative (−) effect on the dependent variable.

[a] Exogenous variables are postulated to be identical in both local and long-distance equations, with the exception of **LD-SUPPLY**, which appears only in the long-distance equation. The actual questions measure perceptions of local or long-distance service as appropriate.

[b] Equation (7) also includes the endogenous variables BILLING (+), LOCAL (+), and LONG (+) as predictor variables.

[c] If the respondent did not use this service in the past 30 days, the variable is coded zero.

[d] Equation (8) also includes the endogenous variables QUALITY (+), BILLING (+), LOCAL (+), and LONG (+) as predictor variables.

Table 2. Two-stage least squares estimates for the residential model

Variable[b]	Estimated coefficients[a]		
	Equation (4)	Equation (5)	Equation (6)
COURTESY	.3112***	.2678***	.2242***
NO-CONTACT	.7682***	...	...
SATISFY	.3749***	...	...
FSTATIC	...	−.2079***	−.2414***
FCONNECT	...	−.0909***	−.1223***
FDIAL	...	−.0865***	−.0514**
FCUTOFF	...	−.1382***	−.1737***
AT & T	...	...	.0460
MCI	...	...	−.1841
SPRINT	...	...	.1157
INTERCEPT	.7843	2.4679	2.5722
F-statistic	50.83***	89.02***	73.63***
R^2	.25	.41	.43
Adjusted R^2	.24	.41	.42

	Estimated coefficient[a]	
	Equation (7)	Equation (8)
BILLING	.1678***	.0052
LOCAL	.5312***	.3175***
LONG	.1463***	.1478**
QUALITY	...	.3654*
NO-CHANGE	.5049***	.3367***
COMPARE	.1796***	.0714*
IMPROVE	.1064***	.1545***
#LOCAL	.0598***	.0115
#LONG	−.0398***	−.0332
DIRECT	.1476	...
NO-DIRECT	.1745	...
OPER	−.0216	...
NO-OPER	−.0007	...
INSTALL	−.1780	...
NO-INSTALL	−.6143	...
REPAIR	.1651***	...
NO-REPAIR	.0611***	...
#HOUSE	...	.0535***
AGE	...	.0643***
INCOME	...	−.0370***
BUSINESS	...	.0433
EMPLOYED	...	−.0627
INTERCEPT	−.5814	−.1215
F-statistic	51.91***	46.57***
R^2	.37	.32
Adjusted R^2	.37	.31

Ellipses indicate variable does not occur in equation.
[a]The coefficients of the six geographic dummy variables are estimated but not reported. The coefficients reported in the table are not standardized.
[b]Variables refer to local or long-distance service as applicable (e.g., col. 2 shows the coefficient of the variable 'static on local calls' and col. 3 shows the coefficient of the variable 'static on long distance calls').
*One-tailed test, $p < .05$.
**One-tailed test, $p < .01$.
***One-tailed test, $p < .005$.

estimation of four quality equations as functions of indices representing the five service-quality dimensions.) In addition, the effects of most variables are in the hypothesized direction, and most are statistically significant (one-tailed tests, $p < .05$).

Performance

The results for the BILLING, LOCAL, and LONG equations are remarkably similar. Customers' assessments of all three services are positively affected by the courtesy of personnel ($p < .005$). COURTESY explains between 5 and 9% of the variance of the dependent variable in each equation.[8] In Parasuraman et al.'s (1988, p. 23), courtesy is part of their assurance dimension and is defined as 'knowledge and courtesy of employees and their ability to inspire trust and confidence'. Hence, the results for COURTESY suggests that *any* contact with telephone service personnel will have an important impact on a customer's assessment of assurance for *all* aspects of telephone service. Results also show that customer's assessments of all three services differ across the seven operating companies participating in this study. The six geographic indicator variables are jointly significant at $p < .05$ and explain about 1% of the variance in each dependent variable.

A customer rates billing service substantially lower if there has been a billing problem ($p < .005$), and the effects of satisfactorily resolving the problem does not entirely offset this impact ($p < .005$). Customer assessments of local and long-distance service are negatively affected by the perceived frequency of static, connection, dial tone, and disconnection service problems ($p < .005$). For both services, a customer attaches the most importance to a static-free line (which explains about 12–15% of the variance in the dependent variable). Together, these results suggest the importance of reliability (or trouble-free service) and responsiveness (willingness to help customers). The service provider cannot entirely regain customer goodwill even if the problem is rectified by courteous personnel. The effects of the long-distance carrier variables on long-distance service rating are jointly, but not individually, statistically significant ($p < .05$). It is interesting to note that MCI customers rate long-distance service lower than AT & T or Sprint. One explanation for this result is that, at the time of the survey, MCI predominantly relied on microwave technology, which can occasionally result in degraded transmission.

Quality

In the residential model, the primary determinants of overall telephone service quality (QUALITY) are the BILLING, LOCAL, and LONG variables (see Table 2). Each variable has a positive, statistically significant effect on overall quality ($p < .005$). Local services is the most important of the three, explaining about 12% of the variance in QUALITY. Customers' assessments of installation service, operator assistance, repair service, and directory assistance seem to be much less important in customers' evaluations of overall quality.

---

[8]The percentage of variance explained is calculated as the square of the standardized coefficient (not reported). Since the predictor variables are not independent, this calculation is only an approximation.

Of installation, operator assistance, repair, and directory assistance services, only the customer's assessment of repair service (REPAIR, NO-REPAIR) is statistically significant ($p < .005$), explaining about 3% of the variance in the dependent variable. One implication of this result concerns the net effect of a repair contact on customers' overall quality assessment. In the QUALITY equation, a repair contact decreases QUALITY by .06. Since the REPAIR coefficient (.17) multiplied by the highest rating (4) is .68, this quality 'penalty' is more than offset by the highest level of repair-service performance. Of course, not all customers give a repair contact the highest rating. One possible reason for the importance of repair service is that it is a relatively unambiguous signal of responsiveness.

Residential customers with no experience with another telephone service provider have higher assessments of overall quality than customers with such experience (NO-CHANGE; $p < .005$).For those customers with alternative carrier experience, quality assessments depends on perceptions of current versus prior telephone service quality ($p < .005$). The variables NO-CHANGE and COMPARE jointly explain about 22% of the variance in QUALITY. Overall quality also depends on whether the customer perceives telephone service to have improved in the past year (IMPROVE); this effect is very small, but statistically significant ($p < .005$). In addition, heavy users of local telephone service (#LOCAL) rate QUALITY higher ($p < .005$) than light users. In contrast, heavy users of long-distance telephone service (#LONG) rate QUALITY lower than light users ($p < .005$). The results for heavy versus light users highlight the role of disconfirmation. Apparently, local service typically provides positive disconfirmation, whereas long-distance service provides negative disconfirmation.

Value

As expected, the most important determinant of perceived service value is QUALITY ($p < .005$), explaining 4% of the variance in VALUE (see Table 2). In addition, a customer's perception of the performance levels of local service (LOCAL) and long-distance service (LONG) affects VALUE directly ($p < .05$) as well as indirectly (through QUALITY), explaining an additional 4% of the variance in VALUE. As before, LOCAL is the most important component. In contrast, BILLING does not affect VALUE except through QUALITY. One explanation for this finding is that customers consider local and long-distance services, but not billing service, as core services or critical signals of service-quality dimensions.

The second most important set of determinants of perceived service value are the customer's disconfirmation experiences. Residential customers' assessments of service value are positively affected by lack of experience with another service provider ($p < .005$), unfavorable experience with another service provider ($p < .05$), and improvements in service in the past year ($p < .005$). However, heavy users of local or long-distance service do not systematically rate VALUE higher or lower ($p < .05$). Together, the disconfirmation variables (NO-CHANGE, COMPARE, IMPROVE) account for about 6% of the variance in customers' assessments of telephone service value. They also indirectly influence service value through QUALITY.

These findings support the notion that customers' perceptions of core, facilitating, and supporting telephone services and their disconfirmation experiences are weighted differently in assessing value than in assessing overall quality. Local and long-distance services (LOCAL, LONG) and disconfirmation experiences (NO-CHANGE, COMPARE, IMPROVE) are weighted more heavily in assessing VALUE.

A joint statistical test indicates that residential customer characteristics (#HOUSE, AGE, INCOME, BUSINESS, EMPLOYED) affect VALUE but do not affect QUALITY. (Note that this hypothesis is implicit in Figure 1). Separate statistical tests indicate that the effects of #HOUSE, AGE, and INCOME on VALUE are small but statistically significant ($p < .005$). The effects of these three variables are in the hypothesized direction. For example, older customers value telephone service more highly.

DISCUSSION

The results of this study support several basic theoretical propositions. Consistent with prior exploratory research concerning service quality, a key determinant of overall service quality is the gap between performance and expectations (i.e. disconfirmation). For residential customers, perceived telephone service quality depended on the disconfirmation triggered by perceived changes in existing service or changes in service providers.

A customer's assessment of overall service quality is also directly affected by perceptions of performance levels. This finding is consistent with the CS/D literature, but it is a new finding for the service-quality literature. It is interesting to note that disconfirmation explains a larger proportion of the variance in service quality than performance, whereas, in prior studies performance explains a larger proportion of the variance in customer satisfaction than disconfirmation (Churchill and Surprenant, 1982).

Customers' assessments of service value are positively related to their evaluations of service quality. However, service quality and value are not identical constructs. For example, disconfirmation experiences were more important in assessing telephone service value than in assessing telephone service quality since disconfirmation was found to affect value directly as well as indirectly (through quality). In addition, customers weight their perceptions of the performance levels of component services differently for service quality than for value. For example, billing, local, and long-distance services were weighted more heavily for value than for quality. Finally, customers' personal characteristics are important in assessing value, but not quality. Thus, perceived service value seems to be a 'richer', more comprehensive measure of customers' overall evaluation of a service than service quality.

Most authors have viewed value as the outcome of a trade-off between a single 'overall quality' construct and sacrifice. However, these results suggest that the customer's value function is more complex. Hence, this study rebuts the simplistic notion underlying many quality-measurement programs, namely that the service provider should focus on maximizing average customer ratings of service quality while minimizing costs (i.e. price). Our research suggests that service providers must offer flexible services that satisfy the different tastes and expectations of each market segment. It also shows that managers can operationalize a model of customers' assessments of service quality and value with survey data. However, it is clear that the specification and operationalization of the model must be carefully tailored to the specific service context. This effort will be rewarded by the many managerial implications that can be derived from estimation results.

Research is needed to further explore the antecedents of customer satisfaction, service quality, and service value. First, there are many measurement and scaling issues to be addressed with respect to these constructs. The present study employs single measures of each model construct, whereas multiple measures would be more appropriate. Second, either experimental or econometric research could be used to further explore the linkages among these constructs. The theoretical linkages described in Figure 1 are considerably more complex than those represented by equations (1), (2), and (3b). For example, a structural equation for customer satisfaction can be integrated into the multistage model. Third, the model should be applied in other contexts (e.g. financial services, retailing, air transportation) to establish its generalizability.

REFERENCES

Anderson, N. H. (1974) 'Information Integration Theory: A Brief Survey'. In *Contemporary Developments in Mathematical Psychology*. Vol. 2 (D. H. Kranz *et al.*, Eds). San Francisco: Freeman, pp. 236–305.

Brunswick, E. (1952) *The Conceptual Framework of Psychology*. Chicago: University of Chicago Press.

Cardozo, R. (1965) 'An Experimental Study of Customer Effort, Expectations and Satisfaction'. *Journal of Marketing Research* **2** (3): 244–249.

Churchill, G. A. Jr. and Surprenant, C. (1982) 'An Investigation into the Determinants of Customer Satisfaction'. *Journal of Marketing Research* **19** (4): 491–504.

Grönroos, C. (1987) 'Developing the Service Offering: A Source of Competitive Advantage'. In *Add Value to Your Service* (C. Surprenant, Ed.). Chicago: American Marketing Association, pp. 81–85.

Hauser, J. R. and Clausing, D. (1988) 'The House of Quality'. *Harvard Business Review* **66** (May–June): 63–73.

Holbrook, M. B. and Corfman, K. P. (1985) 'Quality and Value in the Consumption Experience: Phaedrus Ride Again'. In *Perceived Quality* (J. Jacoby and J. Olson, Eds). Lexington, MA: Lexington, pp. 31–57.

Johnston, J. (1972) *Econometric Methods*. New York: McGraw-Hill.

LaBarbera, P. A. and Mazursky, D. (1983) 'A Longitudinal Assessment of Consumer Satisfaction/Dissatisfaction: The Dynamic Aspect of the Cognitive Process'. *Journal of Marketing Research* **20** (4): 393–404.

Oliver, R. L. (1980) 'A Cognitive Model of the Antecedents and Consequences of Satisfaction Decisions'. *Journal of Marketing Research* **42** (4): 460–469.

Oliver, R. L. (1981) 'Measurement and Evaluation of Satisfaction Processes in Retail Settings'. *Journal of Retailing* **57** (Fall): 25–48.

Oliver, R. L. (1989) 'Processing of the Satisfaction Response in Consumption: A Suggested Framework and Research Propositions'. *Journal of Consumer Satisfaction, Dissatisfaction and Complaining Behavior* **2**: 1–16.

Olshavsky, R. W. (1985) 'Perceived Quality in Consumer Decision Making: An Integrated Theoretical Perspective'. In *Perceived Quality* (J. Jacoby and J. Olson, Eds). Lexington, MA: Lexington, pp. 3–29.

Olshavsky, R. W. and Miller, J. A. (1972) 'Consumer Expectations. Product Performance and Perceived Product Quality'. *Journal of Marketing Research* **9** (1): 19–21.

Olson, J. C. and Dover, P. (1976) 'Effects of Expectations, Product Performance, and Disconfirmation on Belief Elements of Cognitive Structures'. In *Advances in Consumer Research*, Vol. 3 (B. B. Anderson, Ed.) Provo, UT: Association for Consumer Research.

Parasuraman, A., Zeithaml, V. A. and Berry, L. L. (1985) 'A Conceptual Model of Service Quality and Its Implications for Future Research'. *Journal of Marketing,* **49** (4):41–50.

Parasuraman, A., Zeithaml, V. A. and Berry, L. L. (1988) 'SERVQUAL: A Multiple Item Scale for Measuring Consumer Perceptions of Service Quality'. *Journal of Retailing* **64** (1): 12–37.

Phillips, L. W., Chang, D. R. and Buzzell, R. D. (1983) 'Product Quality, Cost Position and Business Performance: A Test of Some Key Hypotheses'. *Journal of Marketing* **47** (Spring): 26–43.

Thaler, R. (1985) 'Mental Accounting and Consumer Choice'. *Marketing Science* **4** (Summer): 199–214.

Tse, D. K. and Wilton, P. C. (1988) 'Models of Consumer Satisfaction Formation: An Extension. *Journal of Marketing Research* **25** (2): 204–212.

Urban, G. L. and Hauser, J. R. (1980) *Design and Marketing of New Products.* Englewood Cliffs NJ: Prentice-Hall.

Zeithaml, V. A. (1988) 'Consumer Perceptions of Price, Quality and Value: A Means-End Model and Synthesis of Evidence'. *Journal of Marketing* **52** (3): 2–22.

Zeithaml, V. A., Parasuraman, A. and Berry, L. L. (1990) *Delivering Quality Service.* New York: Free Press.

17

Buyer Perceived Service Quality in Industrial Networks

Maria Holmlund and Sören Kock

A NEW SERVICE FIRM ON THE MARKET

A service firm building relationships to potential buyers in an industrial market faces several strategic problems. The two major questions are: (1) how to create relationships with potential buyers, and (2) how to determine the quality level of the service offered. The first question focuses on the problem of building relationships – is it possible to break existing relations between potential buyers and their present suppliers; is it possible to become an additional supplier to potential buyers and in that way receive a part of the purchases; or it is possible to approach new buyers that have never bought the product before. The question concerning the level of quality is at least as important for success as how to choose a way of creating relationships. If the quality level is too high, it might result in the firm not being able to cover the production costs. A low-quality level, on the other hand, is likely to result in time- and money-consuming corrections of quality problems as well as dissatisfied lost buyers.

The difficulties in determining the right quality level are obvious both when establishing and maintaining relationships. The costs of finding the right quality level are, however, high. Accordingly and especially for small firms, it is critical to find the right quality level, because necessary large investments in buyer relationships, technical equipment, etc., do not allow a trial-and-error strategy for a longer period of time. The supplier can not only concentrate on correcting the mistakes upon delivery; there has to be quality thinking in the firm as a whole and at all levels.

Earlier studies of perceived service quality in the industrial market are few. The studies that have dealt with service quality have usually been made in the consumer market, or they have dealt with quality aspects in the production process. The importance of service quality, however, can not be denied though, because many studies clearly indicate its importance (Brown *et al.*, 1991; Bazel and Gale, 1987; Grönroos, 1990b; Yamagashi *et al.*, 1988).

Reprinted by permission of the publisher from *Industrial Marketing Management*, Vol. 24, pp. 109–121.

pose of this study are to find different aspects of perceived service quality in industrial context and to determine how buyer perceived service quality uences a supplier's possibilities to build relationships. The supplier in our study is a service firm, whose primary service is laser treatment of metal components in the purpose of improving their durability and extending their lifetime. The supplier creates, together with the buyers, suitable laser applications and possesses highly flexible laser equipment. The supplier, in other words, markets a service, an intangible product, which mainly can be characterized as a process or a series of processes, where among others R&D, testing, and production are included. There are some elements in the laser treatment, which are the same regardless of the buyer, but it is in many ways adapted to the individual buyer's needs and wants. The buyers are themselves actively involved in developing the product because they provide the supplier with specifications and components.

The measuring of quality usually involves everything from suitability for use to zero mistakes in the production. In our study we have chosen to approach service quality from a holistic perspective, and mainly from the buyer's point of view. Service quality is consequently defined as the buyers' perceptions of the service offered by the seller. As several buyers have been interviewed, some of the answers will complement each other, and some will even reflect opposite views. This is, however natural as the perception of service quality is person-and situation-specific, and consequently, can vary at least partly from buyer to buyer and from situation to situation.

Until now, research concerning service quality has been carried out mostly in the consumer market, and it has been assumed either explicitly or implicitly that the service quality dimensions found there can be applied to the industrial market as well. In the consumer market quality is usually divided into a technical ('what') and a functional ('how') dimension (Grönroos, 1990b). These dimensions can further be divided into determinants like reliability, responsiveness, competence, access, courtesy, communication, credibility, security, understanding, and tangibility. Our view is, however, that it is not correct to accept this assumption without a closer evaluation, because there are many major differences within a certain type of market and especially between different types of markets.

The quality concept particularly when establishing relationships is a further cause for this study because service quality is considered to be one of the most vital factors when choosing a supplier. Firms establishing positions in networks, where advanced and adapted technology along side with high transfer capability (Hammarkvist et al., 1982) are of importance, are especially forced to invest considerable resources to find the right level of quality, as it is clearly not the technical aspects of the offer alone that determine the success. A smaller firm with limited resources is even more dependent on finding and developing the right quality level in a reasonable time. These factors motivate a study where the aim is to find different aspects of buyer perceived service quality is a highly developed and adapted technology context.

The theoretical framework is derived from the network approach and the service quality concept. Empirical data has been gathered through in-depth interviews, both in the focal firm, the supplier, and in five buying companies for whom the supplier has developed laser applications. The interviews were carried out between autumn

1991 and spring 1993 with the people who were responsible for developing the contacts with the laser application supplier. These people had positions as technical manager, vice presidents, mechanical engineer, production engineer, and maintenance manager. The buyers were both medium-sized and large companies in a varied line of business – pulp, forest, defense, power plant – and were situated in the same country as the supplier, namely Sweden.

ESTABLISHING RELATIONSHIPS

When a firm builds a position in a network it establishes relationships to other firms who already are embedded in the network. A business network contains: (1) actors, i.e. individuals, firms, departments, organizations, or coalitions of organizations; (2) activities emerging when the actors combine, create, develop, and transfer resources; (3) interactions between the actors that create exchanges and adaptations; (4) relationships aiming at long-term commitments and bonds; and (5) both direct and indirect resources (Häkansson and Johanson, 1992; Kock, 1992).

Hammarkvist *et al.* (1982) state that it is important to choose which network to penetrate. This is the case when the firm chooses to establish relationships in one network where its potential exchange partners are. However, when for example a newly founded firm begins to build relationships to other firms, two situations can arise, the firm can either penetrate one existing network where the potential firms are, or build relationships to firms in separate networks. In the latter case, the established firm connects the previously unconnected networks with each other. Figure 1 illustrates these two situations.

Situation 1

A firm that recently has started a business probably has a relatively limited network, consisting mainly of relationships to some suppliers and some other firms with an interest in the firm. These firms connected to the new firm can be financiers and suppliers of raw materials, machinery, etc. If the firm builds relationships to firms in a network, it will eventually become a part of this network. The network to which the buyers belong will, in other words, expand and include the new supplier and the original network.

Situation 2

The firm is also in this case newly founded and has a similar network to the situation described previously. The firm is about to create a new relationship in buyers in separate networks in different lines of business. These networks can be separate because of differences in the products produced or used production technology. The firm will act as a binding link between the different networks. The networks will be indirectly connected through the firm, which serves the previously separate networks. This kind of situation occurs when a firm has developed a problem solution, a

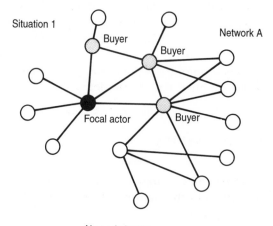

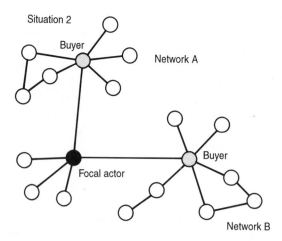

Fig. 1. A focal actor's strategic alternatives when establishing relationships.

product that can be used in many different areas. This creates a more complex situation for a newly founded firm and demands more resources, greater flexibility of the product, more varied social contacts, and more information because the business areas are many and probably differ from each other.

Quality in an industrial network

Quality has traditionally been measured from either the seller's or the buyer's perspective and very little attention has been paid to the dyadic relationships or networks. In a dyadic relationship both the seller's and the buyer's perception of the perceived quality is evaluated, without including the impact of other buyers and their influence. Using a network perspective implies that both direct and indirect influences and relationships are included. It is in other words, a more holistic approach because we analyze not only direct influences on quality by one or two firms, but include also influences from other firms in the network indirectly influencing these firms and their relationship. If, for example, one of the seller's buyers requires ISO certified products, the other buyers of the seller will simultaneously benefit from this requirement.

A network perspective is thus not limited to relationships between one seller and one of its buyers. In most cases the buyers use the purchased product in their production processes to produce products to sell to their buyers, resulting in quality requirements by the buyers' buyers to consequently affect the buyer demands from the seller. In turn the buyers' buyers are selling their products to their buyers extending the quality chain even further. A firm penetrating a network must bear the impact of the actors' embeddedness in mind and consequently a service strategy built on quality must be derived from an evaluation of the needs and wants of not only the buyers to whom it has direct relationships, but also the buyers' buyers, suppliers' suppliers, etc., to whom the firm has indirect relationships. The research and planning undertaken before entering a network must therefore include actors in different positions, otherwise the possibilities to offer the right quality are limited and the firm will not achieve the desired position in the network. In the same way, a firm unable to respond to the demands and requirements of the firms in the network will face a weakened position in the network.

The supplier and the offered service

The focal actor in our study is a service firm establishing relationships to potential buyers in separate business networks, for example, pulp, forest, auto, defense, engineering, and power plant industries. The firm has developed a patented technological innovation within laser technology, which can be used in many fields. The flexibility of this kind of laser treatment of metal components is illustrated by the president who said: 'We have had some kind of cooperation with 21 of the 100 biggest companies in Sweden'.

The novelty with this method is that the powder used to improve the wearing surface is not applied directly onto the metal components, instead it is applied by means of the laser beam on the metal component. Parts of the engine in production processes that are exposed to wear and tear can either be prepared beforehand or after being in use for a while. The advantages for the buyer are more durable production machinery as well as fewer breakdowns. These advantages are highly desirable as they help save a lot of money and minimize delays.

The studied supplier is the only firm on the market selling this kind of laser application method. Other firms have tried to develop materials and applications, which would make it possible to prolong the lifetime of surfaces exposed to intensive wear. Some have even tried to develop a similar method, but these experiments all seem to have failed. Therefore, there are no competitors with exactly the same laser application method. The buyers can of course choose to use the products until they replace them with new ones. The immediate competitors are a few large companies in Switzerland, the United States, and Japan who have specialized in limited applications. In addition to these there are some companies producing substitute surface treatment methods. Other available methods, however, cannot guarantee the same durability and reliability. Their areas of applicability are neither as many as that of the laser application method.

The entrepreneur, who also is the president, owns 63% of the firm and financiers own 37%. The organization is divided into production, R&D and other services. The firm is on one hand technically oriented, because the carrying out of the buyers' technical specifications is very essential, on the other hand the entrepreneur claims to offer services highly adapted to the buyers' needs.

The supplier's quality objectives

Zero mistakes as well as the highest possible technical quality used to be the supplier's goal in whatever was undertaken; now the aim is to offer *the right quality* – from the buyers' point of view. The earlier quality aspiration level was found to be too expensive and the buyers, especially new ones, found the price too high. Achieving a quality level that can be regarded too high is not regarded necessary by any one involved, and it certainly does not justify the attached cost's. A trade-off between costs and the quality level is a guideline when determining what quality level to offer. Simultaneously it constitutes the main problem the supplier faces and has to deal with daily.

The firm's functions are mainly considered to be production, money, personnel, and professionalism. In addition they also consider competence, creativity, quality, and commercialism as key functions. Their opinion is that the main shortages in the firm for the moment lie in the fields of professionalism, commercialism, and money. A possible reason could be that the firm still is too technically oriented, and is trying to reach too high a quality level, which in turn leads to very high costs. Another reason could be that the firm is relatively new, which also applies to the personnel, and that the employees do not yet have enough knowledge about the potential buyers. This fact was underlined by one of the buyers, who found the supplier very skilful in solving technical problems, but clearly lacking in commercial skills when marketing the laser treatments.

The supplier's buyers

It is crucial for the firm to know and learn the buyers' different needs, which can vary a lot as many lines of business are involved. The aim of the supplier has been to build a network of relationships consisting of only positive relationships connecting previously separate networks. Cook and Emerson (1984) and Yamagashi, Gillmore and Cook (1988) claim that power in social exchange networks can consist of three different relationships: positive, negative, or mixed. Positive relationships imply that one relation does not exclude another, or both can exist side by side, for instance that two firms can use the same supplier.

This can occasionally lead to the supplier being forced to renounce potential buyers because they compete with present ones. In other words the supplier deals with and develops relationships with mainly one buyer per line of business. All of the studied buyers correspondingly report that they would break the relation if the supplier established relationships with their competitors. The flexible laser application method that can be used in treating fundamentally all kinds of metal surfaces creates a large potential in spite of this substantial limitation.

The supplier's relation to the buyers

The supplier states that 'it is six times more difficult and more expensive for a new supplier to find buyers than it is for an established supplier. An unknown production technology makes it even more complicated'. A problem the supplier clearly faces is how to show potential buyers what it stands for, and how to motivate the costs necessary for bringing forth a suitable laser application. Developing a suitable application takes place in cooperation with the buyer. The buyer provides the supplier with detailed specifications and the supplier develops and tests different applications in his laboratory. After having developed a possible suitable laser application, full-scale tests are carried out. Sometimes these tests take place in the production facilities of the buyer, occasionally even the end user is involved. Provided the technical quality is good enough production on a regular basis starts. The whole process is very costly, and it can, of course, be stopped whenever the parties want. The terms of the agreement are usually, but not always, stipulated in written contracts. The buyers supply the metal components, and the service of the supplier consists of treating the metal surfaces in laboratories as agreed upon. Together with the buyer, a goal is set to develop a suitable laser application method and to meet the buyer's needs and in the end increase the value of their products.

The supplier also explicitly states that he or she is willing to enter different forms of cooperation with the buyers – for instance joint ventures, licenses, system selling or technical cooperation. Only three to five development projects take place simultaneously as the supplier wants to be able to concentrate on each individual buyer and to learn about the buyer's needs in detail. The potential and actual buyers are divided in segments – groups according to application area and degree of engagement. The personal contacts to the buyers are made systematically, and according to the supplier, good personal contacts are crucial for anyone wanting to get and to stay in touch with buyers in order to create and develop relationships. The entrepreneur has estimated that about 50% of his or her time is spent establishing and maintaining contacts with potential and present buyers.

Establishing new relationships

Establishing relationships is clearly not an easy task. In the interest of the buyer it is often desirable to minimize the number of suppliers in order to decrease the exchange costs (Axelsson and Laage Hellman, 1991). Long-term relationships create a pressure for development (Hammarkvist et al., 1982), which in turn results in investments in bonds and commitment. The evolving bonds make it more difficult and expensive to break the relation. Hedaa (1992) describes four different situations that could arise when a buyer chooses new suppliers.

First, when a buyer is new on the market or has just started to use the particular product, it is natural that new relationships to suppliers are built, i.e. the supplier is given a possibility to reach completely new buyers. New technology can be a further reason for buyers asking for suppliers. Axelsson and Laage Hellman (1991) estimate that 20% to 25% of the engineering industry's technical development occurs within existing relations in Sweden.

Secondly, the buyer wants to change suppliers because he or she, for some reason, is not satisfied with the present supplier and therefore is looking for a new one. The reason can often be found on dissatisfaction with the quality offered, deliveries, adaptations, technology, or price. Dubois (1992) shows in a study carried out in a Swedish manufacturing firm covering 1964 to 1992 that 43 changes have occurred in the relationships to the suppliers of 11 specific components. Of the changes, 25 have been price related, in some cases the variation in price was up to 50%. It is also noteworthy that in 11 of the 25 cases the suppliers were able to come back at a later date. Six of the changes had been made owing to the suppliers' weak ability to deliver, and only three changes were caused by the supplier failing to meet the buyer's need for technical innovations.

Thirdly, we have one group of buyers that consist of those who buy a product but for one reason or another are looking for an additional supplier. One reason might be that the buyer wants to decrease the dependence arising from having only one supplier. By having more than one supplier, the buyer can spread the orders and acquire more general product, price, and market information. Another reason may be that the buyer wants to get a lower price or more competitive payment terms and by adding a new supplier, can keep the supplier aware of the possibility that they can be replaced if they fail in some way or try unreasonably to increase the price. This type of thinking is in congruence with the classical buying philosophy (Axelsson and Laage Hellman, 1991). Using alternative suppliers helps the buying firm to obtain information about prices and innovations and thereby to have better information when making decisions.

Finally, we have the possibility for a supplier to go in and break relationships between a potential buyer and his or her present supplier. Hedaa (1992) says that in a discussion with the sales division of a firm in Finland it came to light that only about 10% of their new relationships came from breaking existing relationships. In order to manage to break existing relationships, the supplier has to have something unique, like a new technology, a new product concept or lower prices to offer the potential buyer.

The studied buyers' cooperation with the supplier

All the buyers in our study mentioned that they were not fully satisfied with their present suppliers, but there were no alternatives until the new laser treatment method was made known. They all faced considerable costs caused by wrong deliveries and corrections. These costs, extra expenses, are not easily estimated because they do not only consist of expenses for corrections and discarded materials but also of indirect and alternative costs like lost working time, repetitive work, inspections, and so on. Therefore all of the studied buyers had more or less actively been searching for a method that would result in fewer quality problems and decreased quality costs.

In spite of great uncertainty in the beginning of the cooperation and high initial costs, the buyers chose to initiate cooperation with the new and relatively unknown supplier, because there were many considerable potential advantages, both technical and economic, with this kind of laser application. It was not the end users who demanded an improvement, quite the contrary, the buyers were prepared themselves to pay the extra costs. The buyers' motives for choosing the supplier of laser application were two-fold; the ability to offer more competitive and durable products to their buyers and the possibility to reduce their own quality costs.

Quality certificates

The awareness of quality that exists in industrial firms is obvious, and more and more companies apply for and are granted quality certificates like ISO. The certificates are used as a competitive mean and assure that quality thinking permeates the whole firm, including suppliers used. A firm aiming at quality and ISO certificates has to use suppliers that have been granted an ISO certificate. This can be an additional driving force for a firm to start looking for suppliers. The competitive advantage that an ISO certificate gives today probably will be eliminated in the future as more or less all firms acquire quality standards.

All of the studied buyers have applied for ISO certificates and were collecting the needed documentation. Consequently the buyers considered themselves having good quality standards and emphasizing quality in general. It was not a problem that the supplier in this case did not have an ISO certificate because the supplier was familiar with ISO standards and requirements. ISO certificates include only technical issues of the product, buyer perceived quality and other unnoticed and hard to measure aspects are left out from the documentation and certification. Buyer perceived quality is much more than technical aspects of the product and therefore not the same as a certificate, but an overall impression of the supplier.

BUYER PERCEIVED SERVICE QUALITY

When measuring buyer perceived service quality in the industrial market, it is in our view essential to include the context in which the firms operate. Market investments, e.g. investments of time and money in bonds, mutual commitments as well as a long-term perspective have to be taken into consideration when examining service quality. Market investments, which have led to bonds, make the firms more or less unwilling to break the relationship as well provide a stable secure ground for product development, change, and information diffusion. In service quality models created for the consumer market (Grönroos, 1983), exit is always an alternative for dissatisfied consumers, as the number of firms offering the same kind of products, is usually quite high and it is easy to switch between products and firms. Naturally this opportunity also exists to some extent in the industrial market, but the loss of made investments tends to be significantly higher, because the heterogeneity of the resources makes the cost of changing supplier high. Furthermore, it can be difficult to find a new supplier.

In Figure 2 the relationship between two actors, a supplier and a buyer, in the industrial market is built on interactions and investments in bonds. Usually, the relationship starts with an interaction, before which the firms stipulate their goals, e.g. what they want to achieve based on perceived needs. The goal of the firm is to gain access to resources controlled by the other firm, e.g., technical competence, money, and raw materials. The actors are said to be attracted to each others' strategic identities. An actor's strategic identity consists of the direct and the indirect resources he or she controls and the buyers' business strategy (Axelsson and Håkansson, 1989). The resources can be divided into personal assets, software assets, hardware assets, organizational assets, and capital assets. Direct resources means that the actor has direct control, i.e. hierarchic power, over the resources, e.g. patents, machines, facilities. Indirect resources can be gained through interactions with other actors in long-term relationships, e.g. raw material, personnel, money (Kock, 1992).

The interactions consist of three types of exchanges: (1) business exchange, (2) social exchange, and (3) information exchange. One or more of these exchanges takes place every time the firms interact with each other, and every interaction leads to investments in different kinds of bonds. Bonds are developed as a consequence of commitments and the use of resources in a specific purpose in order to achieve stability, closeness, security, and long-term relationships with other firms in the network. *Technical bonds* are based on technical adaptations of the product, materials, equipment to the buyer, and can be very hard to break for a new supplier. *Planning bonds* arise when the firms adjust their logistic functions to each other and for example implement just-in-time deliveries and on-line-contact, whereby costs for stock keeping substantially are reduced. *Knowledge bonds* are gradually developed as the firms learn about each other's strengths, weaknesses, needs, problems and possibilities. *Social bonds* take time to develop and are based on individual representatives getting to know and trust each other and can be a complement to

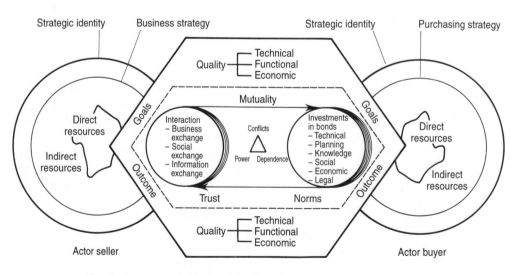

Fig. 2. Quality and relationships in industrial service organizations.

written contracts. *Economic and legal bonds* are made up of contracts, legal ownership, different forms of cooperation, payment terms, etc.

In the relation between the actors, there are also other interorganizational flows like power, dependence and conflicts. Particularly in situations where the firms are specialized and very unequal in size, there is a high risk for one of the firms of becoming highly dependent. Furthermore, different norms are developed, which restrict and guide the actors in the interactions. Within the relationship trust, which is a form of mutual confidence or reliance, will usually gradually evolve. Trust can be regarded as a prerequisite for all kinds of relationships, because the lack of trust often makes it impossible to continue to make exchanges.

The dynamic relationship constitutes of interactions leading to market investments, which lead to new interactions, which lead to further market investments, and so on. This proposal is true, however, only as long as the interacting firms are satisfied with the outcomes of the exchanges. A conformity between the goals and the outcomes are in other words needed. Service quality on the consumer market has been measured in a similar way. Grönroos (1990b) states that consumer perceived service quality can be found in the perceived difference between service expectations and experienced service. In the case that the perceived service matches or exceeds the expectations the buyer will be satisfied with the service. If the service, on the other hand, does not meet with the expectations the buyer will be dissatisfied.

We wish, however, to make a distinction between goals and expectations. An organization with a goal has actively been involved in the setting of the aims for the exchanges. The organization has set the objectives after a decision process based on bounded rationality. Although goals are on the organizational level usually expressed by groups of individuals (Parasuraman *et al.* (1985), expectations can be said to exist on an individual level. Many persons are thus involved in a relationship and everyone does not have to have been actively involved in the setting of the aims. In some cases the relationship can start with interactions on the top level and later spread to the functional level. A person at the functional level, does not have to have explicit goals for interacting although he or she will most certainly have expectations. A conclusion from this reasoning is that goals and outcomes will be based on active explicit behavior concerning the objectives of the relationship based on economic and financial plans. Expectations are more individual assumptions concerning the exchanges.

Goals of the firms

The goals are mainly economic and technical, but also other aspects of the exchanges as the social dimension can be regarded as equally important. The economic goal stipulated by the firm does not necessarily have to be in congruence with neoclassic profit maximization. Instead an actor can try to attain outcomes in line with other kinds of goals and strive for relationships based on mutuality and trust. A prerequisite for lasting relationships is the absence of opportunistic behavior.

The buyer–supplier relationship will include three dimensions concerning the service quality. Parallel to quality goals regarding the technical solution and functional quality there are economic goals. The quality is equivalent to the extent that the outcomes correspond to goals and expectations on each of the three dimensions. A clear correspondence thus emerges between the quality dimensions and the bonds in the relationship. The *technical solution* in the exchange corresponds to technical, knowledge and partly to legal bonds, i.e. contracts stipulating technical specifications. The *functional quality* on the other hand corresponds to knowledge, planning, and social bonds. The *economic quality* consists of economic and partly of legal bonds between the firms.

Economic quality dimension

All business has to be profitable, efficient, effective, and productive; in the long run an actor will not survive unless he or she is profitable. Productivity indicates how efficiently the resources are utilized and can be divided into internal and external efficiency. Improving productivity does not necessarily imply declining quality; on the contrary, quality improvements often lead to improved productivity. This is possible as waste and the repetition of tasks are reduced and as the knowledge of the needs and wants of the buyers increases.

The economic quality dimension implies for the buyer that the relationship has to be profitable. Without profitability, a termination of the relationship is very likely. Profitability means that the buyer can receive compensation at the next step in the activity chain for costs in the exchanges with the supplier. To the supplier the economic quality dimension means that the received price covers total costs, including both internal and external quality failure costs. Total costs that arise in a relationship can be considerably higher than the direct costs, which usually are easier to measure. Total costs also consist of indirect costs, psychological costs, and quality failure costs (Grönroos, 1990a).

Quality failure costs can be divided into four groups (Parasuraman *et al.*, 1991). *Internal quality failure costs* (alterations, inspections, storage, etc.) arise before the transfer to the buyer, when products have to be thrown away. *External quality failure costs* like repairs, guarantees, and complaints are costs arising when taking care of delivered products, which do not meet with the quality standards. *Inspection costs* arise in connection with the evaluation whether the products and processes meet with the specifications. The last type of quality failure costs is *preventive costs of introducing, implementing, and securing a quality system.* Correepondingly, the net price of the supplier for a product can be far below estimated profit because of unobserved extra expenses, costs. Some of the economic aspects of quality, like storage and inspections, are fairly easy to estimate and measure, and others, like possible preventive adjustments, are considerably more difficult to estimate.

Functional quality dimension

Parallel to economic goals, there are other quality goals. The technical solution can be observed and measured with specific technical requirements, like for example durability, precision, and ISO standards, and made explicit in contracts. The functional part of the product and its transfer is less tangible and can not easily be measured or estimated, at least not in quantitative terms. Functional issues are, however, equally important, if not even more important than technical ones. The functional quality dimension can be divided in two aspects, and consists of (1) how the individuals perceive the interactions and (2) how the transfer of the product is carried out. Functional quality thus consists of aspects of personal chemistry and the communication between the involved, if there is trust and commitment in the relationship, as well as how the deliveries are adjusted.

According to our studied buyers it is of utmost importance for the establishing firm to develop a so-called *capital of trust*. The capital of trust can, if properly managed, provide both financial returns and other kinds of returns for everyone involved. The establishing firm has to create and strengthen its trust with buyers, so that the buyer can trust it. It is not possible to any greater extent to urge on this process; it is a question of cumulatively developing trust on the personal level, normally a process lasting many years.

Honesty, mutuality, discretion, openness, ambition, realism, empathy, humbleness, seriousness, professional skill, pride, and communication skills – not necessarily in this order – were some of the crucial factors mentioned in the choice of supplier. It is important to have the courage to inform the buyer of unpleasant things like not being able to deliver on time and explain why. The buyer appreciates honesty like that from the suppliers, because it proves the right kind of attitude. If further enables the avoidance of many problems, costs, and delays, which otherwise tend to arise in connection with delays. It is often possible to somehow solve the problems through discussions and thereby no one has to lose time, money, materials, or even a buyer/supplier. In some cases the buyers actually terminate the supplier relationship if a delay occurs as delivery times are without exception to be kept. Other sanctions like a penalty fee can also sometimes result from delays.

A great deal of the success of a firm not only depends on resources under its direct control but largely on resources obtained through long-term relationships with suppliers. As one of the buyers expressed it 'We shall become the best buyer in the world, thereafter the best supplier in the world'. In other words, the firms have to be aware of their own strengths and weaknesses and have to have the will to improve and develop their business both toward the buyers and the suppliers.

Technical quality dimensions

As our study deals with establishing relationships from a technical service firm's point of view the fulfilment of technical specifications is very important, when the buyers evaluate the service quality. Unless the supplier can deliver a product that technically fulfils the requirement, future business is impossible and he or she can not stay in business in the long run. Technical standards are generally the first and the decisive criteria set by buyers for the suppliers to fulfil. An even quality level, which is reproducible on a large scale with only minor deviations, that is a high repetition accuracy, is the aim for both the supplier and the buyers. The costs for developing this even technical quality are crucial. If short-term thinking prevails in the buying firm, such high initial costs will deter the firm from developing such a technical service quality. Long-term thinking buyers are prerequisites for long-term thinking suppliers, because otherwise technical and financial plans do not motivate the choice and keeping of the supplier. Usually contracts stipulating projects are made that result in so-called project plans. In this way the firms safeguard themselves and are able to terminate the relationship if for example costs should increase unacceptably. Simultaneously the contracts facilitate the evaluation of realized projects.

The studied supplier says that quality implies fulfilling calculations and profit margins and simultaneously offering *value* for the buyer. This corresponds to both an internal and an external dimension regarding quality. For the supplier the follow-up of deliveries is a major problem. The documentation of made tests is done carefully and is by the buyers rated as one of the suppliers greatest competitive advantages.

CONCLUSIONS

It is obvious that economic considerations permeate the exchanges and the quality evaluation, at least in the long run. Buyers can experiment with new promising suppliers, but only to a certain extent, over a reasonable period of time – sooner or later the relationship enters a make-money phase. A termination of the relationship with the supplier does not always have to mean that the buyer finds the relationship a waste of time and money. On the contrary, the relationship can be seen as a stage in the development of a know-how-bank or slack (Oakland, 1989) that every firm has regarding the line of business, technology, and products. The buyer can in a later stage resume with the supplier if premises change and for example the technology of the supplier improves.

Service quality is by the buyers perceived as the fulfilment of technical specifications and around this there is the personal chemistry parallel to economic issues. Working social relations are a must; one cannot compensate this dimension with technology. Service quality must be considered from a holistic perspective consisting of technology, administration, security in deliveries, and a working information flow, etc. Security in deliveries is important because of high costs in a breakdown in the production process. Costs of storage and a feeling of insecurity are some obvious consequences in case of delays and other problems in the deliveries. A failing information flow can lead to a change of supplier, because the situation will become intolerable if the supplier doesn't give the right information, gives false information, or otherwise takes advantage of his position repeatedly.

Service quality is both competence and service, as patents alone do not guarantee success for a very long time – an appropriate balance between technology and market orientation is optimal. Irrespective of line of business the service firms who want to stay on top have to be market-oriented and complement hardware with buyer-adjusted software, that is concentrate on high quality in other aspects than the technical only. The result has to be high-qual–high-tech. Not even where technology seems to dominate can it by itself determine service quality perceived by buyers: it is the perception of all the interactions that counts, and in this, technology is only one part.

In our model describing service quality and relationships in industrial service organization, this is illustrated by dividing buyer perceived service quality into a technical, a functional, and an economic quality dimension. Good service quality is

Table 1. Management checklist for industrial service quality

Economic quality	Functional quality	Technical quality
Profitability	Mutuality	Technical specification
Productivity	Trust	R&D
Initial costs	Social relationships	Testing
Production costs	Communication	Production
Failure costs	Actors' characteristics	Adaptations
Inspection costs	Secure deliveries	Documentation
Storage costs	Adjusted deliveries	Equipment
Guarantee costs	Accessibility	Computer systems
Complaint costs		Administrative routines

formed when the supplier knows the buyers' needs and develops and adjusts the problem solution that it meets these needs. The importance of long-term relationships causes the suppliers and buyers to try to attain cooperation and to share the responsibility over the growth of processes and products (see Table 1).

In our study, buyer perceived service quality has been derived from three different quality dimensions, namely economic, functional, and technical quality. The economic quality dimension consists of different costs ranging from initial costs when establishing a new relationship, production costs when using the product in the production process, failure costs and inspection costs when the technical specifications are not met, storage costs for handling the products, to costs for guarantees and complaints. All these costs form the buyer's profitability for a specific product and a specific relationship. This study has shown that buyers embedded in an industrial network must be able to sell their product to buyers at a profit – this could be called a profit chain.

Functional quality explains how the individuals involved in the relationship perceive each other and how the product is transferred from the seller to the buyer. Mutuality, trust, communication, social relationships, and the actors' characteristics in terms of openness, empathy, professional skills, etc., are important criteria for buyers when they evaluate a seller and his performance. In other words, the buyer must have confidence in the seller. The second aspect with functional quality is the transfer of the product and here the buyers seem to emphasize secure deliveries and accessibility.

The technical quality is evaluated by analyzing if the products are produced in accordance with the technical specifications, how they are adapted to the buyer's needs, and the documentation of production. Furthermore, the seller's machinery, production facilities, cars, computer system, and administrative routines will influence how the buyers perceive the technical quality. Efficient production, implemented quality standards, clean facilities, buyer adapted computer systems, and administrative routines will increase the buyer's feelings of being important to the seller.

We have certified that different exchanges takes place in the interactions between the firms; there are exchanges of information, social contacts, and business. Through interacting the firms invest in relationships, which become long-term. These evolving long-term bonds influence the service quality perceived by the firms and must consequently be considered when studying the buyer evaluation of service quality. The bonds make up the context for the quality evaluation influencing the buyer and his or her evaluation, and to study only separate exchanges without including this context would result in a rather limited description.

The firms have goals for their relationships with the supplier expressed in technical, functional, and financial analyses, which are used when evaluating the service quality. In order to achieve a better problem solution there are goals concerning the technical requirements. Moreover, there are functional aspects of the service quality in the relationship based on honesty, trust and mutuality. The economic aspect is illustrated by one of the respondents when he used the phrase make-money phase as a base for a working relationship – concerns like productivity, efficiency, and effectiveness must always be taken into consideration, and they form a base for all kinds of cooperation and business.

The goals in the service quality dimensions and the outcomes are in the model to be seen as an evaluation of the interactions and bonds taking place in an atmosphere consisting of mutuality, trust, and norms. The service quality perceptions of the firms surround their relationship, and these perceptions control and direct the relationship. The quality perceptions emanate from the goals with the relationship and the outcomes of the exchanges. It is obviously difficult to generalize buyer perceived service quality as it is embedded in a specific context. The concept of service quality is dynamic and alters as the firms get to know each other and as the bonds evolve. In this article we have stressed the economic quality dimension, because earlier studies have not elaborated this issue to any larger extent.

REFERENCES

Axelsson, B. and Häkansson, H. (1989) *Inkop for konkurrenskraft (Purchasing for Competitiveness)*. Lund: Faber.

Axelsson, B. and Laage Hellman, J. (1991) *Inkop en ledningsfraga (Purchasing: A Management Issue)*. Stockholm: Mekanforbundets Forlag.

Brown, S. V., Gummesson, E., Edwardsson, B. and Gustafsson, B.O.(eds) (1991) *Quality in Service: Multidisciplinary and Multinational Perspectives*. Massachusetts: Lexington Books.

Buzell, R. D. and Gale, B. T. (1987) *The PIMS Principles: Linking Principles to Performance*. New York: The Free Press.

Cook, K. S. and Emerson, R. M. (1984) 'Exchange networks and the Analysis of Complex Organizations'. In *Research in the Sociology of Organizations*, Vol. 3. Greenwich, Connecticut: JAI Press, 1–30.

Dubois, A. (1992) '*Changing Purchasing Behavior in a Long Time Perspective*'. Paper presented at the Second Nordic Workshop on Interorganizational Research in Yxtaholm, Sweden, August 21–23.

Grönroos, C. (1983) 'Innovative Marketing Strategies and Organization Structures for Service Firms'. In *Emerging Perspectives on Service Marketing* (L. L. Berry, G. L. Shostack and G. D. Upah, Eds). Chicago: American Marketing Association, p. 21.

Grönroos, C. (1990a) '*Facing the Challenge of Service Competition. Costs of Bad Service*'. Unpublished working paper. Swedish School of Economics and Business Administration, Hesingfors, Finland.

Grönroos, C. (1990b) *Service Management and Marketing: Managing the Moments of Truth in Service Competition*. Massachusetts: Lexington Books.

Hammarkvist, K. O., Häkansson, H. and Mattsson, L. (1982) *Marknadsforing for knokurrenskraft (Marketing for Competitiveness)*. Malmo: Liber.

Hedaa, L. (1992) '*Under Norms of Long Lasting Supplier Buyer Relationships: How Are New Relationships Established*'. Working paper No. 4, Copenhagen Business School, Copenhagen, Denmark.

Holmlund, M. and Kock, S. (1992) '*Quality Based Service as an Establishing Strategy in Business Networks*. Working paper No. 249. Swedish School of Economics and Business Administration. Helsingfors, Finland.

Häkansson, H. and Johanson, J. (1992) 'A Model of Industrial Networks'. In *Industrial Networks: A New View of Reality*. London: Routledge, pp. 28–34.

Kock, S. (1992) '*A Strategic Process for Managing Relationships in Business Networks*'. Working paper No. 240. Swedish School of Economics and Business Administration. Helsingfors, Finland.

Kock, S. (1991) '*A Strategic Process for Gaining External Resources Through Long Lasting Relationships: Examples from Two Finnish and Two Swedish Industrial Firms*'. Economy and Society No. 47, Swedish School of Economics and Business Administration. Helingsfors, Finland.

March, J. G. (1981) 'Decision Making Perspective: Decisions in Organizations and Theories of Choice'. In *Perspective on Organization Design and Behavior*. (A. H. Van de Ven and W. I. Joyce, Eds). New York: John Wiley.

March, J. G. (1988) *Decisions and Organizations*. Cornwall: Blackwell.

Oakland, J. S. (1989) *Total Quality and Management*. Wiltshire: Redwood Press.

Parasuraman, A., Zeithaml, V. A. and Berry, L. L. (1985) 'A conceptual Model of Service Quality and Its Implications for Future Research'. *Journal of Marketing* 47 (Fall): 41–50.

Parasuraman, A., Berry, L. L. and Zeithaml, V. A. (1991) 'Understanding Buyer Expectations of Service'. *Sloan Management Review* (Spring): 34–48.

Yamagashi, T., Gillmore, M. R. and Cook, K. S. (1988) 'Network Connections and the Distribution of Power in Exchange Networks'. *American Journal of Sociology* **93**: 835–851.

Section IV

Service Management

In this section we consider some of the broader issues facing service managers. The first article by Christian Grönroos (1994) charts the development of management thought from its domination by the scientific management principles proposed by Taylor. Grönroos illustrates how the increasing realisation by service firms of the shortcomings of the traditional approaches to management has led to todays more holistic approach to management theory. He suggests that the service management perspective has had an impact beyond the scope of specific service industries, bringing together a variety of other disciplines with a common perspective. The recognition of the value of services as a source of competitive advantage by adding value to the core product extends the scope of service management and has had an important impact on how organisations view the marketing function.

By way of contrast, the second article by Silvestro, Fizgerald, Johnston and Voss (1992) considers the provision of a service management tool through the development of a classification scheme based on service processes. The value of classification schemes to managers has been the subject of some debate. In 1976 Hunt suggested several criteria for determining the strength of a classification approach including the mutual exclusiveness of the categories and their collective exhaustiveness. However, no classification scheme is ever perfect; the purpose of service classification is merely to assist in understanding the service product. As Wright (1995) points out, it is obvious from discussing the characteristics of services that there is great variation between services and that if managers are to respond to them effectively, some form of classification or categorisation is necessary. In the Silvestro article, the authors start by reviewing previous classifications and propose three 'archetypes', professional services, mass services and service shops. They suggest that each gives rise to different management concerns and that strategy, control and performance measurement differ between the three types. This represents additional evidence for non-standard, non-generic management approach to services.

The final two articles in this section consider specific strategic management issues: sustainable competitive advantage and entry mode into new markets. Bharadwaj, Varadarajan and Fahy (1993) review the conditions for sustainable competitive advantage and considers the issues raised with regard to service industries. Taking Porter's (1985) two main generic strategies, the authors consider the management implications of achieving competitive cost advantage and differentiation advantage. These are then discussed in the light of specific features of service organisations which affect the achievement of competitive advantage. Erramilli and Rao (1993), on the other hand, consider the impact of the characteristics of services on organisations choosing an entry mode into new markets. Previous discussions of entry mode have concentrated entirely on manufactured goods and have employed transaction cost analysis (TCA) to explain the choice between wholly owned operations, joint ventures and contractual agreements. This paper points to problems with the TCA framework in general before considering the characteristics of service firms which demand an extension of the model. Focusing on asset specificity as a determinant of service firms' propensity to establish shared-control entry modes, the paper examines the factors that affect service firms' choices in this context.

CONTENTS

18

From Scientific Management to Service Management: A Management Perspective for the Age of Service Competition

Christian Grönroos

INTRODUCTION

Service management is not a well-delineated concept. It is however, used more and more by academics as well as by practitioners. Conferences on service management are arranged, books with the phrase service management as part of the title are published and academic courses called service management are developed. Service management is inevitably establishing itself as a recognized field. However, it is understandable that an outside observer easily feels confused when confronted with the concept. The purpose of this article is to discuss how service management emerged, what it is, and what contributions it offers to management research and practice.

Today, service management is more a perspective than one discipline or one coherent area of its own. It is a perspective that gives firms that face service competition, i.e. that have to understand and manage service elements in their customer relationships in order to achieve a sustainable competitive advantage, more or less similar guidelines to the development of such separate areas as management, marketing, operations, organizational theory and human resources management and TQM. This perspective is described very well be the observation by Schneider and Rentch (1987) that firms that apply service management principals consider 'service as *the* organizational imperative'.

The service management perspective includes some more or less general shifts in the focus of management (Grönroos, 1990a, p. 118):

1. From the product-based utility to total utility in the customer relationship.
2. From short-term transactions to long-term relationships.
3. From core product (goods or services) quality or the mere technical quality of

Reprinted with permission from *International Journal of Service Industry Management*, Vol. 5, No. 1, pp. 5–20
© 1994 MCB University Press

the outcome to total customer-perceived quality in enduring customer relationships.

4. From production of the technical quality of products (goods or services) as the key process in the organization to developing and managing total utility and total quality as the key process.

In addition to this, a number of principles of service management that seem to be fairly commonly accepted are discussed in the lead article of the first volume of the *Journal of Services Industry Management* from 1990 (Grönroos, 1990c).

FACETS OF SERVICE MANAGEMENT

The service management perspective has emerged within several disciplines with a number of somewhat different and yet interrelated angles. One can say that major impacts on this perspective come from at least six different areas: marketing, operations management, organizational theory and human resources management, management, and service quality management, and finally as a sixth area business executives and consultants. The approach by executives and consultants was originally heavily influenced by the Scandinavian experience in turning around and managing service firms, particularly by SAS Scandinavian Airlines System (see Albrecht and Zemke, 1985; Carlzon, 1987). In addition to these areas, there are scattered contributions from other disciplines as well (e.g. economics).

As service management has emerged from so many points of view and not yet merged into one management theory, there is no definition of it that would have been commonly accepted. In fact, most authors seem to avoid in-depth discussion of the definition issue. However, Grönroos (1990a; see also Grönroos, 1988) offers a fairly exhaustive definition of service management:

Service management is:

(1) To understand the utility customers receive by consuming or using the offerings of the organization and how services alone or together with physical goods or other kinds of tangibles contribute to this utility, that is, to understand how total quality is perceived in customer relationships, and how it changes over time;

(2) To understand how the organization (personnel, technology and physical resources, systems and customers) will be able to produce and deliver this utility or quality;

(3) To understand how the organization should be developed and managed so that the intended utility or quality is achieved; and

(4) To make the organization function so that this utility or quality is achieved and the objectives or the parties involved (the organization, the customers, other parties, the society, etc.) are met (Grönroos, 1990a, p. 117).

Albrecht (1988) presents a shorter definition. Some of the information content of the above mentioned definition is of course lost, but it clearly demonstrates some to the key facets of service management:

Service management is a total organizational approach that makes quality of service, as perceived by the customer, the number one driving force for the operations of the business (p. 20).

The shift of focus and the definitions presented above demonstrate the major meaning and significance of service management. Five key facets of the service management perspective can be recognized, viz., overall management perspective, customer focus, holistic approach, quality focus, and internal development and reinforcement:

1. It is an *overall management perspective* which should guide decisions in all areas of management (not only provide management principles for a separate function such as customer service);
2. It is *customer driven* or market driven (not driven by internal efficiency criteria);
3. It is a *holistic perspective* which emphasizes the importance of intraorganizational, cross-functional collaboration (not specialization and the division of labour);
4. Managing *quality is an integral part* of service management (not a separate issue); and
5. *Internal development* of the personnel and reinforcement of its commitment to company goals and strategies and strategic prerequisites for success (not only administrative tasks).

In the major part of this article these five facets of service management will be discussed. However, today the mainstream management focus is still on economies of scale and a striving to decrease the cost of production and of administering the business, in order to minimize the unit cost of the products, accompanied by aggressive traditional marketing and sales campaigns and continuous product development efforts. While there is no contradiction between service management and product development efforts, the overemphasis on cost reduction and economies of scale as well as on traditional marketing activities is challenged as obsolete and even potentially dangerous as general management principles.

FROM 'SCIENTIFIC MANAGEMENT' TO SERVICE MANAGEMENT

The mainstream management principles of today are based on a perspective that emerged during the industrial revolution. They can be traced back to Adam Smith's analysis of the pin factory. In *The Wealth of Nations* (1950/1776) Smith advocated that one should pursue specialization and the division of labour. Later in *Scientific Management* (Taylor, 1947) principles along the same lines were formulated, although Taylor did take into account the well-being of the workforce. Mass production and economies of scale were considered fundamental parts of this management philosophy.

Long-lasting and well-established structures are not easily changed from within. Environmental changes may put enough pressure on the establishment so that marginal corrections of problems are made, but the structure itself lasts. This is what seems to have happened with today's management principles based on the scientific management perspective. The educational level and standard of living of the workforce has increased tremendously and made people much more sophisticated and demanding as employees and consumers; the magnitude of competition has increased and its nature changed which, for example, has made firms much more vulnerable to international competition and has made the competitive edge provided by excellent core products much less effective; the exploding development of information technology has made customers and competitors much more aware of available options and the nature of the new technology makes it possible to achieve results totally different from mass production and standardization which have been the traditional gains of new technology. In spite of all these trends, the grip of the traditional management principles has remained steady.

However, all these trends make old management principles less appropriate and effective. The work environment becomes less encouraging for the employees, technology is not used to create as much job satisfaction for employees and value for customers as possible, enduring customer relationships are not developed and competitive advantages are not achieved. Service firms were among the first to observe the problems created by the old management structure. An interest in studying service-specific issues emerged first among marketing researchers.[1] The development of new models, concepts and tools based on the characteristics of services and of their production and delivery processes started during the 1970s. Following a few earlier doctoral dissertations and articles, the doctoral dissertations by Judd (1965), Johnson (1969) and George (1972) offered a thorough description of the nature of services and of specific problems in services marketing. Wilson's (1972) and Rathmell's (1974) books on professional services and the service sector in general respectively were the first ones exploring marketing problems in service firms. Even if research into services took off at approximately the same time in North America (resulting in, for example, two widely used texts and readings by Lovelock from 1984 and 1988), much of the dominance of services marketing progress shifted to Europe (e.g. Bateson, 1989 in English; Grönroos, 1979 and Gummesson, 1977 in Swedish; Langeard and Eiglier, 1987 in French; Lehtinen, 1983 in Finnish; and in addition, a number of books published in, at least, Austria, Belgium, Denmark, Germany, Italy, The Netherlands, Norway and Spain (see Grönroos, 1990a)).

Among other things, the nature of the customer relationships and of operations and the production and delivery processes were considered different for services by the pioneering researchers, and the quality of services was found to be formed and perceived in such a way that traditional models from manufacturing did not apply. However, researchers interested in services did not predominantly attempt to change old management models and concepts in a marginal fashion in order to fit services. This is especially true for the so-called Nordic School of services with its roots in the mid-1970s (e.g. Grönroos and Gummesson, 1985), where for example, marketing was viewed as an area that cannot be separated from overall management. Instead a totally new approach to the problem of how to manage various aspects of service organizations was taken. This was the beginning of what later, by Richard Normann (1982/1984), was labelled 'service management'.[2]

THE OVERALL MANAGEMENT PERSPECTIVE

Normann (1982/1984) and Grönroos (1982) have shown how a traditional management focus overemphasizing cost reduction efforts and scale economies may become a management trap for service firms and lead to a vicious circle where the quality of the service is damaged, internal workforce environment deteriorates, customer relationships suffer, and eventually profitability problems occur. Growing marketing and sales budgets may slow down the negative trend for some time, but as this normally only means increased persuasion and overpromising, in the long run it only leads to unsatisfied and defecting customers. In the tradition of Adam Smith and scientific management, the traditional management principles are largely based on specialization and the division of labour. From this has frequently followed a short-term, manipulative and transaction-oriented view of market relationships and an adversary relationship between functions within the firm and between the firm and its external partners, such as customer, suppliers and middlemen. Service management is based on a different assumption of how the intraorganizational and interorganizational relationships should be viewed and developed. Teamwork, interfunctional collaboration and interorganizational partnership, and a long-term perspective are, generally speaking, inherent values in service management.

Originally, Normann and Grönroos discussed service firms only, but as it has gradually become evident that services are growing in importance for manufacturers as will, the arguments for a management trap and vicious circles become more generally valid. Grönroos' definition of service management and the notion of service competition clearly imply that not only service firms but all types of organizations may be included.

Service management as an overall management perspective gives high priority to the external efficiency, economies of scale and cost reduction. This combines the overall management perspective of service management with its customer-driven and quality-oriented facets, employee-oriented concerns and its long-term perspective.

CUSTOMER ORIENTATION

As a general lesson from service management, Heskett (1986 and 1987) argues for a focus on 'market economies' instead of emphasizing scale economies too much. By this he means that a competitive edge and profitability are accomplished by a closer market orientation rather than by a focus on large-scale production of more or less standardized products in order to keep unit production costs down. More recently, Sasser and Reichheld have stressed this point in their studies of the economic effects of retaining customers as compared to cost reduction efforts without diminishing customer defection rates (Reichheld, 1993; Reichheld and Sasser, 1990). Their studies show that the decrease of the defection rate by a comparatively small percentage has an impact on profits that would be difficult to achieve by cost reduction efforts. The figures differ greatly from industry to industry but the trend is the same. Additional studies will most probably support these findings. For services businesses where the service outcome and the production and delivery processes can be highly standardized, economies of scale based on a production-line approach as suggested by Levitt (1972) may be possible. McDonald's would be an example of such a case, but as Schlesinger and Heskett (1991) more recently have argued, when facing more pressure from new competitors even firms like McDonald's may have less support from technology-driven standardization of the production and delivery of their services. This does not, of course, mean that economies of scale and cost reduction efforts would be a thing of the past; on the contrary. It means, however, that the major focus cannot be on such efforts any more. 'Market economies' and a genuine interest in the customer become imperative.

Customer loyalty is the cornerstone of successful service management (Heskett *et al.*, 1991). However, a word of warning is needed here. Even if customer retention is important, the firm should strive to keep the right customers from defecting. The recently emerging interest in what we in another context (Grönroos, 1993b) have labelled 'customer relationship economics', has shown that 'customer relationship profitability', to use an expression coined by Storbacka (1993), is not only a function of a stable customer base. As he points out, the firm must not retain the wrong customers, i.e. customers that are not and cannot be expected to become profitable (Storbacka, 1993; see also Barnes and Cumby, 1993). Doing a thorough customer relationship profitability analysis is equally important as efforts directed towards creating a loyal customer base and retaining customers.

Voices have been raised that service management overemphasizes the importance of customer satisfaction and efforts to improve customer perceived quality. Productivity and profitablilty issues may suffer from this alleged myopic view of the importance of service quality and customer satisfaction (Storbacka, 1993). If the service management perspective is applied so that the firm loses track of the importance of productivity and profitability, this criticism is of course valid. In this sense, the critical voices are important, because in the service management literature, productivity and profitability are far too often given only marginal attention. And without proper segmentation and a customer relationship profitability analysis done for each segment of customers, mistakes may easily be made. Large groups of unprofitable customer relationships may easily be tolerated and not even recognized, if total profitability is good enough. This does not, however, decrease the importance of service management in today's competitive situation. Any model or concept can be implemented in a less than satisfactory way.

Research into service management has shown that, contrary to common belief, quality improvement and productivity gains are not necessarily mutually exclusive (e.g. Haywood and Pickworth, 1988). This view is partly due to the fact that most frequently productivity is measured in an unsophisticated way (Steedle, 1988). The influence of scientific management can be seen here as well. Productivity is treated as an internal efficiency issue only, where the impact on perceived quality and customer satisfaction is neglected. Productivity measurement models have also always been developed within a manufacturing context, and there the customer's impact on operations and on quality formation has been ignored. Still, today, how to measure productivity in a service organization is more or less an unsolved problem. Manufacturing models, which inevitably become unsophisticated in service contexts, give wrong signals to management. They are internally oriented, they are short term in nature, they do not give information about long-term productivity, and they seldom measure the productivity of the whole operation. As noted by Pickworth (1987), who uses a restaurant example,

> . . . the issue is whether food-service managers should think of their outputs *as meals produced or customers satisfied*. If customer is the measure, *a quality dimension* is also needed in productivity measurement (p. 43, emphasis added).

The same efforts may, correctly implemented, improve service quality and at the same time have a favourable impact on productivity (e.g. Cowell, 1984). For example, training employees makes them more knowledgeable of the services and the production and delivery processes, and, therefore, they make fewer mistakes and can answer questions asked by customers more quickly. The customer gets faster service and more accurate information. A new technology may remove bottlenecks in operations and speed up the service production and delivery process, a fact that the customers perceive as improved quality.

As far as profitability is concerned, the slowly growing number or studies of customer relationship economics demonstrate, as has been noted previously, that customer retention has a positive effect on profitability. Customer retention again is among other things depending on how well the firm can provide its customers with services. Of course, the core product and price issues are important here, too.

CUSTOMER PERCEIVED QUALITY ORIENTATION

Quality is another area where research into the various areas of service management has had a decisive impact. As noted by Gummesson (1993a), quality has been a black box in management and marketing theories. And in operations and production management quality has been treated as a production problem from an internal efficiency point of view. Especially, research into the marketing of services (e.g. Grönroos, 1982, 1984, 1993a; Gummesson, 1993; Parasuraman *et al.*, 1985) has demonstrated the need for including quality management as an integral part of service management theory.[3] The perceived service quality model (Grönroos 1982, 1993a), the gap analysis model (Parasuraman *et al.*, 1985), the SERVQUAL instrument (Parasuraman *et al.*, 1986, 1994), the Meyer-Mattmuller model (Meyer and Mattmuller, 1987), Lindqvist's index (Lindqvist, 1988), and other quality management models and instruments (e.g. Anderson, 1992; Edvardsson and Gustavsson, 1988; Lemmink and Behara, 1992; Liljander and Strandvik, 1993, and 1994; Stauss, 1993) are examples of what has been developed within the marketing-oriented approach to services. In service operations research quality has been studied as well (cf. Haywood-Farmer and Stuart, 1988; Johnston, 1987).[4] The literature on services by consultants also includes service quality books (e.g. Davidow and Uttal, 1989).

The customer focus of the research into services has had a decisive impact on the general approach to quality management. Service researchers very strongly put forward the view that it is the customer who decides what quality is and that it is customer perceived quality that has to be studied. Subsequently, this view has been supported by, for example, the findings of the PIMS project (Buzzell and Gale, 1987) and by the total quality management (TQM) movement. Customer orientation is a central aspect of TQM programmes. Nevertheless, many such programmes seem to fail.[5] One reason for this may be the fact that marketing is often missing. As Kordupleski *et al.* (1993) observe,

> there is a considerable participation by quality control engineers, manufacturing people, operations managers, human resource people, and organizational behaviour experts. A group notable by its absence is the function closest to the customers – namely, marketing. . . . Why are marketing people not more involved in quality improvement? (p. 83).

Here is a big difference between TQM and service management. TQM has been developed by non-marketing people who only recently have observed that customers are important to the success of the business. The customer-perceived quality focus and quality management models inherent in service management have been developed by marketing and operations as part of the interface between those two areas. Marketing and quality are seen as two sides of the same coin. Hence, the contact with marketing is more natural in service management than in TQM.

LONG-TERM PERSPECTIVE

The long-term perspective inherent in service management has had an important impact on marketing. Services marketing research has demonstrated the importance of long-term relationships instead of short-term deals and campaigns (cf. Grönroos, 1982 and Gummesson, 1987). The emerging interest in customer relationship economics (Storbacka, 1993) and recently published studies of the economic impact of customer retention (Reichheld and Sasser, 1990) support this view. Relationship marketing (cf. Christopher *et al.*, 1991; Grönroos, 1994 and Gummesson, 1993b; see also Berry, 1983) is a new approach to marketing which is quickly growing in importance.

The long-term orientation is clearly in line with current trends in business (cf. Kotler, 1992). Partnerships and networks as will as strategic alliances are formed in international business and in many industries are becoming increasingly important on domestic markets as well. As Frederick Webster (1992) concludes in an analysis of current trends in business,

> there has been a shift from a transaction to a relationship focus (p. 14) . . . and . . . from an academic or theoretical perspective, the relatively narrow conceptualization of marketing as a profit-maximization problem, focused on market transactions, seems increasingly out of touch with an emphasis on long-term customer relationships and the formation and management of strategic alliances. . . . The focus shifts from products and firms as units of analysis to people, organizations, and the social processes that bind actors together in ongoing relationships (p. 10).

In service management, marketing efforts are often considered investments in customers more than marketing expenses. This view is nothing entirely new in marketing. In the network approach to industrial marketing the concepts of market and marketing investments have been introduced (Johanson and Mattsson, 1985). More recently, Slywotzky and Shapiro (1993) also argue for a new attitude towards marketing, where marketing is treated as investments instead of short-term expenses.

> In 1992, US companies spent more than \$700 billion on activities such as selling, advertising, and sales promotion. For many companies, sales and marketing expenditures represent 15% to 20% of each revenue dollar. From that same dollar, about 4% to 10% is devoted to capital budgeting projects. While capital budgeting expenditures are carefully examined and analysed – and treated as investments – the much larger marketing piece is viewed as an annual expense (p. 98).

HOLISTIC APPROACH TO MANAGEMENT

Service management's holistic approach to management has had several effects. In marketing it has clearly demonstrated the need for expanding the notion of who the marketers in a firm are. Gummesson (1991) has introduced the breakthrough concept 'part-time marketers' for the employees outside a traditional marketing department, who normally are not trained as marketers or even appointed as marketers, but who nevertheless take care of customer contacts and thus make an impact on the future purchasing behaviour of the firm's customers. He emphasizes the importance of the part-time marketers by stating that:

> marketing and sales departments (the full-time marketers) are not able to handle more than a limited portion of the marketing *as its staff cannot be at the right place at the right time with the right customer contacts* (p. 72).

It has, thus, been concluded that everyone is a marketer, one way or the other (Grönroos, 1982 and Gummesson, 1990; see also Webster, 1988).

Even more important is the influence that the holistic view of the service management perspective has had as a means of crossing traditional business functions and corresponding academic disciplines. In service marketing research the importance of operations as part of marketing has been observed. The concept 'interactive marketing function' (Grönroos, 1982) has been developed to point out the marketing impact of the service production and delivery process. Langeard and Eiglier (1987) introduced the *servuction* concept which treats service operations in the context of marketing. In his services marketing system, Lovelock (1988) has integrated marketing, operations and human resources management. In operations a similar trend can be observed. The service management perspective has made researchers within the area of production and operations interested in the impact of the operations systems on customers (e.g. Bowen *et al.*, 1990; Chase, 1978, 1991; Collier, 1987; Voss *et al.*, 1985). The textbook on service operations by Sasser *et al.* (1978) was a first major step in this direction, which at Harvard Business School led to an experiment with an academic course combining service operations and services marketing. However, apparently this experiment was not allowed to last very long.

In organizational theory and human resources management a similar trend can be seen. The service management perspective has, for example, created such concepts as the service management system (Normann, 1982) incorporating a marketing and operations view in an organizational theory context, and empowerment (Bowen and Lawler, 1992) which relates human resources management to marketing. Other contributions from this field include publications by Schneider (1980) and Mills (1986).[6]

FOCUS ON INTERNAL DEVELOPMENT

Service management also has an internal focus where the development of the personnel and the creation of employee commitment to the goals and strategies of the firms are key issues. In service marketing research the need for internal marketing has been observed (Grönroos 1982; see also, for example, Barnes, 1989; Berry, 1981; George, 1984, 1990). In 1982 Grönroos formulated the internal marketing concept, according to which the internal market of employees is best motivated for service mindedness and customer-oriented performance by an active, marketing-like approach, where a variety of activities are used internally in an active, marketing-like and co-ordinated way.

Without active and continuous internal marketing efforts the interactive marketing impact on customers will deteriorate, service quality will suffer and customers will start to defect with negative effects on profitability as a result. In this sense internal marketing is a prerequisite for successful external marketing. Internal marketing includes both an attitude management aspect and a communications management aspect (Grönroos, 1990a). In organizational theory and human resources management the same issues have been addressed and for example the above mentioned concept of empowerment has emerged as an element of internal marketing. Generally speaking, internal marketing and HRM represent an interface between marketing and organizational theory that has been emphasized by the service management perspective (cf. Grönroos, 1990b).

Internal marketing is not, of course, anything entirely new in a firm. Internal programmes to make employees committed to various goals have always existed. What is new is the active, market-oriented approach as suggested by the internal marketing concept. Some marketing activities from traditional external marketing may be used together with training and other traditional personnel development activities. At best, internal marketing offers an umbrella for all these and other activities which make the development of personnel a strategic issue.[7]

IN CONCLUSION: WHAT IS SERVICE MANAGEMENT?

As the discussion of service management and its five key facets above demonstrates, service management is not a well-defined area or a single theory of management. Rather it is a management perspective that fits today's competitive situation. Cost reductions and core product quality are still important to success, but to achieve customer satisfaction and a competitive advantage through differentiation of the market offer (cf. Quinn *et al.*, 1990) more value has to be added to the core product. This is done through a variety of services and by turning activities such as deliveries, technical service, claims handling, telephone exchange, invoicing, etc. into customer-oriented, value-adding services.

The service management perspective has had a novel impact on cross-disciplinary research. Volumes including research from various fields are published (Swartz *et al.*, 1992, 1993). International conferences have been arranged, mostly in Europe, on service management (*Proceedings* from the 1st and 2nd International Research Seminars in Service Management 1990 and 1992) and on service quality management (e.g. Kunst and Lemmink, 1992; Brown *et al.*, 1991; Scheuing *et al.*, 1992),[8] where researchers representing marketing, operations, organizational theory, psychology, finance, economics and other disciplines together discuss various aspects of management from a service perspective. In these areas research has taken new directions guided by this common perspective.

The term service management was introduced in Swedish in 1982 and in English in 1984. Since then it has slowly become a term used to indicate a common perspective. But this perspective started to evolve long before this term came into use within disciplines such as marketing, organizational theory and human resources management, and operations. Various disciplines have brought contributions of their own to service management, e.g. service competition, the long-term relationship marketing notion, interactive and internal marketing, the part-time marketer concept and the perceived service quality model (marketing), the service management system, the high-contact/low-contact personnel distinction, empowerment and the notion of people as the major resource of a firm (organizational theory and human resources management), the customer-oriented and outward looking approach to operations, and the front-office/back-office notion (operations management), and service guarantees, the market economics focus and customer retention analysis (management), to mention just a few. However, true cross-disciplinary research is still rare. In the future such research projects will broaden and deepen the service management perspective even more.

NOTES

1. Berry and Parasuraman provide an interesting analysis of the development of services marketing thought in their article 'Building a New Academic Field—The Case of Services Marketing' (Berry and Parasuraman, 1993). See also the article on the evolution of the English-language services marketing literature by Fisk *et al.* (1993).
2. Subsequently, among other things, building on the notion that customer participation in the production and delivery process is a central characteristic of services and service management, Normann has developed this further into an interactive strategy model for any type of business, according to which successful firms not only create value but reinvent it together with their customers (see Normann and Ramirez, 1993).
3. There have been earlier attempts to treat quality in a more explicit way in the microeconomic and marketing literature. In the 1950s researchers such as Abbott (1955), who wanted to add more realism to microeconomic price theory, included quality in their models. Abbott, for example, had an astonishingly modern view of quality: 'The term 'quality' will be used . . . in its broadest sense, to include all qualitative elements in the competitive exchange process – materials, design, service provided, location, and so forth' (p. 4). These models influenced parameter theory (Mickwitz, 1959), a marketing theory which was somewhat similar to but much more developed than the marketing mix approach which since the 1960s has dominated marketing. In this theory quality was an integral element. With parameter theory, quality as anything other than a black box disappeared from the literature.
4. Specific contributions from the area of operations management are not discussed in detail here, as the role of that area in service management is the topic of Robert Johnston's article 'Operations: From Factory to Service Management' (1994).
5. Compare, for example, the disappointing findings in two studies by the consulting firms A. T. Kearney and Arthur D. Little (*The Economist*, 1992). In a study of more than 100 firms in the UK, 80% reported that no significant impact could be observed as a result of TQM, and in a study of 500 US firms, almost two-thirds said that they had achieved no competitive gains.
6. The integration of marketing and operations management with human resources management is further elaborated on in Benjamin Schneider's article 'HRM – A Service Perspective: Towards a Customer-focused HRM' (1994).
7. However, even this umbrella notion of internal marketing is not entirely new. Major changes in management perspectives always require extensive internal attention. It is interesting to notice that Frederick Taylor in his testimony about scientific management before the American congress in 1912 explicitly states that '. . . in its essence, scientific management involves a complete *mental revolution* on the part of the working men engaged in any particular establishment or industry. . . . And it involves the equally

complete mental revolution on the part of those on the management's side. . . . And without this complete mental revolution on both sides scientific management does not exist.' (Taylor, 1947, testimony part, p. 27; emphasis added). Taylor stressed the importance of this internal focus, which, however, seems to have been neglected by his followers. Service management, equally, requires such a mental revolution or, to use a modern metaphor, cultural change. The similarity between Taylor's mental revolution and the attitude management aspect of internal marketing is obvious.

8. Two international service management conferences were arranged in France in 1990 and 1992 by IAE at the University-d'Aix-Marseille. In service quality management three QUIS (Quality in Services) conferences initiated by the Service Research Center at the University of Karlstad have so far been arranged bi-annually since 1988, two in Sweden by the Service Research Center and one in the US by St John's University, and furthermore three international workshops devoted to quality management in services co-sponsored by the European Institute for Advanced Studies in Management have been arranged annually since 1991, in Brussels, Maastricht and Helsinki respectively.

REFERENCES

Abbott, L. (1955) *Quality and Competition.* New York, NY: Columbia University Press.

Albrecht, K. (1988) *At America's Service.* Homewood, IL: Dow Jones-Irwin.

Albrecht, K. and Zemke, R. (1985) *Service America!.* Homewood, IL: Dow Jones-Irwin.

Andersson, T. D. (1992) 'Another Model of Service Quality: A Model of Causes and Effects of Service Quality tested on a Case within the Restaurant Industry. In *Quality Management in Services* (P. Kunst, and J. Lemmink, Eds). Assen, Maastricht, The Netherlands: Van Gorcum, pp. 41–58.

Barnes, J. G. (1989) 'The Role of Internal Marketing: If the Staff Won't Buy It, Why Should the Customer?' *Irish Marketing Review* 4(No. 2): 11–21.

Barnes, J. G. and Cumby, J. A. (1993) 'The Cost of Quality in Service-Oriented Companies: Making Better Customer Service Decisions Through Improved Cost Information'. Research Paper, *ASB Conference 1993.* University of New Brunswick, Canada.

Bateson, J. (1989) *Managing Services Marketing: Text and Readings.* Hinsdale, IL: Dryden Press.

Berry, L. L. (1981) 'The Employee as Customer'. *Journal of Retail Banking* 3(No. 1): 33–40.

Berry, L. L. (1983) 'Relationship Marketing'. In *Emerging Perspectives of Services Marketing* (L. L. Berry, G. L. Shostack and G. D. Upah, Eds). Chicago, IL: American Marketing Association, pp. 25–28.

Berry, L. L. and Parasuraman, A. (1991) *Marketing Services Competing Through Quality.* Lexington, MA: Free Press/Lexington Books.

Berry, L. L. and Parasuraman, A. (1993) 'Building a New Academic Field – The Case of Services Marketing'. *Journal of Retailing* 69(Spring): 13–60.

Bowen, D. E., Chase, R. B. and Cummings, T. G. (Eds) (1990) *Service Management Effectiveness.* San Francisco, CA: Jossey-Bass.

Bowen, D. E. and Lawler III, E. E. (1992) 'The Empowerment of Service Workers: What, Why, How, and When', *Sloan Management Review* 33(No. 3): 31–39.

Brown, S. W., Gummesson, E., Edvardsson, B. and Gustavsson, B. O. (Eds) (1991) *Quality in Services. Multidisciplinary and Multinational Perspectives.* Lexington MA: Lexington Books.

Buzzell, R. D. and Gale, B. T. (1987) *The PIMS Principles. Linking Strategy to Performance.* New York, NY: Free Press.

Carlzon, J. (1987) *Moments of Truth.* Cambridge, MA: Ballinger.

Chase, R. B. (1978) 'Where Does the Customer Fit in a Service Operation'. *Harvard Business Review* 56(November–December): 137–142.

Chase, R. B. (1991) 'The Service Factory: A Future Vision'. *International Journal of Service Industry Management* 2(No. 3): 60–70.

Christopher, M., Payne, A. and Ballantyne, D. (1991) *Relationship Marketing Bringing Quality, Customer Service and Marketing Together.* Oxford: Butterworth-Heinemann.

Collier, D. A. (1987) *Service Management. The Automation of Services.* Englewood Cliffs, NJ: Prentice-Hall.

Cowell, D. (1984) *The Marketing of Services.* London: Heinemann.

Davidow, W. H and Uttal, B. (1989) *Total Customer Service. The Ultimate Service.* New York, NY: Harper & Row.

Edvardsson, B. and Gustavsson, B. O. (1988) *Quality in Services and Quality in Service Organizations—A Model of Quality Assessment.* Center for Service Research, Karlstad, Sweden.

Fisk, R. P., Brown, S. W. and Bitner, M. J. (1993) 'The Evolution of the Services Marketing Literature'. *Journal of Retailing* **69**(Spring): 61–103.

George, W. R. (1972) 'Marketing in the Service Industries'. Unpublished dissertation, University of Georgia.

George, W. R. (1984) 'Internal Marketing for Retailers. The Junior Executive Employee'. In *Developments in Marketing Science* (J. D. Lindqvist, Ed.). Academy of Marketing Science.

George, W. R. (1990) 'Internal Marketing and Organizational Behavior: A Partnership in Developing Customer-Conscious Employees at Every Level'. *Journal of Business Research* **20**(No. 1): 63–70.

Grönroos, C. (1979) *Marknadsföring av tjanster. En studie av marknadsfunktionen i tjänsteföretag,* (Marketing of services. A study of the marketing function of service firms), with English summary, Akademilitteratur/Marknadstekniskt Centrum, Stockholm, Sweden.

Grönroos, C. (1982) *Strategic Management and Marketing in the Service Sector,* Swedish School of Economics and Business Administration, Helsingfors, Finland, (published in 1983 in the US by Marketing Science Institute and in the UK by Studentlitteratur/ Chartwell-Bratt).

Grönroos, C. (1984) 'A Service Quality Model and Its Marketing Implications'. *European Journal of Marketing* **18**(No. 4): 36–44.

Grönroos, C. (1988) 'New Competition in the Service Economy: The Five Rules of Service'. *International Journal of Operations and Product Management* **8**(No. 3): 9–18.

Grönroos, C. (1990a) '*Service Management and Marketing. Managing the Moments of Truth in Service Competition.* Lexington, MA: Free Press/Lexington Books.

Grönroos, C. (1990b) 'Relationship Approach to the Marketing Function in Service Contexts: The Marketing and Organizational Behavior Interface'. *Journal of Business Research,* **20**(No. 1): 3–12.

Grönroos, C. (1990c) 'Service Management: A Management Focus for Service Competition'. *International Journal of Service Industry Management* **1**(No. 1): 6–14.

Grönroos, C. (1993a) 'Toward a Third Phase in Service Quality Research: Challenges and Future Directions'. In *Advances in Services Marketing and Management,* Vol. 2 (T. A. Swartz, D. E. Bowen and S. W. Brown, Eds). Greenwich, CT: JAI Press, pp. 49–64.

Grönroos, C. (1993b) 'From Marketing Mix to Relationship Marketing: Toward a Paradigm Shift in Marketing'. Working Paper, No. 263. Swedish School of Economics and Business Administration, Helsingfors, Finland.

Grönroos, C. (1994) 'Quo Vadis, Marketing? Toward a Relationship Marketing Paradigm'. *Journal of Marketing Management* **10**(No. 4): 347–360.

Grönroos, C. and Gummesson, E. (1985) 'The Nordic School of Service Marketing'. In *Service Marketing – Nordic School Perspectives* (C. Grönroos and E. Gummesson, Eds). Stockholm University, Sweden, pp. 6–11.

Gummesson, E. (1977) *Marknadsföring och inköp av konsulttjänster* (Marketing and purchasing of professional services), Akademilitteratur, Stockholm, Sweden.

Gummesson, E. (1987) 'The New Marketing – Developing Long-term Interactive Relationships'. *Long Range Planning* **20**(No. 4): 10–20.

Gummesson, E. (1991) 'Marketing-orientation Revisited: The Crucial Role of the Part-time Marketer'. *European Journal of Marketing* **25**(No. 2): 60–75.

Gummesson, E. (1993a), *Quality Management in Service Organizations.* New York, NY: ISQA International Service Quality Association.

Gummesson, E. (1993b) *Relationsmarknadsföring. Frön 4 P till 30 R* (Relationship marketing. From 4 P's to 30 R's), Stockholm University, Sweden.

Haywood, K. M. and Pickworth, J. R. (1988) 'Connecting Productivity with Quality through the Design of Service Delivery Systems'. In *Proceedings from an International Conference on Services*

Marketing (E. G. Thomas and S. R. Rao, Eds). Special Conference Series, Vol. V, Academy of Marketing Science/Cleveland State University, pp. 261–273.

Haywood-Farmer, K. M. and Stuart, F. I. (1988) 'Measuring the Quality of Professional Services'. In *The Management of Service Operations* (R. Johnston, Ed.). Kempston: IFS Publications, pp. 207–220.

Heskett, J. L. (1986) *Managing in the Service Economy.* Boston, MA: Harvard Business School Press.

Heskett, J. L. (1987) 'Lessons in the Service Sector'. *Harvard Business Review,* **65**(March–April): 118–126.

Heskett, J. L., Sasser, W. E. and Hart, C. W. L. (1991) *Service Breakthroughs: Changing the Rules of the Game.* New York, NY: Free Press.

Johanson, J. and Mattsson, L-G. (1985) 'Marketing Investments and Market Investments in Industrial Networks'. *International Journal of Research in Marketing* **2**(No. 3): 185–195.

Johnson, E. M. (1969) 'Are Goods and Services Different? An Exercise in Marketing Theory'. Unpublished dissertation, Washington University.

Johnston, R. (1987) 'A Framework for Developing a Quality Strategy in a Customer Process Processing Operation'. *International Journal of Quality & Reliability Management* **4**(No. 4): 35–44.

Johnston, R. (1994) 'Operations: From Factory to Service Management'. *International Journal of Service Industry Management* **5**(1).

Judd, R. C. (1965) *The Structure and Classification of the Service Market,* Dissertation, University Microfilms, Ann Arbor, MI.

Kordupleski, R. E., Rust, R. T. and Zahorik, A. J. (1993) 'Why Improving Quality Doesn't Improve Quality (Or Whatever Happened to Marketing?)'. *California Management Review,* **35**(No. 3): 82–95.

Kotler, P. (1992) 'It's Time for Total Marketing'. *Business Week ADVANCE Executive Brief.* Vol. 2.

Kunst, P. and Lemmink, J. (1992) *Quality Management in Services.* Assen, Maastricht/The Netherlands: Van Gorcum.

Langeard, E. and Eiglier, P. (1987) *Servuction. Le marketing des Services.* Paris: Wiley.

Lehtinen, J. (1983) *Asiakasohjautuva Palveluyritys* (Customer-oriented service firm), Espoo, Finland: Weilin + Göös.

Lemmink, J. and Behara, R. S. (1992) 'Q-Matrix: A Multi-Dimensional Approach to Using Service Quality Measurements'. In *Quality Management in Services* (P. Kunst and J. Lemmink, Eds). Assen, Maastricht, The Netherlands: Van Gorcum. pp. 79–88.

Levitt, T. (1972) 'Production-line Approach to Service'. *Harvard Business Review* **50**(September–October): 41–52.

Liljander, V. and Strandvik, T. (1993) 'Estimating Zones of Tolerance in Perceived Service Quality and Perceived Service Value'. *International Journal of Service Industry Management* **4**(No. 2): 6–28.

Liljander, V. and Strandvik, T. (1994) 'Different Comparison Standards as Determinants of Service Quality'. *Journal of Consumer Satisfaction, Dissatisfaction and Complaining Behaviour* **7** (in press).

Lindqvist, L. J. (1988) *Kundernas kvalitetsupplevelse i konsumtionsfasen* (The quality perception of customers in the consumption phase), Swedish School of Economics and Business Administration, Helsingfors, Finland.

Lovelock, C. H. (1984) *Services Marketing.* Englewood Cliffs, NJ: Prentice-Hall.

Lovelock, C. H. (1988) *Managing Services. Marketing, Operations, and Human Resources,* Englewood Cliffs, NJ: Prentice-Hall.

Meyer, A. and Mattmuller, R. (1987) 'Qualität von Dienstleistungen. Entwurf eines praxisorientierten Qualitätsmodells' (The quality of services. Outline of a practice-oriented quality model). *Marketing.* ZPF, Vol. 3.

Mickwitz, G. (1959) *Marketing and Competition.* Societas Scientarium Fennica, Helsingfors, Finland (available from University Microfilms, Ann Arbor, MI).

Mills, P. K. (1986) *Managing Service Industries: Organizational Practices in a Post-Industrial Economy.* Cambridge, MA: Ballinger.

Normann, R. (1982) *Service Management.* Liber, Malmö, Sweden (published in English in 1984 by John Wiley and Sons, New York, NY).

Normann, R. and Ramirez, R. (1993) 'From Value Chain to Value Constellation: Designing Interactive Strategy'. *Harvard Business Review* **71** (July–August): 65–77.

Parasuraman, A., Zeithaml, V. A. and Berry, L. L. (1985) 'A Conceptual Model of Service Quality and its Implications for Future Research'. *Journal of Marketing* **49**: 41–50.

Parasuraman, A., Zeithaml, V. A. and Berry, L. L. (1986) 'SERVQUAL: A Multiple-Item Scale for Measuring Customer Perceptions of Service Quality'. *Journal of Retailing* **64**(Spring): 12–40.

Parasuraman, A., Zeithaml, V. A. and Berry, L. L. (1994) 'Reassessment of Expectations as a Comparison Standard in Measuring Service Quality: Implications for Future Research'. *Journal of Marketing* **58**(Winter): 111–124.

Pickworth, J. R. (1987) 'Minding the Ps and Qs: Linking Quality and Productivity'. *The Cornell Hotel and Restaurant Administration Quarterly* **28**(No. 1) 40–47.

Proceedings from the 1st International Research Seminar in Service Management, Marketing, Operations, Human Resources Insights Into Services, IAE, Aix-en-Provence, France, June 1990.

Proceedings from the 2nd International Research Seminar in Service Management, Marketing, Operations, Human Resources Insights Into Services, IAE, Aix-en-Provence, France, June 1992.

Quinn, J. B., Dorley, T. L. and Paquette, P. C. (1990) 'Beyond Products Service-Based Strategy'. *Harvard Business Review* **68**(March–April): 58–67.

Rathmell, J. M. (1974) *Marketing in the Service Sector*. Cambridge, MA: Winthrop Publishers.

Reichheld, F. E. and Sasser, Jr W. E. (1990) 'Zero Defections: Quality Comes To Service'. *Harvard Business Review* **68**(September–October): 105–111.

Reichheld, F. E. (1993) 'Loyalty-Based Management'. *Harvard Business Review* **71**(March–April) 64–73.

Sasser, W. E., Olsen R. P. and Wyckoff, D. D. (1978) *Management of Service Operations*. Boston, MA: Allyn and Bacon.

Scheuing, E. E., Gummesson, E. and Little. C. H. (Eds) (1992) *Quality in Services* (*QUIS 2*) *Conference, Selected Papers*. New York, NY: St John's University.

Schlesinger, L. A. and Heskett, J. L. (1991) The Service-Driven Service Company. *Harvard Business Review* **69**(September–October): 71–81.

Schneider, B. (1980) 'The Service Organization: Climate is Crucial'. *Organizational Dynamics*, **9**(No. 2) 52–65.

Schnieder, B. (1994) 'HRM – A Service Perspective: Towards a Customer-focused HRM'. *International Journal of Service Industry Management* **5**(No. 1): 64–76.

Schneider, B. and Rentsch, J. (1987) 'The Management of Climate and Culture: A Futures Perspective'. In '*Futures of Organizations* (J. Hage, Ed.). Lexington, MA: Lexington Books.

Slywotzky, A. J. and Shapiro, B. P. (1993) 'Leveraging to Beat the Odds: The New Marketing Mind-Set'. *Harvard Business Review* **71**(September–October): 97–107.

Smith, A. (1950/1776) *The Wealth of Nations. An Inquiry into the Nature and Cause of the Wealth of Nations*. London: Methuen (the original published 1776).

Stauss, B. (1993) 'Service Deployment: Transformation of Problem Information into Problem Prevention Activities'. *International Journal of Service Industry Management* **4**(No. 3): 41–62.

Steedle, L. F. (1988) 'Has Productivity Measurement Outgrown Infancy?'. *Management Accounting* **70**(No. 2): 15.

Storbacka, K. (1993) *Customer Relationship Profitability in Retail Banking*. Research Report. Swedish School of Economics and Business Administration, Helsinki, Finland.

Swartz, T. A., Bowen, D. E. and Brown, S. W. (Eds) (1992) *Advances in Services Marketing and Management*, Vol. 1. Greenwich, CT: JAI Press.

Swartz, T. A., Bowen, D. E. and Brown, S. W. (Eds) (1993) *Advances in Services Marketing and Management*, Vol. 2. Greenwich, CT: JAI Press.

Taylor, F. W. (1974) *Scientific Management*. London: Harper & Row (a volume of two papers originally published in 1903 and 1911 and a written testimony for a Special House Committee in the US in 1912).

Voss, C. A., Armistead, C. G., Johnston, R. and Morris, B. (1985) *Operations Management in Service Industries and the Public Sector*. Chichester, UK: Wiley.

Webster, Jr. F. E. (1988) 'The Rediscovery of the Marketing Concept' *Business Horizons* **31** (May–June): 29–39.

Webster, Jr. F. E. (1992) 'The Changing Role of Marketing in the Corporation'. *Journal of Marketing* **56** (October): 1–17.

Wilson, A. (1972) *The Marketing of Professional Services.* London, UK: McGraw-Hill.

19

Towards a Classification of Service Processes

Rhian Silvestro, Lin Fitzgerald, Robert Johnston and Christopher Voss

INTRODUCTION

Schmenner[1] argues that, over the years, manufacturers have been unified by their acceptance of a certain terminology to describe generic production processes. Use of these process types has helped to remove the myth that all manufacturing activities and problems are unique. This has facilitated the sharing of ideas and techniques and the development of an understanding of process choice implication on manufacturing strategies. The process typology has also become a powerful tool in the teaching and development of production and operations management.[2,3]

The traditional view has been that the heterogeneity of services means that little communication or learning can take place between different service businesses; as Lovelock[4] states, 'Service industries remain dominated by an operations orientation that insists each industry is different'. A service typology which transcends narrow industry boundaries may lead to some cross-fertilization of ideas and to an understanding of the management methods and techniques appropriate to each service type. Although many service classification schemes have been proposed before, no categorization has been either as pervasive or as useful as the process type classification provided in the production management literature.

A REVIEW OF SERVICE CLASSIFICATIONS

Several production/operations authors have in the past applied manufacturing process types to services. The five generic process types, which have become a part of classic production management[2,5,6] are project, jobbing, batch, line and continuous process operations. The model, illustrated in Figure 1, shows how the five types are positioned along the diagonal on a graph where product volume correlates with product mix[5] to which Wild[7] refers as product variety.

Reprinted with permission from *International Journal of Service Industry Management*, Vol. 3, No. 3, pp. 62–75

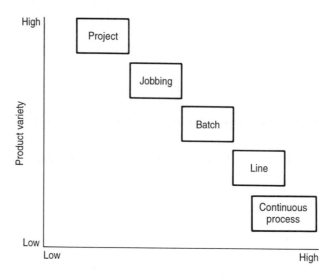

Figure 1. The five generic production process types.

Hill[6] identifies the following additional dimensions which characterize the five process types:

- product range
- customer order size
- degree of product change accommodated
- ability of operations to cope with new developments
- orientation of innovation
- performance criterion
- nature of the process technology
- number and expense of set-ups
- control of quality

Thus, at one extreme, project activities are defined as highly customized, one-off, large-scale and complex activities, such as civil engineering contracts or aerospace programmes. At the other extreme, continuous processing refers to the processing of a basic material, such as petrochemicals, through an automated plant. Between these extremes lie jobbing, batch and line processes. Some production processes will be hybrids sharing the characteristics of more than one of these three process types.[6]

Sasser et al.[8] are an example of authors who claim the transferability of this model to services, providing the following examples of service operations:

- *Project*: management consultancy, banqueting
- *Jobbing*: management development programme, design and installation of a computer system
- *Batch*: computer bureau

- *Line*: preparatory operation in fast food restaurants
- *Continuous process*: not used in service operation.

Such attempts have met with considerable criticism in the service operations literature on the grounds that they 'are insufficient for diagnosing and thinking about (service) systems'[9] and do not take account of one essential characteristic of service industries, that of the inherent variability created by the existence of the customer within the system.[10] The application of the generic production types to service appears to be an unnecessary force-fit of manufacturing concepts to the service sector.

Authors in the service management field have, therefore, responded by proposing service typologies, which they argue differentiate better between the management issues and concerns in different types of service. The six service dimensions below have over the past 15 years become widely recognized and used in the service operations management literature:

1. Equipment/people focus.[11,12]
2. Length of customer contract time.[9,13]
3. Extent of customization.[14–16]
4. Extent to which customer contact personnel exercise judgement in meeting individual needs.[4]
5. Source of value added, front office or back office.[15]
6. Product/process focus.[16]

Thomas[11] and Kotler[12] distinguish between equipment-based and people-based services. Examples of equipment-based services include airlines and vending machines, and examples of people-based services are appliance repair and management consultants. These articles are an attempt to move managers' strategic thinking away from product-oriented terms to talking about services and the characteristics which make services unique.

The classification scheme proposed by Chase[9] has produced some valuable insights for control. Chase suggests classifying services along a continuum from high to low contact, where contact refers to the length of time the customer is in contact with the service. For example, in a management consultancy there is a high degree of interaction between the customer and the processes of service delivery; Chase suggests that the control measures used in such an organization will differ radically from low contact services such as postal services.

Maister and Lovelock[14] add the extent of service customization to chase's classification. Customized activities involve compiling a service package for each customer as in a management consultancy project, for example. At the other extreme standardized activities are non-varying processes; although there may be several routes or choices, their availability is always pre-determined. For example, rail transport systems provide passengers with a wide variety of routes between many locations, but the service offered cannot be tailored (at least in the short term) to meet individual passenger needs. The resulting matrix yields a four-way classification, which the authors label service factory, service shop, mass service and professional service (See Figure 2).

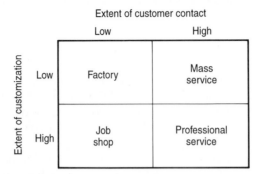

Figure 2. Maister and Lovelock's[14] classification of services 1982.

A review of the literature reveals several more four-way classifications of services, combining various dimensions in two-by-two matrices. Maister[15] distinguishes between value added in the front or back office, mapping it against the degree of customization[4] uses the extent to which customer contact personnel exercise judgement in meeting individual customer needs, against the degree of customization. Johnston and Morris[16] use the degree of product or process focus against the degree of customization. In a product-focused organization the emphasis is on *what* the customer buys, whilst in a process-focused business the emphasis is on *how* the customer buys, that is, the way the service is delivered.

More recently Haynes[17] combines dimensions previously proposed by Schmenner[1] and Schostack,[18] yielding a two-by-two matrix with the following axes: degree of operational complexity and the degree to which the operation is mechanistic or organic. The aim of all three writers, Hayes, Schmenner and Schostack, is to facilitate analysis of service positioning strategies rather than develop service typologies. To this extent the matrices can form useful management tools.

The ambiguity in Schostack's[18] definition of complexity, however, makes it difficult to operationalize. For some operations are complex in the sense that they involve highly sophisticated, difficult takes (e.g. management consultancy, scientific research), while others, simple by this definition, are complex in that the service process involves a multiplicity of choices or routes from which customers can select (such as freight forwarding). This ambiguity seems not to have been resolved by Haynes[17] and is therefore a residual problem, when his classification scheme is applied to service organizations.

The continuum of mechanistic/organic operations is a development of Schmenner's[1] dimension of the degree of customization and interaction between server and customer. This, and the other dimensions presented by Schmenner and Schostack (not captured in Haynes' matrix[17]), labour intensity and divergence respectively, do not seem to add significantly to the six dimensions listed above; labour intensity being essentially similar to equipment/people focus, and divergence being a combination of customization and front line staff discretion.

Another two-by-two matrix is proposed by Wemmerlov,[19] the axes of which are customer contact (again based on Chase's definition, though operationlized slightly differently) and the degree of 'routinization' of the service operation, ranging from fluid to rigid. Wemmerlov[19] (p. 28) is, however, reluctant to operationalize the definition of fluid and rigid operations.

LESSONS FROM THE PRODUCTION OPERATIONS LITERATURE

What emerges from this review of service classifications is a miscellany of different approaches lacking a cohesive framework, which derives benefit from all the dimensions identified. As a result no single classification scheme has proved so robust and useful as the process model in the manufacturing literature. Many services still 'view themselves as unique, and consequently do not promote service operations management techniques with the same vigour as does the manufacturing sector'.[1]

The strength of the manufacturing process model is that it is multidimensional. Several different manufacturing process dimensions are unified in a single model by correlation against production volume. Might it be possible, then, to use a volume measure to unify the disparate dimensions currently used to classify services?

Unfortunately the volume of services or number of service outputs is less meaningful than production volume in manufacturing. In service operations the heterogeneity and intangibility of services means that the measurement of service outputs is less straightforward than that of manufactured products. Moreover, in service operations significant volume increases can be made, and frequently are made, without any change in the service process, as would be expected in manufacturing (indeed this is precisely what the production process model shows). Service organizations may significantly increase the volume of operations by reproducing service operations, for example, using multisite strategies[8,20] *without* requiring a change in the process of provision.

We propose that a more appropriate measure of the volume of service activity is the number of customers processed by an individual service unit per day. Indeed services have been defined as essentially 'customer-processing operations'.[10,21] This includes customer business which may or may not require the presence of a customer. Thus, in a bank, for example, the volume measure includes back-office as well as front-office transactions, because not all services provided for the customer require his/her physical presence.

We propose that the measure of volume be used as a mechanism to integrate the disparate service classifications in the literature into a single service process model. The viability of this ides is tested using empirical data drawn from 11 in-depth case studies carried out as part of a research project funded by The Chartered Institute of Management Accountants. Eleven large, for-profit UK service organizations were studied by means of interviews with management and staff and an examination of company documentation and information flows. The aim was to develop an understanding of the companies' competitive strategies, the nature of the service processes and the consequent tasks and challenges encountered by service managers. (The methodology for gathering the data together with the case studies is documented more fully in ref. 22.)

On the basis of the data in the report the service organizations are categorized against each of the service dimensions as well as the volume measure. The objective is to look for clusters of features, which may lead to an integrated typology, which can be used as a basis for developing an understanding of management issues in service organizations across industry boundaries.

APPLICATION OF SERVICE CLASSIFICATIONS TO 11 FOR-PROFIT ORGANIZATIONS

The definitions of classification dimensions used in this section of the article were based, initially, on the literature. However, some ambiguities were found. For example, contact time was defined by Chase[9] as the length of time the customer is in contact with the service. However, contact time might be seen to be made up of two elements: the frequency of contact and the duration of contact. Thus a service with low frequency and high duration would rank the same as one with high frequency and low duration. Since the frequency of service encounters is likely to coincide with volumes of customers (frequency often being high, when customer volumes are high), we define contact time in terms of the length of customer contact time per transaction.

The service classifications, as defined in the literature, were examined and the definitions developed and refined, so that they could be operationalized and used to rank our sample of 11 service organizations. Our definitions are provided in Table 1.

Having refined the definitions, the next stage was to use data from our case studies of 11 service organizations to classify each company against each of these service dimensions. First, the companies were ranked by the volume of customers processed by a typical unit per day on an ordinal scale as shown in Figure 3.

At one extreme the volume of customers processed per unit per day by the management consultancy and field engineering service was measured in tens; whereas at the other extreme the transport company and transport terminus processed thousands of customers per unit per day.

The company data were then used to rank the organizations along each classification dimension derived from the literature, as defined in Table 1:

1. Equipment/people focus.
2. Customer contact time.
3. Degree of customization.
4. Degree of discretion.
5. Value added front office/back office.
6 Product/process focus.

In the case of the volume measure and customer contact time, the organizations could be ranked on the basis of customer volume and average dwell time statistics provided by the companies. The other dimensions are, however, qualitative rather than quantitative in nature, so a Delphi approach was adopted. The ranking process was for each of the five members of the research team to make an independent judgement of the companies' relative positioning along each dimension on a three-

Table 1. Definitions

1. *Equipment/people focus*
   Equipment-focused services are those where the provision of certain equipment is the core element in the service delivery. People-focused services are those where the provision of contact staff is the core element in service delivery.

2. *Customer contact time per transaction*
   High customer contact is where the customer spends hours, days or weeks in the service system, per transaction. Low customer contact is where the contact with the service system is a few minutes.

3. *Degree of customization*
   A high degree of customization is where the service process can be adapted to suit the needs of individual customers. A low degree of customization is where there is a non-varying standardized process; the customer may be offered several routes but the availability of routes is predetermined.

4. *Degree of discretion*
   A high degree of discretion is where front-office personnel can exercise judgement in altering the service package or process without referring to superiors. A low degree of discretion is where changes to service provision can be made only with authorization from superiors.

5. *Value added back office/front office*
   A back-office-oriented service is where the proportion of front-office (customer contact) staff to total staff is small. A front-office-oriented service is where the proportion of front-office staff to total staff is large.

6. *Product/process focus*
   A product-oriented service is where the emphasis is on what the customer buys. A process-oriented service is where the emphasis is on how the service is delivered to the customer.

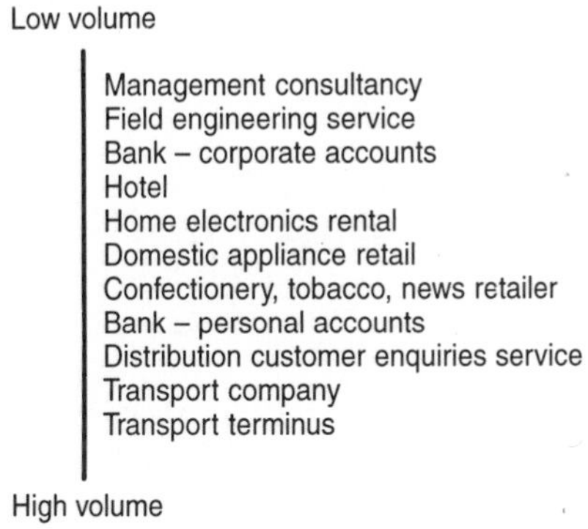

Low volume

Management consultancy
Field engineering service
Bank – corporate accounts
Hotel
Home electronics rental
Domestic appliance retail
Confectionery, tobacco, news retailer
Bank – personal accounts
Distribution customer enquiries service
Transport company
Transport terminus

High volume

Figure 3. Company rankings by volume of customers.

point scale, based on their understanding of the companies. The rankings produced by each team member were tabulated and results compared. There was considerable agreement among the members' ratings. Differences were highlighted and discussed by the team until a rating was unanimously agreed. The results are presented in Table 2.

Table 2. Company rankings

Company	Ranking: number of customers processed per unit per day	Equipment/ people focus	Customer contact time per transaction	Degree of customization	Degree of discretion	Value added back office/ front office	Product/ process focus
Management consultancy	1	People	High	High	High	Front office	Process
Field service	2	People	High	High	High	Front office	Process
Bank corporate	3	People	Medium	High	High	Both	Mix
Hotel	4	Mix	High	Medium	Medium	Both	Process
Rental	5	Mix	Medium	Medium	Medium	Both	Mix
Retail	6	Mix	Medium	Medium	Medium	Both	Mix
Confectioners, tobacconists and newsagents	7	People	Low	Low	Low	Front office	Product
Bank retail	8	Mix	Low	Medium	Medium	Both	Mix
Distribution enquiries	9	Mix	Low	Medium	Medium	Front office	Product
Transport	10	Equipment	High	Low	Low	Back office	Product
Transport terminus	11	Equipment	High	Low	Low	Both	Product

From Table 2, the six classifying dimensions are plotted against the volume ranking for each company. The results are shown in Figure 4. A pattern seems to emerge along the diagonal. As the number of customers processed by a typical unit per day increases, the general trend seems to be:

- Focus moves from a people to an equipment orientation.
- Length of contact time moves from high to low.
- Degree of customization moves from high to low.
- Level of employee discretion moves from high to low.
- Value added moves from front office to back office.
- Focus moves from a process to a product orientation.

The graphical representation of these organizations, plotted against all the dimensions, reveals clusterings of organizations along the diagonal, as identified in Figure 5. In the case of four of the companies (the management consultancy, field service, rental and retail services) the rankings are the same for each of the six dimensions. The corporate banking service appears to be split evenly between the upper two ranks. All the other companies have a predominance of one ranking: in the case of the transport company, for instance, all the characteristics except contact time are in the lower rank.

The clustering of characteristics and their correlation with the volume measure suggests that there may be three service types. We have called them professional, service shop and mass services, using the terminology which has become well-known in the service literature, although traditionally defined in terms of only two classification dimensions. We believe that, by clarifying the classification definitions and bringing several classifications together in a multidimensional and cohesive framework, the three archetypes will become more useful service process descriptions in operations management.

The model, which is analogous to the production process model in the manufacturing literature, is represented in Figure 6. The figure also indicates which companies in our small sample were representative of each service type. As with the production process model, the three categories may overlap; that is to say, some companies may be hybrids which share the characteristics of more than one type. In our sample the corporate bank is an example, sharing some features of a professional service (customization, discretion and people focus) and some of a service shop (contact time, front-/back-office mix, process/product mix).

It is hoped that these three archetypes will prove to be useful in developing an understanding of the management issues and challenges shared by organizations of the same type, even though they operate in quite different lines of business.

CONCLUSION

We propose that there are three types of service process: professional, service shop and mass. Each service type is characterized in terms of six dimensions drawn from the service operations literature. On the basis of evidence from a small sample of

	Management consultancy	Field service	Bank – corporate accounts	Hotel	Rental	Retail	Confectionery, tobacco, news retailer	Bank retail	Distribution enquiries	Transport	Transport terminus
High — People focus	●	●	●	●			●			●	●
Contact time	●	●									
Customization	●	●	●								
Discretion	●	●	●	●			●				
Front office	●	●									
Process focus	●	●	●	●							
Medium — People/equipment			●	●	●	●		●	●		
Contact time				●	●	●		●	●		
Customization			●	●	●	●		●	●		
Discretion				●	●	●		●	●		
Front office/back office			●	●	●	●		●	●		
Process/product			●	●	●	●		●			
Low — Equipment focus							●		●	●	●
Contact time							●			●	●
Customization							●		●	●	●
Discretion							●			●	●
Back office								●	●	●	●
Product focus										●	
	1	2	3	4	5	6	7	8	9	10	11

Volume ranking

Figure 4. Classifying dimensions vs. volume ranking.

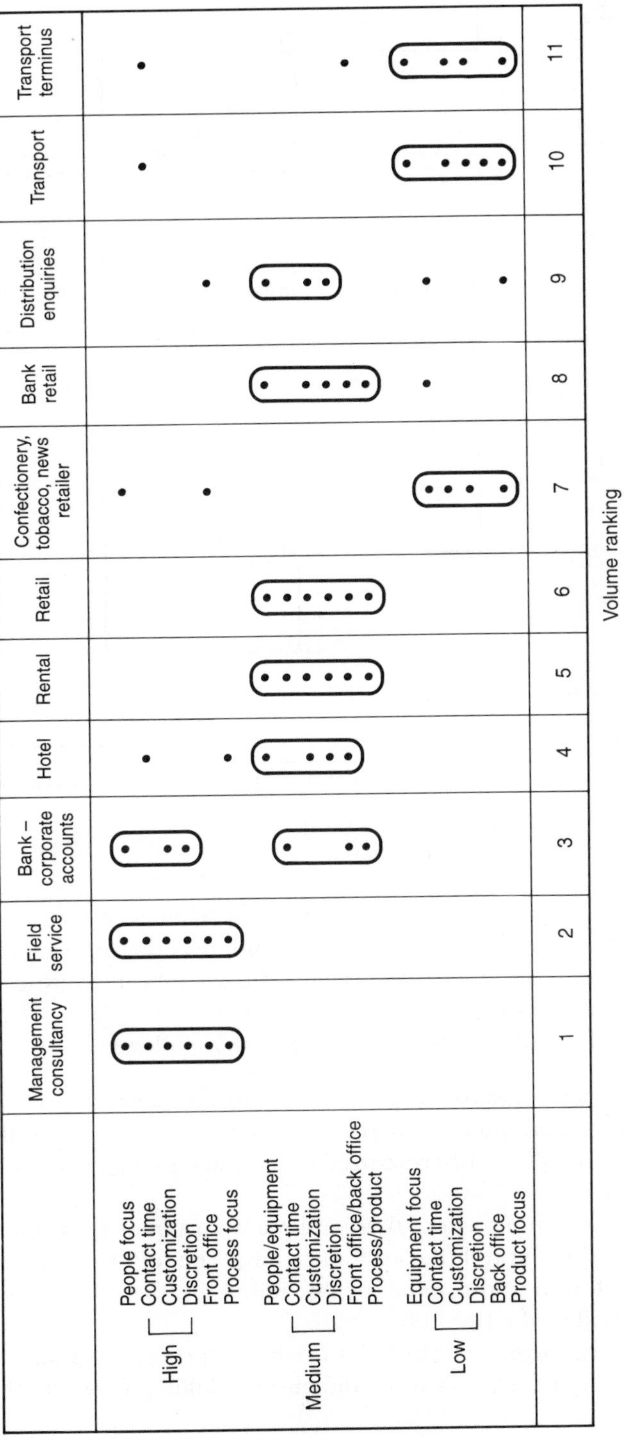

	Management consultancy	Field service	Bank – corporate accounts	Hotel	Rental	Retail	Confectionery, tobacco, news retailer	Bank retail	Distribution enquiries	Transport	Transport terminus
High — People focus / Contact time / Customization / Discretion / Front office / Process focus	● ● ● ● ● ●	● ● ● ● ● ●	● ● ●							●	●
Medium — People/equipment / Contact time / Customization / Discretion / Front office/back office / Process/product			● ● ●	● ● ● ● ●	● ● ● ● ●	● ● ● ● ● ●	● ●	● ● ● ● ● ●	● ● ●	
Low — Equipment focus / Contact time / Customization / Discretion / Back office / Product focus				● ●			● ● ● ●	●	● ●	● ● ● ● ●	● ● ● ●
	1	2	3	4	5	6	7	8	9	10	11

Volume ranking

Figure 5. Organizational clustering.

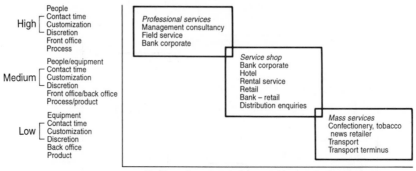

Figure 6. Production services, service shop and mass services.

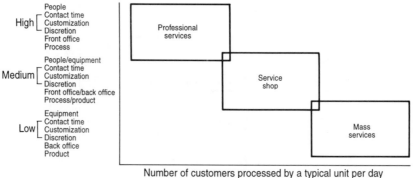

Figure 7. Service processes model.

service organizations these dimensions appear to correlate with volume of customers processed per unit per day. Just as production volume is the unifying mechanism in the manufacturing process model, so it seems this volume measure can be used to integrate the previously disparate service typologies.

Our definitions of the three service archetypes are as follows:

1. *Professional services*: organizations with relatively few transactions, highly customized, process-oriented, with relatively long contact time, with most value added in the front office, where considerable judgement is applied in meeting customer needs.
2. *Mass services*: organizations where there are many customer transactions, involving limited contact time and little customization. The offering is predominantly product-oriented with most value being added in the back office and little judgement applied by the front office staff.
3. *Service shops*: a categorization which falls between professional and mass services with the levels of the classification dimensions falling between the other two extremes.

Our proposed model of service processes, which is analogous to the production process model in the manufacturing operations literature, is represented in Figure 7.

Having adopted the conventional terminology, professional, service shop and mass, perhaps some explanation is called for the absence of the fourth category of services, the service factory. Although this was initially used as a category in several two-by-two matrices (such as in ref. 14 (see Figure 2)), it has rarely been applied as a descriptor of service organizations. Rather the service factory has evolved in the operations literature into a concept which has acquired new connotations. Chase and Erikson[23] use the term to describe service-oriented manufacturing companies, that is, companies which recognize and exploit the competitive opportunities of improving their service performance as well as the quality of their tangible products. The service factory has thus become 'an integrated view of product and service'.[23]

It may be, therefore, that the service factory forges the link between the production process types presented in the manufacturing model and the three service types presented in this article. For the service factory can be characterized both in term of the manufacturing dimensions listed earlier *and* the service dimensions incorporated in our model.

To conclude, we propose that the three types of service process, professional service, service shop and mass service, give rise to different management concerns, and that service strategy, control and performance measurement will differ significantly between the three. The next stage in our research is to see whether the issues which preoccupy managers in our sample of organizations can indeed be differentiated by the service types, which cut across industry boundaries. If so, the aim is to develop some propositions as to the management issues which typify professional services, service shops and mass services.

ACKNOWLEDGMENT

The authors wish to acknowledge the support of The Chartered Institute of Management Accountants for funding the research on which this article is based.

REFERENCES

1. Schmenner, R. (1986) 'How Can Service Businesses Survive and Prosper?'. *Sloan Management Review* (Spring): 21–32.
2. Hill, T. (1983) *Production/Operations Management.* Englewood Cliffs, NJ: Prentice-Hall International.
3. Hayes, R. and Wheelwright, S. (1979) 'Linking Manufacturing Process and Product Life Cycles'. *Harvard Business Review* 57(No. 1, January–February): 133–140.
4. Lovelock, C. H. (1983) 'Classifying Services to Gain Strategic Marketing Insights'. *Journal of Marketing* 47(Summer): 9–20.
5. Buffa, E. (1963) *Operations Management.* Chichester: Wiley.
6. Hill, T. (1985) *Manufacturing Strategy: The Strategic Management of the Manufacturing Function.* London: Macmillan.
7. Wild, R. (1971) *Techniques in Production and Operations Management.* New York: Holt, Rinehart and Winston.

8. Sasser, W. E., Olsen, R. P. and Wyckoff, D. D. (1982) *Management of Service Operations*. Boston: Allyn and Bacon.
9. Chase, R. B. (1978) 'Where Does the Customer Fit in a Service Operation?'. *Harvard Business Review* **56**(No. 4, November–December) 137–142.
10. Morris, B. and Johnston, R. (1987) 'Dealing with Inherent Variability—The Difference between Service and Manufacturing Explained'. *International Journal of Operations & Production Management* **7**(No. 4): 13–22.
11. Thomas, D. R. E. (1975) 'Strategy is Different in Service Businesses'. *Harvard Business Review* **53**(No. 4, July–August): 158–165.
12. Kotler, P. (1980) *Principles of Marketing*. Englewood Cliffs, NJ: Prentice-Hall International.
13. Chase, R. B. (1981) 'The Customer Contact Approach to Services: Theoretical Bases and Practical Extensions'. *Operations Research* **29**(No. 4).
14. Maister, D. and Lovelock, C. H. (1982) 'Managing Facilitator Services'. *Sloan Management Review* (Summer): 19–31.
15. Maister, D. (1983) 'The Defining Qualities of Four Different Managerial Environments'. *Research in Service Operations Management*, Proceedings of the workshop on Teaching and Research in Production and Operations Management, London Business School.
16. Johnston, R. and Morris, B. (1985) 'Monitoring and Control in Service Operations'. *International Journal of Operations & Production Management* **5**(No. 1): 32–38.
17. Haynes, R. M. (1990) 'Service Typologies: A Transaction Modelling Approach'. *International Journal of Service Industry Management* **1**(No. 1).
18. Shostack, G. L. (1987) 'Service Positioning through Structural Change'. *Journal of Marketing* **51**(January).
19. Wemmerlov, U. (1990) 'A Taxonomy for Service Processes and its Implications for System Design'. *International Journal of Service Industry Management* **1**(No. 3).
20. Voss, C. A., Armistead, C. G., Johnston, R. and Morris, B. (1985) *Operations Management in Service Industries and the Public Sector*. Chichester: Wiley.
21. Johnston, R. (1987) 'A Framework for Developing a Quality Strategy in a Customer-processing Operation'. *International Journal of Quality & Reliability Management* **4**(No. 4): 35–44.
22. Fitzgerald, L., Johnston, R., Silvestro, R., Steel, A. and Voss, C. (1989) *Control Information for Management in Service Industries*. Research Report, The Chartered Institute of Management Accountants, London.
23. Chase, R. B. and Erikson, W. J. (1988) 'The Service Factory'. *Academy of Management Executive* **II**(No. 3).

20

Sustainable Competitive Advantage in Service Industries: A Conceptual Model and Research Propositions

Sundar G. Bharadwaj, P. Rajan Varadarajan and John Fahy

During the past two decades, marketing scholars have focused on a broad range of issues pertaining to the marketing of services, as evidenced by two recent reviews of extant literature on services marketing (Fisk, Brown and Bitner, 1993; Swartz, Bowen and Brown, 1992). The emergence of services marketing as a distinct body of literature notwithstanding, there seems to be broad consensus that the boundary delineating services from goods is somewhat fluid. Often significant service components are integral to the consumption/use of tangible goods (e.g. automobiles, household appliances), as are significant tangible elements to the consumption/use of services (e.g. car rentals, air travel). As evidenced by Shostack's (1977) characterization of products (goods and services) in terms of the proportion of physical goods and intangible services they contain, there are few pure goods or services. Recognizing the fluid nature of the boundary delineating services from goods, the molecular model (Shostack, 1977) views all market entities as exhibiting varying levels of tangible and intangible elements, and services as intangibles-dominant market entities. Along similar lines Berry and Parasuraman (1991) suggest that if the source of a product's[1] core benefit is more tangible than intangible, it should be considered a good, and if it is more intangible than tangible, it should be considered a service. In addition to intangibility, inseparability/simultaneity, heterogeneity, and perishability are generally viewed as the distinguishing characteristics of services.

We focus on organizational skills and resources underlying the competitive advantages of service businesses, and the moderating effects of the characteristics of services, service industries, and firms within an industry on the skills and resources underlying a business's competitive positional advantages. Through an extensive body of literature focusing on a broad range of issues pertaining to competitive advantage has been published to date, this article is based on the premise that a

Reprinted with permission from *Journal of Marketing*, Vol. 57, October, pp. 83–99 closed examination of the sources of competitive advantage in the context of service industries can provide unique managerial insights into strategic problems and opportunities that may not be readily apparent from an examination of the sustainable competitive advantage (SCA) related issues at a more aggregate level. As Shostack (1977, p. 75) notes, 'the greater the weight of intangible elements in a market entity, the greater will be the divergence from product marketing in priorities and approach.[2] Recent reviews of literature on services marketing and management also allude to the dearth of strategic emphasis in extant literature (Fisk, Brown and Bitner, 1993; Swartz, Bowen and Brown, 1992). Against this backdrop, we provide insights into the sources of SCA in service industries by reviewing and integrating research on SCA-related issues explored in the fields of marketing, strategic management and industrial organization economics and exploring the implications of the distinctive characteristics of service industries and firms for achieving SCA. The paper is organized as follows: First, an overview of the concept of SCA is presented. Second, a contingency model of SCA in service industries is proposed. Third, the moderating effects of the characteristics of services, service industries, and firms within an industry on potential sources of SCA are explored and the propositions presented. We conclude with a discussion on managerial implications and future research directions.

THE CONCEPT OF SUSTAINABLE COMPETITIVE ADVANTAGE: AN OVERVIEW

In most industries, some firms are more profitable than others, regardless of whether the average profitability of the industry is high or low. The superior performers conceivably possess something special and hard to imitate that allows them to outperform their rivals. These unique skills and assets (resources) are referred to as *sources of competitive advantage* in strategy literature.[2] *Competitive advantage* can result either from implementing a value-creating strategy not simultaneously being implemented by any current or potential competitors (Barney, McWilliams and Turk, 1989; Barney, 1991) or through superior execution of the same strategy as competitors. *Sustainability* is achieved when the advantage resists erosion by competitor behavior (Porter 1985, p. 20). In other words, the skills and resources under-lying a business's competitive advantage must resist duplication by other firms (Barney, 1991). Case in point:

> ServiceMaster is a company that manages support services for hospitals, schools, and industrial companies. It supervises the employees of customers' organizations engaged in housekeeping, food service, and equipment maintenance. The company has been successful in using its unique resources and skills (specifically, system economies and specialized management skills) to raise the quality of its customers' maintenance services and at the same time lowering their costs. Using its data base (a firm specific resource), which covers more than a decade of maintenance history on several million pieces of equipment at thousands of locations, ServiceMaster can determine objectively how its customers' facilities should be maintained, when equipment purchases and maintenance will pay off, and when parts should be replaced. The effectiveness of ServiceMaster's systems are reportedly such that its customers often invest jointly in new equipment and share the resulting productivity gains (see Quinn, Doorley and Paquette, 1990).

Conditions for sustainable competitive advantage

A number of studies have explored the conditions under which a business's competitive advantage is sustainable (cf. Barney, 1991; Coyne, 1985). Barney lists four essential requirements for a resource/skill to be a source of SCA:

- It must be *valuable*;
- It must be *rare* among a firm's current and potential competitors;
- It must be *imperfectly imitable*; and
- There must not be any *strategically equivalent substitutes* for this resource/skill.

Firm resources and skills are considered valuable when they aid a firm in formulating and implementing strategies that improve its efficiency and/or effectiveness. However, if certain resources/skills are possessed by a large number of present or potential competitors, they cannot be a source of SCA. Valuable and rare organizational resource/skills can be sources of SCA only if firms that do not possess these resources cannot obtain them (as a direct consequence of a capability gap (Coyne, 1985), the critical resources being imperfectly imitable (Lippman and Rumelt, 1982; Coyne 1985; Barney, 1986a, 1986b)). The final requirement for a resource/skill to be a source of SCA is that the resource/skill is nonsubstitutable. Substitutability can take two forms. If a competitor cannot duplicate a firm's resources/skills exactly, but can substitute *similar* resources that enable it to formulate and implement identical strategies and use very *different* resources/skills as strategic substitutes (see Barney, 1991), then a resource/skill cannot be a source of SCA.

Coyne (1985) points out that, not only must a firm have a skill or resource that its competitors do not have (i.e. there must be a capability gap), but also the capability gap must make a difference to the customer. In other words, for a business to enjoy a SCA in a product-market segment, the difference(s) between the firm and its competitors must be reflected in one or more product/delivery attributes that are *key buying criteria*. Furthermore, in order for a competitive advantage to be sustainable, both the key buying criteria and the underlying capability gap must be enduring. Additionally, in the face of changes in key buying criteria, the sustainability of a business's competitive advantage would depend on its ability to *adapt* to these changes and/or influence key buying criteria (see Boulding *et al.*, 1993; Hamel and Prahalad, 1991; Treacy and Wiersema, 1993).

A CONCEPTUAL MODEL OF SUSTAINABLE COMPETITIVE ADVANTAGE

A conceptual model of SCA in service industries, which builds on the works by Barney (1991), Coyne (1985, 1989), Day and Wensley (1988), Dierickx and Cool (1989), Lippman and Rumelt (1982), and Reed and Defillipi (1990), among others, is presented in Figure 1. Here a firm's distinctive organizational skills and resources are viewed as the source of a business's competitive advantages in the marketplace.[3] The characteristics of services, service industries and firms within an industry are

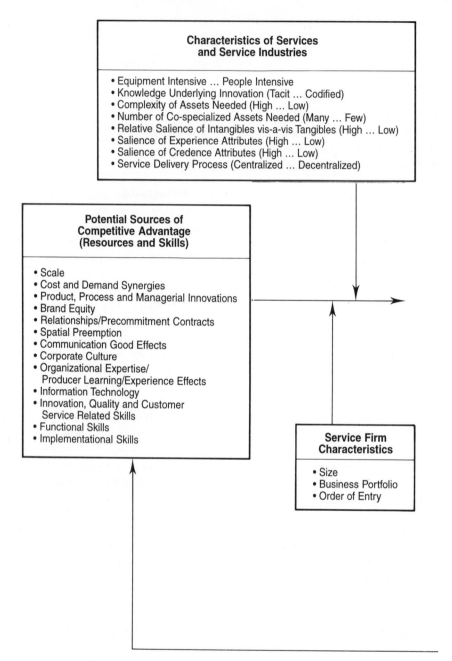

Figure 1. A contingency model of sustainable competitive advantage in service industries.

shown as moderating the skills and resources underlying a business's competitive positional advantages. The sustainability of a business's competitive advantages is viewed as contingent on barriers to imitation of its unique skills and resources. The model further suggests that sustainable competitive advantages are a key to sustained,

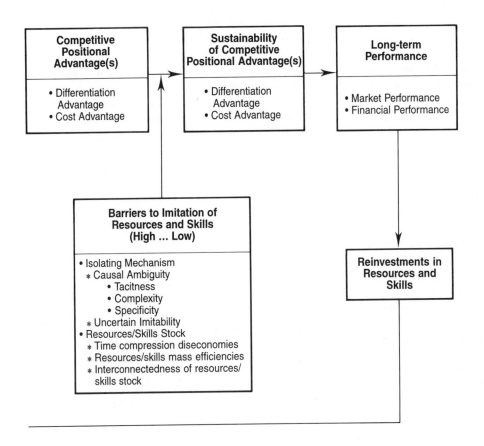

superior long-term performance. Reinvestments in both present and new skills and resources are viewed as critical to strengthening (or preventing erosion of) competitive advantages, A detailed discussion of the constructs central to the model and the proposed links follows.

Sources of competitive advantage

Researchers generally distinguish between two broad sources of competitive advantage – unique resources (assets) and distinctive skills (capabilities). Day and Wensley (1988) characterize superior skills as the distinctive capabilities of a firm's personnel that set them apart from the personnel of competing firms and superior resources as more tangible requirements for advantage that enable a firm to exercise its capabilities.[4] These two broad sets of sources enable a business to perform the various primary and secondary value activities that compose its value chain either at a lower cost or in a way that leads to differentiation. They facilitate the attainment of competitive positional advantages in the form of (1) superior customer value through a differentiated good/service, and/or (2) lower relative cost through cost leadership.[5] Firm-specific skills and resources are also referred to as the 'drivers' of cost and/or differentiation advantages (Porter, 1985). A wide variety of drivers has received attention in the literature, including *resource-based drivers* such as economies of scale and scope, brand equity, and reputation, and *skills-based* drivers such as the skills underlying the innovativeness and superior quality of a business's offerings. Superior skills and resources do not, however, automatically give a business a competitive advantage. They only provide the business an opportunity to *leverage* its skills and resources to achieve competitive cost and/or differentiation advantages. This entails first identifying those skills and resources a company has that have the greatest potential to endow the firm with enduring competitive advantages. Also, as Asker (1989) notes, multiple bases of competitive advantage may be needed for a business to compete successfully. A more detailed discussion on the skills and resources underlying a business's competitive advantage listed in Figure 1 is presented in a later section, along with the propositions.

Competitive positional advantages

Competitive positional advantages can be broadly construed as cost leadership and differentiation advantages. Cost leadership entails performing most activities at a lower cost than competitors while offering a parity product. Differentiation entails customers perceiving a consistent difference in important attributes between the firm's offerings and its competitors' offerings. The advantages, disadvantages, risks, and implementational requirements of cost leadership and differentiation as generic strategy alternatives have been well documented (Porter, 1980, 1985). Shostack's (1987) analysis of the process of service provision in terms of complexity (the number of steps involved in providing the service) and divergence (the executional latitude at each step) and the positioning alternatives that emerge from this analysis – reduced divergence (a standardized, cost-efficient service), increased divergence (greater customization for specific segments), reduced complexity (a stripped down generic service), and increased complexity (addition of services tending toward a multi-service position – provide additional insights into differentiation possibilities in service industries. Each of these positioning alternatives can result in differences in customer's perception of value. For example, a strategy of reduced divergence could lead to some customers perceiving the shift as one that lowers customization and limits their options and hence rejecting a highly standardized service even if it costs less (see Shostack, 1987).

Moderating effects of the characteristics of services, service industries, and firms

In the proposed conceptual model (Figure 1), the following characteristics of services, service industries, and firms within an industry moderate the effects of skills and sources underlying a business's positional advantage.

A. Characteristics of services and service industries
- Equipment intensive . . . people intensive
- Complexity of assets needed (high . . . low)
- Number of co-specialized assets needed (many . . . few)
- Relative salience of intangibles vis-a-vis tangibles (high . . . low)
- Salience of experience attributes (high . . . low)
- Salience of credence attributes (high . . . low)
- Service delivery process (centralized . . . decentralized)

B. Service firm characteristics
- Size
- Business portfolio composition
- Order of entry into market

Though other characteristics merit consideration as moderating factors in the context of specific service industries, the principal focus here is on characteristics that transcend industry boundaries. Such as orientation can be conducive to managerial learning by facilitating identification of and learning from the experience of organizations facing parallel situations in other service industries (see Lovelock, 1983).

Barriers to imitation

Central to the concept of SCA is the notion of durability or non-imitability. A key difference between *entry barriers* and *barriers* to imitation is that though the former are prone to free-riding (because they are the private collective asset of the industry), the latter are endogenous and idiosyncratic (i.e. firm-specific) (Mahoney and Pandian, 1992). Overlapping conceptualizations of barriers to imitation have been proposed by Lippman and Rumelt (1982), Coyne (1985), Rumelt (1984, 1987), and Reed and Defillipi (1990). A map of the broad playing field of barriers to imitation is provided by Rumelt's (1984) treatise on *isolating mechanisms*.[6] Dierickx and Cool's (1989) discussion on *resource/skills* stock provides additional insights into the operation of barriers to imitation.

Isolating mechanisms

These are essentially asymmetries in the skills and assets of competing firms that increase the costs associated with strategic imitation. Engaging in the maintenance of these isolating mechanisms protects the competitive advantages derived from past and/or present managerial actions. Fisher (1989) notes that understanding the relative durability of each isolating mechanism and marketing mix element has important implications for differentiation strategies pursued by service firms. Barriers to imitation are even greater when *causal ambiguity* exists over the factors responsible for a business's superior performance. Three critical characteristics of a firm individually or in combination contribute to causal ambiguity (Reed and Defillippi 1990): *Tacitness* is defined as the implicit and non-codifiable accumulation of skills that result from learning by doing (Polanyi, 1962); (2) *Complexity* results from the interrelationships between various skills and assets (Barney, 1926b; Nelson and Winter, 1982); and (3) *Specificty* entails the transaction-specific skills and assets that are utilized in the production processes and provision of services for particular customers (Williamson, 1985). Any of these can produce ambiguity regarding the firm's actions and outcomes and in turn create barriers to imitation (Reed and Defillippi 1990).

Ambiguity over factors responsible for superior performance acts as a powerful barrier to imitation as will as a deterrent to *resource mobility* (Dierickx and Cool, 1989). Resources that cannot be traded either because (1) their property rights are not well defined or (2) they are idiosyncratic to the firm and have no value outside it constitute *immobile resources* (Dierickx and Cool, 1989). Furthermore, the complexity of firms often makes identification of their key success factors separately may often be an inaccurate representation, because the interaction among the factors can be the cause of a business's success. Therefore, potential imitators may find it hard to develop an unambiguous list of factors responsible for a business's success.

Uncertain imitability results when the creation of new products is inherently uncertain and causal ambiguity about the process of asset stock accumulation (the building of stocks of resources and skills) impedes imitation and/or mobility of a firm's unique resources. Its relevance increases when complex products and administrative structures are involved (Lippman and Rumelt, 1982). The lack of a clear-cut causal explanation between the actions and performance of some large firms is supportive of the notion of uncertain imitability. Though economic theory suggests that the presence of excess profits in any industry can make markets *contestable* (Baumol, Panzar and Willig, 1982) and bring down industry profits to normal levels, the theory of uncertain imitability (Lippman and Rumelt, 1982) suggests high profits may signal the presence of successful firms with difficult-to-imitate capabilities that impede entry attempts.

Resource/skills stock

The imitability of a business's resource/skill stock are related to the characteristics of the *process* by which they are accumulated. Dierickx and Cool (1989) identify three major characteristics: (1) *time compression diseconomies*, (2) *resource/skill mass efficiencies*, and (3) *interconnectedness of resources/skills stock*. Time compression diseconomies refers to the accumulation of certain advantages to firms owning a resource/skill for a long period of time (e.g. firm reputation for quality). A firm may have built a reputation for quality by following a consistent set of production.

quality control, and other policies over time. Such sources of competitive advantage can be neither acquired nor imitated by competitors within a short period of time.

The presence of large amounts of existing stock of resources/skills facilitates further resource/skill accumulation. For example, firms that already have an existing stock of research and development may often by in a better position to make further breakthroughs and add to their existing stock of knowledge than firms who have low initial levels of know-how. The implication here is that when asset mass efficiencies are critical, building stocks of resources/skills by firms that have initial low levels of stock can be difficult. Difficulties in 'catching up' can be even greater when the asset accumulation process exhibits discontinuities; i.e. a critical mass is required (Dierickx and Cool, 1989).

Interconnectedness of resources/skills acts as a barrier to imitation when some firms lack complementary resources/skills that are critical to competing in a product market. For instance, a new entrant to a market with a product (of comparable quality to that of incumbents) encountering difficulties in distributing the product because of no established dealer network would be at a competitive disadvantage.

Performance outcomes

Competitive advantage can be expected to lead to superior marketplace performance (e.g. market share, customer satisfaction) and financial performance (e.g. return on investment, shareholder wealth creation). Accounting ratios and market measures constitute two broad indicators of a business's financial performance. However, they have been criticized for their (1) inadequate handling of intangibles and (2) improper valuation of sources of competitive advantage (i.e. allocating historic and current costs to satisfy tax requirements (Day and Wensley, 1988)). Financial performance measures characterized by a future orientation (e.g. shareholder value creation potential) though not entirely free of shortcomings, are generally viewed as more appropriate for evaluating the desirability of planned investments in defensible positional advantages. However, a detailed discussion of the merits and shortcomings of these measures is beyond our scope here.[7]

Reinvestments in resources and skills

Because the barriers to imitation of a firm's skills and resources are prone to decay in the absence of adequate 'maintenance' expenditure (Dierickx and Cool, 1989), the maintenance of an SCA requires the constant monitoring of and reinvesting in the present sources of advantage, as will as investing in other potential sources of advantage.[8] For example, a business with a reputation for superior quality could experience an erosion in quality as a source of SCA if it fails to continue investing in processes that contributed to the business's reputation for quality. As Porter (1985, p. 20) notes, a firm must offer 'a moving target to its competitors, by reinvesting in order to continually improve its position'.

SOURCES OF SUSTAINABLE COMPETITIVE ADVANTAGE IN SERVICE INDUSTRIES: PROPOSITIONS

This section provides an overview of the skills and resources underlying a business's competitive positional advantages and a number of propositions delineating the moderating effects of the characteristics of services, service industries, and firms within industries on these sources. However, we present no formal discussion in reference to certain potential sources of competitive advantage listed in Figure 1 (superior skills in various functional areas and those relating to innovation, quality, customer service, and implementation) because their importance as determinants of superior performance are widely recognized, transcend goods and service industry boundaries, and have been extensively discussed in business literature.

Scale effects

Given the decentralization of the service production process to a local level in many service industries, the potential for achieving a competitive cost advantage by exploiting economies of scale has traditionally been viewed as modest. Nevertheless, opportunities for exploiting scale economies are significantly greater in equipment-based service industries than in people-based service industries. Service firms can also achieve economies of scale by centralizing service production facilities while decentralizing customer-contact facilities (Upah, 1980) or centralizing certain critical (and/or equipment-intensive) activities and localizing less critical (and/or people-intensive) activities, as exemplified by clinical laboratories performing some tests in dispersed local units and others involving expensive equipment and/or skilled personnel in regional centers (see Porter, 1990). Operating economies can also be realized through reconfigurations such as replacing stand-alone with multi-unit motion picture theatres sharing a centralized projection room, ticket selling booth, and refreshment stand (see Thomas, 1978). Also, as Quinn and Gagnon (1986) note, in a number of service industries, the application of new technologies has allowed firms to realize significant scale economies.

P$_1$: The greater the equipment intensity of a service industry, the greater the importance of economies of scale as a source of competitive cost advantage.

The inseparability of production and consumption of services and the resultant inability to efficiently mass produce services at a central location often necessitates service businesses to make the service available at multiple sites. This in turn necessitates examining the implications of size on cost and differentiation advantages at the operating unit and firm level. Heskett (1987) notes that for service firms operating under a common identity over a wide area, scale economies often are more important at the firm than operating unit level. A manifestation of the relative size (of firms competing in an industry) at the company level is the number of dispersed local units (either company owned or franchised) operating under a common corporate identity. All else equal, economies of scale associated with selection and training of employees, purchased goods and services, investments in specialized technology and R&D to systematize the service delivery process, and shared marketing (e.g. national or large- scale local advertising and sales promotion), billing and logistics-related activities enable a multi-unit service firm to achieve a cost advantage vis-a-vis single-unit and multi-unit service firms with fewer units.

In many service industries, multi-unit firms are better equipped to achieve a competitive differentiation advantage over single-unit firms through *systematization* and *standardization* of the process of delivering services (Porter, 1990). For example, a multi-unit firm that replicates its services at many locations by creating standardized facilities, procedures to guide the behavior of employees, and automating individual service delivery tasks (Levitt, 1976) can achieve a differentiation advantage vis-a-vis single-unit service firms.

P_2: The larger the number of local units of a service firm operating under a common corporate identity within an industry (either company owned or franchised), the greater the potential to exploit scale economies to achieve competitive cost advantage and institute systematization, standardization, and other differentiation features to achieve a differentiation advantage.

When a service product is a multi-attribute benefit bundle characterized by the delivery of certain attributes of the total service from dispersed site locations (e.g. purchase of travelers' checks) and other attributes from a central location (e.g. arranging for replacement of lost travelers' checks), firm size relative to competitors (e.g. market share/customer base) can be a major determinant of the economic viability of investing in certain differentiation features that might endow the firm with a competitive differentiation advantage. Case in point:

An important attribute or key buying criterion in the context of purchasing travelers' checks is the assurance that they will be replaced promptly should they be lost or stolen. A state-of-the-art satellite communication system that allows customers who have lost their travelers' checks to communicate with the firm from any part of the world, an office that is staffed 24 hours a day, 365 days a year by a team of well-trained employees, a supporting information system that allows the staff handling the phone lines to verify the veracity of customers' claims regarding lost travelers' checks on the basis of their responses to a few questions, and a distribution system that is the most intensive and extensive (a worldwide network of branch offices and agents) could conceivably be some of the basic building blocks (firm-specific resources and skills) that allows only one firm in the industry to guarantee that if lost or stolen, its travelers' checks will be replaced within eight hours or less. For a firm with a sizeable share of the market, making substantial investments in satellite communication systems, earth stations, and a state-of-the-art information system to achieve such a differentiation advantage may be an economically viable proposition; for competitors with smaller shares of the market, however, this may not be the case.

Cost and demand synergies

Economies of scope are realized when a firm is able to market entirely new services with little added costs through networks or systems previously established for current services. Communications and information-handling technologies often facilitate distribution of a broader set of services to a more diffused customer base, as well as lower the marginal costs on *old* services, as equipment development and software investments are allocated over a broader line of services (Quinn and Gagnon, 1986). Therefore, relative to single business firms, multi-business firms have the opportunity to (1) reduce costs by sharing activities between businesses; (2) increase revenues by cross-selling to customers of different businesses in the firm's portfolio; and (3) share knowledge and skills. For instance, a multi-business firm such as ServiceMaster – whose subsidiaries include Terminix (termite and pest control service), ChemLawn and True Green (lawn care service), and American Home Shield (appliance insurance service) – has an opportunity to exploit demand synergies by cross-selling of services, and cost synergies by centralizing the accounts processing for various services. More importantly, competitive cost and differentiation advantages associated with synergy are less likely to be imitated, because these are often achieved under a unique set of circumstances as will as on the basis of unique firm specific resources and skill base. Case in point:

> In 1990, when AT&T launched its AT&T Universal Visa and MasterCard credit cards, it had access to the credit histories of 70 million AT&T long-distance customers (a firm-specific resource). By qualifying these potential customers in advance, the firm was in a position to respond quickly to inquiries from households that were good credit risks and lower its vulnerability to bad credit risks (Blattberg and Deighton, 1991). An additional incentive it could offer to its credit card customers (a 10% discount on long-distance calls made over the AT&T network by using its cards), also attributable to a firm-specific resource, could be matched only by some of its larger competitors by entering into alliances with competing long distance carriers such as MCI and US Sprint.

P_3: The greater the cost (demand) interrelationships between a particular service business in a firm's portfolio and other businesses in its portfolio, the greater the cost (demand) synergies as a source of competitive cost and/or differentiation advantage.

Product, process, and managerial innovations

Product, process, and managerial innovations can be used to gain a competitive advantage, to the extent that the technology underlying such innovations remain proprietary. Technology held proprietary through patents, copyright, or secrecy can deter new entrants, as well as achieve a competitive advantage by exploiting economies of scale and scope and/or through differentiation. Teece (1988, p. 48) characterizes *regime of appropriability* as those aspects of the commercial environment, excluding firm and market structure, that govern an innovator's ability to capture the rents associated with the innovation. Relative to goods industries, in service industries, technology suffers from a weak regime of appropriability, which implies that patents can be 'invented around.' For example, though Merrill Lynch obtained a patent for its Cash Management Account (CMA), which integrated four basic investor services into a single account, and holds a dominant share of the market, practically all its major competitors offers a similar service.[9] Trade secrets, an alternative to patents, can offer protection from imitation, provided the secret is kept in the form of *tacit knowledge*. Whereas *codified knowledge* is transferable and more prone to be copied, tacit knowledge, being difficult to articulate, is difficult to transfer or copy (Teece, 1981, 1988). A number of service firms have successfully used information technology to capture tacit organizational knowledge and retain property rights over the resulting innovations. For example, American Express developed an expert system called Authorizer's Assistant to facilitate credit authorization judgments. As a result, a decision that traditionally created a bottleneck (involving the scanning of 13 data bases or necessitating a judgment call) can now be made in a few seconds.

The presence of *cospecialized* assets or the lack thereof also impacts on the imitability of innovations. When commercializing an innovation requires other specialized assets in marketing and/or production, and these assets are specific to the particular innovation, the imitability of the innovation will be impeded to the degree of complexity and number of cospecialized assets needed to put the innovation to work. Even if competing firms were to find it easy to copy the innovation, they might face difficulties in putting together the organizational apparatus needed to bring the innovation to market. A complex set of cospecialized assets may therefore protect the innovation and allow it to continue to yield value (see Teece, 1987). For example, it took more than two years for competitors to respond to American Hospital Supply Corporation's ASAP system, because they needed to computerize their inventory systems first (Vitale, 1988). Though entering certain service businesses could require a firm to possess complex and/or multiple co-specialized assets, entering into other service businesses may not be inhibited by such requirements.

P_4: The greater the complexity of assets needed to market a service, the greater the importance of innovation as a source of competitive advantage.

P_5: The greater the number of cospecialized assets needed to market a service, the greater the importance of innovation a source of competitive advantage.

BRAND EQUITY[10]

Aaker (1991, p. 15) defines brand equity as 'a set of brand assets and liabilities linked to a brand, its name and symbol, that add or subtract from the value provided by a product to a firm and/or that firm's customers'. He distinguishes between five categories of assets that give rise to a brand's equity: (1) brand loyalty, (2) name awareness, (3) perceived quality, (4) brand associations, and (5) proprietary brand assets such as patents and symbols. In the context of marketing of service, Berry and Parasuraman (1991) note that brand equity also could reside in the name of the firm itself. Here, the absence of a tangible physical product on which a brand name can be affixed often necessitates assigning greater prominence to the corporate brand name on the various physical products and facilities used to deliver the service (e.g. displaying an airline's logo and name on airplanes, ground transportation vehicles, baggage handling equipment, ticketing counter, departure and arrival gates, etc.). Strong brand names or symbols impact positively on brand equity, both directly and indirectly, through perceived quality. Brand equity (1) helps differentiate the product from competitors' offerings (Park, Jaworski, and MacInnes, 1986); (2) serves as a proxy for quality and creates positive images in consumers' minds (Oster, 1990; Kamakura and Russell, 1991); (3) prevents market share erosion during price and promotional wars (Kamakura and Russell, 1991; Johnson, 1991); and (4) prevents market share erosion by giving a firm time to respond to competitive threats (Aaker, 1991).

Shostack (1977) suggests that since services are characterized by a greater degree of intangibility, 'tangibilizing' (managing the evidence) must be attempted in order to make the product more salient to customers. The need to tangibilize is inversely related to the level of intangibility of a service. Brand names and symbols used by firms to add tangible aspects to the product help reduce the search costs of consumers (Landes and Posner, 1987), such as Prudential Insurance's use of the Rock of Gibraltar to present a message of strength and stability, and Travelers Insurance's use of an umbrella to convey a message of protection (Aaker, 1991).

P_6: The greater the intangibility of a service, the greater the importance of brand equity as a source of competitive differentiation advantage.

Nelson (1970 and Darby and Karni (1973) suggest that customers take a chance when they purchase an experience good. Unlike search goods, consumers cannot infer through simple inspection whether a product is of high or low quality with experience goods. A major challenge faced by a new entrant in an experience goods market is the need to convince consumers to take a chance on a new product when they are aware of the quality of the incumbent's product because of prior use (Schmalensee, 1982). In general, the likely presence of variability in service quality, not only makes it difficult and riskier for consumers to evaluate the quality of a service, but also makes the consumers' purchase choices more complex (Murray, 1991: Nayyar and Templeton, 1991). Though on one hand, consumers may seek more information to make better choices, since information search is generally expensive (Stigler, 1961), buyers seeking to economize on evaluation costs might be inclined to choose the product with the best brand reputation because it has the lowest evaluation costs (Rumelt, 1987). When buyers cannot easily evaluate the capabilities of the service provider and the quality and value of the service provided (as would be the case with credance goods) brand reputation serves as an important proxy for quality and other key buying criteria that cannot be easily evaluated.

Also, as pointed out by Levitt (1986), when buyers select a particular brand, they are engaging in an act of risk reduction. Through risk can be viewed as a function of the perception of variability in quality, in service industries, firms having strong brand names and symbols are better positioned to mitigate customers' perceptions over variability in quality and therefore differentiate themselves from competition. Moreover, the additional marketing efforts that may be expended in order to overcome consumers' risk perceptions can often lead to a cost asymmetry between a firm owning brands with strong equity vis-a-vis its competitors.

P_7: The greater the experience and credence attributes of a service, the greater the importance of brand equity as a source of competitive cost and differentiation advantage.

Information asymmetries also can be exploited by firms to diversify into new services and provide multiple services to its customers. In reference to service industries, Nayyar (1990) argues that each sampling by experience contributes to the information bank that consumers maintain. In reference to new service introductions he notes:

When the producer of a brand introduces another brand, buyers may draw upon their information bank to form associative evaluations of the likely properties of the new brand. This 'carry-over' of evaluative information tends to reduce information acquisition costs for buyers. Hence it can be expected that customers who have favourable impressions of current service providers will tend to favor such providers when making purchase decisions about other services that these providers may offer (Nayyar, 1990, pp. 515–516).

Furthermore, when appropriate, service providers who have created favorable impressions can attempt to capitalize on ongoing relationships by allocating more effort to convincing their existing customers (rather than new customers) to try their new services. In summary, a firm with a well established brand reputation diversifying into new services that its existing customers may buy from can be expected to enjoy a competitive advantage, because of the lower information acquisition costs to consumers.

P_8: The greater the experience and credance attributes of a *new* service being marketed by a firm, the greater the importance of brand equity as a source of competitive advantage.

Relationships/precommitment contracts[11]

In general, firms can enhance their performance by cultivating new customers and/or retaining their existing customers and selling more to them. Cultivating new customers in generally more expensive than retaining existing customers, particularly in mature markets. Riechheld and Sasser (1990) found a 5% reduction in customer defections to be associated with profit increases ranging from 25 to 85% in the industries they studied. Findings such as these suggest that service firms doing business with their customers from a long term relationship perspective (rather than a single transaction perspective) either through an implicit or explicit precommitment have a greater potential of achieving cost advantages. Precommitment contracts, by removing a portion of the market from the competitive arena and thereby introducing an asymmetry between incumbents and potential entrants, act as entry deterrents (Oster, 1990).

Developing relationships with and retaining customers are central to the concept of *memberships*, which constitute non-contractual approaches to precommitment. Service businesses have successfully employed various methods to 'lock in' customers. Non-contractual switching costs created by airlines through their frequent flyer programs and hotel chains through their honored frequent guest programs are cases in point. The more formalized such relationships are, the greater are the benefits that accrue to the service provider. In return for exclusive privileges for members, valuable information collected about customers can be used to gain scope advantages (by cross-selling other services to customers), as well as to build non-contractual switching costs. For example, American Express reportedly has over 450 items of information on each customer that are used by its direct marketing division to sell consumer products to them (Newport, 1989). Studies focusing on service industries have found that developing relationships with customers (through implicit contracts) has a positive impact on firm performance (Nayyar, 1992; Crosby, Evans and Cowles, 1990; Crosby and Stephens, 1987). Trust provides an alternative means to developing non-contractual precommitments with customers. Trust (i.e. a willingness to rely on an exchange partner in whom one has confidence) has also been shown to be positively associated with commitment to a relationship (Moorman, Zaltman and Deshpande, 1992).

Precommitment contracts can not only deter entry but also prevent customers from exiting existing contracts. For example, in hospital management contracts, incumbent firms have a significant edge in contract renewals because of the substantial costs to hospitals of changing firms (Porter, 1985). The switching costs become higher as (1) the customer gets accustomed to the procedures provided by the system, resulting in a *procedural specificity* (Malone, Yates and Benjamin, 1987); (2) the extent to which this procedural specificity is increased by an *electronic integration* effect (dependency of the customer on a vendor, created by the use of interorganizational or transaction-based systems (Malone, Yates and Benjamin, 1987; Glazer, 1991)); and (3) the customers modify their own internal procedures as a result of using the system (Barrett and Konsynski, 1982; Runge, 1988). Studies in the insurance industry have found that agents who were electronically linked with a particular insurance carrier showed a significant increase in the number of policies written with that carrier compared to agents who were not electronically linked to the carrier (Venkatraman and Zaheer, 1990; O'Callaghan, Kaufmann and Konsynski, 1992). As noted previously, buying services with greater experience and credence qualities involves greater consumer risk taking. Relationships, by nurturing strong social and personal ties with consumers (Czepiel, 1990), allow a firm to offer a greater assurance to customers and lower the perceived risk (see Crosby and Stephens, 1987; Crosby, Evans and Cowles, 1990).

P₉: The greater the experience and credence attributes of a service, the greater the importance of relationships as a source of competitive differentiation advantage.

Spatial preemption

Because demand for many customer services is based on convenience, preemptive identification of ideal service locations is critical to achieving better facility utilization (Allen, 1988). However, though the delivery of certain services could require a firm to invest in multiple service delivery facilities at locations that are convenient to the served market (e.g. facilities for cash withdrawal and deposit), certain other services can be offered from a single centralized location (e.g. credit cards). Clearly, preemption of strategic locations is an important source of competitive cost and differentiation advantage only in the context of the former, as highlighted in reference to the banking industry:

The *simultaneity/inseparability* characteristic of services implies that unlike goods, services are typically produced and consumed at the same time. Therefore, a consumer engaging in a financial transaction such as cash withdrawal must interface with a service deliverer, namely the bank teller. An alternative technological solution to serving this customer need is to install automated teller machines (ATMs). With ATMs in place, serving a customer need such as financial transactions processing does not have to be limited to the regular banking hours of 9.00 a.m. to 3.00 p.m. In effect, the simultaneity characteristic of services is no longer a constraint on the service provider. The service can be made available for 24 hours a day, 365 days a year. Also, to use the service, the consumer does not have to be physically present on the bank premises. The transactions can be processed through ATMs placed at strategic locations off the bank premises.

The first firm that recognized the potential of this alternative technological solution had an array of opportunities to achieve a SCA. First, it had the opportunity to acquire or lease prime real estate at strategic locations (off-bank premises) for placing its ATMs at prices below those that would prevail later in the evolution of the market. (As the market for a resource such as strategic locations for placing ATMs became competitive, the price of this resource would have been bid up until it was equal to the net present value of future above-normal benefits that can be derived from this resource (see Barney, 1986b).) This would have lead to a cost asymmetry between the first firm to make a significant investment in spatial preemption of locations for placement of ATMs and later entrants. Second, under conditions of manufacturing capacity constraints in the supplier industry, by contracting with supplier firms for their entire output of ATMs, the firm could have delayed the availability of ATMs to other competing firms. Because of the response time lag inherent in the supplier industry (i.e. the amount of time that would have elapsed before ATM manufacturers would have been in a position to deliver ATMs to the competitors of the pioneering bank), this source of competitive advantage would have endured for some period of time, though not indefinitely. In other words, even the firm's competitors who also recognized the potential of ATMs as an effective solution to the simultaneity characteristic of services would not have been in a position to immediately neutralize the differentiation advantage enjoyed by the pioneering firm attributable to a unique firm resource (ATMs). In summary, by making preemptive investments in key resources, a perceptive firm could have achieved an *absolute cost advantage* (through preemptive contracts for acquiring or leasing strategic locations for placing ATMs), as well as a *differentiation advantage* (through preemptive contracts to acquire the entire output of ATM manufacturers and spatial preemption of strategic locations). Understandably, the value of supplier industry response lag time as a source of competitive advantage would have diminished over time as manufacturers of ATMs stepped up their output. Hence, firms need to constantly explore new bases of competitive advantage.

P_{10}: The more decentralized the service delivery process, the greater the importance of spatial preemption as a source of competitive cost and/or differentiation advantage.

Communication good effects

The value of certain products (e.g. telephone network services, micro computer services) increases as the number of users or adopters increase. These products, called communication goods (Connor and Rumelt, 1991), serve as a means of standardization, because a large user base brings a large number of complementary goods into being. Case in point:

> The importance of communication good effects as a source of competitive differentiation advantage is highlighted by the evolution of the video cassette recorder (VCR) business. In the early years, when Sony's Betamax and Matsushita's VHS-format VCRs were coexisting, as well as competing to become the industry standard, video rental service businesses stocked an equal number of prerecorded tapes in both formats. As the percentage of households owning VHS format VCRs increased relative to the percentage owning Betamax format VCRs, video rental service businesses modified their inventory mix. In most instances, they stocked multiple copies of video software prerecorded in the VHS format, but only one copy in the Betamax format. Over time, with (1) video software marketers (i.e. movie studios) increasingly offering their ware exclusively in the VHS format, (2) video rental service firms carrying only VHS-format tapes, and (3) most retail outlets stocking only VHS-format blank tapes, the VHS format emerged as the industry standard.

When communication goods are also experience products (such as computer software, disk operating systems), there is a market for both standardization and reputation bonding. Therefore, a particular brand becomes the industry standard and a powerful means of coordination (Rumelt, 1987). Developing or setting industry standards makes a firm's position more sustainable (Porter, 1985). In cases of products in which evaluation is difficult, akin to reputation, the industry standard plays the role of an alternative cue that makes itself more salient to the customer. Therefore,

P_{11}: The greater the experience and credence attributes of a service, the greater the importance of communication good effects as a source of competitive differentiation advantage.

The importance of spatial preemption and communication good effects as potential sources of competitive advantage is also moderated by the order of entry of firms into an industry. Literature on pioneering or first-mover advantage, a major area of research in economics, strategic management, and marketing, suggests that on average, pioneers have higher market shares than late entrants (cf. Robinson and Fornell, 1985; Robinson, 1988).[12] Potential sources of first-mover advantage and disadvantages associated with market pioneering are reviewed by Lieberman and Montgomery (1988) and Kerin, Varadarajan and Peterson (1992). The preceding discussions relating to spatial preemption and communication good effects suggest the following:

P_{12}: Potential opportunities for achieving competitive cost and/or differentiation advantage through spatial preemption are greater for the market pioneer than for later entrants.

P_{13}: Potential opportunities for achieving competitive differentiation advantage through communication good effects are greater for the market pioneer than for later entrants.

Corporate culture

An organization's culture is a complex set of beliefs and ways of doing things that influence the organization's perspective of itself and the world around it. A key element of corporate culture is the set of formal rules and structures that governs the way people relate to one another in the workplace. Another is the set of myths and traditions that help define the ideology of the organization (Mintzberg, 1983). Most of the literature on organization culture and performance of a firm suggests that culture can have a significant positive economic value for a firm (Barney, 1986a; Ouchi, 1981; Deal and Kennedy, 1982). The strong culture hypothesis suggests that firms that have strong distinctive traits, values and shared belief patterns will outperform organizations that are weak on these dimensions (Dennison, 1984). Strong cultures can (1) help attain a shared vision and goal congruence among employees to meet organizational goals (Wilkins and Ouchi, 1983); (2) empower employees to be flexible and achieve organizational goals (Pascale, 1985); and (3) energize the employees of an organization. A recent study reports that firms with cultures that emphasize key managerial constituencies (customers, stockholders and employees) and leadership (at all levels) outperformed by a large margin firms that did not have those cultural traits (Kotter and Heskett, 1992). Another recent study focusing on culture types as determinants of performance (Deshpande, Farley and Webster, 1993) reports that Japanese companies with corporate cultures stressing competitiveness (markets) and entrepreneurship ('adhocracies') outperformed those dominated by internal cohesiveness (clans) or rules (hierarchies). Services being primarily delivered by employees, the 'people' component of service delivery as perceived by customers plays an important role in service differentiation. Hence, a critical factor that endows a service organization with a competitive edge is its employees, and the way they are influenced by the culture of the organization.

P₁₄: The greater the 'people' intensity of a service industry, the greater the importance of culture as a source of competitive advantage.

Organizational expertise/producer learning/experience effects[13]

Organizational learning, or the improvement in skills and abilities achieved through learning within the firm (Weston, Chung and Hoag, 1990), can have at least two beneficial effects. The first is increased efficiency of individual workers or worker groups. Experience curves, an extension of learning curves, are the result of applying the learning curve principle to all value-added costs rather than to just production and labor costs.[14] The presence of experience effects (the average total cost per unit, measured in constant current declining by a constant percentage with every doubling of cumulative experience) have been documented in the context of both equipment-intensive service industries such as telecommunications and electric power utilities and people-intensive service industries such as life insurance (see Abell and Hammond, 1980; Boston Consulting Group, 1972).

A second aspect of organizational learning is team effort. As members of an organization work together over a period of time, the *Williamson principle* can take effect – that is, an organization may realize economies of information interchange through common training and experience, repeated interpersonal interactions, and the possible development of a compact code (Williamson, 1971, 1975). In other words, inside the organization, information flows more efficiently and transaction costs are reduced, and the firm becomes more efficient as experience is gained. Furthermore, firms, by changing task designs to form self-managed cross-functional and cross-trained service groups, could (1) improve the quality of service provided by controlling variance at source (Pasmore, 1988), (2) improve the flexibility of the organization by empowering teams to respond to specific consumer requests (Tansik, 1990), and (3) blend capabilities to solve complicated problems spanning several functional areas speedily and effectively. Enhanced performance resulting from employing teams has been documented in a number of empirical research studies (cf. Johnston *et al.*, 1981).

Organizational learning or expertise can be a source of competitive advantage only when the (1) learning is tacit and not observable in use and (2) underlying knowledge is complex (Winter, 1987). Competitors free riding on a firm's learning and expertise is more difficult under these conditions, as well as when few people are privy to the information and employee mobility is low. However, the characteristics of various service industries do not appear to moderate the role of organizational expertise as a source of competitive advantage.

Information technology[15]

Information technology (IT) refers to the collective means of assembling and electronically storing, transmitting, processing, and retrieving words, numbers, images, and sounds (Gerstein, 1987, p. 5). IT's importance as a source of SCA stems from its potential to impact the transformation of a service firm's value chain (see Porter, 1990). IT can aid in attaining an SCA by (1) providing companies with new ways to outperform rivals, through lowering costs and/or enhancing differentiation; (2) building barriers to entry, building switching costs, and sometimes completely changing the basis of competition; and (3) spawning entirely new businesses (Porter and Millar, 1985). For example, investments in IT allow a business to achieve a differentiation advantage by securing relationships through improved service quality and enhancing its ability to quickly respond to market shifts. Cases in point: A large medical supply company provides on-line order entry terminals and inventory management software for its customers and successfully achieves a competitive differentiation advantage and creates switching costs, thereby reducing buyer power. As customers' systems are integrated with those of suppliers, it becomes more difficult for customers to order from a competitor. Because changing suppliers would entail testing, implementation, and retraining costs, customers exhibit an inclination to remain loyal to their current suppliers. The more sophisticated the ordering system, the less the buyers' power to switch. The Limited, a major retail chain, reportedly is able to respond four times faster than its competition to shifts in customers' preferences by monitoring customer preferences on a daily basis, and transmitting this information to production plants through satellite communication systems (Achrol, 1991). Additional insights into the potential for exploiting IT to achieve a sustainable competitive advantage across a broad spectrum of service industries are provided by the case histories summarized in Table 1.

DISCUSSION

The managerial implications presented in this section are organized around six themes:

1. A firm's skills and resources constitute potential sources of competitive advantage only if they offer benefits desired by customers. As Day and Wensley (1988) point out, assessment of opportunities for competitive advantage must revolve around the analysis of customer benefits. In the absence of such analysis, a firm's attempts to leverage its skills and resources into positional advantages are likely to prove ineffective. Case in point:

> In the market for electronic components and calculators, Texas Instruments (TI) successfully exploited scale effects and experience effects to lower costs, and market the product at a low price. It attempted to pursue a similar strategy with digital watches. However, customers did not view low price as a key buying criterion in the purchase of watches. Features and appearance were viewed as more important. TI's pursuit of a cost leadership strategy in the marketing of digital watches was ineffective, ultimately leading to its withdrawal from the business.

2. The attainment of SCA is not an end in itself, but a means to an end, namely superior long-term financial performance. A corporation is not in business just to achieve an SCA over its competitors, but to create wealth for its shareholders. Actions that contribute to SCA but detract from creating shareholder wealth can be good strategy in the competitive sense, but bad strategy for the corporation (Coyne, 1985). Case in point:

Table 1. Leveraging information technology for achieving competitive advantage in service industries

Potential opportunities for capitalizing on information technology[a]	Case exemplars
A. Spawn new businesses Information technology (IT) has the potential to spawn new businesses in three ways: (a) by making new businesses technologically feasible; (b) by creating derived demand for new products; and (c) creating new businesses within old businesses.	The Internal Revenue Service (IRS), with the objectives of cost saving and improved accuracy, introduced electronic filing of individual tax returns in 1985. Electronic filing coupled with direct deposit has opened the gateway for a variety of new financial service products. As Zuboff (1988) notes, an attempt at automation of an activity has *informated* the industry (i.e. provided as a by-product large quantities of information that were previously unavailable). American Express and IDS Tax Services launched a new business called AmeriTax to exploit this opportunity by offering to provide a variety of specially tailored services for individual tax payers (Venkatraman, 1991).
B. Build switching costs and deter entry IT provides opportunities for firms to introduce switching costs on buyers or channel members, and thereby deter exit, as well as make entry more difficult for new entrants.	Some large medical supply companies provide on-line order entry terminals and inventory management software for their customers. As customers' systems are integrated with those of suppliers, it becomes more difficult for customers to order from a competitor. Because changing suppliers would entail testing, implementation and retraining costs, customers exhibit an inclination to remain loyal to their current suppliers. The more sophisticated the ordering system, the less the buyer's power to switch. McKesson, a large drug distributor, by constantly reinvesting in information technology and enhancing its capabilities, and providing newer and additional services, has not only kept itself ahead of competition, but also has become indispensable to its consumers (Magnet, 1992).
C. Enhance cost and differentiation advantage IT provides firms with an opportunity to achieve a cost advantage by lowering the cost of various activities constituting the value chain, and a differentiation advantage through (a) service customization, and/or (b) value enhancement through bundling of information.	USAA, an insurance firm, by employing IT to image documents, has been able to significantly reduce the amount of paper handling and lower the cost of writing policies. At USAA, use of IT to image documents has enabled one employee to do the work previously done by five employees. Furthermore, when consumers call for information, little time is spent in searching for old paper correspondence, since all prior correspondence is available on the computer network. This enables USAA to provide superior service at a lower cost (Magnet, 1992; Weizer *et al.*, 1991).

Coping with the soaring cost of insurance is a concern shared by insurance companies and its corporate customers alike. Cigna, an insurance carrier, by compiling risk information and sharing this information with its customers, has been in a position to achieve a differentiation advantage. The Cigna Risk Information Service enables its customers to identify their facilities with a disproportionately high frequency of accidents, institute new safety programs at these facilities and thus lower their insurance |

Table 1 continued on next page

Table 1. Leveraging information technology for achieving competitive advantage in service industries *continued*

Potential opportunities for capitalizing on information technology[a]	Case exemplars
	bill. The system's ability to provide Cigna's customers better information about their far-flung operations than they can get using their own customers is reported to have been instrumental in several large firms shifting all or more of their casualty business to Cigna (Petre, 1985).

A recent innovation developed by Federal Express Corporation, a hand-held device that allows couriers to generate optically scannable zip code labels indicating the destination to which a package is to be sent, enables the firm to provide superior service at a lower cost. This process innovation manifests in better service quality (faster and reliable service) by speeding up the sorting process at Federal Express' hub locations and cutting down on the number of misrouted packages (Hawkins, 1992). |

[a]For additional insights into using information technology for competitive advantage, see Porter and Millar (1985).

Fruhan (1972) illustrates the economics of capacity competition in the context of an airline route served by two carriers, in which the dominant carrier, by providing 70% of all the seats available on the route, gains a 80% market share. On the other hand, the smaller carrier with a 30% capacity share is in a position to obtain only a 20% share of the market. Assuming that all other firm controllable market share influencing factors are the same for the two carriers (such as air fare), how does one explain the imbalance between capacity share and market share? Fruhan theorizes that this may be because there is a greater likelihood that the larger carrier is offering a flight at a time closer to the departure time desired by a traveler. In such a hypothetical two-carrier route, if the dominant carrier adopted a retreat strategy (not responding to a minority carrier's capacity additions) it would rapidly find itself losing both market share and profit. On the other hand, if the dominant carrier adopted a matching strategy (responding to the minority carrier's capacity additions by adding capacity to maintain a constant percentage capacity share (i.e., 70% vs. 30%)) it could hold onto its market share position (i.e., 80% vs. 20%). However, this scenario will inevitably lead to a decline in a passenger load factor of both carriers and hence, adversely impact their financial performance.

3. Certain sources of competitive advantage may be more enduring than others. Two additional potential sources of competitive advantage discussed in the previous section are reputation and corporate culture. The development of reputation being socially complex (Reed and Defillippi, 1990) and reputation being a form of a stock (Dierckx and Cool, 1989) developed/earned over time, it is imperfectly imitable (Barney, 1991), and a relatively more enduring source of competitive advantage. Though frequent calls to emulate a particular organization's culture are made, there is evidence to suggest that imitating culture may be difficult.

A. The culture of a successful firm can be difficult to describe (Lippman and Rumelt,

1982) and categorize (Barley, 1983; Gregory, 1983). Because culture in most situations is tacit (Berger and Luckman, 1967), it remains inherently proprietary (Barney, 1986a).

B. Even if culture can be described, it may be intrinsically wound up with a firm's unique history and heritage, making it nearly impossible to imitate (Barney, 1986a; Clark, 1970, 1972).

C. The failure of numerous mergers has been attributed to the clash of cultures and the difficulty in changing them. In the face of organizational rigidities, changing the prevailing culture may often be difficult, and attempts to do so have yielded mixed results (Kanter, 1989).

Scale economies, in contrast, may be less enduring as a source of competitive advantage, to the extent that it is not imperfectly imitable and strategically equivalent substitutes are available. For example, firms can use nimbleness and flexibility to overcome the benefits of scale enjoyed by larger competitors (cf. Peters, 1992). Furthermore, information technology, by facilitating mass customization (and thus effectively offering to customers the cost benefit of mass production and the differentiation benefit of customization), could limit the value of scale economies per se as a source of competitive advantage (see Boynton and Victor, 1991; Zuboff, 1988).

4. Durability of a firm's competitive positional advantages is contingent on its making sustenance and enhancement reinvestments in its present sources of competitive advantage, as well as investments in new skills and resources. Realistically, competing firms in an industry are likely to continuously strive to bridge the resource and skill gaps that place them at a disadvantage relative to their competitors. Furthermore, in a dynamic market environment characterized by changes in consumer preferences, the resources and skills underlying a particular firm's positional advantages are prone to depreciate over time. Under these conditions, ensuring the durability of a firm's sources of competitive advantage may require both *sustenance* and *enhancement reinvestment* in these sources. Also, given the ever-present possibility that a firm's present sources of competitive advantage might over time erode (become competitively neutral), there is a constant need for businesses to focus on developing new and high-order sources of competitive advantage. The need for making substantial sustenance and enhancement reinvestments over the long term to develop and nurture sources of competitive advantage is exemplified by the case of the SABRE system, owned by AMR Corporation, the parent firm of American Airlines. Though the system became operational in 1976, even as late as 1988, AMR Corporation continued to spend significant amounts (approximately $1.225 billion) toward further enhancing the capabilities of SABRE (Hopper, 1990). The importance of making sustenance and enhancement investments is also highlighted by the case of Mead Data Central, a pioneer in document retrieval services that experienced a decline in market share from 95% in the early 1980s to 60% in 1992. West Publishing Company, which entered the market six years later, was able to overcome the pioneering advantages of Mead Data Central by employing a strategy of technology leapfrogging and providing more information, a more user friendly interface, and a lower price. Mead, in contrast, is reported to have stayed with an archaic consumer interface and not provided any new services (Berss, 1993).

5. A critical reassessment of conventional wisdom regarding sources of competitive advantage may be called for in the face of successful new game strategies. The business world is replete with case histories of firms departing from prevalent industry practices in major ways and succeeding in their pursuit of contrarian strategies. Case in point:

> Southwest Airlines, a Dallas-based airline, does many things differently compared to traditional airlines. Though its airfares are significantly lower than those of full service airlines, it does not offer many features that full service airlines do, such as advance boarding passes, in-flight meals, and automatic transfer of luggage to or from other carrier's flights. In order to keep costs low, Southwest generally operates out of secondary airports of the cities it serves rather than major airports. These differences, coupled with a highly productive work force, have enabled Southwest to enjoy a 43% cost advantage over the industry leader, American Airlines (*Business Week*, 1992).

New game strategies entail exploring ways to influence the environment, redefine market boundaries, reshape market behavior to fit the company's strengths, and refute or make irrelevant conventional wisdom regarding key success factors (sources of competitive advantage) (Buaron, 1981). Consider, for example, the service-process matrix (Schmenner, 1986), in which service businesses are classified into the following categories on the basis of the degree of labor intensity and interaction and customization, characterizing a service:

A. Service factor: Low labor intensity – low interaction and customization
B. Service shop: Low labor intensity – high interaction and customization
C. Mass service: High labor intensity – low interaction and customization
D. Professional service: High labor intensity – high interaction and customization.

True to the concept of new game strategies, service firms have gained competitive advantages by being innovative and breaking traditional molds. The restaurant business (service shop) was revolutionized by fast-food restaurants (service factory), and the traditional commercial banking industry (mass service) by some banks offering certain segments, financial and investment advice at the individual customer level (professional service). Inevitably, successful new game strategies necessitate a reassessment of presumed relationships between key variables and resource deployment patterns viewed as normatively conducive to superior performance.

6. The sustainability of a firm's competitive advantages are also impacted by imperfectly competitive markets for skills and resources, luck, and suboptimal decisions made by competitors. It was pointed out previously that spatial preemption of a strategic resource such as geographic locations for installation of ATMs can be a source of competitive advantage and above-normal profits if the price paid for the resource is lower than the benefits derived from it. However, if the market for the resource were perfectly competitive, the price of the resource would be bid up until it was equal to the net present value of its future above-normal benefits. This point of view implies that the achievement of SCA and, consequently, above-normal profits depends crucially on the presence of imperfections in the market for skills and resources. If the markets are perfect, the prices of resources/skills are bid up and the above-normal profits are competed away. The presence of imperfectly competitive markets for resources and skills can occur under the following conditions: (1) some firms are better informed or have special insights than competitors about the future value of a strategy and (2) firms that achieve competitive advantage are lucky (Barney, 1986b). For example, at the end of World War II, two major competitors, Sears and Montgomery Ward were more or less of the same size. Sears envisioned that the end of the war would stimulate pent-up demand for goods and services and invested heavily in the expansion of its retail and catalogue operations.[16] Montgomery Ward, in contrast, envisioned that the end of the war would be followed by a period of austerity and went on a rampant cost-cutting program. Here, a better informed firm (Sears) was able to gain a competitive advantage in the absence of its principal competitor (Montgomery Ward) pursuing a similar strategy and bidding up the price of critical resources/skills.

Given that luck is beyond the control of managers, the alternative strategy open to them is to become better informed than their competition. Two ways of achieving this are (1) environmental analysis and (2) organizational analysis. Barney (1986b) contends that environmental analysis is less likely to systematically generate exceptional advantages because its methods are readily available in the public domain. Organizational analysis, in contrast, which is based on information internal to the firm and not available to competition, is more likely to generate exceptional advantages. Prahalad and Hamel's (1990) examination of the strategies adopted by NEC building on its 'core competencies' is an example in this genre. Firms may be better off relying on such organizational analysis rather than depending on publicly available techniques to identify sources of competitive advantage.

In addition to the existence of an imperfectly competitive market for skills and resources, and/or luck, certain other factors in the market environment could also impact on the sustainability of sources of competitive advantage (Amit and Schoemaker, 1993). It has been suggested that the emergence of new technologies, economic and political trends, competitive actions, and changes in consumer preferences could lead managers to approach future courses of action with 'considerable bias, illusion and suboptimality' (Kahneman, Slovic and Tversky, 1982; Amit and Schoemaker, 1993). The presence of uncertainty also makes managers hold diverse expectations about the potential returns from a source of competitive advantage.[17] Schoemaker (1992) outlines a methodology for linking the strategic vision of the firm with its core capabilities in the presence of market uncertainty and an unpredictable future.

CONCLUSION

In a recent article providing an assessment of the services marketing and management literature spanning a 15-year period, Swartz, Bowen, and Brown (1992, p. 17) highlight the need for developing contingency theories of services marketing and management:

> Several scholars have invested much energy in analyzing the variance *between* the manufacturing and service sectors. . . . However, it is now time to invest more energy in analyzing the substantial variance *within* the service sector. . . . The research requirement, then, is to develop and test propositions about what marketing and management practices are effective for certain types of services under certain conditions.

The contingency model of SCA in service industries and propositions presented here partially address the research needs highlighted by these authors. Building on extant literature, the proposed model provides insights into the moderating effects of the characteristics of services, service industries, and firms within an industry on the skills and resources underlying a service business's competitive positional advantage. However, for many of the constructs presented in the model (e.g. brand equity, communication goods effect, and spatial preemption), psychometric scales are not currently available. Development and validation of psychometric scales for these constructs and empirical testing and further refinement of the proposed model constitute promising future research directions.

ACKNOWLEDGMENTS

The authors thank A. Parasuraman, Leonard L. Berry, the anonymous *JM* reviewers, and Thomas C. Kinnear for their detailed and constructive comments.

NOTES

[1] Unless stated otherwise, the term 'product' is used in the article to encompass both goods and services.

[2] For a discussion on the distinctive competencies/competitive capabilities underlying the superior performance of two superior performers in the banking sector – Wachovia Corporation and Bank One – see Stalk, Evans and Shulman (1992, pp. 68–69).

[3] The skills and resources underlying a business's positional advantages listed in Figure 1 and discussed in this article are intended to be illustrative rather than exhaustive. The principal focus here is on skills and resources that could impact differentially on competitive advantage across service industries.

[4] Finer distinctions of resources and skills are provided by Williams (1992) and Lado, Boyd and Wright (1992).

[5] Though the value chain (a set of interdependent primary and secondary value activities that are connected by linkages) is not explicitly shown in Figure 1, it should be recognized that a business's unique resources and skills lead to competitive positional advantages by enabling it to perform the various value activities either at a lower cost or in a way that leads to differentiation. See Porter (1985) and Stalk, Evans and Shulman (1992) for additional insights into value chains.

[6] An examination of the writings of Rumelt (1984) and Coyne (1985) on barriers to imitation reveals considerable overlap if not synonymity of thought. Implicit in the business system, position, and organizational or managerial quality gaps outlined by Coyne are the various isolating mechanisms identified by Rumelt.

[7] See: McGuire and Schneeweis (1983) and Lubatkin and Shrieves (1986). Additionally, in the case of several resources and skills, their benefits may be in the long term and in some cases the benefits (such as fact information flow, understanding of market trends, fast procedures, and more effective customer service) may be difficult to quantify. In these cases, the use of standard hurdle rates may be inappropriate, and non-traditional criteria may be required (Shank and Govindarajan, 1992).

[8] As evidenced by the links leading into and from the box labeled 'Re-investments in Resources and Skills' (Figure 1), there is an implicit time dimension in the proposed conceptual framework.

[9] It is not clear, however, whether it was Merrill Lynch's patent application, the time it took for competitors to develop the technology needed to offer similar service, the uncertainty created by the legal opposition to the service raised by banks and state governments, or a combination of these factors that gave Merrill Lynch a five-year head start and market exclusively (see *Wall Street Journal*, 1989, 1993; Kerin, Varadarajan and Peterson, 1992).

[10] The discussion presented in this section builds on literature on brand equity in the marketing discipline and on reputation in the management and economics disciplines.

[11] Though the focus of this section is limited to relationships with customers, relationship marketing is more broadly construed in business literature to include relationships with suppliers, channel members, and other organizations as well (i.e. cooperating and partnering with other firms including competitors). For example, see Ohmae (1989).

[12] The validity and generalizability of studies reporting a systematic relationship between order of entry and market share have, however, been questioned in light of their methodological shortcomings, such as operational definition of market pioneer, survivor bias, and sample composition (Kerin, Varadarajan and Peterson, 1992).

[13] Given that organizational expertise and information technology appear to be equally important sources of competitive advantage across all service industries, no formal propositions are presented in the sections devoted to these sources of competitive advantage.

[14] The experience curve doctrine has been criticized for lacking a sound theoretical base. It has been pointed out that it treats a possible effect of achieving a cost advantage (share building) as a cause and what is actually a possible contributing cause of share building (achieving a cost advantage) as an effect (Albert, 1989).

[15] Because several studies published during the last ten years provide excellent insights into the importance of IT as a source of competitive advantage (cf. Benjamin *et al.*, 1984; Cash and Konsynski, 1985; Clemons and Row, 1987; Glazer, 1991; Little, 1990; Porter and Millar, 1985; and Weill, 1992), only a few key issues are highlighted in this section.

[16] The question of whether Sears had special insights or was just lucky is very relevant here. However, the problems currently afflicting the firm are not an issue.

[17] For a more detailed exposition of this viewpoint, see recent literature on behavior decision theory (Amit and Schoemaker, 1993; Klayman and Schoemaker, 1992; Schoemaker, 1990; Zajac and Bazerman, 1991).

REFERENCES

Aaker, D. A. (1989) 'Managing Assets and Skills: A Key to Sustainable Competitive Advantage'. *California Management Review* **31**(Winter): 91–106.

Aaker, D. A. (1991) *Managing Brand Equity: Capitalizing on the Value of a Brand Name.* New York: The Free Press.

Abell, D. F. and Hammond, J. S. (1980) *Strategic Market Planning: Problems and Analytical Approaches.* Englewood Cliffs, NJ: Prentice-Hall, Inc.

Achrol, R. S. (1991) 'Evolution of the Marketing Organization: New Forms for Turbulent Environments'. *Journal of Marketing* **55**(October): 77–93.

Alberts, W. W. (1989) 'The Experience Curve Doctrine Revisited'. *Journal of Marketing* **53**(July): 36–49.

Allen, M. (1988) 'Competitive Confrontation in Consumer Services'. *Planning Review* **17**(January–February): 4–9.

Amit, R. and Schoemaker, P. J. H. (1993) 'Strategic Assets and Organizational Rent'. *Strategic Management Journal* **14**(January): 33–46.

Barley, S. P. (1983) 'Semiotics and the Study of Occupational and Organizational Cultures'. *Administrative Science Quarterly* **28**(September): 393–413.

Barney, J. B. (1986a) 'Organizational Culture: Can It Be a Source of Sustained Competitive Advantage?'. *Academy of Management Review* **11**(July): 656–665.

Barney, J. B. (1986b) 'Strategic Factor Markets: Expectations, Luck and Business Strategy'. *Management Science* **32**(October): 1231–1241.

→ Barney, J. B. (1991) 'Firm Resources and Sustained Competitive Advantage'. *Journal of Management* **17**(March): 99–120.

Barney, J. B., McWilliams, A. and Turk, T. (1989) 'On the Relevance of the Concept of Entry Barriers in the Theory of Competitive Strategy'. Paper presented at the Annual Meeting of the Strategic Management Society, San Francisco.

Barrett, D. and Konsynski, B. (1982) 'Inter-Organization Sharing Systems'. *MIS Quarterly* **6** Special Issue (December): 93–105.

Baumol, W. J., Panzar, J. C. and Willig, R. P. (1982) *Contestable Markets and the Theory of Industry Structure.* New York: Harcourt, Brace, and Jovanovich.

Benjamin, R. I., Rockhart, J. F., Scott Morton, M. S. and Wyman, J. (1984) 'Information Technology: A Strategic Opportunity'. *Sloan Management Review* **25**(Spring): 3–10.

Berger, P. L. and Luckman, T. (1967) *The Social Construction of Reality.* Garden City, NY: Anchor.

Berry, L. L. and Parasuraman, A. (1991) *Marketing Services: Competing Through Quality.* New York: The Free Press.

Berss, M. (1993) 'Logging off Lexis'. *Forbes* (Jan 14): 46.

Blattberg, R. C. and Deighton, J. (1991) 'Interactive Marketing: Exploiting the Age of Addressability'. *Sloan Management Review* **33**(Fall): 5–14.

Boston Consulting Group (1972) *Perspectives on Experience.* USA: BCG, Inc.

Boulding, W., Kalra, A., Staelin, R. and Zeithaml, V. A. (1993) 'A Dynamic Process Model of Service Quality: From Expectations to Behavioral Intentions'. *Journal of Marketing Research* **30**(February): 7–27.

Boynton, A. C. and Victor, B. (1991) 'Beyond Flexibility: Building and Managing the Dynamically Stable Organization'. *California Management Review* (Fall): 53–66.

Buaron, Roberto (1981) 'New Game Strategies'. *McKinsey Quarterly* (Spring): 24–40.

Business Week (1992) 'The Airline Mess' (July 6): 50–55.

Cash, J. I. and Konsynski, B. (1985) 'IS Redraws Competitive Boundaries'. *Harvard Business Review* **63**(March–April): 134–142.

Clark, B. R. (1970) *The Distinctive College: Antioch, Reed, and Swarthmore.* Chicago: Aldine.

Clark, B. R. (1972) 'The Organizational Saga in Higher Education'. *Administrative Science Quarterly* **17**(June): 178–184.

Clemons, E. K. and Row, M. (1987) 'Structural Differences Among Firms: A Potential Source of Competitive Advantage in the Application of Information Technology'. *Proceedings of the Eighth International Conference on Information Systems* (December): 1–9.

Coyne, K. P. (1985) 'Sustainable Competitive Advantage—What It Is, What It Isn't'. *Business Horizons* **29**(January–February): 54–61.

Coyne, K. P. (1989) 'Beyond Service Fads – Meaningful Strategies for the Real World'. *Sloan Management Review* **30**(Summer): 69–76.

Crosby, L. A. and Stephens, N. (1987) 'Effects of Relationship Marketing on Satisfaction, Retention, and Prices in the Life Insurance Industry'. *Journal of Marketing Research* **24**(November): 404–411.

Crosby, L. A., Evans, K. R. and Cowles, D. (1990) 'Relationship Quality in Services Selling: An Interpersonal Influence Perspective'. *Journal of Marketing* **54**(July): 68–81.

Czepiel, John A. (1990) 'Managing Relationships with Customers: A Differentiation Philosophy of Marketing'. In *Service Management Effectiveness* (David E. Bowen, Richard B. Chase, Thomas G. Cummings, Eds). San Francisco, CA: Jossey-Bass Publishers, 213–233.

Darby, M. R. and Karni, E. (1973) 'Free Competition and the Optimal Amount of Fraud'. *Journal of Law and Economics* **16**(January): 67–86.

Day, G. S. and Wensley, R. (1988) 'Assessing Advantage: A Framework for Diagnosing Competitive Superiority'. *Journal of Marketing* **52**(April): 1–20.

Deal, T. and Kennedy, A.E. (1982) *Corporate Cultures.* Reading, MA: Addison-Wesley.

Dennison, D. R. (1984) 'Bringing Corporate Culture to the Bottom Line'. *Organizational Dynamics* **13**(Autumn): 4–22.

Deshpande, R., Farley, J. U. and Webster, F. E. Jr. (1993) 'Corporate Culture, Customer

Orientation and Innovativeness in Japanese Firms: A Quadrad Analysis'. *Journal of Marketing* **57**(January): 23–37.

Dierickx, I. and Cool, K. (1989) 'Asset Stock Accumulation and Sustainability of Competitive Advantage'. *Management Science* **35**(November): 1504–1511.

Fisk, R. P., Brown, S. W. and Bitner, M. J. (1993) 'Tracking the Evolution of the Services Marketing Literature'. *Journal of Retailing* **69**(Spring): 61–103.

Fruhan, W. E. (1972) *The Fight for Competitive Advantage: The Study of the United States Domestic Trunk Carriers.* Boston: Harvard University, Division of Research, Graduate School of Business Administration.

Gerstein, M. S. (1987) *The Technology Connection.* Reading, MA: Addison-Wesley.

Glazer, R. (1991) 'Marketing in an Information-Intensive Environment: Strategic Implications of Knowledge as an Asset'. *Journal of Marketing* **55**(October): 1–19.

Gregory, K. L. (1983) 'Native-view Paradigms: Multiple Cultures and Culture Conflicts in Organizations'. *Administrative Science Quarterly* **28**(September): 359–376.

Hamel, G. and Prahalad, C. K. (1991) 'Corporate Imagination and Expeditionary Marketing'. *Harvard Business Review* **69**(July–August): 81–92.

Hawkins, Chuck (1992) 'Fedex: Europe Nearly Killed the Messenger'. *Business Week* (May 25): 124–126.

Heskett, James L. (1987) 'Lessons in the Service Sector'. *Harvard Business Review* **65**(March–April): 118–126.

Hopper, M. D. (1990) 'Rattling SABRE—New Ways to Compete on Information'. *Harvard Business Review* **68**(May–June): 118–125.

Johnson, D. W., Maruyama, G., Johnson, R., Nelson, R. and Skon, L. (1981) 'Effects of Cooperative, Competitive, and Individualistic Goal Structures on Achievement: A Meta-Analysis'. *Psychological Bulletin* **89**: 47–62.

Johnson, T. (1991) '15 Years of Brand Loyalty Trends'. Paper presented at the Marketing Science Institute Conference on Managing Brand Equity, Austin, TX.

Kahneman, D., Slovic, P. and Tversky, A. (1982) *Judgment Under Uncertainty: Heuristics and Biases.* Cambridge: Cambridge Press.

Kamakura, W. A. and Russell, G. J. (1991) 'Measuring Consumer Perceptions of Brand Quality with Scanner Data: Implications for Brand Equity'. Report No. 91-122, MA: Marketing Science Institute.

Kanter, R. M. (1989) *When Giants Learn to Dance.* New York, NY: Touchstone.

Kerin, R. A., Varadarajan, P. R. and Peterson, R. A. (1992) 'First-Mover Advantage: A Synthesis, Conceptual Framework and Research Propositions'. *Journal of Marketing* **56**(October): 33–52.

Klayman, J. and Schoemaker, P. J. H. (1992) 'Thinking About the Future: A Cognitive Perspective'. *Journal of Forecasting.*

Kotter, J. P. and Heskett, J. L. (1992) *Corporate Culture and Performance.* New York: The Free Press.

Kado, A. A., Boyd, N. G. and Wright, P. (1992) 'A Competency-Based Model of Sustainable Competitive Advantage: Toward a Conceptual Integration'. *Journal of Management* **18**(March): 77–91.

Landes, W. M. and Posner, R. A. (1987) 'Trademark Law: An Economic Perspective'. *Journal of Law and Economics* **30**(October): 265–309.

Levitt, T. (1976) 'The Industrialization of Service'. *Harvard Business Review* **54**(September–October): 42–52.

Levitt, T. (1986) *The Marketing Imagination.* New York: The Free Press.

Lieberman, M. B. and Montgomery, D. B. (1988) 'First-Mover Advantages'. *Strategic Management Journal* **9**(Summer): 41–58.

Lippman, S. A. and Rumelt, R. P. (1982) 'Uncertain Imitability: An Analysis of Interfirm Differences in Efficiency Under Competition'. *The Bell Journal of Economics* **13**(Autumn): 418–438.

Little, J. D. C. (1990) 'Information Technology in Marketing'. Working paper, Massachusetts Institute of Technology.

Lovelock, C. H. (1983) 'Classifying Services to Gain Strategic Marketing Insights'. *Journal of Marketing* **47**(Summer): 9–20.

Lubatkin, M. and Shrieves, R. E. (1986) 'Toward Reconciliation of Market Performance Measures with Strategic Management Research'. *Academy of Management Review* 11(July): 497–512.

Magnet, M. (1992) 'Winners in the Information Revolution'. *Fortune* (November 30): 110.

Mahoney, J. T. and Pandian, R. (1992) 'The Resource-Based View Within the Conversation of Strategic Management'. *Strategic Management Journal* 13(June): 363–380.

Malone, T. W., Yates, J. and Benjamin, R. I. (1987) 'Electronic Markets and Electronic Hierarchies'. *Communications of the ACM* 30(June): 484–497.

McGuire, J. and Schneeweis, T. (1983) 'An Analysis of Alternative Measures of Strategic Performance'. Paper presented at The Third Annual Strategic Management Society Conference, Paris.

Mintzberg, H. (1983) *Power in and Around Organizations.* Englewood Cliffs, NJ: Prentice Hall, Inc.

Moorman, C., Zaltman, G. and Deshpande, R. (1992) 'Relationships Between Providers and Users of Market Research: The Dynamics of Trust Within and Between Organizations'. *Journal of Marketing Research* 29(August): 314–328.

Murray, K. B. (1991) 'A Test of Services Marketing Theory, Consumer Information Acquisition Activities'. *Journal of Marketing* 55(January): 10–25.

Nayyar, P. R. (1990) 'Information Asymmetries: A Source of Competitive Advantage For Diversified Service Firms'. *Strategic Management Journal* 11(November–December): 513–519.

Nayyar, P. R. (1992) 'Performance Effects of Three Foci in Service Firms'. *The Academy of Management Journal* 35(December): 985–1009.

Nayyar, P. R. and Templeton, P. L. (1991) 'Seller Beware: Choosing Generic Competitive Strategies for Service Businesses Under Information Asymmetry'. In *Academy of Management Best Paper Proceedings* (J. L. Wall and L. R. Jauch, Eds), pp. 36–40.

Nelson, P. (1970) 'Information and Consumer Behavior'. *Journal of Political Economy* 78(October): 311–329.

Nelson, R. and Winter, S. (1982) *An Evolutionary Theory of Economic Change.* Cambridge, MA: Harvard University Press.

Newport, J. P. (1989) 'American Express: Service That Sells'. *Fortune* 120(November 20): 44–60.

O'Callaghan, R., Kaufmann, P. J. and Konsynski, B. (1992) 'Adoption Correlates and Share Effects of Electronic Data Interchange Systems in Marketing Channels'. *Journal of Marketing* 56(April): 45–56.

Ohmae, K. (1989) 'The Global Logic of Strategic Alliances'. *Harvard Business Review* 67(March–April): 143–154.

Oster, S. M. (1990) *Modern Competitive Analysis.* New York: Oxford University Press.

Ouchi, W. G. (1981) *Theory Z.* Reading, MA: Addison-Wesley.

Park, C. W., Jaworski, B. J. and MacInnes, D. J. (1986) 'Strategic Brand Concept-Image Management'. *Journal of Marketing* 50(October): 135–145.

Pascale, R. T. (1985) 'Fitting New Employees into the Company Culture'. *Fortune* (May 28): 28.

Pasmore, W. A. (1988) *Designing Effective Organizations: The Sociotechnical Systems Perspective.* New York: John Wiley & Sons.

Peters, T. J. (1992) 'Rethinking Scale'. *California Management Review* 34(Fall): 7–29.

Petre, P. (1985) 'How to Keep Customers Happy Captives'. *Fortune* (September 2): 42–46.

Polanyi, M. (1962) *Personal Knowledge: Towards a Post Critical Philosophy.* London: Routledge.

Porter, M. E. (1980) *Competitive Strategy.* New York: The Free Press.

Porter, M. E. (1985) *Competitive Advantage.* New York: The Free Press.

Porter, M. E. (1990) *The Competitive Advantage of Nations.* New York: The Free Press.

Porter, M. E. and Millar, V. E. (1985) 'How Information Gives You Competitive Advantage'. *Harvard Business Review* 63(July–August): 149–160.

Prahalad, C. K. and Hamel, G. (1990) 'The Core Competence of the Corporation'. *Harvard Business Review* 68(May–June): 79–87.

Quinn, B. J. and Gagnon C. E. (1986), 'Will Services Follow Manufacturing into Decline?' *Harvard Business Review* 64 (November–December), 95–103.

Quinn, B. J., Doorley,T. L. and Paquette, P. C. (1990), 'Beyond Products: Service-Based Strategy'. *Harvard Business Review* 68 (March–April): 58–68.

Reed R. and DeFilippi, R. J. (1990) 'Casual Ambiguity. Barriers to Imitation and Sustainable Competitive Advantage'. *Academy of Management Review,* **15** (January) 88–102.

Reichheld, F. F. and Sasser, W. E. (1990) 'Zero Defections: Quality Comes to Services'. *Harvard Business Review* **68** (September–October): 301–307.

Robinson, W. T. (1988) 'Sources of Market Pioneer Advantages: The Case of Industrial Goods Industries. *Journal of Marketing Research* **25** (February): 87–94.

Robinson, W. T. and Fornell, C. (1985) 'Sources of Market Pioneer Advantages in Consumer Goods Industries, *Journal of Marketing Research* **22** (August): 305–317.

Rumelt, R. P. (1984) 'Towards a Strategic Theory of the Firm'. In *Competitive Strategic Management.* (R. Lamb. Ed.). Englewood Cliffs, NJ: Prentice-Hall, pp. 556–570.

Rumelt, R. P. (1987) 'Theory, Strategy and Entrepreneurship'. In *The Competitive Challenge: Strategies for Industrial Innovation and Renewal.* Cambridge MA: Ballinger Publishing Co., pp. 137–158

Runge, D. A. (1988) *Winning with Telecommunications: An Approach for Corporate Strategists.* Washington, DC: ICIT Press.

Schmalensee, R. (1982) 'Product Differentiation Advantages of Pioneering Brands'. *American Economic Review* **72** (June): 349–365.

Schmenner, R. W. (1986) 'How Can Service Businesses Survive and Prosper?' *Sloan Management Review,* 27 (Spring): 21–32.

Shank, J. K and Govindarajan, V. (1992) 'Strategic Cost Analysis of Technological Investments'. *Sloan Management Review* **33** (Fall): 39–51.

Shoemaker, P. J. H. (1990) 'Strategy, Complexity, and Economic Rent'. *Management Science* **36** (October): 1178–1192.

Shoemaker, P. J. H. (1992) 'How to Link Strategic Vision to Core Capabilities'. *Sloan Management Review* **34** (Fall): 67–81.

Shoestack, G. L. (1977) 'Breaking Free from Product Marketing'. *Journal of Marketing* **41** (April): 73–80.

Shoestack, G. L. (1987) 'Service Positioning Through Structural Change'. *Journal of Marketing* **51** (January): 34–43,

Stalk, G., Evans, P. and Shulman, L. E. (1992) 'Competing on Capabilities; The New Rules of Corporate Strategy'. *Harvard Business Review* **70** (March–April): 57–69.

Stigler, G. J. (1961) 'The Economics of Information'. *Journal of Political Economy* **69** (June): 213–225.

Swartz, T. A., Bowen, D. E. and Brown, S. W. (1992) 'Fifteen Years After Breaking Free: Services Then, Now and Beyond'. In *Advances in Services Marketing and Management: Research and Practice,* Vol. 1 (T. A. Swartz, D. E. Bowen and S. W. Brown, Eds.). Greenwich, CT: Jai Press.

Tansik, D. A. (1990) 'Balance in Service Systems Design'. *Journal of Business Research* **20** (January): 55–61.

Teece, D. J. (1981) 'The Market for Know-How and the Efficient International Transfer of Technology'. *Annals of the American Academy of Political and Social Science* **458** (November): 81–96.

Teece, D. J. (1987) 'Profiting from Technological Innovation: Implications for Integration, Collaboration, Licensing and Public Policy'. In *The Competitive Challenge: Strategies for Industrial Innovation and Renewal,* (D. J. Teece, Ed.). Cambridge, MA: Ballinger Publishing, pp. 185–219.

Teece, D. J. (1988) 'Capturing Value from Technological Innovation: Integration, Strategic Partnering, and Licensing Decisions'. *Interfaces* **18**(May–June): 46–61.

Thomas, D. R. E. (1978) 'Strategy is Different in Service Businesses'. *Harvard Business Review* **56**(July–August): 158–165.

Treacy, M. and Wiersema, F. (1993) 'Customer Intimacy and Other Value Disciplines'. *Harvard Business Review* **71**(January–February): 84–93.

Upah, G. D. (1980) 'Mass Marketing in Service Retailing: A Review and Synthesis of Major Methods'. *Journal of Retailing* **56**(Fall): 59–76.

Venkatraman, N. (1991) 'IT-Induced Business Reconfiguration'. In *The Corporation of the 1990s,* (M. S. Scott Martin, Ed.). New York: Oxford University Press, pp. 122–158.

Venkatraman, N. and Akbar Zaheer (1990) 'Electronic Integration and Strategic Advantage: A Quasi-Experimental Study in the Insurance Industry'. *Information Systems Research* **1**(December): 377.

Vitale, M. R. (1988) 'American Hospital Supply: The ASAP System (A)'. Harvard Business School Case 9-186-005, Revision 1/88, Boston, MA: Harvard Business School Publishing Division.

Wall Street Journal (1989) 'Merrill Lynch CMAs Draw Interest, 1977' (November 3), B1.

Wall Street Journal (1993) 'Merrill's Once Revolutionary CMA Loses Some Force' (January 7), C1, C13.

Weill, P. (1992) 'The Relationship Between Investment in Information Technology and Firm Performance: A Study of the Value Manufacturing Sector'. *Information Systems Research* **3**(December): 307–333.

Weizer, N., Gardner, G. O., Lipoff, S., Roetter, M. F. and Withington, F. G. (1991) *The Arthur D. Little Forecast on Information Technology and Productivity.* New York: John Wiley & Sons Inc.

Weston, J. F., Chung, K. S. and Hoag, S. E. (1990) *Mergers, Restructuring, and Corporate Control.* Englewood Cliffs, NJ: Prentice-Hall.

Wilkins, A. L. and Ouchi, W. G. (1983) 'Efficient Cultures: Exploring the Relationship Between Culture and Organizational Performance'. *Administrative Science Quarterly* **28**(September): 468–481.

Williams, J. R. (1992) 'How Sustainable Is Your Competitive Advantage?'. *California Management Review* **34**(Spring): 29–51.

Williamson, O. E. (1971) 'The Vertical Integration of Production: Market Failure Considerations'. *American Economic Review* **61**(May): 112–123.

Williamson, O. E. (1975) *Markets and Hierarchies: Analysis and Antitrust Implications.* New York: The Free Press.

Williamson, O. E. (1985) *The Economic Institutions of Capitalism.* New York: The Free Press.

Winter, S. G. (1987) 'Knowledge and Competence as Strategic Assets'. In *The Competitive Challenge* (D. J. Teece, Ed.). New York: Harper and Row, pp. 159–184.

Zajac, E. J. and Bazerman, M. H. (1991) 'Blind Spots in Industry and Competitor Analysis'. *Academy of Management Review* **16**(January): 37–56.

Zuboff, S. (1988) *In the Age of the Smart Machine: The Future of Work and Power.* New York: Basic Books.

21

Service Firms' International Entry-Mode Choice: A Modified Transaction-Cost Analysis Approach

M. Krishna Erramilli and C.P. Rao

After a firm decides to enter a certain foreign market, it must choose a mode of entry, i.e. select an institutional arrangement for organizing and conducting international business transactions, such as contractual transfers, joint ventures, and wholly owned operations (Root, 1987).

The choice of the correct entry mode for a particular foreign market is 'one of the most critical decisions in international marketing' (Terpstra and Sarathy, 1991, p. 361). The chosen mode determines the extent to which the firm gets involved in developing and implementing marketing programs in the foreign market, the amount of control the firm enjoys over its marketing activities, and the degree to which it succeeds in foreign markets (Anderson and Gatignon, 1986; Root, 1987; Hill et al., 1990; Terpstra and Sarathy, 1991). In fact, Wind and Perlmutter (1977) describe entry-mode choice as a 'frontier issue' in international marketing.

As service firms assume greater prominence in international business (US Congress, 1986; Cateora, 1990, p. 451), researchers are beginning to ask how service firms effect entry into foreign markets and whether they differ from manufacturers in this respect (Carman and Langeard, 1980; Cowell, 1983; Sharma and Johanson, 1987; Erramilli, 1990). However, for several reasons the international marketing literature offers few concrete answers to these questions.

First, previous investigations examining entry-mode choice have focused almost exclusively on manufacturing firms (see Agarwal and Ramaswami, 1992; Gatignon and Anderson, 1988; Kogut and Singh, 1988; and Hill et al., 1990 for excellent reviews of this literature). Second, most published studies on the international operations of service firms do not directly address the question of entry-mode choice (e.g. Bower, 1968; Gaedeke, 1973; Hackett, 1976; Cowell, 1983; Palmer, 1985; Sharma and Johanson, 1987; and Terpstra and Yu, 1988). Finally, the few studies that do examine the issue provide limited insights, because entry-mode choice is not the

Reprinted with permission from *Journal of Marketing*, Vol. 57, July, pp. 19–38
© 1993 American Marketing Association

focus of their investigations (Weinstein, 1974, 1977; Lo and Yung, 1988) or because they are not driven by well-established theory (Erramilli, 1990; Erramilli and Rao, 1990).

Thus, existing knowledge concerning how firms choose entry modes has emanated almost entirely from the manufacturing sector. However, a growing stream of recent literature suggests that service firms differ from manufacturing firms (Bowen, Siehel and Schneider, 1989; Larsson and Bowen, 1989; Berry, 1980; Lovelock, 1983; Chase and Tansik, 1989) and face unique challenges in their foreign-market entry and expansion process (Carman and Langeard, 1980). This article will strive to demonstrate some peculiar characteristics of service firms (e.g. low capital intensity) that warrant adaptation of the underlying theory used to investigate entry-mode choice. Moreover, case studies on the internationalization of technical consultancy firms by Sharma and Johanson (1987) suggest that results obtained for manufacturing firms are not necessarily generalizable to service firms. Therefore, there exists a strong need to rigorously examine the process by which service firms choose entry modes.

Scope and purpose

This study focuses on the choice of entry modes in the *service* sector and includes a broad range of service industries, spanning both business and consumer services. It covers choice among wholly owned operations, joint ventures, and contractual transfers but not export modes of entry, because the theory employed, transaction-cost analysis (TCA), is not appropriate for comparing exports with foreign direct investment methods (Hennart, 1989).[1] Unlike previous entry-mode investigations, which were generally confined to the activities of large multinational corporations, it includes small and medium-sized firms as well.

As Figure 1 depicts, contractual methods, joint ventures, and wholly owned operations represent increasing degrees of ownership, vertical integration, resource commitment, and risk from the firm's perspective (Root, 1987; Kotler, 1991, p. 413;

Basic modes	Variations	Degree of ownership/ integration	Resource commitment/ risk	Designation
Contractual transfer	Licensing, franchising, correspondent banking	None/little	None/little	Shared-control mode
Joint venture	Partnership, consortium, affiliate	↓	↓	Shared-control mode
Wholly owned operation	Subsidiary, office, branch, project office, representative office	Full	High	Full-control mode

Figure 1. Entry modes in the service sector.
Source: Based partly on Hill *et al.* (1990), Kotler (1991), and Anderson and Gatignon (1986).

Hill *et al.*, 1990). Since wholly owned operations give the firm complete control of foreign production and marketing activities, they are designated *full-control* modes. In all other modes the firm generally has to share control with external entities; therefore, they are labeled *shared-control* modes.

The purpose of this paper is to *investigate how service firms choose between full-control and shared-control entry modes.* There are important reasons for confining the investigation to this binomial choice. When comparing entry modes, the only generalization that could be made with reasonable certainty is that wholly owned operations allow the firm more control than do other arrangements. The differences in control levels between different types of joint ventures and between joint ventures and contractual methods may often be indistinguishable or may be other than expected (Lecraw, 1984). More to the point, the theory employed, TCA, has had less success in explaining the more complex multinomial choice among entry modes. For example, Gatignon and Anderson (1988) concluded that, while TCA is well equipped to explain why firms prefer full ownership to partnership, it does not distinguish well between the different *degrees* of partnership. Similarly, in reporting their investigation of integration in export channels, Klein, Frazier and Roth (1990, p. 204) concede that 'attempting to classify across four different options is difficult'.

Following this introductory session the transaction-cost theory is described, as is the conceptual framework. The paper will argue why conventional TCA needs adaptation, describe the assumptions and approach, explain transaction-specific assets in the service sector, and develop several hypotheses on how the relationship between asset specificity and entry-mode choice is moderated. Then, separate sections will describe the sample and variables, and the model to be tested, followed by a discussion of the estimation process and results. Finally, the results will be summarized, including an understanding of their managerial and theoretical implications, along with the limitations of the study and suggestions for future research.

TRANSACTION-COST ANALYSIS

Applications of TCA have become fairly common in the general marketing literature (Anderson and Weitz, 1986; Anderson and Schmittlein, 1984; Dwyer and Oh, 1988; Heide and John, 1988, 1992), especially in entry-mode investigations (Anderson and Gatignon, 1986; Anderson and Coughlan, 1987; Gatignon and Anderson, 1988; Klein, 1989; Klein, Frazier and Roth, 1990). The theory appears to be especially effective in explaining vertical integration decisions.

A given task could be contracted out to external agents, partners, or suppliers (market-contracting or low-control modes) or it could be internalized and performed by the company's own employees (integration or full-control modes). The particular *governance* structure that is actually utilized in a given situation depends on the comparative transaction costs, that is, the costs of running a system, including the *ex ante* costs of negotiating a contract and the *ex post* costs of monitoring the performance and enforcing the behavior of the parties to the contract (Williamson, 1985).

The TCA approach begins with the assumption that markets are competitive, i.e. that there are many potential suppliers, and that market pressures minimize the need for monitoring and enforcing supplier behavior (Hennart, 1989). Under these conditions, market-contracting arrangements, or low-control modes, are favored because the threat of replacement dampens opportunism and forces suppliers to perform efficiently (Anderson and Coughlan, 1987; Anderson and Gatignon, 1986). When markets fail and the range of suppliers available to the firm is restricted (resulting in 'small-numbers bargaining'), the supplier's tendency to behave opportunistically is reduced only through stringent negotiation and supervision of contractual relationships (Dwyer and Oh, 1988), thereby greatly increasing the transaction costs associated with low-control modes. In such circumstances, the firm can significantly reduce its transaction costs by replacing external suppliers with its own employees, whose behavior it can monitor and control more effectively (Hennart, 1989; Klein, 1989). Thus, market failure is the primary antecedent to the firm's decision to integrate and assume greater control.

From the transaction-cost perspective, the most important determinant of market failure is the presence of *transaction-specific assets* (Williamson, 1986; Klein *et al.*, 1990). Transaction-specific assets are nonredeployable physical and human investments that are specialized and unique to a task (Williamson, 1985, 1986). For example, the production of a certain component may require investment in specialized equipment, the distribution of a certain product may necessitate unique physical facilities, or the delivery of a certain service may be predicated on the existence of an uncommon set of professional know-how and skills.

The *benefits* of integration under market failure (higher control, with attendant reduction of market transaction costs) must, however, be compared with the *costs* of integration. Establishment of an integrated operation entails significant *internal organization* or *bureaucratic* costs, including investments in legal, administrative, and operating infrastructures (Davidson and McFetridge, 1985). The high overhead is thought to diminish the firm's ability to dissolve one type of institutional arrangement and move to another, resulting in high switching costs. As such, control is assumed to carry a high price. Anderson and Gatignon (1986) postulate that, in choosing entry modes, firms make trade-offs between *control* (benefit of integration) and *cost of resource commitments* (cost of integration). Transaction-cost theory predicts that firms integrate when asset specificity is high, because the higher costs of vertical integration are more than offset by the benefits flowing from such an arrangement. When specificity is low, firms refrain from integration because the benefits of control fall short of the costs of attaining it.

CONCEPTUAL FRAMEWORK

Why modify the TCA model?

Although the TCA framework has become a popular theoretical approach to investigating integration issues, there is a growing realization that 'middle-range theoretical extensions ... are needed to enable TCA to address specific classes of situations not adequately addressed in the global specification' (Heide and John,

1988, p. 21). For instance, John and Weitz (1989) augment the transaction-cost framework with motivational variables to better explain sales force compensation. Similarly, Heide and John (1988) extend the model by employing dependence theory to explain how small firms with limited resources safeguard their transaction-specific investments. More recently, Heide and John (1992) have embellished the TCA approach with relational norms to explain buyer control over suppliers.

The authors' application of TCA to the service firm's entry-mode choice has uncovered certain shortcomings which necessitate modification of the basic model. TCA studies usually begin with the assumption that market-contracting or low-control modes represent the default choice for situations characterized by low asset specificity (e.g. Gatignon and Anderson, 1988; Klein *et al.*, 1990). For this assumption to be valid, the following two conditions must hold: (1) the only benefits of integration are a reduction of transaction costs in imperfect markets (thus eliminating all incentives for low-specificity[2] firms to integrate) and (2) the costs of integration are always high. Given these stipulations, low-specificity firms, i.e. firms characterized by low asset specificity, would find the cost-benefit analysis to unambiguously favor low-control ventures.

In practice, however, the first condition does not always hold true, as Anderson and Gatignon (1986) acknowledge. The literature is quite clear in emphasizing that, in addition to reducing transaction costs, firms often have numerous non-TCA motives to integrate. For instance, in their study of US multinational corporations, Stopford and Wells (1972) observed a strong, well-entrenched 'drive for unambiguous control' (p. 107). This occurs because control facilitates global integration and coordination of strategies in muiltinational corporations (Kobrin, 1988; Hill *et al.*, 1990), extends market power (Teece, 1981), obtains a larger share of the foreign enterprise's profits (Anderson and Gatignon, 1986), and overcomes the disadvantages inherent in shared-control ventures (conflicts with partners, partners becoming competitors, etc.) (Contractor and Lorange, 1988).

Similarly, the second stipulation, concerning the high costs of integration, may not be strictly true in the case of many (although not all) service firms. Unquestionably, ownership of overseas *manufacturing* facilities entails considerable resource commitment, risk, and switching costs for most firms. This may not be true, however, for many service firms, especially in the professional and business services sector (e.g. advertising agencies and management consultants). For these firms, the creation of a wholly owned subsidiary is limited to establishing an office, which frequently involves little fixed overhead. Large-scale investments in plants, machinery, buildings, and other physical assets are not required. Even switching costs may be comparatively small, because the true value-generating assets in these types of service firms are often people, and people are relatively mobile.

Not surprisingly, Sharma and Johanson (1987) observed that Swedish technical consultancy service firms bypassed the incremental establishment chain followed by manufacturing firms, because 'resource commitments are of minor significance' for the former. Consequently, the authors believe control can be acquired at comparatively low expense by many service firms. It must be emphasized that there are service firms for which integration entails large-scale investments in physical facilities (hospitals, hotels, airlines, etc.). The authors are merely contesting the general presumption that integration is *always* a high-resource proposition.

It is clear that the assumption that low-specificity firms will automatically resort to shared-control modes is unduly restrictive. If internal organization costs are low enough, such firms can be expected to assume control in order to exploit non-TCA benefits. Therefore, the effect of asset specificity on the firm's choice of integrated versus shared-control modes is contingent on *other factors* that affect the relative costs and benefits of integration. Since the traditional TCA approach does not normally consider this eventuality, there is need to modify it.

Assumptions and approach

The *non-TCA* benefits flowing from integration (such as global integration, market power, and avoidance of conflicts with partners) are available in equal measure to all service firms in this analysis. On the other hand, the magnitude of *TCA-related* benefits (reduction of transaction costs) will vary with the degree of asset specificity, being great for high-specificity firms but approaching zero in the case of low-specificity firms. Because there are strong incentives (both TCA and non-TCA) for firms to assume control, the analysis starts by assuming that service firms prefer maximum control when establishing entry modes. This assumption is not only plausible but actually conforms better to empirical evidence that indicates US multinational companies prefer integration *per se* (Gatignon and Anderson, 1988). More importantly, three-fourths of the respondents to the authors' survey agreed with the statement, 'If circumstances permit, we would always prefer to use a foreign-market entry method that will enable us to have maximum control'. The assumption of full-control modes being the default option is, therefore, realistic. At worst, it is no more deficient than assuming low-control modes are the default choice. Since full-control modes represent the default choice, this *study develops hypotheses predicting circumstances under which firms establish shared-control modes.* This approach is different from traditional TCA studies, which investigate why firms assume greater control.

In keeping with TCA tradition, the assumption is made that the benefits of integration are so immense for high-specificity firms, i.e. firms characterized by high asset specificity, that they will tend to shun shared-control modes in virtually all situations, regardless (within reasonable limits, of course) of costs and other factors. Breaking with tradition, however, the authors assume that low-specificity service firms also have incentives to integrate because of the presence of non-TCA benefits. However, since these firms lack TCA-related motives, they tend to be less fervent than high-specificity firms in retaining control. For instance, to start with, low-specificity firms can be expected to avoid shared-control arrangements with nearly the same intensity as high-specificity firms. But as costs of integration increase, low-specificity firms find shared-control arrangements increasingly more attractive compared to full-control modes. Alternatively, these firms can be expected to move to shared-control arrangements when costs remain constant but their ability to integrate diminishes (for example, because of decreasing firm size). Accordingly, the following two scenarios emerge:

- When internal organization costs are high, or their ability to integrate is low, low-specificity firms are more likely to *prefer* shared-control modes than are high-specificity firms, as predicted by conventional TCA.

- When internal organization costs are low, or their ability to integrate is high, low-specificity firms are nearly as likely to *avoid* shared-control modes as are high-specificity firms.

According to this argument, the transaction-cost framework loses much of its ability to explain the variation in entry-mode choice when costs are low or when the ability to integrate is high (as in the first scenario). However, *the theory becomes increasingly powerful as costs of control-acquisition mount or as the ability to integrate diminishes and low-specificity firms rush to establish shared-control ventures.* Following this line of logic, it is clear that asset specificity alone may not produce significant variation in entry-mode choice. Rather, its efficacy depends upon other factors which drive low-specificity firms to establish shared-control modes. This represents the basic premise of the current study. In the following sections asset specificity will be described in the context of the service sector, and certain moderating factors that influence the relationship between asset specificity and entry-mode choice will be explained.

Asset specificity in the service sector

The literature provides few insights into the origin of transaction-specific investments in the service sector. Consequently, the circumstances under which the service firm's arm's-length relationship with its supplier deteriorates into bilateral dependence are yet to be understood. Perhaps the answer lies in identifying situations in which potential agents, contractors, partners, or suppliers are required to make significant physical and human investments which cannot be productively employed outside the context of the specific transaction under consideration.

One such situation is the marketing of *idiosyncratic* services. An idiosyncratic service is defined as one which is characterized by 'high' levels of professional skills, specialized know-how, and customization.

- *Professional skills.* Professional expertise and skills are acquired only through several years of education and training (e.g. accounting or management consulting). Accordingly, services requiring professional skills will be associated with significant physical and, especially, human investments.
- *Specialized know-how.* Knowledge that is useful in only a narrow range of applications cannot be easily put to use elsewhere. Consequently, the greater the specialized know-how characterizing a service, the less likely it is that associated investments will be utilized outside the current context (e.g. management consulting for a specific industry, such as health care).
- *Customization.* The degree to which the service is customized to one or a few users (e.g. data processing tailored for an individual client company) will also determine the nature and specificity of the investments. Generally speaking, the more customized the service, the greater the attendant transaction-specific assets.

It is proposed that the production and delivery of idiosyncratic services is characterized by high asset specificity, necessitating, as it does, nontrivial, transaction-specific physical and human investments in the value-added chain. A supplier that is asked to provide these services on the firm's behalf will have to make significant investments in acquiring skills, expertise, and know-how that are uncommon and not easily transferable to other situations. Therefore, as the service becomes more idiosyncratic, the asset specificity of transactions increases.

Moderators

TCA predicts that the firm's utility for shared-control modes *diminishes* with increasing asset specificity. The *strength* of this inverse relationship is, however, contingent upon the influence of a number of moderating factors. The authors' hypotheses will focus on the effects of these factors and argue that increasing capital intensity, widening cultural distance between home and host countries, escalating host country risk, the inseparability of production and consumption in services (all of which raise the costs of integration), and decreasing firm size (which diminishes the ability to integrate) cause a significant variation in entry-mode choice by encouraging low-specificity firms to employ shared-control modes. All hypotheses are proposed on the assumption that effects not under consideration are being held constant at some 'average' level.

Capital intensity[3]

Although service firms may be generally less capital-intensive than manufacturing firms, capital intensity varies significantly across service industries (from relatively low levels in consulting firms and advertising agencies to fairly high levels in hospitals, hotels, and airlines). Since the level of capital intensity represents the relative magnitude of fixed investment, increasing capital intensity signifies rising resource commitments and escalating costs of integration.[4] All else being equal, the rising costs make it more difficult to establish wholly owned operations, thereby forcing firms to seek resources of partners and associates in shared-control arrangements. Although previous entry-mode studies have not explicitly considered the effects of capital intensity, Gatignon and Anderson's (1988) finding that the incidence of joint ventures increased with the increasing size of the foreign subsidiary underscores the impact of rising resource commitments on entry-mode choice.

Generally speaking, low-specificity firms are more likely to favor shared-control modes than high-specificity ones. Still, in situations characterized by *low* levels of capital intensity (and hence low costs of integration), low-specificity firms would be reluctant to relinquish control and lose the opportunity to exploit the non-TCA benefits of integration. As capital intensity *increases* (and internal organization costs escalate), however, low-specificity firms find deployment of full-control modes less and less justifiable in relation to the benefits they gain and, consequently, they shift to shared-control modes. High-specificity firms, on the other hand, will insist on integrated modes, regardless of capital intensity, because savings resulting from the reduction of transaction costs will continue to be substantial. The net result is that the differences in entry-mode choice between low- and high-specificity firms become more pronounced with increasing capital intensity. Hence:

H_1: The inverse relationship between asset specificity and service firms' utility for shared-control modes will become stronger with increasing capital intensity.

Inseparability

Many internationally marketed services are 'separable' (Sampson and Snape, 1985), i.e. their production and consumption can be decoupled. These services are frequently produced outside the host country and then transferred to it as a document, disk, or in some other tangible form. Examples include software services, engineering design, and architectural services.

However, a large number of services are produced and consumed simultaneously. *Inseparability* is a feature that distinguishes many service firms from manufacturers (Zeithaml *et al.*, 1985). For instance, the competent delivery of services by hospitals, hotels, consulting firms, and advertising agencies requires the close physical proximity of providers and receivers. Inseparability 'forces the buyer into intimate contact with the production process' (Carman and Langeard, 1980, p. 8) and necessitates close buyer–seller interactions (Gronroos, 1983).

In order to ensure effective delivery of inseparable services, elaborate systems have to be put in place to monitor the performance of employees who deal directly with customers. Inseparable services are conceivably more sensitive to cultural differences and may have to be better adapted to local tastes. Carman and Langeard (1980) also argue that service firms that provide inseparable services face special risks. They have to face customers and produce their services on foreign soil from day one without the benefit of initially exporting to the market and gaining experience.

For all these reasons, inseparability inflicts significant additional costs and risks on service firms which they can either bear themselves or share with their associates. While high-specificity firms find the first option worthwhile, low-specificity firms will more likely opt for the second. Consequently, asset specificity will more effectively distinguish between full- and shared-control choice for inseparable services than for separable ones. Hence:

> H_2: The inverse relationship between asset specificity and service firms' propensity for shared-control modes will be stronger for inseparable services than for separable services.

Cultural distance

Foreign-market entrants often perceive a significant amount of internal uncertainty caused by the *cultural distance* between the firm's home country and the host country. Numerous empirical studies have concluded that cultural distance encourages deployment of shared-control modes (Davidson and McFetridge, 1985; Kogut and Singh, 1988; Gatignon and Anderson, 1988).

To better understand the effect of cultural distance on entry-mode choice in a transaction-cost context, the costs of acquiring information needed to monitor and evaluate the performance of employees in bureaucracies must be considered (Jones and Hill, 1988). Since Kogut and Singh (1988) argue that differences in organizational characteristics increase with increasing cultural distance, such information-acquisition activity will be proportional to the cultural distance of the host country. When management moves to a country that is culturally similar to the home country, it may already possess most of the information to operate in the market; hence, information-acquisition costs will approach zero. However, when management enters an unfamiliar foreign culture, it may have great difficulty in imposing subjective judgment to determine how people should behave and in evaluating hard-to-quantify inputs and results (Gatignon and Anderson, 1988). As a general rule, information-acquisition costs and, therefore, integration costs, can be expected to increase with the increasing cultural distance of the host country.

When specificity is *high*, firms will insist on integrated modes because control continues to be immensely rewarding, even when the host country's culture is extremely disparate. However, when asset specificity is *low*, expanding cultural distance will diminish the firm's desire for control since rising information costs will outstrip integration benefits. The net result is that low- and high-specificity firms increasingly diverge in their entry-mode choices as the host country becomes culturally less and less familiar to the firm. Hence:

> H$_3$: The inverse relationship between asset specificity and service firms' propensity for shared-control modes will become stronger with increasing cultural distance between the home and host countries.

Country risk

High volatility in the external environment of the host country, i.e. high country risk, has been demonstrated to promote the use of shared-control arrangements (Goodnow and Hansz, 1972; Mascarenhas, 1982; Gatignon and Anderson, 1988). In high-risk countries, firms must possess the necessary *flexibility* to shift to a different mode of operation should the original mode be rendered inefficient by unpredictable changes in the environment (Anderson and Gatignon, 1986). Integrated modes are associated with high switching costs and, as a result, are not generally recommended in these environments. Low-control modes, on the other hand, offer the necessary flexibility and are characterized by low switching costs.

Low-specificity firms find little reason to give up control in low-risk countries. However, as countries become riskier and the need for flexibility becomes more important, low-specificity firms will increasingly seek shared-control arrangements. High-specificity firms, on the other hand, will continue to insist on full-control modes regardless of country risk. In fact, TCA argues that these firms will find control even more desirable in high-risk situations. When specificity is high, the frequent changes in the external environment provide more opportunities for suppliers, irreplaceable as they are, to shirk their obligations and to renegotiate contracts to their advantage (Gatignon and Anderson, 1988; Williamson, 1987). The resultant costs of haggling and maladaptation will further enhance the attractiveness of full-control modes in volatile environments and reduce the desire to share control. The net result is that entry-mode choice by low- and high-specificity firms can be expected to differ minimally in low-risk countries but substantially in high-risk countries. Hence:

> H$_4$: The inverse relationship between asset specificity and service firms' propensity for shared-control modes will become stronger with increasing country risk.

Firm size

Frequently, it is the firm's *ability* to integrate that determines its choice of entry modes. The typical argument in the literature is that integration entails significantly higher resource commitments and carries greater risk than shared-control arrangements (see Figure 1). Consequently, larger firms that have a greater ability to expend resources and absorb risks than smaller ones will conceivably be more likely to establish integrated modes. Also, larger firms may have greater bargaining power to negotiate for greater ownership and control in countries with restrictive investment policies (Lecraw, 1984). Empirical studies demonstrate that the firm's ability to marshal resources is a potential determinant of entry-mode choice (Gatignon and Anderson, 1988; Agarwal and Ramaswami, 1992).

Because the benefits flowing from control (both TCA and non-TCA) are immense, high-specificity firms will insist on full-control modes regardless of size. Even when they are small, these firms will scrounge for resources to establish integrated modes. However, low-specificity firms, which do not share the same fervor to preserve control at any cost, will more readily establish shared-control modes when they are small to take advantage of resources pooled by associates. But as they grow larger and their ability to integrate increases, these firms can be expected to become more reluctant to relinquish control. Consequently, the power of asset specificity to distinguish between full- and shared-control modes is greatest when firms are small, but it becomes progressively weaker with increasing firm size. This relationship is hypothesized as follows:

H_5: The inverse relationship between asset specificity and service firms' propensity for shared-control modes will become weaker with the increasing size of the firm.

Figure 2 depicts the conceptual framework for the study. Asset specificity is shown as inversely influencing the service firm's propensity for shared-control modes. This relationship is strengthened (shown by negative sign) or weakened (positive sign) by the five moderators.

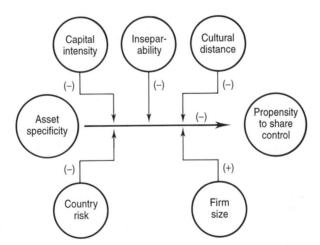

Figure 2. Conceptual framework: asset specificity's influence on service firm's propensity for shared-control modes moderated by various factors. Increasing asset specificity diminishes propensity to share control. The strength of this relationship is determined by the five moderators. (−) indicates the moderator strengthens the relationship; (+) suggests it weakens the relationship.

Hypothesis according to conventional TCA

Although the impact of the increasing costs of integration or of the diminishing capability to integrate on the influence of asset specificity has not been explicitly discussed in the TCA studies reported in the literature, it is likely that conventional TCA would have predicted increasing capital intensity, widening cultural distance, and inseparability to have minimal effects as moderators. This occurs because low-specificity firms are automatically assumed to favor low-control modes and high-specificity firms are expected to insist on full-control ones, regardless of costs or firm capabilities. So H_1, H_2, and H_3 have no bases.

However, conventional TCA would have proposed the same hypothesis as H_4 but for different reasons. Increasing country risk, while having little impact on low-specificity firms, is expected to further heighten the need for control in high-specificity firms. The net result is that the differences in entry-mode choice among low- and high-specificity firms would grow larger in high-risk countries.

On H_5, conventional TCA might have predicted just the opposite. While low-specificity firms are expected to insist on shared-control modes regardless of size, high-specificity firms may favor full-control modes ever more strongly with increasing size. As such, the differences between low- and high-specificity firms are perceived to grow *stronger* not weaker (as predicted) with increasing firm size.

SAMPLE AND VARIABLES

Sample

The unit of analysis used is an *individual foreign-market entr decision* made by a service firm. Data for this investigation was collected through a mail survey of United States service firms engaged in international operations. Despite much effort, no sampling frame for the study could be obtained from any source: government agencies, trade groups, or commercial vendors. Therefore, a systematic sample of service firms known to be engaged in international operations was drawn from various business directories.[5]

To be included in the study, the firm had to belong primarily to a service sector SIC and also had to be in international business. A total of 463 companies, representing a wide variety of service industries, were included in the mail survey. Questionnaires were mailed to managers who were most likely to be involved in the foreign-market entry decision process in their firms, including vice presidents and directors in charge of international operations, presidents, and CEOs. Each respondent was asked to provide data on up to six foreign-market entry decisions with which he/she was very familiar.[6]

Twenty-five questionnaires were returned undelivered, and 43 companies wrote back expressing regret at their inability to participate for various reasons, usually because they were no longer in international business. From the remaining pool of 395 potential respondents, usable responses were received from 175. The response rate of 44.3% compares favorably with rates reported in other surveys involving international marketing executives (e.g. Klein, 1989) and service firms (e.g.

Zeithaml, Parasuraman and Berry, 1985). Respondents did not differ significantly from nonrespondents in industry distribution, mean firm size, or mean sales revenue. Therefore, nonresponse bias, if any, may be negligible.

Of the firms responding, 47 reported serving foreign markets only through export operations, and 14 had insufficient information on some key variables and were dropped from the analysis. The remaining 114 service firms provided data on a total of 381 foreign-market entry decisions, complete in every aspect.[7]

As Table 1 (section A) shows, the number of entries reported by each firm varied considerably. The foreign-market entries included in the sample differ considerably by size of the responding firm (section B, Table 1), when firm size is measured in

Table 1. Characteristics of foreign-market entries in sample

Number of entries in sample = 381

A. Entries per firm		B. Distribution by firm size	
Entries/Firm	No. of firms	Number of employees	Percentage of entries
1	34	a. <500	30.4
2	20	b. 500–1000	3.7
3	15	c. 1001–2000	11.0
4	11	d. 2001–4000	17.6
5	10	e. 4001–10 000	17.6
6	28	f. >10 000	19.7

C. Distribution by industry

Service industry	Percentage of entries
Advertising	13.1
Architecture	2.4
Banking	13.4
Computer software and data processing	15.8
Engineering	10.8
Health care	3.7
Management consulting	21.5
Research and development	3.9
Restaurants and hotels	11.0
Miscellaneous services (accounting, leasing, maintenance, etc.)	4.4

D. Distribution by country of entry		E. Entry modes employed	
Country of entry	Percentage of entries	Entry mode	Percentage of entries
1. English-speaking industrialized	26.5	1. Wholly owned subsidiary	33.2
2. Non English-speaking industrialized	37.5	2. Other wholly owned operation	27.4
3. Others	36.0	3. Joint venture	24.4
		4. Contractual method	15.0

terms of the *number of employees* as reported in the directories consulted. Also, the observations span several service industries (section C, Table 1), although there is heavier representation from professional and commercial service firms. Furthermore, as section D of Table 1 indicates, nearly two-thirds of the reported entries are into industrialized countries, including Australia, Canada, Japan, New Zealand, and the market economies of Europe. Finally, entries associated with wholly owned modes represent about 60% of the sample; the other 40% involve joint ventures and contractual transfers (section E, Table 1).

Variables

The Appendix contains details of measurement and validity assessment of all the variables. The dependent variable, entry-mode choice, is represented by a dichotomous variable that becomes zero for *full-control* modes – since they represent the default or base option in the study (contrary to conventional TCA operationalizations) – and 1 for *shared-control* modes. *Asset specificity* is a 3-item scale measuring the extent to which the service is characterized by professional skills, specialized know-how, and customization. *Capital intensity* of a particular service industry is measured as the ratio of fixed assets to sales revenue. *Firm size* is measured as the number of company employees. *Inseparability* is a dummy variable (1 = inseparable service; 0 = separable service). *Cultural distance* is a composite index representing the host country's cultural distance from the United States. *Country risk* is a dummy variable (1 = entry into high-risk country; 0 = entry into lower-risk country) representing environmental volatility in the host country. Moderator effects are represented as *interactions* between asset specificity and the corresponding moderating variables. All interaction effects are represented by cross products of the main effects (as recommended by Neter, Wasserman and Kunter, 1983).

THE MODEL

The model examines the impact of asset specificity and its interactions on service firm's propensity to establish shared-control entry modes, as opposed to full-control ones. Logistic regression is utilized for estimation of the effects, because it is recommended when (1) the dependent variable is binary, (2) there are qualitative and quantitative independent variables, and (3) underlying assumptions of multivariate normality cannot be met (Cox, 1970; Bali and Tschoegl, 1982; Afifi and Clark, 1984; Kachigan, 1986).

Many recent studies related to entry-mode choice have employed logistic regression models (Davidson and McFetridge, 1985; Gatignon and Anderson, 1988; Kogut and Singh, 1988; Agarwal and Ramaswami, 1992; Kim and Hwang, 1992). The probability of a service firm choosing a shared control entry mode in preference to a full-control one can be modeled as a function of the main effects and the interaction terms as follows:

Probability of choosing shared-control mode

$$= 1/\{1 + exp^{[-Y]}\} \tag{1}$$

where

$$Y = \beta_0 + \beta_1 X_1 + \beta_2 X_2 + \cdots + \beta_p X_p \tag{2}$$

$X_1, X_2, \ldots, X_p$ are the explanatory variables (including asset specificity, the moderators, and interactions between asset specificity and moderators), $\beta_1, \beta_2, \ldots, \beta_p$ are the corresponding coefficients, and β_0 is the intercept term.

The parameters are estimated using maximum likelihood, employing the LOGISTIC procedure of the SAS statistical package (SAS Institute, 1989). The overall efficacy of the model is assessed using the likelihood ratio χ^2, which is twice the difference in log likelihoods for the current model and the intercept-only model. Large χ^2 values and small p values indicate statistical significance. The predictive ability of the model can be gauged by the correct classification rate *in conjunction with* the τ statistic (Klecka, 1980), which represents the percentage reduction in classification errors relative to random selection. A statistically significant parameter indicates the extent to which the corresponding variable contributes to the *utility* of a shared-control mode relative to the full-control option. It does not *directly* signify the *probability* of firms using shared-control modes. Once equation (2) is estimated, the probabilities could be computed for a given situation using equation (1).

The estimated model includes all the main effects, including asset specificity and the moderators and the hypothesized interaction effects. Preliminary analysis led the authors to believe that the relationship between *capital intensity* and *entry-mode choice* is not linear over the range of values considered in the analysis, apparently following the pattern portrayed in Figure 3.

As capital intensity increases from 'low' to 'moderate' levels (i.e. from A to B in Figure 3), the propensity to employ shared-control modes increases, as expected. As it increases further from 'moderate' to 'high' levels (i.e. from B to C in Figure 3), the propensity to share control *diminishes*, contrary to expectations. The reason why firms avoid shared-control modes at high levels of capital intensity is not clear; perhaps

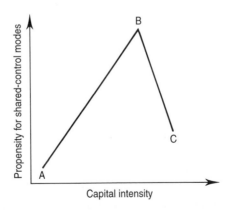

Figure 3. Observed relationship between capital intensity and desire for shared-control modes.

they feel compelled to protect their rather heavy investments by integration. Notwithstanding its origin, this nonlinearity necessitated the inclusion in the model of two quadratic terms, [capital intensity]^2 and asset specificity $\times$ [capital intensity]^2.

ESTIMATION AND RESULTS

Multicollinearity

When such a large number of interaction terms involving one variable are included in the model, the likelihood of serious multicollinearity problems exists. Because some of the correlations among the variables were indeed high, the original variables were rescaled using procedures recommended by Aiken and West (1991). All continuous variables were 'centered' (by subtracting the corresponding variable mean from each value), and dummy variables were recorded using 'weighted effects coding' (Darlington, 1990).[8] Such rescaling, however, does not affect the substantive interpretation of the coefficients (Aiken and West, 1991). An examination of the correlation matrix of the rescaled variables reported in Table 2 indicates that, except for those involving asset specificity and capital intensity, none of the interaction term terms appears to be highly correlated with other variables.

Variance inflation factors for terms included in the model did not indicate serious levels of collinearity. Nevertheless, to assess the stability of the parameter estimates, the full model was reestimated for sixteen different subsamples of 300 observations each, drawn randomly from the original sample. The parameter estimates for the interaction terms, particularly the coefficients for asset specificity $\times$ capital intensity and asset specificity $\times$ [capital intensity]^2, remained remarkably stable over these runs, thereby discounting the possibility of significant multicollinearity problems.

Table 2. Correlation matrix for independent variables

	B	C	D	E	F	G	H	I	J	K	L	M
A	−.29	−.23	−.13	.00	.07	−.34	.32	.39	.21	.05	−.11	.35
B		.93	.19	−.09	−.09	.28	−.60	−.63	−.21	.06	.04	−.12
C			.20	−.10	−.09	.17	−.58	−.65	−.15	.05	.06	−.04
D				−.03	−.16	.26	−.15	−.14	.07	−.03	.00	−.10
E					.37	−.02	.05	.04	−.03	−.02	.11	.02
F						−.04	.03	.05	.01	.10	.18	.07
G							−.13	−.12	−.14	.03	.11	−.52
H								.93	.35	−.07	−.09	.08
I									.29	−.06	−.11	.05
J										.01	−.16	.34
K											.26	−.02
L												−.15

A = asset specificity. B = capital intensity. C = [capital intensity]^2. D = inseparability. E = country risk. G = firm size. H = asset specificity $\times$ capital intensity. I = asset specificity $\times$ [capital intensity]^2. J = asset specificity $\times$ inseparability. K = asset specificity $\times$ cultural distance. L = asset specificity $\times$ country risk. M = asset specificity $\times$ firm size.

Model estimation and fit

Initial runs revealed that the interaction term, *asset specificity* × *cultural distance,* was insignificant. Therefore, this term was dropped, and the full model was reestimated. Table 3 reports that this reestimated model is statistically significant (likelihood ratio $\chi^2_{(12)} = 73.0$, $p = 0.0001$), which suggests that the variables as a group discriminate well between full- and shared control choice. Furthermore, the model correctly classifies 69% of the entry-mode choices which, as the τ statistic suggests, represents an improvement (36% fewer errors) relative to classification based on chance alone. In the light of these results, the model appears to have reasonable explanatory and predictive abilities.

A comparison of the full model with the main-effects-only model reveals that the interactions terms account for a substantial amount of the variation of entry-mode choice (incremental $\chi^2_{(5)} = 52.0$, $p = 0.0001$). This underscores the important role

Table 3. Results of logistic regression

Effect	Label	Parameter estimate	Standard error	Asymptotic t statistic
Dependent variable is *entry-mode choice* (0 = full-control; 1 = shared-control mode)				
Intercept	$b0$	−.143	.166	.86
Asset specificity	$b1$	−1.999	.485	4.12[d]
Capital intensity	$b2$	7.645	2.420	3.16[d]
[Capital intensity]^2	$b3$	11.799	7.532	1.57[b]
Inseparability	$b4$	.150	.096	1.56[b]
Cultural distance	$b5$	.200	.091	2.20[c]
Country risk	$b6$	.238	.333	.72
Firm size	$b7$	−.024	.011	2.18[c]
Asset specificity × capital intensity	$b8$	−12.836	5.916	2.17[b]
Asset specificity × [capital intensity]^2	$b9$	109.00	34.229	3.18[d]
Asset specificity × inseparability	$b10$	−.932	.219	4.25[d]
Asset specificity × country risk	$b11$	−1.072	.661	1.62[a]
Asset specificity × firm size	$b12$	.040	.016	2.50[d]

A. Model Statistics:
N   381
Model χ^2 73.0 with 12 *df* $(p = .0001)$
−2 Log likelihood   437.8
Correct classification %   69
τ .36

B. Contribution of interaction terms:
Incremental χ^2 52.0 with 5 *df* $(p = .0001)$

C. Contribution of asset specificity and its interactions:
Incremental χ^2 57.2 with 6 *df* $(p = .0001)$

$a = p < .10$ (one-tail).
$b = p < .05$ (one-tail).
$c = p < .01$ (one-tail).
$d = p < .005$ (one-tail).

that moderating effects seem to play in entry-mode choice. Finally, as testimony to TCA's efficacy, asset specificity and its interaction effects together account for a very appreciable amount of the explanation (incremental $\chi^2_{(6)} = 57.2$, $p = .0001$).

Hypotheses testing

A hypothesis is supported by the data if the coefficient for the corresponding interaction term is statistically significant and possesses the predicted sign (see Figure 2). Table 3 reports the parameter estimates, standard errors, and asymptotic t statistics. As argued earlier, the service firm's utility for shared-control modes, relative to the full-control option, *decreases* with increasing asset specificity. A minus sign on the coefficient for an interaction term suggests that this inverse relationship is *strengthened* with increasing values of the moderator; a plus sign indicates it is *weakened*. Therefore, barring the coefficient for *asset specificity × firm size*, all interaction terms are predicted to be negatively signed.

To gain further insights into the hypothesized relationships, the probability that service firms employ shared-control modes is estimated for low- and high-specificity situations for different levels of each moderating variable whose interaction with asset specificity was significant (holding the other effects constant at their average levels). Following Aiken and West (1991), 'low (or small)' was defined as one standard deviation below mean; 'medium' as mean; 'high (or large)' as one standard deviation above mean; and 'very high (or very large)' as two standard deviations above mean. The probabilities were then estimated with the help of equations (1) and (2), using these values and the parameter estimates from Table 3. For easy interpretation, these probabilities are shown pictorially in Figure 4. For each level of the moderating variable under consideration, lines are drawn connecting the corresponding probability levels for low- and high-specificity firms. These lines merely connect two discrete points and *do not necessarily depict a direct linear relationship* between asset specificity and probability. However, a downward sloping line suggests that low-specificity firms are more likely to employ shared-control modes than are high-specificity firms; an upward sloping line indicates just the opposite. The steeper the line, the greater the disparity between the two firm types.

Hypothesis 1

Coefficients $b8$ and $b9$ in Table 3, which represent the interaction between asset specificity and capital intensity, are both statistically significant. The minus sign on $b8$ (linear term) suggests that, at lower levels, increasing capital intensity *strengthens* the inverse relationship between *asset specificity* and *entry-mode choice*. However, the plus sign on $b9$ (quadratic term) implies that, at higher levels, rising capital intensity *weakens* this relationship. Thus, while H_1 appears to be supported at lower levels of capital intensity, it is not at higher levels.

To understand this relationship further, Figure 4A could be examined. If H_1 is supported, the line connecting the probability levels for low- and high-specificity firms should be downward-sloping and relatively flat for low levels of capital intensity but should become steeper with increasing capital intensity. This expectation is

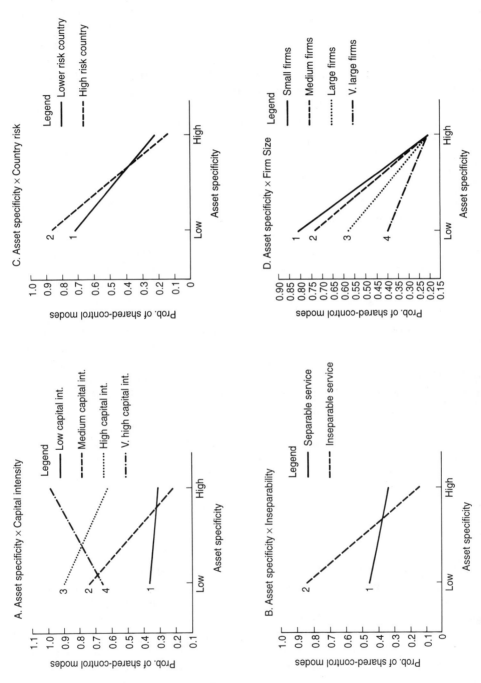

Figure 4. Estimated probability of employing shared-control modes: at low and high levels of asset specificity for different levels of moderators.

fulfilled for 'low' and 'medium' levels of capital intensity (lines 1 and 2). However, as capital intensity increases to 'high' levels, the line becomes *flatter* because, although low-specificity firms intensify their preference for control-sharing, high-specificity firms unexpectedly begin to follow the same pattern (line 3). Finally, at 'very high' levels, the line reverses its slope as high-specificity firms become *more likely* to employ shared-control modes than low-specificity ones (line 4).

In trying to comprehend this complicated relationship, it is helpful to remember that H_1 assumes increasing capital intensity, raises integration costs, and, consequently, enhances the relative utility of shared-control modes. In other words, it assumes a *positive* relationship between *capital intensity* and *entry-mode choice*. This is the relationship that seems to prevail at lower levels of capital intensity, as depicted by the A–B portion of Figure 3. H_1 appears to hold well for these observations.

However, the hypothesis seems to break down when, at higher levels, *capital intensity* and *entry-mode choice* become *inversely* related (see B–C portion of Figure 3). It is for these observations that the relationship between *asset specificity* and *entry-mode choice* appears to become less negative, or even positive, with rising capital intensity.

It can only be speculated as to why high-specificity firms seem to desire *less*, not more, control than low-specificity firms when capital intensity reaches higher levels. It may be merely a sample-specific aberration, since there are relatively few observations in the sample involving highly capital-intensive firms. But if it is not, a more complex phenomenon may be driving the relationship.

Other sources of asset specificity that are not explicitly included in the model, such as advertising intensity, may be affecting the low-specificity firms characterized by high capital intensity. This is not an unreasonable speculation, since most of these firms appear to be from the consumer services industry. Concurrently, it is possible that, faced with high resource commitments in capital-intensive industries, high-specificity service firms may be designing out specificity from otherwise idiosyncratic services in order to take advantage of resources pooled by partners a possibility consistent with suggestions made by Anderson and Gatignon (1986). Again, this seems plausible because many of the high-specificity firms from capital-intensive industries in the sample appear to be relatively small in size. At any rate, H_1 finds only partial support from the data.

Hypothesis 2

The large negative coefficient for the *asset specificity* $\times$ *inseparability* interaction, $b10$ ($p < .005$), is consistent with the hypothesis that the inverse relationship between asset specificity and propensity for shared-control modes is substantially stronger when services are inseparable than when they are separable. Figure 4B sheds more light on this matter. The relatively flat line for separable services implies that low-specificity firms are not very different from high-specificity firms in their desire for shared-control modes (line 1). The line for inseparable services is, however, noticeably steeper (line 2). Two reasons appear to account for this: (1) as predicted by H_2, low-specificity firms substantially increase the use of shared-control arrangements and (2) for reasons more in tune with conventional TCA, high-specificity firms seem to further reduce their use of shared-control modes. The additional demands of inseparable production and consumption of services may be escalating market transaction costs and making control even more imperative in high-specificity situations.

Hypothesis 3

The hypothesized interaction between *asset specificity* and *cultural distance* did not materialize (result not reported). Apparently, *cultural distance* does not raise costs substantially enough for low-specificity firms to divest control. H_3 is not supported by the data. Although the interaction is not significant, the *main* effect of *cultural distance* is significant and positively signed ($b5$ in Table 3). This result suggests that service firms do not differ from manufacturing firms in favoring shared-control modes over full-control options with increasing cultural distance.

Hypothesis 4

H_4 predicted that increasing country risk will strengthen the inverse relationship between *asset specificity* and *entry-mode choice*. Supporting this prediction, coefficient $b11$ is significant ($p < .10$) and negatively signed (Table 3). An examination of Figure 4C reveals that the line for high-risk countries (line 2) is steeper than that for lower-risk countries (line 1). This seems to arise primarily from low-specificity firms growing keener on employing shared-control modes in riskier environments, as predicted by the modified framework. However, there is also some evidence that high-specificity firms further eschew control-sharing arrangements in high-risk countries, in accordance with conventional TCA arguments.

Given the contention that low-specificity firms tend to avoid shared-control modes when country risk is low, the rather high probability of about .7 is indeed puzzling. Further analysis (not reported), however, showed that this probability drops to .3 when capital intensity is *low* and not 'average or medium', as is assumed in all calculations underlying probability estimates reported in Figure 4. This points to a more complex interaction involving asset specificity, country risk, and capital intensity.

Hypothesis 5

The coefficient $b12$ is significant ($p < .05$ level) and *positively* signed (Table 3). The result suggests a *weakening* of the inverse relationship between specificity and propensity for shared-control modes, thereby supporting H_5. If the hypothesis is to be corroborated, the line connecting the probability levels for low- and high-specificity firms should be steep for small firms and get flatter as firms grow larger, as shown in the pattern evident in Figure 4D.

It is noteworthy that the probability of high-specificity firms engaging shared-control modes is virtually unaffected by firm size. However, the probability for low-specificity firms is highest when they are small, but it declines steadily as they grow larger. This result is consistent with the postulate that low-specificity firms prefer full-control modes to start with but shift to shared-control ventures when their ability to integrate diminishes (because of decreasing size). Therefore, H_5 finds strong support. The modified framework presented here appears to more accurately predict the moderating effect of firm size than conventional TCA, which (as described earlier) would have predicted a negative interaction effect.

Summary of results

Of the five hypotheses tested, H_3 (host-country cultural distance) does not find any support. H_1 appears to be supported only as capital intensity increases from low to medium levels (the range over which the expected effect of capital intensity on entry-mode choice apparently prevails). Based on the hypotheses that were more fully supported, there is sufficient basis to believe the existence of the following relationships. Service firms generally tend to favor shared-control modes more when asset specificity is low than when it is high. This tendency *intensifies* (1) when services are inseparable (relative to when they are separable), (2) with increasing country risk, and (3) as firms become smaller. In the concluding section of the paper, some implications of these results will be explored, some limitations will be listed, and a few suggestions for future researchers will be made.

CONCLUSION

Traditional entry-mode investigations have tended to concentrate on the behavior of manufacturing multinational corporations. This study focuses on the entry-mode choice by firms from a wide range of service industries and includes very small to very large organizations. Some effects hitherto not empirically investigated in the entry-mode context, such as inseparability and capital intensity, are tested. Furthermore, because of some unduly restrictive assumptions associated with conventional TCA, a framework is developed that extends the TCA model. The conventional TCA approach actually represents a special case of this paradigm, dealing with situations wherein internal organization costs are high *and* non-TCA incentives to integrate are low.

This paper argues that the relationship between asset specificity and entry-mode choice is moderated by numerous factors that either raise the costs of integration or diminish the firm's ability to establish full-control modes. When costs are low or the ability to integrate is high, firms characterized by low asset specificity are nearly as likely as high-specificity firms to establish full-control ventures. But as costs escalate or ability diminishes, low-specificity firms will increasingly seek out shared-control ventures. While not supporting all of the hypotheses, the results do provide a reasonable basis to suggest that substantial variation in entry-mode choice is caused when low-specificity firms are pressed to share control. Some of the principal implications of the results follow.

Implications

Managerial implications

Managers apparently make cost-control trade-offs in several dimensions in their pursuit of the most efficient mode of entry. It is often claimed that many international marketing decisions are made by managers on a crude, nonsystematic basis (e.g. Aharoni, 1966; Goodnow, 1985). But the findings of this study and others demonstrate that managers do make choices based on considerations of long-term efficiency. The fact that the authors were able to correctly predict at least some of the behavior of service firms, based on efficiency considerations, suggests that 'nonsystematic' does not necessarily mean 'inefficient'.

Managers in the international service sector can draw useful lessons from the study. When entering a foreign market, they frequently have an array of entry modes from which to choose. TCA provides a framework within which these alternatives can be evaluated. Specifically, this research highlights the usefulness of control as a basis for making an entry-mode choice. All costs and benefits of obtaining and retaining control in a specific situation must be carefully weighed against each other. The most efficient mode is the one with highest benefit-to-cost ratio. In this regard, this research identifies situations in which the benefits of control outweigh the costs of control and vice versa.

Analytical implications

For researchers, the results underscore the complexity characterizing entry-mode analysis and suggest that a superficial examination of relationships could be dangerously misleading. Effects are often embedded in or intertwined with others, and researchers need to develop strategies to analytically disentangle the underlying relationships. Furthermore, if these results and recent research (Agarwal and Ramaswami, 1992) are any indications, researchers should be cautious about interpreting main effects alone, because variables seem to interact with each other in complicated ways. It is necessary to envision how a given variable effects entry-mode choice not only directly but also indirectly.

Theoretical implications

From a theory-building standpoint, the results of this study vindicate Boddewyn *et al.* (1986), who concluded that existing theories could be employed, with suitable adaptations, to investigate issues relating to multinational service enterprises. The transaction-cost framework is useful and universally applicable. However, to be more effective as a general theory of entry-mode choice, it must be extended for several reasons: (1) Firms appear to evaluate alternative institutional arrangements using a wider range of integration costs (e.g. inseparability) than previously recognized. At the same time, these costs do not necessarily need be assumed to be high in all situations. (2) Firms appear to be evaluating the merits of acquiring control based not only on reduction of transaction costs but on other non-TCA related considerations as well. Indeed, non-TCA motives, combined with low integration costs, seem to explain why many service firms establish full-control modes, even in low asset-specificity situations. (3) The firm's ability to integrate should be incorporated in future TCA studies as an important determinant of entry-mode choice.

Furthermore, conventional TCA thinking focuses on factors *promoting,* not *repressing,* integration. Although the results on inseparability and country risk support the conventional model, in the sense that some variation in entry-mode choice appears to result from high-specificity firms demanding greater control, a substantial amount of variation appears to be caused by low-specificity firms switching from full-control to shared-control modes in response to rising costs or diminishing ability to integrate. An examination of the results suggests that, relative to the conventional model, the modified framework appears to have more accurately predicted (1) the strengthening of the relationship between *asset specificity* and *entry-mode choice* with increasing costs of integration, and (2) the weakening of this relationship with increasing firm size. Therefore, the modified TCA approach appears to have serious merits and deserves further scrutiny.

Although on the surface the research appears to endorse the acquisition of control for control's sake, this is not accurate. The authors are merely arguing that, given all the *TCA* and *non-TCA* incentives to integrate, it is more constructive to view firms as desiring maximum possible control from the start. The relative merits of relinquishing this control, as opposed to maintaining it in a given situation, could then be examined. Finally, although the modified framework was originally developed to accommodate some peculiar characteristics of service firms, it is really broader in its applicability and can be easily extended to entry-mode investigations in the manufacturing sector or even to problems other than entry-mode choice.

Limitations and suggestions for future research

The study suffers from some important limitations. First, the sample is not representative of the general population of service firms in the United States. Non-random sampling became a necessity, however, when the authors were unable to obtain a comprehensive sampling frame. In this connection, they would like to emphasize one major challenge facing researchers investigating entry-mode issues: Since the unit of analysis in entry-mode studies is usually not the firm itself but rather an individual entry decision made by the firm, researchers should sample from the sum total of all entry-mode decisions made by all firms of a given industry or sector to obtain a truly representative sample. Clearly, this is an arduous task.

Second, this study followed previous studies by employing ownership as the determinant of control. This may not always be appropriate. There is increasing recognition that firms may gain control through nonequity, contractual methods (Dunning and McQueen, 1982; Dunning, 1988; Heide and John, 1992). Therefore, it is possible for a service firm to exercise a degree of control that is unrelated to its equity participation. Future researchers must recognize and incorporate contract-based means of acquiring control. Alternately, a degree-of-control construct should be developed and measured independently of the entry mode employed. In this connection, the work of Killing (1983), Klein (1989), and Geringer and Ebert (1989) may offer a strong basis upon which to build.

In the current study, the authors implicitly assumed that the *actual* level of control employed by the service firm (as indicated by the entry mode used) is its *desired* level. However, 'foreign government restrictions, the dictates of corporate parents, resource scarcity, and contractual commitments' indicate that there may be a significant difference in the two levels (Klein, 1989, p. 258). Discrepancies may occur when firms are *forced to integrate* in countries where market exchange is unfeasible because of lack of indigenous technical capabilities (Contractor, 1984), absence of adequate infrastructure and entrepreneurship (Teece, 1981), or unavailability of suitable partners (Stopford and Wells, 1972; Robinson, 1978).

Since theoretical predictions generally focus on the desired level of control, the efficacy of entry-mode models could be greatly improved by measuring the firm's desired level of control *independently* of the actual entry mode employed. This reinforces earlier arguments for the development of an independent measure for control.

As discussed earlier, there may be several benefits and costs associated with integration that have not been explicitly incorporated in previous transaction-cost investigations. Future researchers could give some thought to improving the framework's predictive power by determining how these other costs and benefits could be measured and included in their investigations.

APPENDIX: MEASUREMENT OF VARIABLES

Entry-mode choice

The dependent variable in this study is dichotomous, equaling 1 when the firm employs a shared-control entry mode and 0 when it uses a full-control entry mode. For each entry decision described, the respondent was given a list of possible entry modes (wholly owned subsidiaries, joint ventures, etc.) and asked to indicate which one best described the method his/her company had used to *initially* enter the foreign market under consideration. Responses were appropriately classified into the full- and shared-control categories, as described in Figure 1.

Asset specificity

Represented by the degree of idiosyncracy that characterizes a service, asset specificity is measured using three items that correspond to the three service attributes: (1) *professional skills*, (2) *specialized know-how*, and (3) *customization* (see definition of idiosyncratic services in the text). Customization was reverse-coded and measured as *standardization* (which, pretests revealed, was less ambiguous for respondents to interpret and describe). Respondents indicated the degree to which each attribute (i.e. professional skills, specialized know-how, and standardization) characterized their service on a 5-point scale (where 1 = no extent, and 5 = great extent). Asset specificity represents the mean of responses for the three attributes.

Cronbach's alpha for the 3-item scale is .64 and, although modest, compares favorably with the alphas of .69 for the 5-item scale of Anderson and Coughlan (1987) and .65 for the 6-item measure of asset specificity of Klein *et al.* (1990).

To further examine the validity of the measure, the mean levels of idiosyncracy associated with services from various industries in the sample were compared. An inspection of the results, presented in Table A-1 (line 1), suggests that consumer services are the least idiosyncratic. However, the across-industry variation, though significant, is not extremely high. Perhaps, this is the result of sample being skewed toward professional and business services. The variation across industries is much more evident when the degree of *customization* characterizing the service as shown in (Table A-1, line 2) is examined. Not surprisingly, consumer services are the least customized (or most standardized) of all services in the sample. The results in Table A-1 appear to be consistent with logic (for example, consumer services are the most standardized) and with information published on the industries (US Congress, 1987).

Table A-1. Across-industry variation of some independent effects

Effect	Service Industry						
	Advertising services (n = 50)	Computer services (n = 60)	Engineering/ architecture services (n = 50)	Management consulting services (n = 82)	Consumer services (n = 58)	Banking services (n = 51)	Miscella- neous services (n = 30)
1. *Idiosyncracy* Mean 'degree of idiosyncracy' associated with industry	4.28[b]	4.28[b]	4.46[a,b]	4.57[a]	3.59[c]	4.34[b]	4.34[b]
2. *Customization* Mean 'degree of customization' associated with industry	3.20[b]	3.33[b]	3.46[b]	4.05[a]	2.03[c]	3.59[ab]	3.70[ab]
3. *Client following* Percentage of entries in industry associated with client following	46.0	25.0	24.0	26.8	0.0	29.41	26.7
4. *Inseparability* Percentage of entries in industry associated with inseparable services	100.0	51.7	22.0	58.5	100.0	58.8	40.0

Notes:
1. n = Number of entries reported in each industry.
2. Idiosyncracy and customization are measured on scales ranging from 1 through 5. Higher means indicate that the characteristic (idiosyncracy or customization) is more dominant. Means with the same letter are not significantly different ($\alpha = .05$).
3. Tests for differences across industries: (1) Idiosyncracy ($F_{(6)} = 22.06$; $p < .001$), (2) Customization ($F_{(6)} = 19.91$; $p < .001$), and (3) Client following ($\chi^2 = 31.9$; $p < .001$), and (4) Inseparability ($\chi^2 = 110.7$; $p < .001$).

Capital intensity

This is the ratio of fixed assets to sales revenue for the industry to which the service firm belongs. This measure was borrowed from Kim and Lyn (1987), because of contextual similarity (they use it to predict foreign direct investment flows) and data availability. Data for the computation of the ratios are obtained from *Industry Norms and Key Business Ratios* (*1985–86 edition*) published by Dun and Bradstreet Information Services. The publication reports information for 'typical' firms in each SIC. The fixed-assets to sales-revenue ratio computed for the typical firm is taken as representative of the capital intensity of the particular industry. Capital intensity ratios ranged from a low of about .04 for advertising agencies to a high of .76 for hotels.

Inseparability

In international marketing and trade, the inseparability issue is best seen as a *tradeability* problem (e.g. Sapir, 1982; Sampson and Snape, 1985; Boddewyn *et al.*, 1986). Separable services are tradeable or exportable; inseparable services are not. Therefore, respondents were asked whether or not it is possible to export their service ('Is it possible to serve your overseas clients/customers by producing your service here in the US and then "exporting" the service?'). A positive response suggested a separable service, a negative response an inseparable service. INSEPARABILITY is defined as a dummy variable (0 = separable service; 1 = inseparable service). Table A-1 describes the proportion of inseparable services characterizing each industry. Inseparability appears to dominate advertising and consumer services. On the other hand, engineering and architectural services appear to be most amenable to separation.

Cultural distance

This is a measure of the cultural distance between the United States and the host country. Based on information provided by 88 000 respondents from 66 countries. Hofstede (1980) developed indices to measure four dimensions of national culture: power distance, uncertainty avoidance, individuality, and masculinity/feminity. Using these indices, Kogut and Singh (1988) computed cultural distances between the United States and other countries as follows:

$$(\text{Cultural distance})_j = [(I_{ij} - I_{iu})^2 / V_i]/4$$

where I_{ij} stands for the index for the ith cultural dimension and jth country, V_i is the variance of the index of the ith dimension, u indicates the United States, and Distance$_j$ is cultural distance of the jth country from the United States. The authors use this index of cultural distance with considerable success to test their hypothesis on the entry-mode choice of foreign firms entering the United States.

Country risk

This study uses the same measure of country risk that Gatignon and Anderson (1988) had employed in their study. High-risk countries are identified based on the classification system developed by Goodnow and Hansz (1972). In terms of the time frame within which the entry-mode decisions studied here were made, the classification scheme is not greatly outdated. Country risk in this study is represented by a dummy variable that takes on a value of 1 when entry is into high-risk countries and 0 when it is into any other country. As a result, it contrasts entries into high-risk countries with entry into lower-risk ones. High-risk countries include Algeria, Argentina, Bahrain, Bangladesh, Bolivia, Cameroon, Chad, China, Egypt, Gabon, Hungary, India, Indonesia, Iran, Nigeria, Peru, the Philippines, Saudi Arabia, Tanzania, Thailand, Turkey, and the United Arab Emirates.

Firm size

Following Gatignon and Anderson (1988) number of employees was adopted as the measure of firm size. The size of a service firm is measured by its number of employees, as reported in the directories consulted. For firms whose employment figures were unavailable, the median employment estimates (computed from the sample) for other firms in their industries were used.

ACKNOWLEDGMENTS

The authors thank Barbara Coe, Subhash Jain, Essam Mahmoud, and Jeffrey Sager for their helpful comments on earlier versions of this paper. They also gratefully acknowledge the suggestions made by William Darden and Tracy Murray on the original research project that resulted in this manuscript. In addition, they are deeply obliged to three anonymous *JM* reviewers for their contributions.

NOTES

[1] It is appropriate to use transaction costs to compare exports with foreign direct investment (FDI), since these two modes involve production in different locations. The choice between exports and FDI is less of a transaction-cost problem and more of a production-cost problem. This is supported by prevalent thinking on why firms would exploit their ownership-specific advantages using FDI rather than exports: the advantages of host-country production vis-a-vis home country production.

[2] For the sake of convenience and brevity, firms characterized by low asset specificity will be hereafter referred to as 'low-specificity' and those characterized by high asset specificity as 'high-specificity' firms.

[3] The authors are grateful to an anonymous JM reviewer for bringing the capital-intensity issue to their attention.

[4] For instance, the fixed investment of the 'typical' advertising agency (SIC 7311) is only \$36 347, but it increases to \$4 694 874 for a 'typical' hospital (SIC 8062), according to Dun and Bradstreet's *Industry Norms and Key Business Ratios (1985–86 Edition)*.

[5] (a) *Consultants and Consulting Organizations Directory* (1984), Janice McLean, Ed. Detroit, MI: Gale Research Company; (b) Dun and Bradstreet's *Million Dollar Directory* (1986). Parsippanny, NJ: Dun & Bradstreet Inc.; (c) *Standard & Poor's Register of Corporations* (1986). New York: Standard & Poor; (d) *Standard Directory of Advertising Agencies* (1985–86). New York: National Register Publishing Co.

[6] Respondents provided detailed data on one decision and some very basic data on five others.

[7] The practice of using multiple observations from individual firms is common in entry-mode studies (Gatignon and Anderson, 1988; Davidson, 1982; Davidson and McFetridge, 1985).

[8] The authors are grateful to Leona Aiken, Arizona State University, for suggesting 'weighted effects coding' as a technique to reduce collinearity. In this method, the zero in the original dummy variable is replaced by a value calculated as follows (Darlington, 1990):

$$- \frac{\text{Weight of cell identified by the variable}}{\text{Weight of base cell}}$$

REFERENCES

Afifi, A. A. and Clark, V. (1984) *Computer-Aided Multivariate Analysis*. Belmont, CA: Lifetime Learning.

Agarwal, S. and Ramaswami, S. (1992) 'Choice of Foreign Market Entry Mode: Impact of Ownership, Location and Internalization Factors'. *Journal of International Business Studies* 23(1st Quarter): 1–27.

Aharoni, Y. (1966) *The Foreign Investment Decision Process*. Boston, MA: Harvard Graduate School of Business Administration, Division of Research.

Aiken, L. S. and West, S. G. (1991) *Multiple Regression: Testing and Interpreting Interactions*. London: Sage Publications.

Anderson, E. and Schmittlein, D. C. (1984) 'Integration of the Sales Force: An Empirical Examination'. *Rand Journal of Economics* 15(Autumn): 385–395.

Anderson, E. and Gatignon, H. (1986) 'Modes of Entry: A Transactions Cost Analysis and Propositions'. *Journal of International Business Studies* 17(Fall): 1–26.

Anderson, E. and Weitz, B. A. (1986) 'Make or Buy Decisions: A Framework for Analyzing Vertical Integration Issues in Marketing'. *Sloan Management Review* 27(Spring): 3–19.

Anderson, E. and Coughlan, A. T. (1987) 'International Market Entry and Expansion via Independent or Integrated Channels of Distribution'. *Journal of Marketing* 51(January): 71–82.

Ball, C. A. and Tschoegl, A. E. (1982) 'The Decision to Establish a Foreign Bank Brank or Subsidiary: An Application of Binary Classification Procedures. *Journal of Financial and Quantitative Analysis* 17(September): 411–424.

Berry, L. L. (1980) 'Service Marketing is Different'. *Business* 30 (May–June): 24–29.

Boddewyn, J. J., Halbrich, M. B. and Perry, A. C. (1986) 'Service Multinationals: Conceptualization, Measurement and Theory'. *Journal of International Business Studies* 17(Fall): 41–57.

Bowen, D. E., Siehel, C. and Schneider, B. (1989) 'A Framework for Analyzing Customer Service Orientation in Manufacturing'. *Academy of Management Review* 14(1): 75–95.

Bower, M. (1968) 'Personal Service Firms Venture Abroad'. *Columbia Journal of World Business* 3 (March–April): 49–58.

Carman, J. M. and Langeard, E. (1980) 'Growth Strategies of Service Firms'. *Strategic Management Journal* 1(January–March): 7–22.

Cateora, P. R. (1990) *International Marketing*. Homewood, IL: Richard D. Irwin, pp. 410–412.

Chase, R. B. and Tansik, D. A. (1989). 'The Customer contact model for organization design'. *Management Science* 9: 1037–1050.

Contractor, F. J. (1984) 'Choosing Between Direct Investment and Licensing: Theoretical Considerations and Empirical Tests'. *Journal of International Business Studies* 15(Winter): 167–188.

Contractor, F. J. and P. Lorange, P. (1988) *Cooperative Strategies in International Business.* Lexington, MA: Lexington Books.

Cowell, D. W. (1983) 'International Marketing of Services'. *The Service Industries Journal* 1(November): 308–328.

Cox, D. R. (1970) *The Analysis of Binary Data.* London: Methuen & Co.

Darlington, R. B. (1990) *Regression and Linear Models.* New York: McGraw-Hill.

Davidson, W. H. (1982) *Global Strategic Management.* New York: John Wiley and Sons.

Davidson, W. H. and McFetridge, D. G. (1985) 'Key Characteristics in the Choice of International Technology Transfer Mode'. *Journal of International Business Studies* 16(Summer): 5–21.

Dunning, J. H. (1988) *Explaining International Production.* London: Unwin Hyman.

Dunning, J. H. (1989) 'The Study of International Business: A Plea for a more Inter-disciplinary Approach'. *Journal of International Business Studies* 20(Fall): 411–436.

Dunning, J.H. and McQueen, M. (1982) 'The Eclectic Theory of the Multi-national Enterprise and the International Hotel Industry. In *New Theories of Multinational Enterprise* (A. M. Rugman, Ed.). New York: St Martin's.

Dwyer, R. F. and Oh, S. (1988) 'A Transaction Cost Perspective on Vertical Contractual Structure and Interchannel Competitive Strategies'. *Journal of Marketing* 52(April): 21–34.

Erramilli, M. K. (1990) 'Entry Mode Choice in Service Industries'. *International Marketing Review* 7(5): 50–62.

Erramilli, M. K. and Rao, C. P. (1990) 'Choice of Foreign Market Entry Mode by Service Firms: Role of Market Knowledge'. *Management International Review* 30(2): 135–150.

Gaedeke, R. M. (1973) 'Selected U.S. Multinational Service Firms in Perspective'. *Journal of International Business Studies* 4(Spring): 61–67.

Gatignon, H. and Anderson, E. (1988) 'The Multinational Corporation's Degree of Control Over Foreign Subsidiaries: An Empirical Test of a Transaction Cost Explanation'. *Journal of Law, Economics, and Organization* 4(Fall): 305–336.

Geringer, M. J. and Ebert, L. (1989) 'Control and Performance of International Joint Ventures'. *Journal of International Business Studies* 20(Summer): 235–254.

Goodnow, J. D. (1985) 'Developments in International Mode of Entry Analysis'. *International Marketing Review* 2(Autumn): 17–30.

Goodnow, J. D. and Hansz, J. H. (1972) 'Environmental Determinants of Overseas Market Entry Strategies'. *Journal of International Business Studies* 3(Spring): 33–60.

Gronroos, C. (1983) *Strategic Management and Marketing in the Service Sector.* Marketing Science Institute Report, pp. 83–104, May.

Hackett, D. W. (1976) 'The International Expansion of U.S. Franchise Systems: Status and Strategies'. *Journal of International Business Studies* 7(Spring): 67–75.

Heide, J. B. and John, G. (1988) 'The Role of Dependence Balancing in Safeguarding Transaction-Specific Assets in Conventional Channels'. *Journal of Marketing* 52(January): 20–35.

Heide, J. B. and John, G. (1992) 'Do Norms Matter in Marketing Relationships?'. *Journal of Marketing* 56(April): 32–44.

Hennart, J.-F. (1989) 'Can the "New Forms of Investment" Substitute for the "Old Forms?" A Transaction Costs Perspective'. *Journal of International Business Studies* 20(Summer): 211–234.

Hill, C. W. L., Hwang, P. and Kim, W. C. (1990) 'An Eclectic Theory of the Choice of International Entry Mode'. *Strategic Management Journal* 11(2): 117–128.

Hofstede, G. (1980) *Culture's Consequences: International Differences in Work-Related Values.* Beverly Hills CA: Sage Publications.

John, G. and Weitz, B. (1989) 'Salesforce Compensations: Compensation: An Empirical Investigation of Factors Related to Use of Salary Versus Incentive Compensation'. *Journal of Marketing Research* 26(February): 1–14.

Jones, G. R. and Hill, C. W. L. (1988) 'Transaction Cost Analysis of Strategy-Structure Choice'. *Strategic Management Journal* 9(2): 159–172.

Kachigan, S. K. (1986) *Statistical Analysis: An Interdisciplinary Introduction to Univariate and Multivariate Methods.* New York: Radius Press.

Killing, J. P. (1983) *Strategies for Joint Venture Success.* New York: Praeger.

Kim, S. W. and Lyn, E. O. (1987) 'Foreign Direct Investment Theories, Entry Barriers, and Reverse Investments in U.S. Manufacturing Industries'. *Journal of International Business Studies* 18(Summer): 53–66.

Kim, W. C. and Hwang, P. (1992) 'Global Strategy and Multinationals' Entry Mode Choice'. *Journal of International Business Studies* 23(1st Quarter): 29–53.

Klecka, W. R. (1980) *Discriminant Analysis*. Beverly Hills, CA: Sage Publications.

Klein, S. (1989) 'A Transaction Cost Explanation of Vertical Control in International Markets'. *Journal of the Academy of Marketing Science* 17(Summer): 253–260.

Klein, S., Frazier, G. and Roth, V. J. (1990) 'A Transaction Cost Analysis Model of Channel Integration in International Markets'. *Journal of Marketing Research* (May): 196–208.

Kobrin, S. J. (1988) 'Trends in Ownerships of American Manufacturing Subsidiaries in Developing Countries: An Inter-Industry Analysis'. *Management International Review* (Special issue): 73–84.

Kogut, B. and Singh, H. (1988) 'The Effect of National Culture on the Choice of Entry Mode'. *Journal of International Business Studies* 19(Fall): 411–432.

Kotler, P. (1991) *Marketing Management: Analysis, Planning, Implementation, and Control*. Englewood Cliffs, NJ: Prentice-Hall, p. 413.

Larsson, R. and Bowen, D. E. (1989) 'Organization and Customer: Managing Design and Coordination of Services'. *Academy of Management Review* 14(2): 213–233.

Lecraw, D. J. (1984) 'Bargaining Power, Ownership, and Profitability of Transnational Corporations in Developing Countries'. *Journal of International Business Studies* 15(Spring/Summer): 27–43.

Lo, T. W. and Yung, A. (1988) 'Multinational Service Firms in Centrally-Planned Economies: Foreign Advertising Agencies in the PRC'. *Management International Review* 28(1): 26–32.

Lovelock, C. H. (1983) 'Classifying Services to Gain Strategic Marketing Insights'. *Journal of Marketing* 47(Summer): 9–20.

Mascarenhas, B. (1982) 'Coping With Uncertainty in International Business'. *Journal of International Business Studies* 13(Fall): 87–98.

Neter, J., Wasserman, W. and Kutner, M. H. (1983) *Applied Regression Models*. Homewood, IL: Richard D. Irwin.

Palmer, J. D. (1985) 'Consumer Service Industry Exports: New Attitudes and Concepts Needed for a Neglected Sector'. *Columbia Journal of World Business* 20(Spring): 69–74.

Robinson, R. C. (1978) *International Business Management: A Guide to Decision Making*. Hinsdale, IL: The Dryden Press.

Root, F. R. (1987) *Foreign Market Entry Strategies*. New York: AMACOM.

Sampson, G. P. and Snape, R. H. (1985) 'Identifying the Issues in Trade in Services'. *The World Economy*, 171–182.

Sapir, A. (1982) 'Trade in Services: Policy Issues for the Eighties'. *Columbia Journal of World Business* 17(Fall): 77–83.

SAS Institute (1989) *SAS/STAT User's Guide, Version 6, 4th ed., Vol. 2*. Cary, NC: SAS Institute Inc.

Sharma, D. D. and Johanson, J. (1987) 'Technical Consultancy in Internationalization'. *International Marketing Review* 4(Winter): 20–29.

Stopford, J. M. and Wells, L. T. Jr. (1972) *Managing the Multinational Enterprise*. New York: Basic Books.

Teece, D. J. (1981) 'The Multinational Enterprise: Market Failure and Market Power Considerations'. *Sloan Management Review* 22(Spring): 3–17.

Teece, D. J. and Yu, C.-M. (1988) 'Determinants of Foreign Investment of U.S. Advertising Agencies'. *Journal of International Business Studies* 19(Spring): 33–46.

Teece, D. J. and Sarathy, R. (1991) *International Marketing*, 5th edn. New York: The Dryden Press.

United States Congress, Office of Technology Assessment (1986) *Trade in Services: Exports and Foreign Revenues—Special Report*, OTA-ITE-316. Washington, DC: U.S. Government Printing Office.

United States Congress, Office of Technology Assessment (1987) *International Competition in Services*, OTA-ITE-328. Washington, DC: US Government Printing Office.

Weinstein, A. K. (1974) 'The International Expansion of U.S. Multinational Advertising Agencies'. *MSU Business Topics* **22** (Summer): 29–35.

Weinstein, A. K. (1977) 'Foreign Investments by Service Firms: The Case of Multinational Advertising Agencies'. *Journal of International Business Studies*, **8** (Spring/Summer), 83–91.

Williamson, O. E. (1985) *The Economic Institutions of Capitalism.* New York: The Free Press.

Williamson, O. E. (1986) *Economic Organization: Firms, Markets and Policy Control.* New York: New York University Press.

Williamson, O. E. (1987) 'The Economics of Organization: The Transaction Cost Approach'. *American Journal of Sociology* **87** (3): 548–577.

Wind, Y. and Perimutter, H.V. (1977) 'On the Identification of the Frontier Issues of International Marketing'. *Columbia Journal of World Business* **12** (Winter): 131.

Zeithaml, V. A., Parasuraman, A. and Berry, L. L. (1985) 'Problems and Strategies in Services Marketing'. *Journal of Marketing* **49** (Spring): 33–46.

Section V

Services Marketing in Context

This section considers some contextual examples of service marketing in order to give the reader some feel for the breadth of service marketing research activity. Increasingly, service marketers are finding that generic principles require some re-examination and customisation as they are adopted within particular service contexts. Financial services, for instance, have always been regarded as a special case of service marketing, primarily because the product is so varied, so resistant to definition and so reliant upon the future. Very often purchase is made without any personal contact or any dimension of a delivery experience. The paper by Knights *et al.* (1994) is included here because it raises some interesting issues about the applicability of adopting a marketing orientation where consumers are generally disinterested, and display high levels of inertia. The authors assert this has the effect of encouraging a product led approach. They point to the limitations apparent in the financial services context of responding to consumer needs and in particular the tendency for the pursuit of profit to displace the satisfaction of consumer need.

The second article in this section by Arnould and Price (1993) considers the delivery of an extraordinary service experience characterised as extreme hedonic consumption. The authors use a multi-day river rafting trip in Colorado to investigate the true meaning of the extraordinary experience which takes place over an extended period. It is a remarkable article for a number of reasons. First and primarily, it provides an encapsulation of service consumption, including planning and expectations, the trip experience and post trip evaluations and reflections. This approach, with its implicit longitudinal element, provides a number of unusual insights into how both consumers and guides develop a reflective narrative which is used as a basis for evaluation. The second important feature of this work is the way in which the authors have woven together qualitative and quantitative measures to present a rich analysis of the experience. The third important feature of the article is the outcome, which points to a number of questions regarding the appropriateness of the expectation–performance framework in understanding the nature of extraordinary performance. Finally the article points in a new direction for services research, concentrating upon the whole story, a predominantly gestalt approach to service consumption which may require a new vocabulary from service marketing researchers.

The work of Edvardsson (1992) is notable for two main reasons: the context and the methodology. Airlines have been used on many occasions as examples of service breakdowns yet this particular service industry is also a good example of the range and complexity of the overall service experience. Luggage handlers, airport staff, traffic control and check-in assistants all contribute to our overall experiences yet only a small number of these tasks are under the direct control of the airline. When a service breakdown occurs, attribution is often directed at the airline who are frequently in a position of engaging in recovery for another service provider and this article highlights some of the complexities inherent in this service sector. The second important attribute of this article is the use of the critical incident technique which is finding increased application in services research (see Bitner, Booms and Mohr, 1994, Gabbott and Hogg, 1996, amongst others). The technique has many interesting features, not least in the ability to span both qualitative and quantitative approaches to the same problem, thereby providing opportunities for empiricist and interpretavist researchers alike.

The final article by Szmigin (1993) is a contextual analysis of service quality. Using business-to-business services, Szmigin concentrates upon the role of expectations in the development and maintenance of long-term relationships. A distinction is drawn between hard, soft and outcome quality, where hard and soft quality is synonymous with technical and functional quality (following Grönroos) while outcome quality is considered to be the determinant of the long-term health of the relationship. The crux of the article is the importance of these three quality dimensions to different types of relationship. What follows is a comprehensive analysis of relationship form and management which reviews the critical issues for business to business services in the maintenance of long-term relationships. Overall the article provides some useful considerations for business to business marketers and highlights the proximity between service quality and relationship marketing on building success.

CONTENTS

22

The Consumer Rules? An Examination of the Rhetoric and 'Reality' of Marketing in Financial Services

David Knights, Andrew Sturdy and Glenn Morgan

INTRODUCTION

Over recent years the financial services have been subject to considerable disruption in their traditional ways of doing business. The boundaries between banks, building societies and insurance companies have begun to disappear as government policy and economic deregulation has forced them into competition with one another. Political re-regulation, though largely self-administered, has shaken the insurance industry to its roots, resulting in regular revelations of highly respectable companies suffering the humiliation of hefty fines from the regulators for non-compliance with the Financial Services Act (FSA).[1] Admittedly, the new regulations have not been entirely constraining. In conjunction with other stimulants, they have encouraged banks and building societies to be more strategic in their pursuit of fee income from insurance and investment products, if only to compensate for declining profits in their traditional fields of business activity.

As service organizations, the objective towards which the financial services are directed in accommodating these and various other changes, such as the growth of new information technologies,[2-4] is the consumer. More precisely, they have been concerned to improve their service to the customer for purposes of promoting profitable sales. In doing so, they have begun to embrace a market- rather than product-led approach to their business.[5-7] The focus, it is claimed, is on identifying the pattern and content of consumer 'needs' and (re-)designing products and targeting their distribution so as to exploit this knowledge profitability. In short, the marketing concept combined with market segmentation is seen to be the emerging model for business activities in financial services.

The marketing concept is often cited as underpinning progressive marketing practice both in the literature and by practitioners. Recognizing that it has been the

Reprinted with permission from *European Journal of Marketing*, Vol. 28, No. 3, pp. 42–54 focus of some definitional debate[8-11] our concern here is with the restricted but common usage of the marketing concept as focused on establishing and satisfying (responding to) consumer 'needs' profitably. As elsewhere in marketing theory, this assumes that consumers have identifiable 'needs' prior to consumption and that they act on them. It implies that such 'needs' should be incorporated into products and services delivery either to the extent that it is profitable to do so or because in competitive markets where 'sovereign' consumers can make informed 'choices', those companies which respond to 'needs' will necessarily be profitable as a result.[12]

Within the context of the UK personal financial services market and in relation to relevant literature, we challenge some of the assumptions about consumer 'needs' and highlight the tension with the marketing concept between responding to 'need' and achieving profitability. First, it is argued that consumer 'need' is a category for ordering and making sense of behaviours which are the outcome of producer/consumer relationships (e.g. the sale) rather than a property of individuals, as is conventionally assumed. Accordingly, in the context of many financial services, but particularly life products, individuals are transformed into consumers only at the point of sale when their lives are reconstituted as a problem (need) to be resolved (satisfied) by the product on offer. Research to identify 'needs' prior to consumption is then highly artificial since it is abstracted from the circumstances in which 'needs' are created and sustained. Second, and contrary to the conventional view within financial services of an increasing competitive climate prompting a greater market/customer orientation, we highlight how competitive pressures also limit this tendency by reinforcing managerial concerns with costs and profitability. Here, high cost/low profitability consumer segments and hence their 'needs', are selected out through pricing and targeting. Relatedly, and reinforcing established critiques of the concept of consumer sovereignty,[13] there is considerable consumer inertia in relation to many financial services which allows for, and even encourages, a (profitable) product-led approach to the market.

Although primarily theoretical, this article draws selectively on empirical data gathered over a number of years through links with financial services companies in academic research and practical involvement in the industry. The article is organized as follows: first, the literature documenting and often prescribing an increased market orientation in financial services and the conditions of its emergence are briefly reviewed. Our critique of this approach is then presented, first in relation to the concept of need itself and second with regard to the pre-eminence of profit in marketing practice. The article is not seeking to deny the 'sea swell' of change in the direction of marketing in financial services but merely to curtail the excessive claims regarding its success and, more importantly, its potential. We turn now therefore to an examination of the growth of marketing applications in this sector of the economy.

THE MARKETING ORIENTATION IN UK FINANCIAL SERVICES

The UK financial services sector (i.e. banks, building societies, insurance companies and their distributors) is perceived as having been highly undeveloped and reluctant to adopt the marketing concept.[14-16] It has been characterized as supply orientated – principally concerned with operational risk and financial issues and, in marketing terms, product led. A range of well-established products would be sold, 'hard' in some areas such as life assurance, or left to be 'bought' in others.[5,6,14,17] Relatedly, marketing activities, ideas and departments within companies were limited in their scope and afforded low status in relation to other business 'disciplines' such as accounting and actuarial work.[18] An early exception to this generalization was the retail banks which, according to Clarke *et al.*[16] (p. 10), were by 1988 entering the 'final' evolutionary stage of marketing development – the 'marketing control' era – where the marketing concept drives the whole organization.

The new competitive climate, however, is forcing a transition in the direction of accelerating the development of marketing practices throughout the whole sector. Companies are increasingly adopting a strategic marketing orientation where the emphasis is on consumer 'needs' – their identification and the tailoring of products and services for purposes of satisfying them profitably[16,17,19-21]. The transition is recent and rapid, indicated by a survey of companies' self-perceptions which recorded 53% as being 'market-orientated' compared with 2% five years earlier.[17] Similarly, another survey found that 48% of the sample companies had established their marketing departments only in the last five years.[18] Also market research and segmentation techniques in product development (i.e. tailoring products to specific market segments) have proliferated in recent years.[6,22] For example, more companies are using information technology in the application of relatively modern forms of segmentation such as 'lifestyles' in focusing on customer needs.[19,23,24] Speed and Smith[7] claim that 'market segmentation has become accepted and followed as a strategy in the financial services industry (p. 376). More specifically, banks and building societies have been expanding their product range and distribution channels by cross-selling tailored, targeted and, often, branded products and services.[6,24,26] It is this strategy of 'farming' the customer base that is most closely associated with the increasing emphasis on consumer 'needs' and segmentation.

Despite this groundswell of activity, one needs to be cautious of the extent and quality of the changes that are deemed to be taking place, for they are reminiscent of earlier claims that the industry was subscribing to the marketing concept.[15,27] Marketing literature, let alone practice, in this field still remains undeveloped particularly in relation to consumer behaviour.[28] Financial services continue to lag behind other sectors in the use of strategic and other marketing techniques, including segmentation.[5,17] For example, Davison *et al.*[18] show that 72% of their financial services sample had no market research function and 16%, no marketing department in 1989.[29] Although the paucity of market research may be partly a consequence of the relative ease with which competitors can imitate one another's products in financial services, such findings suggest a considerable variation in the extent of marketing development and practice.

This variation has often been the focus of literature which seeks to measure and categorize marketing developments implicitly as a 'progressive' force. Larger companies are found to be more 'advanced'[11,14] and it is possible to provide evolutionary accounts of marketing in the sector. In this context, Thwaites and Lynch[6] (p. 440; see also ref. 11) constructed three company typologies of approaches to marketing among building societies, suggesting that a developmental pattern existed from 'marketing myopics', through 'departmental promoters' and 'advanced functionalists' towards the ideal of 'guiding philosophers'. As many as 40% of building societies were seen to fit the latter category where marketing informed and stimulated every activity, and not just the marketing function. In providing evidence of the character and variability of marketing practices, such research is valuable. However, the unexplained evolutionary and prescriptive assumptions underlying the research require critical examination. Typologies of this kind suggest a trajectory in which there is an inevitable logic of development from one stage to the next as organizations move closer to the ideal prescribed by the researcher. Any constraining or counterveiling pressures are often underplayed or bypassed and the concept of marketing itself is presumed to be 'progressive' and unproblematic even though, as we seek to show, there may be some tensions in its application to this sector of industry. Before focusing on these issues, we offer a brief examination of the conditions in which the transition towards a more comprehensive use of the marketing concept is emerging.

The conditions of emergence

There are a number of accounts which outline the key factors associated with the emergence of the current form of heightened competition and of an increased marketing orientation.[5,14,16,19] There is no attempt here to duplicate the detail contained therein; the aim is merely to provide a brief overview. First, a series of (de-/re-) *regulatory changes* reflected in the legislation of the early 1970s and late 1980s have transformed internal sector boundaries, intensified competition, stimulated market demand and generated a greater concern with consumer protection (e.g. selling to 'need'). Associated *ideological changes* towards neo-liberalism have raised the value of 'consumer sovereignty' in society with consequences for organizations and their relationships with 'external' customers. This has helped to raise the legitimacy of marketing as a specialism in relation to other managerial/professional groups.[30] Other changes in the *socio-economic* profile of the population have stimulated demand in some areas and generated 'new' financial services 'needs'. This includes the continued 'demassification' of society to increasingly diffuse groupings (or market segments) with different lifestyles.[31,32]

Increased personal income in the 1980s combined with market saturation of certain core products saw the development of 'new' products and increased segmentation. Indeed, in the marketing theory of product life-cycles, market saturation is a classic condition for segmentation.[33,34] More recently, the economic recession and housing 'crisis' have focused managerial attention more acutely towards costs and profitability as well as new markets. At the same time, and partly as a consequence of increased marketing, government regulation and the attention of the media and consumer groups, it is claimed that financial services consumers are becoming more financially literate, sophisticated and discerning (i.e. 'sovereign') in their choice of product, service and company. Finally, innovations in information technology (IT) have facilitated increased and more flexible use of data in service distribution and new product development.[4,35,36]

In addition to the largely acknowledged factors listed above, two further conditions relating to company practices help to account for the nature and growth of marketing in financial services. First, forms of segmentation are inherent to traditional banking and insurance activities. Actuarial and credit scoring techniques, like those of market segmentation, are derived from early statistical classification of people and behaviour.[37] They are used to measure, classify and locate risks. The first forms of market segmentation used such information to target 'good' risks for motor and life insurance, for example. This tradition of 'segmentation selection' has helped to shape contemporary market segmentation with its focus on the costs and profitability of products and segments.

Second, through targeted advertising in particular, the marketing (and production) practices of manufacturing companies since the 1960s have helped to structure the diversified market for personal consumption in ways which provide the basis for the segmentation strategies deployed by financial service companies.[32,38,39] Furthermore the development, dissemination and promotion of marketing techniques and approaches, combined with those associated with strategy and accounting knowledges, are conditions as well as consequences of changing marketing practice.[37]

While no doubt necessary, the dissemination of new knowledges and techniques cannot be seen as a sufficient condition for their widespread adoption. According to historical accounts of the growth of marketing activity, the most crucial stimulus is intensified competition for industry, in general[33,40] and financial services, in particular.[8] The key, if not distinctive (see ref. 5, p. xii), characteristic of the recent changing climate of regulation and competition has been the erosion of technical product boundaries in markets which, in many senses, may be seen as oversupplied. These and other competitive factors have not only contributed to the increasing attention given to diverse consumer 'needs', but also have helped to shape the way in which market segmentation strategies are implemented.[37]

LIMITATIONS IN RESPONDING TO CONSUMER NEEDS

As has been intimated, there is a general view that current competitive conditions have forced financial service companies to develop or modify their products, customer service and methods of distribution in accordance with a prior assessment of consumer 'needs' or preferences.[5,15,41] However, we are sceptical of claims that consumer 'needs' predominate. First, our scepticism revolves around the very concept of 'need' so readily and unproblematically adopted by marketing theorists and practitioners. We believe the concept to be problematic within marketing as a whole but especially with respect to those aspects of financial services (e.g. life insurance, pensions and other long-term savings products) where the consumer is often inert or inactive as a buyer until the actual point of sale. Second and relatedly, we argue that even if the problems surrounding the concept of 'need' were resolvable, suppliers of financial services would be heavily constrained from satisfying consumers 'needs' by the higher priority of selling profitable products. In short, competition may also act to limit the extent to which perceived needs are addressed.

The concept of 'need'

The concept of 'need' has a long history within the field of industrial psychology where it was originally seen to fill the conceptual gap between stimulus and response in behaviourist theory. The stimulus was seen to elicit a response if the individual had a need that could be satisfied by such a response. It was particularly adopted in motivation theory when the presumed causal relationship between job satisfaction and work productivity/performance failed to be confirmed in several empirical studies.[42]

While there is not space here to enter into a long philosophical debate about our epistemological and ontological misgivings with the concept of 'need',[43] it is appropriate to point to its inadmissible essentialist and individualistic nature. Largely because of a preoccupation with 'scientific' respectability, marketing is dominated by a reduction of its field (i.e. human behaviour) to a set of measurable variables, and 'need', like all marketing concepts, falls into this paradigm and is operationalized so as to remove the sense of ambiguity, uncertainty or precariousness in its meaning.

Through this process, 'need' is made really to exist as an essential feature of the individual psyche which is itself seen to have autonomous existence. But, in effect, the belief in its existence serves to influence the exercise of power (e.g. advertising, selling and marketing) by producers in such a way as to reproduce the kinds of behaviour in consumers that sustain the belief. It also reinforces an individualistic perception on the part of consumers that anxieties, frustrations and desires can be satisfactorily managed through buying products that are deemed to fulfil deeply held 'needs'. The irony in all this is that while holding assumptions which disregard the social construction of reality,[44] the concept of 'need' is ultimately validated precisely because of such constructions, albeit supplemented by powerful practices on the part of producers and distributors. Marketing then claims to be satisfying a range of consumer 'needs' which it plays a large, though not exclusive, part in creating.

It may be suggested that conventionally we attribute need to individuals as a *post hoc* rationalization to account for and render rational and meaningful some recurrent behaviour we have observed. 'Need', then, is not a property of the customer so much as a category for ordering and making sense of behaviours which are a complex outcome of the producer/distributor/consumer relationship. This is the case in any consumption process but even more so with respect to insurance and associated products in financial services, where individuals are transformed into consumers only at the point of sale when their lives are reconstituted as a problem (need) to be resolved (satisfied) by the product on offer. If 'needs' are socially constructed within effective sales encounters, the process is accomplished by the sales person with particular products in mind (i.e. those available for sale); it is then somewhat exaggerated to argue that financial services now *respond* to consumer 'needs'. They do so only insofar as the 'need' that the salesperson has been active in constructing, can be apparently satisfied from within the product range on offer.

Of course, the original design of products may well have been developed by using various market research techniques to secure a better 'fit' between product and what a sample of the population anticipate people might want. But these techniques can never simulate consumer behaviour since, by definition, they are abstracted from the actual circumstances of consumption. Moreover, if consumers do not often know what they want prior to the construction of a problem or 'need' in the sales encounter, then such market research has a marginal role to play. This takes us to our second reason for being sceptical of the claims regarding the centrality of consumer 'needs' in the distribution of financial services – the concern to sell profitable products to profitable consumers.

The pre-eminence of profit

While we recognize the concept of need to be problematic as illustrated, this in itself would not preclude financial services companies from developing a stronger orientation to the consumer. But, as we have intimated, profit acts as a constraint on, as well as an incentive for, such practices. In one sense, this is an obvious point. Indeed, it is clear from the earliest discussions of a market-led approach that consideration of cost and profitability limit the possible diversity of products and services offered to the consumer (ref. 33, p. 401). This is underplayed if not neglected in the marketing literature at a time when, owing to intensified competition, the tension surrounding the potential conflict between profit and responding to consumer 'needs' has heightened.

Selecting profitable consumers has been a concern of financial services companies in a variety of forms such as the exclusive bank account or the pricing of 'bad' risks out of the market through strict insurance underwriting. With increased competition, and, in banking, the push for cross-selling, market segmentation has simply added another technique which can make this search for the profitable consumer more precise and effective. As one bank insurance director expressed it:

> We are actually encouraging – largely as a result of targeting – this search for the 'holy grail', the good customer who never makes a claim – we're giving him(sic) such competitive premiums but what's it doing at the other end of the book . . . we're seeing cases now where the choice is not which insurer, but do I insure? The premium increases are such that it is becoming beyond some people's means.

The more this increases, however, the less plausible becomes the rhetoric of responding to consumer 'needs', since the qualification has to be added that they must be low-risk or high-priced 'needs'.[45–49]

The preoccupation with profitability does not merely restrict those to whom financial services companies sell their products but also what they are prepared to sell. In insurance and investment, the demands of the Financial Services Act to give 'best advice' (i.e. selling to 'need') from across the whole range of a company's products resulted in products being withdrawn from the range simply on the basis of their low profitability. Even where such questionable practices are not adopted, sales staff are often in a position to sell those products that attract higher rates of commission and policing 'best advice' has not seriously affected commission-based selling.[50,51]

The selection of 'profitable' products and consumers and the concomitant 'selecting out' of others can, in part, be attributed to managerial short-termism or the continued predominance of 'non-marketing' management groups' priorities within organizations[17] such as those of financial accountants, actuaries, underwriters and sales managers.[30] Moreover, it could be argued that profitability, in the long term at least, is more likely to result from addressing consumers' 'needs' than by neglecting them. This is particularly the case where 'repeat' business or 'cross-selling' depends on consumer satisfaction with a company's service. It is sometimes explicit in the literature when, for example, high company performance is seen to be linked with the practice of relationship marketing,[21] albeit with a high net worth (i.e. more 'active' and profitable) customer base. Thus, the apparent neglect in the marketing literature of the cost constraints on a marketing orientation may well stem from the assumption that there is no tension involved. This is because it is assumed that high levels of competition in financial services will 'protect' consumers from the tendencies of companies seeking to determine or ignore their 'needs'. Only those companies which satisfy the consumers' 'needs' will survive, it is argued. But the competition argument is dubious even in areas of consumption such as consumer commodities because of the tendency of retailers not to stock comparable models of the same product.[30] In the long-term business aspects of financial services especially, it has little impact because, on the whole, the consumer is inactive and/or indifferent.

Set against the claims of increasing consumer sophistication, there is some consensus in the literature that the key factors for most consumers remain simply a confidence in the security of the organization and, in particular, convenience of purchase.[25,28,51,53–55] Even in the relatively transparent and price sensitive market of motor insurance, convenience of supply is the primary consideration.[56] Through the provision of a range of packaged and branded products conveniently available in high street networks and numerous other channels of distribution, it might be argued that the financial services companies are responding to these consumer 'needs'.

The apparent preference for convenience and confidence is typically understood as a product of consumer ignorance resulting from the complexity and non-comparability of financial services. However, an alternative account is that it reflects not so much consumer preference or ignorance, but, a lack of interest in, or even an indifference towards, financial services – an attitude which is reinforced by the complexity of products in this field. Even in terms of service provision or delivery, there remains considerable 'inertia' – consumers do not tend to 'vote with their feet'.[51,52] As Watkins[53] notes, with some exceptions, such as consumers switching from bank accounts to interest bearing building society accounts in the 1980s:

> There is little hard evidence of substantial shopping around by the majority of buyers in choosing financial services, nor of switching between suppliers on a large scale . . . (p. 48).

This is particularly evident in insurance.[56] Indeed consumers' lack of interest in insurance is given as one reason why there is little use of market research (an essential element of the marketing orientation) in this area (refs. 18, 41, p. 146). In life assurance especially, despite years of successive educational campaigns from the industry and increased marketing activity and media attention, the adage that it is not bought but must be sold because of 'ignorance of the product and distaste for the message' (i.e. associations with death)[15] remains relevant. This 'requirement' for a sales push/product-led rather than market-led approach highlights the active role of sales and marketing in helping to construct consumer 'needs' and shape preferences across financial services. This is, once again, typically neglected or underplayed in the marketing literature for it directly contradicts the notion of an active and sovereign consumer.[13,57]

At the very least then, widespread consumer inertia reduces the incentive for companies to design products primarily on the basis of prior 'needs' analysis. Rather, for many companies there are only the mass and the more active or sophisticated high net worth markets and life stages within them. Indeed, it is claimed that the financial services market is, as yet, less differentiated than other sectors.[58] This is also acknowledged by some practitioners. For example, one bank insurance director described the packaging of standard products for convenience and presenting/selling them as if they specifically met the consumers' 'needs' as 'mass marketing to units of one (consumer)' and as an ideal to be sought. Moreover the banks' strategy to 'farm' the captive customer base by life-long cross-selling is informed more by the resulting cost savings (claimed to be as much as three to seven times cheaper than selling to new customers) than responding to diffuse needs.

This is not to argue crudely that companies simply exploit customers. Rather, it is to raise questions about the claims that competitive pressures have led companies to respond to consumer 'needs'. Competition can work on companies in at least two ways: to offer better products and services in order to increase or maintain market share, and to contain costs in order to survive or maximize profitability. In both cases needs may be conveniently bypassed as 'costly' consumers are avoided and consumer inertia provides the opportunity or rationale for adopting a profitable product-led approach. Until such time as consumers do become more sophisticated 'financially self-disciplined subjects',[44] such strategies may well be appropriate in this sector.

CONCLUSIONS

In this article we have sought to examine critically the concept of need deployed in marketing and the claims of an increasingly market-led approach within UK retail financial services. As with earlier marketing developments in the USA and particularly with respect to manufactured goods, heightened competition has encouraged increasing managerial attention to consumer needs. But consideration of costs and profitability are also intensified by competition. While it is acknowledged in the general marketing literature that such concerns place a limit on the scope for responding to needs, it is rarely the focus of academic attention. Cost considerations encourage a ('profitable') product-led approach, whereby segmentation techniques are used to *select out*, where possible, 'unprofitable' products and consumer segments almost irrespective of consumer need. Moreover, such practices are made possible and reinforced not only by the dominance of 'accounting' interests within management, but also by the comparative inertia evident among financial services consumers. The marketing concept assumes consumers to be knowledgeable and interested in the products on offer – therefore, if companies respond to consumers' needs, increased market share will necessarily follow. As we have argued, such a view neglects the way in which needs are as much a consequence as a condition of marketing and other supplier activities rather than a property of individuals which is identifiable prior to consumption. In addition and in financial services especially, it overlooks the possibility that consumers continue to be comparatively indifferent to the product, and to a lesser extent to the nature of service delivery.

It appears that the increased marketing (as well as other media and consumer pressure group activity) in financial services is, somewhat paradoxically, raising the interest or 'sophistication' of some (e.g. the middle and professional classes) consumers.[13] Such a development is reinforcing the pressure to become more market-led. An example of this is the provision by some banks of independent financial advice to high net-worth customers. However, and more generally, to the extent that profit retains a primacy over attention to 'needs' and products are sold as if they have been tailored ('mass marketing to units of one'), there is a danger that increased consumer awareness combined with expectations of a 'personal service' will provoke consumer resistance and/or demands for customized products. Or it is possible that, as the regulators seem to be advocating, a 'professional' or advice-based model rather than a 'sales' approach is more appropriate to the future of financial services. In which case, marketing would have to take a 'back seat' or undergo a dramatic transformation in the direction of assisting the process of financial education rather than advancing the effective and profitable consumption of products.

ACKNOWLEDGMENTS

The authors would like to acknowledge the special editors and anonymous reviewers for their helpful comments on an earlier version of this article. We would also like to thank Helen Dean as secretary of the Financial Services Research Centre (FSRC). The research was supported by the TS-funded FSRC at UMIST.

NOTES AND REFERENCES

1. For example, such respectable companies as Scottish Widows, Guardian Royal Exchange, and Sun Alliance have suffered fines as a result of investigations by the Life Assurance and Unit Trust Regulatory Organization (LAUTRO).
2. Kerfoot, D. and Knights, D. (1993) 'Management, Manipulation and Masculinity'. *Journal of Management Studies* **31**(4): 659–679.
3. Knights, D. and Willmott, H. (1993) 'It's a Very Foreign Discipline: Expenses Control in a Mutual Life Insurance Company'. *British Journal of Management* **4**(4): 1–18.
4. Sturdy, A. J. (Ed.) (1989) *Managing Information Technology in Insurance.* Harlow: Longman.
5. Ennew, C. T., Watkins, T. and Wright, M. (Eds) (1990) *Marketing Financial Services.* Oxford: Heinemann.
6. Thwaites, D. and Lynch, J. E. (1992) 'Adoption of the Marketing Concept by UK Building Societies'. *Service Industries Journal* **12**(4): 437–462.
7. Speed, R. and Smith, G. (1992) 'Retail Financial Services Segmentation'. *Service Industries Journal* **12**(3): 368–383.
8. *Journal of the Academy of Marketing Science* (1992) Special 20th Anniversary Issue, **20** (No. 4, Fall).
9. Hunt, S. D. (1992) 'Marketing Is . . .'. *Journal of the Academy of Marketing Science* **20** (No. 4, Fall): 301–312.
10. Bennett, P. D. (1988) *Dictionary of Marketing Terms.* Chicago, IL: American Marketing Association.

11. Hooley, G. J., Lynch, J. E. and Shepherd, J. (1990) 'The Marketing Concept: Putting Theory into Practice'. *European Journal of Marketing* **29**(9): 7–24.
12. Kotler, P. (1984) *Marketing Management*, 5th edn. Englewood Cliffs, NJ: Prentice-Hall.
13. Smith, N. C. (1987) 'Consumer Boycotts and Consumer Sovereignty'. *European Journal of Marketing* **21**(5): 7–19.
14. Morgan, N. and Piercy, N. (1990) 'Marketing in Financial Services Organizations. Policy and Practice'. In *Managing and Marketing Services in the 1990s* (R. Teare, L. Moutinho and N. Morgan, Eds). London: Cassel.
15. Newman, K. (1984) *Financial Marketing and Communications*. Eastbourne: Holt, Rinehart and Winston.
16. Clarke, P. D., Edward, P. M., Gardner, E. F., Feeney, P. and Molyneux, P. (1988) 'The Genesis of Strategic Marketing Control in British Retail Banking'. *International Journal of Bank Marketing* **6**(2): 5–19.
17. Hooley, G. J. and Mann, S. J. (1988) 'The Adoption of Marketing by Financial Institutions in the UK'. *Service Industries Journal* **8**(4): 488–500.
18. Davison, H., Watkins, T. and Wright, M. (1989) 'Developing New Personal Financial Products: Some Evidence of the Role of Market Research'. *International Journal of Bank Marketing* **7**(1): 8–15.
19. Joseph, L. and Yorke, D. A. (1989) 'Know Your Game Plan: Market Segmentation in the Personal Financial Services Section', *Quarterly Review of Marketing* **15**(1): 8–13.
20. Within this framework, Speed and Smith[21] identify three interrelated dimensions of strategic marketing in financial services – an emphasis on customer selection, internal operations or an overall strategic orientation.
21. Speed, R. and Smith, G. (1993) 'Customers, Strategy and Performance', *International Journal of Bank Managing* **11**(5): 3–11.
22. Ennew, C. T. (1990) 'Marketing Strategy and Planning'. In *Marketing Financial Services* (C. T. Ennew, T. Watkins and M. Wright, Eds). Oxford: Heinemann, pp. 60–79.
23. Wells, W. D. (1975) 'Psychographics – A Critical Review'. *Journal of Marketing Research* **12** (May): 196–213. Reprinted in Ennis, B. M. and Cox, K. K. (Eds) (1988) *Marketing Classics*, 6th edn. London: Allyn & Bacon.
24. Lewis, B. R. (1990) 'Bank Marketing'. In *Marketing Financial Services* (C. T. Ennew, T. Watkins and M. Wright, Eds). Oxford: Heinemann, pp. 157–177.
25. McGoldrick, P. J. and Greenland, S. J. 'Competition between Banks and Building Societies in the Retailing of Financial Services'. *British Journal of Management* **3**(1): 169–179.
26. Sturdy, A. J. (1992) 'Banks a Lot (Banks, General Insurance and the Consumer)'. *Post Magazine*, 4 December.
27. Watson, I. (1982) 'The Adoption of Marketing by the English Clearing Banks'. *European Journal of Marketing* **16**(3).
28. McKechnie, S. (1992) 'Consumer Buying Behaviour in Financial Services: An Overview'. *International Journal of Bank Marketing* **10**(5): 4–12.
29. The absence of specific marketing departments in this case was not considered as a reflection of a highly advanced 'stage' of development involving the diffusion of marketing throughout the organizations surveyed.
30. Wittington, R. and Whipp, R. (1992) 'Professional Ideology and Marketing Implementation'. *European Journal of Marketing* **26**(1): 52–63.
31. Baudrillard, J. (1988) In: *Selected Writings* (M. Procter, Ed.). Oxford: Polity Press.
32. Featherstone, M. (1991) *Consumer Culture and Postmodernism*. London: Sage.
33. Smith, W. R. (1956) 'Product Differentiation and Market Segmentation as Alternative Strategies'. *Journal of Marketing*, July: 3–8. Reprinted in Ennis, B. M. and Cox, K. K. (Eds) (1988) *Marketing Classics*, 6th edn. London: Allyn & Bacon.
34. Zollinger, M. (1985) *Marketing Bancaire*. Paris: Dunod.
35. Dyer, N. and Watkins, T. (Eds) (1988) *Marketing Insurance: A Practical Guide*. London: Kluwer.
36. Knights, D. and Murray, F. (1994) *Divided Managers: Organizational Politics and IT Management*. Chichester: Wiley.
37. Sturdy, A. J., Knights, D. and Morgan, G. (1993) 'Marketing the Soul: The Subjectivity of

Segmentation and the Segmentation of Subjectivity'. Paper presented at 11th European Group on Organisation Studies Colloquium, Paris.

38. Curtis, T. (1988) 'The Information Society: A Computer Generated Caste System?' In *The Political Economy of Information* (V. Mosco and J. Wasko, Eds). Madison, WI: University of Wisconsin Press.

39. Goldman, R. (1992) *Reading Ads Socially.* London: Routledge.

40. Engel, J. F., Fiorillo, H. F. and Cayley, M. A. (Eds) *Market Segmentation – Concepts and Applications.* New York: Holt, Rinehart and Winston.

41. Watkins, T. and Wright, M. (1986) *Marketing Financial Services.* London: Butterworths.

42. Vroom, V. H. (1964) *Work and Motivation.* New York: John Wiley & Sons.

43. Knights, D. and Willmott, H. (1974) 'Humanistic Social Science and the Theory of Needs'. *Interpersonal Development* **12**(1): 213–222.

44. Knights, D. (1988) 'Risk, Financial Self-discipline and Commodity Relationships'. *Advances in Public Interest Accounting* **2**. New York: JAI Press, pp. 47–69.

45. It is somewhat ironic that techniques originally developed in nineteenth-century studies on the plight of the poor such as the family life-cycle[46,47] and what is now termed 'geodemographics'[48,49] are effectively being used to select-out similar groups from financial services.

46. Rowntree, B. S. (1901) *Poverty: A Study of Town Life.* London: Macmillan.

47. Wells, W. D. and Gubar, G. (1966) 'The Life Cycle Concept in Marketing Research'. *Journal of Marketing Research* **4** (No. 4, November).

48. Booth, C. (Ed.) *The Life and Labour of the People of London.* London: Macmillan, pp. 1889–1902.

49. Rothman, J. (1989) 'Geodemographics (Editorial)'. *Journal of Market Research* **31**(1): editorial and pp. 139–150.

50. Grey, C. and Knights, D. (1990) 'Investor Protection and the "Cowboy" Stereotype: A Critical View'. *Managerial Finance* **16**(5): 29–30.

51. Mitchell, J. and Weisner, H. (1992) 'Savings and Investments – Consumer Issues'. Occasional Paper to OFT, Office of Fair Trading, London.

52. Knights, D., Morgan, G. and Sturdy, A. J. (1993) 'Quality for the Consumer in Bancassurance?'. *Consumer Policy Review* **3**(4): 232–240.

53. Watkins, T. (1990) 'The Demand for Financial Services'. In *Marketing Financial Services* (C. T. Ennew, T. Watkins and M. Wright, Eds). Oxford: Heinemann.

54. Carter, R. L., Chiplin, B. and Lewis, M. K. (1986) *Personal Financial Markets.* Oxford: Philip Allan.

55. Ennew, C. T. (1992) 'Consumer Attitudes to Independent Financial Advice'. *International Journal of Bank Marketing* **10**(5): 13–18.

56. Evans, P. and Gumby, J. (1992) 'Going for Broke?' *Post Magazine* (28 May) 9–12.

57. DuGay, P. and Salaman, G. (1992) 'The Cult(ure) of the Consumer'. *Journal of Management Studies* **29**(5): 615–633.

58. Jayasinghe, S. and Yorke, D. A. (1991) 'A Technique to Evaluate Secondary Data on Personal Financial Services to Identify Potential Customer Segments'. Occasional Paper, Manchester School of Management, UMIST.

FURTHER READING

Beane, J. P. and Ennis, D. M. (1987) 'Market Segmentation: A Review'. *European Journal of Marketing* **21**(5): 20–42.

Berger, P. and Luckmann, T. (1967) *The Social Construction of Reality.* Harmondsworth: Penguin.

Stanley, T. J. Moschis, G. P. and Danko, W. D. (1987) 'Financial Service Segments – The Seven Faces of the Affluent Market'. *Journal of Advertising Research* **27**(4): 52–67.

23

River Magic: Extraordinary Experience and the Extended Service Encounter

Eric J. Arnould and Linda L. Price

River rafting is a growing component of the Colorado leisure services industry. Thousands of people take rafting trips every year for tens of thousands of client-days. Multiday rafting trips on the Colorado, Green, Yampa, Arkansas, and others are river outfitters' most resource-intensive service offerings. River outfitters discuss the river rafting experience with a sense of reverence and mystery – a singular quality some call 'river magic'. Our findings tell of the experience of multiday commercial river rafting. Our research is unique in (1) focusing on key elements in delivering temporally extended, extraordinary experiences, (2) representing different participant perspectives in the service encounter, (3) detailing the emergent interplay of consumer and service provider behaviors in the delivery of service outcomes, and (4) integrating and cross-validating data collected by multiple methods.

The rafting story begins by describing the pretrip planning process. Answers to how people decide on a river rafting adventure, descriptions of their pretrip expectations and accounts of their planning and pretrip imagery display little deliberation. Although it costs much time and money, people do not appear to think about it carefully. Sometimes a family member or friend arranged the trip, and they 'just went'. More often consumers choose it because it is something they've 'always' wanted to do, but search is minimal and pretrip expectations vague. Often consumers articulate the desire for 'something beyond their imagination' or just letting everything be what it is, denying specific expectations. Many of these reports imply a desire for something different, without articulating what it might be. Some reports carry a theme of 'getting away from it all', where 'it all' ranges from Nintendo to job-related stress. In anticipation of the trip, consumers say they expect that the environment will be clean and natural, guides will be competent and knowledgeable, other people will be friendly and pleasant, and they will 'not get killed'. They expect to have fun.

Our story then moves to the trip experience and posttrip descriptions and reflections. As the trip unfolds, we learn that the setting, guides, and other people on the trip are important in articulating the narrative of the experience. The guide is an impresario who facilitates the enactment of vaguely familiar cultural scripts, helping participants to transform experiences into treasured, culturally construed memories of personal growth, challenges overcome, teamwork, and perseverance (Abrahams, 1986; Bruner, 1986; Featherstone, 1991, pp. 132–133, 143; Kapferer, 1986). The successful narrative of friendship with guides and strangers that are profound and intimate. It includes a deep connection to the land and the river. The narrative is held up as proof of the work of self, family, and humanity, and demonstrates what is really important in life. In short, the story is a romance (Campbell, 1987; Urry, 1990), a triumph over natural forces achieved through trust and mutual reliance.

The experience is extraordinary, offering absorption, personal control, joy and valuing, a spontaneous letting-be of the process, and a newness of perception and process (Csikszentmihalyi, 1990). It is recalled easily for years after, but, because of its considerable emotional content, it is difficult to describe. People sometimes report that it changed them forever. It is magical. As such, satisfaction with river rafting, a hedonic encounter between customer, guide and 'nature', does not seem to be embodied in attributes of the experience such as amount of time spent freezing in wet clothes, uncomfortable toilet facilities, bad food, or any summary index of specific attributes of the trip. Rather, satisfaction is embodied in the success of the narrative, an interactive gestalt orchestrated by the guide over several days' journey into the unknown.

The guide role is a demanding one fraught with illusion and role conflict. In contrast to familiar transports of fancy provided by performing artists and theme parts, river guides offer commercially a magic that comes from an interpersonal dynamic developed over an extended interval of time in a seemingly authentic environment. They give their customers something they do not know how to ask for, but something that makes customers very happy.

The story we tell is emergent. We did not find it in the literature, but we can document theory and research that support the importance and plausibility of our account. Before we tell our story, we briefly review some relevant literature. This review emphasizes several features. Using the literature, we describe characteristics of extraordinary experience, speculate about why it evokes vague script expectations and complex evaluations of satisfaction, discuss salient features of services that deliver extraordinary experience, and elaborate on the role of the service provider in articulating this experience over an extended temporal framework.

LITERATURE REVIEW

Extraordinary experience

Hedonic consumption experience has received some attention in the literature (Havlena and Holbrook, 1986; Hawes, 1978; Hirschman, 1984; Hirschman and Holbrook, 1982; Holbrook et al., 1984; Holbrook and Hirschman, 1982; Unger and Kernan, 1983). Although largely ignored by consumer researchers, other researchers identify a special class of hedonic consumption activities – intense, positive, intrinsically enjoyable experiences. Concepts that map this domain include peak experience (Maslow, 1964), peak performance (Klausner, 1968; Privette, 1983), flow (Csikszentmihalyi, 1985), and extraordinary experience (Abrahams, 1986). Certain qualities unify these experiences, including the merging of action and awareness, attention or clear focus, personal integration, personal control, awareness of power, joy and valuing, and a spontaneous (uninhibited) letting-be of process (Csikszentmihalyi, 1975, 1990; Csikszentmihalyi and LeFevre, 1989; Privette, 1983).

Intensity and the relational mode of the experience differentiate these concepts from one another. The term we use, 'extraordinary experience', entails a 'sense of newness of perception and process' (Privette, 1983, p. 1366; see also Abrahams, 1986). By contrast with flow, extraordinary experience is triggered by unusual events and is characterized by high levels of emotional intensity and experience. By contrast with peak experience and peak performance (Celsi, Rose and Leigh, 1993), extraordinary experience implies neither superior levels of effort nor an independent relational mode. In fact, an important trigger for this experiential state is interpersonal interaction (Abrahams, 1986).

Vague Expectations and Complex Satisfaction

What are the distinguishing characteristics of extraordinary experience? Specifically, how and what type of expectations do consumers form and how do they evaluate the experience? Much of consumer research posits a model of choice and satisfaction based on defined expectations and subsequent performance of a consumer alternative in terms of those expectations (Fiebelkorn, 1985; Oliver and DeSarbo, 1988). This disconfirmation paradigm, however, is based on two important assumptions. First, it assumes consumers have expectations. Second, it assumes satisfaction is a function of deviations between expected product or service performance and actual performance. It is questionable whether consumers evaluate extraordinary experience in terms of well-defined expectations or rate subsequent performance in terms of them.

Expectations

Expectations (including beliefs, evaluative criteria, attitudes, and activity sequences) for extraordinary experiences are likely to be vague. Why? First, consumers of extraordinary experience may desire intense emotional outcomes, for example, joy or absorption, but not know what consumption alternatives produce them. The rarity and intensity of emotions associated with extraordinary experiences may mean information sources such as documentary films, word of mouth, and promotional materials provide limited cues for linking outcomes to consumption alternatives. Moreover, emotions are subjective, fluctuating across individuals and social situations (Denzin, 1983; Holbrook and Hirschman, 1982), which makes them challenging for consumers to predict. Since extraordinary experience emerges from the dynamic interaction of participants, it is difficult to predict one's own behavior and others' responses from behavior in ordinary contexts. The emotional content of these interactions is epiphenomenal (Denzin, 1983).

A second reason scripts are apt to be vague is that extraordinary experience is spontaneous and unrehearsed (Abrahams, 1986). Spontaneity distinguishes extraordinary events from everyday routines and contributes to the perception of the event as extraordinary. Consumers value and protect these qualities. Lying (1990, pp. 861–862) reports that many rock climbers and sky divers 'regard the experience as ineffable . . . some believe that talking about edgework should be avoided because it contaminates one's subjective appreciation of the experience'.

In a search for authenticity, consumers of extraordinary experience surrender their expectations to the 'immediate encounter with being' (Redfoot, 1984, p. 295). Perceived ineffability of extraordinary experiences makes consumers unwilling to anticipate or rehearse them.

Performance

A prevailing view is that satisfaction can be described with a summary index of a product or service's performance on various attributes. In contrast, satisfaction with extraordinary experience is emergent across the temporal frame of the experience (Deighton, 1992; Gergen and Gergen, 1988; Howard, 1991). Popular movies depicting extraordinary experience, such as *City Slickers* and *K2*, illustrate this point. They highlight unpleasant and life-threatening events. But in each case a triumphant moment – saving the cattle herd and attaining the summit – leads to emphatic positive reevaluation of all the negatives that might otherwise dominate evaluation of the experience.

Satisfaction is also interpreted within the broader narrative context of the consumer's life (Botterill, 1987; Deighton, 1992). People are concerned with having experiences that tell about the self – define, develop, and change it (Sarbin, 1986). Consumers use extraordinary experiences to give agency and coherence to their stories about the self. Thus, consumers of intense martial arts training may interpret physical injury or fear as contributing positively to self-growth, efficacy, and authenticity (Donohue, 1991).

In summary, for extraordinary experiences we speculate that expectations are likely to be vague. Moreover, evaluation of the experience evolves within the context of the overall story. Hence, the disconfirmation paradigm commonly evoked in consumer research is not a useful metaphor for interpreting satisfaction with extraordinary experiences.

Delivering extraordinary experience

Commercial delivery of hedonic experiences has received little attention in marketing (for exceptions see Durgee, Holbrook and Sherry (1991), Holbrook (1990), Holbrook and Zirlin (1985), and O'Guinn and Belk (1989)). Commercial delivery of *extraordinary* experiences has received no attention. However, important keys to understanding service delivery come form the services literature. This literature emphasizes the importance of setting, process, and provider–client relationships in determining consumer satisfaction (Bitner, 1990, 1992; Bitner, Booms, and Tetreault, 1990; Czepiel *et al.*, 1985; McCallum and Harrison, 1985;

Mohr and Bitner, 1991). Each of these elements plays an important role in delivering extraordinary experience. However, the service quality literature has primarily focused on evaluation of technical and functional elements (Parasuraman, Zeithaml, and Berry, 1985, 1988). Similarly, most evaluations of white water rafting have focused primarily on client-days, perceived crowding, safe runs, and quality of the water (Heywood, 1987; Hollenhorst and Olson, 1990; Roggenbuck *et al.*, 1991; Shelbey, Bregenzer and Johnson, 1988).

Research from a variety of disciplines and contexts, including research on the delivery of hedonic outcomes, suggests services providing extraordinary experience must emphasize process elements that have received less attention in marketing literature. Among these are affect, narrative, and ritual understandings.

Affect

Service establishments must monitor and control the emotions employees convey (Hochschild, 1983; Peters and Austin, 1985; Rafaeli and Sutton, 1987). For example, Disney World coaches prospective employees on how to look like they are having fun (Martin 1986; Romm, 1989); McDonald's stresses the importance of displaying enthusiasm and a sense of humor (Boas and Chain, 1987); waitresses at Route Diner strive to boost their tips by being 'especially friendly' (Paules, 1991, p. 27). Classical ballet dancers' expression of emotion becomes the focal point for the hedonic experience (King and Straub, 1984; cited in Holbrook (1987), p. 166). We speculate that engineering affect is central to successful delivery of extraordinary experiences.

The engineering of hedonic outcomes should take place behind the scenes, below the line of visibility (Shostack, 1987). 'Disney World is carefully designed to promote a frontstage view and to suppress backstage information from public awareness' (Johnson, 1981, p. 159). For the desired affective response, provider emotions must be perceived as authentic (Hochschild, 1983; Rafaeli and Sutton, 1987; Romm, 1989) – spontaneous responses to environment, activities, and social interaction (Abrahams, 1986), rather than directed process. In this sense, commercial delivery of extraordinary experience creates a dilemma – to be effective, it must transcend the purposive, task-oriented, and commercial nature of the ordinary service interaction.

Narrative

Service encounters facilitate enactment of familiar, if implicit narrative understandings (Abrahams, 1986; Holbrook, 1987; Shott, 1979; Spradley and Mann, 1975; Sutton and Rafaeli, 1988; van Maanen and Kunda, 1989). Service delivery at McDonald's enacts a number of core American values (Kottak, 1982); service encounters at convenience stores endorse the American norm of efficiency (Sutton and Rafaeli, 1988). Cocktail waitresses learn a generative framework for conventionalized, sexual joking that contributes to their success in extended, commercial interactions (Spradley and Mann, 1975). Much of the hedonic satisfactions of vacation theme parks derives from performers' successful condensations and expressions of the total park experience consistent with consumers' unarticulated and vague cultural narratives (Durgee *et al.*, 1991). Disney World packages history, fantasy, and the future into conventional plots, conveying idealized American cultural values (Johnson, 1981; King, 1981). In many of these contexts, customers and providers have well-developed narrative expectations because of extensive experience in such settings. By contrast, novel service encounters providing extraordinary experience will likely 'require participants to engage in considerable trial and error before they reach tacit agreement or develop norms about which scripts should guide [their] actions' (Sutton and Rafaeli, 1988, p. 474; Bettenhausen and Murnighan, 1985). As a dramaturgical perspective suggests, meaning emerges during the process of interaction; communication of evolving expectations of outcomes plays a key role in satisfactory experience (Grove and Fisk, 1992).

Ritual

The relationship between extraordinary experience and ritual is likely to be complex. Although individuals articulate extraordinary experience as unique and ineffable, at an etic level these experiences exemplify culturally embedded rituals that are played out across generations (Abrahams, 1986). Because all experiences address the 'ongoingness of life as it is registered through the filter of culture' (Abrahams, 1986, p. 55), ritual aspects become salient even in enacting what the individual participants define as authentic, unique, and extraordinary. Two general classes of ritual (rites of passage and rites of integration) characterize delivery of extraordinary experience.

The metaphor of the *pilgrimage* based on van Gennep's (1960) formulation of rites of passage provides a useful basis for understanding satisfaction. In particular, it helps us understand the sequencing of events in the delivery of extraordinary experience and how overall satisfaction is linked to underlying cultural scripts.

The pilgrimage incorporates the three essential features – separation, transition, and reintegration – but, unlike many rites of passage, a pilgrimage is typically voluntary. Pilgrims leave their homes and disengage from their ordinary lives. They enter the sacred precincts; their stay is a phase of transition. One of the most common activities in the transitional phase of a rite of passage is stripping of markers of rank and status. Stripped initiates experience a fellowship with other corituralists who, like themselves, perceive themselves in their basic, common humanity. The transitional phase is punctuated by shared performances by pilgrims who experience a sense of what Turner (1969, 1974) calls 'communitas'. They return home transformed and are reintegrated into their community.

A pilgrimage may also be viewed as a *rite of intensification* (Coon, 1958). A rite of intensification increases the emotional intensity of links among persons widely scattered and dissimilar in ordinary life but who share a common mythohistorical orientation. The pilgrim returns, not transformed as in the basic formulation of rites of passage, but affirmed, renewed, or even cured of his/her ailments (Moore, 1980).

Viewing the commercial delivery of extraordinary experience as a *rite of integration* is another potentially useful tool for understanding. Rites of integration are defined as 'planned social interactions that consolidate various forms of cultural artifacts (language, displayed emotions, gestures, symbols, and the physical setting) with the objective of achieving "a temporary sense of closeness" between "potentially divergent" subsystems' (Siehl, Bowen, and Pearson, 1993; see also Mills and Morris, 1986; Trice and Beyer, 1991). Certain service encounters have a feeling of a relationship rather than merely a transaction. These transactions can be described as 'boundary open', resembling a meeting between friends. In boundary open transactions service providers are expected to be actively involved and share their feelings. Siehl *et al.* (1993) hypothesize that less tangible services are more likely to be boundary open. In them, process dimensions that communicate responsiveness, empathy, and assurance become increasingly important influences on customers' satisfaction. Extraordinary experience is likely to involve boundary open transactions.

Provider–customer relationships in delivering extraordinary experience

Previous research has revealed that service employees hold special relationships with customers (Mars and Nicod, 1984; Spradley and Mann, 1975), customers are active participants in service outcomes (Mills and Morris, 1986; Rafaeli, 1989; Sutton and Rafaeli, 1988), and provider–customer independence is high (McCallum and Harrison, 1985). However, research on service encounters has concentrated on comparatively brief transactions (Bitner, 1990; Bitner *et al.*, 1990; Fiebelkorn, 1985; Surprenant and Solomon, 1987; Zeithaml, Berry and Parasuraman, 1987). Virtually no literature examines temporally extended service provider roles. One distinguishing feature of extended encounters is long transactions that provide more time for the customer to react to the emotional behavior of an employee (Sutton and Rafaeli, 1988, p. 483). Further, Americans' underlying scripts for 'slow times' have more 'scenes' (Nisbett and Ross, 1980, p. 34) that emphasize interpersonal exchanges and the display of emotions (Sutton and Rafaeli, 1988, p. 477). Because of Americans' script expectations about lengthy transactions, there will be pressures for extended encounters to become affectively charged, boundary open relationships. Due to the defining qualities of extraordinary experiences discussed above, we might reasonably expect that customer–provider interdependence, and active customer participation in the successful delivery of extraordinary experiences, will be even more pronounced than in other kinds of extended service encounters.

In summary, service encounter research increasingly recognizes that service experience is inherently interpretive, subjective, and affective (Czepiel *et al.*, 1985; Klaus, 1985; McCallum and Harrison, 1985; Parasuraman *et al.*, 1988). Enriched views of the service encounter relate service satisfaction to script expectations, dramaturgy, and ritual enactments. Although the marketing literature is silent on the delivery of extraordinary experience, literature from related research streams offers possible insights into individual and cultural narratives that underlie extraordinary experience. This research suggests service establishments may orchestrate effective, narrative, and ritual content through the skills, engagement, emotions, and dramatic sense of service providers.

DESCRIPTION OF RESEARCH ACTIVITY

A combination of factors motivated the research. First, one of us has had a memorable experience with rafting that left an impression that satisfaction with the experience is complex: How could so many awful things add up to a positive experience? Much later, serendipitous conservations with an outfitter led to an invitation to study river rafting. Our early conversations led us to believe that river rafting is a different kind of service encounter than has been previously studied, and is one that lends itself to multimethod data collection.

In order to find our story, and then tell it, we engaged in extensive data collection over a two-year period using a variety of techniques. Table 1 outlines the sequence of data collection activities, the rationale guiding these efforts, and summary features of the data. The table illustrates iteration between data collection techniques. Techniques were combined, often within the same temporal frame and physical setting, such as the participant observation, focus group, and surveys conducted in May 1990. At each stage we revised and elaborated fundamental constructs and validated findings in a variety of ways. Further, we could move beyond the limitations of each technique by probing systematically, through the incorporation of different methods, for both convergent and divergent data.

Table 1 also illustrates the focus of data collection. Overall, data collection aimed to gather multiple participant perspectives as well as multiple temporal perspectives. Data were gathered from outfitters, guides, and participants. Data were also gathered before, during, immediately after, and well after the experience. The table shows how we tried to apprehend expectations, critical consumption incidents, and postconsumption evaluation through a variety of procedures. In the first research season we gathered data from multiple customers of a single outfitter. In the second research season we gathered data from guides and customers of several different outfitters.

Finally, Table 1 summarizes features of interest for the data analyzed here. In general, we conducted exploratory research with small samples allowing us to advance and amend evolving interpretations. We deployed larger samples and more formal instruments to survey variation in phenomena of demonstrated significance to participants. The table also shows that we expanded the scope and formality of our data gathering over the two seasons as we refined our measures and constructs.

FINDINGS

Table 2 provides an overview of the primary analyses and categories of findings at each step in the research process. Table 2 illustrates that certain experiential qualities and themes showed up consistently throughout the data collection process. Other findings were pronounced in some of the data, but barely apparent in other data. Experiential themes that developed over the course of the first season, and were cross-validated between methods, were further refined and validated in the second season.

Although different methods, data, and analyses were used, a coherent story

Table 1.   Research sequence and focus

Date	Method	Focus	Summary sample/data features
1/90	Written protocols	Experiential view of river rafting	Convenience sample, $n = 35$
2/90	On-site depth interviews	View of commercial provision of river experience; input for preseason guide survey	Outfitters, $n = 2$; field notes and photo accounts; collection of promotional and training materials
4/90	Drop-off/ mail-back survey	Description of guide expectations and characteristics; input for script for guide focus group	Census of guide trainees for one outfitter, $n = 8$
5/90	Participant observation	Commercial river experience; revision of script for guide focus group; input for customer pre- and post-river-trip surveys	Field notes and photo accounts; two researchers, separate rafts; trip with guide trainees
5/90	Focus group	Guide approach to service delivery, training, management, setting; input for customer pre- and post-river-trip surveys	River guides, $n = 8$; two-hour focus group; notes transcribed; two facilitators
5/90	Pretrip and posttrip surveys	Consumer expectations and reasons; experiential themes; salient attributes; pretest consumer surveys	Teens and counselors, $n = 17$; pretrip survey administered at put-in; posttrip survey collected Monday following three-day weekend trip; triangulation with participant observation for trip
5/90	Participant observation	Guide/customer and group dynamics; consumer experience of multiday river rafting; revision of customer surveys	Field notes and photo record; two researchers separate rafts; trip with teens and counselors
6/90– 8/90	Pretrip customer surveys	Reported pretrip decision factors and expectations; reported pretrip planning; recreational interests and participation, demographics	$n = 19$, telephone precontact of group leaders, mailed to arrive within a week to 10 days of departure; of the 36 groups, responses were received from 13, or 36%; responses were received from more than one participant in six of the groups
6/90– 8/90	Posttrip customer surveys	Reported best and worst experiences; element of satisfaction; perceptions of river guide; develop measures of experiential themes; examine relationships	$n = 43$, mailed to be waiting after trip, with follow-up mailing after two weeks; of 54 groups, mailings to three were undeliverable; responses were received from 26 groups, or 51%

Table 1 continued on next page

Table 1.   Research sequence and focus *continued*

Date	Method	Focus	Summary sample/data features
7/90	Participant observation	Contrast one-day with multiday rafting experience; peak season river trip	Field notes and photorecord, one researcher, one day
9/90	Focus group	Multiple consumer perspec–tives; how experience remembered; texture of themes; differentiate from other experiences	Past season river consumers, $n = 4$; 90 minutes, videotaped and then transcribed; member check of draft of account with one member of focus group
11/90– 1/91	Member check	Incorporate perspective of outfitter on findings	Two 90-minute interviews with outfitter; two researchers
1/91	Mail survey	Postseason guide perspective on what customers value, what makes a trip work; difficult encounters, river crew experience	Census of guides of one outfitter; of 19 surveys mailed, five returned as undeliverable, seven responses for response rate of 50%
4/91	On-site depth interviews	Perspective of different outfitters in remote river area; setting; input on customer surveys	Four interviews, about 60 minutes each; field notes and photo record; two researchers
5/91	Drop-off, pick-up surveys	Preseason guide skills and expectations; training; input on customer surveys	Census of guides of three outfitters hired as of 5/91, $n = 34$
6/91– 7/91	Participant observation	Perspective on experience – new rivers, 'typical' trips, different outfitter, use of 'duckies', elaborate understanding of narrative and ritual themes	Three-day trip and four-day trip; taped field notes and photo record; one researcher on each trip – other served as member check; interview with river guide one week later served as member check
6/91– 8/91	Pretrip drop-off and collect surveys	Expectations and decision factors; trip planning; background and interests; demographics	Stratified random sample, multiday river trip clients of three outfitters in Dinosaur National Monument, $n = 211$ (97 matched with posttrip); fewer than five unusable, distributed on hour shuttle ride en route to put-in, sealed, collected, mailed back
6/91– 8/91	Posttrip drop-off collect postcard, mail-back survey	Validate refined measures of experiential themes; elaborate guide role, setting; facets of experience; transcendence of commercial	Stratified random sample of multiday river trip clients of three outfitters in Dinosaur National Monument, $n = 137$ (97 matched with pretrip); postcard served as validity check and allowed follow-up mailing to nonrespondents; response rate on mail-back survey of 55%

Table 2.   Data analysis and categories of findings

Date	Method	Primary analyses	Categories of findings
1/90	Written protocols	Text analyses, key word search, summary statistics	Extraordinary experience; components of satisfaction
2/90	On-site depth interviews	Text analysis of transcribed field notes; sequential photo analysis	Consumer complaints; outfitter motives, feelings; descriptions of guides and clients; descriptions of equipment, settings; stories of transformation and 'river magic'
4/90	Drop-off/ mail-back survey	Simple frequencies; text analysis of open-ended responses	Variance in background and experience; guide motives, feelings; guide expectations of service delivery factors; selection of occupation and outfitter
5/90	Participant observation	Text analysis of transcribed field notes; sequential photo analysis	Guide/customer dynamics; guide skills; setting; experiential qualities of extraordinary experience; components of satisfaction
5/90	Focus group	Text analysis; key word search	Guides' role conflicts; transcendence of the commercial; themes
5/90	Pre-river-trip and post-river-trip surveys	Simple frequencies; text analysis of open-ended responses	Expectations; components of satisfaction; elements of extraordinary experience; experiential themes
5/90	Participant observation	Text analysis of transcribed field notes; key word search; notes of two researchers compared for convergence and divergence	Themes and rituals; guide characteristics; narrative components of satisfaction and experience
6/90–8/90	Pretrip customer surveys	Frequencies, cross-tabulations, t-tests, ANOVA, and correlations; reliability analyses; text analysis, key word searches, and counts on open-ended word responses	Pretrip expectations; word-of-mouth influence; prepurchase search
6/90–8/90	Posttrip customer surveys	Frequencies, cross-tabulations, t-tests, ANOVA, and correlations; select factor analyses; correlations; text analysis, key word searches, and statistics on open-ended responses	Measures of experiential themes: validity of themes; emotion work of guides; components of satisfaction
7/90	Participant observation	Text analysis and sequential photo analysis	One-day trip themes; group dynamics; guide role

Table 2 continued on next page

Table 2.   Data analysis and categories of findings *continued*

Date	Method	Primary analyses	Categories of findings
9/90	Focus group	Text analysis and key word search and statistics on transcribed video	Expectations; experiential themes; guide/customer dynamics and transcendence of the commercial; pilgrimage script, reentry
11/90–1/91	Member check	Text analysis of notes; solicitation and incorporation of feedback into report	Guide weaknesses and variability among guides; guide role conflicts
1/91	Mail survey	Frequencies; text analyses of open-ended responses	Guide role conflict; postseason understandings of themes
4/91	On-site depth interviews	Text analysis and sequential photo analysis	Outfitters' positioning strategies and approach; history and stories of commercial provision of river rafting in Dinosaur National Monument, knowledge of setting; day-to-day operations
5/91	Drop-off, pick-up surveys	Frequencies, cross-tabulations, *t*-tests, ANOVA, and correlations; select factor analyses; correlations; text analysis, key word searches, and statistics on open-ended responses	Preseason perceptions of guide roles, client service topics in training; guide motives
6/91–7/91	Participant observation	Text analysis, key word search and statistics; sequential photo analysis	Narrative components of experience; group dynamics; guide use of ritual
6/91–8/91	Pretrip drop-off and collect surveys	Frequencies, cross-tabulations, *t*-tests, ANOVA, and correlations; select factor analyses; correlations; text analysis, key word searches, and statistics on open-ended responses	Prepurchase search; planning and character of pretrip imagery for first-time river rafters; pretrip expectations
6/91–8/91	Posttrip drop-off, collect postcard, mail-back survey	Frequencies, cross-tabulations, *t*-tests, ANOVA, and correlations; select factor analyses; correlations; text analysis, key word searches, and statistics on open-ended responses	Measures of experiential themes and relationship to satisfaction; guide success factors; relationship between pretrip expectations and satisfaction

emerged about the experience of river rafting. Rather than organize around the sequence or type of data, findings are organized around the story to be told. Descriptions of findings are cross-referenced to Table 2 by the data provided in parentheses after each reported finding. In general, findings from the second season validate and extend the findings from the first season. Care has been taken to protect participant anonymity by disguising names in the reporting of results. A brief introduction to the setting for a multiday river rafting trip is provided in Table 3. Unfamiliar river rafting terminology is included in a glossary, Table 4. Next, we explore the pretrip planning process, experiential themes emergent over the course of the trip, and, finally, posttrip recollections of the experience.

PRETRIP PLANNING PROCESS

Prospective customers expressed minimal, varied and veiled feelings and expectations about the experience, the guides, other people, safety, comfort, emotions, and the setting (5/90, 6/90–8/90). We find hints in pretrip comments of themes that would emerge more strongly during the trip and in informants'

Table 3.   River rafting: the setting

Outfitters:
Most rafting firms are family-run businesses located in rural towns. Their capital investment consists primarily of warehouse/dormitory buildings and rafting equipment amounting to about $200 000. Outfitters' largest recurrent cost is for liability insurance covering the 2–25 guides employed. The business is highly seasonal; there is a maximum five-month window for commercial trips bracketed by cold weather and flood water in the spring, then low water in the late summer. Business is further constrained by federal regulations on river access.

Clients and trips:
A trip brings together clients and guides, typically numbering from six to 25 persons on a 3–12-day excursion down one of Colorado's white water rivers. Groups meet in the chilly morning hours either at the outfitters' headquarters or at the put-in. At the put-in the rafts are set up and gear is stowed. Guides explain the fundamentals of equipment, gear, safety, and paddling as clients listen in nervous anticipation.

A typical day:
A typical day begins as the sun lights up the red wall of a majestic canyon summit high above the riverside campsite. At dawn, guides prepare breakfast, clients crawl from their tents and visit the 'groover' (a primitive toilet make from an ammunition box). With numb fingers, guides and clients pack, stow, and tie down gear in the raft. The cold, muddy water sings by. Guides invite clients to pilot a 'duckie' (one-person, inflatable rubber kayak). For several hours people paddle through an ever-changing landscape of breathtaking geological contrasts. They chart courses and negotiate their way down roaring giddy rapids. The trip is exhilarating and restful by turns. Occasionally, guides find eddies where they tie up to climb up the canyons to wonder at native American pictographs, archaeological sites, or early settlers' camps. About noon, there is a lunch break. Guides prepare a light meal; people chat and explore the tumbled boulders and cottonwood thickets around the lunch site.

   The afternoons are much like the mornings. Usually the trip ties up at a prearranged camping spot around 4.00 pm. Clients and guides form a human chain to unload the boats; clients pitch tents, change out of wet clothes, and explore the area. Guides and clients prepare a hot dinner. After dinner guides may orchestrate games and stories; some clients may read the natural history literature that guides typically pack along. After relaxing around a fragrant campfire, enjoying the slice of star-spattered sky overhead, people normally retire by 9.00 pm, but guides often stay up later taking care of camp details and unwinding.

Table 4.   Glossary of river terms

Boatman	The guide's preferred term for themselves; it lacks commercial connotations
Day bag	A small Dungee bag used for carrying supplies needed during the day when the other bags are stowed and tied down
Dry bag	*See* Dungee bag
Duckie	An open, rubber, inflatable kayak
Dungee bag	A rubberized, waterproof duffle bag, closed by rolling one end over and over and clipping the ends together
Fan hole	Drop-off of water running over a flat rock; watched for in order to avoid wrapping the raft around the unseen rock or boulder
Maytagged	Getting caught in a recirculating hole
Wrapped	Getting a raft hung up on a boulder in such a way that both ends of the boat are caught in the current and the middle is caught over the rock or boulder
Groover	Metal ammunition can, lined with plastic and used as a toilet; the name comes from effect of the can's edges on one's derriere
Oarboat	A raft that is rowed by a guide
Oarers	Rafters who merely sit on the boat while a guide rows
Paddle boat	A boat that is rowed by the customers under guide supervision
Paddler	A rafter who takes charge of rowing the boat under a guide's supervision
Put-in	A spot along the river bank where the rafts are set up, gear stowed, and from where the trip is launched
Recirculating hole	Imagine a whirlpool turned on its side; caused by the force of water dropping down forcefully over a rock ledge; dangerous for a swimmer to be caught in
River kill	Left-over food
Strainer	A pile-up of logs, sticks and other debris, usually by a river bank; extremely dangerous for duckies or individuals since the force of the water makes it difficult to extricate oneself from one
Take-out	A spot along the river bank where the rafts are broken down, gear unloaded, and the trip ends
Trip	A load of clients and one or more guides who travel together for as little as a few hours to as much as a few days

retrospective reports. Included are hints of the themes of pilgrimage, intensification and rediscovery of self, and communion with nature and others.

Expectations of the experience

Ambiguous and protected expectations of the experience are well illustrated in excerpts from field notes recorded during a trip with a group of alternate high schoolers and their counselors (5/90): 'One kid mentions that he's just started expecting the worst so he won't be disappointed. I ask what's the worst thing he's imagined happening. He says, not coming back. Then he tells me he wouldn't mind falling out, that would be a rush.'

One possible explanation for the vagueness of expressed expectations is that consumers may be motivated to imagine what their trip will be like, but ill equipped with expertise to construct such images. Another possible explanation is consumers' desire to preserve the spontaneous and unrehearsed characteristics of extraordinary experience (Abrahams, 1986). Written protocols reflecting back on the experience of river rafting suggest that limited expectations contribute to satisfaction with the experience (1/90): 'So much of the experience is the thrill of the unknown. Beyond all it is at least exhilarating. . . . Similar to a symphony when you must read several bars ahead of what you are already playing.'

Expectations of the guides

Customers rarely anticipated the affective role of the guides in orchestrating their experiences. Instead, customers hoped guides would be 'friendly', 'competent', 'safe', and 'knowledgeable'. A single, more experienced customer did express the hope that the guide would 'be genuinely interested in rafters, their interests and facilitate having fun'.

Expectations of others

Most inexperienced rafters have little sense of the importance of other rafters in constructing a satisfactory, shared river experience. Instead, customers hoped other rafters would be 'friendly', 'sharing', 'considerate', and 'sociable'. The same, more experienced rafter quoted above expressed a more sophisticated understanding of the camaraderie and sense of teamwork that, in fact, contribute to satisfaction in stating, 'Relaxed, honest, having fun and concerned about each other: releasing inhibitions is essential – being oneself; be paddlers not oarers'.

Comfort and safety

Inexperienced customers articulate simple, general desires for safety: 'knowing our daughter is safe'; 'that I don't drown'. Most fail to anticipate many factors that could affect their safety. Their concerns carry an undercurrent of fear of rafting – that this is something they might die doing. Such fears contribute to perception of the experience as extraordinary and set the stage for a rite of intensification that extends and renews the self.

Expectations about the environment

Consumers' expressed expectations about the natural environment are vague, but they are also romantic and consensual. In the first season's data the theme of a wild, clean, natural, isolated, and 'noncommercial' setting appeared explicitly in all but two of the pretrip expectations about the river and surroundings (6/90–8/90), for example: 'clean, with no signs of civilization, other than ourselves, to be intruding on the pristine environment'; 'clean, undisturbed by commercial ventures'. When expectations are specific, they are frequently wrong, as in these excerpts from a pretrip survey (6/91–8/91): 'clear blue river with large rapids'; 'grassy with a lot of trees and spacious. I want a good view with mountains'. In fact, Colorado River basin rivers are typically greenish brown and muddy, the canyons narrow, flora parched and spiny, and views obstructed by canyon walls.

A number of commercial cues reinforce consumer expectations of immersion in a pristine, uncivilized environment (2/90, 5/90, 4/91). Included are the logo used by one of our outfitters incorporating a Native American war shield, eagle feathers, and a motif of crossed arrows. Native Americans are popularly imagined as living in harmony with nature. Perhaps more significant, advertising brochures feature photographs of clients in scenic, wild settings. Supply lists provided by outfitters emphasize the absence of amenities, and the necessity of impact-free camping. These lists also stress that ready access to medical care and telecommunications is impossible. These and other cues build expectations of an almost sacred pilgrimage into a world 'untouched by civilization' (Belk, Wallendorf and Sherry, 1989).

Expectations about feelings

The feelings consumers reported expecting often derived from their beliefs about nature, for example, 'sense of isolation, serenity' and 'to be in the great outdoors and to go back to nature'. Consistent with our sense that consumers do not know what feelings to expect, comments such as 'river experiences' and just 'have fun' were common.

For the second season, data sampled a broader range of trips and outfitters. Expectations were collected closer to the actual trip, en route to the put-in (6/91–8/91). Still, expectations about guides, other rafters, and feelings were vague. Again, pretrip expectations about the natural environment were consensual and romantic. Of course, the richer experiential base of the enlarged sample yielded more variety, but the standard template remained the same. For example, in response to the question of expected feelings, one respondent wrote 'gratitude and surrender. "I wish to hear the silence of the night. . . . " Thoreau'. As suggested by first season findings, many of the feelings that people expected to experience related to the environment, but, without question, the most common response was 'to have fun' or a close variant. The theme of fear was much more pronounced in the second season's data, as illustrated in the following responses to what clients wanted in comfort and safety: 'that I come home alive' and 'that no one is negligent. Everyone is aware of existing dangers'.

We have observed that themes of personal growth and intensification of self emerge over the course of trips. We sought in the second season to explore whether people had pretrip expectations about personal growth and renewal. To minimize coaching we used a simple prompt 'I want to learn . . . '. Most responses could be described as skill acquisition expectations, for example 'how to read rapids and navigate them' or 'a little about rafting and camping'. A minority provided more existential responses: 'I can accomplish anything', 'more about myself, (strengths and weaknesses), and more about nature', 'what is really important in life (or start to learn)'. Even though the themes of personal growth and intensification are only vaguely articulated in pretrip commentary, among a minority of consumers there is some testimony for these themes at this early stage in the experience.

A more thorough investigation into pretrip planning in the second season revealed that people often choose a river trip in hopes of finding something different. Two verbatims illustrate this point: 'as a family vacation of more than just going somewhere, but doing something different' and 'new experience away from what I know'. In addition to the theme of doing something different, a related description revolved around doing 'something I've always wanted to'. In these descriptions the expectation of a life adventure is captured: 'I have just always felt that white water rafting would be exciting and fulfilling'. The combination of expressed expectations emphasizing newness and adventure evokes the theme of pilgrimage, leaving the familiar and known behind. These comments may also suggest why the narrative qualities of the experience, its storylike qualities, dominate in consumer reports of satisfaction. The only other frequently stated reason for trip selection focused on going at someone else's invitation or recommendation. Again the comments are unreflective, for example, 'My dad said let's go rafting. I said O.K. So here we are'; 'Well, my father gave me the pamphlet and he said, "Pick one", so I did'. In spite of these offhand comments, in both cases informants' posttrip comments reflect the discovery and renewal of self: 'I can do lots of things I never dreamed I could do. I gained a lot of self-confidence'; '[I learned] how to put confidence into myself'. Satisfactory meanings evolve over the course of the trip from these vague narrative expectations.

The experience of river rafting

Three main organizing themes associated with satisfying raft trips emerged early in our research. As we accumulated repeated traces of the themes across different methods we were able to name and interpret the fabric of these themes. The themes – communion with nature, communitas or connecting to others, and extension and renewal of self – link rafting to extraordinary experience. Participant observation field notes trace the evolution of these themes over the course of individual multiday rafting trips. In part, these experiences are guided by service providers; in part, they seem to be produced from unarticulated narrative expectations that clients already 'know' in some unspecified way.

Communion with nature

Weaving through all our data is an emergent feeling of rejuvenation associated with a sense of communion with nature. Two episodes from transcribed notes from one river trip suggest the guides' reverent feelings toward nature. At a particularly stupendous point in one canyon, a guide threw his arms wide and said to everyone within shouting distance, and no one in particular, 'You have to believe in something in a place like this'. The second episode occurred on the last night of a trip. An especially early start was planned for the next morning and the day would be very long. Most clients retired early, but the guides stayed up 'to watch the [full] moon come up over the canyon wall'. They sat on the beach with a few die-hard clients and waited until well after midnight for the full moon to rise.

Numerous examples from transcribed field notes illustrate an active role played by the guides in providing cues to facilitate consumers' communion with nature. For example, one of us wrote 'I remember at some point in the day someone had asked Mel [a guide] about the times in which we would do things. She said we'd get up when the sun got up and go to bed when the sun went down. We'd basically be on "river time". She had joked with me about getting rid of my watch. She says only the guides are allowed to have watches on the trip' (6/91).

Other rituals passed down through generations of river guides convey beliefs about the enduring power of nature and humans' vulnerability to immeasurable natural forces. At one point in the Yampa River, above a series of wild rapids, is a place called 'kissing rock'. Guides instruct clients in the tradition of kissing the rock in order to ensure safe passage of the 'dangerous' rapid below. Our photographs show paddlers of all ages kissing the rock. Thus, what is important is not so much what guides know, but the feeling and values they embody and communicate to customers.

Responding to these cues and the stunning natural setting, another excerpt from transcribed field notes (7/91) illustrates the sense of communion with nature rafting customers can create for themselves.

> And at the top of this hike there was a beautiful fresh spring waterfall. And it was fabulous. And it felt so good for everybody because everybody's been in dirty water since yesterday when we embarked on this trip . . . one of the college girls organized a group shot. . . . And in that group shot there was a clear intermingling of groups that included hugging and having arms around people who I think under other conditions would be considered strangers. . . . And it was a really wonderful shared moment. And we were all huddling in there and at the same time sharing space with each other so that no one was hogging the water.

Water provides a catalyst for a profound experience of nature for some; the impressive geology of the canyons provides this catalyst for others, as shown in this excerpt from participant observation field notes (6/91):

> After lunch, after cleanup, Mel organized a little hike up the cliff behind us to a site where there were model fossils of rock. I sort of got started early, as I wanted to. The others came along in a bit – single file. Mel talked a little about the geology. We showed off the fossils, talked a little about the fossil corals, rim rock and further up, krinoid stems. As she talked about those, people looked on appreciatively.

The trip orchestrates many opportunities for the participants to commune with nature. Some participants are affected by the water, others by geology, still others are moved by the wildlife, old settler's camps, starlit beaches, or the remains of Native American dwellings. The trip allows participants to share their experiences of nature; it operates for some as a sacred passage.

Communitas

A second theme prevalent in all our data is an evolving feeling of communion with friends, family, and strangers. This sense of communion, or communitas in Turner's (1974) dramaturgical framework, is illustrated below. Feelings of linkage, or belonging, of group devotion to a transcendent goal are facilitated by proximity forced by the narrow canyons, small camping areas, boats, and teamwork associated with rafting itself. The emergence of communitas varies in degree with the characteristics of the group coming into the trip. Nonetheless, it emerges in subtle ways over time. Guides impose rules and order on the trip from the beginning that prefigure the development of community. Excerpts from participant observation field notes of the teen trip (5/90) evoke this:

> A girl comes to ask the head chaperone, Rick [head of the group] whether she should take off her ring. It's loose, she explains. I notice she has hickies on her neck. Rick says yeah take it off. What about her friends with loose rings. I say take 'em off 'cause of blisters. Blisters? From rowing, I explain. She gets a glimmer of understanding on her face and goes off to tell her friends.

> People are invited to leave some gear behind in the cars and to pack other stuff out of the way for the day by Peter, by Tom [guides], and also by the head chaperone, so he gets the message. Peter announces there is rain gear for all of the boats. So is there a kind of homogenization, throwing off old roles implicit here? Kids load bags with cigarettes and other junk.

In a rite of passage, the creation of communitas typically begins with a casting off of goods that differentiate members in favor of shared goods (Turner, 1969; van Gennep, 1960). Thus, here the kids are urged to leave stuff behind and are informed that there is a uniform, that is, the life jacket and the rain gear, for all. Of course, there is resistance, too, and kids pack their bags with good emblematic of every day personae, for example, cigarettes, bandanas, and so on.

Guides invite the production of community, but people already seem to be prepared to perform in a communitarian way. Remarkably, some of the kids on the teen trip seemed to be acting in terms of a script favorable to the creation of community at the put-in. Thus, several girls offer to leave behind the 'friendship' rings emblematic of boyfriends who are not part of the group but remain in the everyday world at home.

Guides reinforce teamwork themes in a variety of ways. Field notes and photographs from each of the trips shows teamwork in loading and unloading supplies (e.g. passing 'dry bags' up and down the bank through a chain of clients), tying gear into the boats, cooking and doing dishes, and participating in campfire activities. Guides sometimes attempt to facilitate the development of community by leading people through various team-building games over the course of the trip. One set of transcribed participant observation field notes (6/91) said,

> The next game we played was a trust game where we stood in a tight circle and the person went in the middle, and went stiff and closed their eyes and we then sort of rocked them around the circle. Each person in turn did this. Bev hesitated at first, saying that she wasn't going to do this one, but finally she did . . . So this was an evening in which hair was much more let down . . . this was sort of a turning point I think in terms of the creation of community on the trip.

The lingering impact of these games is illustrated from the second morning of another set of transcribed participant observation field notes (7/91): 'I have to admit that that silly name game that we played last night probably has a lot to do with having loosened everybody up . . . there were several references all day long to names from the game and motions from the game . . . And that's weird because it's as if people were just looking for a way to do that'.

Norms of cooperation are further reinforced by helping behaviors among guides and between different outfitters on the many occasions when novice paddlers lose their paddles, boats become grounded, or rafts flip. In these and other instances guides provide cues to channel cooperative activity. Some clients seek out ways to help; other need guidance. Few refuse to become involved. Thus, guides invite and clients voluntarily transcend their passive role as service recipients (spectators) to take an active role in the production of community.

As the trips progress the opportunities for group experience accumulate. One excerpt from field notes provides an example of a playful context in which both the theme of communion with nature and that of communitas are evident:

> To create this waterfall faucet means that people have to block off the water with their bodies at several juncture points on this little stream so that the water accumulates. And then somebody stands under the place where the trickle of water is going down. And it creates a gushing waterfall that comes over on top of them. And I guess what was interesting about this was two things. First, it's real dependent on lots of bodies participating on the whole thing to make it happen. And it also meant getting real close together. 'Cause you have to put your bodies real close together in the little part of the stream where you're trying to block off the water. And that was – it was really fun.

After negotiating each stretch of white water, crews congratulate themselves and are typically congratulated by the guides. In one case, in the aftermath of an accident in which a boat turned over and everyone helped to right it, discussion often returned to whether equipment had dried out as in this excerpt from participant observation notes: 'It was a quiet morning in camp. People revived the discussion of things being wet. People were heard to exclaim, "Hey that pretty well dried out!" and "How are your sleeping bags, are they pretty well dried out?" and things of that nature'.

Participant observation research provided numerous illustrations of the evolution of community over the course of a three-day trip. Our photographs record some dramatic examples. One features a picture of four of the six high school girls braiding each other's hair into identical French braids. These girls were not friends when the trip began. What drove their emergent sense of identify was shared recognition of a common problem: their fear of the river, including shampooing their hair in it. This photograph was taken on the final day of the trip.

Participants' embodiments of communitas become particularly evident and striking as leave-taking approaches. Field notes from the final day of one four-day river trip reveal this evolution:

> Allen [a customer], at one point, said that we should all get together and do this again next year. That we should come as a group. And I think that's not something I had heard before. But it's real clear that he'd come to think of us as a group of people that belonged together as a good team. And that's funny because Becky and Rex, and really all of us were all so different from each other. And come from much different backgrounds and orientations and everything else. I mean Allen and Jane are the perfect yuppie couple. And Becky and Rex both chew tobacco. So it's quite a contrast.

Field notes from the end of this trip disclose the depth of emotional attachments formed among the members of the trip. There were lots of staged photographs of subsets of people who had not known one another at the beginning of the trip that symbolized the sense of community that had developed:

> So, one of the last parts of this ending here was that one of the people in the group of eleven suggested that everybody get into the bags that we had packed our stuff in. And so, many of us, absent Kate and Dennis and some of the people who weren't quite brave enough to jump into that shot, jumped into the bags and crowded together into a group shot . . . one of the guides who hadn't gone along on the trip took a picture with my camera and several other cameras were involved in taking pictures of that shot.

Communitas developed not only among the customers but between customers and the guides. In most of the field note illustrations provided, the guides were fully integrated into the experience as members of the team. Consistent with our conceptualization of the experience as a rite of intensification, photographs illustrate that affectionate, playful construction of a community that does not separate guides from clients, young from old, or rich from poor. People report thinking of the guide, not in service provider terms, but as a friend. Participant observation notes from the end of a trip (7/91) depict the emotionally charged, boundary open relationships that develop: 'It's real clear that Jeff [one of the guides] made an impact on people. And that a lot of people would come up to him and say, you made this trip for me . . . the people from Carbon wanted Jeff to come up and interview with the school in Carbon, because they thought he'd be a fabulous addition . . . and other people also were trying to make some kind of more permanent contact, at least with Jeff'.

Personal growth and renewal of self

A third theme evidenced in our data is a rediscovered sense of self. Rafting provides a simple, encapsulated world that offers participants 'a sense of place and purpose, a rationale for behavior', and guides for action (Donohue, 1991, p. 14). Our data help explain outfitter's apocryphal stories of successful East Coast accountants and business executives giving up their plush jobs for the life of a river guide after just one encounter with a wild, Western river.

Tangible elements of material culture, the physical evidence of which Bitner *et al.* (1990) speak, is of importance in personal growth and self-renewal. Consistent with many clients' articulated expectations, guides help clients acquire new skills. Demonstrating the use of safety equipment, paddling techniques, methods of tying down equipment, encouraging the use of the duckies and attempts to guide the paddle boats, cooking on a camp fire, and so on are among the myriad ways in which guides use props to 'provide new challenges' and 'make things fun'.

Progressive mastery over novel things and tools begins at the put-in and continues throughout the trip, as this excerpt from day 1 of participant observation field note suggests (5/90):

When the troops [a dozen alternate high school students and their chaperones] arrive, Peter, the trip leader, takes charge. Kids are set off to pack and do a pretty good job of it, all breaking into twos to pack. The head chaperone, Rick, says some have never camped before. When they are about packed he has 'em carry the bags down. I note one kid checks in with Tom, one of the guides, to see if it's packed right. Before putting in, Peter gave a safety speech; did the thing about bouncing someone in a life-jacket to demonstrate how tight it should be. All stood around in a semicircle to watch this and listened to discussion of how to pull someone out of the water. There were 6–7/boat. Paddling not a big strength as yet. Noticed how people were willing to participate in it right away. People began to joke about paddling skills, began to be competitive with other boats right away. 'Let's ram the boat' kinds of stuff were said. Most of the kids were pretty willing to take guide (or steering) duty and tried to guide the boat under the guides' instructions.

Transcribed field notes from participant observation on day 4 of a trip illustrate the evolution and articulation of skill acquisition (6/91): 'Sandy [a guide] relinquished the oars to me today for the first time. I rode all the way to Warm Springs, about seven miles. . . . I noticed that at first Ike, then later Will, took a turn on the oars in the other boat as we rode on down the stream'.

Learning how to pack a rubberized dry bag, how to attach a life jacket, how to use it in an emergency, and how to manipulate a paddle provide tangible manifestations of the new skills and control the novice rafters gain from the first moments. As the trip progresses, skills are perceived to have been sharpened by the increasing speed, facility, and success with which rapids, loading and unloading, cooking chores, and unexpected incidents like drenched gear are negotiated.

Another part of the personal growth process is learning the new jargon that accompanies the boatman's skills and life-style. Naming and labeling are fundamental cultural processes; terminology provides cultural categories that stabilize the flux inherent in brute experience (Douglas and Isherwood, 1979, pp. 64–70). Thus, learning terms that seem arcane at first – 'put-in', 'oar boat', 'dungee bag', 'day bag', 'duckie', 'recirculating hole', 'fan hole', 'strainer', 'getting maytagged', 'groover', 'river kill', 'take-out' and so on – provide markers of personal control over experience (see Table 4).

Guides coach and communicate, by example and direct experience, something more than new skills. Most important is the notion that action on the river is charged not only with great serenity, but with imminent danger, that is, river magic, that transcends normal activity. Guides cater to clients' physical and existential fears about rafting; they also acknowledge clients when they overcome danger. A particularly overt example comes from participant observation notes of the teen trip. In anticipation of running some big rapids:

> Peter [a guide] gave a lecture in which he said everyone was doing really well and he knew a lot of people hadn't done something like this before . . . Peter ended with a story about fear [overcome]. [That evening] Ryan gave me back the quote [i.e. the supporting comment] more or less: 'Come to the edge, come to the edge'. 'No, we are afraid to come to the edge'. So they came to the edge. We pushed them off and they flew Mr. A pitched in, 'That's the gist of it'.

Clients internalize the sense of danger and obstacles overcome, contributing to a sense of personal intensification and renewal (Donohue, 1991; Klausner, 1968). Most clients have a safe, danger-free trip; however, many trips arouse life-and-death fears. Many trips include one or more accidents that people experience as truly 'close calls', or brushes with death. On the teen trip, an inappropriately clothed girl fell in the water and suffered early symptoms of hypothermia. On a trip during the second season, a raft overturned, a guide suffered a gashed forehead, clients lost eye glasses and caps, and camping equipment was drenched. On another trip someone's duckie became stuck in a 'strainer' and he was rescued from potentially serious trouble. Thus, field notes contain numerous references to 'the danger withstood' (Gergen and Gergen, 1988). The fear aroused by such experiences helps crystallize one's sense of self (Donohue, 1991). Reinforced with guides' and other rafters' stories of close calls, clients emerge with a sense of mastery and enhanced agency.

Recollections of the experience

Transcribed field notes (7/91) convey a sense of exhaustion and reentry into the everyday world: 'One of the things that we joked about as we were sitting around at the take-out, Russ reiterated how he thought that a scotch and soda, a cold, cold

Pepsi Cola, or cold Coca Cola with some ice cubes in it would really be something to be looking forward to and then perhaps a scotch and soda on ice after that'.

A client (9/90) reflecting back on his feelings at the end of the trip, remarked: 'I don't think you feel like you want to immediately go on another raft trip. What you're really interested in is having a shower, and a nice hot shower, and get in some dry clothes, and a martini'.

Also reflected in the reentry to the everyday world is a sense of being hit with the routines, noises and other features of everyday life. A focus group participant reflected on end-of-trip feelings talked about the 'yuk' mail. Then she continued in a more reflective vein: 'You let your perception all open up. All these defenses that we have, and take for granted, that we don't even think about them in the city, where you block out sounds, and you block out a lot of things. You haven't done that for a while. All of a sudden you come back. And that's one reason that we get hit so quickly'.

In one sense the trip ends at the take-out. But, as our data reflect, many years after a river trip, the memory lingers. Vivid recall of the experience is evidenced throughout retrospective reports, with comments such as that it 'made a lasting impression' or 'was an overwhelming experience'. One participant notes, 'Although it has been a long time, probably eight years, once I began writing, the feelings and sensations come right back'. Respondents vividly remember their rafting experience but find it difficult to describe. A consistent theme was, 'You almost have to do it to really understand the experience'. One participant said, 'It is easier for me to describe the intense moments experienced in rafting and these are perhaps more alive memories. Those longer periods of quiet solitude, which are just as vivid in my mind and heart, are somehow more difficult to put into words'.

Participants do not appear to want to engage in very much *cognitive* recall of the experience. It is as if river magic is best preserved if the associated feelings and sensations are not examined too closely. Comments from the client focus group (9/90) exemplify this resistance: 'You know, I've treated the trip as something to be enjoyed . . . I happen to be in academia. And so, what you need to do is get away from that atmosphere and do something else. And a raft trip is a way of doing that. So it's enjoyable and that's exactly how I look upon it. No point in making it all complicated'.

Evident in all of our data is that the experiences are productive of emotional outcomes, and in retrospect are often described in terms of these outcomes, as the following quotation shows (1/90): 'It is an experience that combines a multitude of feelings and emotions that could differ depending on a person's likes and dislikes and their fears'.

The narrative qualities of the experience and articulation of the interwoven themes of communion with nature, communitas, and extension and renewal of self become more pronounced with time and retelling.

Communion with nature

Posttrip responses to what were the best things that happened on the trip (6/90–8/90) contained numerous references to 'great scenery', 'natural environment', and the 'solitude of the canyons'. One rafter observed, 'The solitude in the vastness of the canyon was uplifting and exciting'. Nearly half of respondents (49%) mentioned natural environmental features as one of the best things that happened on their trip.

A particularly rich articulation of the communion with nature that derives from rafting in a river canyon was provided by a participant in our focus group (9/90): 'But in the river, there's something about the canyon and the river and the narrowness. There's a limited, you're not just limited by no noise from the city, or not, you know, bus stops and all. But you're limited by the wall or the beach . . . And go to look . . . up at the stars and you know, identify a few of the stars, that you know you can identify because the rest of them are blocked out, It just ah . . . in every way . . . '

First-season quantitative analyses provided statistical support for the relationship between a feeling of communion with nature and reported satisfaction with the trip. A seven-item scale (alpha = .84) measured communion with nature (scale items are included in the Appendix). The correlation of the 'communion with nature' scale and a six-item measure of overall trip satisfaction (alpha = .90) was .70 ($p < .001$).

Long afterward, the memory of the absorption in nature and the newness of perception associated with the trip linger. Recollections of what it is like to go river rafting (1/90) carry these themes: 'As the river carves its way through majestic canyons one can feel the inner sense of fulfillment that only nature can bring out'. 'It gives you a chance to see things one wouldn't see unless they partook in the experience. It is an experience that allows you to witness the beauty and the immense power of our natural environment'.

Data from the second season echo the theme of communion with nature. Comments suggest the newness of perception and melding with nature characteristic of this experience. When asked to describe the river and surroundings, people wrote: 'Stark, but beautiful. There was a grandness and awsomeness in the sheer walls and steadily changing slopes of the river and the rocks. It was unhurried and restful'. 'Peaceful, I felt at times like a child seeing things for the first time. I was in awe. Sometimes we tend not to appreciate our own country. We want to visit outside the USA. Colorado is wonderful'.

Quantitative analyses from second-season data again support the importance of communion with nature in trip satisfaction. On the basis of our experiences during the first season we revised slightly our measure of communion with nature (scale items for season 2 are included in the Appendix). Correlation of the revised six-item scale (alpha = .86) with overall trip satisfaction (alpha = .93) was .61 ($p < .001$).

Communitas

In the first season, one-third of posttrip responses (6/90–8/90) made mention of interactions with others as one of the best things that happened on the trip. Examples include 'our family being together', 'friendships you would form', and 'comradeship'.

Vivid articulation of the communion with others that derives from rafting in a river canyon were provided by focus group verbatims (9/90) in response to a moderator's probe about the 'most appealing aspect' of rafting: 'Even people you didn't know, you met them and you get to know them real well on the river, and then you maybe never see them again. But for those few days, you know, you shared something in a really intimate way'.

A sense of communitas is not produced merely by shared experience. Shared 'edgework' (Lyng, 1990), such as working a craft through dangerous rapids, more quickly creates a sense of communion, one that differs somewhat from that built up over the course of the trip. Another verbatim from the focus group suggests this dynamic: 'And so there's a bonding that occurs pretty quickly I think, when you come through an experience that frightens you, or intimidates you or excites you. Guess everyone's emotional levels are going pretty high, and it's through teamwork that you're going to get through this experience. And when you come through it on that other side of the rapids, you're a little bit closer than you were when you went in'.

In the first season, we developed the communitas scale on the basis of repeated comments from outfitters, guides, and river trip participants to the effect that being with family and connecting with others gives a 'new perspective on life' and helped participants see 'what really matters'. One outfitter emphasized how she developed her rafting business partly because of the unique ability of the river experience to change interpersonal dynamics and transform individual perspectives: 'Among peer groups, it really changes around patterns of interaction, urban leader may be pushed onto the back burner . . . it is a learning experience beyond anything I've ever gone through. Day three on the water is the dramatic changing point. . . . This is the fastest transition period we've found for any outdoor kind of experience, this day three thing. You get a lot of leaders among the adult trips'.

Quantitative analyses support the relationship between communion with others and reported satisfaction with the trip. Communitas was measured by a four-item scale (alpha = .82; scale items are provided in the Appendix). The correlation of the scale and the six-item measure of overall trip satisfaction is .71 ($p < .001$).

Long afterward, unguided retrospective reports of going river rafting include this theme of communitas (1/90): 'When you're with friends, very few things can compare to the bond you create because it's a team sport. You overcome the scary spots together and then laugh together as the water splashes at you'. 'You develop a team attitude and form close bonds with raft partners'.

Posttrip survey responses in the second season of research provided even richer articulations of communitas, again stressing the rapid sense of communion with strangers very different from oneself (6/91–8/91). For example, when asked what they had learned, one participant said: 'I learned that group success sometimes requires sacrificing of self. I learned that people from varied backgrounds are very much the same and can and do have fun together'.

Posttrip survey responses also pointed to the incorporation of guides into the community, supporting interpretation of this service encounter as a boundary open transaction. These responses to guides are typical of posttrip comments: 'Like a true friend after only a couple of hours'. 'Let us in on her personal life, told great stories, well educated on surroundings, the type of person I would like for a sister'.

Quantitative results from the second season of research again supported the role of communitas in trip satisfaction. By the end of the first season we had an improved understanding of the nature of feelings of community. Correlation of a significantly revised six-item scale (alpha = .90) measuring sense of community with overall trip satisfaction was .55 ($p < .001$).

Personal growth and renewal of self

First-season posttrip responses to the question of the best things that happened on the trip (6/90–8/90) contain allusions to self-discovery as well as numerous references to feelings of adventure, challenge, and excitement. Examples include 'discover internal strengths', 'proving to myself I could handle the trip (camping/rapids)' or 'surviving overturned raft'. The progressive mastery over novel things and tools is suggested by this verbatim about 'duckies' given as a response to the 'best part of the trip': 'The fun of kayaking down rapids like Crystal and Spector and ending up right side up at the end and feeling like I was somewhat in control!'

Focus groups (5/90, 9/90) provided rafters with an opportunity to express more fully feelings of self-discovery, awareness, achievement, and personal transformation, that is, the impact of a ritual of intensification on sense of self. A river guide trainee summarized the impact of his past few weeks on the river in the following terms (5/90): 'Learned bunch of things. How tired you can be doing physical work. How selfish and petty one can be when we're outside of our comfort zones. To find these things out, and reiterate from time to time keeps us humble. Being able to assess a situation slowly gives you the concrete things. Discover what you like and don't like'.

From the client focus group (9/90) we heard these comments: 'Yeah, I mean in my case it was definitely a skills-building activity. Where you start out and you're a little bit uncomfortable and you kind of establish a better comfort zone or a wider comfort zone'. 'The thing that I enjoyed the most was the risk involved, and the fact that you were able to overcome the risk at the end. . . . It's the fact that, wow, I really did do that. And you feel real positive when you get all done. . . . And I guess the next best part, [is] to know that you can rely on most people'.

Comments from the focus group (9/90) substantiated field observations about the importance of the guide in orchestrating personal growth and renewal: 'And he seemed very confident and built all our confidence up around him. And I think it really helped near the end of the trip when he let us take turns guiding. And we'd all sit in the back of the boat and try and give commands and try to get the boat to go certain directions. And it was so hard for us, and we'd screw things up so much that by the time we sat back in our position as paddlers, we had a lot more respect for Doug, because we felt like, oh, this job is hard'.

Quantitative analyses support the relationship between personal growth and renewal of self and reported satisfaction with the trip. A six-item scale (alpha = .84) measured personal growth and renewal (scale items are provided in the Appendix). The correlation between this scale and a seven-item measure of overall satisfaction is .65 ($p < .001$).

Recollections of river rafting (1/90) depicted themes common to positive experience including absorption and integration, personal control, joy and valuing, and spontaneous letting-be of the process. In addition to the themes illustrated below, the theme of 'newness of perception and process' characteristic of extraordinary experience was evident. These themes provide an environment for a rite of intensification instrumental in experiencing personal growth: 'Going river rafting is a natural high. It is you and the water . . . all your problems are forgotten and one can use their body and feel all the muscles work in harmony'. 'The only sounds you hear are the water splashing and its flow through the rapids and a few yells and screams of pleasure from companions. You feel the water pushing underneath and around the raft. And the feel of humidity and wetness all around. Your body is under the control of the rapids and you ride the raft'.

Recollections of going river rafting (1/90) contain mentions of renewed self-awareness, rejuvenation, skill enhancement, testing limits, and personal achievement: '[You] develop a personal enrichment especially if you encounter a situation in which you become frightened and overcome the obstacle of the situation. And finally, long after its done, even years later, you'll find your mind escaping/returning back to the journey and reliving the thrill and when you encounter a situation in life where you're afraid or unsure the river experience often enables you to overcome it because you are inevitably more self-assured'.

Posttrip survey responses in the second season included a prompt on what clients felt they learned from their rafting experience. In contrast to pretrip expectations, which were primarily skill acquisition related, only a few posttrip responses could be so characterized. Even in those cases, the use of exclamation marks suggests some greater accomplishment. For example, one client who expected to learn 'how to live in the outdoors', reported after his trip that he learned 'I can "captain" a raft!' In general, what clients reported learning was very different from what they initially reported wanting to learn. Obviously, if we had asked instead 'Did you learn boat skills as you expected?' they would probably have responded yes. However, what stuck in their minds was other things, and the verbatims read like a compendium of life wisdoms: 'It is better to try and fail, rather than to not try at all'; 'So much worry over stupid things in the world'; or 'Patience, understanding'.

Quantitative analyses from second-season posttrip responses again supported the importance of personal growth and renewal in overall trip satisfaction. Based on our first-season research experiences, the same six-item scale (alpha = .91) measured personal growth and renewal (items are included in the Appendix). The correlation of this measure with overall trip satisfaction was .62 ($p < .001$).

Links between themes

Evident in both research seasons and across different research methods was the close linking of the themes. The link with nature and the separation from 'civilization' plays a role in the creation of communitas: 'What you really do is just for the sheer enjoyment of being together. And this is a way of insuring that, because we don't get together very often in that kind of an experience without taking the time to do something away from the helter skelter activity of daily living. So it [rafting] forces you to do it more than anything else'.

Several other focus group comments substantiate the relationship between isolation in a natural environment and the creation of communitas: 'We were removed from all those other peripheral things and so we were able to focus on our friendship and concentrate on each other and our interaction with each other was much better than we would've been able to do in another setting'.

Similarly, verbatims about learning to trust, to lead, to get along with others, and to be part of a team suggest a close connection between a sense of communitas and personal growth. The close interplay between self, nature, and others is evidenced in verbatims again and again. Many verbatims already provided play on how the rediscovered self emerges in the natural setting and through interactions with others.

Quantitative analyses in the first season suggested that the three experiential themes are highly correlated, ranging from .64 to .71 ($p < .001$). Because of the small sample size for posttrip survey responses in the first season ($n = 43$), it was not appropriate to factor analyze the items for the three experiential themes to establish unidimensionality. Ordinary least squares (OLS) regression with the three experiential themes as predictor variables and overall trip satisfaction as the dependent variable yields an adjusted R^2 of .57 ($F = 16.57$, $p < .001$). Because of potential multicollinearity among the three predictor variables, interpreting the individual betas and t-values may be problematic. However, OLS results are fairly robust for these levels of correlation between the predictor variables and for the level of R^2 reported (Mason and Perreault, 1991).

With the larger sample size available in season 2 posttrip survey responses, we confirmed that the three themes are related but separate components of rafting satisfaction. Because of our experience during season 1, the revised item pool generated for season 2 data collection seemed effective in capturing the constructs. Very little adjustment to the hypothesized scales was required in season 2. On the basis of initial reliability analyses two items were dropped from the personal growth scale (from eight back to six) and two items were dropped from the communitas scale (from eight to six). Next, an unconstrained principal components factor analysis yielded three factors with eigenvalues greater than one. Together, these three factors explain 66% of the variance. All items loaded on the expected factor and no cross-loadings exceeded .40. The rotated factor solution is included in the Appendix. Of course, the themes are related, with correlations ranging between .52 and .57. The OLS solution with overall satisfaction as the dependent variable and the three experiential themes as predicted variables results in an adjusted R^2 of .46 ($F = 34.05$, all t-values are significant at $p < .05$).

The narrative of a rafting experience

Looking across the pretrip planning process to the culmination of the trip in a series of affectively charged recollections, we are struck by the importance of the entire narrative in understanding the experience. Consequently, the disconfirmation paradigm is not a particularly useful metaphor for interpreting satisfaction with this experience. Significant deviations from even vaguely articulated expectations are common, and the link between confirmation of expectations and satisfaction is weak.

Deviations from expectations

In advance of the trip, it is difficult for clients to grasp the taken-for-granted world of river rafting aficionados and the romance they experience in their outdoor life.

Similarly, outfitters do not always anticipate the gap between the assumptions of clients and the realities of river trips. In short, outcomes differ from expectations. Unanticipated realities are commonly expressed in posttrip comments (6/90–8/90). Examples include 'I didn't expect to have wet feet for six days', 'I was disappointed at the flat water on a three day trip. I was hoping for more white water' (long stretches of flat water between rapids), 'the necessity of washing in muddy river water, the lack of privacy', 'sleeping on the hard ground', and so on.

Guides and outfitters are frequently indifferent to aspects of the trip that subsequently surprise clients. For example, a wealthy client and his family were disappointed to discover that the water in the Green River was not, in fact, green, but rather a muddy brown, and that the scenery was desert rather than lush forest. They demanded the outfitter arrange for helicopter transport out of the wilderness area. Dissuaded, the family was 'ecstatic' at the end of their trip, and later wrote to the outfitter to explain that the trip had brought them together (field notes; 2/90).

Weak link between expectations and satisfaction

Satisfaction may have little if anything to do with confirmation of expectations. The client focus group (9/90) hints at a weak link between expectations and satisfaction. At one point a client explains that 'the rapids were a little better than I'd imagined they would be'. As the conversation develops, it turns out this is an understatement. The whole raft turned over on a rapid; he was first trapped underneath, and then 'went almost a mile through two other major rapids on his own'. This even provoked the couple to unusual action, 'We came home and made some arrangements. With our lives and affairs'. Their concluding remarks suggest, 'But in any event, it was a, it was a very exciting trip', and 'It was wonderful. On the way home we were already thinking of what one [i.e. river] next'. Thus, satisfaction may derive from having survived an unexpected challenge.

Weak links between expectations and satisfaction may be due to the complexity of satisfaction with extraordinary experience. One participant's description of her reactions to the experience captures the complexity particularly well (1/90):

> For me, river rafting is a horrible thing, I am scared to death of water. . . . I have to admit – it was the most exciting thing I've done in a long time. I never felt safe, but I did start to feel like I wasn't in complete danger. For the first 15 to 20 minutes it was pure terror. . . . By the end of the day – I'd been thrown all over the raft. I was soaking wet, I was very drained because I'd been tense all day long, but I felt very invigorated . . . it is challenging, exciting, thrilling, exhausting, and I'd recommend it highly.

Data from season 2 allow an explicit comparison between pretrip expectations and posttrip responses on several features of the trip including setting, guides, people, feelings, safety, and learning. In each category, deviations from expectations were common, and many have detailed in previous sections. The rivers and setting were majestic, but 'brown' and 'desolate', not 'green' and 'lush'. The guides were more than informative and skilled, they were friends and members of a team. The people were not just friendly, but bonded together in a rite of intensification. People did not just learn how to oar the raft, but learned about themselves and life. Some additional illustrations of the complexity of the narrative come from comparing feelings people expected with feelings they reported having. Typical pretrip and posttrip responses are illustrative:

Expected: Satisfaction.
  Actual: Big mood swings. Bad mood to being in awe.
Expected: Exhilaration, peacefulness.
  Actual: Some frustration, exhilaration, and mostly ratification. I felt a sense of accomplishment that I finished something which was very challenging. The experiences I had will last forever; going under the waterfall, the rock climbing, leading my boat through the rapids, just everything.

DISCUSSION AND IMPLICATIONS

Experiences, like tales, fetes, potteries, rites,
dramas, images, memoirs, ethnographies,
and allegorical machineries, are made; and
it is such made things that make them.
[Geertz, 1986, p. 380]

White water river rafting provides a dramatic illustration of complex features of delivering 'extraordinary experience'. Because of the complexity of the domain and the difficulty of acquiring rich and representative data, multiple methods were employed to articulate the lived meaning of this experience from both the guides' and the consumers perspectives. No data set stands on its own as sufficient evidence of the narrative. Each data set can be criticized on one or more criteria (Arnould and Wallendorf, 1993). Together, however, they converge to tell a story about 'river magic'.

River rafting is a unique recreational form, but its power lies in the romantic cultural scripts that evolve over the course of the experience – the opportunity to participate in rites of intensification and integration and to return to an everyday world 'transformed'. Although the form is unique, the cultural script is exceedingly common and increasingly sought (Cohen, 1989; Krippendorf, 1987; MacCannell, 1989). White water river rafting is viewed in individuals' narratives as an unforgettable, affectively charged experience. Consistent with research on extraordinary experiences, river rafting provides absorption and integration, personal control, joy and valuing, a spontaneous letting-be of the process, and a newness of perception and process. Dimensions of extraordinary experience manifest themselves in the themes of harmony with nature, communitas, and personal growth and renewal. These experiential themes are evidenced across all the data; they evolve and are woven together over the course of the trip. Together, the three themes are significant in explaining overall satisfaction. Both qualitative and quantitative results support the value of viewing the themes as an interactive gestalt instead of trying to separate the contributions of the three themes.

In the current historical and cultural context, it can be argued that these three themes are deeply frustrated values that American consumers seek and prize. For many consumers intense, positive experiences crystallize selfhood, provide life meaning and perspective, confer awareness of one's own morality, reduce anxiety, and improve fear coping (Abrahams, 1986; Celsi *et al.*, 1993; Donohue, 1991; Ewert, 1988; Ewert and Hollenhorst, 1989; Solomon, 1988). Some authors think the value placed on intense, positive experiences is a reaction against the commercialization of meaning and segmentation and specialization of roles in the workplace (Csikszentmihalyi, 1990; Cushman, 1990; Ewen, 1988; Giddens, 1991, p. 9). In services ranging from fast food to birthing classes, providers could, and sometimes do, stress one or more of these three themes. Although it may seem a stretch to promise a renewed sense of self from stopping at McDonald's for breakfast, several award-winning advertisements do just that. Incorporation of these themes in service provision may be both unexpected and highly satisfying for consumers.

The subtle role of the guide in orchestrating delivery of an extraordinary experience is revealed in field notes, photos, and focus groups. Emotional outcomes associated with extraordinary experience are embedded in relationships between customer and service provider. Previous research has discussed neither the interactive dimension of extraordinary experiences nor the association between extraordinary experience and commercial service encounters. Our findings suggest that guides, partly at their own invitation, are inducted into the community as friends and team players. The rite of intensification into which the guide is bound by the experience of clients changes the nature of interaction in fundamental ways, shifting it into a boundary open transaction between provider and customer that transcends commercial interaction. The guide exemplifies a service role of increasing importance as more and more people buy experiences to give their lives meaning (Ewert and Schreyer, 1990).

We have drawn attention here to the role of guides in providing expressive models that 'socialize' river rafting participants into intrinsically meaningful experiences over the course of the river trip (Csikszentmihalyi, 1981, pp. 338–339). At the same time we have suggested that participants in river rafting experiences bring their own preconscious scripts to these travel 'performances' (Adler, 1989). These scripts prepare them for a pilgrimage, orchestrated by the guides, into a sacred place where pilgrims and guides are bonded together. For many the river trip is a rite of intensification that emotionally links people widely scattered and dissimilar in ordinary life. The pilgrim returns affirmed and renewed. The experience itself is vividly recalled but difficult to describe because of its emotional content and perceived distinctiveness.

There is a complex relationship between client expectations and satisfaction with extraordinary experience. The narrative of the experience is central to overall evaluation. For these experiences, participants may access an array of culturally informed, preconscious scripts or narrative themes (e.g. overcoming adversity through personal initiation or the quintessentially romantic story of the self-perfecting self, as in the novels of Herman Hesse or Carlos Castenads (Campbell, 1987). Or their expectations may be loosely formed. Or they may protect expectations of hedonic outcomes from reasoned anticipation. Finally, consumers invited to enact unfamiliar scripts may experience as much satisfaction as, or greater satisfaction than, with familiar scripts. In each case, satisfaction may have little to do with whether the experience unfolds as expected. These findings are at odds with a disconfirmation paradigm of service satisfaction.

To say merely that people like to be surprised would understate the import of our findings. The important point is that people may be unable or unwilling to articulate the meanings they really seek from many service encounters and especially service encounters that offer something 'extraordinary'. Therefore, deciphering the unarticulated meanings that people seek becomes more important to service provision that recording articulated expectations. Mechanically linking managerial decisions to stated consumer expectations does not necessarily lead to increased customer satisfaction.

In summary, many of the reported findings may have implications for a broad array of services and consumption activities. Recognizing the danger of over-generalizing beyond the current context, future research should explore the relevance of our research findings to other service and consumption experience contexts. First, our findings argue for more attention to the temporal moments of a consumption experience when assessing satisfaction. Theory and research on a range of other service encounters is beginning to suggest that knowing the story and the ending can be crucial in distinguishing between particularly satisfying and particularly unsatisfying interactions (Bitner *et al.*, 1990; Deighton, 1992). Second, our findings argue for more attention to underlying cultural scripts in examining consumption experiences and satisfaction with those experiences. The universalizing of the particular and the particularizing of the universal are evident in the experience of river rafting but might easily be mapped to other consumption experiences as well (Kapferer, 1986, p. 191). Confirmation of particular expectations may be far less important than conformance of an experience to an often unarticulated cultural script. Finally, our findings argue for more attention to boundary open transactions where the demarcation between service provider and client are blurred (at least from the client's perspective). More research is needed to explore the implications of exchanges that transcend commercial interactions for behaviors such as tipping, repeat purchase, and service provider role stress.

APPENDIX

Measures

Table A1.   Construct measures: experiential themes

Season 1	Season 2
Harmony with nature: I felt	
1. Harmony with nature	1. Same
2. Like I explored new worlds	2. Same
3. I escaped into a different world	3. Same
4. Satisfied with wilderness scenery	4. I got a new perspective on nature
5. Freedom from obligations	5. Same
This rafting trip	
6. Was like getting away from it all	6. Same
7. Make me fell like I was in a different world	

Table A1.   Construct measures: experiential themes *continued*

Season 1	Season 2
Communitas: I felt 　1. Satisfied with being part of a team 　2. Closer to friends/family 　3. I got a new perspective on life 　4. I rediscovered what really matters	1. In harmony with others 2. I interacted well with others 3. I made new friends 4. My skills were appreciated by others 5. Needed by the group 6. I pulled my weight
Personal growth and renewal: I felt 　1. A sense of adventure or risk 　2. Personally challenged 　3. An adrenalin rush 　4. I learned new things 　5. I mastered new skills 　6. I tested my limits	1. Same 2. Same 3. Same 4. Same 5. Same 6. Same

Table A2.   Unconstrained factor solution: principal components analysis with varimax rotation

	Factor 1	Factor 2	Factor 3
Harmony with nature:			
1	.13	.16	.64
2	.17	.12	.76
3	.18	.27	.81
4	.36	.20	.65
5	.16	.16	.68
6	.13	.23	.76
Communitas:			
1	.02	.76	.34
2	.11	.83	.21
3	.21	.71	.28
4	.35	.74	.29
5	.34	.79	.13
6	.38	.67	.04
Personal growth:			
1	.72	.19	.27
2	.83	.19	.14
3	.76	.29	.11
4	.74	.09	.26
5	.77	.15	.22
6	.87	.24	.14

$n = 126$.

ACKNOWLEDGMENTS

We wish to thank Bill and Jaci Dvorak, Patrick Tierney, Lisa Penaloza, Rick Perdue, and four reviewers for their useful recommendations.

REFERENCES

Abrahams, R. D. (1986) 'Ordinary and Extraordinary Experience'. In *The Anthropology of Experience* (V. W. Turner and E. M. Bruner, Eds). Urbana: University of Illinois Press, pp. 45–73.

Adler, J. (1989) 'Travel as Performed Art'. *American Journal of Sociology* **94**(6): 1366–1391.

Arnould, E. J. and Wallendorf, M. (1993) 'Market-oriented Ethnography'. Working paper, Department of Marketing, California State University, Long Beach, 90840.

Belk, R. W., Wallendorf, M. and Sherry, J. F. (1989) 'The Sacred and the Profane in Consumer Behavior: Theodicy on the Odyssey'. *Journal of Consumer Research* **16** (June): 1–38.

Bettenhausen, K. and Murnighan, J. K. (1985) 'The Emergency of Norms in Competitive Decision-making Groups'. *Administrative Science Quarterly* **30** (September): 350–372.

Bitner, M. J. (1990) 'Evaluating Service Encounters: The Effects of Physical Surroundings and Employee Responses'. *Journal of Marketing* **54** (April): 69–82.

Bitner, M. J. (1992) 'Servicescapes: The Impact of Physical Surroundings on Customers and Employees'. *Journal of Marketing* **56** (April): 57–71.

Bitner, M. J., Booms, B. H. and Tetreault, M. S. (1990) 'The Service Encounter: Diagnosing Favorable and Unfavorable Incidents'. *Journal of Marketing* **54** (January): 71–84.

Boas, M. and Chain, S. (1976) *Big Mac: The Unauthorized Story of McDonalds.* New York: Dutton.

Botterill, D. T. (1987) 'Dissatisfaction with a Construction of Satisfaction'. *Annals of Tourism Research* **14**(1): 139–140.

Bruner, E. M. (1986) 'Ethnography as Narrative'. In *The Anthropology of Experience* (V. W. Turner and E. M. Bruner, Eds). Urbana: University of Illinois Press, pp. 139–158.

Campbell, C. (1987) *The Romantic Ethic and the Spirit of Modern Consumerism.* Oxford: Blackwell.

Celsi, R., Rose, R. L. and Leigh, T. W. (1993) 'An exploration of high-risk leisure consumption through skydiving', *Journal of Consumer Research* **20** (June): 1–23.

Cohen, E. (1989) '"Primitive and Remote" Hill Tribe Trekking in Thailand'. *Annals of Tourism Research* **16**(1): 30–61.

Coon, C. (1958) *Caravan: The Story of the Middle East.* New York: Holt, Rinehart.

Csikszentmihalyi, M. (1975) *Beyond Boredom and Anxiety: The Experience of Play in Work and Games.* San Francisco: Jossey-Bass.

Csikszentmihalyi, M. (1981) 'Leisure and Socialization'. *Social Forces* **60** (December): 332–340.

Csikszentmihalyi, M. (1985) 'Reflections on Enjoyment'. *Perspectives in Biology and Medicine* **28** (Summer): 489–497.

Csikszentmihalyi, M. (1990) *Flow: The Psychology of Optimal Experience.* New York: Harper & Row.

Csikszentmihalyi, M. and LeFevre, J. (1989) 'Optimal Experience in Work and Leisure'. *Journal of Personality and Social Psychology* **56**(5): 815–822.

Cushman, P. (1990) 'Why the Self Is Empty: Towards a Historically Situated Psychology'. *American Psychologist* **45** (May): 599–611.

Czepiel, J. A., Solomon, M. R., Surprenant, C. F. and Gutman, E. G. (1985) 'Service Encounters: An Overview'. In *The Service Encounter: Managing Employee/Customer Interaction in Service Businesses* (J. A. Czepiel *et al.*, Eds). Lexington, MA: Lexington, pp. 3–16.

Deighton, J. (1992) 'The Consumption of Performance'. *Journal of Consumer Research* **19** (December): 362–372.

Denzin, N. K. (1983) 'A Note on Emotionality, Self, and Interaction'. *American Journal of Sociology* **89** (September): 402–409.

Donohue, J. (1991) 'Dancing in the Danger Zone: The Martial Arts in America'. Paper presented at the annual meeting of the Association for Consumer Research, Chicago.

Douglas, M. and Isherwood, B. (1979) *The World of Goods.* Harmondsworth: Penguin.

Durgee, J. F., Holbrook, M. B. and Sherry, J. F., Jr. (1991) 'The Delivery of Vacation Performances'. In *Highways and Buyways: Naturalistic Research from the Consumer Behavior Odyssey.* (R. W. Belk, Ed.). Provo, UT: Association for Consumer Research, pp. 131–140.

Ewen, S. (1988) *All Consuming Images.* New York: Basic.

Ewert, A. (1988) 'Reduction of Trait Anxiety through Participation in Outward Bound'. *Leisure Sciences* 10(2): 107–117.

Ewert, A. and Hollenhurst, S. (1989) 'Testing the Adventure Model: Empirical Support for a Model of Risk Recreation Participation'. *Journal of Leisure Research* 21(2): 124–139.

Ewert, A. and Shreyer, R. (1990) 'Risk Recreation Trends and Implications for the 1990s'. Paper presented at Outdoor Recreation TRENDS Symposium III. Indianapolis.

Featherstone, M. (1991) *Consumer Culture and Postmodernism.* Newbury Park, CA: Sage.

Fiebelkorn, S. (1985) 'Retail Service Encounter Satisfaction: Model and Measurement'. In *The Service Encounter: Managing Employee/Customer Interaction in Service Businesses* (J. A. Czepiel et al., Eds). Lexington, MA: Lexington, pp. 181–193.

Geertz, C. (1986) 'Making Experiences, Authoring Selves'. In *The Anthropology of Experience* (V. W. Turner and E. M. Bruner, Eds). Urbana: University of Illinois Press, pp. 373–380.

Gergen, K. J. and Gergen, M. M. (1988) 'Narrative and the Self as Relationship'. In *Advances in Experimental Social Psychology*, Vol. 21 (L. Berkowitz, Ed.). San Diego, CA: Academic Press, pp. 17–56.

Giddens, A. (1991) *Modernity and Self-Identity: Self and Society in the Late Modern Age.* Stanford, CA: Stanford University Press.

Grove, S. J. and Fisk, R. P. (1992) 'The Service Experience as Theater'. In *Advances in Consumer Research*, Vol. 19 (J. F. Sherry, Jr. and B. Sternthal, Eds). Provo, UT: Association for Consumer Research, pp. 455–461.

Havlena, W. J. and Holbrook, M. B. (1986) 'The Varieties of Consumption Experience: Comparing Two Typologies of Emotion in Consumer Behavior'. *Journal of Consumer Research* 13 (December): 394–404.

Hawes, D. K. (1978) 'Satisfactions Derived from Leisure-Time Pursuits: An Exploratory Nationwide Survey'. *Journal of Leisure Research* 10(4): 247–264.

Heywood, J. L. (1987) 'Experience Preferences of Participants in Different Types of River Recreation Groups'. *Journal of Leisure Studies* 19(1): 1–12.

Hirschman, E. (1984) 'Experience Seeking: A Subjectivistic Perspective of Consumption'. *Journal of Business Research* 12: 115–136.

Hirschman, E. and Holbrook, M. B. (1982) 'Hedonic Consumption: Emerging Concepts, Methods, and Propositions'. *Journal of Marketing* 46 (Summer): 92–101.

Hochschild, A. R. (1983) *The Managed Heart.* Berkeley and Los Angeles: University of California Press.

Holbrook, M. B. (1987) 'O, Consumer, How You've Changed: Some Radical Reflections on the Roots of Consumption'. In *Philosophical and Radical Thought in Marketing* (A. F. Firat et al., Eds). Lexington, MA: Lexington, pp. 137–177.

Holbrook, M. B. (1990) 'Presidential Address: The Role of Lyricism in Research on Consumer Emotions: Skylark, Have You Anything to Say to Me?' In *Advances in Consumer Research*, Vol. 17 (M. Goldberg et al., Eds). Provo, UT: Association for Consumer Research, pp. 1–18.

Holbrook, M. B., Chestnut, W., Oliva, T. A. and Greenleaf, E. A. (1984) 'Play as a Consumption Experience: The Roles of Emotions, Performance, and Personality in the Enjoyment of Games'. *Journal of Consumer Research* 11 (September): 728–739.

Holbrook, M. B. and Hirschman, E. (1982) 'The Experiential Aspects of Consumption: Consumer Fantasies, Feelings, and Fun'. *Journal of Consumer Research* 9 (September): 132–140.

Holbrook, M. B. and Zirlin, R. B. (1985) 'Artistic Creation, Artworks, and Esthetic Appreciation: Some Philosophical Contributions to Nonprofit Marketing'. In *Advances in Nonprofit Marketing*, Vol. 1 (R. W. Belk, Ed.). Greenwich, CT: JAI Press, pp. 1–54.

Hollenhorst, S. and Olson, D. (1990) 'Trends in Organizational and Institutional Use of Wilderness: The Case of the Boundary Waters Canoe Area Wilderness'. Paper presented at Outdoor Recreation TRENDS Symposium III, Indianapolis.

Howard, G. S. (1991) 'Culture Tales: A Narrative Approach to Thinking, Cross-cultural Psychology and Psychotherapy'. *American Psychologist* **46** (March): 187–197.

Johnson, D. M. (1981) 'Disney World as Structure and Symbol: Re-creation of the American Experience'. *Journal of Popular Culture* **15**(1): 157–165.

Kapferer, B. (1986) 'Performance and the Structuring of Meaning and Experience'. In *The Anthropology of Experience* (V. W. Turner and E. M. Bruner, Eds). Urbana: University of Illinois Press, pp. 188–206.

King, M. J. (1981) 'Disneyland and Walt Disney World: Traditional Values in Futuristic Form'. *Journal of Popular Culture* **15**(1): 116–140.

King, S. and Straub, P. (1984) *The Talisman*. New York: Viking.

Klaus, P. G. (1985) 'Quality Epiphenomenon: The Conceptual Understanding of Quality in Face-to-Face Service Encounters'. In *The Service Encounter: Managing Employee/Customer Interaction in Service Businesses* (J. A. Czepiel *et al.*, Eds). Lexington, MA: Lexington, pp. 17–33.

Klausner, S. Z. (Ed.) (1968) *Why Man Takes Chances: Studies in Stress-Seeking/* Garden City, NY: Doubleday.

Kottak, C. (1982) *Cultural Anthropology*. New York: Random House.

Krippendorf, J. (1987) *The Holiday Makers: Understanding the Impact of Leisure and Travel.* Oxford: Heineman Professional.

Lyng, S. G. (1990) 'Edgework: A Social Psychological Analysis of Voluntary Risk Taking'. *American Journal of Sociology* **95**(4): 851–886.

MacCannell, D. (1989) *The Tourist: A New Theory of the Leisured Class.* New York: Schocken.

Mars, G. and Nicod, M. (1984) *The World of Waiters.* London: Allen & Unwin.

Martin, W. B. (1986) *Quality Service: The Restaurant Manager's Bible.* Ithaca, NY: Cornell School of Hotel Administration.

Maslow, A. (1964) *Religions, Values, and Peak-Experiences.* Columbus: Ohio State University Press.

Mason, C. H. and Perreault, W. D., Jr. (1991) 'Collinearity, Power, and Interpretation of Multiple Regression Analysis'. *Journal of Marketing Research* **28** (August): 268–280.

McCallum, J. R. and Harrison, W. (1985) 'Inter-dependence in the Service Encounter'. In *The Service Encounter: Managing Employee/Customer Interaction in Service Businesses* (J. A. Czepiel *et al.*, Eds). Lexington, MA: Lexington, pp. 35–48.

Mills, P. K. and Morris, J. H. (1986) 'Clients as "Partial" Employees of Service Organizations: Role Development in Client Participation'. *Academy of Management Review* **11**(4): 726–735.

Mohr, L. A. and Bitner, M. J. (1991) 'Mutual Understanding between Customers and Employees in Service Encounters'. In *Advances in Consumer Research*, Vol. 18 (M. Solomon and R. Holman, Eds). Provo, UT: Association for Consumer Research, pp. 611–617.

Moore, A. (1980) 'Walt Disney World: Bounded Ritual Space and the Playful Pilgrimage Center'. *Anthropological Quarterly* **53** (October): 207–218.

Nisbett, R. E. and Ross, L. (1980) *Human Inference: Strategies and Shortcomings of Social Judgment.* Englewood Cliffs, NJ: Prentice-Hall.

O'Guinn, T. C. and Belk, R. W. (1989) 'Heaven on Earth: Consumption at Heritage Village, USA'. *Journal of Consumer Research* **16** (September): 227–238.

Oliver, R. L. and DeSarbo, W. S. (1988) 'Response Determinants in Satisfaction Judgments'. *Journal of Consumer Research* **14** (March): 495–507.

Parasuraman, A., Zeithaml, V. A. and Berry, L. L. (1985) 'A Conceptual Model of Service Quality and Its Implications for Future Research'. *Journal of Marketing* **49** (Fall): 41–50.

Parasuraman, A., Zeithaml, V. A. and Berry, L. L. (1988) 'SERQUAL: A Multiple-Item Scale for Measuring Consumer Perceptions of Service Quality'. *Journal of Retailing* **64**(1): 12–40.

Paules, G. F. (1991) *Dishing It Out: Power and Resistance among Waitresses in a New Jersey Restaurant.* Philadelphia: Temple University Press.

Peters, T. J. and Austin, N. (1985) *A Passion for Excellence.* New York: Random House.

Privette, G. (1983) 'Peak Experience, Peak Performance, and Flow: A Comparative Analysis of Positive Human Experiences'. *Journal of Personality and Social Psychology* **45**(6): 1361–1368.

Rafaeli, A. (1989) 'When Cashiers Meet Customers: An Analysis of the Role of Supermarket Cashiers'. *Academy of Management Journal* **32**(2): 245–273.

Rafaeli, A. and Sutton, R. I. (1987) 'Expression of Emotion as Part of the Work Role'. *Academy of Management Review* **12**(1): 23–37.

Redfoot, D. L. (1984) 'Touristic Authenticity, Touristic Angst and Modern Reality'. *Qualitative Sociology* **7** (Winter): 291–309.

Roggenbuck, J. W., William, D. R., Bange, S. P. and Dean, D. J. (1991) 'River Float Trip Encounter, Norms: Questioning the Use of the Social Norms Concept'. *Journal of Leisure Research* **23**(2): 133–153.

Romm, D. (1989) '"Restauration" Theater: Giving Direction to Service". *The Cornell Hotel and Restaurant Association Quarterly* **29** (February): 31–39.

Sarbin, T. R. (1986) *Narrative Psychology: The Storied Nature of Human Conduct.* New York: Praeger.

Shelby, B. Bregenzer, S. and Johnson, R. (1988) 'Displacement and Product Shift: Empirical Evidence from Oregon Rivers'. *Journal of Leisure Research* **20**(4): 274–288.

Shostack, G. L. (1987) 'Service Positioning through Structural Change'. *Journal of Marketing* **51** (January): 34–43.

Shott, S. (1979) 'Emotion and Social Life: A Symbolic Interactionist Analysis'. *American Journal of Sociology* **84** (May): 1317–1334.

Siehl, C. Bowen, D. E. and Pearson, C. M. (1993) 'Service Encounters as Rites of Integration: An Information Processing Model'. *Organization Science* **3** (November): 537–555.

Solomon, J. (1988) *The Signs of Our Time.* New York: Harper & Row.

Spradley, J. P. and Mann, B. J. (1975) *The Cocktail Waitress: Woman's Work in a Man's World.* New York: Knopf.

Surprenant, C. and Solomon, M. (1987) 'Predictability and Personalization in the Service Encounter'. *Journal of Marketing* **51** (April): 86–96.

Sutton, R. and Rafaeli, A. (1988) 'Untangling the Relationship between Displayed Emotions and Organizational Sales: The Case of Convenience Stores'. *Academy of Management Journal* **31**(3): 461–487.

Trice, H. M. and Beyer, J. M. (1991) 'Cultural Leadership in Organizations'. *Organization Science* **2** (May): 149–169.

Turner, V. W. (1969) *The Ritual Process.* Chicago: Aldine.

Turner, V. W. (1974) 'Social Dramas and Ritual Metaphors'. In *Dramas, Fields, and Metaphors.* Ithaca, NY: Cornell University Press, pp. 23–59.

Unger, L. S. and Kernan, J. B. (1983) 'On the Meaning of Leisure: An Investigation of Some Determinants of the Subjective Experience'. *Journal of Consumer Research* **9** (March): 381–392.

Urry, J. (1990) *The Tourist Gaze: Leisure in Contemporary Societies.* Beverly Hills, CA: Sage.

van Gennep, A. (1960) *The Rites of Passage,* trans. Monika B. Vizedom and Gabrielle L. Caffee, Chicago: University of Chicago Press.

van Maanen, J. and Kunda, G. (1989) 'Real Feelings: Emotional Expression and Organizational Culture'. In *Research in Organizational Behavior,* Vol. 11. (L. L. Cummings and B. M. Staw, Eds). Greenwich, CT: JAI Press, pp. 43–104.

Zeithaml, V. A., Berry, L. L. and Parasuraman, A. (1987) 'Communication and Control Processes in the Delivery of Service Quality'. Marketing Science Institute Working Paper, Report No. 87-100. Cambridge, MA: Marketing Science Institute.

24

Service Breakdowns: A Study of Critical Incidents in an Airline

Bo Edvardsson

INTRODUCTION

Many executives see quality as the cornerstone or driving force for improving competitiveness, customer satisfaction and profitability. Since the service sector is of such importance for the community – in the Organization for Economic Co-operation and Development (OECD) countries about 70% are employed in the service sector – it is essential to create a basis for developing quality in services. By this I mean both methods for studying quality in services and empirical results which will reveal the somewhat special nature of quality issues in services.

Quality defects cause service companies considerable costs. What it costs is not quality but lack of quality. Getting it right from the start, the zero fault strategy, has become the lodestar for the leading companies. In service companies it is estimated that as much as 35% of the staff are employed in 'correcting the mistakes made by the others'.[1] Crosby sees three factors as being particularly important for profitability. First, high quality means that the company can charge a higher price. Second, high quality entails lower costs and thus higher income. Third, those companies which are known for high quality have a considerable advantage when it comes to image. This gives them a competitive edge. Thus quality development leads not only to reduced costs and increased productivity but also to more satisfied customers, and all these factors improve profitability.

To be able to study quality in service companies, one must first be aware of the characteristic features of services and service production. Service is not a uniform concept.[2,3-6] There are great differences between different kinds of services, between, for instance, cleaning and security services, educational services, health care services and consultancy services. Despite these major differences as regards the degree of standardization or labour and capital intensity, etc., services have certain features in common. The most important of these, from a management perspective, are that:

● The customer often participates directly and actively in the production process as co-producer;

Reprinted with permission from *International Journal of Service Industry Management*, Vol. 3, No. 4, pp. 17–29
© 1992 MCB University Press

- Services are often abstract, which makes them difficult for the supplier to explain and for the customer to assess;
- Many non-standardized services are very closely linked with the service provider as an individual, his knowledge, behaviour, commitment and approach, etc.;
- Services are often made up of a sub-system of services, and quality depends on how the customer perceives the whole.

The fact that services often arise in the interaction between individuals and that the customer often participates in the production process, leads to special quality management problems. One aspect of this is that the service producer is unable to control all the conditions and factors affecting quality, with the result that the quality may be uneven.

The interaction between the company's employees and the customer is usually termed the moment of truth[7] or the service encounter.[3,8] The service arises in the interaction between customer and staff. Each situation is unique, provided that the contact between the actors is not automatized. The customer's perception of these encounters is a crucial component in the evaluation of the quality of the service.[9,10]

Service quality may be said to be of two kinds:[11] the quality of a 'normal' service and the quality of the 'exception', i.e. when critical incidents occur. It is only when the customer fails to get what he had expected that he becomes aware of what he usually gets.[12]

The customer has certain service level expectations. Parasuraman et al.[13] make a distinction between adequate and desired service level. Separating the desired an adequate service level is a zone of tolerance. 'The zone of tolerance expands and contracts like an accordion. It can vary from customer to customer and, potentially, from one situation to the next for the same customer' (p. 42). In deviant situations – moments of truth below the tolerance zone – quality perceptions are formed which remain in the customer's long-term memory. They also provide the service supplier with a golden opportunity to turn dissatisfaction into something positive by skilful and professional handling of the situation. If he fails to do this, the result may be great dissatisfaction and a broken relationship. Further, he may gain a negative reputation in the market.

The customer may reconsider his attitudes and expectations on the basis of negative critical incidents caused by defective details in service delivery. To improve quality and build up trustful and strong customer relations, it is important therefore to attend to faulty details which result in negative critical incidents in service production.[4,14]

For an incident to be defined as critical, the requirement is that it can be described in detail and that it deviates significantly, either positively or negatively, from what is normal or expected. In this study we consider only negative critical incidents, i.e. customer encounters which do not proceed normally but create friction, irritation and dissatisfaction.

DISCUSSION OF METHODS

Since services are processes, a method of describing the process aspect of service production and of providing detailed information about critical incidents is needed.

The critical incident technique (CIT) captures part of the process, in some cases a very small part. The method enables us to investigate and gain a greater understanding of situations where quality fails, i.e. where a critical incident occurs. CIT was presented for the first time by Flanagan[15] in an article in the *Psychological Bulletin*. Flanagan developed the technique to define the critical requirements for certain key positions in the American Air Force. It has since been used in a variety of contexts, including the study of quality failures in the service field.[10,16–18]

Data on critical incidents can be collected in several ways. It is essential to gain access to[19] and 'get close' to the phenomenon to be studied. Among the data collection techniques which can be used are personal interviews, focus group interviews and direct or participatory observation. It is most important and at the same time difficult to gain access to the phenomena being studied.[19] As argued by Olsen[20] only the actors, in this case customers and staff, are able to describe their experience of critical incidents in service processes. I agree with the conclusions in the extensive research by Andersson and Nilsson,[21] that the personal interview is usually preferable due to 'depth' and 'richness' in the data collected.

Flanagan maintains that is is not collecting the data which is most problematic but interpreting them and developing systems of classification. I would like to stress the importance of theoretical sensitivity in making interpretations.[22] Another key concept is pre-understanding, which may consciously steer interpretation, but at the same time an understanding of the context may aid interpretation and lead to an even greater understanding. The emphasis on interpretation means that the researcher adopts a phenomenological/hermeneutic approach: ' . . . the phenomenologist is committed to understanding social phenomena from the actor's own perspective. He or she examines how the world is experienced. The important reality is what people perceive it to be' (ref. 23, p. 2). Ödman[24] makes the distinction that phenomenology focuses on 'the immediate phenomena of human experience, such as thinking and feeling' while hermeneutics 'is more context directed'.

The main advantage of CIT is that it generates detailed process descriptions of critical incidents as those interviewed, e.g. customers, perceive them. The customer has the opportunity of describing the situation in his own words. The accounts given describe microprocesses in the relationship between the service producer and the customer. The weakness of the method is primarily that the interviewer can filter, misrepresent or unconsciously misunderstand the respondent, which is true for all 'verbal' methods.

To ensure as good responses as possible, it is essential for the interviewer to be fully conversant with the service and the service company being studied. At the same time there is a danger that the interviewer's pre-understanding or preconceived opinions may steer the collection of the data. To obtain good validity, it is necessary to describe, as unambiguously as possible, what is meant by critical incident in the study in question, preferably providing exemplification. Further, it is essential to ask about individual, specific incidents which the interviewee remembers well and to ask follow-up questions to ensure the interviewee has given a both comprehensive and detailed account of the incident in question. The account should be written down directly and even read back to the interviewee to check that it is correct and complete.

To help the interviewer, a simple model of a critical incident – e.g. cause, course and result – may be used as a sort of interview guide. The analysis and interpretation of the accounts generated is an ongoing process. The incidents are classified, and gradually a pattern and thus a classification scheme emerges. It does not seem to be a good idea to use a previously established set of categories for classifying critical incidents, as Stauss and Hentschel[25] do.

The analysis is inductive and partly subjective as in all qualitative research. When it is felt that a sufficient degree of saturation and stability has been attained in the data, no more data are collected. The incidents may be classified in several ways. How this is done purely practically is primarily determined by the purpose of the survey and the researcher's interests. He may wish to emphasize typical incidents, particularly 'living' descriptions which are highlighted or limited, but recurrent factors, e.g. those which cause critical incidents or are the source of them.

The collection of the data raises several issues which must be resolved in the light of the aim and purpose of the study. These include, for instance, the place where the interviews are to be conducted, the topicality of the incident, who should be selected to provide information, and who should conduct the interviews. When, for example, students collect data, it is crucial that they understand both the point of the study and CIT and that detailed situation-related instructions for collecting data have been prepared and learnt. Andersson and Nilsson[21] describe the correct procedure.

'Individual interviews should be conducted on the basis of previously determined models. Having stated the goal, the point of the interview, and having taken up the question of anonymity, etc., the interviewer asks about incidents when especially efficient/inefficient behaviour has been observed' (p. 30). 'Naturally there is no general form for collecting critical incidents. Interview questionnaires must be devised for each particular survey in accordance with the preconditions and aim' (p. 31).

DATA COLLECTION AND ANALYTICAL MODEL

During the autumn of 1989 four students under my supervision made a survey of critical incidents in an airline. The study highlighted the cause, course and result of these critical incidents (Figure 1).

Only negative critical incidents were studied. The sample consisted of 320 business passengers and 80 employees representing front staff. The selection of interviewees and critical incidents was based on certain criteria. The requirement as regards the business passengers was that they had experienced the incident themselves and that it has occurred during the last two years while they were travelling on business. The respondents were selected at random at four different airports. The data were collected at different times over the course of a month. The respondents were each

Figure 1.   Model of a critical incident.

asked to give information about two critical incidents. As regards airline staff, the requirement was that they worked in the front office and had been employed for at least six months, and that the incidents had occurred during the last two years. Furthermore, the critical incident was to be seen from the perspective of the business passenger.

Interviewing both employees and customers in order to compare their views is quite rare. The advantage of including both customers and employees is that it enables the researcher to identify possible differences in their attitudes to ordinary problems in the service offering.[26]

The method used to collect the data was the personal interview where the respondent was asked to recount in detail, in his own words, a critical incident he had experienced. The interviews were conducted at four airports with two students acting as interviewers and two others keeping a record. The accounts were between a half and one page in length.

The students classified the critical incidents independently of each other. Where differences occurred, they were resolved through discussion. Flanagan claims that the decisive test of whether an incident may be adjudged a fact is whether the observation is 'objective' in terms of the probability that different interviewers would arrive at the same result. In our case the majority, or about 90% of the critical incidents, were classified in the same way.

The analysis began with a careful scrutiny of the accounts of the critical incidents. This revealed certain clear patterns in the material, which make it possible and meaningful to classify the incidents in accordance with the model. The causes of the critical incidents could be divided into source (= where) and type (= what). During the course of the critical incident a certain tendency as regards passivity or activity on the part of the two parties, the customer and the service provider, could be distinguished. The result of the critical incident as regards customer relations could be classified as a strengthened, unchanged, weakened or broken relation with the airline.

The critical incidents were classified into main categories and sub-categories. An example of a main category is air transport, which concerns critical incidents occurring at the airport or on board the aircraft; the sub-categories here are: delayed flight, cancelled flight, delayed luggage, overbooking and lack of information.

I have chosen to present the results in table form and by means of some illustrative examples. The results of the interviews with business passengers are presented first, followed by employees' accounts.

RESULTS – BUSINESS PASSENGERS

Cause

The most common source of critical incidents in the view of the business passengers interviewed is related to air transport, i.e. what happens at the airport or on board the aircraft (Table 1). The conditions causing the critical incident are ranked on the following descending scale: delays (114), cancelled flights (112), delayed or damaged luggage (26), overbookings (14) and other sources (8). The first two factors account for 82% of the dissatisfaction. When it comes to ground transport, the critical incidents are often the result of the airport taxi being late or not coming at all.

Course

Table 2 shows that in most cases the business passengers said that they were passive, i.e. they did not do anything to try and resolve the problems resulting from the critical incident. They appeared to have confidence in the employees, expecting them to sort out the problems. This seems quite natural. Most people deem it impossible to do anything about the weather or technical problems with an aircraft.

Results

Table 3 shows that in 80% of the cases the critical incidents studied resulted in unchanged customer relations. In 16% of the cases the critical incidents resulted in a weakened and in 4% of the cases in a strengthened relationship as perceived by the

Table 1.   Business passengers' perception of the source of critical incidents

	Number	Proportion (%)
Air transport	274	85.6
Ground transport	32	10.0
Other incidents	14	4.4

Table 2.   The actions of the business passengers

	Number	Proportion (%)
Active	76	23.8
Passive	244	76.2

Table 3.   The effect of the critical incident on the business passengers' relations with the airline

	Number	Proportion (%)
Relation broken	8	2.5
Relation weakened	42	13.1
Relation unchanged	256	80.0
Relation strengthened	14	4.4

business passengers. Thus the airline was in many cases able to deal with the situation in a satisfactory manner from the customer's viewpoint. In the following section a number of individual incidents are presented in order to illustrate the problems of facing an airline. The low proportion of broken relations may presumably be explained by the fact that the airline has in principle a monopoly.

AN EXAMPLE OF A CRITICAL INCIDENT INVOLVING DELAY

Delays are the most frequent causes of critical incidents in air transport. In this specific instance the business passenger was delayed by a 'technical fault'. The staff were alert and exercised their authority to issue vouchers. However, dissatisfaction arose because insufficient information was given about the delay. The expression 'technical fault' was felt to be very diffuse and created much irritation. The situation resulted in a weakening of the relations with the airline. The business passenger claimed that 'if the airline explained why the plane was delayed, it would increase the passenger's willingness to accept the situation'.

AN EXAMPLE OF A CRITICAL INCIDENT INVOLVING A CANCELLED FLIGHT

The next most common cause of critical incidents after delays is cancelled flights. Cancellation is often due to technical faults or bad weather. The situation described below occurred when a business passenger's flight was cancelled because of a technical fault. The passenger was convinced that the reason for the cancellation was that there were too few passengers booked on the flight. The process can be briefly described as follows: initially, insufficient information was provided as to the cause of the delay; when the flight was later cancelled, the businessman was very annoyed. He had lost valuable time for work and the staff 'did not care' and their attitude was 'disgraceful'. The incident resulted in a negative attitude towards the airline. The man pointed out that time was most important to him as a businessman. 'If the airline cancels too many planes, in the end you lose patience and take the train instead.'

AN EXAMPLE OF A CRITICAL INCIDENT RELATING TO THE AIRPORT TAXI

The airline provides ground transport such as airport buses and taxis for its passengers. The critical event in question was caused by a lack of service on the part of the taxi company. The passenger missed his flight because the taxi which had been ordered earlier did not come. The result was that the businessman was unable to attend an important meeting with a customer, and his relationship with the airline was weakened. The staff did not attempt to assist him to resolve the problem by arranging alternative transport. The ironic comment from the passenger was telling: 'It is exciting every time I order an airport taxi'. The airline did not accept responsibility for the situation, and the passenger received no compensation for the inconvenience.

RESULTS – AIRLINE STAFF

Cause

The staff believed that 72% of the critical incidents arose in connection with air transport (Table 4). The 58 critical incidents related to 'Air transport' are ranked on the following descending scale: delayed or damaged luggage (26), cancelled flights (14), delays (12), overbookings (4) and other sources (2). The first two factors account for 69% of the dissatisfaction. When it comes to ground transport, the critical incidents are often the result of the airport taxi being late or not coming at all.

Course

Table 5 indicates that 85% of the staff said they were active in trying to resolve the critical incidents. They felt they were helpful and tried to reduce irritation by compensating business passengers with vouchers.

Table 4.   Staff perception of the source of critical incidents

	Number	Proportion (%)
Air transport	58	72.5
Ground transport	12	15.0
Other incidents	10	12.5

Table 5.   The staff view of their actions

	Number	Proportion (%)
Active	68	85.0
Passive	12	15.0

Results

Table 6 shows that as much as 20% of the critical incidents – by the staff interviewed – resulted in a strengthened relationship between the business passengers and the airline. This may be compared with the customers' view (see Table 3) where we find that only 4% perceived the relationship to be strengthened.

Table 6.   The effect of the critical incident on the business
passenger's relations with the airline (according to staff)

	Number	Proportion (%)
Relation broken	0	0
Relation weakened	16	20
Relation unchanged	48	60
Relation strengthened	16	20

AN EXAMPLE OF A CRITICAL INCIDENT CONCERNING LUGGAGE

From the staff viewpoint lost luggage is the factor which is though to create most
critical incidents for business passengers. In the case in question the passenger
checked in his luggage in the usual manner. On arrival at his destination the suitcase
had disappeared. The passenger, who was extremely annoyed, started to abuse the
staff, calling them all kinds of names. The staff felt that the result of the incident was
a very dissatisfied passenger, with weakened relations with the airline as a result.
However, the suitcase turned up and was taken to the owner by taxi.

AN EXAMPLE OF A CRITICAL INCIDENT CONCERNING A CANCELLED FLIGHT

According to staff, cancelled flights are a common cause of irritation among business
passengers. In this case the cancellation was due to bad weather. On the particular
occasion in question four planes were due to depart at the same time but only one
could take off. The course of the incident may be described as follows. The
passengers were informed via loudspeakers that those who had international flights
were to go on board first. Chaos broke out and several business passengers who did
not have international tickets rushed to the counter and the tumult resulted in a
VDU falling to the floor. However, the passengers received no information and they
finally realized that they had no chance of getting on the flight. The staff learnt,
among other things, that a well-organized queue system was necessary in such cases.

ANALYSIS

The survey shows that there is a considerable difference between the ways business
passengers and staff perceive the causes and handling of critical incidents. The chi-
square test based on 'Cause' (air transport, ground transport and other incidents)
show that there is a statistically significant difference. The chi-square value is 9.82 and
the p value .0074. If we look at the subcategories making up 'Air transport' (delayed

luggage, cancelled flight, delays and other sources) our data show a statistically significant difference between the two groups. The chi-square value is 47.52 and the p value $< .00000$. The former saw delays and cancellations as the most common problems, while the latter thought that the majority of the critical incidents were caused by delayed or damaged luggage.

We also find a statistically significant difference between the business passengers' and the staff's perception of the critical incidents effect on the customers' relationship with the airline (broken, weakened, unchanged or strengthened). The staff interviewed are more positive than the business passengers. The chi-square value is 24.94 and the p value .000004.

It emerges from the study, then, that collecting information from the front line staff will not enable us to grasp the customers' perceptions of quality failures. This does not mean, however, that information from front line staff is valueless. Several researchers, e.g. Schneider and Bowen[27] and CEOs such as Carlzon[28] maintain that the 'psychological closeness' between front line staff and customers means that there is much valuable information on customer needs, wishes and expectations to be gathered from the service company's contact staff. On the other hand, there is also research which shows that customers and staff have different views about what creates dissatisfaction.[26,29] My results indicate how important it is to collect data about lapses in quality directly from the customer in order to gain an understanding of quality defects and to develop quality in the right areas.

The study also shows that staff are now aware of the importance of clear and correct information when critical incidents occur. The customer needs to know why there is a problem and what the likely outcome is, the latter in order to be able to decide how to act. It is a matter of providing the customer with the opportunity of being able to influence his own situation (compare the discussion on perceived control, in refs. 2, ch. 3, p. 30). Instead of announcing the cancellation of a flight due to a technical fault over the loudspeaker system, the situation could be dealt with in the following way: the captain, or another reliable person, goes into the departure lounge and meets the passengers. He apologises for the delay and explains what has happened: a punctured nose-wheel or damaged rudder, etc. Then he provides an estimate of how long it is likely to take to repair the damage, informs passengers of alternative means of transport: changing flights, bus or train, etc. and perhaps provides some form of compensation for the delay: a cup of coffee for instance.

One of the conclusions to be drawn from the study is that the airline should train its own staff in the techniques of communication and how to relate to customers when critical incidents occur. Several of those interviewed did not believe the information they received. 'They're lying again when they say it is a technical fault. There are in fact too few passengers, and the flight will lose money. But they won't admit that'.

Further, several of those interviewed felt the information to be insufficient and late (not enough information about 'why things are as they are and about what is going to happen'). Credible, clear and rapid information emerges as an important source of customer perceived quality. The study shows that reliable core services, confidence-inspiring, i.e. knowledgeable and motivated staff, who show empathy and are able to communicate with and look after customers, and deal with complaints in critical situations, are the most important quality creating resources.

Another result of the study is that the undertakings given in publicity material, etc.

are not always fulfilled and this produces irritation and perhaps heightens the customer's dissatisfaction in critical situations. The airline is marketed as the quickest and most time-saving means of transport. The customer should perhaps be informed via the publicity material that technical faults sometimes occur, leading to delays and that the weather may also lead to delays or cancellations. The marketing of services should not only clarify and make concrete the features and value of the service but also steer customer expectations so that they are at the 'right level' in relation to what the service provider can achieve. In this way it might be possible to prevent critical incidents or, perhaps more importantly, reduce dissatisfaction when a critical incident does occur.

In those situations where the business passenger is affected by delays, the results of the study highlight the importance of committed and knowledgeable staff who have the authority to act. If the customer is met with initiative and commitment, a negative situation can be turned into something positive. Even in this respect some form of education and practical training is necessary to provide staff with a greater understanding of what shapes customers' expectations and perception of quality. This should contribute to more professional crisis management.

In order to maintain a high level of service, it would seem necessary to develop more customer-oriented complaint management. Interviews with business passengers and the airline's complaints department indicate that complaints procedures are often felt to be complicated and time-consuming by passengers.

Finally, better co-ordinated activities between the airline and the companies providing ground transport is required. The offering or service system should be so designed that the different customer needs are satisfied. The core service is often described in terms of the flight. But a number of support services are required to meet the needs of the customer in connection with the flight. Transport to and from the airport is an essential part of the total service package and is often experienced as an integrated part of the core service.

DISCUSSION AND SUGGESTIONS FOR FURTHER RESEARCH

In the introduction I observed that the aim of the article was to contribute to a greater understanding of how to manage critical incidents. The study shows that CIT is a useful tool, and that is provides interesting and meaningful information about customers. It is also a helpful tool when it comes to involving staff in further quality work.

Furthermore, it is perfectly satisfactory to allow students to collect data, provided they are given an opportunity to learn about the purpose of the study and about CIT, are given clear instructions and work closely with a supervisor. The difficulty with CIT is primarily associated with classifying and interpreting the incidents. This can, of course, be done in more than one way, and different researchers would probably reach different conclusions, but the core content should be the same. To prevent preconceived ideas and predetermined interpretative frameworks from steering the analysis, the classification should be carried out by two people separately. Differences of classification can be resolved by discussions, which may result in new categories being established.

In an article in the *Journal of Marketing*, Bitner *et al.*[10] report the results of a number of American studies of service quality in which CIT has been used. The analysis is based on data from 700 incidents in three service areas: airlines, hotels and restaurants. In Edvardsson[18] I report the results of a survey of 205 service-related critical incidents in sales processes in mechanical engineering companies in Sweden. Both these studies show similar results to those in this article. CIT has proved to be a useful and suitable method of identifying and analysing defects in service quality. The importance of committing oneself to the customer and of providing clear and 'truthful' information is a recurrent result. This is also supported by Stauss and Hentschel,[25] who interviewed 321 garage customers in Germany. Altogether data on 599 positive and negative incidents were collected. The results showed, among other things, that negative critical incidents affected customer behaviour and, in the first place, led to complaints, reduced willingness to return to the company and to the spread of negative comments about the company in question by ten people on average.

Placing the customer in the centre makes customer care and complaint management an important aspect of quality development. However, in most companies marketing is primarily concerned with identifying and attracting new customers. It is only recently that attention has also been directed to looking after existing customers in a purposeful and systematic manner. In this context CIT has proved to be a useful tool for determining why the customer is satisfied or not with a certain service or service company. Facts about customer dissatisfaction and the causes of critical incidents are an important part of the basis for continuous quality improvement.

I would therefore like to stress the importance of the following for quality development:

- Highlighting the personal quality of the staff.
- Being actively considerate towards existing customers.
- Being sensitive to signals of dissatisfaction by 'reading' customers and thus discovering quality defects before the customer complains, and making it easier for the customer to complain.
- Looking after the customer and correcting faults which have arisen.
- Providing generous compensation.
- Providing clear, rapid and 'truthful' information.

Service quality is a matter of controlling details in the service delivery. Thus quality development means improving all the parts of the service chain and seeing the whole. Far too many companies work on the detail 'the encounter with the customer' but really they should be studying critical incidents in the whole production chain. From the customer's perspective it is essential that the whole service process functions properly.

An important task for management-oriented quality research is to study the service chain in detail and identify critical points in the process. This should provide a basis for changes in the chain in an effort to achieve zero faults, i.e. the non-occurrence of critical incidents. Both new and better methods of analysis are needed for this as well as more in-depth and systematic empirical research focusing on the microprocesses. I believe it would be very useful to take critical incidents at different stages in the service chain and interview both customers and the staff involved about the same critical incident. The more we know about critical incidents in the whole service chain, the better the basis for further and continuous quality development.

REFERENCES

1. Crosby, P. B. (1980) *Quality is Free.* New York: New American Library.
2. Grönroos, C. (1990) *Service Management and Marketing Managing the Moments of Truth in Service Competition.* Lexington, MA: Lexington Books.
3. Edvardsson, B. and Thomasson, B. (1989) *Kvalitetsutveckling i privata och offentliga tjänsteföretag.* Stockholm: Natur och Kultur (in Swedish).
4. Edvardsson, B. and Thomasson, B. (1991) *Kvalitetsutveckling – ett managementperspektiv,* Lund: Studentlitteratur (in Swedish).
5. Gummesson, E. (1991) 'Service Quality – A Holistic View'. In *Service Quality Multidisciplinary and Multinational Perspectives* (S. W. Brown, E. Gummesson, B. Edvardsson and B. O. Gustavsson, Eds). New York: Lexington Books.
6. Gummesson, E. (1991) 'Kvalitetsstyrning i tjänste- och serviceverksamheter. Tolkning av fenomenet tjänstekvalitet och syntes av internationell forskning'. Forskningsrapoort Centrum för tjänsteforskning – CTF, Högskolan i Karlstad (in Swedish).
7. Normann, R. (1983) *Service Management.* Lund: Liber.
8. Czepiel, J., Solomon, M. R. and Surprenant, C. F. (1985) *The Service Encounter.* New York: Lexington Books.
9. Bitner, M. J. (1988) 'A Model of Service Encounter and Marketing Mix Effects', paper presented at the QUIS – seminar, Service Research Center, CTF, Karlstad.
10. Bitner, M. J., Booms, H. B and Tetreault, M. S. (1990) 'The Service Encounter: Diagnosing Favorable and Unfavorable Incidents'. *Journal of Marketing* 54(1).
11. Berry, L., Zeithaml, V. and Parasuraman, A. (1985) 'Quality Counts in Services Too'. *Business Horizons* (May–June).
12. Levitt, T. (1984) *Lysande marknadsföring.* Stockholm: SvD förlag (in Swedish).
13. Parasuraman, A., Berry, L. L. and Zeithaml, V. (1991) 'Understanding Customer Expectations of Service'. *Sloan Management Review* (Spring).
14. Edvardsson, B. (1990) 'Management Consulting towards a Successful Relationship'. *International Journal of Service Industry Management* (No. 3).
15. Flanagan, J. C. (1954) 'The Critical Incident Technique'. *Psychological Bulletin* 51 (July).
16. Bitner, M. J., Jody, D., Nyquist, J. D. and Booms, B. H. (1985) 'The Critical Incident as a Technique for Analyzing the Service Encounter'. In *Services Marketing in a Changing Environment* (T. M. Bloch, G. D. Upah and V. A. Zeithaml, Eds). Chicago: American Marketing Association.
17. Bitner, M. J. (1990) 'Evaluating Service Encounters: The Effect of Physical Surrounding and Employee Responses'. *Journal of Marketing* 54 (No. 2).
18. Edvardsson, B. (1989) 'Critical Incidents in Customer Relationships. A Study of Mechanical Engineering Companies'. *The Service Industry Journal* (No. 4).
19. Gummesson, E. (1988) *Qualitative Methods in Management Research.* Lund: Studentlitteratur Chartwell-Bratt.
20. Olsen, M. (1992) 'Kvalitet i banktjänster'. Service Research Center – CTF, University of Karlstad, Karlstad, Diss. (In Swedish).
21. Andersson, B. -E. and Nilsson, S. -G. (1966) *Arbets-och utbildningsanalyser med hjälp av Critical Incident Metoden.* Göteborg: Akademiförlaget (in Swedish).
22. Glaser, B. (1978) *Theoretical Sensitivity.* Mill Valley, CA: The Sociology Press.
23. Taylor, S. and Bogdan, R. (1984) *Introduction to Qualitative Research Methods.* New York: Wiley.
24. Odman, P. -J. (1985) 'Hermeneutics'. In *The International Encyclopedia of Education* (T. Husén and N. Postlethwaite, Eds). Oxford: Pergamon Press.

25. Stauss, B. and Hentschel, B. (1991) 'Attribute-Based Versus Incident-Based Measurement of Service Quality: Results of an Empirical Study in the German Car Service Industry'. Paper presented at Workshop on Quality Management in Services, Brussels, 16–17 May.
26. Andersson, G. (1985) 'Kritiska händelser i banken'. Paper presented at the Second Nordic Meeting on Service Management. University of Lund, Lund (in Swedish).
27. Schneider, B. and Bowen, D. E. (1984) 'New Service Design, Development and Implementation and the Employee'. In *Developing New Services* (W. R. George and C. E. Marshall, Eds). Chicago: American Marketing Association.
28. Carlzon, J. (1987) *Moments of Truth.* Cambridge, MA: Ballinger.
29. Folkes, V. S. and Kotsos, B. (1986) 'Buyers' and Sellers' Explanations for Product Failure: Who Done It?' *Journal of Marketing* **50** (April).
30. Bateson, J. (1985) 'Perceived Control and the Service Encounter'. In *Services Marketing in a Changing Environment* (T. M. Bloch, G. D. Upah and V. A. Zeithaml, Eds). Chicago: American Marketing Association.

FURTHER READING

Brown, S. W., Gummesson, E. Edvardsson, B. and Gustavsson, B. O. (1991) *Service Quality Multidisciplinary and Multinational Perspectives.* New York: Lexington Books.
Edvardsson, B. (1988) 'Kritiska händelser i försäljningsprocessen – En studie av tjänstekopplade kritiska händelser inom verkstadsindustrin'. In *Management i Tjänstesamhället* (B. Edvardsson and E. Gummesson, Eds). Lund: Liber (in Swedish).
Nyquist, J. D., Bitner, M. J. and Booms, B. H. (1985) 'Identifying Communication Difficulties in the Service Encounter: A Critical Incident Approach'. In *The Service Encounter* (J. Czepiel, M. Solomon and C. Surprenant, Eds). Lexington, MA: Lexington Books.

25

Managing Quality in Business-to-Business Services

Isabelle T. D. Szmigin

This article puts forward the case for analysing service business clients' expectations of quality. It proposes that an ongoing survey of clients' expectations can play a useful role in the beneficial development and running of client/supplier relationships. A classification that encapsulates three aspects of quality is suggested which can act as the basis for an ongoing review of client/supplier relationships relevant to most business-to-business services. The three elements of the classification scheme are defined as 'hard', 'soft' and 'outcome' quality.

A relationship cycle is proposed which suggests the likely paths typical relationships may follow. It highlights problem areas and opportunities where attention to the client's needs and to the 'hard' and 'soft' quality elements, in particular, could help keep the relationship alive.

It is suggested that three factors underpin an understanding of the buyer's quality requirements in a business relationship:

1. An understanding of clients' perceptions of quality.
2. Clients' different quality priorities.
3. Clients' changing priorities, both over the duration of the relationship and within any given decision-making unit.

Thorough investigation of these areas could enable businesses to manage their relationships more profitably.

THE SHIFT FROM TRANSACTIONAL TO RELATIONSHIP MARKETING

Many service businesses depend on the successful formation and continued management of a buyer/supplier relationship. This may seem obvious for services of an inherently long-term nature, such as retail and corporate banking and advertising

Reprinted with permission from *European Journal of Marketing*, Vol. 27, No. 1, pp. 5–21
© 1993 MCB University Press

agencies, but it is also true of many other services as diverse as hairdressing and plumbing. All these will benefit from the development of a mutually satisfactory relationship, managed over time.

Gronroos[1] compares the relationship approach to marketing with the traditional transactional approach. The latter he identifies as being primarily focused on the marketing mix, where marketing specialists are the only people to have an impact on the customers' views of the firm and on their buying behaviour. Gronroos points to the service and industrial sectors as areas where the marketing mix approach does not adequately identify the range of resources and activities that appear in customer relationships at various stages of the customer relationship life cycle. Using examples such as waiters, air stewardesses, telephone receptionists and design engineers, he makes the point that marketing activity is spread throughout the entire organization and that its customers take an active part in the service production process.

The relationship approach to marketing revolves around the creation, maintenance and development of customer relationships, where the objectives of customers and sellers are met through various exchanges between the two sides, possibly with a variety of personnel from both. It recognizes the importance of businesses keeping existing customers and cross-selling to them rather than viewing customers as a series of discrete transactions. George[2] recognizes that one of the most important factors for success in relationship marketing will be a service marketing orientation among employees throughout the depth and breadth of an organization.

This is, if anything, even more vital for business-to-business services, where each side of the relationship may involve a number of diverse people from within, and even beyond, the organization. An advertising agency account team, for example, may include specifically trained and experienced account handlers who are used to the marketing role but also creative people, media buying specialists, planners and market researchers. It may also include receptionists and accounts personnel who may come into contact with the client and have an opportunity to help or hinder the relationship.

In the traditional professional service, such as accounting and the law, the client team may have no person specifically trained in the marketing role. Account handling is generally dealt with by a number of different professionals who manage the relationship and their company's day-to-day marketing, including cross-selling of services. Customers and sellers are many-headed.[3] This method reflects what has long been known about organizational buying behaviour. Both customers and sellers are likely to have complex decision-making units and the influences on any decision may even go beyond such units. Though it may not always be possible to identify the traditional roles of buyer, user, influencer, decision maker and gatekeeper of Webster and Wind,[4] the buying and selling centres in services are complex entities worthy of further consideration.

This may also go some way towards explaining the slow adoption of marketing by professional service firms in an increasingly deregulated market. This has been well documented[5] but, in many cases, it may not be so much due to the reactionary approach of such services as to marketing's reluctance to recognize that such firms have already adopted a form of relationship marketing which may be open to improvement but not to unnecessary reorganization.

THE INDUSTRIAL SECTOR AND RELATIONSHIP MARKETING

It is in the industrial sector where the literature on buyer/seller relationships is best developed: forces such as total quality management (TQM) and just-in-time (JIT) delivery have led both suppliers and clients to look closely at what are the best kind of relationships for them. In 1975, Guillet de Monthoux[6] outlined the bases for relationships in this sector when he used the analogy of courtship through marriage and even divorce to highlight the relationship process. His work not only revealed the potential benefits of a long relationship, especially in terms of the barriers it can provide against competition, but also some other aspects of the psychology of working within a relationship. For example, de Monthoux's research revealed that buyers, as well as suppliers, perceive the relationship as an investment in time and money and thus are unlikely to switch suppliers because of some short-term competitive advantage. Indeed, in some instances, buyers would prefer to engage in training programmes for their existing suppliers when problems occur. This is an important point because it highlights the willingness of some buyers to be involved in a process that may improve the relationship for both sides.

Once a relationship has reached this point, communications may actually increase between the buying and selling firms to further stabilize and build the relationship.[7] Barrett[8] takes this one step further when he quotes the hypothesis put forward by Homan, in 1954, that 'it is not people we like whom we interact with, rather we like the people we interact with'.[9] Barrett goes on to say that interactions develop into friendships, creating stronger partners. Part of this is possibly the Hawthorne effect at work: the very act of taking notice of us may improve the relationship and engender team spirit.[10]

The importance of developing buyer/seller relationships in the field of industrial products and services cannot be overestimated. These relationships may take many different forms and clearly involve costs as well as benefits. Dwyer et al.[11] suggest that the benefits of such a relationship include reduced uncertainty, exchange efficiency and social satisfaction, and it can insulate the seller from price competition. Costs can, however, outweigh the benefits. For example, a bad fit of customer and seller may lead to protracted negotiation. More generally, there is the opportunity cost of alternative exchanges or relationships. This may account for the reluctance of some firms to enter into such a relationship.

Relationships have to be managed and this takes time, money and commitment from the seller. Customers may find themselves wanting to commit themselves to a relationship but find sellers unwilling or unable to do so. Parasuraman et al.[12] found both consumer and business service customers wanting closer relationships with service providers but being disappointed. They point out that relationship building is 'process intensive'. It is the ongoing, day-to-day management of the relationship which is costly and time consuming and does not necessarily produce immediate results.

UNDERSTANDING QUALITY IN THE SERVICES SECTOR

There now exists a substantial body of research in the area of services quality, and Lewis[13] provides a substantial review. Different views have developed regarding customer evaluation of quality and the likely dimensions of quality. Le Blanc and Nguyen[14] have identified three principal schools of thought:

1. Quality may be implied through the tangible elements of the service, largely the physical environment.
2. Quality can be perceived through contact personnel, their attitudes and behaviour.
3. Perceived quality may be derived from the service encounter or the actual process of buying the service.

It is likely that consumers may also perceive quality in combinations of the above and that some services may be more likely to be judged by one method rather than another. Different types of transaction may be judged by different criteria within the same business. For example, in addition to the meal itself, quality in a restaurant may well be a combination of all three of the factors mentioned above: the ambience of the restaurant, largely received through the physical environment; the waiters as contact personnel; and the actual process, including getting your meal on time. Incidents that may occur during your stay in the restaurant are all likely to affect the overall evaluation of the service experience. On the other hand, a transaction from an automatic teller machine may only require that the process is satisfactory, i.e. the machine is working, does not require too much of the user and dispenses the money accurately. People are not involved in the transaction and the environment, usually a street or within a shop, is out of the control of the service management.

In business-to-business services, rather than looking for some objective measure of quality, it may be managerially more useful to identify the subjective components of quality of the service that are likely to satisfy the consumer – i.e. what is it about the service that satisfies them. This would be a large and costly task for retail services and, indeed, the likely heterogeneity of customers for many services might mean the variety of results would not make the exercise worthwhile. Here, pursuing some standard measuring scale such as SERVQUAL[15] certainly seems the most fruitful line of research to date. However, in business-to-business services, individual studies may yield a number of useful strategic results, both for the businesses concerned and also as the basis for further broader research.

IDENTIFYING THE CLIENT'S QUALITY AND SATISFACTION COMPONENTS

Gronroos[16] proposed two types of service quality: technical and functional. They both contribute to the perceived service quality. Gronroos points out that technical quality, e.g. a bank paying invoices promptly or transferring money from one account to another, etc., can be done by any bank, but that it is often the functional quality – attitudes, accessibility, appearance of the bank, service-mindedness of the contact personnel – that may ultimately influence a customer's choice of bank with which to do business. In other words, a certain level of technical quality would generally be assumed by potential clients. Technical quality can often be assessed in an objective manner, as any technical dimension of a product might be, whereas functional quality is perceived in a much more subjective way.

The make-up of quality along the technical and functional dimensions outlined by Gronroos has been furthered by other writers on services. Morgan[17] refers to process elements of service quality, i.e. how the service is delivered, staff/customer interaction, and outcome elements, i.e. what is actually received by the customer. Edvardsson[18] added integrative quality – the ease with which different portions of the service delivery system work together – and outcome quality – whether or not the actual service product meets both service standards of specifications and customer needs/expectations.

The Gronroos dual aspect of technical and functional quality is particularly well suited to act as a framework for the study of business service relationships. It could prove useful both for defining customer needs and for supplying corrective measures. As writers on organizational buying have already recognized,[19,20] purchasing is not a purely rational process and, as already pointed out, some clients get very close to their suppliers and work better with this kind of association. Recognizing such requirements could be particularly advantageous for firms able and willing to supply such a relationship.

However, discussions with service companies have revealed that the terms 'functional' and 'technical' are difficult to differentiate, while the terms 'hard' and 'soft' are easy to visualize for most managers. Indeed, work by Peters and Waterman[21] and Lessem,[22] where the term 'hard' has been used for features such as strategy, structure or systems and 'soft' for skills, staff or style, has in some ways made such terms easier to introduce in discussions with managers.

The terms 'hard' and 'soft' are used here therefore to refer to those quality elements identified by Gronroos as 'technical' and 'functional'.

Before looking at the implications of the above in more detail, it is worth introducing a third quality component at this point. This is basically the result of the relationship which will be referred to as 'outcome quality' as outlined by Edvardsson.[18] Outcome quality is different from hard quality in as much as a company may perform excellently in the hard area and still not achieve the desired goal or outcome. A merchant bank may perform well in all areas expected of it in a takeover bid, but the shareholders may still vote against the bid. A lawyer may present a superb case but the court can still rule against the client. An advertising agency may put together an advertising campaign which meets the brief in all particulars but it may still not achieve the company's objectives. One of the important aspects that differentiates outcome quality from the other two areas of quality mentioned is that it cannot always be controlled by the companies in the relationship. It is susceptible to outside pressures and environmental conditions, but it is still a part of the overall quality on which a supplier will be judged and which will relate to overall satisfaction with the relationship.

During the period of a business relationship it is likely that both aspects of quality, the hard and soft, are likely to be tested; invoices may not always be paid promptly, a bank transfer may go astray. These are usually errors rather than the norm and are likely to be perceived as such by the client, as long as they do not become too frequent, when they probably would begin to affect the overall relationship. Similarly, at the beginning of a relationship with a new client, service personnel may be keen to be as helpful as possible but, as time goes on and new business needs to be won, long-standing customers can be taken for granted and soft quality may decline.

Over time, the client's requirements regarding the relationship may well change.

Business objectives, changes in personnel, differing competitive situations, may all lead to changes in what is required from the supplier. Successful management of the relationship over time does depend to a large extent on successfully understanding and managing the client's changing requirements with regard to hard and soft quality.

Hard and soft quality affect the day-to-day running of a relationship and they affect one another. If the soft aspects of the relationship are going well, it is likely that some hard errors will be allowed and vice versa. The long-term health of a relationship will ultimately depend on outcome quality, although this may be balanced by the hard and soft input. If day-to-day service is going badly, however, the relationship may well be curtailed before outcome quality has an opportunity to influence the relationship. Similarly, companies do not often sack their legal advisers or merchant bank if they fail in one project when the hard and soft aspects of the transaction were perceived by management to be of a high quality. But a number of outcome quality failures may change their perceptions of the relationship, however satisfactory the day-to-day running of the relationship is.

Figure 1 attempts to chart the various interactions involved in relationship quality and their importance of the maintenance of a successful long-term relationship. The term 'process satisfaction' is suggested to convey the day-to-day running of a business relationship, where the various interactions between the client and the service firms, and within these firms, help to build up or to erode the relationship. These are essentially the hard and soft quality components.

The idea of process satisfaction builds on the importance of the internal customer as part of the process, and introduces the external customer as part of this same process. Gummeson[23] illustrates the importance of the internal process by referring to Kaoru Ishikawa who, in the 1950s, used the slogan 'the next process is your customer' to reduce barriers of sectionalism. This is equally appropriate in relationships where one has to manage not only the internal processes, but also those between different levels in the relationship of client and supplier. A well-known example is the chief executive who will only talk to his direct counterpart even if his query can be dealt with satisfactorily at a lower level. If supplier and buyer cannot agree on workable lines of communication, the process satisfaction has to diminish.

Obviously, any service business is ultimately trying to effect satisfactory outcome quality and the strategic and tactical decisions taken by the client and supplier will influence the outcome. Further study of the subjective nature of satisfaction in business services could prove of particular usefulness for the following:

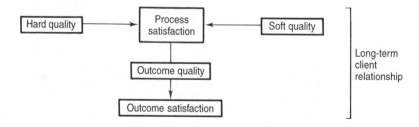

Figure 1.   The role of satisfaction and quality in the long-term relationship.

1. The understanding and provision of the client's quality requirements.
2. The ongoing management of the client/supplier relationship.
3. Choosing and targeting segments with a satisfaction profile best suited to the supplier.

This article highlights the importance and role of the areas of service quality outlined above and, particularly, the way that attention in these areas can assist in the ongoing management of a relationship. Their role in segmentation requires further research and will not be directly discussed here. A key point is for suppliers to be aware of the differences highlighted between hard and soft and outcome quality, and of the role each might play in the management of *different* relationships.

UNDERSTANDING AND PROVIDING THE CLIENT'S QUALITY REQUIREMENTS

Different clients have different requirements in the balance between hard and soft quality. It is in the supplying company's interests to identify what that balance is and, at the same time, to pinpoint any specific requirements that need to be met. While this can be done informally, there are more benefits from a structured system for identifying specific clients' needs. When both client and supplier are party to the process, they become aware of, and more focused on, this aspect of the relationship: the vendor, particularly in terms of trying to supply what is required; while buyers must realistically consider what provides them with most value in the relationship. This can then act as a starting-point for further discussion, and also as a point to refer back to if things go wrong or changes occur in either side of the relationship. It is not intended to be an audit. The supplier firm may wish to do that anyway but rather as a regular contact point to compare perceptions and to eliminate, where possible, gaps between the perceptions of one side and the other.

Michell[24,25] has already achieved a great deal in identifying the realities of problems in long-term relationships in his work with advertising agencies and clients. This work is highly relevant to the topic of quality in relationships, under discussion here. Michell looked at the composition of agency/client advertising decision-making units and examined those factors which contributed to advertisers switching advertising agencies in the UK and in the USA.[24] In this study, he found that dissatisfaction with agency performance rested largely on three factors – creativity, campaign results, and client service. This last item covered account management, marketing advice and generally being 'close to the client'. If one accepts that creativity is essentially the advertising agency's product, it seems reasonable to suggest that, broadly, these three factors cover hard, soft and outcome quality – i.e. creativity, client service and campaign results respectively. Clearly, different service businesses will have different factors falling into these three groups but, by initially looking for these three groupings of quality, one can begin to assess the balance required by clients.

It is not the purpose of this article to chart the specific processes used to identify clients' specific quality requirements, and it is envisaged that a future article will examine this in detail. However, at this stage, it is worth saying a few general words on the method. One checklist is unlikely to do justice to the variability in most business services clients' quality requirements. Initially, prompts may be used to help clients decide what is, or is not, important to them in terms of hard and soft factors. This is not always easy, as some clients do not feel comfortable with having to define or even admit to what really matters to them, especially in the soft areas. However, in beginning this process, a watertight checklist is not necessary. It is probably better to identify some quality requirements along the way and add them to the list with mutual agreement. Though no one wants to spend their time searching for new problems regular debriefing meetings can pick up many such points once the concept has entered the consciousness of the main contact personnel.

At some point, a list of important hard and soft quality factors is drawn up, which should be agreed by both client and supplier. Especially important at this time is agreement about what statements mean: replying to letters promptly, for example, needs some kind of time scale included.

MANAGING QUALITY IN THE SUPPLIER/CLIENT RELATIONSHIP

The shift from a transactional to a relationship focus brings problems that, as yet, have not been fully explored in the literature. The problems are essentially to do with managing a relationship over time so that both parties gain satisfaction. Many of the likely problems can be seen in terms of hard and soft quality. I have highlighted the problems that can come about when the quality of the relationship is perceived by the customer as high. When personal relationships have developed, and soft quality generally is perceived to be high, issues may be brushed over or even ignored that really should question the continuance of the relationship.

When a relationship has developed with a supplier (or buyer) there is sure to be resistance at the prospect of terminating that relationship, even when there are very good reasons to do so. The very act of developing a relationship over time means that to leave it can be painful for one or both of the parties.

Once a relationship has developed, there may be less information readily available against which to judge a partner's performance, simply because the business may now have no other similar suppliers with which to compare. This may lead to an acceptance of less, in terms of quality, simply because of a lack of alternatives to assess the supplier against.

Interestingly, consideration of how a service relationship matures over time has received little attention to date. Again, it is in the area of perceived quality and customer satisfaction that a supplier can judge how best to manage an ongoing relationship within the bounds of the alternatives available. Any relationship changes over time. It is critical for buyers and sellers to recognize change and act on it where necessary. Changes comes in many forms, and any industry or service will be subject to particular forces, but there are some general currents to which organizations should pay heed. Identified below are three concepts drawn from the business literature that could help to chart change within a relationship:

1. The transaction life cycle.
2. The experience cycle.
3. The customer activity cycle.

Following a brief discussion of each of these, a fourth cycle is proposed – the relationship cycle – with a view to identifying the typical routes a relationship in the business services area may take over time.

The transaction life cycle

Services, just like products, can move through life cycles. The ability to recognize that what you were marketing two years ago is no longer perceived in the same way by its original market is vital, both for maintaining existing relationships and for developing new ones.

Mathur's transaction life cycle,[26] although originally developed for the industrial products market, is equally applicable to services. Mathur describes the introduction of a radically new type of hardware. The vendor has to supply not only the hardware, but also the know-how, to enable buyers to realize the full benefits of their purchase. At this stage, the vendor is marketing a system but, as the new packages catches on, competitors enter the market with similar packages. Now some concentration on market segments may follow. Gradually, buyers learn and improve on how the hardware can be used, and the software no longer becomes an essential purchase. Some players may concentrate on the provision of specialized software, thus, in Mathur's terms, providing a service and, as they refine their services, also providing a class of services after time. Similarly, competitors will enter the market specializing in different areas of hardware, generally reducing the barriers to entry and adding to the features and refinements of the hardware. This is the emergence of a product class.

The process of 'desystemization' can continue with the hardware and software coming to be regarded as commodity items by an increasing number of purchasers. Figure 2 shows how the process can go full circle, as mature commodities can be packaged with new or existing software to provide a new cluster of benefits; this, Mathur describes as decommodization or systemization.

The basic outline of the transaction life cycle can find many parallels in business services, e.g. the continuing repackaging of airline services for business travellers and financial services for small businesses, and also the more sophisticated financial instruments offered by corporate banks. The message for management regarding the relationship is, however, not easy to accept – especially the fact that such cycles indicate changes in the power balance of the relationship, usually from the supplier's favour to the buyer's. Here the shifts come about because of how the service is changing in the marketplace. The know-how for a commodized service will be of far less importance and the outcome quality should be assured as far as it is in the vendor's power to do so. Both hard and soft process elements must have particular attention paid to them, as shortcomings in these areas are going to be far more noticeable. Strategically, the power base of the relationship is unlikely to rebalance unless research and development by the vendor resystemize the current offering.

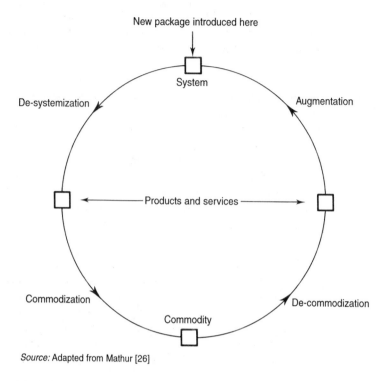

Source: Adapted from Mathur [26]

Figure 2.   The transaction life cycle.

The experience cycle

Another danger to relationships arises when the supplier makes the mistake of believing that the benefits offered to their customers on day one of the relationship will have equal value to the customer on day 100. Just as products and services evolve, so do customers, and their experience of a particular service over time means they will grow in sophistication and self-confidence in their use of it. They are likely to need less support from the relationship and may become increasingly price sensitive. Termed the 'customer experience effect' by DeBruicker and Summe,[27] this threat is ever present in a relationship but can be managed as long as the vendor company is carefully watching the development of the relationship, changes in personnel, specific requirements, etc. and not leaving the responsibility for management to one person who may lose sight of change because he or she has become too close to the customer. Regular checks on the state of the relationship should throw up changes of this nature.

Customers often begin to unbundle the services they previously bought as a system as they gain experience and need less support. In particular, one would expect the need for soft quality to diminish and so the ties of the relationship will weaken. Firms needing services such as legal services, public relations and market research on a regular basis may decide, after a certain level of experience has been reached, to end a long-standing relationship and provide all or part of the service themselves by employing expert personnel and buying the remaining components on an *ad hoc* basis from a number of sources, feeling confident that they now have the experience so to do.

For the supplying company, the customer experience effect requires a decision at a strategic level. If the company's strengths lie in offering a full service relationship and a current customer no longer requires this, it may well be better to end the relationship and find alternative customers who will value this aspect of the company's offering. It is not a requirement for every company to change its strategy in line with its customers. Having said this, a supplier facing a combination of the customer experience effect and the transaction life cycle may have little choice but to go with the flow of the market.

The customer activity cycle

Vandermerwe[28] stresses the importance of understanding a customer's activity cycle as a holistic experience over time. Service customers, she says are not only buying advertising, legal services, treasury bills, they are aiming to maximize what they get from the experts over the period of the relationship. One might say that this is the process satisfaction, as compared to the outcome satisfaction, of the results of the service. Vandermerwe shows how critical points may be mapped over an activity cycle of the relationship which may act an an indicator for the selling company, in terms of

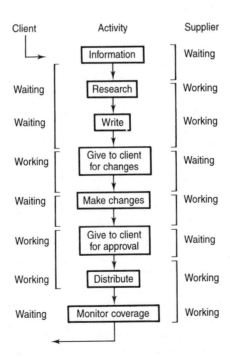

Figure 3.   Press release activity cycle.

when different types of activity may be required. This corroborates the point made earlier that, while everyone is looking for successful outcome quality, one cannot ignore the various stages required to achieve this, some more difficult to negotiate than others; quite different requirements may be made of the relationship depending on what stage the activity has reached.

Figure 3 depicts an activity cycle drawn up to show the stages in a public relations company's press release writing and approval process. The centre line charts the various processes that have to be undertaken; if appropriate, suggested or probable timings between each stage could be inserted. On either side of the main process centre line specific actions can be placed – likely problems, etc. for the client on one side and for the supplier company on the other. Charting the customer activity cycle (see Figure 3) in this way can be useful at both the planning and review stages for both sides of the relationship. It can also prove useful for generally looking at ways of improving the process and identifying where contact should be kept up when the inevitable lulls in activity reduce the essential need for meeting.

On this activity cycle the starting-point for action is when the client gives the necessary information to the agency. There then follows a process where, for much of the time, one or other side is 'waiting' while the other is 'working'. Charting the activity in this way not only aids planning generally but, when times are added to the various phases, a business can identify where there are long time lags and review whether they can improve the process. During the client's 'waiting time', it may be just as well to keep them appraised of what is happening, while the supplier's 'waiting time' should be carefully managed so that other work can be carried on while, at the same time, encouragement is given to clients if necessary, to ensure the process keeps going at the required pace. One can build into process cycles such as this relatively simple actions, such as ensuring the notification of the client as soon as it is known a deadline will not be met. Keeping a close eye on the process can avoid misunderstandings on both sides of the relationship.

Service companies might consider charting their own relationships according to activity to identify, for example, whether there are critical points that regularly occur among clients or where there are points where the need for hard or soft quality may be more in evidence.

The relationship cycle

The relationship cycle proposed here suggests that, in most relationships, the expectations of either side and the satisfaction derived from the relationship are rarely completely in tune. If the expectation and reality are too far apart the relationship is likely to flounder unless one side is brought closer to the other.

To examine the relationship cycle, it is necessary to view both sides of the relationship and look to identify likely crisis points. Figures 4 and 5 chart two scenarios of the cycle which may occur in service relationships. The two lines indicate the buyer's and seller's view of the relationship; the lines are basically an amalgam of expectations about, and satisfaction derived from, the relationship. In reality, expectations and satisfaction will enjoy a different balance at different stages of a relationship: at the beginning, expectations, by definition, must almost

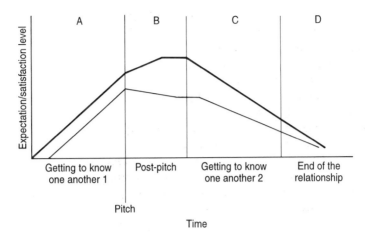

Figure 4.   The relationship cycle – the relationship ends.

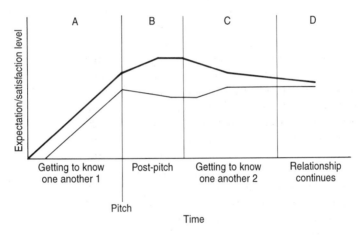

Figure 5.   The relationship cycle – the relationship continues.

outweigh satisfaction, whereas later in the relationship the parties are more likely to know what to expect and be satisfied or not. Generally, if one is not satisfied, one's expectations lower and, therefore, the important elements of this cycle are the direction in which it is going and the closeness of the buyer and seller lines. Overall, the horizontal axis should be seen as generally tracking both parties' expectation/satisfaction level.

A key point in the cycle is the pitch which is common in services from accounting to advertising, although less so in corporate banking where a number of banks are often retained after proving themselves on a particular task. However, one way or another, there is a moment where speculative discussion between two parties who are getting to know one another changes into a buying/selling situation; if not, the parties either drift apart or keep in sporadic touch with one another.

The basic scenarios are:

1. The relationship thrives.
2. The relationship dissolves either from the supplier's or the customer's choice.

One overriding contribution towards the continuation of the relationship would seem to be that the closer the two sides are to meeting, in terms of what they expect from the relationship, the more likely it is that the relationship will be successful. This equilibrium does not necessarily have to be at a particularly high point if both sides are satisfied, although it should be said that this leaves the door open for others to lure customers away with better offers. Clearly, over the course of any relationship, the two lines will at times be nearer or further apart. However, the relationship is least likely to prosper when the expectation/satisfaction lines for each side are far apart for some time.

The thick lines in Figures 4 and 5 depict the buyer side of the relationship and the thin line the vendor. During phase (A) both sides are getting to know one another without having to make a commitment. The nearer together the lines are at this point reflects the closeness of perceptions of what the relationship should look like – therefore, this is a very important time for both sides. Both buyer and seller have this time to begin to get to know the other and assess whether they are right for one another in terms of a long-term relationship.

An important point comes at the pitch line. Once both parties have agreed to work with one another, this is the first major opportunity for divergence between their perceptions of the relationship. A customer who has decided to embark upon a relationship may have their expectations raised quite rapidly; largely due to post-pitch euphoria. Meanwhile, the vendor knows they now have to provide all that was promised in the pitch for the relationship to thrive. If the two sides do not move closer together in phase (C), the second period of getting to know each other, the relationship is probably doomed to disaster – i.e. (D).

(C) is a critical period of time, as each side is reappraising the relationship; the closer both sides can get to one another here, the more chance they have of a successful partnership. It is during this time that pursuing the client's hard and soft quality needs may help improve the relationship. There may be little to show in terms of pure results (outcome quality), but the supplier has this time to make sure that they have a clear understanding of the client's requirements and expectations of the relationship. If the seller does not ensure satisfaction in terms of hard and soft quality, then process satisfaction will suffer and, at this stage, the client has little else on which to judge the relationship.

For most relationships to thrive there has to be some realignment of each side's expectations/satisfaction level. This is generally an ongoing process as changes in each side's needs, such as those outlined earlier in this article, are inevitable. A successful cycle, however, could be such as outlined in Figure 5. Here the key difference from the previous diagram is that the two sides realign their expectation/satisfaction level post-pitch such that a workable equilibrium is reached. Obviously, as the activity cycle continues, there will be many other opportunities to lose that equilibrium and sometimes the cessation of a relationship can be best for both parties.

In a business-to-business service, quality issues may well be apparent at the beginning of the relationship, especially if the buyer has specific quality requirements of a long-standing and/or company-wide nature. But, as a problem, quality is much more likely to become an issue at some point or points during the relationship. Being aware of this likelihood, and managing the consequences rather than taking a defensive stance, may further help the relationship if both sides can agree to a solution. The following are some situations which give rise to changed hard/soft quality problems:

1. Change in top management.
2. Change in company objectives.
3. Change in the decision-making unit.
4. Change in specific objectives relating to the supplier/client relationship.
5. Change in personnel on the supplier side.
6. Reduced interest shown by supplier to buyer, possibly for one of the reasons above, e.g. change in company objectives.

The above should act as markers for those times when a supplier might consider reviewing his client's requirements. From one point of view it requires supplier management to regularly check specific relationships for signs of strain or boredom in the relationship but it also goes beyond this to a somewhat more difficult problem for management – that of 'knowing thyself'. Too often, unattractive clients are kept in a relationship but given a reduced service. This is not good for client or supplier and a slipshod ethos can soon find its way into other areas of a company's business. Regularly checking that the supplier/client fit is still good for both parties is an important part of the hard/soft management concept, and suppliers should not fear the possibility of extracting themselves from relationships that are no longer worthwhile.

CONCLUSION

The trend in business today is clearly towards relationship marketing. In business services, successful management should lead to a profitable relationship for both buyer and seller. While the outcomes of any relationship are clearly crucial, managing the process such that the client is satisfied with the service over time has to be the prime responsibility of the seller. One method of enhancing this process satisfaction is to manage the hard and soft quality requirements of the client. Not only can this improve existing relationships, it may help to identify the best type of clients with which to work.

Putting these ideas into action has already begun with some success. A future article will review the findings from some of the clients who agreed to be involved in the quality study which will be reported. Already it is clear that the results of such a review may be far reaching and could have implications for how firms organize themselves and their internal communications for best advantage within a relationship.

REFERENCES

1. Gronroos, C. (1990) 'Relationship Approach to Marketing in Service Contexts: The Marketing and Organizational Behavior Interface'. *Journal of Business Research* **20**: 3–11.
2. George, W. R. (1990) 'Internal Marketing and Organizational Behavior: A Partnership in Developing Customer-Conscious Employees at Every Level'. *Journal of Business Research* **20**: 63–70.
3. Gummesson, E. (1987) 'The New Marketing – Developing Long-Term Interactive Relationships'. *Long Range Planning* **20**: 10–20.
4. Webster, F. E. and Wind, Y. (1972) 'A General Model for Understanding Organizational Buying Behavior'. *Journal of Marketing* (April): 12–19.
5. Morgan, N. A. (1990) 'Communications and the Reality of Marketing in Professional Service Firms'. *International Journal of Advertising* **9**: 283–293.
6. Guillet de Monthoux, P. B. L. (1975) 'Organizational Mating and Industrial Marketing Conservatism – Some Reasons Why Industrial Marketing Managers Resist Marketing Theory'. *Industrial Marketing Management* **4**: 25–36.
7. Landeros, R. and Monczka, R. M. (1989) 'Cooperative Buyer/Seller Relationships and a Firm's Competitive Posture'. *Journal of Purchasing and Materials Management* (Fall): 9–18.
8. Barrett, J. (1986) 'Why Major Account Selling Works'. *Industrial Marketing Management* **15**: 63–73.
9. Homan (1954), cited in Hakansson, H. and Wootz, B. (1979) 'Framework of Industrial Buying and Selling'. *Industrial Marketing Management* **8**: 28–39.
10. Mayo, E. (1949) 'Hawthorne and the Western Electric Company'. *The Social Problems of an Industrial Civilization.* London: Routledge, pp. 60–76.
11. Dwyer, F. R., Schurr, P. H. and Oh, S. (1987) 'Developing Buyer–Seller Relationships'. *Journal of Marketing* **51** (April): 11–27.
12. Parasuraman, A., Berry, L. L. and Zeithaml, V. A. (1991) 'Understanding Customer Expectations of Service'. *Sloan Management Review* (Spring): 39–48.
13. Lewis, B. (1989) 'Quality in the Service Sector: A Review'. *International Journal of Bank Marketing* **7**(5): 4–12.
14. LeBlanc, G. and Nguyen, N. (1988) 'Customers' Perceptions of Service Quality in Financial Institutions'. *International Journal of Bank Marketing* **6**(4): 7–18.
15. Parasuraman, A., Zeithaml, V. A. and Berry, L. L. (1988) '"SERVQUAL" A Multiple Item Scale for Measuring Consumer Perceptions of Service Quality'. *Journal of Retailing* **64** (No. 1, Spring): 12–40.
16. Gronroos, C. (1984) 'A Service Quality Model and Its Marketing Implications'. *European Journal of Marketing* **18**(4): 36–44.
17. Morgan, N. A. (1991) 'Corporate Legal Advice and Client Quality Perceptions'. *Marketing Intelligence & Planning* **8**(6): 33–39.
18. Edvardsson, B., Gustavsson, B. O. and Riddle, D. J. *An Expanded Model of the Service Encounter, with Emphasis on Cultural Context*, Research Report 890:4, CTF Services Research Centre, University of Karlstad, Sweden.
19. Sheth, J. N. (1973) 'A Model of Industrial Buyer Behavior'. *Journal of Marketing* **37**: 50–56.
20. Lazo, H. 'Emotional Aspects of Industrial Buying'. In *Dynamic Marketing for a Changing World* (R. S. Hancock, Ed.) Proceedings of the 43rd National Conference. Chicago, IL: American Marketing Association, pp. 258–265.
21. Peters, T. J. and Waterman, R. H., Jr. (1982) *In Search of Excellence.* New York: Harper and Row.
22. Lessem, R. (1989) *Global Management Principles.* Englewood Cliffs, NJ: Prentice-Hall.
23. Gummeson, E. (1990) 'Marketing-Orientation Revisited: The Crucial-Role of the Part-Time Marketer'. *European Journal of Marketing* **25**(2): 60–75.
24. Michell, P. C. N. (1987) 'Auditing of Agency-Client Relations'. *Journal of Advertising Research* (December/January): 29–41.
25. Michell, P. C. N. (1988) 'The Influence of Organizational Compatibility on Account Switching'. *Journal of Advertising Research* (June/July): 33–38.

26. Mathur, S. 'Competitive Industrial Marketing Strategies'. *Long Range Planning* **17**(4): 102–109.
27. DeBruicker, F. S. and Summe, G. L. (1985) 'Make Sure Your Customers Keep Coming Back'. *Harvard Business Review* (January/February): 92–98.
28. Vandermerwe, S. (1990) 'The Market Power Is in the Services: Because the Value Is in the Results'. *European Marketing Journal* **8** (No. 4, December): 464–473.

Index

Note: Most references are to services. The word *services* is therefore generally omitted as a qualifier.